INTERNATIONAL LAW AND THE ENVIRONMENT

International Law and the Environment

Patricia W. Birnie
Alan E. Boyle

CLARENDON PRESS · OXFORD

Oxford University Press, Walton Street, Oxford OX2 6DP
Oxford New York Toronto
Delhi Bombay Calcutta Madras Karachi
Kuala Lumpur Singapore Hong Kong Tokyo
Nairobi Dar es Salaam Cape Town
Melbourne Auckland Madrid
and associated companies in
Berlin Ibadan

Oxford is a trade mark of Oxford University Press

Published in the United States
by Oxford University Press Inc., New York

© Patricia Birnie and Alan Boyle 1992

First published 1992
Paperback reprinted (with corrections) 1993, 1994

British Library Cataloguing in Publication Data
Data available

Library of Congress Cataloging in Publication Data
Birnie, Patricia W.
International law and the environment/Patricia W. Birnie.
Alan E. Boyle.
Includes bibliographical references and index.
1. Environmental law, International.   I. Boyle, Alan E.
II. Title.
K3585.4.B57   1992   341.7'62—dc20   92–24779
ISBN 0–19–876282–8
ISBN 0–19–876283–6

Printed and bound in Great Britain by
Biddles Ltd, Guildford & King's Lynn

PREFACE

This book is an attempt to assess the present state of international law concerning the protection of the world's natural environment. Our view of what constitutes an environmental problem is necessarily a broad one, reflecting the development of the subject, and encompassing not only pollution but sustainable development and conservation of natural resources and ecosystems. We have not, however, sought to examine in detail all aspects of these problems, nor is this book a work of policy analysis, but rather our aim is to explore the basic principles, structure, and effectiveness of the international legal system as it relates to the environment, while selecting for closer scrutiny a number of topics where the role and impact of international law have been most evident.

It is hoped that what emerges will provide the reader with a clearer and more coherent picture of the remarkable developments in international law which contemporary concern for the state of the global environment has brought about. A better understanding of this subject is, the authors believe, an essential element of progress in protecting the world's environment, at a time when the United Nations Conference on Environment and Development evidences growing anxiety concerning the health of the planet and the use of its resources.

The writing of this book would not have been possible without the assistance and advice of many people. The library staff of the London School of Economics, the Institute of Advanced Legal Studies, Queen Mary and Westfield College, the Tarlton Law Library of the University of Texas, the Marshall Wythe Law Library of the College of William and Mary and the International Maritime Organisation bore the main burden of our research. The UNCED Secretariat, the Foreign and Commonwealth Office, IMO, UNEP, the Environmental Law Centre of the IUCN, the Natural Heritage Institute, the Advisory Committee on Pollution of the Sea, FAO, Unesco, the World Wide Fund for Nature, and the secretariats of many of the conventions cited, including the Conventions on International Trade in Endangered Species, and on Conservation of Migratory Species of Wild Animals, the International Whaling Commission, the Council of Europe, the Commission of the European Community, the UN Economic Commission for Europe and the Oslo/Paris Commission, were most helpful in providing additional information and documentation.

Our students in various universities and many colleagues, in London and elsewhere, have knowingly or unknowingly given us much helpful inspiration, insight, and information during our long immersion in matters environmental. To them all we are most grateful. Especial thanks are due in the case of Patricia Birnie to the Rockefeller Foundation for inviting her to start on this work in 1987 as a resident scholar in the fabled environment of the Bellagio Study and Conference Centre, and to the British Academy and the Nuffield Foundation for financial support which enabled her to visit UNEP's Headquarters, the Council of Europe, the IUCN Environmental Law Centre, and a number of Convention Secretariats. Alan Boyle is similarly indebted to the Marshall Wythe Law School of the College of William and Mary, Williamsburg, Virginia, and the Law School of the University of Texas at Austin, for their invitations to spend the 1987–8 academic year as a visiting professor, and whose generous support enabled his research to begin.

Our special thanks are also due to Julie Herd and Sophia Oliver, at Queen Mary and Westfield College, and Michelle Mangion and Josephine Aquilina, at the IMO International Maritime Law Institute in Malta, for their dedication in typing a long and involved manuscript; to our ever cheerful and efficient researchers George Kasoulides, Katherina Kummer, Mark Laskay, and Mary Munson; to our publisher for tolerating a work, that like the subject itself, must frequently have seemed about to expand beyond all boundaries of time and space; and to Caroline Boyle, without whose uncomplaining patience and invaluable practical help this book would never have seen the light of day.

Each author wrote separate parts of the book, but all chapters have been read and redrafted by the authors jointly, and such errors and misconceptions as may remain are our collective responsibility. We have tried to take account of developments up to 1 January 1992, but it has been possible to incorporate some reference to the conclusions of the UNCED conference held at Rio in June 1992. Parts of Chapters 3, 4, and 9 have previously appeared in the *British Yearbook of International Law* and the *Journal of Environmental Law* and we are grateful to Oxford University Press for permission to reproduce them.

This book is dedicated to past, present, and future generations of our students.

P.B.
A.B.

Malta
30 March 1992

CONTENTS

ABBREVIATIONS

AFDI	*Annuaire Français de Droit International*
AIR	*All India Reports*
AJIL	*American Journal of International Law*
ALJR	*Australian Law Journal Reports*
ALR	*Australian Law Reports*
Ann. Inst. DDI	*Annuaire de L'institut de droit international*
Ann. Suisse DDI	*Annuaire suisse de droit international*
AUJILP	*American University Journal of International Law and Politics*
AULR	*American University Law Review*
AYIL	*Australian Yearbook of International Law*
BFSP	*British and Foreign State Papers*
BJIS	*British Journal of International Studies*
Boston CICLJ	*Boston College International and Comparative Law Journal*
BYIL	*British Yearbook of International Law*
Burhenne	*International Environmental Law: Multilateral Treaties*, ed. W. Burhenne (Berlin, 1974).
CJIEL and P	*Colorado Journal of International Environmental Law and Policy*
CJTL	*Columbia Journal of Transnational Law*
CLB	*Commonwealth Law Bulletin*
CLP	*Current Legal Problems*
CMLR	*Common Market Law Review*
Cornell ILJ	*Cornell International Law Journal*
CWILJ	*California Western International Law Journal*
CWRJIL	*Case Western Reserve Journal of International Law*
CYIL	*Canadian Yearbook of International Law*
Dalhousie LJ	*Dalhousie Law Journal*
Den. JILP	*Denver Journal of International Law and Politics*
Duke LJ	*Duke Law Journal*
Earth LJ	*Earth Law Journal*
ECHR	*European Court of Human Rights*
ECJ Rep.	*European Court of Justice Reports*
EHRR	*European Human Rights Reports*
ELQ	*Environmental Law Quarterly*
ELR	*European Law Review*
Ency. of Pub. Int. L.	*Encyclopaedia of Public International Law*
Envtl. Consvn.	*Environmental Conservation*
EPL	*Environmental Policy and Law*
FNI	*Fishing News International*
GYIL	*German Yearbook of International Law*

Hague YIL	*Hague Yearbook of International Law*
Harv. ELR	*Harvard Environmental Law Review*
Harv. ILJ	*Harvard International Law Journal*
Harv. LR	*Harvard Law Review*
HRLJ	*Human Rights Law Journal*
HRR	*Human Rights Reports*
ICJ Rep.	*International Court of Justice Reports*
ICLQ	*International and Comparative Law Quarterly*
Idaho LR	*Idaho Law Review*
IJECL	*International Journal of Estuarine and Coastal Law*
ILA	*International Law Association*
ILC	*International Law Commission*
ILM	*International Legal Materials*
ILR	*International Law Reports*
Ind. JIL	*Indian Journal of International Law*
Int. Affairs	*International Affairs*
Int. Org.	*International Organisation*
Ital. YIL	*Italian Yearbook of International Law*
IUCN Bull.	*International Union for the Conservation of Nature Bulletin*
Jap. Ann. IL	*Japanese Annual of International Law*
JEL	*Journal of Environmental Law*
JLS	*Journal of Law and Society*
JMLC	*Journal of Maritime Law and Commerce*
Jnl. of Bus. Admin.	*Journal of Business Administration*
JPEL	*Journal of Planning and Environmental Law*
J. Space L.	*Journal of Space Law*
LNTS	*League of Nations Treaty Series*
LOSB	*Law of the Sea Bulletin*
McGill LR	*McGill Law Review*
MLR	*Modern Law Review*
ND	*New Directions in the Law of the Sea*, ed. Lay, Welch, Churchill, and Simmonds, 11 vols., and looseleaf service (Dobbs Ferry, NY, 1974–)
NILR	*Netherlands International Law Review*
NLB	*Nuclear Law Bulletin*
NRJ	*Natural Resources Journal*
NYIL	*Netherlands Yearbook of International Law*
NYJIL and Pol.	*New York Journal of International Law and Policy*
NY Law School LR	*New York Law School Law Review*
NZLR	*New Zealand Law Reports*
ODIL	*Ocean Development and International Law*
OGTLR	*Oil and Gas Taxation Law Review*
OJEC	*Official Journal of the European Community*
OLR	*Oregon Law Review*
OPN	*Ocean Policy News*
OsHLJ	*Osgoode Hall Law Journal*
PCIJ	*Permanent Court of International Justice Reports*

Proc. ASIL	*Proceedings of the American Society of International Law*
RBDI	*Revue belge de droit international*
Rev. jurid. de l'env.	*Revue juridique de l'environnement*
RGDIP	*Recueil général de droit international public*
RIAA	*Reports of International Arbitration Awards*
Ruster and Simma	*International Protection of the Environment,* ed. B. Ruster and B. Simma, 30 vols., and looseleaf service (Dobbs Ferry, NY, 1975–)
SALJ	*South African Law Journal*
SCal. LR	*Southern California Law Review*
SCC	*Supreme Court Cases (India)*
SDLR	*San Diego Law Review*
Stanford JIL	*Stanford Journal of International Law*
Sydney LR	*Sydney Law Review*
TILJ	*Texas International Law Journal*
UBCLR	*University of British Columbia Law Review*
UKTS	*United Kingdom Treaty Series*
UNCLOS	*United Nations Convention on the Law of the Sea, 1982*
UNGAOR	*United Nations General Assembly Official Records*
UN Jurid. YB	*United Nations Juridical Yearbook*
UN Leg. Ser.	*United Nations Legislative Series*
UNTS	*United Nations Treaty Series*
U. Penn. LR	*University of Pennsylvania Law Review*
UTLJ	*University of Toronto Law Journal*
Vand. JTL	*Vanderbilt Journal of Transnational Law*
VJIL	*Virginia Journal of International Law*
VUWLR	*Victoria University of Wellington Law Review*
Yale LJ	*Yale Law Journal*
Ybk of the AAA	*Yearbook of the Hague Academy of International Law*
YEL	*Yearbook of European Law*
YIEL	*Yearbook of International Environmental Law*
ZAORV	*Zeitschrift für Ausländisches und Öffentliches Recht und Völkerrecht*

TABLE OF CASES

TABLE OF MAJOR TREATIES
AND INSTRUMENTS

Only those treaties and instruments which are cited frequently in the text or are of particular significance are listed here. References to other treaties will be found in the footnotes. 'Not in force' indicates that the treaty had not come into force by 31 December 1991.

1902   Convention for the Protection of Birds Useful to Agriculture (Paris), 102 *BFSP* 969. In force 20 April 1908.

1909   Treaty between the United States and Great Britain Respecting Boundary Waters Between the United States and Canada (Washington), 4 *AJIL* (Suppl.) 239. In force 5 May 1910.

1911   Treaty for the Preservation and Protection of Fur Seals (Washington), 104 *BFSP* 175. In force 15 December 1911.

1931   Convention for the Regulation of Whaling, 155 *LNTS* 349. In force 16 January 1935.

1933   Convention Relative to the Preservation of Fauna and Flora in their Natural State (London), 172 *LNTS* 241; *UKTS* 27 (1930), Cmd. 5280. In force 14 January 1936.

1940   Convention on Nature Protection and Wild-Life Preservation in the Western Hemisphere (Washington), 161 *UNTS* 193. In force 1 May 1942.

1944   United States—Mexico Treaty Relating to the Utilization of Waters of the Colorado and Tijuana Rivers and of the Rio Grande, 3 *UNTS* 313. In force 8 November 1945.

1945   Charter of the United Nations (San Francisco), 1 *UNTS* xvi; *UKTS* 67 (1946), Cmd. 7015; 39 *AJIL Suppl.* (1945) 190. In force 24 October 1945.

1946   International Convention for the Regulation of Whaling (Washington), 161 *UNTS* 72; *UKTS* 5 (1949), Cmd. 7604. In force 10 November 1948. Amended 1956, 338 *UNTS* 366. In force 4 May 1959.

1947   Convention of the World Meterorological Organization (Washington), 77 *UNTS* 143; 1 *UST* 281, *TIAS* 2052; *UKTS* 36 (1950), Cmd. 7989. In force 23 March 1950.

1948   Convention on the International Maritime Organization (Geneva), 289 *UNTS* 48; *UKTS* 54 (1950), Cmnd. 589; 53 *AJIL* (1948), 516. In force 17 March 1958. Amended 1964, 1965, 1974, 1975, 1977, 1979.

        Universal Declaration of Human Rights, UNGA Res. 217A (III).

1963   Agreement Supplementary to the Paris Convention of 1960 on Third Party
        Liability in the Field of Nuclear Energy (Brussels), *UKTS* 44 (1975), Cmnd.
        5948; 2 *ILM* (1963), 685. In force 4 December 1974. Amended 1964 *UKTS*
        44 (1975) Cmnd. 5948, in force 4 December 1974; 1982, *UKTS* 23 (1983),
        Cmnd. 9052, in force 1 August 1991.

        Agreement Concerning the International Commission for the Protection of
        the Rhine Against Pollution (Berne), 994 *UNTS* 3. In force 1 May 1965.

        Convention on Civil Liability for Nuclear Damage (Vienna), Misc. 9 (1964),
        Cmnd. 2333; 2 *ILM* (1963), 727. In force 12 November 1977. 1983
        Protocol, not in force.

        Treaty Banning Nuclear Weapon Tests in the Atmosphere, in Outer Space
        and Under Water (Moscow), 480 *UNTS* 43; *UKTS* 3 (1964), Cmnd. 2245;
        14 *UST* 1313, *TIAS* 5433. In force 10 October 1963.

1964   Agreement Concerning the River Niger Commission and the Navigation and
        Transport on the River Niger (Niamey), 587 *UNTS* 19. In force 12 April
        1966.

        Convention for the International Council for the Exploration of the Sea
        (Copenhagen). *UKTS* 67 (1968), Cmnd. 3722. In force 22 July 1968.

        Agreed Measures for the Conservation of Antarctic Fauna and Flora, Misc.
        23 (1965) Cmnd. 2822.

1966   UN Covenant on Civil and Political Rights, 6 *ILM* (1967), 368. In force 23
        March 1976.

        UN Covenant on Economic, Social and Cultural Rights, 6 *ILM* (1967), 360.
        In force 3 January 1976.

1967   Treaty on Principles Governing the Activities of states in the Exploration and
        Use of Outer Space, Including the Moon and Other Celestial Bodies, 610
        UNTS 205; *UKTS* 10 (1968), Cmnd. 3519; 18 *UST* 2410, *TIAS* 6347; 6
        ILM (1967), 386. In force 10 October 1967.

        Treaty for the Prohibition of Nuclear Weapons in Latin America
        (Tlatelolco), 22 *UST* 762, *TIAS* 7137; 6 *ILM* (1967), 521. In force 22 April
        1968.

        Convention on the Conduct of Fishing Operations in the North Atlantic
        (London), 6 *ILM* (1967), 760. In force 26 September 1976.

1968   African Convention on the Conservation of Nature and Natural Resources
        (Algiers), 1001 *UNTS* 4. In force 16 June 1969.

        Convention on Jurisdiction and Enforcement of Judgments in Civil and
        Commercial Matters (Brussels), *OJEC* L 304/77 (1978); EC 46 (1978),
        Cmnd. 7395; 8 *ILM* (1969), 229. In force 1 February 1973.

        European Convention for the Protection of Animals During International
        Transport, 788 *UNTS* 185; *UKTS* 31 (1974), Cmnd. 5613. In force 20
        February 1971. Additional Protocol of 1979, *ETS* 103.

        Treaty on the Non-Proliferation of Nuclear Weapons (Washington, London,
        Moscow), 729 *UNTS* 161; 21 *UST* 483, *TIAS* 6839. In force 5 March 1970.

1969   TOVALOP Agreement, 8 *ILM* (1969), 497.

Convention on the Law of Treaties (Vienna), 8 *ILM* (1969), 679. In force 27 January 1980.

Agreement for Cooperation in Dealing with Pollution of the North Sea by Oil (Bonn), 704 *UNTS* 3; *UKTS* 78 (1960), Cmnd. 4205; 9 *ILM* (1970), 359. In force 9 August 1969. Replaced by 1983 Agreement (q.v.)

International Convention on Civil Liability for Oil Pollution Damage (Brussels), 973 *UNTS* 3; *UKTS* 106 (1975), Cmnd. 6183; 9 *ILM* (1970), 45. In force 19 June 1975. 1976 Protocol, *UKTS* 26 (1981), Cmnd. 8238; 16 *ILM* (1977), 617. In force 8 April 1981. 1984 Protocol, IMO Doc Leg./ Conf. 6/66, not in force.

International Convention Relating to Intervention on the High Seas in Cases of Oil Pollution Damage (Brussels), *UKTS* 77 (1971), Cmnd. 6056; 9 *ILM* (1970), 25. In force 6 May 1975. 1973 Protocol *UKTS* 27 (1983), Cmnd. 8924; 68 *AJIL* (1974), 577. In force 30 March 1983.

1971   Convention on Wetlands of International Importance (Ramsar), 996 *UNTS* 245; *UKTS* 34 (1976), Cmnd. 6465; 11 *ILM* (1972), 963. In force 21 December 1975. Amended by Protocol of 1982, 22 *ILM* (1983), 698, in force 1986; 1987 amendments, not in force.

CRISTAL Agreement, 10 *ILM* 137 (1971).

Agreement Concerning Cooperation in Taking Measures Against Pollution of the Sea by Oil (Copenhagen), 822 *UNTS* 311. In force 16 October 1971.

Convention Relating to Civil Liability in the Field of Maritime Carriage of Nuclear Material (Brussels) Misc. 39 (1972), Cmnd. 5094. In force 15 July 1975.

Convention on the Establishment of an International Fund for Compensation for Oil Pollution Damage (Brussels), *UKTS* 95 (1978), Cmnd. 7383; 11 *ILM* (1972), 284. In force 16 October 1978. Amended 1976, 16 *ILM* (1977), 621, not in force; 1984 Protocol, not in force.

1972   Convention for the Prevention of Marine Pollution by Dumping from Ships and Aircraft (Oslo), 932 *UNTS* 3; *UKTS* 119 (1975), Cmnd. 6228; 11 *ILM* 262 (1972). In force 7 April 1974. Amended by protocols of 1983, *UKTS* 59 (1989), Cm 889, in force 1 September 1989; 1989 Protocol, not in force.

Convention on International Liability for Damage Caused by Space Objects, 961 *UNTS* 187; *UKTS* 16 (1974), Cmnd. 5551; 24 *UST* 2389, *TIAS* 7762. In force 1 September 1972.

Convention for the Conservation of Antarctic Seals (London), 29 *UST* 441, *TIAS* 8826; 11 *ILM* 251 (1972), 251. In force 11 March 1978.

Convention on the International Regulations for Preventing Collisions at Sea, *UKTS* 77 (1977), Cmnd. 6962. In force 15 July 1977. Amended 1981 *UKTS* 68 (1984), Cmnd. 9340, in force 1 June 1983; 1987, in force 19 November 1989; 1989, in force 19 April 1991.

Declaration of the United Nations Conference on the Human Environment (Stockholm), UN Doc. A/CONF/48/14/REV.1.

Unesco Convention Concerning the Protection of the World Cultural and Natural Heritage, *UKTS* 2 (1985), Cmnd. 9424; 27 *UST* 37, *TIAS* 8225; 11 *ILM* (1972), 1358. In force 17 December 1975.

Convention on the Prevention of Marine Pollution by Dumping of Wastes and other Matter (London), 26 UST 2403, *TIAS* 8165; *UKTS* 43 (1976), Cmnd. 6486; 11 *ILM* (1972), 1294; In force 30 August 1975. Amended 1978, in force 11 March 1979; 1980, in force 11 March 1981; 1989, not in force.

1973   Convention on International Trade in Endangered Species of Wild Fauna and Flora (Washington), 993 *UNTS* 243; *UKTS* 101 (1976), Cmnd. 6647; 12 *ILM* 1085 (1973). In force 1 July 1975.

International Convention for the Prevention of Pollution by Ships (MARPOL) (London), *UKTS* 27 (1983), Cmnd. 8924; 12 *ILM* (1973), 1319. Amended by Protocol of 1978 (q.v.) before entry into force.

Agreement on the Conservation of Polar Bears (Oslo), 27 *UST* 3918, *TIAS* 8409; *ILM* 13 (1974), 13. In force 26 May 1976.

1974   Nordic Convention on the Protection of the Environment (Stockholm), 13 *ILM* (1974), 511. In force 5 October 1976.

Convention on the Protection of Marine Environment of the Baltic Sea Area (Helsinki), 13 *ILM* 546 (1974), 546. In force 3 May 1980.

Convention for the Prevention of Marine Pollution from Land-Based Sources (Paris), *UKTS* 64 (1978), Cmnd. 7251; 13 *ILM* 352 (1974), 352. In force 6 May 1978. Amended by Protocol of 1986, 27 *ILM* (1988), 625, in force 1 February 1990.

International Convention for the Safety of Life at Sea, 1184 *UNTS* 2; *UKTS* 46 (1980), Cmnd. 7874; *TIAS* 9700. In force 25 May 1980. Amended 1981, in force 1 September 1984; 1987, in force 30 October 1988; 1988 (1), in force 22 October 1989; 1988 (2), in force 29 April 1990; 1988 (3), not in force; 1989 (1), not in force; 1989 (2), in force 12 April 1990.

1976   Convention for the Protection of the Mediterranean Sea Against Pollution (Barcelona); Protocol Concerning Cooperation in Combating Pollution of the Mediterranean Sea by Oil and Other Harmful Substances in Cases of Emergency; Protocol for the Prevention of Pollution of the Mediterranean Sea by Dumping from Ships and Aircraft, 15 *ILM* (1976), 290. In force 12 February 1978. 1980 and 1982 Protocols (q.v.).

Convention on Conservation of Nature in the South Pacific (Apia), Burhenne, 976: 45. In force 28 June 1980.

ILO Convention No. 147 Concerning Minimum Standards in Merchant Ships (Geneva), 15 *ILM* (1976), 1288. In force 28 November 1981.

European Convention for the Protection of Animals Kept for Farming Purposes (Strasbourg), ETS No. 87; *UKTS* 70 (1979), Cmnd. 7684. In force 10 September 1978.

Convention on the Protection of the Rhine Against Chemical Pollution (Bonn), 1124 *UNTS* 375; 16 *ILM* (1977), 242. In force 1 February 1979.

Convention for the Protection of the Rhine from Pollution by Chlorides (Bonn), 16 *ILM* (1977), 265. In force 5 July 1985.

Convention on the Prohibition of Military or Any Other Hostile Use of Environmental Modification Techniques (Geneva), 31 *UST* 333, *TIAS* 9614; 16 *ILM* (1977), 88. In force 5 October 1978.

1977 Convention on Civil Liability for Oil Pollution Damage Resulting from Exploration for and Exploitation of Sea-bed Mineral Resources (London), 16 *ILM* (1977), 1450. Not in force.

Protocols I and II Additional to the Geneva Conventions of 12 August 1949 and Relating to the Protection of Victims of International Armed Conflicts, 1125 *UNTS* 3; 1125 *UNTS* 609; 16 *ILM* (1977), 1391. In force 7 December 1978.

1978 Protocol Relating to the Convention for the Prevention of Pollution from Ships (MARPOL), 17 *ILM* 546 (1978), 546. In force 2 October 1983. Annex I in force 2 October 1983. Annex II in force 6 April 1987. Annex V in force 31 December 1988. Refer to IMO for amendments.

Convention on Future Multilateral Co-operation in the North-West Atlantic Fisheries. Misc. 9 (1979), Cmnd. 7569. In force 1 January 1979. Amended 1979, Misc. 9 (1980), Cmnd. 7865.

Regional Convention for Cooperation on the Protection of the Marine Environment from Pollution (Kuwait), 1140 *UNTS* 133; 17 *ILM* (1978), 511. In force 1 July 1979. Protocols 1978, 1989, 1990 (q.v.).

Protocol Concerning Regional Cooperation in Combating Pollution by Oil and Other Harmful Substances in Cases of Emergency (Kuwait), 17 *ILM* (1978), 526. In force 1 July 1979.

Treaty for Amazonian Cooperation (Brasilia), 17 *ILM* (1978), 1045. In force 2 February 1980.

Convention on Standards of Training, Certification and Watchkeeping for Seafarers, *UKTS* 50 (1984), Cmnd. 9266. In force 28 April 1984.

United States–Canada Agreement on Great Lakes Water Quality with Annexes, 30 *UST* 1383, *TIAS* 9257. In force 27 November 1978. Amended 1983, *TIAS* 10798.

1979 Convention on the Conservation of Migratory Species of Wild Animals (Bonn), 19 *ILM* (1980), 15. In force 1 November 1983.

Convention on the Conservation of European Wildlife and Natural Habitats (Berne), *UKTS* 56 (1982), Cmnd. 8738; *ETS* 104. In force 1 June 1982.

Convention on Long-Range Transboundary Air Pollution (Geneva), *UKTS* 57 (1983), Cmd. 9034; *TIAS* 10541; 18 *ILM* (1979), 1442. In force 16 March 1983. Protocols of 1984, 1985, 1988, and 1991 (q.v.).

Agreement Governing the Activities of States on the Moon and Other Celestial Bodies, 18 *ILM* (1979), 1434. In force 11 July 1984.

Convention for the Conservation and Management of the Vicuna (Lima), Burhenne 979: 94. In force 19 March 1982.

European Convention for the Protection of Animals Used for Slaughter (Strasbourg), *ETS* 102. In force 11 June 1982.

1980   Protocol for the Protection of the Mediterranean Sea against Pollution from Land-Based Sources (Athens), 19 *ILM* (1980), 869. In force 17 June 1983.

Convention on the Physical Protection of Nuclear Material (Vienna) 18 *ILM* (1979). In force 8 February 1987.

Convention on the Conservation of Antarctic Marine Living Resources (Canberra), *UKTS* 48 (1982), Cmnd. 8714; *TIAS* 10240; 19 *ILM* (1980), 837. In force 7 April 1981.

Convention on Future Multilateral Co-operation in North-East Atlantic Fisheries, Misc. 2 (1980), Cmnd. 8474. In force 17 March 1982.

1981   African Charter on Human Rights and Peoples' Rights (Banjul), 21 *ILM* (1982), 52. In force 21 October 1986.

Convention and Protocol for Cooperation in the Protection and Development of the Marine and Coastal Environment of the West and Central African Regional (Abidjan) and Protocol concerning Co-operation in Combating Pollution in Cases of Emergency, 20 *ILM* (1981), 746. In force 5 August 1984.

Protocol between the government of Canada and the government of the USSR on Settlement of Canada's Claim for Damage Caused by COSMOS 954, 20 *ILM* (1981), 689.

Convention for the Protection of the Marine Environment and Coastal Area of the South-East Pacific (Lima), *ND* (Looseleaf), Doc. J. 18. In force 19 May 1986.

Agreement on Regional Cooperation in Combating Pollution of the South-East Pacific by Hydrocarbons or Other Harmful Substances in Cases of Emergency (Lima), *ND* (Looseleaf), Doc. J. 18. In force 14 July 1986.

1982   Memorandum of Understanding on Port State Control of Ships (Paris), 21 *ILM* (1982), 1.

Regional Convention for the Conservation of the Red Sea and Gulf of Aden Environment (Jeddah), and Protocol Concerning Regional Co-operation in Combating Pollution by Oil and Other Harmful Substances in Cases of Emergency, 9 *EPL* 56 (1982). In force 20 August 1985.

Protocol (to the 1976 Barcelona Convention) Concerning Mediterranean Specially Protected Areas (Geneva), *ND* (Looseleaf) Doc. J. 20. In force 23 March 1986.

World Charter for Nature, UNGA Res. 37/7, 37 UNGAOR Suppl. (No. 51) at 17, UN Doc. A/37/51 (1982).

Convention for the Conservation of Salmon in the North Atlantic Ocean (Reykjavik), EEC *OJ* (1982) No. L378, 25; Misc. 7 (1983), Cmnd. 8830. In force 10 October 1983.

UN Convention on the Law of the Sea (Montego Bay), Misc. 11 (1983), Cmnd. 8941; 21 *ILM* (1982), 1261. Not in force.

1983   Convention for the Protection and Development of the Marine Environment of the Wider Caribbean Region (Cartegena de Indias) and Protocol Concerning Co-operation in Combating Oil Spills in the Wider Caribbean Region, 22 *ILM* (1983), 221; *UKTS* 38 (1988), Cm 399. In force 11 October 1986. 1990 Protocol (q.v.).

Protocol (to the 1981 Lima Convention) for the Protection of the South-East Pacific Against Pollution from Land-Based Sources (Quito), Burhenne, 983: 54. In force 23 September 1986.

Agreement Between Canada and Denmark on Co-operation Relating to the Marine Environment, 23 *ILM* (1984), 269. In force 26 August 1983.

Agreement for Co-operation in Dealing with Pollution of the North Sea by Oil and Other Harmful Substances, (Bonn) Misc. 26 (1983), Cmnd. 9104. In force 1 September 1989.

Agreement between the United States and Mexico on Co-operation for the Protection and Improvement of the Environment in the Border Area, 22 *ILM* (1983), 1025, with Annexes I–IV of 1987, 26 *ILM* (1987), 16, and Annex V of 1990, 30 *ILM* (1991), 678. In force 16 February 1984.

1984   Protocol (to the 1979 Geneva Convention) on Long-Term Financing of the Co-operative Programme for Monitoring and Evaluation of the Long-Range Transmission of Air Pollutants in Europe, 24 *ILM* (1985), 484. In force 28 January 1988.

1985   Convention for the Protection of the Ozone Layer, (Vienna), *UKTS* 1 (1990), Cm. 910; 26 *ILM* (1987), 1529. In force 22 September 1988 (1988 Protocol (q.v.)).

South Pacific Nuclear Free Zone Treaty (Raratonga), 24 *ILM* (1985), 1442. In force 11 December 1986.

Convention for the Protection, Management and Development of the Marine and Coastal Environment of the Eastern African Region (Nairobi); Protocol Concerning Protected Areas and Wild Flora and Fauna in the Eastern African Region; Protocol Concerning Co-operation in Combating Marine Pollution in Cases of Emergency in the Eastern African Region, Burhenne, 385: 46; *ND* (looseleaf) Doc. J. 26. Not in force.

Protocol (to the 1979 Geneva Convention) on the Reduction of Sulphur Emissions, (Helsinki), 27 *ILM* (1988), 707. In force 2 September 1987.

ASEAN Agreement on the Conservation of Nature and Natural Resources (Kuala Lumpur), 15 *EPL* (1985), 64. Not in force.

1986   Single European Act, EC 12 (1986), Cmnd. 9758; *UKTS* 31 (1988), Cm. 372; 25 *ILM* (1986), 506. In force 1 July 1987.

Convention on Early Notification of a Nuclear Accident, (Vienna), Misc. 2 (1989), Cm. 565; 25 *ILM* 1370 (1986), 1370. In force 27 October 1986.

Convention on Assistance in the Case of a Nuclear Accident or Radiological Emergency, (Vienna) Misc. 3 (1989), Cm. 566; 25 *ILM* (1986), 1377. In force 26 February 1987.

Agreement Between Canada and the United States on Transfrontier Movements of Hazardous Waste (Ottawa), *TIAS* 11099.

Convention for the Protection of the Natural Resources and Environment of the South Pacific Region (Noumea); Protocol for the Prevention of Pollution of the South Pacific Region by Dumping; and Protocol Concerning Co-operation in Combating Pollution Emergencies in the South Pacific Region, 26 *ILM* (1987), 38. In force 18 August 1990.

European Convention for the Protection of Vertebrate Animals Used for Experimental and other Scientific Purposes (Strasburg), *ETS* No. 123; Misc. 4 (1986), Cmnd. 9884. Not in force.

1987   European Convention for the Protection of Pet Animals (Strasbourg), *ETS* No. 125. Not in force.

Protocol (to the 1985 Vienna Convention) on Substances that Deplete the Ozone Layer, (Montreal), *UKTS* 19 (1990), Cm. 977; 26 *ILM* (1987), 1550. In force 1 January 1989. Amended 1990, *OJEC* No. C11 (1991), 21.

1988   Convention on the Regulation of Antarctic Mineral Resource Activities (Wellington), Misc. 6 (1989), Cm. 634; 27 *ILM* (1988), 868. Not in force.

Protocol (to the 1979 Geneva Convention) Concerning the Control of Emissions of Nitrogen Oxides or Their Transboundary Fluxes (Sofia), Misc. 16 (1989), Cm. 885; 27 *ILM* (1988), 698. In force 14 February 1991.

Protocol to the 1969 American Convention on Human Rights in the Area of Economic, Social and Cultural Rights (San Salvador), 28 *ILM* (1989), 156. Not in force.

Joint Protocol Relating to the Application of the 1963 Vienna Convention and the 1960 Paris Convention, Misc. 12 (1989), Cm. 774. Not in force.

1989   Convention on the Control of Transboundary Movements of Hazardous Wastes and Their Disposal (Basel), 28 *ILM* (1989), 657. In force 24 May 1992.

International Convention on Salvage (London), IMO/LEG/CONF.7/27 (1989). Not in force.

ILO Convention No. 169 Concerning Indigenous and Tribal Peoples in Independent Countries, 72 *ILO Off. Bull.* 59 (1989); 28 *ILM* (1989), 1382. Not in force.

Convention on Civil Liability for Damage Caused During Carriage of Dangerous Goods by Road, Rail and Inland Navigation Vessels (Geneva). Not in force.

Protocol (to the 1981 Lima Convention) for the Conservation and Managements of Protected Marine and Coastal Areas of the South-East Pacific (Paipa), *ND* (looseleaf), Doc. J. 35. Not in force.

Protocol (to the 1981 Lima Convention) for the Protection of the South-East Pacific Against Radioactive Pollution (Paipa), *ND* (looseleaf), Doc. J. 34. Not in force.

1

International Law and the Environment

1. INTRODUCTION

(1) What is International Environmental Law?

A number of preliminary problems arise in any attempt to identify 'international environmental law'. First, some legal scholars dislike the use of the term 'international environmental law', because they consider that there is no distinct 'environmental' body of law with its own sources and methods of lawmaking deriving from principles peculiar or exclusive to environmental concerns. Rather, such relevant laws as do now exist originate from the application of principles generated by classical international law and its sources, which are considered in the second part of this chapter.[1]

The problem with this approach, as one writer points out, is that 'the traditional legal order of the environment is essentially a *laissez-faire* system oriented toward the unfettered freedom of states. Such limitations on freedom of action as do exist have been formulated from perspectives other than the specifically environmental'[2] and have emerged in an *ad hoc* fashion. None the less, a distinct body of law does now exist for protection of the environment, which we will endeavour to identify in this work. We, therefore, will use the expression 'international environmental law' simply to encompass the corpus of international law relevant to environmental issues, in the same way that use of the terms 'Law of the Sea', 'Human Rights Law', and 'International Economic Law' is widely accepted, without intending thereby to indicate the existence of a new discipline based exclusively on environmental perspectives and strategies, though these play an important role in stimulating legal developments in this field, as we shall establish. It has become common practice to refer to international environmental law in this way.[3]

---

[1] Brownlie, *Principles of Public International Law* (4th edn., Oxford, 1990), for example, has no chapter on this topic and there is no reference to 'environment' in the index.
[2] Schneider, *World Public Order of the Environment: Towards an Ecological Law and Organization* (Toronto, 1979), 30.
[3] See e.g. Kiss and Shelton, *International Environmental Law* (Dordrecht, 1991); Kiss, 2 *Rev. jurid. de l'env.* (1982), 149–53; Teclaff and Utton (eds.), *International Environmental Law* (New York, 1974).

(2) What is Meant by 'the Environment'?

A second problem concerns the meaning of the term 'environment'. Defining this presents important preliminary difficulties. None of the major treaties, declarations, codes of conduct, guidelines, etc. referred to throughout this work attempts directly to define the term. No doubt this is because it is difficult both to identify and to restrict the scope of such an ambiguous term, which could be used to encompass anything from the whole biosphere to the habitat of the smallest creature or organism. Dictionary definitions range from 'something that environs' to 'the whole complex of climatic, edaphic, and biotic factors that act upon an organism or an ecological community and ultimately determine its form or survival; the aggregate of social or cultural conditions that influence the life of an individual or a community'[4] or, simply, 'surroundings; surrounding objects, region or circumstances'.[5] The Declaration of the United Nations Stockholm Conference on the Human Environment (UNCHE) merely refers obliquely to man's environment 'which gives him physical sustenance and affords him the opportunity for intellectual, spiritual, moral and social growth' adding that 'both aspects of man's environment, the natural and the man-made, are essential for his well-being and enjoyment of basic human rights'.[6] The World Commission on Environment and Development (WCED) relies on an even more succinct approach; it remarks that 'the environment is where we all live'.[7] One of the few bodies to proffer a definition is the European Commission, in developing the European Community's Action Programmes on the Environment. It defines the term as 'the combination of elements whose complex inter-relationships make up the settings, the surroundings and the conditions of life of the individual and of society as they are and as they are felt'.[8]

The 1980 Convention on Conservation of Antarctic Marine Living Resources (CCAMLR) does not define the Antarctic environment but does identify both the marine living resources forming part of the Antarctic marine ecosystem to which it applies and defines that ecosystem as 'the complex of relationships of marine living resources with each other and with their physical environment'.[9] Some conventions come close to a definition but only

---

[4] Webster's *New World Dictionary* (3rd College edn., Cleveland, 1988), 454.

[5] *Concise Oxford Dictionary* (5th edn., Oxford, 1972), 406.

[6] Preamble, para. 1, Report of United Nations Conference on the Human Environment 1972, A/CONF. 48/14/Rev. 1 (New York, 1972), 3, and see further *infra*, Ch. 2.

[7] WCED, *Our Common Future* (Oxford, 1987), p. xi. The WCED's Legal Expert Group on Environmental Law did not define the term; see Munro and Lammers, *Environmental Protection and Sustainable Development* (Dordrecht, 1986).

[8] Council Regulation (EEC) No. 1872/84 of 28 June 1984 on Action by the Community Relating to the Environment, OJ L. 176 (1984), 1.

[9] Article 1, paras. 2 and 3.

in order to narrow the term down to fit their particular purposes. The 1988 Convention on the Regulation of Antarctic Mineral Resource Activities (CRAMRA), defines damage to the Antarctic environment or dependent or associated ecosystems, as 'any impact on the living or non-living components of that environment or those ecosystems, including harm to atmospheric, marine or terrestrial life . . .'.[10] But generally even conventions limited to the 'marine environment' avoid defining that term, as is the case in the 1982 United Nations Convention on the Law of the Sea (UNCLOS), although Malta had proposed that the term 'comprises the surface of the sea, the air space above, the water column and the sea-bed beyond the hightide mark including the biosystems therein or dependent thereon'.[11] It seems, however, at least to have been generally understood at the Third UN Law of the Sea Conference that 'marine environment' did include both the atmosphere and marine life.[12] The Ozone Convention defines adverse effects on the environment to include "changes in the physical environment or biota, including changes in climate, which have significant deleterious effects on human health or on the composition, resilience and productivity of natural and managed ecosystems, or on materials useful to mankind'.[13] Most conventions avoid the problem, however, no doubt because, as Caldwell remarks 'it is a term that everyone understands and no one is able to define'.[14]

(3) Environment and Development: What is 'Sustainable Development'?

It was perceived at the time of the Stockholm Conference that progress on environmental protection was inextricably linked, especially for developing states, with progress in economic development.[15] The UNCHE Declaration recognized this need and provided for it in several of its principles. Problems soon emerged, however, because of the political and economic implications of restricting industrial, agricultural, fisheries, and other developmental activities in order to protect the environment from pollution or to conserve resources, and though they continue to arise for all states they do so in an increasingly acute form for developing countries whose incomes are everywhere declining. Their attempts in the 1970s to create a New International Economic Order based on a Charter of Economic Rights and Duties of states were embodied in the UN General Assembly Resolutions considered in Chapter 3 and in the second part of this Chapter, but these made no reference to and took little account of the impacts of development on the environment.

---

[10] *Infra*, p. 100. This convention is unlikely to enter into force.
[11] Nordquist (ed.), *The United Nations Convention on the Law of the Sea: A Commentary* (Dordrecht, 1991), 42–3.
[12] Ibid., and see Article 194(5), and *infra*, Ch. 7.
[13] Article 1, para. 2; see *infra*, p. 100.
[14] Caldwell, *International Environmental Policy and Law* (1st edn., Durham, NC, 1980), 170.
[15] *Development and Environment*, Founex Report (Paris, 1972).

In the 1980s, however, strategies were promulgated which, though primarily aimed at environmental protection, did take account of the need for development whilst recognizing that the environment could not in all cases sustain unlimited development. The International Union for Conservation of Nature's World Conservation Strategy[16] adopted in 1980 was premised on sustainable utilization of species and ecosystems. The World Charter for Nature adopted by the General Assembly in 1982[17] aimed, *inter alia*, at optimal sustainable productivity of all resources coupled with conservation and protection.

In 1987, the World Commission on Environment and Development (WCED) synthesized these aims in pointing to the need to ensure 'sustainable development' and to provide mechanisms to increase international co-operation to this end. It defined 'sustainable development' as 'development that meets the needs of the present without compromising the ability of future generations to meet their own needs'[18] and UNEP has since added that it requires 'the maintenance, rational use and enhancement of the natural resource base that underpins ecological resilience and economic growth' and 'implies progress towards international equity'.[19]

It follows that goals of economic and social development now have to be defined in all states in terms of sustainability.[20] The role of law in achieving sustainable development has been little discussed but is crucial in regulating use of resources and the biosphere. New concepts are emerging such as the inherent rights or interests of future generations, of equitable utilization, and the 'precautionary principle'.[21] The problem of achieving 'sustainable development' is, however, easier to identify than to resolve and is essentially one of negotiating balanced solutions taking account of both developmental and environmental factors in the particular context of the problem in issue, and of the wider environmental impacts of the possible solutions. International law cannot provide the answers to this dilemma but it can, in its constitutional role, provide mechanisms for negotiating the necessary accommodations, settling disputes, and supervising implementation of treaties and customs, and in its regulatory, prescriptive role can embody the necessary protective measures and techniques in conventions, codes, and standards, and provide flexible procedures for amending and updating these as required, in the light of technological developments and advances in scientific and other informa-

---

[16] World Wildlife Fund/United Nations Environment Programme/IUCN (Gland, 1980), on which, see *infra*, Ch. 11. The Strategy has now been revised and published as *Caring for the Earth: A Strategy for Sustainable Living* (London, 1991), stressing the need for sustainable development.

[17] UNGA Res. 37/7, 9 Nov. 1982, 22 *ILM* (1983), 455.

[18] WCED, *Our Common Future*, 43; see also 43–65.

[19] UNEP Governing Council Decision 15/2 of May 1989, Annex II, GAOR, 44th Session Suppl. No. 25 (A/44/25).

[20] But see Handl, 1 *YIEL* (1991), 24–8.

[21] See Munro and Lammers, *Environmental Protection* for further examples, and see *infra*, Chs. 3 and 5.

tion. As this work illustrates, active use has been made of international law in both these ways. Moreover, international law can also be used to secure harmonization and development of national environmental law, facilitate compensation for environmental damage, and provide for offences, penalties and other sanctions to be employed under national law against individuals and companies whose activities are harmful to the environment. International organizations of all kinds—the UN and its specialized agencies, global and regional bodies of all forms, and numerous *ad hoc* commissions—now provide forums for this process of lawmaking and a broad regulatory framework has been developed. The International Maritime Organisation's (IMO) conventions, codes, and guidelines provide good examples of accommodation of economic and environmental interests, as do the many fishery commissions and their constitutive conventions. The 1982 UNCLOS provides a framework for these in requiring that maximum sustainable yield of stocks be maintained but allowing this to be qualified by environmental and economic factors, including the economic needs of coastal fishing communities and the special requirements of developing states, as well as various ecological considerations.[22] None the less, this goal is proving difficult to attain in practice, even for the developed states that form the European Community.[23]

Sustainable development is a seductively simple concept, basic to human survival and, though it cannot yet be said to be a norm of international law, as one leading commentator has pointed out 'it is a notion around which legally significant expectations regarding environmental conduct have begun to crystallise'[24] and which he considers might in time even become a peremptory norm of international law (*jus cogens*). The problems of its content, however, will remain.

In an endeavour to find solutions to the complex problems of securing sustainable development in a wide spectrum of environmental issues, a United Nations Conference on Environment and Development (UNCED)[25] was convened in 1992. Its Preparatory Commission attempted to identify both the problems and the solutions in relation to virtually every aspect of the environment on which developmental progress adversely impacts, to identify and evaluate, *inter alia*, the role being played by international law in this process, and to strengthen and develop it further. It was originally planned to conclude

---

[22] United Nations Convention on the Law of the Sea (New York, 1983), Article 61, paras. 3 and 4; see also FAO Doc. COFI/91/3, Feb. 1991, *Environment and Sustainability in Fisheries*; Elder, *Sustainable Use of Marine Resources*, Law of the Sea Institute, *Proceeding of the 25th Annual Conference* (Malmo, 1991) publication forthcoming.

[23] Churchill, *Fisheries in the European Community: Sustainable Development or Sustained Mismanagement*, Law of the Sea Institute Proceedings, supra n. 72.

[24] Handl, 1 *YIEL* (1991), 25. See further, *infra*, 122–4.

[25] Preparations for the United Nations Conference on Environment and Development on the Basis of General Assembly Resolution 44/228: *Report of the Secretary General of the Conference*, UNCED Prep. Com. Doc. A/Conf. 151/PC/5, 28 June 1990.

several new conventions relating to key issues on which currently no global convention exists—climate change, bio-diversity, and land-based sources of pollution—and to promulgate an 'Earth Charter'. UNCED also aimed to improve co-ordination between the many organizations (see Chapter 2) whose roles and programmes conflict or overlap in areas where sustainable development is required.

But even before the conference opened, the range and complexity of the economic and social problems involved in achieving these goals proved virtually insurmountable.[26] It is questionable whether international law can do more than provide certain general principles and frameworks at this stage, given the developmental concerns of developing states. However, as we shall see, international law has played a dynamic role in developing environmental protection, despite the political, social, and economic problems inherent in this field, and will continue to do so in the future, whether or not further conventions are concluded.[27] A particularly important role in the context of sustainable development is that international law, if supported by consensus among states concerned in a particular issue, can facilitate equitable distribution of the economic and other benefits and burdens of regulation and ensure parity of sacrifice among those states, as in IMO conventions.

(4) Developmental Concerns: Is there a 'Common Future' for Developed and Developing States?

It will not be possible to use this formidable array of techniques to address some of the remaining problems, however, unless new ways are found of facilitating the participation of developing states in the regulatory process. The Brundtland Commission assumed a 'common future' for all states which could be arrived at through achievement of sustainable development. The divisions emerging at UNCED, however, call this assumption into question. Whereas many Western states, including the European Community, now support further environmental controls, developing states accord priority to development and have made it clear in the UNCED Preparatory Commission that they are not prepared to accept further environmental controls, without such financial assistance and transfer of technology as is necessary to offset the economic restrictions otherwise involved.

Some steps have been taken in this direction through the institution of a Global Environmental Facility by the World Bank and the provision of financial assistance under Protocols to the Ozone and Wetlands Conventions and the Convention on Protection of the Marine Environment of the

---

[26] 11 *Network '92* (Oct. 1991), 1; *Ocean Policy News* (Oct. 1991), 1–6.
[27] For a good résumé of the role of International Environmental Law in this field, see Sand, *Lessons Learned in Global Environmental Governance* (Washington, DC, 1990).

Mediterranean (see Chapters 2, 10, and 12), but these fall far short of what is demanded by developing states, which are, therefore, beginning to formulate law-making strategies of their own. Some, for example, propose that charges should be levied for use by developed states of the biological resources (including flora and tropical forests), located in developing states. It is notable that generally fewer developing states become signatories or parties to environmental treaties. One exception is the 1982 UNCLOS to which far more developing states have become signatories and which has been ratified, with only one exception, exclusively by developing states because of its perceived economic benefits. Not only do these states expect to benefit from the internationalized exploitation of deep sea-bed resources but from the new sovereign rights over the resources of the Exclusive Economic Zone and from the opportunity this provides for extracting financial, economic, social, and technological concessions from developed states in return for access to those living and non-living resources.

(5) Is there a Common International Environmental Law?

One must ask whether in the context of a world community as diverse in interests and economic development as that which now exists, there can be a global environmental law that protects the interests of all states, or even the interest states have in common. Areas of international commons have diminished as national jurisdiction has been extended over vast areas of ocean; few developing states are numbered among the Consultative Parties of the Antarctic Treaty or are even party to it and its related treaties; no developing states participate as such in the use of outer space. There do, however, remain many issues of common interest—the need to ensure wise and equitable use of living and non-living resources, which requires avoidance of over exploitation of the former and over-rapid or wasteful depletion of the latter; to preserve wildlife that crosses boundaries and which can, therefore, be captured or enjoyed in more than one state, whether developed or developing, and whether on land, in the sea or in the air; to maintain freedom of navigation and protect the marine environment from all sources of pollution; to ensure equitable use of rivers that flow through more than one state; and to preserve the climate and atmosphere that sustain life itself, to mention but a few of the shared concerns addressed in this work. But greater involvement of developing states in conventions or codes concerning these issues, or in active implementation of conventions, such as UNEP's Regional Seas Conventions (Chapter 7), to which they are party, is likely to be dependent on further financial and technical and technological inducements or stimulation of greater public awareness in such states of their common interest in shared resources and surroundings and of the threats posed by environmental degradation, or over-exploitation, or both.

(6) Does Existing International Law Protect the Environment?

This is obviously an important question to which there is no easy or single answer. As this work will indicate, in some cases the measures developed are inadequate in scope or in application or in enforcement—as in the case of UNEP's regional seas conventions (Chapter 7), in measures taken under many fisheries conventions and in many national maritime zones (Chapter 13), or in the enforcement of wildlife conventions (Chapter 12). In others some success can be recorded, as with the London Dumping Convention (Chapter 8).

International environmental law is at a very early stage of development and has evolved at a time when the heterogeneity of the international community has rapidly intensified and when, simultaneously, economic problems have correspondingly increased and the developmental needs and aspirations of the poorer states have accordingly become urgent. Given these problems, the progress made in developing a body of international law with a purely environmental focus is, in our view, a remarkable achievement despite the strains the rapidity of developments has imposed on the international legislative process.[28] As far as measuring the effectiveness of these regimes is concerned much depends on the criteria used; effectiveness has multiple meanings: it may mean solving the problem for which the regime was established (for example, avoiding further depletion of the ozone layer); achievement of goals set out in the constitutive instrument (for example, attaining a set percentage of sulphur emissions); altering behaviour patterns (for example, moving from use of fossil fuels to solar or wind energy production); enhancing national compliance with rules in international agreements, such as those restricting trade in endangered species.[29] Effectiveness is largely determined by the nature of the problem at which the solution is directed. This is in large part due to the flexibility of international law-making processes, of which considerable advantage has been taken, and their ability to incorporate new concepts and techniques.[30] It has been pointed out, however, that sustainable development evinces a strictly utilitarian, non-preservationist view of environmental protection,[31] which is likely to inhibit the scope for further development of a truly 'environmental' legal system.

---

[28] Handl, 1 *YIEL* (1991), 3.

[29] Young, Demko, and Ramakrishna, *Global Environmental Change and International Governance* (Dartmouth, 1991), Summary and Recommendations of a Conference held at Dartmouth College, Hanover, NH., June 1991, at 8–9 and *passim*.

[30] For examples of innovatory techniques used in standard setting and implementation now developed, see Sand, *Lessons*, 5–20 and 21–34 respectively.

[31] Handl, 1 *YIEL* (1991), 24.

2. SOURCES OF INTERNATIONAL LAW IN AN ENVIRONMENTAL PERSPECTIVE

Crucial to an assessment of the current state of international environmental law is an understanding of the sources from which it derives. Since international environmental law can be assumed to be the aggregate of all the rules and principles aimed at protecting the global environment and controlling activities within national jurisdiction that may affect another state's environment or areas beyond national jurisdiction, it involves questions of sovereignty, jurisdiction, regulation, and state responsibility and liability.[32] It can also involve individuals' responsibility under municipal laws and decisions of national courts. We are, however, primarily concerned here with international law sources. These, of course, are the same as those from which all international law emanates, since environmental law is no more, or less, than a specialized branch of that general law. But it can be said, as this chapter will illustrate, that environmental law is particularly rich in illustrations of both the problems posed by taking a narrow view of the traditional sources of international law and of the solutions adopted in what is increasingly being referred to as a divided[33] or a multicultural world,[34] or both. Indeed, given the vast increase in the number of states, from fifty to about 170, since the establishment of the United Nations in 1945, the emergence of new states in Eastern Europe, and the diversity of political, racial, and religious systems as well as of relative size and strength, it has been asked whether it is even possible to maintain the proposition that any universal international law can exist in modern international society,[35] and if so what is now the nature and content of such law, and how, and by what techniques, we now identify this.[36] It is now well established and widely accepted that newly independent states have to take the previously Eurocentric international law as they find it but that they can then seek to change and influence its development. This they have done, successfully ensuring that international environmental law has taken account of their developmental interests from the time of the 1972 United Nations Conference on the Human Environment and its Declaration

---

[32] Brazil, 'International Environmental Law', *Australian IL News* (1985), 315–26.
[33] Cassese, *International Law in a Divided World* (Oxford, 1986), esp. 171–99.
[34] Dupuy (ed.), *The Future of International Law in a Multicultural World* (The Hague, 1984); Mosler, in TMC Asser Institute (ed.), *International Law and the Grotian Heritage* (The Hague, 1985), 173–85; Dinstein, *NYJIL and Pol.* (1986–7), 1–32; Friedman, *The Changing Structure of International Law* (1964), 121–3.
[35] Green, 23 *CYIL* (1985), 3–32; Jennings, in Bos and Brownlie (eds.), *Liber Amicorum for Lord Wilberforce* (Oxford, 1987), 187–97.
[36] Jennings, 37 *Ann. Suisse DDI* (1981), 59–88.

of Principles (UNCHE) onwards.[37] Their influence is increasingly apparent in the development of new strategies and approaches to the evolution of international environmental law today.

There has been increasing recognition of the need to protect the global environment as a whole and in particular to lay down new principles and rules to govern certain priority issues, such as preventing marine pollution by oil and toxic discharges and dumping; controlling emission of gases that damage the ozone layer; regulating the transboundary movement of hazardous wastes; and preserving endangered species, and of ensuring that these rules can be readily amended as knowledge develops and situations change. This has required that international law be developed more quickly, in a more flexible manner than in the past, and that it adopts new concepts and principles, recognizing the interdependence of both the ecosystems of which the global environment consists and of the international community of states itself in relation to preservation on a sustainable basis. The framework of environmental treaties, principles, and codes that has been developed in the last twenty years reflects these imperatives but there is increasing resort to a so-called 'soft' law[38] approach, either through the use of framework or 'umbrella' treaties or of non-binding declarations, codes, guidelines, or recommended principles, as we shall see.

This does not, of course, mean that traditional sources are not also used and before examining the 'soft' approach, we must first identify these traditional sources, which produce the so-called 'hard' law, and the extent to which these have been both used and adapted for environmental purposes. We will then consider the forms and uses of the 'soft' approach, whether it can ever be transformed into 'hard' law and, if so, the extent to which this has happened or is happening today, and, finally, whether 'soft' law is itself a new vehicle for development of customary international environmental law.

(1) Traditional Sources[39]

Treaties and custom have historically been the main methods of creating binding international law. These were favoured by states supporting the

---

[37] 1972 Stockholm Declaration, n. 6, and see further, Ch. 2.

[38] For general discussion of 'soft Law', see Gruchalla-Wesierski, 30 *McGill LJ* (1984), 37; Chinkin, 38 *ICLQ* (1989), 850; Bothe, 11 *NYIL* (1980), 65; Tammes, in *Essays on International and Comparative Law in Honour of Judge Erades* (The Hague, 1983), 187–95; Seidl-Hohenveldern, 163 *Rec. des cours* (1980), 164; Sonio, 28 *Jap. Ann. IL* (1985), 47; Riphagen, 17 *VUWLR* (1987), 81. Notably more has been written about 'soft law' in an economic than in an environmental law context. See further, *infra*, pp. 26–30, and Baxter, 29 *ICLQ* (1980), 549–65.

[39] For a good succinct account of sources, a discussion of the term itself, and analysis of Article 38 of the ICJ Statute, see Brownlie, *Principles of Public International Law*, 1–31; see also Parry, *The Sources and Evidences of International Law* (Manchester, 1965); for an Eastern European view, see Danilenko, in Butler (ed.), *Perestroika and International Law* (Dordrecht, 1990), 61,

'positivist' approach to international law which postulated that states could not be bound without the clear expression of their consent. However, these sources were augmented in 1920 in the Statute of the Permanent Court of International Justice, subsequently replicated in Article 38(1) of the Statute of the International Court of Justice (ICJ).[40] Though this article was drafted before the rapid growth in the number and diversity of states or the emergence of environmental consciousness, it lays down the generally accepted sources of international law to be applied by the ICJ, namely, international conventions (treaties), whether general or particular; international custom; general principles of law; and, as secondary sources, judicial decisions and the teachings of the most highly qualified publicists. These sources have been shown to have both advantages and disadvantages as a basis for developing international law.

Questions, of course, remain concerning whether these sources are exhaustive of the possible sources of law and we must, therefore, also examine other candidates that have been suggested from time to time such as General Assembly Resolutions, treaty provisions arrived at by general consensus among the majority of states, specific Declarations of Principles adopted by the UN or by *ad hoc* UN and other conferences, and the proposals of the International Law Commission. Many commentators consider, however, that these have to be embodied in treaties or custom before they become binding on states. It should also be noted at the outset that there is a dearth of judicial decisions on contentious issues of international law, and very few which directly raise environmental issues. One consequence is that commentators tend to place too much reliance on those cases that do exist.

(a) Treaties[41]

Treaties are now the most frequent method of creating binding international rules relating to the environment.[42] Essentially they are agreements in whatever form between states, or between states and international organizations, governed by international law. They can be called by a variety of names, including treaty, convention, protocol, covenant, pact, act, etc. There are no

which recognizes the need for more rapid generation of new international legal norms in a changing international society but none the less concludes that these changes have not resulted in a reform of constitutional principles governing lawmaking. For more detailed discussion, see Cassese, *International Law, passim*; Macdonald and Johnston (eds.), *The Structure and Process of International Law* (Dordrecht, 1983); see also van Hoof, *Rethinking the Sources of International Law* (Deventer, 1983).

[40] Text in Brownlie, *Basic Documents in International Law* (3rd edn., Oxford, 1983).

[41] See generally Brownlie, *Principles of Public International Law*, 603–835; McNair, *Law of Treaties* (London, 1961); Sinclair, *The Vienna Convention on Treaties* (2nd edn., Manchester, 1984); van Hoof, *Rethinking the Sources*, 185–92, esp. on 'The "New" Law', 189–91; Reuter, *Introduction to the Law of Treaties* (London, 1989).

[42] Socialist and developing countries particularly favour this method according to Tunkin, 24 *Ind. JIL* (1984), 24.

rules prescribing their form but the 1969 Vienna Convention on the Law of Treaties[43] lays down rules for treaties concluded after the date of its entry into force in 1980, on such matters as entry into force, reservations, interpretation, termination, and invalidity. States which sign a treaty are expected, pending ratification, not to do anything that undermines its objects and purposes. Unless they specifically agree to be bound by signature, it is not until states have formally deposited their instrument of ratification (which generally requires approval by national parliamentary or other internal processes) and any other requirements for entry into force have been fulfilled (for example, a specific number of ratifications or ratification by certain named states), that the treaty enters into force and becomes binding on its parties on the basis of the underlying principle of customary law that *pacta sunt servanda* (treaties are made to be kept). The treaty-making process is thus generally somewhat slow and delays frequently occur before a treaty enters into force. This is not always the case, however; the rapid entry into force of the 1985 Vienna Convention for Protection of the Ozone Layer and its Montreal Protocol indicates that multilateral treaties can provide an efficient means of urgent global or regional law-making when necessary.

Some agreements are executed in a simplified form, by exchange of notes or letters, and become binding on signature without need for reference to parliaments; others may be concluded at the administrative level in the form of Memoranda of Understanding (MOU).[44] They can be much more quickly concluded to deal with urgent issues.

Though treaties do not *ipso facto* bind third states they can do so if they clearly express an intent that their benefits or obligations may do so and the state concerned expressly accepts this; in the case of obligations this must be done in writing. Certain provisions may also, of course, affect other states or may become part of customary international law by the processes described in the following section. To be capable of so doing the ICJ has ruled in the *North Sea Case Continental Case* that: 'It would in the first place be necessary that the provision concerned should, at all events potentially, be of a fundamentally norm-creating character such as could be regarded as forming the basis of a general rule of law.'[45]

This would potentially include a number of general environmental principles, such as those laid down in the 1982 UNCLOS, which are increasingly incorporated into regional treaties and state practice, but is less likely to apply to such highly specific requirements as those prescribed in the Protocols to the 1979 Geneva Convention on Long-Range Transboundary Air Pollution

---

[43] Whilst not all provisions of this convention have attained the status of customary law, all are of great significance and influence. See further Sinclair, *Vienna Convention*.

[44] Aust, 35 *ICLQ* (1986), 787–812; 1982 Paris Memorandum on Port state Control, *infra*, 270.

[45] *ICJ Rep.* (1969), 3, para. 72.

concerning, *inter alia*, sulphur dioxide emissions.[46] It is common practice, moreover, to separate such technical standards from the basic provisions of the treaty, in order to allow for ease of amendment in the light of technical or scientific experience. They will instead usually be found in protocols or annexes, as in most marine pollution conventions, or in schedules, as in the 1946 International Convention for the Regulation of Whaling (ICRW).[47] The provisions of protocols or annexes of this kind are not always binding on all the parties to a treaty; in many cases states are free to opt out by objecting within an appropriate time after adoption or subsequently.[48] Thus it should not be assumed that every treaty provision is capable of transformation into customary law, even if widely followed.

Treaties do not necessarily lay down clear, detailed, or specific rules capable of being instantly enacted into municipal law; sometimes they are no more than a 'framework', laying down only very general requirements for states 'to take measures' or enact 'all practicable measures', as do the UNEP regional seas treaties or the 1979 Convention on Long-Range Transboundary Air Pollution.[49] These require further action by states to prescribe the precise measures to be taken, which can include concluding more specific conventions, adding protocols to existing conventions, or enacting national legislation. Treaties can also be concluded in the form of an 'umbrella' instrument consisting of a framework convention linked to one or more protocols dealing with specific issues. The 1976 Barcelona Convention on Protection of the Mediterranean Sea, for example, requires states to ratify at least one of its accompanying protocols on co-operation in combating oil spills, dumping of wastes, protection of the marine environment from landbased sources of pollution, or protection of specially sensitive areas. Another example of the "framework" approach is the 1979 Bonn Convention on Conservation of Migratory Species of Wild Animals which requires *inter alia* conclusion of agreements between 'Range states' and the listing of species on its appendices for its effective operation.[50]

The 1969 Vienna Convention on the Law of Treaties liberalized treaty-making in a number of ways. In particular, it upheld the 'universality of treaties' in relation to its rules on reservations.[51] Unless a treaty effectively prohibits reservations, such as the 1982 UNCLOS,[52] or permits only certain kinds of reservations, as does the 1946 International Convention for the Regulation of Whaling, any state may make a reservation that is not incompatible with the treaty's objects and purposes even if the treaty does not specifically permit reservations. The treaty enters into force between the state making the reservation and any other states parties that have not objected to it

---

[46] See Ch. 10.   [47] See Chs. 7, 8, 12, and 13.
[48] Contini and Sand, 66 *AJIL* (1972), 41 and 49.
[49] See Chs. 7, 8, and 10, and on the principle of due diligence, 92–4.
[50] See Ch. 12, 70–5.   [51] Articles 19–23.   [52] Articles 309–10.

doing so, though the effect of the reservation itself will vary according to the response of other parties.[53] The possibility of making reservations encourages wider participation in treaties; it is partly their impermissibility under the 1982 UNCLOS (albeit for good and specific reasons) that has so far prevented this treaty achieving the sixty ratifications required for entry into force. On the other hand, reservations, especially in the form of 'objection procedures' permitting parties to opt out of amendable regulations, also undermine the effectiveness of treaties, by enabling states to protect their economic and other interests. This weakness is especially pertinent to environmental protection treaties; states can and do opt out of stricter controls negotiated under the 1973 Convention on Trade in Endangered Species (CITES) and the ICRW, for example.[54]

So far as interpretation of treaties is concerned, the Vienna Convention's provisions[55] include all three major schools of thought on the subject—the literal, the 'effective', and the teleological approaches.[56] Thus, the ordinary meaning of the words to be interpreted must first be sought but in their broad context in the convention. The interpretation must be compatible with the objects and purposes of the convention, which means that an interpretation must be adopted, so far as is possible, which makes the convention effective, a particularly valuable rule in the case of treaties with environmental objectives. Lastly, if the wording is ambiguous, recourse may be had to the *travaux préparatoires* (preparatory documents) to verify the interpretation derived from the above processes.

The 1969 Vienna Convention also recognized in the controversial concept of *jus cogens* the notion that there are certain basic norms of international law which represent such fundamental values that no state can opt out of their observance.[57] The Convention does not, however, give any indication as to what these norms might now be: the obligation to preserve the environment might be one, following its enunciation in the UNCHE Declaration and its manifestation in numerous treaties, strategies, declarations, and resolutions of the General Assembly and other international bodies and conferences. Some writers go so far as to suggest that a right to a clean and healthy environment is another such principle, though this is less well supported by the necessary evidence of acceptance by the international community of states as a whole. The significance of *jus cogens* is further considered in Chapter 4.

---

[53] For a clear explanation of this complex problem, see Brownlie, *Principles of Public International Law*, 608–10; *Reservations to the Genocide Convention Case*, *ICJ Rep.* (1951), 15; *Anglo-French Continental Shelf* Arbitration *Case* (1978), Cmnd. 7438, at 32–50; and Bowett, 48 *BYIL* (1977), 67.

[54] See Ch. 12.

[55] Articles 31–3.

[56] Sinclair, *Vienna Convention*, 114–58.

[57] Articles 53, 64, 71; Brownlie, *Principles of Public International Law*, 512–15.

(b) Custom[58]

Although treaties are the most frequently used method of international environmental law-making, some writers consider that states may prefer customary law-making for a number of reasons. The burdensome procedures of treaty ratification are absent, and customary rules may more easily acquire universal application, since acquiescence will often be enough to ensure that 'the inactive are carried along by the active',[59] a particular advantage in environmental matters. The introduction of new concepts into environmental law, such as 'inter-generational equity', 'common concern', 'common heritage', 'sustainable development', and others referred to later, exemplify the attempts of conservationist states and NGOs to use this form of customary law-making in order to advance changes in the nature and scope of national sovereignty as regards protection of the environment and the exploitation of natural resources.[60] On the other hand, however, many states, including those which accord particular priority to developmental issues, tend to emphasize their own sovereignty, and the importance of persistent objection in preventing the crystallization and application of particular customary rules to the objecting state.[61] Although most writers consider that it is not necessary for a state to have expressly or impliedly consented to a rule of customary law that *has* crystallized as such in order to be bound by it, the creation of new customary rules does in the end depend on some form of consent, whether express or implied, and this remains a limitation of some importance on the use of customary law. Moreover, it is often difficult to determine whether or not a new custom has crystallized into international law, and, if so, at what point. Thus the identification of customary law always has been, and remains, particularly problematical, requiring the exercise of skill, judgment, and considerable research.

Article 38(1) of the ICJ Statute instructs the Court to apply 'international custom, as evidence of a general practice accepted as law'. This formulation is often criticized on the ground that it inverts the actual process whereby state practice supported by *opinio juris* (the conviction that conduct is motivated by a sense of legal obligation, not merely of comity) provides the evidence necessary to establish a customary rule. Thus, in a recent case, the ICJ observed that it was 'axiomatic that the material of customary international law is to be looked for primarily in the actual practice and *opinio juris* of states'.[62] Both conduct and conviction on the part of the state are thus required before

---

[58] Brownlie, *Principles of Public International Law*, 4–11; Akehurst, 43 *BYIL* (1974–5), 1–53; Meijers, 9 *NYIL* (1978), 3–26.

[59] Meijers, 9 *NYIL* (1978), 4.

[60] Handl, 1 *YIEL* (1991), 31.

[61] See Brownlie, *Principles of Public International Law*, 10–12; Charney, 56 *BYIL* (1985), 1–24.

[62] *Libya–Malta Continental Shelf Case*, *ICJ Rep.* (1985), 29–30.

it can be said that a custom has become law; in the absence of any clear statement of intent, as is generally the case, state practice must be examined for evidence of the underlying consent. At least there must be evidence of both an objective element and a subjective (psychological) element before it can be said that the custom has formed and become binding whether universally, regionally, or as between particular states involved in its formation.

It is, however, becoming increasingly difficult, in a world of over 170 states of diverse cultures, policies, interests, and legal systems to identify any universal practice. Their approaches and aims are difficult to reconcile even on questions of general principle, let alone specific details of policy. Even without these new problems, customary law in most cases takes a considerable time both to crystallize and therefore to change. Nowadays, deciding what has crystallized into custom involves examination not only of states' authoritative statements, unilateral and multilateral declarations, legislative and other acts, court decisions and actions in international organizations relevant to particular issues, but also their policies and conduct in the numerous other international forums created this century. These include the United Nations and its fifteen specialized agencies, amongst which we must especially mention for our purposes, the International Maritime Organisation (IMO), the Food and Agriculture Organization (FAO), the World Health Organization (WHO), United Nations Educational, Scientific, and Cultural Organization (Unesco), and the International Atomic Energy Agency (IAEA). Some of these, for certain limited purposes, can take binding as well as non-binding decisions. Also relevant are *ad hoc* bodies such as the United Nations Environment Programme (UNEP); regional pollution prevention commissions; fisheries commissions, established both under the auspices of the FAO and *ad hoc*; numerous wildlife protection bodies established by specific treaties; and the many international conferences, convened both by UN or other agencies and interested governments, at the global, regional, subregional, and bilateral levels.[63] These bodies produce a wide variety of instruments, ranging from treaties, some of which never enter into force, through executive agreements, to Codes of Practice, Recommendations, Guidelines, Standards and Declarations of Principles, generally adopted in the form of resolutions that are not *per se* or *ab initio* binding.

None of these instruments fits neatly into any of the established sources referred to in Article 38(1) of the ICJ Statute. They are often referred to as 'soft law', as opposed to the binding 'hard law' represented by custom, treaty, and established general principles of law. Though the term is misleading in that soft law instruments are not *per se* 'law', it is a convenient term for describing the sometimes *de lege ferenda* status of such instruments and we shall, therefore, use it in that sense in our discussion later in this chapter. It

---

[63] See further, Ch. 2.

will suffice to note at this point that in as novel, rapidly developing, and uncertain a field as international environmental law, 'soft law' is much used, both pending the development of 'hard law' and because it has certain inherent advantages. Agreement on 'hard law' may require a degree of scientific certainty concerning the precise need for action (or precautionary action) on problems such as depletion of living resources, 'acid rain', or climate change that has in some cases been difficult to achieve. It has been pertinently remarked that deciding which of these vehicles has crystallized into customary law is in many areas not just a matter of inquiry but of policy choice, a consideration of great importance in the development of environmental law.[64] It has also been pointed out that 'although the acts of states on the real-world stage often clash, the resultant accommodations have an enduring and authoritative quality because they manifest the latent stability of the system' and that 'the role of *opinio juris* in this process is simply to identify which acts out of many have legal consequence'.[65] As illustrated throughout this work, because of the socio-economic implications of many environmental questions, states' interests frequently clash, but none the less in the common interest of protecting whatever aspect of the environment is involved, accommodation has been arrived at on most issues, sometimes expressed in treaties, sometimes in new customary law, sometimes through adoption of new principles or 'soft law' codes.

Most, but not all, lawyers now agree that we should not take too narrow a view of what constitutes state practice for the purpose of identifying customary law.[66] The ICJ itself has taken account, *inter alia*, of unilateral declarations, such as the Truman Proclamation on the Continental Shelf,[67] France's declaration that it would not conduct further nuclear tests,[68] and the consensus achieved at the Third United Nations Conference on the Law of the Sea (coupled with subsequent practice based thereon).[69] An interesting recent example concerns the status of the joint Ministerial Declarations adopted at the end of the series of conferences held on the protection of the North Sea. After remarking that the status of such declarations is a controversial issue, Van der Mensbrugghe[70] concludes that these North Sea Declarations are not legally binding instruments: non-compliance does not entail international responsibility or resort to judicial tribunals. But they do have to be carried out in good faith and they may have legal significance in that policies adopted therein may later be cast in legal form at the appropriate national, regional, or

---

[64] Jennings, 37 *Ann. suisse DDI* (1981), 67.

[65] D'Amato, 81 *AJIL* (1987), 102.

[66] See the résumé of views in Akehurst, 43 *BYIL* (1974–5), 1–11.

[67] *North Sea Continental Shelf Case*, *ICJ Rep.* (1969), 32–3, 47, 53; text of Proclamation in 40 *AJIL* (1946), Suppl., 45.

[68] *Nuclear Tests Cases*, *ICJ Rep.* (1974), 253, 267, *et seq.*

[69] *Libya–Malta Continental Shelf Case*, *ICJ Rep.* (1985).

[70] Van der Mensbrugghe, 5 *IJECL* (1990), 15–22.

international level. They may also give rise to estoppel and negate the argument that the issues are of purely domestic concern. One can only agree with his conclusion that the proliferation of instruments of this kind, which is especially remarkable in the environmental field, 'creates a rather confused situation that impairs the normativity of rules'.[71]

The *PCIJ* took account of omissions to act,[72] and more recently, the ICJ has relied on the practice of organs of international organizations, composed of state representatives, and of the UN Secretariat itself.[73] The acts of individuals are more difficult to categorize in the custom-creating process. Here it is more a question of states' reaction to acts of their nationals— whether they approve or authorize them or reject or prosecute them—that is significant. Thus though individuals may form non-governmental pressure groups, such as Greenpeace, the Sierra Club, Friends of the Earth, or the World Wide Fund for Nature, that actively campaign for development of or change in the law to protect the environment, and often with some political success—as in the case of suspension of ocean dumping of low-level radioactive waste (see Chapter 8) or the cessation of trade in ivory derived from elephants (see Chapter 13)—it is the adoption of their proposals by states or the significance attributed to them by international courts that is determinative.

Another point of significance to the development of international environmental law is that the ICJ, in the *Nicaragua* case, reiterated that 'the shared view of the parties as to the content of what they regard as the rule is not enough. The Court must satisfy itself that the existence of the rule in the *opinio juris* of states is confirmed by practice'.[74] However, it added that it is not expected that practice be perfectly consistent or conform rigorously to the rule in issue in order to establish its customary status, though inconsistent conduct must have been treated by the states concerned as a breach of that rule, not as an indication of a new rule. Attempts to justify inconsistent conduct as a legitimate exception to the rule serve, on this view, merely to confirm it. This case also recognized that the embodiment of a rule in a treaty (in this case the UN Charter) does not replace its continued existence as a rule of customary international law or prevent its continued development.[75]

Finally, it should be observed that the attempts of the International Law Commission to codify international law are generally regarded as providing evidence of what the existing law is. Thus its reports on the Law of the Sea, on water resources, and, most recently, on state responsibility and liability are much relied upon by writers, as illustrated especially in Chapters 4 and 6.

---

[71] Van der Mensbrugghe 5, *IJECL* (1990), 21.
[72] *Lotus Case, PCIJ*, Ser. A, No. 10 (1927), 28.
[73] *Nottebohm Case, ICJ Rep.* (1955), 4; *Paramilitary Activities in Nicaragua Case* (Merits), *ICJ Rep.* (1986), 14, 98.
[74] *Nicaragua Case, ICJ Rep.* (1986), paras. 184–6.
[75] *Ibid.* 92–6, paras. 174–9.

(c) Status of UN General Assembly Resolutions and Declarations

Ascertaining the *opinio juris* necessary for the creation of customary law remains a problem, given the variety of manifestations of state conduct from which it may be inferred and of forums in which states' views may be expressed. There has been long-standing disagreement and debate concerning the possibility of resort to resolutions of autonomous international bodies, especially of the United Nations, as instruments for international law-making, and in particular as proof of the *opinio juris* of states. Since membership of the UN now comprises most states constituting the international community, resolutions of the General Assembly may be said to be generally representative of world opinion. Three problems arise, however, in according binding status to such resolutions. First, except in relation to a few special issues,[76] Article 10 of the UN Charter gives the Assembly power only to make recommendations—it has no *prima facie* legislative power. Secondly, resolutions can be adopted by simple or weighted (three-quarters) majority vote according to whether they relate to procedural or substantive matters respectively—unanimity is not required. Thirdly, a practice has grown up of adopting resolutions by consensus, without resort to any vote at all: the President asks whether any state has any objections to the proposed resolution, and, none being voiced, the President (often after allowing further time to attempt to negotiate a consensus), declares the resolution adopted by consensus. States are not expected to raise any objections unless they are vital to their interests (there is strong psychological pressure on them not to do so if the vast majority support the resolution). Some states may nevertheless retain serious reservations to such resolutions, which, though they do not express them at that point, may be expressed before or after their formal adoption. Care thus has to be taken, in evaluating the legal status of resolutions, to ascertain the views of states as revealed in their statements before or after the adoption of the resolution, even in relation to resolutions that have achieved apparent consensus.

Despite these reservations, however, it has to be acknowledged that though resolutions are not *per se* binding, they may become so in the light of the subsequent conduct of states. It is a matter of controversy whether the resolution itself provides the *opinio juris* for a custom which, taken with the *subsequent* practice of states, constitutes the binding obligation, or whether the opinions expressed in the debate and the support expressed by voting for or abstaining on the resolution are evidence of *opinio juris*. Although many lawyers continue to maintain that resolutions *per se*, without clear subsequent state practice evidencing *opinio juris*, can never be regarded as part of

---

[76] e.g. the UN budget, Article 17; establishment of subsidiary organs, Article 22.

customary law,[77] others hold the opposite view[78] or position themselves in between saying that unanimously supported resolutions create strong expectations of conforming conduct and that by these means the votes and views of states in international organizations come to have some legal significance, especially when resolutions are repeated or acquiesced in by a large number of states with sufficient frequency.[79]

None the less, in the *Nicaragua* case, the ICJ concluded, in the context of the obligation not to use force, that *opinio juris* may, 'though with all due caution', be deduced from, *inter alia*, the attitude of the parties and states towards certain General Assembly resolutions and, in particular, from a resolution adopted without a vote and expressed in the form of a Declaration of Principles according to the UN Charter.[80] Consent to such a resolution expressed in the Court's view not merely consent to the reiteration of the treaty commitment laid down in the Charter but represented acceptance of the validity of the rules concerned, separately from the relevant Charter provisions. It is thus possible for a rule or principle of customary law, embodied in a treaty, such as the UN Charter, to be different in its precise content and not subject to all the constraints concerning its application that are prescribed in the treaty. On this view the attitudes of states expressed in the debates of the UN or other international bodies and their voting on resolutions (including their abstention) may be regarded as constituting the *opinio juris* required to confirm the customary rule as set out in the Resolution or Declaration. The validity in customary international law of the rule concerned in the *Nicaragua* case was further confirmed by the fact that states had frequently referred to it as a fundamental or cardinal principle of international law, and that the International Law Commission had expressed the view during its work on the codification of treaties that it was a 'conspicuous example of a rule in international law having the character of *jus cogens*'.[81] The

[77] MacGibbon, in Cheng (ed.), *International Law: Teaching and Practice* (London, 1982), 10–25 maintains that this is so however often the Resolution is repeated since 'however many times nothing was multiplied by nothing the result was still nothing' (p. 17). See also Stone, letter dated 27 June 1980 from the Permanent Representative of Israel to the United Nations addressed to the Secretary General, UN Doc A/35/316 S/14045, 3 July 1980, at 5–14.

[78] There is a large literature on this subject, but see esp. Joyner, 11 *CWILJ* (1981), 446–78, who considers that both the law and the law-creating procedures are dynamic and subject to revision and should not be restricted by rigid interpretation, and Skubiszewski, 61 *Ann. Inst. DDI* (1986), 29–230.

[79] Higgins, whilst of the opinion that resolutions do have more than recommendatory significance, goes no further than to say that if adopted unanimously or without the negative vote of the states most concerned, they raise strong expectations of conformity to their requirements: Higgins, *The Development of International Law through the Political Organs of the United Nations* (Oxford, 1963); id., *Proc. ASIL* (1965), 116; id., 54 *AJIL* (1970), 37–48; id., in Cheng, *International Law*, 27–44.

[80] UNGA Res. 2625 (XXV) 24 Oct. 1970, Declaration of Principles of International Law concerning Friendly Relations and Co-operation among states in accordance with the Charter of the United Nations; text in Brownlie's *Basic Documents* (3rd edn.), 32.

[81] *Nicaragua Case, ICJ Rep.* (1986).

Court also relied on the 1975 Helsinki Final Act[82] to the same effect, as evidencing *opinio juris*, since the states concerned therein iterated their *undertaking* to refrain from the use or threat of force 'in their international relations in general'. The *Nicaragua* case is not without its critics; it has been contended that the court completely reversed the normal process for formation of custom based on actual state practice accompanied by a psychological element of legal conviction, that is, that it took account of state practice only after first using the UN resolutions as evidence of the *opinio juris*.[83]

As we shall see, law-making in the environmental field now includes a large number of UN resolutions and declarations, starting with the 1972 Stockholm Declaration on the Human Environment,[84] the significance of which will become fully apparent in subsequent chapters. The importance of such instruments or enunciations of principles is that they authorize, even if they do not oblige, states to act upon the basis of the principles concerned; they are, to put it another way, 'directly enforceable in interstate relations', and potentially of significant law-making effect, even though they will often require further elaboration through treaties or state practice.[85]

(d) General Principles of International Law[86]

These also are a controversial source but one that is important in the current development of international environmental law since there now exist an increasing number of instruments expressed as 'Declarations of Principles', ranging from the UNCHE Declaration itself, through such documents as the World Charter for Nature to UNEP's various sets of Principles on, for example, the use of shared natural resources.[87] We have to ask whether these are the kinds of principles referred to in the ICJ Statute or whether a narrower view limiting the role of general principles to identification of common legal maxims is all this that is intended.

Both the statutes of the *PCIJ* and the ICJ instructed the Court to apply

---

[82] Declaration of the Conference on Security and Co-operation in Europe, Helsinki, 1975 on which see Ch. 2, nn. 116–7. Ott, *Public International Law in the Modern World* (London, 1986), 286 considers that though the Declaration does not create binding law, it appears to have been intended to restate and apply existing law, of which it is partly declaratory.

[83] See in particular D'Amato, 81 *AJIL* (1987), 101.

[84] See *infra*, pp. 45–7.

[85] Brownlie, *Principles of Public International Law*, 19; Van der Mensbrugghe, 5 *IJECL* (1990), 15–22.

[86] Brownlie, *Principles of Public International Law*, 15–19; Cheng, *General Principles of International Law* (London, 1953). See also Bos and Brownlie, *Liber Amicorum*, 259–85; Lammers, in Kalshoven, Kuypers, and Lammers, *Essays on the Development of the International Legal Order* (Alphen den Rijn, 1980), 53–75; Mosler, TMC Asser Institute (ed.), *International Law and the Grotian Heritage*, 173–85, and *infra*, pp. 124–7.

[87] UNGA Resolution 37/7, Nov. 1982, text in 10 *EPL* (1983), 30–1; Draft Principles of Conduct in the Field of the Environment for the Conduct of States on the Conservation and Harmonious Utilization of Natural Resources Shared by Two or More States; UNEP/I.G. 12/2, 8 Feb. 1978, text in 17 *ILM* (1978), 1098, and see *infra*, Ch. 2.

'the general principles of law recognized by civilized nations'. Quite apart from the problem of interpreting the outdated reference to 'civilized nations' in the context of the membership of modern international society, it is unclear whether the principles referred to are merely those commonly applied in all municipal legal systems, such as the maxims relied on to ensure a fair and equitable legal process—*audi alteram partem, res judicata*, etc.—or whether they also include 'principles' recognized by international law itself—for example, the prohibition on the non-use of force; basic principles of human rights; the freedom of the seas; the need for good faith evidenced in the maxim *pacta sunt servanda*. The ambiguity arises from the need to compromise, which arose in the 1920s when the Statute of the *PCIJ* was being developed. One group on the relevant preparatory committee thought that the traditional sources of custom and treaty should be expanded to enable the Court to apply 'the rules of international law as recognised by the *legal conscience* of civilised nations',[88] based on the concept that certain principles existed in so-called 'natural law', principles of 'objective justice' that could be identified by all rational human beings. The purpose of this group has been described as revolutionary, namely to place as a 'wedge between the crevices of existing law principles derived from Western civilization',[89] since the principles would not rest on the free will of states. The rival group adopted the traditional 'positivist' approach, namely that the Court should apply only rules and principles derived from the will of states. This view has been supported in more recent times by lawyers from developing countries and Eastern European states adopting so-called Socialist policies. The compromise adopted, found in the above Statutes, was regarded by this group as referring only to general principles accepted by all nations in *foro domestico*, as already exemplified above.

One authority, however, concludes that Article 38 does not codify an existing unwritten rule on general principles, but endeavours to establish a new secondary source, which has never since been protested, leaving it to the Court, not states, to enunciate the relevant principles by induction.[90] This gives the Court a creative role within certain limits and is thought by some to avoid any possibility of a *non liquet* because of gaps in the law. Such an approach could be helpful in developing international environmental law, perhaps eventually leading to the acceptance of principles of precautionary action, sustainable development, equitable utilization of shared resources, etc. It allows some scope for constructing new principles by means of analogy with national systems in order to fill gaps in fields in which legal development is at an embryonic stage, as in environmental law, but such powers should be viewed and used with caution since national law is not necessarily consistent

---

[88] Cassese, *International Law*, 170, citing Lord Phillimore; emphasis added.
[89] Ibid. 171.   [90] Ibid. 171–2.

with state practice at the international level, as, for example, in the case of principles concerning liability, as emphasized in Chapter 4.

In practice, the Court has not, in the few cases where it has relied on general principles, considered in detail the practice of domestic courts but has endeavoured to extract concepts from them by legal deduction or general jurisprudence, and has used such general principles more to support conclusions drawn on other bases than as a basis of decision in their own right.[91] Tribunals have not mechanically borrowed from domestic law but have invoked 'elements of legal reasoning and private law analogies in order to make the law of nations an able system for application in the judicial process'.[92] This has occurred mostly in the fields of procedure and evidence since state practice can hardly evolve the rules for international courts to apply in this respect.

Although some writers consider that general principles as a source of international law have virtually fallen into desuetude, others give the concept a more substantive content. The International Court's practice suggests that it will also take cognizance of general principles that can be deduced or generalized from treaty and customary law or that have been instituted by states to establish basic standards of behaviour for international society. In this albeit limited sense, general principles still have considerable relevance and significance for international environmental law. The fact remains, however, that in the jurisprudence of the ICJ such principles have again not been relied on as the sole basis of a decision but have been invoked in support of decisions arrived at by reference to a variety of sources.[93] This seems to have been the case in the ICJ's recent decisions on delimitation of the continental shelf and exclusive economic or fishery zones, in which it has invoked 'equitable principles', not as rules of law but as a means of facilitating an equitable solution.[94] Given the resource allocation implications of these decisions, and the resulting obligations of conservation and preservation which arise, this reasoning may have some significance for international environmental law, as do earlier cases in which other general principles have been invoked. As early as 1937, the PCIJ in the *Diversion of Water from the Meuse* cases[95] considered that equitable principles might be derived from 'general principles of law recog-

---

[91] Ibid. 174. Relevant cases include the *Chorzow Factory Case* (Indemnity) (Jurisdiction), *PCIJ*, Ser. A, No. 8/9 (1927), 31; *Corfu Channel Case, ICJ Rep.* (1949), 18; *South West Africa Case* (Second Phase), *ICJ Rep.* (1966), 294–9.

[92] Lammers, in *Essays on the Development of the International Legal Order.*

[93] Brownlie, *Principles of Public International Law*, 16; he cites as preferable Oppenheim's view that the idea is to permit the Court to apply 'the general principles of municipal jurisprudence' in so far as they are applicable to relations between states.

[94] *Libya–Malta Continental Shelf Case, ICJ Rep.* (1985), 13; *Gulf of Maine Case, ICJ Rep.* (1984), 246. For an account of this trend, see Birnie, in Blake (ed.), *Ocean Boundaries* (London and Sydney, 1987), 15–37, and *infra*, pp. 126–7.

[95] *PCIJ* Ser. A/B No. 70 (1937), 4, 73, 76.

nised by civilized nations'. In the *Chorzow Factory* case[96] the court enunciated the general principles of state responsibility and reparation, including the principle of *restitutio in integrum*, and in the *Free Zones* cases[97] the court made some reference to the doctrines of abuse of rights and good faith. In the *South West Africa* case (Second Phase),[98] one judge considered that elements of natural law were inherent in general principles and could be a foundation of concepts of human rights; the nascent concepts of a right to a clean and healthy environment and of inter-generational rights (see Chapters 3 and 5) could develop further in this way. None the less, it has to be recognized that the most frequent use of general principles derives from the drawing of analogies with domestic law concerning rules of procedure, evidence, and jurisdiction and these are only marginally useful in an environmental context.

(e) Judicial Decisions

There is some controversy concerning the reference in the ICJ Statute to judicial decisions as a 'subsidiary means' for determining rules of law[99] because of the important and often innovatory role inevitably fulfilled by the ICJ and other international tribunals in pronouncing on matters of international law. Though judicial decisions cannot be said to be a formal source as such, since the court does not ostensibly make the law but merely identifies and applies it, they clearly provide authoritative evidence of what the law is. While there is no doctrine of precedent in the ICJ or in other international courts, including arbitral tribunals,[100] these courts will not lightly disregard their own pronouncements, though they may find ways of distancing themselves from earlier decisions. Thus a body of jurisprudence accumulates, particularly in the case of the ICJ, and contributes to the progressive development of international law. Important ICJ judgments for the process of international law-making include the *Reparation for Injuries* case[101] (interpreting the UN Charter and state practice and establishing the international personality of the United Nations and hence of other international organizations); the *Genocide* case[102] (clarifying the status of reservations to treaties); and the *Norwegian Fisheries* case,[103] which, *inter alia*, established both the role of persistent objection in preventing the formation of new custom during the period of crystallization, and the need for acceptance or acquiesence in new

---

[96] *Supra*, n. 91, and see *infra*, pp. 139–60.

[97] *Free Zones Case* (Second Phase), Final Order, *PCIJ*, Ser. A, No. 24 (1930), 12, and *Free Zones Case* (Merits), Ser. A/B, No. 46 (1932) 167.

[98] *Supra*, n. 91, on which see Ch. 5 n. 43.

[99] ICJ Statute, Article 38(1)(d); see Fitzmaurice, *Symbolae Verzijl* (1958), 174.

[100] For an analysis of the significance and interrelationship of the different kinds of tribunal and their decisions, see Brownlie, *Principles of Public International Law*, 19–24.

[101] *Reparation for Injuries Suffered in the Service of the United Nations Case, ICJ Rep.* (1949), 174.

[102] *Reservations to the Genocide Convention Case, ICJ Rep.* (1951), 15.

[103] *Anglo-Norwegian Fisheries Case, ICJ Rep.* (1951), 131.

unilateral claims that encroach upon existing rights in international areas. Moreover, other ICJ and arbitral decisions are directly relevant to environmental issues.[104]

As well as the ICJ and arbitral tribunals, there are a number of other Courts whose decisions will be considered here. These include the European Court of Human Rights,[105] the European Court of Justice,[106] and national courts.[107] Though decisions of these bodies are not all of equal weight and significance they may throw light on sources and legal doctrines and provide evidence of state practice. The United States Supreme Court in particular has had occasion to consider a number of international environmental issues concerning conservation.[108] From time to time states also establish tribunals by agreement amongst themselves for particular purposes, such as the International Military Tribunal set up in 1945 at Nuremberg to try war criminals[109] or, more recently, the Iran–United States Claims Tribunal,[110] which have dealt with significant points of law. The 1982 UNCLOS, if and when it comes into effect, will establish a new International Tribunal on the Law of the Sea and panels of experts to consider cases concerning, *inter alia*, pollution, scientific research, and conservation of fisheries, which will undoubtedly in time contribute to the jurisprudence in these fields.[111]

(f) The Writings of Publicists

The ICJ Statute also cites 'the teachings of the most highly qualified publicists of the various nations' as a 'subsidiary means for the determination of rules of law'. The works and views of some writers have been referred to in the ICJ and other tribunals and are especially cited by those preparing opinions or briefs, such as law officers and counsel preparing memorials to present to the ICJ; arbitrators and, especially, municipal courts less familiar with the concepts and practice of international law are, however, more inclined to give weight to writers than is the ICJ, although dissenting ICJ judges are more disposed to do so.[112] Reports of international codification bodies can also provide sources significant as *lex ferenda* and are much quoted and relied on for this purpose. These include the reports and articles drafted by the International Law Commission, which is charged with furthering the codification and progressive development of the law, the Harvard Research Drafts and the reports and resolutions of the Institute of International Law, and the Inter-

---

[104] See Ch. 3.   [105] See Ch. 5.   [106] See Chs. 2 and 4.   [107] See Ch 5.

[108] For details, see *infra*, pp. 194–6, and Chs. 12 and 13.

[109] See Charter of the International Military Tribunal, annexed to Agreement for the Prosecution and Punishment of Major War Criminals of the European Axis, 8 Aug. 1945; text in 39 *AJIL* (1945), Suppl., 258; *Brownlie, Principles of Public International Law*, 561–3.

[110] Iran–US Claims Tribunal Reports; Lillich (ed.), *The Iran–United States Claims Tribunal* (Charlottesville, Va., 1984).

[111] See *infra*, pp. 179–86.

[112] See Brownlie, *Principles of Public International Law*, 25.

national Law Association.[113] Some UN reports and drafts, including those of specialized agencies, and, at the regional level, reports and recommendations of the European Commission having a bearing on legal topics could also be significant.

(2) Non-Traditional Sources: 'Soft Law'

So-called 'soft law' is a highly controversial subject. Some lawyers harbour such strong dislike of the appellation that they refuse even to mention it, especially in connection with sources.[114] Generally, what distinguishes law from other social rules is that it is both authoritative and prescriptive and in that sense binding. In this strict sense law is necessarily 'hard'; to describe it as 'soft' is a contradiction in terms.

None the less, in the case of international law, given the lack of any supreme authoritative body with lawmaking powers, it has always been difficult to secure on a universal basis the consent otherwise necessary to establish binding rules. Given as we have seen, the political, cultural, and religious diversity of contemporary international society, it has become increasingly difficult to secure widespread consent to new rules, whether by treaty or custom. Securing agreement even on issues of urgent importance is fraught with difficulty, results in compromises and ambiguities, and is seldom global in scope, as we shall see. These constraints on the lawmaking process present particular problems in relation to development of the universal standards for environmental protection that are now widely perceived to be required to deal with urgent problems such as conservation of particular species of wild fauna and flora and their protection against various threats to their survival, and prevention of pollution of the seas and atmosphere from a variety of sources. As we have seen, it is difficult, especially in the short term, to develop the precise constraints required through customary law processes. In today's heterogeneous society there are problems of identifying not only the practice of states but the *opinio juris* when there are so many modes for expressing it.[115] Treaties are a more useful medium, but many either do not enter into force, or, more frequently, do so for only a limited number of parties which do not necessarily include the states whose involvement is most vital to the achievement of their purposes. This is especially true of environmental issues, whose regulation may require modification of economically profitable conduct. Thus there are problems in negotiating treaties that lay down clear and specific rules which will secure wide ratification without

---

[113] Ibid. See *infra*, Chs. 4, 6, 7, 13.

[114] Brownlie's *Principles of Public International Law*, neither includes the phrase in the chapter on sources nor is it listed in the index. But cf. authors cities *supra*, n. 38.

[115] Jennings, 37 *Ann. Suisse DDI* (1981), 61–6.

reservations. Treaties thus present problems as vehicles for changing the law as opposed to codifying it. Their relation to customary law is unclear, as we have illustrated, and it is increasingly difficult in relation to unratified treaties and non-parties, as well as for customary law, to distinguish between what is *lex lata* and what is *lex ferenda*.

Increasing use is made, therefore, of half-way stages in the lawmaking process, especially on environmental and economic matters, in the form of codes of practice, recommendations, guidelines, resolutions, declarations of principles, standards, and so-called 'framework' or 'umbrella' treaties which do not fit neatly into the categories of legal sources referred to in Article 38(1)(c) of the ICJ Statute. These are clearly not law in the sense used by that article but none the less they do not lack all authority. States expect that they will command respect and there is a strong expectation that they will be adhered to in the longer as well as the short-term. It is these instruments that have attracted the description 'soft law'. Jennings, though not using the term, has remarked that the old tests of law are increasingly irrelevant since much of the new law is not custom in the orthodox sense: 'it is recent, it is innovatory, it involves topical policy decisions, and it is the focus of contention'.[116] The term 'soft law' is perhaps unfortunate since it insinuates that the approach is lacking in significance or that it is not law, and is thus regarded by many lawyers as only a 'second best' approach.[117] Others welcome it on the grounds that particular techniques suit particular situations at a given time and these new techniques take account of the differences in international society to either screen or harmonize them so as to allow the promulgation of common aims and standards.

'Soft law' is by its nature the articulation of a 'norm' in written form, which can include both legal and non-legal instruments; the necessary abstract norms in issue which have been agreed by states or in international organizations are thus *recorded* in it, and this is its essential characteristic; another is that a considerable degree of discretion in interpretation and on how and when to conform to the requirements is left to the participants. Its great advantage over 'hard law' is that, as occasion demands, it can either enable states to take on obligations that otherwise they would not, because these are expressed in vaguer terms, or conversely, a 'soft law' form may enable them to formulate the obligations in a precise and restrictive form that would not be acceptable in a binding treaty. Despite the fact that states retain control over the degree of commitment, the very existence of such an instrument encourages the trend towards hardening the international legal order; not all 'soft' instruments necessarily themselves become 'hard' law nor is that an inherent aim of each one, but several have. One such example is the partial hardening of UNEP's Cairo Guidelines and Principles for the Environmentally

---

[116] Ibid. 67.   [117] Gruchalla-Wesierski, 30 *McGill LJ* (1984), 58, 62.

Sound Management of Hazardous Waste[118] in the 1989 Basel Convention on the Control of Transboundary Movements of Hazardous Wastes.[119]

The 'soft law' approach allows states to tackle a problem collectively at a time when they do not want too strictly to shackle their freedom of action. On environmental matters this might be either because scientific evidence is not conclusive or complete but none the less a cautionary attitude is required,[120] or because the economic costs are uncertain or over-burdensome. Though enforcement presents difficulties, it does not follow that all elements are unenforceable; some may, for example, rapidly become part of customary law, others are found in treaties. Flexibility is, as we shall see in relation to almost all environmental regulation, essential in modern international society. State sovereignty has to be respected but at the same time the inevitability of increasing co-operation in regulating the many problems that cross state boundaries, such as those concerning migratory species, waste disposal, discharge of effluents, rivers, the oceans (especially semi-enclosed seas) has to be acknowledged and manifested.

It is not surprising, therefore, that international environmental law provides numerous examples of the 'soft law' approach; these are illustrated in almost all of our chapters. They include several UNEP initiatives, deriving from the basic principles set out in the UNCHE Declaration of Principles. UNEP's main long-term programme, the Montevideo Programme for the Development and Periodic Review of Environmental Law, integrated into the broader UN System-Wide Medium Term Environment Programme (SWMTEP), includes in its three projects not only development of international agreements but also international guidelines, principles, and standards, and the provision of assistance for the national legislation and administration necessary to develop and apply these as indicated in Chapter 2. Much of this will be a continuation of the process of 'norm setting, norm-applying, and norm-reviewing' that has dominated UNEP's programmes.[121] UNEP has also published ten sets of guidelines in addition to the Stockholm Declaration. As well as the Cairo Guidelines and the Principles of Conduct on Shared Natural Resources, already referred to, they include Provisions for Co-operation between States in Weather Modification;[122] Conclusions on Offshore

---

[118] UNEP Environmental Law Guidelines and Principles, Decision 14/30 of the Governing Council of UNEP of 17 June 1987. See *infra*, Ch. 8.

[119] Adopted and opened for signature 22 March 1989; see *infra*, Ch. 8.

[120] See e.g. the Declaration adopted by the 1990 Third North Sea Ministerial Conference which incorporated the 'precautionary principle', accepting that states may need to take measures before clear scientific proof of harmful effects is obtainable, on which see *infra*, pp. 95–8.

[121] Sand, 'Environmental Law in the United Nations Environmental Programme', in Dupuy (ed.), *The Future of International Law of the Environment* (The Hague, 1984), 51–88; see also Contini and Sand, 66 *AJIL* (1972), 37–59.

[122] Decision 8/7/A of the Governing Council of UNEP of 29 Apr. 1980.

Mining and Drilling[123] (now included in a Protocol to the Kuwait Regional Convention for Protection of Marine Environment); the World Charter for Nature,[124] a Provisional Notification Scheme for Banned and Severely Restricted Chemicals;[125] the Montreal Guidelines for the Protection of the Marine Environment Against Pollution from Land-based Sources;[126] Goals and Principles of Environmental Impact Assessment;[127] and the London Guidelines for the Exchange of Information on Chemicals in International Trade.[128] The diversity of titles for the categorization of guidelines is in itself interesting and indicative of the flexibility involved. They have been increasingly accepted and implemented, though their progress is somewhat chequered.[129]

The International Maritime Organisation (IMO), though not officially using the term, has also made much use of the 'soft law' approach in addition to adopting numerous conventions.[130] Of particular importance and influence is the International Maritime Dangerous Goods (IMDG) Code[131] produced in co-operation with other United Nations bodies. This was introduced by resolution of the IMO Assembly in 1965, has been constantly updated and amended in response to developments in both the shipping and chemical industries and sets out its requirements in great detail, classifying dangerous goods and laying down marking, labelling, packaging, and documentation requirements. Special procedures have been developed to form the basis of implementation of the code in either national legislation or operational instructions. The Code is widely observed and though state practice probably falls short of the requirements of customary law, it constitutes an indispensable part of the current regulatory regime for carriage of goods by sea, supplementing parts of IMO Conventions, for whose effective implementation it is essential. The IMO Assembly recommended the IMDG Code to governments for adoption as a basis of national regulation; over forty-five states have enacted it, including all major shipowning states. The Code and

---

[123] Conclusions of the Study of Legal Aspects concerning the Environment related to Offshore Mining and Drilling within the limits of National Jurisdiction, Decision 10/14/VI of the Governing Council of UNEP of 31 May 1982.

[124] UN GA Res. 37/7 of 28 Oct. 1982, drafted in collaboration with IUCN and Zaire.

[125] Adopted by the Governing Council of the UNEP in decision 12/14 of 28 May 1984.

[126] Decision 13/18/II of the Governing Council of UNEP of 24 May 1983.

[127] Decision 14/25 of the Governing Council of UNEP of 17 June 1987.

[128] Decision 14/27, ibid.

[129] For details see Birnie, in Butler, Perestroika, 185–9. For criticism of this approach, see Sand, 'Environmental Law', and Brown-Weiss, 11 ELQ (1984), 495–581, passim.

[130] See Chs. 2 and 7.

[131] See Birnie, in Butler, Perestroika, 189–90; Mensah, 'International Regulatory Regimes on the Carriage of Dangerous Goods by Sea', unpub. paper presented at the Ninth International Symposium on the Transport and Handling of Dangerous Goods by Sea and Inland Waterways (TDG-9) held at Rotterdam, Netherlands, 13–17 Apr. 1987; id., in Cheng, International Law, 147–65. IMO Doc. MSC/Cr. 497, 26 July 1988, Ref. T33.06 indicates its wide implementation.

related Recommendations are in effect the essential frame of reference in this field, used by courts as the criteria for determining questions of negligence, responsibility, liability, and compensation.

Although 'soft law' is elusive and difficult to define, and has been described by one writer as no more than 'a convenient shorthand to include vague legal norms',[132] it is clear that it is more than that and has an important contribution to make in establishing a new legal order in such a fast-growing and unsettled field as international environmental law. Such guidelines and norms manifest general consent to certain basic principles that are acceptable and practicable for both developed and developing countries. To this extent, if followed by state practice, they can also provide evidence of the *opinio juris* from which new customary laws and principles develop, and, whilst permitting diversity, contribute to harmonization of environmental law and standards at the global level.[133] The term does at least usefully encapsulate an increasingly used methodology of either moving more slowly towards the formalization of obligations or of setting goals for conduct that though informal, are intended to have some authoritative status. Although as one writer has remarked, 'perhaps nothing is won by recourse to the term or concept of "soft law"', nothing appears to be lost either, provided there is a common understanding of its meaning.

3. CONCLUSIONS

Though many writers and environmentalists are critical of international law's ability to provide adequate protection for the environment and to respond sufficiently quickly to the changes required as scientific knowledge advances, much of this criticism is misconceived, as will be illustrated in our analysis of the emergent regimes governing the main environmental issues. It is true that the law has developed on a sectoral basis and does not, therefore, of itself reflect the interdependence of the various issues and their solutions, but this failing does not derive solely from the inherent nature and structure of international law—municipal legal systems have also not been developed on a holistic basis so far as environmental protection is concerned. International law offers many vehicles for the necessary developments—custom, treaty, 'soft law' principles, which can be used in a variety of ways to develop and revise the law to meet new environmental perspectives. Development does not have to be slow; progress depends on the willingness of states to resort to these processes. The speed with which they do so depends not only on the social, economic, and political implications which it is the responsibility of govern-

---

[132] Gruchalla-Wesierski 30 *McGill LJ* (1984), 44.

[133] *New Directions in Environmental Legislation and Administration Particularly in Developing Countries*, UNEP Environmental Law and Machinery Unit (Nairobi, 1989), *passim*, esp. 18.

ments to weigh against environmental demands, but also on the availability and reliability of scientific information concerning the need for legal measures. 'Soft' law solutions are often in these circumstances preferred, but as the following chapters establish, there has in the two decades since the Stockholm Conference been a remarkable growth not only in legal measures of environmental protection in the form of treaties, but also in new legal concepts and principles which increasingly call into question traditional boundaries between 'public' and 'private' international law, and between national and international law.

It will be the task of the international community acting not only through the international conferences, commissions, and other bodies established by environmental treaties but especially through the international organizations discussed in the next chapter, to co-ordinate these multifaceted measures to ensure, when appropriate, a more integrated approach consistent with the objective of sustainable development. As we shall see in Chapter 2, the UN, its specialized agencies, and other concerned bodies have already developed a number of major strategies which provide the framework for this. It is thus up to states to make imaginative use of the sources of international law, to adopt any further measures and establish any institutions that may be required, and to create the new international environmental order for which the 1992 United Nations Conference on Environment and Development has set the agenda.

2

International Organizations and the Formulation of Environmental Law and Policy

1. INTRODUCTION: ORIGIN OF INTERNATIONAL ORGANIZATIONS

International organizations provide an essential forum for international co-operation in relation to environmental issues. In this context they have two important roles to play: environmental policy-making and the development of international environmental law. It is important to observe, however, that these two roles are distinct, and that the powers of particular organizations in regard to each function will vary. While it is now common practice for a wide range of international organizations to develop environmental policies through long-, medium-, or short-term strategies and action plans, the development of law is usually only one element of these and does not fall within the powers of every organization endowed with environmental responsibilities.

Participation in international organizations at global, regional, subregional levels or for functional, issue-related purposes has been a major manifestation of international co-operation since the early nineteenth century. The Congress of Vienna in 1815 and the series of conferences which followed it were the precursors of the political co-operation that takes place today in the UN.[1] Co-operation for functional, administrative purposes began with the Rhine Commission, established by the Congress of Vienna; its wide powers and effective organs and systems remain a model for such bodies to this day and were followed by innovative public unions—the Universal Postal Union, the International Telegraphic Union, the International Railway Union, the World Health Council, and many others which were instituted as states became aware that they could not operate effective postal, telegraphic, railway services or quarantine systems without international co-operation since all these activities cross borders or have repercussions in other countries. The same realization has now developed in relation to environmental concerns and is resulting in a similar response. The Hague Peace Conferences, convened in

---

[1] For a good account of this period, see Claude, *Swords into Plowshares* (New York, 1984), ch. 1; Goodrich, *The United Nations in a Changing World* (New York, 1974), 1–22.

1898 and 1907, represent another major development in the institutional-ization of international co-operation. They adopted numerous conventions on the laws of war and on the peaceful settlement of disputes, and contributed a spirit of idealism that is similarly reflected in the present universal concern to preserve the environment.

All three of these nineteenth century developments have contributed to and are reflected in modern international institutions—their political role derives from the Congress approach, their regulatory role from that of the Hague Conferences, and their constitutional powers have resulted from a synthesis of the experience in that respect of the early public unions. The League of Nations incorporated all these strands within one body, the prime aim of which was to use its powers to avoid war. It was unsuccessful, partly because its members lacked the will to act collectively for this purpose and avoided their obligations by availing themselves of loopholes in its constituent Covenant; but partly also because, apart from certain internal committees, it lacked the means to address the widespread economic and social problems resulting from the First World War.[2] The only functional organization estab-lished in relation to it was the International Labour Office, although the nineteenth-century public unions continued *ad hoc*, exercising the powers conferred upon them by their constituent treaties. Nevertheless it can be seen from this brief early history that the role and form of international organ-izations have from the outset been responsive to the needs of contemporary international society.

2. THE UNITED NATIONS AND THE ENVIRONMENT

(1) General Background

The advent of the UN in 1945 greatly changed the international system.[3] Lessons were learned from pre-Second World War experience. First, the UN's aims and purposes were expressed in its Charter[4] in far wider terms than those of the League. They include commitments 'To achieve inter-national co-operation in solving international problems of an economic, social, cultural or humanitarian character and in promoting and encouraging respect for human rights and for fundamental freedoms for all ...' and 'To be a centre for harmonizing the action of nations in the attainment of these

---

[2] For analysis of the functioning of the League of Nations, see Hinsley, *Power and the Pursuit of Peace* (Cambridge, 1967), 309–22, and Walters, *A History of the League of Nations* (London, 1960).

[3] For a full account of the United Nations and related agencies, see Bowett, *The Law of International Institutions* (4th edn., London, 1982); Kirgis, *International Organisations in their Legal Setting* (St Paul, 1977); R. J. Dupuy (ed.), *A Handbook on International Organisations* (Dordrecht, 1988).

[4] Repr. in Brownlie, *Basic Documents in International Law* (3rd edn., Oxford, 1983), 1–31.

common ends'.[5] The Charter secures the sovereign equality of all the UN's members and requires them to fulfil their Charter obligations in good faith.[6] The need to protect the environment at the international level had not then been appreciated, however, and the UN and the Specialized Agencies were given no specific mandate to do this. But, as we shall see, their wide powers have enabled them by broad interpretation of their constituent documents to take on this task within the context of their social, economic, and humanitarian responsibilities.

Secondly, the UN was equipped with a range of organs: a General Assembly, a Security Council, an Economic and Social Council (ECOSOC), a Trusteeship Council, a Secretariat, the International Court of Justice (as its principal judicial organ and successor to the Permanent Court of International Justice), and an International Law Commission (ILC), charged with codification and progressive development of the law, though in practice it has ceased to distinguish between these roles. There are also five UN regional economic commissions—for Africa (ECA), Latin America (ECLA), Western Asia (ECWA), Asia and the Pacific (ESCAP), and Europe (ECE)—most of which now have environmental programmes. The ECE has been particularly active in this respect. The 1979 Geneva Convention on Long-Range Transboundary Air Pollution and its Protocols (see Chapter 10) were negotiated under its auspices and it has prepared a Draft Charter on Environmental Rights and Obligations and other international instruments on various environmental matters.[7] Thirdly, the powers of the decision-making organs—the General Assembly, Security Council, and Economic and Social Council—were expressed in wider terms, and the voting procedures for decision-making by these organs were more flexible than the unanimity required in the League of Nations.

Finally, impetus was given to the status and influence of the UN by the International Court of Justice in its advisory opinion in the *Reparation for Injuries* case,[8] where it held that although not expressly provided for in the UN Charter, the organization had international personality in its own right and the capacity to act as such upon the international plane. By virtue of the functions required of it under the Charter, the members must be assumed to have endowed it with the legal competence necessary to enable it effectively to discharge these functions. This did not mean that the UN was to be equated with a state, or had *supra*-national powers but that it was a subject of international law, capable of possessing international rights and duties, with capacity to maintain the former by bringing claims.

All major international institutions will usually have some degree of person-

---

[5] Articles 1(3) and 1(4).   [6] Article 2, paras. 1 and 2 respectively.
[7] See Chossudovsky, *East–West Diplomacy for Environment in the United Nations* (New York, 1989); ECE, *The ECE and Sustainable Development* (New York, 1990). See also 1991 ECE Convention on Environmental Impact Assessment in a Transboundary Context, *infra*, pp. 105–6.
[8] *Reparation for Injuries Case, ICJ Rep.* (1949), 174.

ality to act internationally, separately from their member states, including organizations that have proved important to development of international environmental law. These include UN specialized agencies such as the International Maritime Organisation (IMO) and the Food and Agriculture Organization (FAO), as well as the European Communities (EC), the Council of Europe (CE), the Organization of African Unity (OAU), the Organization of American States (OAS), and the International Union for Conservation of Nature (IUCN).[9] The extent of their power to act independently depends in each case on the tasks required of them by their constituent instrument. This can be either a treaty or agreement, as in the case of UN specialized agencies, or a resolution of another body or conference, as in the case of UNEP. It should be noted, however, that although the United Nations Environment Programme was not instituted as an independent organization but as an autonomous unit within the UN Secretariat, it does not follow that it lacks international legal personality since it is required to fulfil certain tasks on the international plane.

(2) Express and Implied Powers of the UN and Other International Organizations

It follows from the above that international organizations may, depending on the aims of the organization as expressed in its constituent treaty, have power to enter into certain kinds of international treaties.[10] Comprehensive organizations, such as the UN, may by liberal interpretation and resort to the doctrine of implied powers, claim general treaty-making powers. The EC, on the other hand, on the basis of its original treaty had powers to do so only in purely economic fields; none the less, broad interpretation of these and other capacities has enabled it to participate, *inter alia*, in treaties on fishery and wildlife conservation[11] and on pollution[12] and its powers to act on environmental matters have now been clarified by the adoption in 1986 of the Single European Act,[13] and the Maastricht Accord of 1991.

When an organization has permanent organs these have considerable scope to interpret the provisions of the constituent instrument, including the powers of action that must necessarily be implied both from what is expressed therein and from its objects and purposes.[14] In the *Reparation for Injuries* case the ICJ approved this doctrine of implied powers in advising that 'the rights and

---

[9] For discussion of further examples and their limitations, see Brownlie, *Principles of International Law* (4th edn., Oxford, 1990), 682.

[10] The ILC has tried to codifiy the law governing such treaties in the 1985 Vienna Convention on the Law of Treaties between States and International Organisations or between International Organisations, 25 *ILM* (1986), 543–92.

[11] 1980 Convention on Future Multilateral Co-operation in North-East Atlantic Fisheries; see *infra*, Ch. 13.

[12] 1979 Paris Convention for the Prevention of Marine Pollution from Land-based Sources; see *infra*, Ch. 8.

[13] Single European Act, *UKTS* 31 (1988), Cmd. 372.

[14] See Brownlie, *Principles*, 689–91, for further discussion of this point.

duties of an entity such as the Organization must depend upon its purpose and functions as specified or implied in its constituent documents and developed in practice'.[15] In holding that in international law the UN 'must be deemed to have those powers which, though not expressly provided in the Charter, are conferred by necessary implication as being essential to the performance of its duties', the Court linked this doctrine to that of the principle of effectiveness, that is, that an institution must be deemed to have those powers that are necessary to enable it effectively to carry out its purposes. As most states are anxious to protect their sovereignty and equality and generally seek to restrict the independent powers of international organizations, whose actions they may challenge if *ultra vires*, it is often in issue whether action should properly be taken at the international, regional, or national level or whether international action is 'necessary' at all. This question arises frequently in the UN and other bodies such as the European Community in relation to environmental measures and may either restrict the adoption of measures or inhibit their scope and status—the series of guidelines, etc. promulgated by UNEP, which are discussed later in this chapter, illustrate this point. The UN has recently sought to bring issues such as climate change within its scope by designating them as matters of 'common concern' (see Chapter 3 for discussion of the implications of this new concept). The EC has sought to clarify this problem, in its series of Action Programmes on the Environment, by allocating particular actions to the appropriate level, with emphasis on the national level. Challenges to proposed action may be referred by states to dispute settlement procedures, including the ICJ or ECJ if provided for under the relevant constituent treaty. The UN General Assembly and Security Council, moreover, can seek Advisory Opinions of the ICJ on interpretation of the Charter; states, the European Commission, and in certain circumstances (if their rights are involved), even individuals can also refer cases concerning interpretation of the EC's constituent treaties to the European Court of Justice for a ruling. Most 'constitutional' treaties do not provide for compulsory reference of disputes to courts or tribunals, however: at best they offer it as an *ad hoc* option if parties agree (see Chapter 4).

It seems likely that organizations will increasingly seek to extend their roles into environmental spheres by broad interpretation of their powers as programmes on this topic proliferate and a wide variety of organizations, directly and indirectly involved, take up the challenge. Like the EC, a great many organizations have in this way added an environmental protection dimension to their activities where previously they had no such role, such as the World Bank, the Organization for Economic Co-operation and Development (OECD), the International Atomic Energy Agency (IAEA), and even the General Agreement on Tariffs and Trade (GATT).

---

[15] *Supra*, n. 8.

(3) Decision-Making Powers

(a) Binding Decisions

Decisions in international organizations are taken by vote; the number of votes required for adoption of binding decisions is determined by the constituent instrument. In the League of Nations unanimity was required for all decisions but it is now more common for decisions to be taken by majority or weighted majorities, as in some specialized agencies, or for different kinds of decisions on different kinds of subject-matter to be subjected to one or other procedures. Voting procedures in the UN Security Council (SC) provide an example of the latter system. SC decisions require the affirmative vote of nine of its fifteen members, but are also subject to the veto power of each of the five permanent members, except when they relate to procedural issues. In the EC, distinctions are drawn between decisions, directives, regulations, and resolutions, and unanimity has generally been required, but since the 1986 Single European Act an increasing range of powers under various provisions of the EC treaties can now be exercised by majority vote.

The fishery conventions and pollution control conventions discussed in Chapter 4 commonly provide for amendments to the substantive convention to be made by unanimous vote, but amendments of attached schedules or annexes of regulations may be made by more flexible vote—usually a two-thirds or three-quarters majority. Non-binding recommendations can often be adopted by a simple majority, even when they address substantive issues. This enables international bodies to influence the conduct of all states participating in the institution concerned, even if they cannot be compelled to act in a particular way, and contributes to the process of lawmaking.

Many organizations within the UN system and even some outside it, such as the International Whaling Commission (see Chapter 12), now frequently do not vote at all but try to adopt decisions or resolutions by consensus. This involves the continuation of negotiations in an endeavour to reach a compromise which will be reasonably acceptable to all, so that even states with some objections will not press them by insisting on a vote but will content themselves with making statements on their position before or after the adoption of the decision. In this way, although the resultant resolution or measure will generally, in order to attract consensus, be expressed in more general or 'constructively' ambiguous terms, the expectation is that it is more likely to be put into practice by all states affected than if it was adopted by a divisive vote.

(b) Non-Binding Decisions

Most constituent instruments differentiate between binding decisions and non-binding decisions, a practice that goes back to the Rhine Commission of

1815. A simple majority usually suffices for adoption of the latter, which are generally expressed as resolutions or recommendations. Different organs may have power to take different kinds of decisions as in the UN, where, under Article 24(1) of the Charter, only the Security Council can decide on matters of international peace and security and the General Assembly is empowered by Article 11 only to make recommendations on the general principles of co-operation relating to such questions. It should be noted in this connection that some commentators are now interpreting 'security' as including 'environmental security'.

The General Assembly can, however, under Article 10, also discuss any questions or any matters within the scope of the Charter, which include its stated aims and purposes, or relating to the powers of UN organs, and can make recommendations on these either to the Security Council or to member states. It expresses its recommendations in the form of resolutions and has adopted a considerable number on environmental issues especially following its adoption by resolution of the Declaration of Principles on the Human Environment adopted by the Stockholm Conference in 1972.[16] The Conference itself had been convened by resolution of the General Assembly. The legal significance of these resolutions is discussed below. The role of the UN's Economic and Social Council (ECOSOC) in environmental matters is rapidly expanding, given the policy of sustainable development advocated by the World Commission on Environment and Development[17] and the economic and social implications of achieving this. It has power under Article 62 of the Charter to initiate studies on these matters and to make recommendations thereon to the General Assembly, to member states, or to concerned specialized agencies. It can also make recommendations for purposes of promoting respect for and observance of human rights and fundamental freedoms for all, which, as we have remarked, might eventually be expanded to include environmental rights. Although ECOSOC has only recommendatory powers, the Charter in Article 67 refers to these as 'decisions', although they still require only a majority of the members present and voting for their adoption.

The United Nations itself is required to make recommendations for the co-ordination of the policies and activities of the specialized agencies and, as appropriate, initiate negotiations for creation of new ones: it could thus in the future create an institution with overall responsibility for environmental pro-

---

[16] See *Report of the United Nations Conference on the Human Environment (UNCHE)*, Stockholm, 5–16 June 1972 (New York, 1973), UN Doc. A/CONF. 48/14/Rev 1. The Declaration of Principles, Action Plan, and Resolution on Institutional and Financial Arrangements are repr. in 11 *ILM* (1972), at 1416, 1421, and 1466 respectively. They were adopted in UNGA Res. 2997 (XXVII) 1972 by a vote of 116 in favour, none against, with 10 abstentions.

[17] World Commission on Environment and Development, *Our Common Future* (Oxford, 1987), esp. 43–66.

tection but has not yet done so, having instead instituted the United Nations Environment Programme (UNEP) as an autonomous unit within the UN Secretariat. The UN's co-ordinating role is mainly discharged by the General Assembly, which can, however, delegate to ECOSOC, as it has done in respect of various environmental issues. ECOSOC can also take appropriate steps to obtain regular reports from the specialized agencies, another useful role in the environmental sphere.[18] ECOSOC, until recently, has given priority to purely economic matters, in deference to the wish of its majority of developing states for a new international economic order (NIEO), but the close relation now perceived between environment and development and the need to preserve the former in order to sustain the latter is likely to lead to a much more active role being played by ECOSOC in the future.

Constituent instruments of the various types of international bodies considered in subsequent chapters similarly distinguish between the unanimity or weighted majorities required for amendment of the founding treaty or important or binding decisions taken under it and the simple majorities required for resolutions that, *ab initio* at least, are purely recommendatory and non-binding. As we shall see in Chapter 4, this has important implications for the adoption of environmental regulations under various multilateral treaties.

3. THE UNITED NATIONS ENVIRONMENT PROGRAMME (UNEP): FOUNDATION, ROLE, AND POWERS[19]

(1) Significance and Influence of the UN Conference on the Human Environment (UNCHE) 1972[20]

Environmental concerns appeared on the agenda of a wide variety of existing international organizations even before the UN Conference on the Human Environment at Stockholm in 1972. By 1970 various aspects of atmospheric pollution were already within the ambit of WHO, WMO, ICAO, IAEA, FAO, Unesco, the OECD, and NATO's Committee on the Challenges of Modern Society (CCMS). The marine environment was covered by the IMCO (now IMO), FAO, Unesco, WHO, IAEA, OECD, and the CCMS; water pollution and water resources development by WMO, FAO, Unesco, and OECD; land use and conservation of natural resources by FAO and Unesco (through its IOC); urban environmental problems by WHO, FAO, and Unesco, and

---

[18] UN Charter, Article 64.

[19] For an account of its work to date, see Petsonk, 5 *AUJILP* (1990), 351–92.

[20] For a good account of this, see Caldwell, *International Environmental Policy: Emergence and Dimensions* (2nd edn., Durham, 1990, esp. chs. 2 and 3; for an account of the simultaneous meeting held by NGOs and a comparison of the two, see Stone, *Did we Save the Earth at Stockholm?* London, 1983); for a legal analysis of its achievements, see Sohn, 14 *Harv. ILJ* (1973), 423–515.

regulation and standard-setting in relation to selected pollutants by IAEA, OECD, IMCO (IMO), Unesco (IOC), WHO, OECD, and the CCMS. Various other UN bodies, including regional economic commissions, such as the ECE, were involved in specialized aspects of these problems and NGOs also were active on several aspects.[21] Clearly, however, there was a lack of co-ordination of these activities. A body with a clearer environmental focus was required.

Many more organizations began to pay increased attention to environmental matters as a result of the UNCHE. The General Assembly resolution convening the Conference stated that there was 'an urgent need for intensified action at national and international level, to limit, and where possible, to eliminate the impairment of the human environment'.[22] It noted that this was necessary for sound economic and social development. The concern for sustainable development later expressed in the 1987 Brundtland Report thus existed from the outset of the UNCHE although not articulated in precisely those terms. A meeting of experts on environment and development had taken place at Founex in 1971 and had produced a report which drew particular attention to the developmental aspects of the problem.[23] The report greatly facilitated the participation in the UNCHE of developing countries which, until that point, had been wary of taking part for fear that strict regulations might be adopted that would impede their industrial advance, an advance which had already taken place in industrialized countries without such impediments.

The General Assembly Resolution convening the Conference also laid down that it should be the means of stimulating and promoting 'guidelines for action by national governments, and international organizations on broad topics of general significance'. Its mandate was thus expressed in broad policy terms; it was not intended that it should create new law although any 'guide-lines for action' might include some indication of the ways in which this might in future be developed. Eighty-six governments submitted preliminary national reports, which in many instances forced them for the first time to face the intricacies and interrelationships of these problems and the inadequacies of existing laws and institutions for dealing with them, at the international as well as the national level.

One hundred and thirteen states participated in the UNCHE; the USSR and other Eastern bloc states did not do so because East Germany was not

---

[21] Working document, 'US Priority Interests in the Environmental Activities of International Organisations', produced in 1970 by the Committee on Environmental Affairs, US Department of State, cited in Petsonk, 5 *AUJILP* (1990), 351.

[22] UNGA Res. 2398 (XXIII) of 3 Dec. 1968; UNGA Res. 2581 (XXIV) of 15 Dec. 1969.

[23] *Development and Environment: Report and Working Papers of a Panel of Experts Convened by the Secretary-General of the United Nations Conference on the Human Environment*, held at Founex, Switzerland, 4–12 June 1971 (Paris, 1972).

invited to attend, although West Germany was.[24] The USSR did, however, subsequently participate in the UNEP and its programmes.

(2) The Conference Measures

The conference established four major elements of the UN environment programme: an Action Plan for environmental policy; an Environment Fund to be established by voluntary contributions from states; new UN machinery in the form of UNEP, consisting of a Governing Council, a Co-ordination Board (since disbanded), and a Secretariat; and a Declaration of twenty-six principles on the human environment 'to inspire and guide the peoples of the world in the preservation and enhancement of the human environment', Principles 8–14 of which related to the interests of developing states.

The Action Plan consisted of 106 recommendations. These included proposals for three elements: first, a Global Assessment Programme, known as Earthwatch. This was to consist of a Global Environmental Monitoring Service (GEMS) and an International Referral Service (IRS), later renamed INFOTERRA. The aim of these was to obtain information; to give warning of environmental crises; to stimulate scientific research; to evaluate and review this and other data; to link by computer nationally held information. The last aim was later reduced to the more modest and achievable one of linking national sources of information only. There was, however, even in 1972, no plan to establish a global data bank. The second set of proposals concerned natural resources management such as setting goals, planning, consultation, promotion of agreements. The third consisted of supporting measures such as training and education, and provision of information.

In the resolution establishing the Environment Fund, the General Assembly bore in mind that co-operative proposals in this field must have due respect for the sovereign rights of states and be in conformity with the Charter and principles of international law.[25] The costs of the UNEP Governing Council and the Secretariat are borne mainly on the regular budget of the UN but some secretariat costs and programme costs are borne by this fund, which is based on the pledging of voluntary sums by UN Members; only part of the costs of the secretariat staff are borne by the UN budget. It started with a modest $20 million, much of which was not paid up initially. By 1975, 108 projects had been approved at a cost of US $21,897,000 and UNEP had contributed US $14,200,000 to these. States have since consistently proved reluctant to contribute the sum proposed by UNEP as necessary to meet its

[24] The Conference was open to members of the UN and its specialized agencies: West Germany although not at this time a member of the UN was a member of the World Health Organization.
[25] UNEP's financial arrangements were instituted by UNGA. Res. 2997 (XXVII) of 15 Dec. 1972, repr. in 12 *ILM* (1973), 433.

budget, the costs of its programme, and programme support costs. Its budget was severely cut in the early 1980s under the UN policy of maximum budgetary restriction then introduced; in 1987–9 it was only US $25,846,300. It is unlikely that UNEP will be able greatly to expand its activities in the near future[26] unless there is a radical change of policy by UN member states; there is, however, now some evidence that this may be occurring in the light of the global concern relating to harm to the ozone layer, transboundary movement of hazardous waste, the effects of global warming and possible climate change, and the leading role accorded to UNEP on all these issues, as indicated in Chapters 8 and 10.

The new UN machinery originally also consisted of three elements. The UNCHE established a 'small' (*sic*) Secretariat (UNEP), headed by an Executive Director, to act as 'a focal point for environmental action' and co-ordination within the UN system,[27] 'to promote international co-operation in the field of the environment and to recommend, as appropriate, policies to this end; [and] to provide general policy guidance for the direction and co-ordination of environmental programmes within the United Nations system'.[28] It was located in Nairobi on the initiative of developing countries[29] and was the first UN body to be placed in a developing state. It was hoped that this would encourage such states to participate in its programme. UNEP was to serve as a catalyst in developing and co-ordinating an environmental focus in the programmes of other organizations, rather than initiating or mandating environmental programmes on its own account. It has no supranational powers; it does not have even the independent status of the specialized agencies, each of which has its own constituent treaty and enabling powers. UNEP has no such treaty to interpret or make effective. Rather, as its first Executive Director stressed, it was the role of UNEP to 'complexify', that is, 'to remind others of, and help them to take into account, all the system interactions and ramifications implied in their work'.[30] It was, in his view, the continuing lack of this cross-sectoral, cross-disciplinary view that had led to many environmental problems. Development of environmental law was not included in the priority areas of the initial UNEP programme, which were divided into seven: human settlements and habitats; the health of people and their environment; terrestrial ecosystems, their management and control; environment and development; oceans; energy; and natural disasters. These have been subject to revision and UNEP has developed an increasingly

---

[26] Proposed Budget for Programme and Programme Support Costs of the Environment Fund for the Biennium 1988–9, UNEP/GC. 14/21, 2 Mar. 1987.

[27] See UNGA. Res. 2997, at II, para. 1.

[28] Ibid. paras. 2(a)–(b).

[29] See Caldwell, *International Environmental Policy*, 71–83.

[30] UNEP Governing Council, 'Introductory Statement by the Executive Director', 15 Apr. 1975, UNEP/GC/L. 27, 10; see also *The Proposed Environment Programme: Note by the Executive Director*, UNEP/GC/31, 11 Feb. 1975, 1–4.

vigorous role in promoting the development of international environmental law as illustrated throughout this work.

The second component of the UNEP machinery is the Governing Council. This now consists of fifty-eight member states, which are not required to be members of the UN, but are elected by the UN General Assembly for a three-year term on the basis of equitable geographic distribution. It is responsible to and reports to the General Assembly, through the ECOSOC, on the programme's activities. It used to meet annually but now meets biennially and is charged with the tasks, *inter alia*, of promoting international environmental co-operation and recommending policies to this end; providing policy guidance for the direction and co-ordination of environmental programmes in the UN system; reviewing the world environment situation; and promoting the contribution of relevant scientific and other professional communities to the acquisition, assessment and exchange of environmental knowledge and information and to the technical aspects of the formulation and implementation of environmental programmes within the United Nations system.[31]

In establishing the Secretariat, the UN decreed that one of the tasks of its Executive Director was the provision, at the request of all parties concerned, of advisory services for the promotion of international co-operation in the environmental field and the performing of such other functions as may be entrusted to UNEP.[32] As early as its second session, the Governing Council recognized that solutions to many environmental problems are dependent on the existence of adequate law relating to the environment.[33] Effective action on the environment in fact presupposes the conclusion of new agreements and conventions, implementation of recommendations and agreed rules and efforts to find new solutions in the legal field, including new forms of co-operation and regulation. A crucial link in its environmental strategy was the development of environmental law, but UNEP was given no explicit mandate to do this.

Rather it has assumed that in delegating the above tasks to it the UN General Assembly has drawn upon its own authority to encourage progressive development of international law and to promote solutions to international economic, health, and related problems.[34] On this basis, the Governing Council has requested the Executive Director to draw up various conventions and guidelines.[35] Groups of legal and related experts have been established for this purpose.[36] These groups have produced ten sets of guidelines, a series

---

[31] UNGA Res. 2997, at I, para. 2.
[32] Ibid. at II 2(e) and (j) respectively.
[33] *The Proposed Environment Programme*, 54–6, esp. 54, paras. 209–10.
[34] UN Charter, Articles 13(1)(a), 55(b).
[35] See Petsonk, 5 *AUJILP* (1990), 355, n. 17.
[36] For details of these, see *Environmental Law in the United Nations Environment Programme (UNEP)*, United Nations Environment Programme Environmental Law Unit (Nairobi, 1991). See also Petsonk, 5 *AUJILP* (1990), *passim*, esp. 356–62.

of eleven conventions and protocols protecting various regional seas (see Chapter 7), two major global conventions on the transboundary movement of hazardous waste and on the ozone layer (see Chapters 8 and 10), and they have undertaken preparatory work, with other UN bodies, for the drafting of a convention on climate change (see Chapter 10).

The third component, co-ordination, has become increasingly important and difficult since so many agencies have developed environmental pro-grammes and activities. An Environmental Co-ordination Board was initially established for this purpose under the chairmanship of the UNEP Executive Director. It was to meet periodically to ensure co-operation and co-ordination among all bodies concerned in the implementation of environmental pro-grammes, and to report annually to the Governing Council. It was discon-tinued and its role allocated to the UN's Administrative Committee on Co-ordination (ACC), established by ECOSOC in 1946, which convenes biennial meetings of the heads of the specialized agencies, etc. under the chairmanship of the UN Secretary General. UNEP now, however, provides the secretariats of the two principal UN co-ordinating committees for en-vironmental and developmental matters, namely, the Designated Officials for Environmental Matters (DOEM), under the ACC, and the Committee of International Development Institutions on the Environment (CIDIE).[37] UNEP, the World Bank (IBRD), the UN Development Programme (UNDP), and eleven other intergovernmental financial institutions are represented on the latter; though the World Bank is not a member of DOEM it has recently established a Global Environmental Facility (GEF) on which developing states can draw to ameliorate the adverse effects on their development of pursuing environmental protection measures.[38]

However, UNEP has taken various initiatives in arranging joint programmes and inter-agency meetings and consultations—bringing together the heads of various secretariats concerned with marine pollution, for example—and has itself been brought into many consultation meetings on the initiative of other organizations.[39] Its recent activities in relation to the protection of the ozone layer, transport of hazardous wastes, and climate change illustrate this aspect of its activities. It has observer status at many other organizations, ranging from the IMO to the International Whaling Commission. There is much

---

[37] *Co-ordinating Mechanisms in the United Nations System*, background paper, No. 4, World Resources Institute, (Washington, 1991).

[38] IBRD, Resolution 91–5 (1991), 30 *ILM* (1991), 1758. See also World Bank, 'Establishment of the Global Environment Facility', ibid. 1739; Thacher, *Global Security and Risk Management: Background to Institutional Options for Management of the Global Commons and Environment* (Geneva, 1991), 36; World Bank, *The World Bank and the Environment* (Washington, DC, 1991), 101–4.

[39] Thomas, *The United Nations Environment Programme: Constraints and Strategy in the Context of 1992*, Proceedings of the 31st Annual Meeting of the International Studies Association, Washington, DC, 10–14 Apr. 1990, *passim*.

informal consultation with both intergovernmental and non-governmental bodies involved in environmental matters.

(3) Declaration of the United Nations Conference on the Human Environment[40]

The Declaration lays down twenty-six disparate principles, not all of which directly address environmental issues. The Declaration includes several different groups of principles: two proclaiming rights (Principles 1 and 21); four concerning conservation of resources (Principles 2–5); two on pollution (Principles 6 and 7); eight on developmental issues (Principles 8–15); nine on specific non-legal topics (Principles 16, 20, 23, and 26); and one on state responsibility (Principle 22). After a somewhat rhetorical and theoretical preamble which makes no mention of the need for legal developments but does stress the need for co-operation between nations and action by international organizations in the common interest on problems that affect 'the common realm', the Declaration, under the heading 'Principles', adds that it 'states the common conviction that 'Man has a fundamental *right* to freedom, equality and adequate conditions of life, in an environment of quality that permits a life of dignity and well-being, and he bears a solemn responsibility to protect and improve the environment for present and future generations.'[41] Despite the statement of this as a right, neither the introductory language, the formulation of the Declaration, first as a UN Conference Resolution but later endorsed in a General Assembly Resolution, nor the kind of machinery and mandate established to implement these principles suggest that this vaguely expressed right has any legal significance *strictu senso*. For that we must look to subsequent state practice, *opinio juris*, inclusion in treaties, and some hardening of the 'soft law' status, as indicated in Chapter 5.

None the less, the Declaration represents, in UN practice, a formalization used only when principles of special importance are being laid down,[42] though it is not typical of this genre in that Principle 1 is stated merely as a 'common conviction', rather than requiring that states 'shall' act to secure it. Although the same considerations apply to the other right asserted in the Declaration, namely, in Principle 21, that 'states have, in accordance with the charter of the United Nations and the principles of international law, the sovereign right to exploit their own resources pursuant to their own environmental policies which right is coupled with a corresponding responsibility to ensure that

---

[40] *Report of the UNCHE*, 3–5; for an evaluation of the legal significance of this Declaration, see Sohn, 14 *Harv. ILJ* (1973), 423. For the 1992 Rio Declaration, see Ch. 14.

[41] Principle 1, emphasis added.

[42] See Legal Memorandum of the Office of Legal Affairs, UN Doc. E/CN-4/L.610, quoted in part in 34 UN ESCOR supp. No. 8 at 15, UN Doc. E/3616, Rev. 1 and E/CN-4 1832, Rev. 1. (1962), and cable from UN Office of Legal Affairs (16 Nov. 1981), UN *Jurid. YB* (1981), 149 and arguments in relation thereto advanced by Kirgis, Editorial Comment, 84 *AJIL* (1990), 526–7.

activities within their jurisdiction or control do not cause damage to the environment of other states or of areas beyond the limits of national jurisdiction', this has some grounding in pre-existing customary law. This provision is further discussed in Chapter 3, and, unlike Principle 1, is widely assumed to have become part of customary law.[43]

Principles 2–5 also state that the natural resources of the earth '*must* be safeguarded for the benefit of present and *future generations*'[44]—thereby introducing at least the interest of future generations, if not their rights, a proposal discussed further in Chapter 5—and that 'the capacity of the earth to produce vital renewable resources also *must* be maintained and, if practicable, restored or improved'.[45] It states man's responsibility to 'safeguard and wisely manage' the imperilled '*heritage* of wildlife and its habitat'[46] but only requires that nature conservation be 'stressed' in economic development planning, thus accepting the right of continued exploitation of natural resources,[47] and adds that non-renewable resources must be so used as to avoid their exhaustion and to ensure benefit for all mankind. The legal consequences of these principles are discussed in Chapters 11, 12, and 13; in particular several treaties have been developed to protect living resources, for example those on Wetlands of Importance to Wildfowl; Polar Bears; Trade in Endangered Species; Conservation of Antarctic Marine Living Resources; Conservation of Migratory Species of Wild Animals and on Conservation of the Habitats of Wild Flora and Fauna, which are discussed in Chapter 12, and the numerous fisheries conventions discussed in Chapter 13.

Principles 6 and 8 address pollution. The first requires a halt in the discharge of toxic substances or of other substances and of the release of heat, in such quantities or concentrations as to exceed the environment's capacity to render them harmless in order to ensure that irreversible damage is not inflicted upon ecosystems. It was thus particularly significant in at last introducing in an international instrument the concept of preservation of the environment on an ecosystem basis, as had long been proposed by conservationists. Principle 7, though not specifically defining 'pollution', uses the definition developed at that date by GESAMP (Group of Experts on the Scientific Aspects of Marine Pollution)[48] in requiring states to 'take all

---

[43] UNGA Res. 2996 (XXVII) of 1972; see *infra*, Ch. 3 n. 41.
[44] Principle 1; emphasis added; see *infra*, Ch. 5 and Brown-Weiss, 11 *ELQ* (1984), 495–581, esp. 499–502, 502–8.
[45] Principle 3, emphasis added.
[46] Principle 4, emphasis added.
[47] Principle 5.
[48] The group is jointly sponsored by FAO, the IAEA, IMO, the UN, Unesco (IOC), WHO, and the WMO (UNEP is now another sponsor) but is organized by the IOC (International Oceanographic Commission), in which the UK and United States, which have subsequently withdrawn from Unesco, still participate. See Tomczak, 8 *Marine Policy* (1984), 311; Van Heijnsbergen, 5 *EPL* (1979), 11.

possible steps to prevent pollution of the seas by substances that are liable to create hazards to human health, harm to living resources and marine life, to damage amenities or to interfere with other legitimate uses of the sea'. The merits of this definition are considered in Chapter 3; it has provided the basis of various conventions concluded since 1972, subject to some modifications.

Though Principle 21 enunciates the *right* of states to exploit their resources pursuant to their own policies, it subjects this to their responsibility not to cause harm, and, therefore, must also be considered in conjunction with Principle 22, which requires states 'to develop further' the international law on liability and compensation for pollution and other environmental damage to areas beyond their jurisdiction caused by activities within their jurisdiction or control. As the gaps and ambiguities in the existing law concerning state responsibility and the development of Principle 22 since 1972 are discussed at length in Chapters 4 and 5, we shall not pursue these points here. It will suffice to observe that it was those very deficiencies that underlay the formulation of Principle 22 and that there is some difference in phraseology between Principles 21 and 22 in relation to coverage of areas beyond national jurisdiction. In restricting Principle 22 to 'victims of pollution and other environmental damage', the drafters may inadvertently have limited its application in relation to the 'areas beyond national jurisdiction' referred to in Principle 21.

(4) UNEP's Role in Developing International Environmental Law[49]

In its 1975 Environment Programme, in which it first spelt out its objectives for the development of international environmental law, UNEP stated that its intentions were to contribute towards the development and codification of a new body of international law to meet new requirements generated by environmental concerns and by the strategy based on the UNCHE Declaration; to facilitate co-operation in developing the law on state responsibility in accordance with the Principles of that Declaration; to contribute to development of international law at national and regional levels; to promote protection of the international commons and their regulation from an environmental viewpoint; to establish guidelines and procedures for avoidance and settlement of disputes; and to study institutional structures related to the environment with the aim of devising efficient new mechanisms or improving the old.

UNEP's strategy for achieving this programme, as laid down in 1975,[50] was based on co-ordinated action, with close collaboration between governments and intergovernmental bodies, involving as well as the UN bodies, IGOs and

---

[49] Petsonk, 5 *AUJILP* (1990), 351 provides the most detailed and up-to-date account; see also *Environmental Law in the UNEP*; Kiss, *AFDI* (1982), 784–93; Bacon, 12 *CYIL* (1974), 255.
[50] *'The Proposed Environment Programme'*.

NGOs, universities, international law societies of all kinds, and individual experts. It intended to assemble a data base for use in formulation of general principles, rules, and instruments, especially to foster the UNCHE Principles. It would do this in specific contexts, such as state responsibility and liability for damage and natural resources shared by two or more states, to promote agreements on global concerns such as weather and climate modification and sea-bed exploitation, and also in given geographical contexts, such as rivers and river basins, enclosed and semi-enclosed seas, trans-frontier pollution, ground waters, etc. At a more general level, it planned to encourage international organizations and other forums to take the legal aspects into account in their work; to conduct comparative studies of relevant national laws in order to identify ideas and rules adaptable to international environmental law; and to develop voluntary international co-operative arrangements for specific issues in order to facilitate legal developments on these. Finally, UNEP undertook to provide technical assistance to developing countries for the development of their environmental legislation.

This ambitious programme had been only partially achieved by the end of UNEP's first decade and the results were not considered satisfactory by the states attending the tenth anniversary commemorative meeting of the UNCHE in Nairobi in 1982. The Nairobi Declaration[51] adopted there expressed concern and called for intensification of efforts at all levels not only to achieve the original objectives but to take account of new perceptions, especially on transboundary problems. This Declaration sets out reasons for this failure. It is expressed in highly general terms, but directed particular attention to the problems of developing countries, the need for more equitable distribution of technical and economic resources, and use of appropriate technologies and environmentally sound methods of exploitation. It also stressed the need to prevent rather than repair damage. The only specific reference to legal developments, however, is a statement that 'timely and adequate legislative action is important' in regard to ensuring that multinational enterprises take account of environmental responsibilities in adopting production methods and technologies and when exporting.

A more positive view is, however, taken of UNEP's lawmaking role by UNEP itself. Much has happened in the current decade following an 'In-depth Review of Environmental Law' completed in 1981, which surveyed and assessed the relevant activities and plans of all international bodies and organizations dealing with environmental law, both inside and outside the UN system.[52] That year also a 'Programme for the Development and Periodic Review of Environmental Law' (hereafter referred to as the Montevideo

---

[51] Nairobi Declaration on the state of the Worldwide Environment, adopted 19 May 1982 by UNEP Governing Council, Tenth Session, held in Nairobi, 20 May–2 June 1982; UNEP Doc. UNEP/GC 10/INF. 5 of 19 May 1982, repr. in 21 *ILM* (1982), 676–8.
[52] UNEP Report No. 2 (1981).

Programme)[53] was drafted in Montevideo by a group of legal experts convened by UNEP. It was adopted by the Governing Council in 1982 and integrated into the UN System-Wide Medium-Term Environment Programme (SWMTEP) for 1984–9.[54] The Montevideo Programme was to be implemented partly by the UNEP Environmental Law Unit, and by other elements of UNEP, or jointly with other UN bodies, international and regional organizations, and intergovernmental NGOs including IUCN.

The Montevideo Programme can be grouped loosely into three categories: (i) conclusion of international agreements; (ii) development of international principles, guidelines, and standards; (iii) provision of international assistance for national legislation and administration. There is much overlap and interrelationship between these categories. However, UNEP has now made considerable progress under all these heads:[55] a large number of treaties has been concluded under its auspices,[56] various guidelines have been produced[57] and much international assistance has been provided in the drafting of national environmental legislation.[58] A meeting of governmental environ-

[53] *Report of the Ad Hoc Meeting of Senior Government Officials Expert in Environmental Law*, UNEP/GC 10/5/Add. 2, Annex, Ch. 11 (1981).

[54] Now superseded by *The United Nations System-Wide Medium Term Environment Programme 1990–95*, UNEP (Nairobi, 1988).

[55] See *Environmental Law in the UNEP*, and Petsonk, 5 *AUJILP* (1990), esp. at 356–65, and case studies therein; Bacon 12 *CYIL* (1974), 255; Luard, *The United Nations: How it Works and What it Does* (London, 1979), 63; Struthers, 12 *Den. JILP* (1983), 269; Heard, 18 *Va. JIL* (1978), 269; Utton, 12 *CJTL* (1973), 56.

[56] These include the so-called 'Regional Seas Conventions', on which see *infra*, Ch. 7. UNEP's Oceans and Coastal Areas Programme Activity Centre (OCAPAC) is responsible for the regional seas conventions and UNEP provides Secretariat facilities for several of these. See also the 1979 Convention on the Conservation of Migratory Species of Wild Animals 1979, *infra*, Ch. 12; the 1985 Vienna Convention for the Protection of the Ozone Layer, *infra*, Ch. 10; and the 1989 Basel Convention on the Control of Transboundary Movements of Hazardous Wastes and their Disposal, *infra*, Ch. 8.

[57] These include Principles of Conduct in the Field of the Environment for the Guidance of states in the Conservation and Harmonious Utilisation of Natural Resources Shared by Two or More States 1978, on which see Adede, 43 *Albany LR*, (1978–9), 488 and id., 5 *EPL* (1979), 66–76; Provisions for Co-operation between States in Weather Modification, 1979, with Draft Guidelines for National Legislation Concerning Weather Modification; Conclusions on Legal Aspects Concerning the Environment related to Offshore Mining and Drilling Carried Out Within the Limits of National Jurisidiction, 1987; the Montreal Guidelines for the Protection of the Marine Environment against Pollution from Land-based Sources, 1985; Provisional Notification Scheme for Banned and Severely Restricted Chemicals, 1984; Guidelines for Assessing Industrial Environmental Impact and Environmental Criteria for Siting of Industry, 1980; the London Specialized Guidelines for the Exchange of Information on Chemicals in International Trade, 1989; the Cairo Guidelines and Principles for the Environmentally Sound Management of Hazardous Waste 1987; Goals and Principles of Environmental Impact Assessment, 1987. Most of these have been published in UNEP's Environmental Law Guidelines and Principles series. UNEP also participated in preparation of the World Charter for Nature, 1982 and production of Guidelines for Transport and Preparation for Shipment of Live Wild Animals and Plants (Under the CITES).

[58] Forty-one developing countries, had, on request, received such assistance by 1989; see *New Directions in Environmental Legislation and Administration Particularly in Developing Countries*,

mental lawyers held at Rio in 1991 to review the Montevideo Programme concluded that it had generally been successfully implemented and had encouraged the development of environmental law.[59] A range of additional subjects for possible future action by UNCED was also identified.

We shall examine in other chapters the effectiveness of UNEP's law-making strategies. Their approach has been based on first formulating the scientific positions, then developing legal strategies, and in the process building political support with an important role accorded to negotiation of 'soft law' guidelines, principles, etc. In the support-building process many compromises have to be arrived at especially in the interests of maintaining the 'sustainable development' policy propounded by the World Commission on Environment and Development. Thus the conventions are replete with constructive ambiguities in relation both to definitions and terms and the more controversial issues are generally left to the 'soft law' processes, the procedures and status of which are often made deliberately obscure. Thus the General Assembly only asked states to 'use' the UNEP Principles on Shared Natural Resources as 'guidelines and recommendations in formulating conventions'; the Weather Modification Provisions were for 'consideration in the formulation and implementation of programmes and activities' relating to that field;[60] the Offshore Mining Conclusions were to be considered 'when formulating national legislation or undertaking negotiations for the conclusion of international agreements'.[61] In promulgating the World Charter for Nature the General Assembly was more peremptory: it stated that 'the principles set forth in the present Charter *shall* be reflected in the law and practice of each State, as well as at the international level', though this phraseology alone does not render this Charter binding.[62] The Montreal Guidelines on Landbased Pollution were addressed to 'states and international organizations', which were asked to 'take them into account' in the process of developing appropriate agreements and national legislation.[63] The Cairo Guidelines on Waste Management were merely addressed to states 'with a view to assisting them in the process of developing *policies*' for this purpose[64] and the London Guide-

UNEP Environmental Law and Machinery Unit (Nairobi, 1989). See also *Environmental Law in the UNEP*, 36–40. UNEP has published a 'Directory of Principal Governmental Bodies dealing with the Environment' and a 'Manual of Environmental Legislation', and assists the IUCN Environmental Law Centre in Bonn to maintain copies of relevant foreign legislation. An International Register of Potentially Toxic Chemicals (IRPTC) Legal File is maintained on the current legal control status of about 500 toxic chemicals, as well as an Index of Species Listed in Legislation. Similar information on relevant topics is provided by IMO, FAO, and WHO amongst others.

[59] UNEP/Env. Law/2/3 (1991).
[60] UNEP G/C Decision 8/74 of 29 Apr. 1980.
[61] UNGA Res. 37/217 of 20 Dec. 1982.
[62] UNGA Res. 37/7 of 28 Oct. 1982. See *infra*, Ch. 3.
[63] UNEP GC Decision 13/18 (II) of 24 May 1985.
[64] UNEP GC Decision 14/30 of 17 June 1987, emphasis added.

lines on Information Exchange on Traded Chemicals were presented to them to '*help* them in the process of increasing chemical safety in all countries'.[65] None the less, the distinction between 'hard' and 'soft' law becomes blurred as states act on these recommendations and constant watch has to be kept on state practice and re-evaluation made of the status of all these guidelines in the light of that practice.

One of the most thorough reviews conducted to date of UNEP's role in the legal field[66] concluded that its catalytic role had on the whole been positive, despite a preference of its appointed legal experts to draft only general provisions and a lack of sufficiently widespread use of developing country experts. It was more successful in its regional approach. The Treaties and Protocols concluded within its Regional Seas Programme have introduced some innovatory concepts such as Protected Areas, and Specially Sensitive areas for which higher standards of protection are instituted. The 1979 Bonn Convention on Migratory Species, concluded under UNEP auspices, also includes several innovations (see Chapter 12). The Cairo Guidelines provided the basis for rapid negotiation of the 1989 Basel Convention for the Control of Transboundary Movement of Hazardous Waste, when an urgent need for it arose. Procedural provisions laid down in the guidelines on environmental impact assessment have resulted in refinement and adoption of these practices on a wider basis and their inclusion in the 1991 ECE Convention on Environmental Impact Assessment. Finally, the conclusions on offshore mining have led to the addition of a protocol to the Kuwait Convention.

UNEP has also instigated new institutional developments: commissions, secretariats, regular conferences of the parties, standing committees, etc. have been established under many of its conventions, including the Migratory Species, Ozone, Transboundary Movement of Waste and Regional Seas Conventions. It has endeavoured to pinpoint and strengthen the national infrastructure for implementation of environmental law; it has identified and published lists of national 'focal points' and provided technical assistance and advice at this level. None the less, few of the conventions (except most of those covering Regional Seas) are subscribed to by all the states concerned in the problem addressed or, if they are, are not fully and effectively implemented by them. There remains a huge task still to be performed by this small secretariat. It has also co-operated with WMO in the Inter-governmental Negotiating Committee (INC) established by the UN General Assembly to prepare a 'framework' convention on climate change for the UNCED Conference in 1992. UNEP was also involved in the organization of UNCED itself and in other possible legal developments such as proposals for an Earth Charter, biodiversity convention, and a global convention on land-based

---

[65] UNEP GC Decision 14/27 of 17 June 1987, emphasis added.
[66] Ramakrishna, 24 *Ind. JIL* (1984), 346–72; see also the works cited *supra*, n. 49.

pollution. World opinion remains divided, however, on the value of trans-forming it into a specialized agency comparable to FAO or IMO.

(5) Subsequent UN Environmental Conferences

Following the success of the UNCHE, in the subsequent decade the UN convened a series of strategic conferences on issues related to those raised at Stockholm.[67] UNEP participated in most of these and organized some of them in co-operation with other international bodies involved in the subject-matter concerned. The UN conferences on population, water, food, habitat, and desertification did not lead to any substantive legal developments. Though all ended in adoption of declarations or resolutions these were of a policy-oriented, target-setting nature, or were merely statements of intent. However, some institutional advances did result, for example, the estab-lishment of the Habitat Secretariat in Nairobi and the International Fund for Agriculture and Development in Rome. The adoption by the General Assembly in 1974 of the Declaration on Establishment of a New Economic Order, followed by adoption of the Charter of Economic Rights and Duties of states, which proclaimed, *inter alia*, states' full and permanent sovereignty including possession, use, and disposal thereof, over all its wealth, natural resources, and economic activities were significant in establishing the devel-opmental concerns of developing states during this period of rapidly emerging environmental concern. The legal status of these instruments is considered in Chapter 3. They have generated a parallel growth in the international law of development and the concept of a right to development[68] which it is one of the tasks of UNCED to synthesize with the environmental law developments in order to achieve sustainable development.

In 1988 UNEP, in consultation with the UN Economic Commission for Africa (ECA) and the Organization for African Unity (OAU), convened an African Environmental Conference.[69] Whilst this did not lead to any legal

---

[67] These included the World Population Conference (Bucharest, 1974); World Food Conference (Rome, 1974) involving FAO; Habitat Conference (Vancouver, 1976); International Women's Year Conference (Mexico City, 1975); Desertification Conference (Nairobi, 1977); Water Conference (Mar del Plata, 1977); Conference on Long-term Sustainable Development (Nairobi, 1982); Conference on New and Renewable Sources of Energy (Nairobi, 1981). The General Assembly also convened two special sessions in 1974 and 1975 to study the problems of raw materials, development and the optimum use of the world's natural resources. On the 1992 UNCED Conference, see Ch. 14.

[68] For the progress of the international law of development, see Bulajic, *Principles of International Development Law* (Dordrecht, 1986); Garcia Amador, *The Emerging International Law of Development* (New York, 1990); Makarczyk, *Principles of a New International Economic Order* (Dordrecht, 1988); Snyder and Slinn (eds.), *International Law of Development: Comparative Perspectives* (Abingdon, 1987).

[69] African Environmental Conference, Cairo, 16–18 Dec. 1988, Report of the Executive Director of the United Nations Environment Programme. That this was attended by the ECA, UNFPA, FAO, Unesco, Habitat, WMO, IMO, ILO, UNDP, WHO, UNCHR, WFP, WCED,

developments it did result in an action programme and institutionalization of the Conference Bureau with a view to holding triennial conferences, which provides a future opportunity for such developments at the regional level in relation to the many environmental problems of this area, including desertification and species depletion.

4. UN SPECIALIZED AGENCIES INVOLVED IN DEVELOPMENT OF INTERNATIONAL ENVIRONMENTAL LAW

As space does not permit an exhaustive account of the constitutional powers, organs, roles, and procedures of all the UN specialized agencies, only agencies particularly relevant to development of environmental law and policy are discussed below.

(1) The International Maritime Organisation (IMO)[70]

IMO is as important in its particular fields of interest—maritime safety and protection of the marine environment—as is the UNEP at global level. Originally known as IMCO (Intergovernmental Maritime Consultative Organization), it is a UN specialized agency established by a United Nations Maritime Conference held in 1948, primarily, at that date, for purposes of improving safety at sea rather than preventing vessel-source pollution. The constituent convention took ten years to enter into force during which period the problem of vessel-source pollution of the sea, particularly from oil carried by tankers, had begun to attract attention. The first convention on this, the International Convention for the Prevention of Pollution of the Sea by Oil (OILPOL)[71] had been concluded *ad hoc* in 1954; its administration and promotion were transferred to IMO when it became operative in January 1959. Thus from its inception the IMO has in practice been concerned with both maritime safety and marine pollution. It now has 133 member states and one associate member.

The governing body of IMO is its Assembly, which now meets biennially and consists of all the member states. There is also a thirty-two member IMO Council which in the interim exercises the Assembly's functions in supervising the business of the organization. This has a Facilitation Committee to expedite simplification and minimization of documentation in international maritime traffic. The IMO also has a Secretariat, located in the United Kingdom.

as well as six intergovernmental organizations (including the EC) and 6 NGOs shows how wide-ranging such issues are across the international organizational system.

[70] See Mankabady, *The International Maritime Organisation*, 2 vols. (2nd edn., London, 1986).
[71] See Ch. 7.

The IMO is involved in a great deal of technical work deriving from its numerous conventions, codes, advisory, and technical assistance activities. This is carried out through several committees. The most important is the Maritime Safety Committee (MSC) which has established a number of subcommittees. Their subject-matter gives a good idea of the range of IMO's interests: safety of navigation; radio communications; life-saving appliances; standards, training, and watch-keeping; carriage of dangerous goods; ship design, and equipment; fire protection; stability, load lines, and fishing vessel safety; containers and cargoes; bulk chemicals. There is also now, of particular importance to development of international environmental law, a Marine Environment Protection Committee (MEPC) which is concerned wholly with IMO's activities in preventing pollution. As legal issues arise from much of the work of the organization there is also a Legal Committee. Finally, a Committee on Technical Co-operation assists in development of IMO activities in this field.

In pursuit of its twin objectives of safety and pollution prevention, IMO has promoted the adoption of thirty Conventions and protocols to date and a large number of codes of practice and recommendations. Conventions are usually first worked on in a committee or subcommittee; a draft is produced which is submitted to a conference to which all states within the UN system (including its agencies) are invited; thus non-member states of IMO are included. The text, when adopted, is presented to governments for ratification but IMO conventions do not enter into force until certain prerequisites are fulfilled. These generally include ratification either by a specified number of countries, or, if the convention is particularly important, by a certain percentage of world shipping, calculated by the gross registered tonnage of ratifying states, generally 50 per cent.

Though, as discussed in Chapter 1, conventions generally bind only their parties, and codes and recommendations are non-binding, in the case of IMO conventions many have legal significance beyond this simple categorization since standards set by them, for example, for safety and for oil pollution discharges, are widely accepted and implemented and are assumed by many commentators to represent (as relevant) the standards referred to in Part XII of the 1982 United Nations Law of the Sea Convention (UNCLOS), the violation of which generates certain specified enforcement powers on the part of port and coastal states.[72] In this context IMO's Codes, such as the universally accepted International Maritime Dangerous Goods Gode,[73] can equally be significant to the extent that they represent widely accepted standards. Much of this (and other IMO codes) is implemented in states'

---

[72] See Ch. 7.

[73] *Carriage of Goods: Status of Adoption and Implementation of the International Maritime Dangerous Goods Code* (IMDG), IMO DOC. MSCG. 497, 26 July 1988, Ref. T3306.

domestic legislation and can be used by domestic courts as evidence of standards, the breach of which gives rise to responsibility for damage and compensation.[74] The IMO Codes and Conventions have not yet been tested in this context in international courts, however, though they are likely to be so once the UNCLOS enters into force and establishes new international dispute settlement machinery.

Among the most important IMO Conventions[75] for environmental purposes are the Conventions on Safety of Life at Sea 1974 (SOLAS), the basic instrument dealing with maritime safety; on the International Regulations for Preventing Collisions at Sea 1972; on Standards of Training, Certification, and Watchkeeping 1978 (concluded in co-operation with ILO); on Prevention of Pollution from Ships 1973–78 (MARPOL); on Intervention on the High Seas in Cases of Oil Pollution Casualties 1969; on Civil Liability for Oil Pollution Damage 1969 (CLC); on the Establishment of an International Fund for Compensation for Oil Pollution Damage 1971 (IOPCF); and on Liability in the Field of Maritime Carriage of Nuclear Material. In 1990, following the *Exxon Valdez* disaster in Alaskan waters IMO concluded an International Convention on Oil Pollution Preparedness Response and Cooperation (OPRRC).

In developing these conventions and codes the IMO works closely with the UN and other UN Specialized Agencies such as the International Labour Organisation (ILO); World Health Organization (WHO); Food and Agriculture Organization (FAO), and other international bodies such as the UNEP, the United Nations Conference on Trade and Development (UNCTAD), and UNCITRAL (United Nations Commission on International Trade Law). A large number of intergovernmental and non-governmental organizations have observer status at its meetings,[76] ranging from the International Union for Conservation of Nature (IUCN), through industry bodies such as the International Chamber of Shipping (ICS) and the Tanker Owner's Voluntary Association concerning Liability for Oil Pollution (TOVALOP), to non-governmental associations such as the Friends of Earth (FOE) and the Advisory Committee on Pollution of the Sea (ACOPS). This enables them to submit and receive papers and statements at IMO meetings and to meet and lobby government delegates, and thus to have a significant impact on the

---

[74] Mensah, '*International Regulatory Regimes on the Carriage of Dangerous Goods by Sea*', paper presented at the Ninth International Symposium on the Transport and Handling of Dangerous Goods by Sea and Inland Waterways (TDG 9), Rotterdam, Netherlands, 13–17 Apr. 1987.

[75] For a list of IMO Codes and Conventions, see IMO, *Basic Facts About IMO*, 16–20; id., *Focus on IMO* (June 1989); see also 'A Summary of IMO Conventions', ibid. (Mar. 1987). For fuller discussion of the IMO conventions and codes, see Abecassis and Jarashow, *Oil Pollution from Ships* (2nd edn., London, 1985), and *infra*, Ch. 7.

[76] For a list of the 44 bodies with consultative status, see *Review of List of Non-Governmental Organisations in Consultation Status*, IMO Doc. A 16/32(b), 11 July 1989. They are expected to make a significant contribution to the IMO's work.

negotiating process during development, entry into force, and amendment of IMO conventions.

(2) The International Labour Organisation[77]

The ILO, whose headquarters are located in Geneva and which has over 150 members, was established in 1919, for purposes of improving working conditions and promoting the economic and social welfare of workers by building up a code of labour standards, which, of course, directly affect the working environment, working through an annual International Labour Conference, a forty-eight-member Governing Body, the International Labour Office, and a secretariat. ILO has also held regular Maritime Conferences, backed by a Joint Maritime Commission, to develop conventions and recommendations to improve the working conditions and training of seafarers. By promoting the safer and more efficient operation of ships these instruments contribute indirectly to protection of the environment against collisions and accidental oil and chemical discharges. The ILO works closely with the IMO through a Joint IMO/ILO Committee on Training. This produced the first draft of the International Convention on Standards of Training, Crewing, and Watchkeeping on Ships, though the treaty was concluded through IMO and is subject to IMO procedures. The ILO's 1976 Convention on Minimum Standards on Merchant Ships[78] requires IMO co-operation for its implementation. It is one of the Conventions, along with some IMO conventions, whose requirements are inspected by North-West European states under the innovatory Paris Memorandum of Understanding on Port state Inspection (MOU) when ships enter their ports (see Chapter 7). Recently, ILO has turned its attention to the fishing and offshore oil industries, adopting a convention on fisherman's competency certificates and reporting on standards for offshore platforms in response to technological advance.

The ILO has several remarkable features: first, its tripartite system of delegations, which are made up of four persons, namely, representatives of governments (2), employers (1), and workers, that is, trade union representatives (1), who vote independently on adoption of conventions; secondly, its tripartite Conference of forty-eight members composed of twenty-four

[77] For its role and processes generally, see Bowett, *International Institutions*, 108–9. For a succinct summary of the ILO's role in maritime affairs which is particularly pertinent to environmental protection, see Price, *A Tribute to Fifty Years' Work for Seafarers: The International Labour Organisation's Seafarers Code*, pub. Merchant Navy and Airline Officers Association (n.d.).

[78] ILO Convention no. 147; other ILO conventions contributing to better operating standards and reduction of substandard ships include those on the Minimum Age of Seafarers; Officers Competency Certificates; Crew Accommodation on Board Ship; Prevention of Occupational Accidents to Seafarers. ILO has also made recommendations concerning proper training for oil tankers, bulk carriers, chemical carriers, use of container ships and roll-on/roll-off vessels. At present most seafarers are casual and untrained.

governmental, twelve employers', and twelve employees' representatives; and thirdly, its system for endeavouring to ensure that its conventions are ratified by states and incorporated into national law. Under this, the convention text is adopted not by governments but by the tripartite ILO conference and signed only by its President and the ILO Director-General. ILO member states are then obliged to submit it to their parliaments and report annually to ILO on the convention's progress. Governments which have not observed conventions they have ratified can be reported by non-governmental organizations to the ILO which can establish an investigative Commission of Inquiry to examine the allegations. Results are communicated to the government concerned, which can appeal the issue to the International Court of Justice.

These procedures are seldom invoked, however, and there is little evidence, for example, that the convention procedures result in better ratification of the ILO conventions than of IMO ones; ratification, even by major maritime states, is not numerous and some have never entered into force, largely because of the economic costs of bringing this about. On the contrary, the less confrontational negotiating process of the IMO, which endeavours to balance the interests of protection of the marine environment and the freedom of commercial navigation is generally regarded as producing a more widely acceptable result: its conventions are more widely implemented and its codes more widely practised than those of the ILO. The ILO thus introduced new implementation and enforcement techniques in its 1976 Minimum Standards Convention: Article 1 requires parties to ensure that their national laws are 'substantially equivalent' to various parts of fifteen conventions, including some IMO conventions, listed in an Annex. It is implied that a state ratifying the 1976 Convention does not need to ratify these, nor is ratification of them implied by adhering to the 1976 Convention. Like IMO Conventions, this convention, however, required ratification by a fixed number of states, which must include 25 per cent of the world's GRT for entry into force; it also provides for limited inspection in port, and for this purpose it is listed in the Paris MOU.

(3) Food and Agriculture Organization (FAO)[79]

The FAO, which has 158 members, and whose headquarters are located in Rome, is another relevant UN specialized agency working closely with others involved in environmental issues. Its aims are to counter poverty, malnutrition, and hunger, including problems of agriculture, desertification, and deforestation as well as conservation and development of fisheries and land resources.

---

[79] See generally *FAO: What it is and What it Does: How it Works*, FAO (Rome. n.d.); and *Directory of FAO Statutory Bodies and Panels of Experts*, FAO (Rome); Talbot, *The Four World Food Agencies in Rome*, (Ames, 1990).

The FAO Conference meets biennially, but a Council of forty-nine states meets between sessions. One of the five committees that reports to it is the Committee on Fisheries (COFI), open to all member states. In the development of environmental law, FAO's role in promoting fishery management is particularly important. COFI reports and related sub-committee reports provide a rich source of information on global and regional fisheries, the activities of relevant global and regional fisheries commissions, and the development of the law relating to them. The legal division of FAO's secretariat also fulfils an indispenable role in collecting, analysing, and commenting on national legislation, declarations, etc. relating, to fisheries and fisheries jurisdiction.[80] It also provides advice, assistance, and consultants to developing states on fishery management and on drafting national legislation.

COFI's terms of reference, require it, *inter alia*, to review the work programmes of fisheries commissions (including the European Community), the implementation of fisheries conventions, and international fishery problems. It can then make recommendations, report to the Council, and offer advice to the Director General. It has produced several influential reports, including for example, one by the Advisory Committee of Experts on Marine Resources Research (ACMRR), the findings and recommendations of whose Working Group on Marine Mammals strongly influenced governments and NGOs in calling for the International Whaling Commission to use its powers to regulate whaling more effectively.[81] COFI also advises other UN bodies and programmes, including Unesco's International Oceanographic Commission (IOC). However, no progress has ever been made on its allotted task of deciding whether or not it is desirable to prepare and submit to FAO member states a global international convention to ensure effective international co-operation in fisheries on a world-wide scale. Its member states have never displayed any interest in this goal. Linkages between regional and other fisheries bodies thus remain pragmatic and informal (see Chapter 13). Secretariats of these bodies frequently send observers to each other's meetings (for example, the EC and FAO, the IWC, ICCAT, ICES, NEAFC) or the representative of an FAO member state which is represented at other bodies may be authorized to represent FAO also. By these means, and because FAO meetings and the wide-ranging international aspects of its work bring together global experts in the fields concerned, FAO exercises an important indirect influence on the development of fisheries law, although FAO as such has no mandate to do so. The primary role in promulgating and enforcing the necessary regulations, however, still lies with the regional bodies. FAO has itself established several regional fishery bodies but these are

---

[80] e.g. Moore, *Legislation on Coastal State Requirements for Foreign Fishing*, FAO Legislative Study No. 21, (Rev. 3) (Rome, 1989).
[81] Advisory Committee on Marine Resources Research (ACMRR) Working Party on Marine Mammals, (1977) FAO Fish. Rep. (194).

concerned primarily with developing the fisheries of developing states, although recently conservation and enforcement have attracted more attention.

FAO now has an Assistant Director General for Environment and Sustainable Development and a high level Steering Group on this topic. It seems likely that it will in future exert more influence in this field.

(4) United Nations Educational, Scientific, and Cultural Organization (UNESCO) and the International Oceanographic Commission (IOC)[82]

UNESCO has very wide and generalized terms of reference and promotion of research and co-operation in the fields of natural and social science is only one part of its activities. It also provides technical assistance to developing states in respect of training and transfer of appropriate technology and supports various independent research bodies, including the IOC. Unesco has a fifty-one-member Executive Board that meets biannually, but its 158 members meet only biennially in a General Conference; it also has eight regional offices. The diffuseness of its aims and policies has lead to criticism and the withdrawal of the United States and UK, but this does not apply to the IOC, which both states still support and with which they co-operate. This fulfils a vital role in co-ordinating and developing international marine science research programmes.

The IOC supports many programmes of scientific research[83] of great relevance to the regulatory role of international pollution control commissions referred to in Chapter 4. These include GIPME (Global Investigation of Pollution of the Marine Environment), and GESAMP (Group of Experts on the Scientific Aspects of Marine Pollution), which produced an early working definition of 'pollution'. Suitably adapted, this definition is used in most relevant conventions and declarations and has facilitated production of the Annexes to the London Dumping Convention, the 1973/78 MARPOL and various regional conventions (see Chapters 7 and 8). GESAMP also evaluates IMO's IMDGC (International Maritime Dangerous Goods Code) and the effects of offshore activities on the marine environment, of disposal of radio-active waste at sea and many associated aspects of pollution. It provides a major stimulus for environmental action, especially through its Reports on the state of the Marine Environment. Its most recent report, in 1990, concludes that pollution of the seas is rising and is likely to lead to stricter regulation by various pollution commissions. The UNCHE specifically requested GESAMP annually to examine and revise UNEP's Review of Harmful Chemical Substances and the environmental risks posed; this operates in a manner similar to the IMDGC.

[82] See *Man and his Environment: An Overview of Unesco's Involvement* (Paris, 1979).
[83] The activities of the IOC are documented in its irregular publication, 'The International Marine Science (IMS) Newsletter'.

Of most interest for international environmental law, however, is UNESCO's negotiation and administration of the 1972 Convention for the Protection of the World Cultural and Natural Heritage.[84] As UNESCO's Constitution also requires it to preserve the world's cultural heritage, it promoted the conclusion of this convention which, *inter alia*, requires states to conserve elements of the world heritage (which can include natural areas of outstanding environmental interest) situated within their territory and provides both the procedural means and some funds for this purpose (see Chapter 12). The parties also recognize the duty of the international community to conserve heritage of a universal character.

UNESCO has also adopted various recommendations relevant to this issue[85] which define the principles and standards governing national action and list the required measures. The Rules of Procedure concerning Recommendations to member states and International Conventions covered by Article IV(4) of the UNESCO constitution that 'formulate principles and norms for the international regulation of any particular question', require member states 'to take whatever legislative steps may be required in conformity with the constitutional practice of each state and the nature of the question under consideration... to apply the principles and norms aforesaid within their respective territories.'[86] These norms do not require ratification; member states are merely invited to apply them and are left the choice of means for doing so. Recommendations of the General Conference have the weight of its authority behind them and aim to influence the development of national law and practice. These and the texts of conventions are developed through a series of procedures, including studies and reports, designed to intensify the commitment of states at each stage. If the proposed action is approved by the General Conference, the Director General will usually be instructed to report further, and member states will have the opportunity to comment before a draft text is put forward for adoption by the Conference. Conventions require a two-thirds majority for adoption; recommendations a simple majority only.

---

[84] Adopted on 16 Nov. 1972 by the General Conference of Unesco at its seventeenth session held in Paris; text in 11 *ILM* (1972), 1358, and Lyster, *International Wildlife Law* (Cambridge, 1984), 208–38. See also *Conventions and Recommendations of Unesco Concerning the Protection of the Cultural Heritage*, Unesco (Paris, 1983) (hereafter 'Unesco'), at 75–94. This includes the texts of the 1954 Convention for the Protection of Cultural Property in the Event of Armed Conflict and of the 1970 Convention on Means of Prohibiting and Preventing the Illicit Import, Export and Transfer of Ownership of Cultural Property. See further, *infra*, Ch. 12.

[85] Unesco, 101–239; particularly relevant are recommendations adopted in 1962 concerning the Safeguarding of the Beauty and Character of Landscapes and Sites; in 1972 concerning the Protection, at National Level, of the Cultural and Nature Heritage and in 1968 concerning the Preservation of Cultural Property Endangered by Public or Private Works; texts in Unesco, 129–36, 167–79, 151–63 respectively.

[86] Article 1(b) of Unesco constitution.

(5) The World Health Organization (WHO)[87]

WHO conducts some of its activities on a regional and subregional basis, through regional WHO offices and associated research centres. Its main aim, stated in Article 1 of its constitution, is 'The attainment by all peoples of the highest possible level of health.' As the 'health of the environment' affects the health of people, WHO has an interest in controlling environmental factors that adversely affect health, such as use of drugs, chemicals, and the effect of these and other pollutants on water quality standards. It develops and administers the International Health Regulations and collects and disseminates information on this issue. Developments concerning establishment of a right to health have added to the importance of its work (see Chapter 5).

It also has an interest in the preparations currently taking place for a convention on biological diversity and it has assisted and co-operated with the International Council for the Exploration of the Sea (ICES) in preparing reports on levels of marine pollution. It thus makes a major contribution to international standard setting, helping to draft and provide consultants on relevant regulations.[88] This requires international co-operation with other bodies such as the IMO, ILO, UNEP, and the IAEA.

(6) The World Meteorological Organizations (WMO)[89]

WMO has 160 member states and territories; its Congress meets every four years but an Executive Council of thirty-six members meets inter-sessionally. Its headquarters are in Geneva. WMO operates through six technical commissions in exclusively scientific investigations and is backed by six regional meteorological associations. It facilitates the co-operation necessary to monitor and forecast changes in weather and climate and the effects of human activity thereon. Its role is thus of vital importance in evaluating the effect of global warming and possible world climate change. It has, with UNEP, organized two major World Conferences on this topic and it worked closely with the UN and UNEP, under the auspices of the Intergovernmental Panel on Climate Change, on preparations for the 1992 United Nations Conference on Environment and Development. Earlier it was consulted during development of the 1977 Convention on Environmental Modification.[90] It also collaborates with Unesco (IOC/GESAMP) and the IAEA and IMO.

---

[87] Caldwell, *International Environmental Policy*, 108–9; 242–6; Bowett, *International Institutions*, 114–16.
[88] De Kooning (ed.), *Setting Environmental Standards: Guidelines for Decision Making* (Geneva, 1987).
[89] WRI background paper, No. 2.
[90] 1977 Convention on the Prohibition of Military or any other Hostile use of Environmental Modification Techniques, *infra*, Chs. 3 and 10.

(7) International Bank for Reconstruction and Development (IBRD) and International Monetary Fund (IMF)[91]

These two partner organizations and their affiliated agencies, the International Finance Corporation (IFC) and the International Development Association (IDA) (which provides finance on concessionary terms), complement each other's activities in promoting economic growth. They represent the principal source of funding for this purpose. The IBRD and IDA's main organ is a shared Board of Governors—one from each of the 151 member states—which meets annually or as required by members and holds its meetings in conjunction with the IMF Board. The states contributing most to the Bank's capital appoint five of its twenty-two executive directors, and it is predominantly controlled by the developed industrialized economies of the Western World.

The IBRD provides funding by giving long-term capital loans for reconstruction and development projects, or to promote reforms that will lead to economic growth, especially in developing countries. Some of these may pose potential environmental hazards, such as power stations, dams, pipelines, the building of roads through forests, or forest industries. The IBRD has become increasingly aware of this side-effect of its policies and endeavours increasingly to structure and 'condition' loans in such a way that development which it funds is ecologically sound, although it is not always successful, given that its primary role is promotion of development. It has introduced major reforms, establishing an Office of Environmental Affairs to provide studies of the environmental effects of its policies, long-term planning, training, and co-ordination with other parts of the Bank. It has also introduced environment divisions into its regional offices. The Bank has now called for its loans to be based on coherent environmental strategies in its borrower countries. It has prepared Environmental Issues Papers for almost all of these, outlining their environmental problems and strategies for addressing them. These are followed by specific Environmental Action Plans, which themselves provide the basis for guidelines for Environmental Assessments aimed at ensuring that development proposals are environmentally sound. It co-operates closely with UNEP, FAO, UNDP, and, on the Tropical Forest Action Plan, with the World Resources Institute. The IBRD has recently established a Global Environmental Facility (GEF) to assist developing states to bear any additional costs incurred as a result of adopting environmental measures.[92]

Regional development banks face similar problems.[93] In 1980 these banks,

---

[91] Bowett, *International Institutions*, 109–12; WRI background paper, No. 2; World Bank, *The World Bank and the Environment* (Washington, DC, 1991).

[92] *Supra*, n. 38.

[93] These include the EEC's European Development Fund, Inter-American Development

in conjunction with IBRD, UNDP, UNEP, the OAS, and the EEC, formed CIDIE (Committee of International Development Institutions on the Environment) and adopted a Joint Declaration of Environmental Policies and Procedures Relating to Economic Development.[94]

(8) International Atomic Energy Agency (IAEA)[95]

The IAEA has 113 member states, meeting annually in a General Conference, and a Board of Governors of thirty-five members, which must include the ten members most advanced in the technology of atomic energy or production of its source materials, and representatives of the eight major UN regions, if not already included.

Although this agency is associated with the UN and operates like a specialized agency, it is an independent intergovernmental organization without specialized agency status. It is responsible for promoting international co-operation in the peaceful uses of nuclear energy and is also empowered to set standards, which, though not mandatory, are widely adopted in state practice. Its role in this respect is considered in more detail in Chapter 9.

IAEA also has a Safeguards Committee to lay down guidelines for use in concluding the Safeguard Agreements required under the 1968 Treaty on Non Proliferation of Nuclear Weapons (NPT) and an International Safety Advisory Group. Its Committee on Assurances of Supply advises the Board on ways of achieving supplies of nuclear materials in conformity with non-proliferation requirements. The Department of Technical Co-operation overviews the environmental implications of this aspect of IAEA's work.

5. UN SEMI-AUTONOMOUS BODIES[96]

A number of other bodies have functions which are relevant to the development of environmental policy and law within the UN system. The most important are those whose work is closely related to that of the ECOSOC but which are located for administrative purposes within the UN Secretariat. These include the United Nations Institute for Training and Research (UNITAR); the United Nations Conference on Trade and Development (UNCTAD); the United Nations Development Programme (UNDP); and the United Nations Industrial Development Organization (UNIDO). Their role is referred to as appropriate elsewhere in this work.

Bank, Asian Development Bank, Caribbean Development Bank and the Arab Bank for Economic Development in Africa; WRI background paper, No. 2.
[94] 19 *ILM* (1980), 837–8.   [95] *Infra*, Ch. 9.
[96] Caldwell, *International Environmental Policy*, 102–4.

6. INTERGOVERNMENTAL ORGANIZATIONS (IGOS)
OUTSIDE THE UN SYSTEM

Though there are many examples of fishery and pollution commissions referred to in subsequent chapters, most of these IGOs operate at the regional or subregional level. Only a few, such as the International Whaling Commission, or the meetings of parties established under the Convention on Trade in Endangered Species, the London Dumping Convention, the Basel Convention for the Control of Transboundary Movements of Hazardous Wastes and the Ozone Convention, are global in scope. The International Union for Conservation of Nature (IUCN), includes governments among its members, but is non-governmental in character and will be considered under that category. It is apparent from the scarcity of global examples that the regional or subregional local level is usually more appropriate. At the regional and subregional levels, there is now a wide and varied range of relevant intergovernmental bodies.[97] It is impossible in this chapter to discuss them all; attention will be devoted to those that are either the most successful in achieving their goals or offer techniques that are innovatory and therefore of particular interest. Many of these bodies are discussed elsewhere in this work in relation to particular sources of pollution or of resource conservation.

It should be noted that there is no international definition of a region.[98] Co-ordinating factors can include geographical propinquity, shared economic goals, shared resources, security interests, shared political aims, shared seas or rivers. It can only be concluded that no one set of criteria can accommodate all arrangements and that to be workable such associations must correspond to the physical, ecological, economic, social, and political characteristics of the participating states.[99] The complexity and interrelationship of environmental problems generally requires that all these aspects be involved.

(1) Continental Groupings

Bodies such as the Organization of American states (OAS), the Organization of African Unity (OAU), the League of Arab States, and the European Community have all had to address environmental issues, although in most cases these have had a low priority compared to the political and economic problems of the areas in question.

(a) The OAS and OAU[100]

The 1940 Convention on Nature Protection and Wild Life Preservation in the

---

[97] Ibid. 94–100, 129–67, and see *infra*, Ch. 4.
[98] For discussion of this, see Ch. 7 n. 20.
[99] Caldwell, *International Environmental Policy*, 129–30.   [100] Ibid. 97–8.

Western Hemisphere (see Chapter 12) was sponsored by the Pan American Union, the predecessor of the OAS. It is a largely hortatory treaty; no specific measures are required to be taken and no further action was taken on it. The OAS has not subsequently evinced close concern for environmental issues, though it has undertaken evaluation of new development projects in conjunction with UNEP.

An African Convention Relative to the Preservation of Flora and Fauna in their Natural State was concluded in 1933 during the colonial period in Africa and was replaced in 1968 by the African Convention for Conservation of Nature and Natural Resources concluded under the auspices of the OAU, which provides a secretariat (see Chapter 12). It too has lain dormant although recently there has been discussion on updating it. In 1981 the Council of Ministers of the OAU did, however, strongly recommend the adoption of the World Charter for Nature, proposed by Zaire, which was duly approved by the UN. The OAU has also adopted the Lagos Plan of Action 1980–2000, allocating priority to various environmental considerations within the socio-economic planning process. UNEP's 1988 African Environmental Conference is also likely to have stimulated further interest in the region, as also will the preparation of national reports for the 1992 UN Conference on Environment and Development.

Unlike the OAU, OAS, and League of Arab States, which have contributed little to the development of international environmental law to date, the European Communities are rapidly developing a more effective environment programme, albeit its implementation is erratic.

(b) The European Communities

This organization of twelve European states, whose headquarters is in Brussels, merits extended treatment since uniquely amongst the organizations discussed so far in this chapter, the EC has organs and powers, which, if its members are so determined, could be used to create a strict environmental protection regime,[101] although at its inception the objectives laid down in Articles 2 and 3 of its founding treaty, the Treaty of Rome,[102] were wholly economic and developmental.

Thus at first the EC had to rely on broad interpretation of certain articles in the Treaty of Rome as a basis for introduction of environmental measures, including the Preamble which called for improvement of living and working conditions, Articles 2, requiring 'harmonious' development of economic activities and 'balanced' expansion, 36, allowing restriction of trade for reasons of public health and protection of animals and plants. It adopted three 100 on approximation of laws and 235 on gap-filling

---

[101] See, for an outline of these, Lasok and Bridge, *Introduction to the Laws and Institutions of the European Communities* (5th edn., London, 1991).

[102] Treaty of Rome, *UKTS* 15 (1979), Cmnd. 7480; 298 *UNTS* 11.

five-year Action Plans on the Environment between 1973 and 1987, a fourth for 1987–92 following the adoption in 1986 of the Single European Act, and a fifth in 1992, which seeks to promote greater social responsibility among consumers, industry and public bodies, and places more emphasis on economic measures rather than regulation. Article 130R of the Single European Act establishes an environment policy whose objectives are to preserve, protect, and improve the quality of the environment; to contribute towards protecting human health and to ensure a prudent and rational utilization of national resources, provided, that EC environmental activities do not interfere with national policies regarding energy resources. Though the Single Act also endorses preventive action, the 'polluter pays' principle, rectification of environmental damage at source, and integration of an environmental dimension into *all* Community policies, it also requires that the environmental conditions and the economic development of regions must be taken into account as well as the potential benefits and costs of taking or not taking 'action'. These provisions could be used by member states to block more stringent environmental regulation, as could the so-called principle of subsidiarity, which allows the Community to act only if carrying out tasks which may be more effectively undertaken in common than by member states acting separately.

Despite these limitations, there is no doubt that the EC's unique powers provide it with opportunities unrivalled by any of the other organizations discussed in this section to develop regional environmental law.[103] Its Action Plans provide a structure for such development though political and socio-economic problems have inhibited their coherent application; the need for consensus in the Council of Ministers has required a pragmatic approach to the adoption of regulations and directives, but these are now quite wide ranging and cover many aspects of pollution and resource conservation.[104] The EC has also participated in global and regional environmental institutions and agreements and its environmental policies are of increasing international significance for issues such as climate change, ozone depletion, transboundary movements of hazardous waste, and trade in endangered species.

What differentiates the EC from all other international organizations is its institutional structure. This comprises an Assembly or parliament, a Commission, a Council of Ministers and a Court of Justice. The European Parliament is now, uniquely among such regional bodies, directly elected. It was originally an advisory, supervisory, and deliberative body with few legislative powers, but it acquired certain additional powers under the Single

---

[103] For an exhaustive survey of the policy and lawmaking role of the European Communities, see, Johnson and Corcelle, *The Environmental Policy of the European Communities* (London, 1989); Johnson, *The Pollution Control Policy of the European Communities* (London, 1979); Haigh, *European Community Environmental Law in Practice*, 4 vols. (London, 1986).

[104] For examples, see Johnson and Corcelle, *Environmental Policy*, and Haigh, *European Community Environmental Law in Practice*, *passim*.

European Act of 1986, and its role will be further enhanced under the Maastricht Agreement of 1991. It has the right to be consulted, and in practice the Commission informally sends all proposals to it in advance of meetings of the Council of Ministers. It can also appoint rapporteurs to investigate problems on its behalf, and this has led to discussion and reports on a range of important environmental problems. On the other hand, the Parliament remains a body of relatively limited power, and real authority within the Community, including lawmaking, has until now rested largely with the Commission, the Council and the Court.

The Commission consists of Commissioners appointed by the member states who, once appointed, act independently of their member governments. Commissioners are allocated to specialized Directorates-General (D-G); D-G XI is concerned with 'environment, consumer protection and nuclear safety'. But the Commission has no legislative powers: it is the initiator and co-ordinator of Community policy, and, as the executive agency of the Community, the guardian of its treaties. It must ensure that the Treaty provisions are applied and it can take action against defaulters informally or by giving 'reasoned opinions'; failure to respond satisfactorily to these can lead to the issue being referred to the European Court of Justice (ECJ). These enforcement procedures are rather stronger than those available to any other administrative body operating in the environmental field. The Commission plays a major role in evolving detailed policies to achieve the general aims of the treaties and, following the UNCHE, worked hard to secure agreement on the introduction of a Community environmental policy, despite initial objections from member states, which at first saw it as an intrusion into matters which in their view fell properly within national jurisdiction. These objections have only gradually been overcome, and have resulted in many compromises and the expression of Community policy in rather broad terms. A new European Environment Agency was proposed in 1989, but its powers will mainly allow it only to provide scientific, technical, and economic information and to assist the Commission in preparing environmental policies, action plans and legislation and assessing their implementation and results.

Another important role of the Commission is that, either alone or with the President of the Council, it represents the EC in a broad range of international negotiations with third states concerning, for example, fisheries and some aspects of pollution and protection of endangered species. The Community in its own right has adhered to a number of environmental conventions discussed in later chapters,[105] and in meetings of the parties to these

---

[105] e.g. the 1973 Convention on International Trade in Endangered Species (CITES), the 1974 Paris Convention for the Prevention of Marine Pollution from Land-based Sources; the 1976 Barcelona Convention on the Protection of the Mediterranean Sea against Pollution; the 1976 Convention on the Protection of the Rhine against Pollution from Chlorides; the 1979 Berne Convention on the Conservation of European Wildlife and Natural Habitats, on which see Chs. 6, 8, 12.

it is represented by the Commission. The Commission is thus involved in a wide range of international regulatory activities and in their implementation through the various regulations and directives adopted by the Community, such as those establishing quality objectives for surface water intended for abstraction as drinking water; those controlling disposal of certain forms of waste or chemicals, or barring import and export of whales and seals or their products. The regulation introducing a common system for implementing the CITES[106] is of particular value although the removal of frontier controls *within* the Community in 1992 could undermine some of its effectiveness. Lastly, the Commission's responsibility for administration of various Community funds enables it to facilitate acceptance of environmental policies by softening their economic impact, for example, by aiding restructuring of the fishing, shipping, and agricultural industries.

The Council of Ministers is the Community's principal decision-making body, composed of one ministerial representative of each member state, the minister varying with the subject in issue, for example, environment or fisheries. On occasion, the Council may be composed of heads of government of EC member states. Such summit meetings have sometimes included environmental issues on their agenda. Most of the Council's important powers have in the past been exercised by unanimous vote. Two articles of the Single European Act (Articles 100A, 130S) allow for resort to qualified majority voting on certain environmental issues, however. Although Article 130S allows the Council only to act unanimously on a proposal from the Commission and after consulting the Parliament and the Economic and Social Committee, it is also empowered to define the matters on which decisions are to be taken by qualified majority. In practice the latter power has not yet been exercised, and is not the radical departure it seems. In contrast, Article 100A allows measures to harmonize national laws to be decided by qualified majority where they have as their objective the 'establishment and functioning of the internal market'. This article extends to matters of health, safety, and environmental protection, and it has been the basis for the adoption of a number of more recent environmental regulations and directives by majority vote.

The legislative measures available to the Council are regulations, which have direct legal effect in all member states; directives, which bind member states to implement them within their territory in a manner appropriate to their situation, often within a fixed but extended time-limit; and decisions, which bind only the states or persons to whom they are addressed. The Council can also adopt non-binding recommendations. Member states' record of compliance with directives and decisions is on the whole good, although

---

[106] Regulations 3626/82 and 1970/92.

most have at some time, despite their treaty obligations, been referred to the European Court for delay, and have even in some cases defied the court's adverse judgment. In the end the Community's procedures do generally bring about compliance.[107] On the other hand, the possibility of resort to the ECJ means that member states are particularly reluctant to allow adoption of any measures which might present difficulties of compliance, and there is thus a tendency to avoid, neutralize, or postpone them.[108]

The European Court of Justice is another unique institution. It is composed of twelve judges appointed by agreement of member states, and can annul measures taken by the Commission, Council, or member states that are incompatible with the constituent treaties. The Court's procedures can be initiated by Community institutions, member states, or, in some cases, individuals concerned. The Court, which has been very active, can also pass judgment, at the request of national courts, on the interpretation or validity of Community laws. Unfortunately, there are no procedures for enforcing the Court's judgments; reliance is placed on the member states' obligation under the treaties and general principles of international law to carry out their obligations in good faith.

The EC offers a model of environmental regulation which other regions might follow to advantage. Yet there are few regions with the necessary identity of interests and shared willingness to pool their sovereign powers in a comparable manner, and none with the same level of economic development. Moreover, the EC's potential has not in practice been fully realized internally, and externally its policies on resource exploitation, agriculture, and industrial development have proved serious obstacles to effective international co-operation and regulation of various environmental problems, as will be evident in later chapters. Thus its environmental record is not as good as the strength of its powers might suggest.

(c) Council of Europe (CE)[109]

The CE was established in 1948, before the EC, and quickly evinced an interest in environmental issues, pursuant to its aim of 'achieving a greater unity between its members for the purpose of safeguarding and realising the ideals and principles which are their common heritage and facilitating their

---

[107] For a case study of the UK's record of compliance with EC environmental legislation, see Haigh, *EEC Environmental Policy and Britain* (2nd edn., London, 1987); see also id., 4 *Cornell LR* (1989), 453–62.

[108] For detailed examples, see Johnson and Corcelle, *Environmental Policy, passim.*

[109] *Manual of the Council of Europe: Structure, Functions and Achievements* (London, 1970). The activities of the European Committee for the Conservation of Nature and Natural Resources are reported in the CE's *Naturopa Journal.*

economic and social progress.' It has twenty-three members, accords consultative status to over 200 NGOs, and is thus more broadly based than the EC. The international status of some affiliated NGOs, moreover, brings in wider trans-frontier influences. All member states are represented in the main organ, the Committee of Ministers, which acts on behalf of the Council and meets in closed session, and in the Parliamentary (consultative) Assembly, the deliberative organ which meets in open session. It also has a Secretariat located at its headquarters in Strasburg.

The Committee of Ministers does not possess the binding powers, legislative competence, or enforcement mechanisms available to the EC, however. There is a European Court of Human Rights but unless and until protocols instituting environmental rights are added to the European Convention on Human Rights, this plays little role in environmental issues. The Committee of Ministers, meeting biannually, considers the actions required to further the Council's aims, concludes conventions and agreements, promulgates common policy and makes recommendations. It can ask member governments to inform it of action taken. In practice, ministers do not use this forum to take important political decisions but to discuss matters of European co-operation; much authority to act has been delegated to special deputies but major new conventions are opened for signature at Committee meetings, and committees, working groups, etc. monitor and follow up the progress of these. The Council has, however, convened several European Ministerial Conferences on the Environment.

The Parliament merely discusses issues and relies on the resultant publicity for effect. It has discussed many environmental topics, including fisheries and pollution. Being without responsibility, it can be forward looking and promote bold proposals, often opposed by the Committee of Ministers. The expansion of the EC and adoption of its Action Plans on the Environment has removed much of the potential of the CE's role in the environmental field but all twelve EC members are also CE members and the EC itself adheres to some of the Council's conventions, including the important 1979 Berne Convention on the Protection of European Wildlife and Natural Habitats.[110] It also works closely with European local authorities on pollution problems and fisheries. The Parliament can appoint rapporteurs to investigate particular problems, the conclusions of which it then considers and makes recommendations upon. It has done this, for example, on fisheries, pollution, substandard ships, and nuclear accidents. It endeavours to confine its attention to problems that other bodies are not considering but obviously this is not always possible and it can be seen that there is overlap, not only with the EC but with IMO, ILO, FAO, and regional fishery and pollution commissions.

---

[110] See Ch. 12.

(2) Cross-Continental Groupings

(a) Organization for Economic Co-operation and Development (OECD)[111]

The OECD, whose headquarters are in Paris, has twenty-four member states, including not only European states but also Canada, Japan, and the United States. It is more limited in its scope than the organizations referred to above. Recognizing the interdependence of the industrialized world, its objectives are to promote economic growth, help less developed states within and outside the OECD, and encourage world-wide growth in trade. On this basis, and because its members undertake under Article 2 of its constitution to 'promote the efficient use of their economic resources' and in scientific and technological fields to encourage research, the OECD has been able to develop an environmental programme.

It acts through a Council, an Executive Committee of fourteen member states, a secretariat, and various committees, covering the environment, energy, fisheries, and scientific and technological policy. The Council can take decisions that bind members only if they so agree but in any event provides a forum for crystallization of principles that can and have been adopted into national laws. It has also established an autonomous International Energy Agency (IEA) and Nuclear Energy Agency (NEA) to facilitate co-operation in these fields and encourage harmonization of policy and practices in radioactive waste management. It co-operates, as appropriate, with ECE, WHO, IAEA, and UNEP. OECD abandoned preparation of a draft convention on movement of hazardous waste when UNEP took its initiative on this topic at the global level in 1988 (see Chapter 8).

OECD established an Environment Committee in 1970 in which member states discuss common problems and make recommendations for national policy.[112] It co-operates, *inter alia*, with the EC; the European Commission has observer status at OECD meetings. OECD analyses the national environment policies of its members and their economic implications and provides guiding principles. Thus it has made proposals for assessing and improving environmental quality; scrutinizes the environmental and health hazards presented by chemicals; evaluates the environmental implications of various means of energy production; and advises on waste disposal. It has been particularly concerned with finding solutions to transboundary pollution

---

[111] *OECD and the Environment* (Paris, 1986) provides information and a bibliography of relevant OECD documents. Council acts have covered resource management, air, water, energy, waste, chemicals, cross-directorate issues—transfrontier pollution, transport, noise, state of the environment, and such problems as coastal management, radioactive waste, and multinational enterprises.

[112] It produces detailed reports on 'The State of the Environment' in member states. These cover not only the topics referred to *supra* in n. 111 but also inland water, land, forest, and wildlife resources.

problems for which, as early as 1972, it developed, *inter alia*, the influential 'polluter pays' principle,[113] now followed also by the EC,[114] although this principle has been compromised in other civil liability treaties in favour of limited liability. Finally, it organizes studies and seminars. Its seminar on the economic consequences of oil spills that followed the stranding of the *Amoco Cadiz* provided scientific analysis of oil pollution impacts and their economic consequences and has led to better evaluation of the nature of the damage occurring, including environmental consequences and provided better methods of assessment and compensation (see Chapter 7). It has also undertaken extensive studies on transport of hazardous wastes.

The OECD has also contributed to conservation of fisheries by reviewing policy; facilitating adaptation to changing economic conditions; producing annual statistics on the fish catches of its members; and forecasting production and marketing and promoting co-operative research. This information is useful in particular for co-operation with the EC, which is provided for in a supplementary protocol and whose members are also members of OECD. Its constituent treaty allows it, moreover, to enter into agreements not only with its member states but also with non-members and international organizations. Most recently OECD has involved itself in the climate change debate.

(b) North Atlantic Treaty Organization (NATO): Committee on the Challenges on Modern Society (CCMS)[115]

Basically a defensive military alliance involving Canada, the United States, and various European states, NATO developed an environmental programme in 1969 by establishing the CCMS to examine methods of improving inter-allied co-operation in creating better environments in their societies. It has produced several reports on coastal and inland waters, pollution, air pollution, and planning by using the method of 'pilot' studies whereby groups of member and non-member states and concerned international organizations are led by one 'pilot' country. They form the basis of council resolutions on action and member states are required to submit follow-up reports within 2 years on measures taken to implement them. There is some scepticism concerning the value of this process, its overlap with the programmes of bodies referred to above, and lack of clear purpose. Its impact on the lawmaking process has been negligible, although participation of members has been good. Its future, in the post 'Cold War' situation, is uncertain but its existence provides an

---

[113] See Ch. 3.

[114] It was adopted in the EC's first Action Programme on the Environment, adopted 22 Nov. 1973, OJEC No. C112 of 20/12/73; for comments on this, see the Report of the House of Lords 'European Communities Committee on the Polluter Pays Principle', 10th Rep. 1982–3, HL 131 (1983) and the House of Lords debate thereon, Hansard, vol. 444, No. 32 of 14 Nov. 1983, at cols. 1089–112.

[115] See, Nato, *Facts and Figures*, NATO Information Service (Brussels, 1971).

interesting dimension to environmental co-operation. NATO has recently reaffirmed its role and further studies are planned.

(c) Conference on Security and Co-operation in Europe (CSCE)[116]

The CSCE was established in 1975 as a forum for promoting peace and security in Europe, and with the intention of facilitating confidence-building measures of international co-operation. All European states are members, as are Canada and the United States. The Conference adopted the Helsinki Final Act, at its first meeting in 1975, as a non-binding instrument which nevertheless committed the parties to various measures including co-operation on matters of environmental protection and the rational use of resources 'in the interests of present and future generations'. The Final Act recognized the existence of a duty in accordance with international law to ensure that activities carried out within the territory of its parties do not cause degradation of the environment, and it designated the UN Economic Commission for Europe to act as the framework for co-operation on matters of air and water pollution control, protection of the marine environment, land use, nature conservation and human settlements.[117] The first substantive achievement of these commitments was the negotiation under ECE auspices of the 1979 Geneva Convention on Long-Range Transboundary Air Pollution, and its protocols.[118]

Subsequent meetings of CSCE parties have progessively expanded the organization's policy on environmental protection. The Vienna meeting in 1986 recognized the need for 'preventive action' to protect the environment and strengthen co-operation with regard to air pollution, ozone depletion, climate change, marine pollution, transboundary movement of hazardous waste, and natural resource conservation. The Sofia meeting of 1989 recommended the elaboration of conventions on the transboundary effects of industrial accidents and the pollution of international watercourses and lakes, and called for efforts to harmonize management of hazardous chemicals. These recommendations have, as recommended in the Helsinki Final Act, again been referred to ECE for negotiation and drafting of the necessary instruments. In 1991 a Convention on Environmental Impact Assessment in a

---

[116] CSCE, Final Act (Helsinki, 1975), Cmnd. 6198; CSCE, Concluding Document (Madrid, 1980–3), Cmnd. 9066; CSCE, Concluding Document (Vienna, 1989); Report on Conclusions and Recommendations of the Meeting on the Protection of the Environment (Sofia and Vienna, 1988–90); Charter of Paris, 1991, 30 *ILM* (1991), 193; Valletta Meeting on the Peaceful Settlement of Disputes, 1991, Principles for Dispute Settlement and Procedure for the Peaceful Settlement of Disputes; Madrid Conference, Final Resolution Concerning the Establishment of the CSCE Parliamentary Assembly, 1991, ibid. 1345; Berlin Meeting of CSCE Council, 1991, Survey of Conclusions, ibid. 1349.

[117] See further, *infra*, p. 91, n. 46. On the legal status of the Final Act as a non-binding instrument, see Russell, 70 *AJIL* (1976), 246–9; Schachter, 71 *AJIL* (1977), 296.

[118] See further, Ch. 10, and Chossudovsky, *East–West Diplomacy for Environment in the United Nations*, (New York, 1989).

Transboundary context was also adopted by ECE. The Charter of Paris, adopted by the CSCE in 1990 following the demise of communist regimes in Eastern Europe, commits the organization to respect for human rights, democracy, and the rule of law, and for the first time emphasizes the 'significant' role of a well-informed society in enabling the public and individuals to take initiatives to improve the environment. A draft ECE Charter on Environmental Rights was subsequently proposed which would give substantial support to the development of a human rights approach to protection of the environment at a procedural level. This is considered further in Chapter 5.

CSCE environmental policy has thus become the subject of quite radical evolution and it has, after a long period of limited activity, begun to generate significant lawmaking activity within Europe. As indicated in Chapter 3, the 1991 Convention on Environmental Impact Assessment is the first attempt to give detailed content in treaty form to general rules concerning transboundary environmental co-operation and risk management. Moreover, the Charter of Paris also lays stress on the need to encourage clean and low-waste technology, and on the importance of effective implementation of environmental agreements and systematic evaluation of compliance. Another more recent development within CSCE is the creation of a range of institutions intended to give the organization an institutional structure consistent with its new role at the centre of European security. These include the establishment of a Parliamentary Assembly charged with the task of assessing implementation of CSCE objectives, and initiating the adoption of further measures, including those relating to the environment. A weak set of principles and procedures for the peaceful settlement of disputes were also adopted by the CSCE Council in 1991, and a 'Conflict Prevention Centre' was established.

(3) Scientific Research Organizations

A number of international organizations exist to provide scientific advice and research on matters of environmental importance. One of the more interesting is the International Council for Exploration of the Seas (ICES).[119]

ICES is a unique body based in Copenhagen, founded informally by scientists in 1902 but put on a treaty basis in 1967. It now has eighteen members and is open to any state approved by its members though its scope is limited to the Atlantic Ocean and adjacent seas. Its aim is to promote, encourage, and organize research and investigation for the study of the sea, especially its living resources, and to disseminate the results. It has a co-

---

[119] For its founding and history, see Went, *Seventy Years Agrowing* (Charlottenlund, 1972). See also Tambs-Lyche, 2 *Marine Policy* (1978), 127–32; Parrish, ibid. (1979), 232–7.

ordinating, not a managerial or lawmaking, role but contributes to the latter by supplying advice on request or by formal agreement to such bodies as the FAO, IMO, Unesco, WHO, UNEP, the EC, the North-East Atlantic Fisheries Commission and the Helsinki, Oslo, and Paris Commissions since it has interpreted its mandate broadly to cover not only fisheries but pollution from various sources. Though it has no regulatory role, it can come to conclusions and make recommendations, drawing attention to management and legislative needs, indicating whether species or pollutants should be added to regulatory annexes.

It has a very small secretariat (Bureau) and a Council that meets annually taking by vote decisions that are executed by the Bureau. Its meetings are attended by delegates, experts, invited observers from non-member states and international organizations, and scientists invited personally. It works through an elaborate committee structure with work programmes on fisheries and pollution. Its work on fisheries is hampered by uncertainties of data, by lack of agreement on the total allowable catch and on allocation, and distribution of quotas and by poor enforcement. None the less, it has achieved an excellent reputation for offering fair and impartial advice and has published a large number of influential reports. Its use of a grid system for the purpose of collecting information has enabled a detailed picture of fisheries and environmental factors to be built up for the relevant commissions.

In 1919, the International Commission for the Scientific Exploration of the Mediterranean Sea was instituted, followed in 1949 by the establishment of the General Fisheries Council for the Mediterranean (GFCM), sponsored by FAO. These have been less active bodies than ICES in practice although there is now renewed interest in their undertaking a more active role.

Another important non-governmental group is the International Council of Scientific Unions (ICSU), which has various environmental programmes and co-operates with WMO and Unesco in scientific studies relating to possible climate change and in organizing scientific conferences calling for policy decisions from governments.[120] Unesco's Intergovernmental Oceanographic Commission (IOC) plays an active role at the international level in structuring and co-ordinating marine scientific research projects and has increasingly involved developing countries in joint research programmes. It is notable that the United States and UK, which have withdrawn from Unesco, continue to participate in and support the work of the IOC. Scientific research is conducted at the regional level through intergovernmental functional commissions, such as those dealing with land-based pollution, pollution from dumping, and fisheries discussed in later chapters.

---

[120] Tolbert, in Churchill and Freestone (eds.), *International Law and Global Climate Change: International Legal Issues and Implications* (London, 1991), 95.

7. NON-GOVERNMENTAL ORGANIZATIONS

(1) Role of NGOs in General

Modern non-governmental organizations have existed for over 100 years, since their creation in Europe, particularly in the United Kingdom, by Victorian naturalists and philanthropists though the interest of naturalists goes back to the sixteenth century.[121] NGOs have proliferated in modern times. Over fifty now attend meetings of the International Whaling Commission (IWC), for example, but the legal developments analysed in this work have been influenced by the activities and pressure of many private industrial organizations as well as those established purely for purposes of environmental protection, both old and new. Japanese fishermen's unions attend IWC meetings alongside conservationist NGOs. Friends of the Earth (FOE) and the International Chamber of Shipping (ICS) both have observer status at IMO. NGOs' aims and activities are diverse and often entwined. Some are basically international professional bodies, often in the scientific field, such as the International Council of Scientific Unions (ICSU); some have exclusively educational or research purposes, such as the World Resources Institute (WRI) and the International Institute for Environment and Development (IIED); others are campaigning organizations advocating particular courses of action, such as Friends of the Earth (FOE), Greenpeace International, the Sierra Club, the National Audubon Society, the Nordic Union for the Prevention of Oil Pollution of the Sea; and the World Wide Fund for Nature. Some mix various interests on their committees, such as the Advisory Committee on Pollution of the Sea (ACOPS); others, such as the Dutch Noord Zee Werkgroep and ACOPS, also provide forums for discussion through convening regular conferences. Some are purely national, others regional, yet others fully international.

The effectiveness of NGOs varies greatly according to their seriousness of purpose, depth of research, skills in political advocacy, means of exercising pressure, and narrowness of focus. They have become increasingly effective through achieving consultative status at international and regional organizations where their representation and the personal lobbying of their representatives may, if to the point and well researched, influence the negotiating process when conventions and resolutions are in process of drafting or adoption. Their activities at the IWC, IMO and CITES and LDC meetings illustrate this. Increasingly they have 'networked' their activities, for example

---

[121] McCormick, *The Global Environmental Movement* (London, 1989), esp. 1–24. Some of the earliest NGOs were formed to protect birds, the first in 1867. The movement to save whales began at the Eighth International Zoological Congress in 1910. See also 'The Stirring of Awareness', 19 *IUCN Bulletin* (1986, Special Issue), 5.

at IWC meetings, where NGOs meet daily to co-ordinate their policies and actions. Many NGOs active in Europe have since 1974 co-ordinated their activities on European issues through the European Environment Bureau (EEB),[122] established in Brussels. Over sixty NGOs concerned with the EC's environmental policies have formed a coalition and through this bureau receive information on current activities in the EC and concert their recommendations and representations to the EC. The EEB holds workshops, comments critically on EC measures, and convenes conferences at which NGO, EC, and international organizational and government representatives can meet. It also issues reports and facilitates wide-ranging contacts among delegates and national government officials.

The IMO has listed thirty-nine industrial NGOs and six environmental NGOs that have consultative status with it. They range from the International Chamber of Shipping (ICS), through the TOVALOP (Tanker Owners Voluntary Agreement concerning Liability for Oil Pollution) and CRISTAL (Contract Regarding an Interim Supplement to Tanker Liability for Oil Pollution) (see Chapter 7) to the Advisory Committee on Pollution of the Sea (ACOPS) and Friends of the Earth (FOE).

(2) International Union For the Conservation of Nature (IUCN)

One of the most important NGOs operating at the international level, which merits special mention, is the International Union for the Conservation of Nature (IUCN), also known as the World Conservation Union.[123] This is a federative membership organization, founded in 1948, consisting primarily of governments or their agencies but also including scientific, professional, and conservation bodies such as the World Wide Fund for Nature (WWF) with which it has a close association. In this respect it is unique among environmental bodies. By its fortieth anniversary in 1988 it included 61 states and 128 government agencies, 383 national and 33 international NGOs, and a few affiliated members. The diversity of its membership is remarkable.

IUCN has a small secretariat located in Gland, Switzerland, and an Environmental Law Centre in Bonn, in the Federal Republic of Germany. It convenes a triennial General Assembly of its members, as a deliberative forum and for the passing of resolutions which members present to government and relevant bodies, but it operates mainly through numerous standing commissions and committees. The former include Ecology, National Parks, and Protected Areas; Environmental Policy, Law and Administration; Species Survival and Environmental Planning. IUCN lacks real powers, however; its resolutions do not bind and it has no enforcement mechanisms.

---

[122] See European Environmental Bureau's annual reports on 'Activities'.
[123] See *IUCN Bulletin* (1988, Special Issue).

Nevertheless, it has played a catalytic role in initiating new legal developments.[124] It early perceived the need to link environment and development and prepared the IUCN/WWF/UNEP World Conservation Strategy, published in 1980, in which FAO and Unesco also collaborated. This lays down principles for conservation of living resources and for legal developments which will enable their sustainable utilization.[125] A revised Strategy for the 1990s has now been prepared. It identifies the needs of sustainable development, identifies the main issues, sets targets within a framework of a mutually supportive efforts but at the time of writing omits to identify the role of law in securing its goals; it is to be hoped that this will be remedied in the final version. Although IUCN's mission is now primarily to provide knowledge and leadership for sustainable development by publishing studies, issuing its *Bulletin* and organizing meetings, it helps governments develop international declarations and conventions, sometimes providing first drafts through its Law Centre. It has worked on a Convention on Preservation of Biological Diversity and an Earth Charter or Declaration for adoption by the UNCED, and has previously contributed to the 1972 World Heritage Convention, the 1973 Convention on Trade in Endangered Species, the 1971 Convention on Wetlands of International Importance, and the 1979 Convention on Conservation of Migratory Species of Wild Animals.[126] It seeks, as far as possible, to fill gaps in legal developments, or to co-operate with other organizations in preparing drafts, or in commenting on them.

8. CONCLUSIONS

In this chapter we have been able to provide no more than a brief synopsis of the powers, organs, scope, and roles of some of the multifarious organizations most involved in the advancement of international environmental policy and law. We have not considered in any detail the functions and effectiveness of various pollution, fisheries, or wildlife commissions established by a large number of multilateral and bilateral co-operation treaties. The role of these bodies is considered more fully in Chapter 4, and subsequently in relevant chapters. We must ask, however, given the title of this chapter, whether there is either organization of international environmental lawmaking activity or a serious role to be played by international bodies—as opposed to *ad hoc* diplomatic conferences and the development of custom through state practice—and indeed whether a lawmaking 'process' in the sense a series of events with some consequential impacts on change and development is in operation at all.

---

[124] See 'Towards a Convention', 21 *IUCN Bulletin* (1990), 29.
[125] See *infra*, pp. 428–30.   [126] See Ch. 12.

It seems that organizations are increasingly involved in developing strategies, such as UNEP's Action Plans or IUCN/WWF/UNEP's World Conservation Strategy, the report of the UN World Commission on Environment and Development, or the General Assembly Resolution on the Environmental Perspective to the Year 2000, and setting broad goals—such as sustainable or rational or equitable exploitation or development—and laying down broad general principles, but that, apart from the European Community, no organization has been equipped with the powers directly to affect state behaviour in a legally binding way. Even the regulations of the fisheries and pollution commissions have to be enacted into national law by individual member states before they become binding, albeit the obligation to do so has been established in their constituent convention or subsequent protocols. The role of most organizations relates more to production of 'soft law' through non-binding codes and guidelines than to Conventions, though the IMO and UNEP are especially active in both fields and most specialized agencies and the UN itself have concluded some conventions. There is growing evidence that the 'soft law' approach is having a considerable influence on state practice in developing international environmental law, as other chapters of this work amply illustrate.[127]

International organizations make a valuable contribution as part of the lawmaking process but they are not in themselves *the* process. Their most obvious and indispensable role is that they provide a permanent forum in which state members can engage in a continuous negotiating process to arrive at the compromises necessary to propel the law forward in a world consisting of states at very different stages of economic and social development and representing many different legal, cultural, and religious systems and values. The availability of their machinery is a very important part of the lawmaking process. They can also provide, through the existence of their permanent institutions, means of supervising, monitoring, and prompting implementation of their codes and conventions. This is done more by reminder and comment then active or binding enforcement measures, although the EC has these at its disposal to a greater extent than other bodies.

They can also provide the means for drafting appropriate instruments and for articulating resolutions. There now exists, however, a bewildering and somewhat chaotic array of bodies at the global, regional, and subregional level. A recent article listing international coverage of marine affairs in developing regions illustrates the problem in a particularly clear manner.[128] Numerous small commissions have also been established under bilateral agreements. Certainly mechanisms exist in all their infinite variety to regulate pollution and even to some extent to co-ordinate the activities of states and concerned

---

[127] See e.g. Chs. 3, 7, and 9.
[128] Kwiatkowska, 14 *Marine Policy* (1990), 385 at 396–8; 419–20.

organizations on environmental issues, but as most lack power to bind or to enforce, their success depends on the willingness of states effectively to use the mechanisms now available to them.

The problems of co-ordination have not yet been properly addressed. Meetings of heads of agencies or the secretariats, as organized by the ACC or UNEP through the DOEM or CIDIE are insufficient for this purpose. More co-ordination and reduction of overlap is surely required from the bottom up as well as the top down. The task now is to provide this rather than to add more conventions and organizations. Since the UNCHE, too many existing organizations have considered that they must engage in the environmental lawmaking process and have endeavoured to corral various parts on this within their own boundaries. It is unfortunate that the UN, in approving the Stockholm resolution, established the UNEP as a weak 'focal point', without giving it the powers to take a strong co-ordinating role, and that its Environmental Co-ordination Board was disbanded in favour of the UN's ACC. The UN could still itself take a more positive leading role but has seemed so far disinclined to do so though ECOSOC has the potential and powers for this purpose. The UN's World Charter for Nature, WCED's report, and the 'Environmental Perspective to the Year 2000 and Beyond' are expressed in such general terms that they do not go beyond setting the most broad of strategic goals.[129] This, of course, is important and has symbolic significance but has little immediate impact on the legislative process: if they have to be effected through the loose network of organizations outlined in this chapter, it is likely to be many years before their aims are achieved.

The precise impact of international organizations, at whatever level, on state legislative practice is thus difficult to assess. It requires more detailed research than is possible in this work. It is noticeable that North Sea states, among the most advanced in the world, although able and willing to produce for the recent International North Sea Ministerial Conferences a 'Quality Status Report' on the state of pollution levels in that area, did not produce a comparable Quality Status Report on the institutional and legislative regime of an area that is probably better equipped with environmentally active bodies than any in the world. It was left to an NGO privately to commission legal experts in each North Sea state to produce such reports.[130] It is NGOs and academics also who monitor and comment most closely on the performance of these organizations. International organizations have had a considerable influence on changing attitudes and even, in some cases, such as the IMO, on changing the law but have been less effective in producing radical change in their own structure or in national laws. But, as pointed out in Chapter 4, they

---

[129] Wood, 12 *ELQ* (1985), 977–99.

[130] They were commissioned by Greenpeace UK but had not been published at the time of writing; see also the detailed study of UK practice in implementing EC legislation provided by Haigh, *EEC Environmental Policy and Britain*.

can also play a most useful role in law enforcement, lawmaking and dispute settlement, under the various multilateral treaty regimes which now regulate different sectors of environmental protection.

The UNCED in 1992 has undertaken a major review of the whole UN and related institutional system, and its policies for global environmental governance,[131] with a view to possible restructuring. Its aim has been to ensure, *inter alia*, that international institutions can meet the needs of developing states in particular in a flexible fashion and develop the necessary legal regime and measures to help achieve sustainable development. It is to be hoped that it can by this process streamline the present system to avoid the duplication of effort that clearly now exists and enhance co-ordination among all the institutional processes reviewed here. The most notable institutional development endorsed by the Conference is the creation of a Commission for Sustainable Development which will oversee implementation of UNCED policy and 'Agenda 21', the programme of future action adopted by the Conference.

[131] UNGA Res. 44/228 of 22 Dec. 1989; UNGA Res. 45/211 of 21 Dec. 1990.

3

The Structure of International Environmental Law I: Rights and Obligations of States

1. INTRODUCTION

In this chapter we consider the main rules of international law concerning the protection of the environment.[1] Some customary rules have been codified and developed to a limited extent in UNEP principles,[2] in the 1982 UN Convention on the Law of the Sea (UNCLOS)[3], and in the work of bodies such as the International Law Commission (ILC), the International Law Association (ILA), and the World Commission on Environment and Development (WCED), and in UNCED's 1992 Rio Declaration on Environment and Development.[4] The subject is still developing, however, and in certain important respects the rules themselves remain controversial.

---

[1] See generally, Kiss, in Macdonald and Johnston (eds.), *The Structure and Process of International Law* (Dordrecht, 1983), 1069; Schneider, *World Public Order of the Environment* (London, 1979), ch. 3; Handl, *Proc. ASIL* (1980), 223; Caldwell, *International Environmental Policy* (2nd edn., Durham, 1990), ch. 4; Brownlie, 13 *NRJ* (1973), 179; Birnie, 3 *BJIS* (1977), 169; Bleicher, 2 *ELQ* (1972), 1; Springer, *The International Law of Pollution: Protecting the Global Environment in a World of Sovereign States* (London, 1981); Teclaff and Utton (eds.), *International Environmental Law* (New York, 1974); Bothe (ed.), *Trends in Environmental Policy and Law* (Gland, 1980); Kiss, *Droit international de l'environnement* (Paris, 1989); Munro and Lammers (eds.), *Environmental Protection and Sustainable Development: Legal Principles and Recommendations* (London, 1986); Kiss, 32 *GYIL* (1989), 241; Birnie, in Carroll (ed.), *International Environmental Diplomacy* (Cambridge, 1988), 95; Magraw (ed.), *International Law and Pollution* (Philadelphia, 1991); Handl, 1 *YIEL* (1990), 3; Neuhold, Land, and Zamenek (eds.), *Environmental Protection and International Law* (London, 1991).

[2] See Principles of Conduct in the Conservation and Harmonious Utilization of Natural Resources Shared by Two or More States, 1978, UNEP/IG.12/2; Principles of Environmental Impact Assessment, 1987, 17 *EPL* (1987), 36; Montreal Guidelines on the Prevention of Marine Pollution from Land-Based Sources, 1985, 14 *EPL* (1985), 77.

[3] See Chs. 7, 8, and 13.

[4] ILC, Sixth Report on International Liability for Injurious Consequences of Acts Not Prohibited by International Law, UN Doc/A/CN.4/428 (1990), Articles 1–33; ILC Draft Articles on the Non Navigational Uses of International Watercourses, *Report of the ILC to the General Assembly*, UN GAOR, 45th Session, A/45/10 (1990), 137; ILA, Helsinki Rules on International Rivers, 1966, *Report of the 52nd Conference*, 484; ILA, Montreal Rules on Water Pollution, 1982, *Report of the 60th Conference*, 531; ILA, Montreal Rules on Transfrontier Pollution, 1982, *Report of the 60th Conference*, 1; WCED, Draft Convention on Environmental Protection and Sustainable Development, in Munro and Lammers, *Environmental Protection and Sustainable Development*.

(1) The Contribution of Customary Law

Older rules of customary law had relatively little to say on matters of environmental significance.[5] At most, states could be required to act with reasonable regard for the rights of others in the exercise of high seas freedoms, to co-operate in the equitable utilization of shared resources such as international rivers, and to prevent serious transboundary injury to their neighbours. The generality of these rules limited their value as a means of settling environmental disputes or of providing normative standards of behaviour for states faced with increasingly complex environmental problems such as climate change or the loss of species and ecosystems. These older rules placed few limitations on the freedom of states to utilize their own territory or to exploit common areas such as the high seas. They were mainly useful in affording reparation for transboundary injury, as in the *Trail Smelter* arbitration,[6] or in allocating property rights over resources, as in the *Lac Lanoux*[7] and *Behring Sea Fur Seals* arbitrations.[8]

Moreover, as these latter cases showed, the effective implementation of such customary rules was often dependent on negotiation between the states concerned, facilitated in some cases by more formal institutional arrangements such as river commissions or fisheries commissions.[9] These categories represent the earliest examples of the regulation of environmental problems by treaty. In most cases, however, the object of such agreements was confined to ensuring the maximum utilization of an exploitable resource held in common or shared by a number of states. Only in that limited sense were they concerned with nature conservation or the natural environment. Only gradually did the existence of a wider common interest in the conservation of resources, wildlife, or ecosystems gain international recognition both in treaty law and in customary international law.[10]

(2) The Role of Multilateral Lawmaking by Treaty

Since the Stockholm Conference in 1972, international institutions including UNEP, IUCN, and IMO have played an increasingly important role in

---

[5] Brownlie, 13 *NRJ* (1973); Birnie, 3 *BJIS* (1977); Kiss, in Macdonald and Johnston, *Structure and Process*.

[6] 33 *AJIL* (1939), 182, and 35 *AJIL* (1941), 684. See *infra*, n. 38.

[7] 24 *ILR* (1957), 101. See *infra*, Ch. 6.

[8] 1 *Moore's Int. Arbitration Awards* (1898), 755. See Birnie, *International Regulation of Whaling*, i (New York, 1985), 93–104, and *infra*, pp. 493–5.

[9] e.g. the International Joint Council established under the 1909 US–Canadian Boundary Waters Treaty, *infra*, Ch. 6; for fisheries commissions, see Koers, *International Regulation of Marine Fisheries: A Study of Regional Fisheries Organizations* (London, 1973), and see further, *infra*, Ch. 13.

[10] See Chs. 11 and 12.

facilitating the elaboration of more detailed and specific rules of environmental law. Multilateral treaties covering subjects such as marine pollution, protection of the atmosphere, wildlife conservation, international watercourses, and other issues are the major source of these new rules.[11] The emphasis in these treaties is different from older rules of customary law. They focus instead on the prevention of environmental harm and the conservation and sustainable development of natural resources and ecosystems. This change can be observed very clearly in the fisheries conservation and marine pollution provisions of the 1982 UNCLOS, but it is not confined to the law of the sea.[12] The development of international environmental law by multilateral treaty is important for three reasons.

First, it gives some practical content to existing rules of customary law in many cases and enables the primary obligations of states to be identified with greater clarity and developed in a more flexible way through diplomatic conferences and intergovernmental commissions, as we shall see in Chapter 4. The 1973 MARPOL Convention and the 1972 London Dumping Convention are good illustrations of this process. Both conventions have in effect became internationally agreed standards for the conduct of states in preventing marine pollution.[13] While there are a variety of factors which may induce states to conclude environmental agreements, including domestic political needs, the consequent interplay of treaty law and customary obligations has proved to be a central feature of the development of a more sophisticated system of international environmental regulation.[14]

Secondly, these treaties afford a basis for international supervision of standards of environmental protection and sustainable development which customary law alone could not provide. Where formerly the enforcement of international environmental law had to rest on interstate claims and the principle of state responsibility, intergovernmental institutions are now in many cases able to supervise or influence the implementation of treaty obligations.[15] Although the effectiveness of some of these institutions is questionable, they do show that the present structure of international en-

---

[11] See e.g. 1973 MARPOL Convention, *infra*, Ch. 7; 1979 Geneva Convention on Long-Range Transboundary Air Pollution, *infra*, Ch. 10; 1985 Vienna Convention for the Protection of the Ozone Layer, ibid.; 1972 London Dumping Convention, *infra*, Ch. 8; 1989 Basel Convention on the Control of Transboundary Movement of Hazardous Wastes, ibid.; 1973 Convention on International Trade in Endangered Species of Wild Fauna and Flora, *infra*, Ch. 12; 1979 Bonn Convention on the Conservation of Migratory Species of Wild Animals, ibid.; 1979 Berne Convention on the Conservation of European Wildlife and Natural Habitats, ibid.; 1991 Protocol to the Antarctic Treaty on Environmental Protection.

[12] See Chs. 7 and 13.

[13] See *infra*, pp. 92–4.

[14] Kiss, 32 *GYIL* (1989), 240; Birnie, in Carroll, *International Environmental Diplomacy*; Hahn and Richards, 30 *Harv. ILJ* (1989), 421; Gehring, 1 *YIEL* (1990), 35. The legal effect of treaties and their relationship to customary law is considered *supra*, Ch. 1.

[15] See Ch. 4.

vironmental law has moved decisively in favour of a model which emphasizes the fiduciary or custodial relationship of states with the environment. No longer is that relationship best described in terms of tort or property.[16]

Thirdly, this system, like human rights law, now facilitates the protection of community interests, not merely those of states *inter se*. While it retains in many respects the features of an interstate system of rights and obligations, the emergence of environmental obligations owed to the international community as a whole, or '*erga omnes*', is clearly implied in treaties protecting common areas such as the high seas.[17] The concept of the common heritage of mankind represents a parallel development in the management of mineral resources beyond the jurisdiction of individual states.[18] Moreover, the management by a state of its own environment is now increasingly a matter for international scrutiny, independently of any transboundary effects. This can most clearly be observed in a number of multilateral treaties concerned with conservation, trade in hazardous waste, and human rights,[19] and in attempts to regulate areas of 'common concern', such as the ozone layer, the global climate, tropical forests, or world heritage areas.[20] 'Common concern' is the term first used by the UN General Assembly to justify treating the global climate as a unity, regardless of national sovereignty over subjacent airspace and land territory. Its most important implication is that it places the protection of these areas or phenomena on the international agenda and makes them the legitimate object of international attention, overriding the reserved domain of domestic jurisdiction or the possible contention that they relate to matters within the exclusive sovereignty of individual states. The need for a community interest in the enforcement of international environmental law has been recognized, too, by the ILC in its controversial work on international crimes and by attempts to broaden the standing of states to bring international claims.[21] These are in some cases tentative developments, of uncertain legal status, but they do point increasingly to a globalization of international environmental law. It is no longer simply a system of transboundary relations among neighbours.[22]

---

[16] Cf. *The Trail Smelter* arbitration, *supra*, n. 6, and the *Lac Lanoux* arbitration, *supra*, n. 7.

[17] 1982 UNCLOS, Articles 192, 194; 1972 London Dumping Convention; Kiss, 175 *Recueil des cours* (1985), 99.

[18] See *infra*, pp. 120–2; and Kiss, 175 *Recueil des cours* (1985).

[19] See in particular 1968 African Convention on the Conservation of Nature and Natural Resources, *infra*, Ch. 12; 1971 Convention on Wetlands of International Importance, ibid.; 1979 Berne Convention on the Conservation of European Wildlife and Natural Habitats, ibid.; 1989 Basel Convention on the Control of Transboundary Movements of Hazardous Waste, *infra*, Ch. 8, and on human rights, *infra*, Ch. 5.

[20] UNGA Res. 43/53 (1988); 1985 Vienna Convention for the Protection of the Ozone Layer; 1972 Convention for the Protection of World Cultural and Natural Heritage, and see *infra*, Chs. 4 and 10.

[21] See Ch. 4.   [22] Kiss, 32 *GYIL* (1989).

(3) Dispute Settlement and Enforcement

The increasingly global or multilateral character of much environmental law has greatly influenced the choice of methods of dispute settlement and enforcement.[23] The 1982 UNCLOS is exceptional in offering a developed system of judicial supervision in respect of the marine environment, accessible in some cases by individuals and corporations, as well as by states. Although states are free in other environmental cases to refer disputes to the ICJ or *ad hoc* arbitration, they have only rarely done so in this context and there is also nothing directly comparable to regional human rights tribunals such as the European Court of Human Rights or the Inter-American Court, which can hear both interstate complaints and individual petitions. There are various reasons for this reluctance to resort to judicial machinery, considered further in Chapter 4, but it is partly explained by reference to the multilateral character of many environmental problems. As Gehring observes, 'every dispute about an individual actor's compliance with the norms of a legal system also has a collective aspect because the parties, as a group, will primarily be interested in protecting the stability of the legal regime.'[24] The main consequence of this concern for collective interests is the prominence of intergovernmental commissions, 'meetings of parties', and other institutions both in developing international regulation and in ensuring compliance and resolving conflicts of interest by diplomatic or political means.

Despite its collective character, however, the present system of international environmental law also differs from human rights law in that it remains primarily concerned with the rights and obligations of states; the role of individuals, corporations, and NGOs as subjects of international law has received only minimal recognition in this context. The right to a decent environment which is contemplated in Principle 1 of the Stockholm Declaration continues to be no more than a putative human right, part of the so-called third generation of economic and social rights which lack the formal endosement of the international community.[25] Similarly, although the 1972 Stockholm Declaration on the Human Environment and the 1982 World Charter for Nature also refer to the responsibility of individuals for protecting the environment, such declarations do not in themselves constitute legal obligations or render individuals subject to the processes of international law. Only in facilitating individual access to civil remedies for transboundary pollution, or in giving some recognition to the extraterritorial criminal jurisdiction of states for global pollution has international law extended beyond states as its primary subjects.[26] Apart from these limited exceptions, corporations, like individuals, also remain in principle the subject of rights and

---

[23] See Ch. 4.   [24] Gehring, 1 *YIEL* (1990), 51.   [25] See Ch. 5.   [26] Ibid.

obligations only in national law. Thus it is only indirectly, by influencing the behaviour of states, that international law can at present control the activities of the multinational enterprises and companies which constitute a major source of global environmental impact. Moreover, while corporations and NGOs may have observer status or informal access to intergovernmental environmental bodies, and exercise considerable influence on the process of treaty negotiation and international regulation, the primary actors remain states.[27]

(4) The Existence of an 'International' Law of the Environment

The main argument in this and the following chapters is that a system of rules and principles of international environmental law does exist. Its component parts have emerged gradually, through a process of incremental development in the fields of pollution control and conservation of the natural environment. The evidence for this assertion is considered subsequently in more detail; in some cases it is weak or contradictory, and the need for further development apparent. In others, states have not pressed their strict legal rights to the full but have preferred equitable solutions. Thus there are significant qualifications and modifications to be made in applying the rules and principles considered here, despite the evident consensus which exists on many of the main issues.

The most significant qualification concerns the different priorities of southern hemisphere less-developed countries and their demands for 'special consideration'. For many of these countries poverty is perceived as the main 'environmental' problem. Their concerns have been a central feature of environmental diplomacy since the Stockholm Conference.[28] Attempts to reconcile the competing priorities of north and south have been made in various ways, notably by UNEP, IUCN, and the WCED, through the concept of sustainable development,[29] through economic incentives such as trust

---

[27] Cassese, *International Law in a Divided World* (Oxford, 1986), 103; Brownlie, *Principles of Public International Law* (4th edn., Oxford, 1990), 67. But see Benedick, *Ozone Diplomacy* (Cambridge, Mass., 1991), and Charney, *Duke LJ* (1983), 748, who emphasize the involvement of industry in the negotiation of environmental agreements.

[28] Report of the UN Conference on the Human Environment (Stockholm, 1972), UN Doc. A/CONF/48/14/Rev. 1; UNGA Res. 3002 XXVII (1972); Sohn, 14 *HILJ* (1973), 423; Kindt, 20 *VJIL* (1979), 313; Biswas, in Dupuy (ed.), *The Future of the International Law of the Environment* (Dordrecht, 1985), 389–400; Caldwell, *International Environmental Policy*, ch. 3; Anand, *International Law and the Developing World* (Dordrecht, 1987), ch. 6.

[29] *Development and Environment: Report and Working Papers of a Panel of Experts Convened by the UNCHE* (Founex, 1971), *supra*, Ch. 2; WCED, *Our Common Future* (Oxford, 1987), chs. 2 and 3, endorsed by UNGA Res. 42/186 and 187 (1987); 1982 World Charter for Nature, endorsed by UNGA Res. 37/7; UNEP GC Res. 14/14 (1982); and GC Res. (1989), 19 *EPL* (1989) 120; and see *infra*, Ch. 11.

funds,[30] through alterations in the lending policies of the World Bank and other capital providers,[31] and through the negotiation of different—usually lower—standards of environmental regulation and resource exploitation for developing countries in treaties such as the Ozone Convention or the 1982 UNCLOS.[32] The UN General Assembly has also been careful to formulate the 'right to development' in terms which require respect for principles of international law concerning friendly relations and co-operation.[33] Moreover, the emphasis which some states have placed on sovereignty over natural resources and freedom to pursue policies of economic growth must be seen in its proper context. UN resolutions, the Stockholm Declaration, and other international instruments have consistently recognized that although states have permanent sovereignty over their natural resources and retain the right to determine their own environmental policies, they are not free to disregard protection of the environment of common spaces or of other states.[34] Nevertheless, development needs remain a major obstacle to stronger environmental regulation for developing and developed economies alike. A second, but far less significant qualification is the need to make special provision for the rights of indigenous peoples in negotiating conservation and wildlife protection treaties.[35]

Most of the precedents on which this chapter is based are from the northern hemisphere industrialized states, and reflect environmental concerns appropriate to their stage of economic development. There are obvious dangers in assuming that such precedents necessarily have comparable global force. This does not mean that the international environmental law considered here represents only a regional system of law, nor does it imply that its rules have no relevance to the problems of the third world. But in a system of

[30] See e.g. 1972 Convention for the Protection of the World Cultural and Natural Heritage, Articles 15–18, on which see infra, 462–63; 1990 Protocol to the Vienna Convention for the Protection of the Ozone Layer and UNEP's Environment Fund, established by UNGA Res. 2997 XXVII (1972); World Bank, Global Environmental Facility, Annual Report (Washington, DC, 1991), 61.

[31] 1980 Declaration on Environmental Policies and Procedures Relating to Economic Development, 19 ILM (1980), 524; 1989 OECD Recommendation Concerning an Environmental Checklist for Development Assistance, 28 ILM, (1989), 1314; Statute of the European Bank for Reconstruction and Development, 1990, Article 2(1); World Bank, Annual Report (Washington, DC, 1991), 59–64; Muldoon, 22 TILJ (1987), Panel on Environment, Economic Development and Human Rights, 1988 Proc. of the ASIL, 40.

[32] See also Stockholm Declaration, principles 8–12, and 23, and infra, Chs. 8 and 10.

[33] UNGA Res. 41/128.

[34] UNGA Res. 3281 XXIX (1974), Charter of Economic Rights and Duties of States; 1972 Stockholm Declaration on the Human Environment, Principle 21; 1982 UNCLOS, Article 193; infra, 91–92.

[35] See e.g. 1946 International Convention for the Regulation of Whaling, schedule, adopted July 1983, para. 13; 1973 Agreement on the Conservation of Polar Bears, Article 3; 1989 ILO Convention 169 Concerning Indigenous and Tribal Peoples in Independent Countries; 1985 Nairobi Protocol Concerning Protected Areas and Wild Fauna and Flora in the Eastern African Region, Article 12. See also McGoldrick, 40 ICLQ (1991), 658.

international law founded primarily, though not exclusively, on the consent of states, it does emphasize the importance of seeking evidence of third world practice and of securing third world participation in treaty regimes, including especially those of global significance, such as the 1985 Ozone Convention, the 1982 UNCLOS, the proposed Climate Change Convention, or the 1979 Bonn Convention on the Conservation of Migratory Species.[36]

2. CUSTOMARY LAW AND GENERAL PRINCIPLES CONCERNING TRANSBOUNDARY POLLUTION AND ENVIRONMENTAL HARM

International law does not allow states to conduct activities within their territories, or in common spaces, without regard for the rights of other states or for the protection of the global environment. This point is sometimes expressed by reference to the maxim *sic utere tuo, ut alienum non laedas* or 'principles of good neighbourliness', but the contribution of customary law in environmental matters is neither as modest nor as vacuous as these phrases might suggest. Two principles enjoy significant support: a duty to prevent, reduce, and control pollution and environmental harm, and a duty to co-operate in mitigating environmental risks and emergencies. Two further principles, the 'polluter pays' principle, and the principle of equal access and non-discrimination, are also of increasing significance in the development of environmental law at national level.

(1) A Duty to Prevent, Reduce, and Control Environmental Harm

(a) The Customary Principle

It is beyond serious argument that states are required by international law to take adequate steps to control and regulate sources of serious global environmental pollution or transboundary harm within their territory or subject to their jurisdiction. This is a principle of harm prevention, not merely a basis for reparation after the event, although in its judicial applications it has usually taken the latter form. Support for such an obligation can be found in a small number of arbitral and judicial decisions, and in more contemporary sources.[37] In the well-known *Trial Smelter* arbitration,[38] a tribunal awarded damages to the United states and prescribed a regime for controlling future

---

[36] See Hague Declaration, 1989, 19 *EPL* (1989), 78; Helsinki Declaration on the Protection of the Ozone Layer, 1989, ibid. 137, and *infra*, Chs. 7 and 10.

[37] See Dupuy, in OECD, *Legal Aspects of Transfrontier Pollution* (Paris, 1977), 345; Smith, *State Responsibility and the Marine Environment* (Oxford, 1988), 36 ff., 72 ff.; Handl, 26 *NRJ* (1986), 405, 427 ff.; Kirgis, 66 *AJIL* (1972), 290, 315; Quentin-Baxter, II *Yearbook ILC* (1980), pt. 1, 246–62.

[38] *Supra*, n. 6. See Read, 1 *CYIL* (1963), 213; Rubin, 50 *OLR* (1971), 259; Kirgis, 66 *AJIL* (1972); Smith, *State Responsibility*, 72 ff.; Quentin-Baxter, II *Yearbook ILC* (1981), pt. 1, 108 ff.

emissions from a Canadian smelter which had caused air pollution damage. It concluded that 'no state has the right to use or permit the use of its territory in such a manner as to cause injury by fumes in or to the territory of another', and that measures of control were necessary.[39] The judgment of the International Court of Justice in the *Corfu Channel* case supports a similar principle, although the context is rather different and its application to the environment more doubtful. Here the court held Albania responsible for damage to British warships caused by a failure to warn them of mines in territorial waters, and it indicated that it was 'every state's obligation not to allow knowingly its territory to be used for acts contrary to the rights of other states'.[40] This judgment does not suggest what the environmental rights of other states might be, and its true significance may be confined to a narrower point about warning other states of known dangers, considered below.

While the significance of these few judicial precedents should not be overrated, there is ample evidence of continued international support for the broad principle that states must control sources of harm to others or to the global environment. In particular, Principle 21 of the 1972 Stockholm Declaration on the Human Environment is important, because it affirms both the sovereign right of states to exploit their own resources 'pursuant to their own environmental policies' and their responsibility 'to ensure that activities within their jurisdiction or control do not cause damage to the environment of other states or to areas beyond the limits of national jurisdiction'. Although, as Professor Sohn has observed, the first part of this principle comes 'quite close' to asserting that a state has unlimited sovereignty over its environment, the totality of the provision, including its emphatic reference to responsibility for environmental damage, was regarded by many states present at the Stockholm Conference, and subsequently by the UN General Assembly, as reflecting customary international law.[41]

---

[39] 35 *AJIL* (1941), 716. This finding relied on the *Alabama Claims* arbitration (1872), Moore, 1 *International Arbitrations*, 485, and Eagleton, *Responsibility of States in International Law* (1928), 80, for the general proposition that 'A state owes at all times a duty to protect other states against injurious acts by individuals from within its jurisdiction', and on the evidence of US Federal case law dealing with interstate air and water pollution, which it held 'may legitimately be taken as a guide in this field of international law ... where no contrary rule prevails', 35 *AJIL* (1941), 714. Reliance on domestic case law by analogy was *not* required by the *compromis*, which called for application of US law and practice only in respect of issues of proof of damage, indemnity, and the regime of future operations of the smelter, ibid. 698. The use of domestic law analogies is better treated as an invocation of 'general principles of law' referred to in Article 38(1) of the Statute of the ICJ. For criticism of the tribunal's approach, see Rubin, 50 *OLR* (1971), 267; Goldie, 14 *ICLQ* (1965), 1229, and for explanation, see Read, 1 *CYIL* (1963).

[40] *ICJ Rep.* (1949), 22. See also *Nuclear Tests* Case (*Australia* v. *France*) *ICJ Rep.* (1974), 388, per de Castro; *Lac Lanoux* arbitration, 24 *ILR* (1957), 101, 123; and Brownlie, *State Responsibility* (Oxford, 1983), 182.

[41] Sohn, 14 *HILJ* (1973), 491 ff. Several states declared that Principle 21 accorded with existing international law: see Canadian and US Comments in UN Doc. A/CONF.48/14/Rev. 1, at 64–6. UNGA Res. 2996 (XXVII) (1972) asserts that Principles 21 and 22 of the Stockholm

(b) The Significance of Stockholm Principle 21

Principle 21 has remained a highly influential statement in the subsequent development of law and practice in environmental matters,[42] notably in United Nations resolutions,[43] in UNEP principles,[44] and in multilateral treaties such as the London Dumping Convention, the Geneva Convention on Long-Range Transboundary Air Pollution, the Ozone Convention, or the Basel Convention on the Transboundary Movement of Hazardous Wastes. Its normative character is also recognized in Articles 192, 193, and 194 of the 1982 UNCLOS.

Whereas older formulations of the 'no harm' principle, in cases such as *Trail Smelter*, had dealt only with transboundary harm to other states, many of these later conventions point to international acceptance of the proposition that states are now required to protect global common areas, including Antarctica and those areas beyond the limits of national jurisdiction, such as the high seas, deep sea-bed, and outer space.[45] Article 194(2) of the 1982 UNCLOS makes the same point, when it calls for states to prevent pollution spreading beyond areas where they exercise sovereign rights. At the Stockholm Conference itself, the United States submitted that Principle 21 did not in any way diminish an already existing international responsibility for damage to other states or areas beyond national jurisdiction;[46] the UN General

Declaration 'lay down the basic rules governing the matter'. One hundred and twelve states voted for this resolution, none opposed. Eastern bloc states did not attend the Stockholm Conference and abstained on Res. 2996, but have supported subsequent treaties recognizing the normative character of Principle 21. See also CSCE Final Act, *infra*, n. 46; 1992 Rio Declaration, *infra*, Ch. 14.

[42] Bothe, *Trends in Environmental Policy and Law*, 366 ff.; Dupuy, *Legal Aspects of Transfrontier Pollution*, 345 ff. and 356; Arechaga, 159 *Recueil des cours* (1978), 272 f.; Handl, 74 *AJIL* (1980), 525; Springer, in Carroll, *International Environmental Diplomacy*, 45.

[43] UNGA Res. 2849 XXVI (1971); 2995 XXVII (1972); 2996 XXVII (1972); 3281 XXIX (1974); 34/186 (1979).

[44] Principles of Conduct in the Field of the Environment Concerning Resources Shared by Two or More States, Principle 3, UNEP/IG/12/2 (1978), *infra*, pp. 114–7.

[45] Sohn, 14 *HILJ* (1973); Smith, *State Responsibility*, 76 ff.; Fleischer, in Bothe, *Trends in Environmental Policy and Law*, 321; Charney, in Francioni and Scovazzi (eds.), *International Responsibility for Environmental Harm* (Dordrecht, 1991), 149; Pineschi, in eid. (eds.), *International Law for Antarctica* (Milan, 1987), 187. See also 1967 Outer Space Treaty; 1979 Moon Treaty; *infra*, Ch. 10; 1972 London Dumping Convention, *infra*, Ch. 8; 1982 UNCLOS, Articles 145, 209; 1988 Convention for the Regulation of Antarctic Mineral Resource Activities; 1991 Protocol to the Antarctic Treaty on Environmental Protection. Although Antarctica is subject to territorial claims by seven states, these were placed in abeyance by the 1959 Antarctic Treaty and the continent has since been open to all states participating in the treaty system for the purposes of scientific exploration. The 1991 Protocol would prohibit mineral exploitation for 50 years. Thus in practice it is not treated as an area of exclusive territorial sovereignty; injury to its environment is more analogous to injury to the high seas.

[46] Report of the UN Conference on the Human Environment, UN Doc. A/CONF/48/14/Rev. 1, (1972), para. 327. See also CSCE, Final Act, 1975: 'Acknowledging that each of the participating states, in accordance with the principles of international law, ought to ensure, in a

Assembly subsequently affirmed that in the exploration, exploitation, and development of their natural resources, 'states must not produce significant harmful effects in zones situated outside their national jurisdiction.'[47] An important consequence of this changed perspective is that the obligation is no longer solely bilateral in character but benefits the international community as a whole.[48] This point is emphasized by the ILC's treatment of 'massive pollution of the atmosphere or of the seas' as an international crime in respect of which all states are 'injured states'.[49]

Moreover, whatever the earlier significance of *Trail Smelter* and other judicial precedents may have been, Principle 21, as it has been applied in subsequent lawmaking, requires states to do more than make reparation for environmental damage. Its main importance is that it recognizes the duty of states to take suitable preventive measures to protect the environment.[50] Even in the *Trail Smelter* case, Canada was ordered by the tribunal to take measures to prevent future injury, and this is the primary purpose of most modern environmental treaties, including the Ozone Convention, the MARPOL Convention, the London Dumping Convention, and those dealing with land-based pollution. That the rule is now primarily one of prevention and control is indicated most clearly by Article 194 of the 1982 UNCLOS:

1. States shall take, individually or jointly as appropriate, all measures consistent with this Convention that are necessary to prevent, reduce and control pollution of the marine environment from any source, using for this purpose the best practicable means at their disposal and in accordance with their capabilities, and they shall endeavour to harmonise their policies in this connection.
2. States shall take all measures necessary to ensure that activities under their jurisdiction or control are so conducted as not to cause damage by pollution to other states and their environment...[51]

The same approach is found in Article 2(1) of the 1991 ECE Convention on Environmental Impact Assessment, which provides that: 'The parties shall, either individually or jointly, take all appropriate and effective measures to prevent, reduce and control significant adverse transboundary environmental impact from proposed activities.' What these provisions imply is a general obligation on the part of states to act with due diligence.

(c) Due Diligence and Harm Prevention

In general terms, 'due diligence' requires the introduction of legislation and administrative controls applicable to public and private conduct which are capable of effectively protecting other states and the global environment, and

spirit of co-operation, that activities carried out on its territory do not cause degradation of the environment in another state or in areas lying beyond the limits of national jurisdiction.'
[47] UNGA Res. 2995 XXVII (1972).
[48] Charney, in Francioni and Scovazzi, *International Responsibility*, and see *infra*, Ch. 4.
[49] See Ch. 4.
[50] Dupuy, in OECD, *Legal Aspects of Transfrontier Pollution*, 372.   [51] See Chs. 7 and 8.

it can be expressed as the conduct to be expected of a good government.[52] The advantages of this standard of conduct are its flexibility and the fact that it does not make the state an absolute guarantor of the prevention of harm.[53] Considerations of the effectiveness of territorial control, the resources available to the state, and the nature of specific activities may all be taken into account and justify differing degrees of diligence.[54] Article 194 of the 1982 UNCLOS indicates how these considerations allow the concerns of developing states to be accommodated, although less flexibility is allowed where the harm is to other states than in cases affecting common spaces.[55] Similarly, Article 2 of the 1972 London Dumping Convention requires parties to take effective measures 'according to their scientific, technical and economic capabilities . . .'. The view that special allowance is to be made for developing countries in determining the content of their legal obligations is also reflected in Principle 23 of the Stockholm Declaration.

The major disadvantage of this general formulation of due diligence is that it is relatively unhelpful in environmental matters because it offers little guidance on what legislation or controls are required of states in each case. Something more is needed to give it concrete content and predictability. For this purpose a useful approach is to look to internationally agreed minimum standards set out in treaties or in the resolutions and decisions of international bodies such as IMO or IAEA.[56] Such 'ecostandards' can be very detailed and precise, as for example in the case of the 1973 MARPOL Convention.[57] An alternative approach allows for a developing standard of diligence by reference to the use of 'best available technology' or similar formulations, such as 'best practicable means'.[58]

[52] OECD, *Legal Aspects of Transfrontier Pollution*, 385 f.; Dupuy, ibid. 369 ff.; Smith, *State Responsibility*, 36–42.

[53] OECD, *Legal Aspects of Transfrontier Pollution*, 380; Dupuy, ibid. See in particular 1982 UNCLOS, Annex III, Article 4(4): 'The sponsoring state or states shall pursuant to Article 139, have the responsibility to ensure, within their legal systems that a contractor so sponsored shall carry out activities in the Area in conformity with the terms of its contract and its obligations under this Convention. A sponsoring state shall not, however, be liable for damage caused by any failure of a contractor sponsored by it or to comply with its obligations if that state party has adopted laws and regulations and taken administrative measures which are, within the framework of its legal system, reasonably appropriate for securing compliance by persons under its jurisdiction.'

[54] See generally *Alabama Claims* arbitration, *supra*, n. 39, 485; *Case Concerning Diplomatic and Consular Staff in Tehran*, ICJ Reports (1980), 29–33; *Corfu Channel Case*, ICJ Reports (1949), 89, Judge ad hoc Ecer; Dupuy, *Legal Aspects of Transfrontier Pollution*, 375 f.; Smith, *State Responsibility*, 38–41.

[55] For examples of this 'double standard' in practice, see *infra*, Chs. 8 and 10.

[56] Contini and Sand, 66 *AJIL* (1972), 37; Dupuy, in Bothe, *Trends in Environmental Policy and Law*, 369; Birnie, in Carroll, *International Environmental Diplomacy*, 98 ff.; Arechaga, 159 *Recueil des cours*, (1978), 272 f.

[57] See Ch. 7. On IAEA standards, cf. Ch. 9.

[58] See e.g. 1974 Paris Convention for the Prevention of Marine Pollution from Land-based Sources, Article 4(3) and BAT standards adopted by the Paris Commission, *infra*, Ch. 8; 1979 Geneva Convention on Long-Range Transboundary Air Pollution, Article 6; 1982 World Charter for Nature, para. 11; Handl, 26 *NRJ* (1986), 464.

The technique of resorting to standards of this kind for the purpose of defining obligations of conduct is employed by several multilateral treaties. The 1982 UNCLOS in effect incorporates by reference both the MARPOL Convention and the London Dumping Convention by requiring states to give effect to generally accepted international rules and standards, whether or not they are independently binding on parties.[59] Other examples of the same technique of incorporation by reference to internationally accepted standards are found in the Basel Convention on Transboundary Movement of Hazardous Wastes.[60] In some cases states are given more latitude and need only 'take account of international standards', but even this formulation gives some guidance as to content of their general obligation of diligence.[61]

Moreover, quite apart from their incorporation by treaty, such international standards may acquire customary force, if international support is sufficiently widespread and representative. The MARPOL Convention may be one example of this transformation process.[62] IAEA guidelines for the dumping of radioactive waste at sea are arguably another.[63] Thus whether or not they are found in legally binding instruments, it is now often possible to point to specific standards of diligent conduct which in turn can be monitored by international supervisory institutions or employed by international tribunals to settle disputes.

Treaty formulations overwhelmingly favour the due diligence interpretation of states' primary environmental obligations,[64] and, as we shall see in Chapter 4, the most convincing interpretation of the state responsibility precedents is that in most cases this standard now reflects customary law.

(d) Absolute Obligations of Prevention

An alternative interpretation of Principle 21, which itself is ambiguous on the matter, stresses the fact of harm, rather than the conduct of the state in bringing it about or failing to prevent it.[65] Another way of making the same point is to postulate a duty of diligence so demanding that it amounts to an absolute obligation of prevention or an obligation of 'result' rather than of conduct.[66] Since it is not plausible to interpret the typical treaty formulation requiring states to 'prevent, reduce and control' pollution in this absolute sense, the more onerous interpretation of Principle 21 is mainly significant in determining the incidence of state responsibility in customary law for un-

---

[59] Articles 210 and 211. See *infra*, Chs. 7 and 8.   [60] See Ch. 8.
[61] e.g. 1982 UNCLOS, Articles 207 and 208, *infra*, Ch. 8.   [62] See Ch. 7.
[63] See *infra*, pp. 323–5. See also IMO's International Maritime Dangerous Goods Code.
[64] See e.g. 1982 UNCLOS, Article 194; 1979 Convention on Long-Range Transboundary Air Pollution, Article 2; 1985 Convention for the Protection of the Ozone Layer, Article 2; 1972 London Dumping Convention, Article 1; and for international watercourses, see *infra*, Ch. 6.
[65] Springer, in Carroll, *International Environmental Diplomacy*, and *infra*, Ch. 4.
[66] Smith, *State Responsibility*, 41; II *Yearbook ILC* (1977), pt. 2, 11–30.

avoidable or unforeseeable environmental damage, which by definition could not have been prevented or controlled. One problem with these more onerous interpretations, however, is that they may place unacceptable burdens on the freedom of states to permit harmful activities within their own borders and to pursue their own environmental policies. For this reason some commentators limit this version of the obligation to harm caused by ultra-hazardous activities, of which nuclear reactors are an obvious example.[67] An extreme view, that such activities may become impermissible, has led the ILC to develop a novel regime based not on the notion of breach of obligation but requiring compensation for harm as part of an equitable balance of interests allowing the polluting activity to continue.[68] The conclusion that obligations of harm prevention however defined can make the activity itself impermissible is widely regarded as misconceived, however: as Brownlie observes, 'it is the content of the relevant rules which is critical, and a global distinction between lawful and unlawful activities is useless', and unsupported by state practice or international jurisprudence.[69]

A further objection to absolute obligations of prevention is that they concentrate more on shifting the burden of proof and the burden of responsibility for loss back to the polluter than on the diligent control of dangerous activities, since conduct will be irrelevant to the performance of such obligations. Thus even if arguments for an absolute standard of prevention are accepted as a basis for state responsibility for environmental injury, in practice the elaboration of standards of diligent conduct remains an essential complementary principle[70] and a better basis for international regulation of the environment.

(e) Foreseeability of Harm and the 'Precautionary Principle'

As we have seen, the rule that states must not cause or permit serious or significant harm to other states or to common spaces is not simply one of responsibility for injury *ex post facto*. It is now necessarily primarily an obligation of diligent prevention and control, and in this sense, it can be said that international law already adopts a 'precautionary approach'. This inter-

---

[67] e.g. Jenks, 117 *Recueil des cours* (1966), 105, and see *infra*, Ch. 4.

[68] See Quentin-Baxter, II *Yearbook ILC* (1981), pt. 1, 112–22; ibid. (1982), pt. 1, 60, para. 39; ibid. (1983), pt. 1, 206, paras. 19–22; and Barboza, UN Doc. A/CN.4/428 (1990), para. 10, and draft articles 17, 20.

[69] Brownlie, *State Responsibility*, 50; see also Akehurst, 16 *NYIL* (1985), 8; Boyle, 39 *ICLQ* (1990), 12–14, but cf. Magraw, 80 *AJIL* (1986), 305. Nor does the conclusion that some environmentally risky activities are prohibited, such as dumping at sea of high level radioactive waste (*infra*, Ch. 8), or atmospheric nuclear tests (*infra*, Ch. 9) necessarily imply that states are obliged to do more than adopt appropriate laws and exercise the necessary administrative controls. What it does imply is that states must not authorize or conduct such activities.

[70] See Barboza, 2nd Report on International Liability, II *Yearbook ILC* (1986), pt. 1, 159, paras. 63–9; 4th Report, UN Doc. A/CN.4/413, (1988), 34, paras. 103–11. Draft Article 8 amounts to an obligation of diligent control.

pretation of the 'no harm' principle leaves open for determination the point at which preventive or precautionary measures must be taken, however, a question which can only be answered by reference to the foreseeability or likelihood of harm and of its potential gravity.

Some indication of the position in customary law is afforded by the *Corfu Channel*[71] case, in which the ICJ stressed the importance of establishing Albania's actual knowledge of the risk to British warships as a condition of its responsibility for damage. Foreseeability, rather than actual foresight, is required by the ICL's articles on 'International Liability'.[72] These draft articles apply to activities which cause or create a risk of transboundary harm when the state knows or has the means of knowing that such an activity is being conducted or is to be conducted in its territory or jurisdiction. The clear inference is that the obligation of diligent control arises only once the risk is foreseeable.

Moreover, the emphasis which modern treaties place on prior environmental impact assessment of projects likely to affect other states or areas beyond national jurisdiction shows that states are not free to close their eyes to the possible consequences of activities they authorize.[73] The object of prior assessment is to enable 'appropriate' measures to be taken to mitigate or prevent pollution before it occurs. Article 206 of the 1982 UNCLOS is typical of a number of conventions in the way it formulates this obligation:

> When states have reasonable grounds for believing that planned activities under their jurisdiction or control may cause substantial pollution of or significant and harmful changes to the marine environment, they shall, as far as practicable assess the potential effects of such activities on the marine environment and shall communicate reports of the results of such assessments [to IMO].

A similar practice is envisaged in ILC draft articles, in UNEP 'Principles', and by the 1991 ECE Convention on Environmental Impact Assessment.[74] Apart from the incorporation of such obligations in numerous treaties, state practice also favours this requirement in some major jurisdictions,[75] as does

---

[71] *Supra*, n. 40.

[72] See Barboza, 4th Report, UN Doc. A/CN.4/413, (1988), 25; 5th Report, draft Article 3, UN Doc. A/CN/423 (1989), and 6th Report, draft Article 2, UN Doc. A/CN.4/428 (1990), which lists categories of 'activities involving risk'.

[73] See *infra*, n. 125, and Chs. 6 and 8.

[74] ILC, Draft Articles on 'International Liability', Article 11, UN Doc. A/CN.4/428 (1990); UNEP, Principles of Environmental Impact Assessment, 1987; id., Principles of Co-operation in the Utilization of Natural Resources Shared by Two or More states, 1978, *infra*, pp. 114–7; Irwin, 13 *EPL* (1984), 51; Bonine, 17 *EPL* (1987), 5. See also *infra*, n. 127 for adoption by OECD and the ILA.

[75] EEC, Council Directive 85/337, OJ 1985 L 175, 40; Germany, 1990 Act Concerning Environmental Impact Assessment; Canada, 1980 Environmental Assessment Act (Ontario); US, 1969 National Environmental Policy Act, 42 USC ss 4321–47. This act applies only to US government agency projects, but includes those conducted abroad. See *Wilderness Society* v. *Morton* 463 F. 2d 1261 (1972); Grad, *Treatise on Environmental Law*, ii (New York, 1990), ch. 9; 'Comment', 131 *U. Penn LR* (1982), 353. See *infra*, n. 125 for treaty provisions.

the practice of a number of international lending agencies, such as the World Bank.[76] The latter's annual report explains that the Bank's project assessments 'are meant to ensure that development options are environmentally sound and sustainable' and that 'any environmental consequences are recognised early in the project cycle and are taken account of in project design'. It can fairly be assumed that a state, and possibly also an international organization such as the World Bank, whose activities have caused serious environmental injury, will find it difficult to deny responsibility on grounds of non-foreseeability if it has not conducted such an assessment. To that extent prior assessment may already be obligatory as a matter of customary law. It is also possible to argue that it forms part of the obligation of transboundary co-operation and consultation considered in the next section.

But this does not answer the question what kind of risk is necessary to bring obligations of harm prevention into play. Some states have asserted that they are not bound to act until there is clear and convincing scientific proof of actual or threatened harm. As we shall see in Chapter 10, this argument has been used at various times to delay the negotiation of measures to tackle the risk of global climate change, acid rain, and ozone depletion. While this approach may reflect the formulation of international law in the *Trail Smelter* case, it makes no allowance for scientific uncertainty in matters of prediction, and ignores the very different context of that case. A more realistic approach, when the question is one of prevention of foreseeable harm, not responsibility for actual harm, is to lower the threshold of proof. While still entailing some element of foreseeability, this would require measures of prevention at an earlier stage, when there is still some room for uncertainty. Expressions such as 'reasonably foreseeable' or 'significant risk' allow both the magnitude of harm and the probability of its occurrence to be taken into account.[77]

It is in this context that some interpretations of the so-called 'precautionary principle' have acquired special importance. The 1990 Bergen Ministerial Declaration on Sustainable Development defines this principle to mean that:

Environmental measures must anticipate, prevent and attack the causes of environmental degradation. Where there are threats of serious or irreversible damage, lack of full scientific certainty should not be used as a reason for postponing measures to prevent environmental degradation.[78]

---

[76] World Bank, Operational Directive on Environmental Assessment, 1989; id., *Environmental Assessment Sourcebook* (Washington, DC, 1991), 62, and see generally, *supra*, n. 31. World Bank practice is summarized in *The World Bank and the Environment* (Washington, DC, 1991), 66–72.

[77] See Munro and Lammers, *Environmental Protection and Sustainable Development*, 78–80; Barboza, *5th Report on International Liability*, UN Doc. A/CN.4/423 (1989), draft Article 2; Freestone, in Churchill and Freestone (eds.), *International Law and Global Climate Change* (London, 1991), ch. 2.

[78] 20 *EPL* (1990), 100. See generally Gundling, 5 *IJECL* (1990), 29; Freestone, in Churchill and Freestone, *International Law*; Hey, 'The Precautionary Approach and the LDC', annexed to LDC 14/4, 4 Sept. 1991.

The Ozone Convention is perhaps the best example of the application of this approach, which has also been applied to dumping at sea, the transboundary movement of waste, and endorsed by intergovernmental commissions responsible for controlling land-based sources of marine pollution and by the International North Sea Conference.[79] But the difficulty of persuading states to respond to predictions of global climate change indicates that it cannot be assumed there is international consensus on this use of the 'precautionary principle'.[80]

A stronger version of the precautionary principle goes further by reversing the burden of proof altogether. In this form, it becomes impermissible to carry out an activity unless it can be shown that it will not cause unacceptable harm to the environment. Examples of its use in this sense include the resolution suspending disposal of low-level radioactive waste at sea without the approval of the London Dumping Convention Consultative Parties, the suspension of industrial dumping in the Oslo Commission area without prior justification to the Oslo Commission, and the moratorium on whaling.[81] The main effect of the principle in these situations is to require states to submit proposed activities affecting the global commons to international scrutiny, although it is doubtful whether these few rather exceptional examples at present support the conclusion that prior consent of this kind is required by international law.

Despite its attractions, the great variety of interpretations given to the precautionary principle, and the novel and far-reaching effects of some applications suggest that it is not yet a principle of international law. Difficult questions concerning the point at which it becomes applicable to any given activity remain unanswered and seriously undermine its normative character and practical utility, although support for it does indicate a policy of greater prudence on the part of those states willing to accept it.

(f) Environmental Harm or 'Pollution' as the Object of Prevention

Most interpretations of the principle under discussion refer to an obligation to prevent harm or damage and usually assume that this must reach some level of seriousness before it becomes wrongful.[82] The ILC prefers to use the term 'appreciable' to qualify the degree of harm or pollution. Apart from obvious difficulties of definition and assessment of this threshold in individual cases,

---

[79] See Ch. 8 n. 9, and Ch. 10, and see Hey, 'The Precautionary Approach'.

[80] See Freestone, in Churchill and Freestone, *International Law*, 21, but cf. UNCED, Prepcom, UN Doc. A/CONF.151/PC/WG11/Misc. 4 (1991), and Ministerial Declaration of the Second World Climate Conference, 1990.

[81] See Chs. 8 and 12. Also 1988 Convention for the Regulation of Antarctic Mineral Resource Activities, *infra*, Ch. 4.

[82] *The Trail Smelter* arbitration, 35 *AJIL* (1941), 716, talks of 'serious injury'; UNGA Res. 2995 XXVII (1972) refers to 'significant harmful effects'; ILC draft articles on 'International Liability', UN Doc. A/CN.4/428 (1990) and on 'International Watercourses', II *Yearbook ILC* (1984), pt. 1, 112 use the term 'appreciable injury', which is thought to mean less than serious.

other formulations, such as Principle 21 of the Stockholm Declaration, omit any qualifying reference to the level of harm or damage, and cast some doubt on the general assumption.[83]

More problematical is the view that this threshold is essentially relative and conditional on equitable considerations or a balance of interests.[84] This approach has the effect of converting an obligation to prevent harm into an obligation to use territory equitably and reasonably or into a constraint on abuse of rights.[85] There is some support for equitable balancing as a test of the permissibility of pollution of shared resources, such as international watercourses, and some writers would apply the same approach or a test of reasonableness to the obligation to prevent transboundary harm.[86] While states may choose to regulate transboundary pollution in this way,[87] neither the international case law nor treaty definitions of harm or damage support thresholds determined by equitable balancing outside the context of international watercourse law or living resources.[88] The only balancing of interests in *Trail Smelter* related not to the question whether Canada was in breach of its obligation but to the determination of a regime for the future operation of the smelter.[89]

Nor is the case for making the customary threshold of serious harm dependent on a balance of interests a strong one.[90] The notion that states must act with due diligence to prevent serious harm is a formula which already allows for flexibility in individual cases and excludes *de minimis* pollution. To add more variables would be subversive of efforts to establish minimum standards of environmental protection and prove too favourable to the polluter. Only if the obligation of prevention is an absolute one might it then be justifiable to resort to equitable manipulation of the threshold of harm in order to mitigate the rigours of an otherwise extreme rule.

---

[83] e.g. Principle 21 of the 1972 Stockholm Declaration and instruments based on it: see e.g. Article 194, 1982 UNCLOS; Article 30, Charter of Economic Rights and Duties of states, (1974) *infra*, pp. 113–4; Principle 3, 1978 UNEP Principles of Conduct Concerning Resources Shared by Two or More States, *infra*, pp. 114–7. Views differ on whether omission of an explicit threshold is intended to change earlier practice: cf. Springer, in Carroll, *International Environmental Diplomacy*, 51; Handl, 26 *NRJ* (1986), 412 ff., and Pallemaerts, *Hague YIL* (1988), 206.

[84] Handl, 13 *CYIL* (1975), 156; id., 26 *NRJ* (1986), 405; Quentin-Baxter, II *Yearbook ILC* (1981), pt. 1, 112–19; McCaffrey, II *Yearbook ILC* (1986), pt. 1, 133–4.

[85] On abuse of rights, see *infra*, pp. 125–6.

[86] Quentin-Baxter, 2nd Report on 'International Liability', II *Yearbook ILC* (1981), pt. 1, 108 ff.; McDougal and Schlei, 64 *YLJ* (1955), 690 ff., and see *infra*, Ch. 8.

[87] Handl, 26 *NRJ* (1986), 447, argues that states have done so in the 1979 Geneva Convention on Long-Range Transboundary Air Pollution but only for pollution *not* exceeding the customary threshold of serious harm enshrined in Principle 21. This seems doubtful, however: see *infra*, pp. 393–5.

[88] Bleicher, 2 *ELQ* (1972), 28; Handl, 13 *CYIL* (1975), 177–80, agrees but argues that *Lac Lanoux* and precedents relating to international watercourses support a balancing test in that context. See also id., 26 *NRJ* (1986), 421–7.

[89] Read, 1 *CYIL* (1963).

[90] Handl, 26 *NRJ* (1986), 416–21.

Another possible limitation on the principle that harm must be prevented focuses on the type of interest protected, or on the type of harm which must occur. The *Trail Smelter* arbitration took a narrow view. Its concentration on property loss in the United States places no value on wider environmental interests such as wildlife, aesthetic considerations, or the unity of ecosystems.[91] The same focus on damage to property or personal injury is found in Article 1 of the 1972 Space Objects Liability Convention.[92] This approach is clearly outdated and inappropriate. In contrast, Principle 21 of the Stockholm Declaration talks of responsibility for damage to the 'environment' of other states or areas beyond national jurisdiction. Similar phraseology is used in Article 194(2) of the 1982 UNCLOS, which suggests that ecological effects are now included in the no-harm principle. This interpretation is borne out by Article 194(5), which requires pollution control measures to protect and preserve 'rare or fragile ecosystems as well as the habitat of depleted, threatened or endangered species and other forms of marine life'. Definitions of 'the environment' in the Antarctic Mineral Resources Convention[93] and the Ozone Convention[94] point to the same general conclusion. The former refers to 'any impact on the living or non-living components' of Antarctica, including harm to atmospheric, marine, or terrestrial life, 'beyond that which is negligible'. The latter defines 'adverse effects' to include 'changes in climate which have significant deleterious effects on human health, or on the composition, resilience and productivity of natural and managed ecosystems or on materials useful to mankind.'

Determining the scope of international obligations where there is no injury to health or property has, however, proved difficult in disputes concerning nuclear accidents and in the *Nuclear Tests* cases,[95] where there was evidence of radioactive fall-out but no proof of harm. But Canada's later success in recovering the costs of removing debris and cleaning up areas affected by the Cosmos 954 crash[96] may suggest that the no-harm principle does protect a state's natural environment; this conclusion would also be consistent with the award of environmental protection and restoration costs under some marine pollution treaties, and with ILC proposals.[97] What does seem tenable is that

---

[91] Rubin, 50 *OLR* (1971), 272–4. On this issue the tribunal was required to follow US law. US tort law is now more generous in allowing for ecological loss: see *Commonwealth of Puerto Rico v. SS Zoe Colocotroni*, 456 F. Supp. 1327 (1978) and Halter and Thomas, 10 *ELQ* (1982), 5, discussed *infra*, Ch. 7 n. 166.

[92] Christol, *The Modern Law of Outer Space* (New York, 1982), 91–100.

[93] Article 1(15).   [94] Article 1(2).

[95] *Nuclear Tests Cases (Australia v. France)*, *ICJ Rep.* (1974), 253; Handl, 69 *AJIL* (1975), 50. See further, *infra*, p. 361.

[96] 'Claim for Damage Caused by Soviet Cosmos 954', 18 *ILM* (1978), 902; Christol, *The Modern Law of Outer Space*; and on the Chernobyl accident, see *infra*, Ch. 9.

[97] ILC, draft Article 2 on 'International Liability', 1990; 1984 Protocol on Civil Liability for Oil Pollution Damage; 1989 International Convention on Salvage. See *infra*, pp. 292–7, but cf. nuclear civil liability treaties, *infra*, Ch. 9.

while material injury of some kind is a necessary element of the primary obligation,[98] this is not necessarily confined to the loss of resources or amenities of economic value to man, but can extend to the intrinsic worth of natural ecosystems. However, what precisely is meant by 'the environment' for this purpose may depend in each case on the wording of individual treaties.[99]

An alternative approach is simply to define harm in terms of 'pollution'. Although several formulations are used, modern treaty definitions of pollution are considerably wider than the *Trail Smelter* approach.[100] The unifying feature of all current definitions is their focus on a detrimental alteration in quality, but this can be expressed narrowly, in terms of impact on resources or amenities useful to man, or more broadly, in terms of environmental conservation or amelioration.[101] The former approach is represented by the definition of marine pollution adopted by the Group of Experts on Scientific Aspects of Marine Pollution (GESAMP) which refers only to 'harm to living resources, hazard to human health, hindrance to marine activities including fishing, impairment of quality for use of sea water and reduction of amenities'.[102] The latter is found in most subsequent definitions of marine pollution, including the 1974 Paris Convention for the Prevention of Marine Pollution from Land-based Sources and the 1982 UNCLOS. The important point is that these, although similar to the GESAMP definition, also include harm to marine ecosystems, endangered species, and other forms of marine life. As Tomczak observes, this makes the definition independent of actual or intended human usage of the sea and its contents, and focuses instead on the interdependence of human activity and nature. This broader formulation presents a much more clearly environmental[103] perspective, which now predominates in definitions favoured by OECD and the ILA.

Pollution is not defined simply in terms of its effects, however. All definitions confine the term to the introduction by man of substances or energy, whether directly or indirectly into the environment. It is the relationship between these substances and their effects which together constitute pollution. This has several implications. First, it means that over-use of resources, however harmful, is not 'pollution'. Some other concept must be found for this problem. Secondly, despite the apparent breadth of conventional defini-

---

[98] Handl, 69 *AJIL* (1975), 50. In this respect the no-harm principle is at least an exception to the proposition advanced by some writers and adopted by the ILC that harm is not a necessary condition of state responsibility. See Boyle, 39 *ICLQ* (1990), 16.

[99] cf. the broader scope of the 1991 Protocol to the Antarctic Treaty on Environmental Protection with Article 194(5) of the 1982 UNCLOS.

[100] See e.g. 1982 UNCLOS, Article 1(4); 1974 Paris Convention on Prevention of Marine Pollution from Land-based Sources, Article 1; 1979 Geneva Convention on Long-Range Transboundary Air Pollution, Article 1; 1977 OECD Recommendation C(77) 28 (Final) on Implementing a Regime of Equal Access and Non Discrimination.

[101] See Springer, 26 *ICLQ* (1977), 531; Tomczak, 8 *Marine Policy* (1984), 311; Springer, *International Law of Pollution* (Westport, Conn., 1983).

[102] Tomczak, 8 *Marine Policy* (1984), 317.   [103] Ibid. 319–21.

tions, what constitutes pollution will often be limited in practice by reference to the substances whose discharge states have specifically agreed to control. Thus the annexes of prohibited or controlled substances found in treaties concerned with air pollution or land-based sources of pollution are crucial in determining what it is states are meant to regulate.[104] The annexes can be amended, however, so the general concept of pollution serves mainly as a residual category which can be invoked when necessary to deal with additional substances.

Moreover, threshold values do remain important. In some cases any level of discharge will be presumed harmful. A good example of this category is the treaty prohibition of any disposal of high level radioactive material into the global commons.[105] More often, it is only when discharges reach a certain level of seriousness, either in volume or in the context of their location, that they will constitute pollution. Treaties on land-based sources of marine pollution show considerable diversity in the range and volume of toxic emissions treated as pollution in different seas.[106] An extreme case is Principle 6 of the Stockholm Declaration, which refers to the discharge of toxic substances 'in such quantities or concentrations as to exceed the capacity of the environment to render them harmless.' Here the damage must be irreversible. Few treaties dealing with toxic substances have found this approach acceptable, however.

Thus, we can see that what 'pollution' means is, like the term 'environment', significantly dependent on context and objective. While it is possible to talk of an obligation to prevent pollution, or to protect the environment, such an obligation has a very variable content, and there is little point attempting a global definition. The meaning which these terms have acquired will become more apparent in later chapters.

(2) Transboundary Co-operation in Cases of Environmental Risk

(a) The General Principle

A second principle, now widely acknowledged, is that states are required to co-operate with each other in mitigating transboundary environmental risks. In part, this principle can be supported by reference to the law relating to the use of shared natural resources, as we shall see in Chapters 6 and 11. A requirement of prior consultation based on adequate information has a substantial pedigree of international support in this context and is a natural counterpart of the concept of equitable utilization of a shared resource.[107] The *Lac*

---

[104] See Chs. 8 and 10.   [105] See p. 359.   [106] See pp. 310–14.

[107] Riphagen, in Bothe, *Trends in Environmental Policy and Law*, 343; Bothe, ibid. 391; Handl, 14 *RBDI* (1978), 55–63; Levin, *Protecting the Human Environment* (New York, 1977); Utton, 12 *CJTL* (1973), 56; Kirgis, *Prior Consultation in International Law* (Charlottesville, Va., 1983). See *infra*, pp. 114–7, and pp. 528–30.

Lanoux arbitration[108] shows how the principle has been applied in the law of international watercourses. Here the tribunal held that France had complied with its obligations under a treaty and customary law to consult and negotiate in good faith before diverting a watercourse shared with Spain. The Court noted that conflicting interests must be reconciled by negotiation and mutual concession.[109] This implied that France must inform Spain of its proposals, allow consultations, and give reasonable weight to Spain's interests, but it did not mean that it could act only with Spain's consent: 'the risk of an evil use has so far not led to subjecting the possession of these means of action to the authorisation of states which may possibly be threatened'.[110] Spain's rights were thus of a procedural character only; it enjoyed no veto and no claim to insist on specific precautions. It was for France alone to determine whether to proceed with the project and how to safeguard Spain's rights.[111] The obligation to negotiate is a real one, however, not a mere formality.[112]

Despite doubts surrounding the term 'shared resource', these procedural requirements—in effect an international right to a fair hearing, and a formula for minimizing the risk of harm—are fully reflected in the ILC's codification of the law of international watercourses and in the 'Principles of Conduct' relating to shared natural resources adopted by UNEP in 1978.[113] These make it clear that effects on the environment, as well as on the resources of other states, are among the matters which must be taken into account in policies towards shared resource use.[114] UNEP's principles also require states to make environmental assessments before engaging in activities with shared resources likely to create a risk of significant environmental effects in other states.[115]

Thus although the concept of 'shared natural resources' and the legal implications of the term itself have proved controversial, the basic principle that states must co-operate in avoiding adverse effects on their neighbours through a system of impact assessment, notification, consultation, and negotiation appears generally to be endorsed by the relevant jurisprudence, the declarations of international bodies, and the work of the ILC. Moreover, as the *Lac Lanoux* arbitration and the *Nuclear Tests* cases indicate, it also enjoys some support in state practice.[116]

---

[108] *Supra*, n. 7. On the question whether this award is based solely on the 1866 Treaty of Bayonne, or also on customary law, see *infra*, Ch. 6. n. 171.

[109] 24 *ILR* (1957), 119.

[110] Ibid. 126.   [111] Ibid. 140–1.

[112] See *North Sea Continental Shelf Cases*, *ICJ Rep.* (1969), 46–7, paras. 83–5; *Icelandic Fisheries Cases*, ICJ Rep. (1974), 32 ff.; Barboza, *5th Report on International Liability*, UN Doc. A/CN.4/423, (1989), 40 ff.; ILC, *Report to the UN Gen. Assembly*, 42nd Session, UNGAOR A/42/10 (1987), 63 ff., and see further, *infra*, pp. 235–41.

[113] See *infra*, pp. 114–7, and pp. 234–41.   [114] Principle 13.   [115] Principle 4.

[116] On the *Nuclear Tests Cases*, see the French note of 19 Feb. 1973, in NZ Ministry of Foreign Affairs, *French Nuclear Testing in the Pacific* (Wellington, 1973), 42. On state practice, see generally Kirgis, *Prior Consultation*.

(b) Application to Transboundary Risks

The Stockholm Conference recognized in 1972 that

co-operation through multilateral or bilateral arrangements or other appropriate means is essential to effectively control, prevent, reduce and eliminate adverse environmental effects resulting from activities conducted in all spheres, in such a way that due account is taken of the sovereignty and interests of all states.[117]

In endorsing this principle, the UN General Assembly noted that it should not be construed as enabling other states to delay or impede programmes and projects of exploration, exploitation, and development of natural resources within the territory of states, but that it did require the exchange of information 'in a spirit of good neighbourliness'.[118] At the time, agreement could not be reached on more detailed rules and these formulations fall short of explicitly requiring consultation and negotiation with other states, but the broad contours of 'good neighbourliness' can be identified in subsequent legal developments.

These suggest first, an extension of the basic principles of the *Lac Lanoux* case to the management of transboundary or global environmental risks posed by hazardous or potentially harmful activities, including nuclear installations near borders,[119] continental shelf operations,[120] long-range transboundary air pollution,[121] and marine pollution from land-based sources or dumping.[122] In each of these situations some measure of prior notification and consultation has been called for in bilateral, regional, or global treaty regimes. Where global common areas are affected, negotiation with any one state may be inappropriate, however, and the basic principle is modified to provide for notification and consultation to take place through institutions acting for the international community. Chapter 8 provides the best examples of this development: it does show that states are no longer free to put common areas or shared natural resources at risk without taking account of the interests of others.[123]

Secondly, international practice and the various environmental strategies of UNEP, IUCN, and other organizations have tended to emphasized that prior

[117] Stockholm Declaration, 1972, Principle 24.

[118] UNGA Res. 2995 XXVII (1972).

[119] See *infra*, pp. 361–4.

[120] 1983 Canada–Denmark Agreement for Co-operation Relating to the Marine Environment, 23 *ILM* (1984), 269; 1988 Kuwait Protocol Concerning Marine Pollution Resulting from Exploration and Exploitation of the Continental Shelf, 19 *EPL* (1989), 32; 1981 UNEP Principles Concerning the Environment Related to Offshore Drilling and Mining Within the Limits of National Jurisdiction, 7 *EPL* (1981), 50.

[121] 1979 Geneva Convention on Long-Range Transboundary Air Pollution, Articles 5, 8, *infra*, Ch. 10.

[122] See *infra*, Ch. 8.

[123] See Ch. 8, esp. pp. 314–6, and pp. 327–9.

notification, consultation, and negotiation must take place on an adequate basis of information. For this reason, environmental monitoring and prior impact assessment have become necessary additional components of most comprehensive schemes of environmental risk management. These latter features are especially important in anticipating harm to the global commons, such as the high seas or Antarctica.[124] UNEP guidelines also call for prior assessment in the case of any activity likely to have a significant effect on the environment, and there is growing evidence of this requirement in treaties and state practice.[125] Of particular significance are Articles 204–6 of the 1982 UNCLOS which codify obligations of monitoring, reporting, and prior assessment in respect of the risks or effects of substantial marine pollution or significant harmful effects on the marine environment. These provisions are widely followed in regional treaties,[126] although the record of states in implementing these agreements has not been a good one, as we shall see in Chapter 8.

The work of regional organizations and international codification bodies lends further support to the principle of transboundary co-operation in cases of significant environmental risk. Impact assessment, prior notification, consultation, and negotiation are all called for in OECD and ILA principles on transfrontier pollution,[127] and in the UN Economic Commission for Europe's 1991 Convention on Environmental Impact Assessment in a Transboundary Context. This Convention applies to a range of proposed activities, including oil refineries, power stations, nuclear installations, smelters, and waste disposal installations 'that are likely to cause significant adverse transboundary impact'. It is the first multilateral agreement to make detailed provision for transboundary procedural obligations in cases of environmental risk. It requires each party to establish an environmental impact assessment procedure that permits public participation and the preparation of environmental

---

[124] 1982 UNCLOS, Articles 204–6; 1988 Convention for the Regulation of Antarctic Mineral Resource Activities; 1991 Protocol to the Antarctic Treaty on Environmental Protection.

[125] e.g. 1982 UNCLOS, Article 206; 1988 Convention for the Regulation of Antarctic Mineral Resource Activities, Article 4; 1991 Protocol to the Antarctic Treaty on Environmental Protection, Article 2(2); 1983 Convention for the Protection and Development of the Marine Environment of the Wider Caribbean Region, Article 12; 1986 Convention for the Protection of the Natural Resources and Environment of the South Pacific Region, Article 16; 1983 US–Mexico Agreement to Co-operate in the Solution of Environmental Problems in the Border Area, Article 7; 1985 ASEAN Agreement on Conservation of Nature and Natural Resources, Articles 14, 19, 20; and on international watercourses, *infra*, Ch. 6. In effect, the 1972 London Dumping Convention also requires prior environmental impact assessment before the grant of permits: *infra*, pp. 327–9. See also Barboza, *5th Report on International Liability*, UN Doc. A/CN.4/423 (1989), 26–33, and *supra*, nn. 74–5.

[126] See *infra*, Ch. 8.

[127] OECD Council Recommendations C(74) 224 (1974), para. 6; C (77) 28 (1977), paras. 8–10; C(78) 77 (1978); C(79) 116 (1979), collected in, *OECD and the Environment* (Paris, 1986); ILA, *Report of the 60th Conference* (1982), 1, Montreal Rules on Transfrontier Pollution, Articles 4–6. See also 1992 Rio Declaration, *infra*, Ch. 14.

impact assessment documentation. Other states likely to be affected must be notified and given the opportunity to enter into consultations and make representations on the environmental assessment, which must be taken into account in any final decision on the proposed activity. The Convention also provides for activities not listed to be the subject of prior assessment if the parties agree, and it sets criteria to assist in making this judgment, based on the size, location, and effects of the proposed project. An inquiry procedure is established to settle disputes concerning the likelihood of any listed activity having significant adverse transboundary impact.

Finally, the ILC's proposed articles on 'International Liability' also address the procedural obligations of states in cases where there is an 'appreciable' risk of transboundary injury arising from ultra-hazardous activities or dangerous substances.[128] Subject to one qualification considered below, these articles follow closely the main principles indicated here and are in these respects comparable to the Commission's draft articles on the use of international watercourses, which in its view reflect well-established international practice.[129]

It does not follow, however, that identical procedural obligations will apply to every case of environmental risk. First, the risk must be significant or appreciable. This, as we have seen, implies both a degree of probability and a threshold of seriousness of harm, although it seems that the risk does not have to be ultra-hazardous in character.[130] Secondly, as with the obligation of diligent control, much will depend on the circumstances of each case. Procedural obligations in regard to nuclear power, for example, have been narrowly construed, and applied only to border installations, despite the continental implications of accidents at reactors such as Chernobyl.[131] The practice of consultation and notification in respect of activities which affect only common spaces is also limited in scope.[132]

Lastly, it must be recalled that these procedural rules usually lead only to an obligation to negotiate in good faith. They do not impose substantive limitations on the activities which states may undertake, nor do they require states to refrain from acting if negotiations prove unsuccessful. At most, the object of negotiation is to provide the opportunity for accommodating any

[128] ILC, UN Doc. A/CN.4/428 (1990), Articles 7, 11–14, and commentary at 21, para. 32.

[129] Barboza, ibid. 20. On the ILC's articles for international watercourses, see infra, Ch. 6.

[130] ILC Draft Articles on International Liability, supra, n. 128, Article 2, and commentary, ibid. paras. 15–21; id., Draft Articles on International Watercourses, Article 12, Report to the UN Gen. Assembly, 44th Session, UNGAOR A/44/10 (1989), 35; 1982 UNCLOS Articles 206, 210(5); 1991 ECE Convention on Environmental Impact Assessment in a Transboundary Context.

[131] See infra, pp. 361–4. However, Appendix III of the 1991 ECE Convention requires the parties to consider activities located close to an international frontier, 'as well as more remote proposed activities which could give rise to significant transboundary effects far removed from the site of the development.'

[132] See infra, pp. 314–6 and pp. 327–9.

conflict of rights and interests which may exist, not to stifle initiative.[133] In particular, states are not debarred from creating sources of risk to others, even where, as in the case of nuclear installations, these involve the possibility of serious injury. Thus, in the view of one judge in the *Nuclear Tests* cases until damage occurs 'each state is free to act within the limits of its sovereignty'.[134]

But those limits now clearly include both controls on sources of risk and procedural obligations aimed at minimizing their potential for harm. The ILC rapporteurs have followed this trend in their reports on 'International Liability', but unlike other formulations they also envisage an obligation to negotiate a specific regime aimed at preventing, minimizing, and compensating possible injury. This approach is more than procedural; while not prohibiting all risk creation, it requires the negotiation of an equitable balance of interests as the price for undertaking risky activities.[135] All relevant factors, including the possibility of alternative sites and the adequacy of safety measures, would have to be considered in effecting a solution. In an extreme case, where harm can neither be avoided nor adequately compensated, the state of origin must refuse authorization for the activity unless the operator proposes less-harmful alternatives.[136]

Although a logical extension of the obligation to consult and take account of the interests of others, the equitable utilization of a state's own territory which this approach implies goes well beyond most of the precedents dealing with the risk of transboundary harm, and it is not followed in other attempts at codification of environmental law.[137] The closest analogy is with those few cases which require the prior consent of states likely to be affected[138] or of international institutions.[139] But, as we have seen, prior consent remains an exceptional rule in state practice; like the *Lac Lanoux* case, most treaty regimes give neighbouring states or international institutions no veto over the conduct of environmentally risky activities. Nevertheless, the ILC's proposal does have the merit that it would force states to take fuller account of the transboundary or global costs of their activities, something which, as the chapter on nuclear risks shows, the present rules signally fail to achieve.

[133] See esp. Chs. 6, 8, and 9; UNGA Res. 2995 XXVII (1972); and 1991 ECE Convention, Article 6.

[134] *Infra*, Ch. 9 n. 120; *Nuclear Tests Cases* (Jurisdiction) (*Australia* v. *France*) *ICJ Rep.* (1974), 386–90, per de Castro (dissenting). See also id. (interim measures), *ICJ Rep.* (1973), 131, per Ignacio Pinto (dissenting), but cf. the New Zealand response to this argument, *infra*, Ch. 9 n. 121.

[135] 1990 Draft Articles 17–20. See also Quentin-Baxter's 'Schematic Outline', II *Yearbook ILC* (1983), ii, pt. 1, 223, section 6.

[136] 1990 Draft, Article 20. Support for this view is offered by Handl, 7 *ELQ* (1978), 35, but see *infra*, Ch. 9 n. 120, for opposing views.

[137] See e.g. 1991 ECE Convention, *supra*, n. 130, and ILA, Montreal Rules on Transfrontier Pollution, *supra*, n. 4. The ILA's approach is criticized by Quentin-Baxter, II *Yearbook ILC* (1983), pt. 1, 209.

[138] e.g. 1989 Basel Convention on the Control of Transboundary Movements of Hazardous Waste, *infra*, pp. 336–8, and port visits by nuclear ships, *infra*, Ch. 9 n. 117.

[139] *Supra*, n. 81.

(c) Emergency Notification and Assistance

A further application of the obligation of co-operation concerns accidents and emergencies likely to cause transboundary harm. Here state practice and case law support an obligation to give timely notification to states at risk, so that they can take appropriate protective measures. As we saw earlier, the *Corfu Channel* case[140] provides an early example of judicial application of this duty to warn. In that case British warships were damaged by mines in Albanian waters. Giving judgment on this point for the United Kingdom, the Court noted: 'The obligations incumbent upon the Albanian authorities consisted in notifying for the benefit of shipping in general, the existence of a minefield in Albanian territorial waters and in warning the approaching British warships of imminent danger to which the minefield exposed them'.[141] Although the context of this case involved interference with freedom of maritime communication, the Court expressly based its conclusion on additional grounds of more general application, namely, elementary considerations of humanity and the obligation, referred to earlier, that a state should not knowingly allow its territory to be used for acts contrary to the rights of other states.[142] As we have seen, these include the right to protection from environmental harm. For this reason, it is legitimate to view the *Corfu Channel* case as authority for a customary obligation to give warning of known environmental hazards.

Treaties and state practice support this conclusion. It is unequivocally applied to marine pollution by the 1982 UNCLOS and by other treaties now widely ratified.[143] A Convention on Early Notification of Nuclear Accidents, and a network of bilateral agreements apply the same rule to transboundary releases of radioactivity,[144] and it is found in treaties and the ILC's draft articles dealing with pollution of international watercourses,[145] in the ILA Montreal Rules on Transfrontier Pollution,[146] and in OECD principles.[147] In all of these instruments the object of notification is the same: states should be given sufficient information promptly enough to enable them to minimize the damage and take whatever measures of self-protection are permitted by international law.

Modern treaties tend also to require states to make contingency plans for

---

[140] *Supra*, n. 40.   [141] Ibid. 22.

[142] Quentin-Baxter's view, at II *Yearbook ILC* (1980), pt. 1, 258, that this dictum refers only to innocent passage and not to acts which harm other states seems unjustifiably narrow.

[143] 1982 UNCLOS, Articles 198, 211(7), and others cited, *infra*, p. 283. See also 1989 Basel Convention on the Control of Transboundary Movement of Hazardous Wastes, Article 13.

[144] See *infra*, pp. 364–5.

[145] e.g. 1976 Convention on the Protection of the Rhine Against Chemical Pollution, Article 11; ILC, Draft Articles on 'International Watercourses', Article 25, II *Yearbook ILC*, (1984), pt. 1, 120; *infra*, Ch. 6.

[146] *Supra*, n. 4, Article 5.

[147] Council Recommendation C(74) 224 (1974), Annex, Part F.

pollution emergencies and to co-operate in their response. A typical example of this is Article 199 of the 1982 UNCLOS. Practice in this respect is well developed in the maritime field.[148] A multilateral convention and a network of bilateral agreements also facilitate emergency co-operation in cases of nuclear accidents.[149] Only in the law of the sea, however, have states assumed a power to intervene unilaterally to forestall accidental harm emanating from outside their territory,[150] although in other cases the defence of necessity may provide some basis for emergency measures of ecological protection taken in violation of the sovereignty of other states.[151] Such measures must be the only means of protecting an essential interest of the state from a grave and imminent peril and must not seriously impair the essential interests of the other state affected.[152]

Where accidents do pose an environmental risk for other states or the global commons, the obligation of due diligence, considered earlier, will additionally require the source state to take whatever measures are necessary to forestall or mitigate their effects. Thus states do not discharge their duty merely by seeking to prevent accidents, or by giving notification of an emergency.[153] It is in this context that treaty obligations to maintain contingency plans and respond to pollution emergencies must be seen: they are part of a state's duty of diligence in controlling sources of known environmental harm.

(3) The 'Polluter Pays' Principle

The 'polluter pays' principle is essentially a principle of economic policy for allocating the costs of pollution, rather than a legal principle, but it has certain implications for the development of international environmental law. OECD's definition of the principle is that the polluter should bear the expenses of carrying out measures decided by public authorities to ensure that the environment is in 'an acceptable state', or 'in other words the cost of these measures should be reflected in the cost of goods and services which cause pollution in production and or in consumption'. Such measures must not be

---

[148] See *infra*, pp. 283−5.   [149] See *infra*, pp. 365−7.

[150] 1969 Brussels Convention Relating to Intervention on the High Seas in Cases of Oil Pollution Casualties; 1982 UNCLOS, Article 221; see *infra*, pp. 285−8.

[151] ILC, Draft Articles on 'State Responsibility', (Part 1), Article 33, II *Yearbook ILC* (1980), pt. 2, 30, and commentary at 34−52. Bilder, 14 *Vand. JTL* (1981), 63 ff., suggests a broader principle of unilateral action to protect a state from environmental damage caused by another's breach of duty not to cause serious harm to other states.

[152] See Jagota, 16 *NYIL* (1985), 269, and Brown, 21 *CLP* (1968), 113.

[153] ILC, 1990 Draft Articles 7 and 8 on 'International Liability', id., Draft Articles on 'International Watercourses', *infra*, Ch. 6 n. 208. The *Corfu Channel Case* refers only to notification of the danger, but this must be read in the context of that case: notification would of itself have been sufficient to avert the disaster.

accompanied by subsidies causing significant distortions in international trade and investment.[154]

The primary object of such a principle is economic, not environmental: the elimination of hidden subsidies is a necessary part of the process of economic liberalization and free trade in developed economies. Uniform implementation will thus ensure better allocation of resources and avoid distortions in trade and investment. The 'polluter pays' principle has been endorsed and adopted by OECD, although not binding on OECD member states, who are left free to determine how far it should be implemented. In 1973, however, the EEC adopted a programme of action which endorsed the principle.[155] Article 25 of the 1986 Single European Act has now provided a legal basis as part of EEC environmental competence: 'Action by the Community relating to the environment shall be based on the principles that preventive action should be taken, that environmental damage should as a priority be rectified at source and that the polluter should pay.' As such it has a legal force which OECD recommendations lack. The principle has been implemented by a number of European states, using a variety of tax measures, charges, and liability provisions of national law.[156] It has also influenced the formulation of international measures intended to tackle problems of marine pollution.[157]

Beyond the developed world, however, there is less evidence of widespread support for or adoption of the principle. The Stockholm Declaration does not refer to it, and indeed Principle 12 calls instead for developed states to help bear the additional costs of environmental protection measures taken by less developed states, for whose economic needs and special position the declaration makes full allowance. The Conference did recommend, however, that environmental standards should not be directed towards gaining trade advantages.[158] The Montreal Protocol to the 1985 Ozone Convention, considered further in Chapter 10, is a recent example of the application of Principle 12 to an international agreement involving developed and developing states, and the issue is a recurrent topic in international negotiations involving the less developed countries. The 'polluter pays' principle has, however, been

---

[154] OECD, Recommendations C(72) 128 (1972); C(74) 223 (1974); repr. in OECD, *OECD and the Environment* (Paris, 1986), and C(89) 88 (1989), 28 *ILM* (1989), 1320.

[155] Declaration on an Environmental Action Programme, 1973, and EC Council Recommendation on the Application of the 'polluter pays' principle, 1974.

[156] See OECD, *Economic Instruments for Environmental Protection* (Paris, 1989). On liability, see *infra*, pp. 201–6. The UK has imposed pollution charges for watercourse discharges and pesticides and higher taxes for leaded petrol. See in particular, Pesticides (Fees and Enforcement) Act, 1989.

[157] See 1990 Convention on Oil Pollution Preparedness Response and Co-operation, Preamble, which refers to the 'polluter pays' principle as a 'general principle of international environmental law', and *infra*, p. 292. OECD recommendation C(81) 32 (Final) recommends that the principle should be taken into account in assessing and allocating liability for oil pollution spills.

[158] Recommendation 103(e).

endorsed by the Conference on Security and Co-operation in Europe.[159] Moreover, the 1992 UNCED Conference declared that the polluter should 'in principle' bear pollution costs, 'with due regard to the public interest and without distorting international trade and investment', and that national authorities should endeavour to internalize environmental costs.[160] As a policy, therefore, the 'polluter pays' principle has gained significant endorsement, and it represents an important strategy for controlling environmentally harmful activities by emphasizing responsibility for their true economic costs and complementing the more obvious regulatory measures adopted under regional and global treaties.

(4) Equal Access and Non-Discrimination

These principles are primarily concerned with making national remedies available to transboundary complainants, and in that context they are considered in Chapter 5. The principle of non-discrimination may imply more than affording equal access to foreign plaintiffs in judicial or administrative proceedings, however. As defined by OECD, it entails giving equivalent treatment to the domestic and transboundary effects of polluting activities, and requires that polluters causing transfrontier pollution should be subject to legal standards no less severe than would apply to pollution with domestic effects only. In effect, transfrontier pollution should not, under this principle, exceed levels that would be considered acceptable if occurring within the country of origin.

This is not a restatement of Stockholm Principle 21 or the no-harm rule considered earlier, since the standard required of the state of origin is not that of due diligence but only one of equivalent treatment. Quite apart from its potential bias in favour of polluting states with lower standards of regulation, this approach has other difficulties. Does it, for example, mean that a state with high environmental standards cannot export pollution to a state with lower standards, under whose law the levels of pollution involved may not be unlawful, or is it sufficient if the receiving state's law is complied with?

There is evidence that a failure to take account of extraterritorial effects in determining the permissibility of polluting activities may lead to judicial review before national courts in some European jurisdictions, including France and Germany, and Article 2 of the 1974 Nordic Convention on the Protection of the Environment requires parties to equate domestic and transboundary nuisances when considering the permissibility of environmentally harmful activities. It is more doubtful, however, whether such a failure entails the breach of an international obligation, or constitutes a standard for state responsibility in international law. Bilateral and multilateral treaties have

---

[159] *Report of the Meeting on the Mediterranean*, CSCE/RMP.6, 1990.   [160] *Infra*, Ch. 14.

generally not followed the model of the Nordic Convention but have adopted the stronger approach of setting international standards for transboundary pollution control, and, for the various reasons considered here, this does seem preferable to one based on non-discrimination. The principle is, it is suggested, of importance only in the context of transboundary access to civil and administrative proceedings for private individuals.[161]

3. CONSERVATION AND UTILIZATION OF NATURAL RESOURCES AND COMMON SPACES

Rules of international law protecting the environment from pollution are complemented by other principles which affect the conservation and utilization of natural resources. Customary international law has traditionally protected natural resources indirectly by determining the basis on which property rights in a resource are allocated among states. More recently it has done so directly by imposing on states obligations of conservation, sustainable development, and ecological protection intended to avoid over-exploitation and permanent loss of some categories of internationally significant resources. These principles are of particular significance to the conservation of living resources, but they also affect the use of air, water, and common spaces. In this chapter, therefore, the term 'resources' is given a particularly broad meaning to encompass all those components of the natural biosphere which international law in general protects from excessive exploitation.

(1) The Legal Status of Natural Resources and Common Spaces

(a) Permanent Sovereignty over Natural Resources

In general, it was assumed in the early development of international law that natural resources were allocated to sovereign states according to the boundaries established to delimit their respective land territory and territorial seas.[162] Control of these resources depended on the acquisition of territorial sovereignty. Resolution of disputes concerning such resources thus often took the form of boundary delimitations, as in the *Norwegian Fisheries* case,[163] or alternatively centred on the status of a resource as shared or common property falling outside the exclusive control of any one state, as in the *Behring Sea Fur Seals* arbitration[164] or the *Icelandic Fisheries* case.[165] No distinction existed in

---

[161] See OECD Recommendation C(74) 224, Annex, in OECD, *OECD and the Environment* (Paris, 1986), 144; Rehbinder and Stewart, *Environmental Protection Policy* (New York, 1988), 169–70; Pacteau, in OECD, *Legal Aspects of Transfrontier Pollution* (Paris, 1977), 203, and see further, *infra*, pp. 197–8, for consideration of the 1974 Nordic Convention on Protection of the Environment and the private law implications of the principle.

[162] Brownlie, 162 *Recueil des cours* (1979), 272–86.   [163] *ICJ Rep.* (1951), 116.

[164] See *supra*, n. 8, and Ch. 12.   [165] *ICJ Rep.* (1974), 3. See Ch. 13.

this respect between sovereignty over living resources, or non-renewable resources such as minerals.[166] Once a resource fell within the category of exclusive property, such as tropical forests, international law placed few limitations on its use.

The principle of permanent sovereignty over natural resources which developed after 1945 into a rule of international law was mainly a response by newly independent developing states to the problem of foreign ownership of their mineral resources, notably oil. Their efforts resulted in the adoption in 1962 by the UN General Assembly of resolution 1803 XVII.[167] It proclaimed 'The right of peoples and nations to permanent sovereignty over their natural wealth and resources', and the preamble recommended that 'the sovereign right of every state to dispose of its natural wealth and resources should be respected ... in accordance with their national interests.'

The resolution draws no distinction between living and nonliving resources and makes no reference to any duty of conservation, although it does recognize the desirability of promoting international co-operation for the economic development of developing countries and the benefits 'derivable' from the exchanges of technical and scientific information in the development and use of resources. It also stresses the important part which the UN and other international organizations are called upon to play in that connection. It further provides that states' 'free and beneficial' exercise of sovereignty must be promoted by 'the mutual respect of states based on their sovereign equality'. These considerations may influence the conclusion of agreements between states; nevertheless, by emphasizing their apparently untrammelled sovereignty over natural resources, the resolution implies that any restrictions would for the most part require agreement between the states concerned. Whilst not *per se* binding, it has had considerable effect on the development of international law. Some states regard it as declaratory of existing rules; it has also been cited and relied on as evidence of the existing law on the subject and referred to as such by international arbitral tribunals.[168]

Following further similar resolutions, the General Assembly met in special session in 1974, two years after the Stockholm Environment Conference, and adopted a 'Declaration on the Establishment of a New International Economic Order' (NIEO),[169] reaffirming permanent sovereignty over natural resources and the right to nationalize them. This was followed by adoption of the Charter of Economic Rights and Duties of States. Article I of which provided

---

[166] See e.g. 1958 Continental Shelf Convention, which defines 'natural resources' as consisting of 'the mineral and other non-living resources of the sea-bed and subsoil, together with living organisms belonging to sedentary species ...'.

[167] See also UNGA Res. 2158 (XXI) (1966) laying down a programme of action.

[168] Brownlie, 162 *Recueil des cours* (1979); *Texaco* v. *Libya*, 53 *ILR* (1977), 389; *BP* v. *Libya*, ibid. (1973), 297. See generally Schachter, *Sharing the World's Resources* (New York, 1977), 124.

[169] UNGA Res. 3201 (S–VI) (1974).

that: 'Every state has the sovereign and inalienable right to choose its economic system as well as its political, social and cultural systems in accordance with the will of its people, without outside interference, coercion or threat in any form whatsoever'.[170] Article 2 further lays down that 'Every state has and shall freely exercise full permanent sovereignty including possession, use and disposal, over all its natural resources.'

In reality, however, these resolutions, and the strong support given by developing states to the concept of permanent sovereignty, were primarily directed at asserting the right to nationalize or control foreign-owned resources and industries, free from some of the older rules which protected foreign investments. Despite their categorical pronouncements, they have not constrained the development of treaties and rules of customary international law concerning conservation and environment protection that qualify this sovereignty. This can be observed in the rules applicable to shared natural resources, and the resources of common spaces, notably the high seas. Moreover, as we shall see, the concept of permanent sovereignty has not prevented international law from treating conservation issues within a state's territory as questions of common concern in which the international community possesses a legitimate interest. Treaties such as the 1972 World Heritage Convention, the 1973 CITES Convention, 1979 Berne Convention on the Conservation of European Wildlife, the 1968 African Convention on the Conservation of Nature, and the 1985 ASEAN Convention on the Conservation of Nature and Natural Resources exemplify this point.[171] In these various ways it is possible to envisage, as some writers have done, new concepts of 'international property' and resource utilization based on different notions of economic security, ecological protection, and common interest, involving a redefinition of sovereignty itself, so that it is no longer a basis for exclusion of others, but entails instead 'a commitment to co-operate for the good of the international community at large.'[172]

(b) Shared Natural Resources

'Shared natural resources'[173] represent an intermediate category; the resources do not fall wholly within the exclusive control of one state, but neither are they

---

[170] UNGA Res. 3281 XXIX (1974). The US and a number of other Western states voted against this resolution or abstained. See Brownlie, 162 *Recueil des cours* (1979), 267–9; White, 24 *ICLQ* (1975), 542; Chatterjee, 40 *ICLQ* 669; *Texaco* v. *Libya*, 53 *ILR* (1977). Brownlie notes that Article 1 is well founded in existing international law and is virtually identical with Articles 2(1) and 2(4) of the UN Charter.

[171] See Chs. 11–12.

[172] Handl, 1 *YIEL* (1990), 32. See also Fawcett, 123 *Recueil des cours* (1968), 237, 239; Brownlie, 162 *Recueil des cours* (1979), 282; Kiss, 175 ibid. (1982), 229 ff.; Schachter, *Sharing the World's Resources*, and see further *infra*, Chs. 12 and 13.

[173] See generally Brownlie, 162 *Recueil des cours* (1979), 289 ff.; Riphagen, in Bothe, *Trends in Environmental Law and Policy*, 343.

the common property of all states. The essence of this concept is a limited form of community interest, usually involving a small group of states in geographical contiguity, who exercise shared rights over the resources in question. Examples considered in later chapters include international watercourses, regional airmasses, and migratory species.

A succession of UN General Assembly resolutions has recognized the general principle that states do not have unlimited sovereignty with regard to shared resources. In 1973, Resolution 3129 xxviii called for adequate international standards for the conservation and utilization of natural resources common to two or more states to be established and affirmed that there should be co-operation between states on the basis of information exchange and prior consultation. It called for UNEP to report on implementation of the resolution. Article 3 of the 1974 Charter of Economic Rights and Duties of States[174] set out the same principle more fully: 'In the exploitation of natural resources shared by two or more countries each state must co-operate on the basis of a system of information and prior consultation in order to achieve optimum use of such resources without causing damage to the legitimate interests of others.' Although the stress in this charter as a whole still lay with the use of resources for the economic benefit of developing states, Article 3 clearly qualified the sovereignty states enjoy with regard to shared resources. However, the terms 'optimum use' and 'legitimate interests' are not defined and we have to look elsewhere in treaties and customary law for their content. These resolutions formed the basis for the adoption by the Governing Council of UNEP in 1978 of the 'Principles of Conduct, etc. in the Conservation and Harmonious Utilization of Natural Resources Shared by Two or More States'.[175] The General Assembly took note of these 'Principles', including the statement that they are 'without prejudice to the binding nature of those rules already recognized as such in international law', and it called on states to use them as 'guidelines and recommendations' in the formulation of bilateral or multilateral conventions, in such a way as to enhance the development and interests of all states, in particular developing countries.[176]

The Assembly's reluctance to give its full endorsement to the 'Principles', and the use of language which avoids the implication of existing legal obligation, stems from the controversy and opposition earlier resolutions on the subject had aroused.[177] This does indicate that the rules contained in the 1978 Principles cannot necessarily be regarded as settled law, nor as enjoying

---

[174] *Supra*, n. 170.
[175] 17 *ILM* (1978), 1091. See Sand, in Dupuy, *The Future*, 51–72; Adede, 5 *EPL* (1979), 66; Callary, 1 *EPL* (1975), 71; Lammers, *Pollution of International Watercourses* (Dordrecht, 1984), 335–8.
[176] UNGA Res. 34/186 (1979).
[177] Five states voted against UNGA Res. 3129; 43 abstained, and 77 voted for. See also II *Yearbook ILC* (1983), pt. 1, 195, and Adede, 5 *EPL* (1979). The WCED Experts Group preferred the term 'transboundary natural resources': see *infra*, Ch. 11 n. 22.

the support of all states, although as we shall see in later chapters they do in many respects reflect international law and the practice of a significant number of countries. Nevertheless, they have not subsequently lost their controversial character. At the time of their adoption several countries declared that the 'Principles' confirmed the sovereign right to exploit their own resources in accordance with national laws and policy, subject only to an obligation not to cause injury to others; continued opposition to the concept of 'shared natural resources' has led to the removal of all reference to it in the ILC's codification of the law relating to international watercourses.[178] Moreover, the most notable omission from the 'Principles' and from UN resolutions concerns their failure to define what resources should be treated as shared. The Executive Director of UNEP indicated his belief that at least the following are 'shared natural resources': river systems, enclosed and semi-enclosed seas, air sheds, mountain chains, forests, conservation areas, and migratory species.[179] Another proposed definition refers to 'an element of the natural environment used by man which constitutes a biogeophysical unity, and is located in the territory of two or more states.'[180] The working group which drafted the 'Principles' did not discuss the issue or reach any conclusions, however.

The 'Principles' themselves endorse the view that shared resources are subject to obligations of transboundary co-operation and equitable utilization.[181] The requirements of co-operation are comparable to those considered earlier in section 2 of this chapter and follow closely the rules applied to shared watercourses in the *Lac Lanoux* arbitration and state practice, which are considered further in Chapter 6. Principle 4 also calls for states to make environmental impact assessments before engaging in any activity with respect to resources which may significantly affect the environment of another state sharing the resource. Principle 3 affirms responsibility for ensuring that adverse environmental effects on other states or on areas beyond national jurisdiction are avoided or reduced to the maximum extent possible, particularly where the utilization or conservation of the resource may be affected, or public health in other states endangered. The 'Principles' also call for states to consider establishing joint commissions for consultations on environmental problems relating to the protection and use of shared resources, and they recognize a duty to inform other states likely to be affected in cases of emergency or by 'sudden grave natural events', related to shared resources. Principles 13 and 14 adopt the principles of non-discrimination and equal access, considered further in Chapter 5. In many respects therefore, the legal principles applicable to transboundary pollution are also relevant to the broader context of natural resources shared by a number of states.

---

[178] UNEP IG/12/2 (1978), para. 15, and see *infra*, Ch. 6, nn. 35–6.
[179] UNEP/GC/44 (1975), para. 86.   [180] UNEP/IG/12/2 (1978), para. 16.   [181] Principle 1.

The main purpose for regulating the use and conservation of a shared resource is to ensure a balance of interests between the parties concerned. The concept of equitable utilization has been employed in arbitral awards, ICJ decisions, treaties, and the work of the ILC and other codification bodies in resolving conflicts of interest affecting shared resources.[182] UNEP's 'Principles' have thus adopted a well-established concept of international law when they rely on equitable utilization as the basis of co-operation, although to regard all fifteen principles as a definition of this concept is to give it an unusually wide interpretation. No attempt is made in the UNEP 'Principles' to determine what constitutes an equitable allocation of a shared resource among the parties concerned, however, or to settle questions of priority and geographical inequity which have proved in practice to be the most contentious questions affecting such resources. Equitable utilization is best understood in the context in which it is employed; reference should be made to chapters on international watercourses, protection of the atmosphere, and marine living resources for examples of its application.

(c) Common Property

Common property, in international law, refers primarily to areas beyond national jurisdiction, of which the high seas and superjacent airspace are the most important examples. These common spaces are open for legitimate and reasonable use by all states, and may not be appropriated to the exclusive sovereignty of any one state.[183] As we have already seen, the principles of international law which require states to prevent and control pollution and environmental damage have been extended to protect these common spaces, which are now regulated by a series of multilateral treaties for this purpose.[184]

The common property doctrine also extends to most of the living resources of these areas, including fish and mammals found in the high seas. These have always been regarded as common property, a view confirmed in the 1895 *Behring Sea Fur Seals* arbitration[185] and subsequently codified by treaty. Birds and other species of wildlife that inhabit common spaces or migrate through them are similarly regarded. Once living resources are held in common in this way, no single user can have exclusive rights over them, nor the right to prevent others from joining in their exploitation.[186] Such living resources do, however, become exclusive property once reduced into possession by capture or taking. The common property doctrine is not to be confused with the more

---

[182] See *infra*, pp. 126–7.

[183] 1958 Geneva Convention on the High Seas, Articles 1–2; 1982 UNCLOS, Articles 87, 89. See also 1967 Outer Space Treaty, Article 2, and *infra*, Ch. 10.

[184] See Chs. 7, 8, and 10.

[185] *Supra*, n. 8, and see further, pp. 492–5.

[186] Christy and Scott, *The Commonwealth in Ocean Fisheries* (2nd edn., Baltimore, 1972), ch. 2, and see *infra*, Ch. 11.

recent 'common heritage' concept, a specialized regime applied to certain mineral resources, nor with 'shared natural resources', where, as indicated above, rights are shared by a limited number of states.

An important factor contributing to the classification of living resources as common property is that they have generally been so plentiful that the cost of asserting and defending exclusive rights exceeds the advantages to be gained. A regime of open access in these circumstances has generally been to everyone's advantage. However, as Hardin has observed,[187] the 'inherent logic of the commons remorselessly generates tragedy', as the availability of a free resource leads to over-exploitation and minimizes the interest of any individual state in conservation and restraint. Common property resources cannot effectively be protected without the support of all states taking the resource; this has generally been difficult to obtain once resource exploitation has become established.[188] As resources become less plentiful, and particular stocks or species accordingly become more valuable, perceptions of the costs and benefits of exclusivity change. This occurred in relation to high seas fisheries from the 1950s onwards, resulting in increasing pressure for states to extend their jurisdiction over the resources of the sea and of the sea-bed beneath.[189]

Extension of the limits of coastal states' exclusive jurisdiction over fisheries led to numerous conflicts with those distant water states asserting high seas freedoms. In the *Icelandic Fisheries* cases in 1974, the ICJ made significant observations on the character of high seas fishing resources as common property. While affirming that established fishing states continued to have high seas rights beyond the twelve-mile limit of coastal state fisheries jurisdiction, the Court found that all the states concerned had an obligation of reasonable use which required them to take account of the needs of conservation and to allow coastal states preferential rights in the allocation of high seas stocks. There was, in the Court's view, an obligation on all parties to negotiate in good faith with a view to reaching an equitable solution.[190]

This decision is important for two reasons. First, it opened the way for a much more radical transfer to coastal state jurisdiction of much of the world's fishing resources, effected by the 3rd UN Conference on the Law of the Sea and quickly adopted by coastal states in the form of 200-mile exclusive fisheries or economic zones.[191] Thus marine living resources are now for the most part no longer common property, although significant exceptions to this

---

[187] *Science*, 162 (1968), 1243–8. See also Wijkman, 36 *Int. Org.* (1982), 511, and *infra*, Ch. 13.
[188] See Chs. 4 and 13.
[189] See e.g. *Norwegian Fisheries Case, ICJ Rep.* (1951), 116; 1958 Geneva Convention on the Continental Shelf, Article 2(4); 1964 London Fisheries Convention; 1976 US Fishery Conservation and Management Act, ss. 101–3, 401, and see *infra*, Ch. 13.
[190] *ICJ Rep.* (1974), 3; Churchill, 24 *ICLQ* (1975), 82, and see further, *infra*, Ch. 13. On the principle of 'reasonable use', see *infra*, pp. 124–5.
[191] See Ch. 13.

are found in the form of highly migratory species, other stocks which straddle both coastal zones and the high seas, and surplus stocks located within national maritime zones but available for exploitation by other states.[192] Moreover, transferring resources from common property has in many cases meant not that they fall under the exclusive jurisdiction of any one state, but constitute shared stocks straddling national maritime jurisdictions, and to which the principle of equitable utilization will still apply.[193] Thus there remains a substantial international interest in the conservation of these resources even within national maritime boundaries.

Secondly, the *Icelandic Fisheries* cases indicated for the first time that states had a duty in customary law not merely to allocate common resources equitably, but also to conserve them for future benefit in the interests of sustainable utilization. Conservation in this sense has become the basis of a number of multilateral fisheries agreements, starting with the 1958 Geneva Convention on Fishing and Conservation of the Living Resources of the High Seas. It is also recognized in the 1982 UNCLOS and in a number of wildlife agreements, and accords with the more recent emphasis on sustainable utilization or development identified by the World Conservation Strategy and the Brundtland Commission.[194]

There remain problems, however, in implementing conservation measures to restrain over-exploitation and ensure sustainable utilization, whether these are based on common property or exclusive jurisdiction solutions. The concept of 'conservation'[195] remains closely related to Man's need for resources, and the dominant goal is still seen as maintaining these at a level which will best supply human needs on a sustainable basis. Moreover, whether expressed as an obligation of reasonable use, equitable utilization, or conservation, the customary rules, though a useful guide, are often too vague and general to be of practical use. It is, in such circumstances, of vital importance that the activities of all states with regard to common spaces and common property resources be subjected to internationally agreed and prescribed regimes of conservation and environmental control. These are generally best constituted and implemented through treaties, supervised by intergovernmental commissions or similar bodies which can regularly promulgate the necessary rules in a flexible and sustained manner, easily adaptable to changing scientific knowledge and advice and changing economic, social, and political circumstances.[196] The protection of common spaces, and the conservation of their living resources is thus a complex issue in which scientific, moral, ethical, political, economic, social, and technological issues are inextricably intertwined and on which these interests do not always coincide.

---

[192] 1982 UNCLOS, Articles 62(2), 63, 64, 66. See also Articles 69, 70, which confer rights on landlocked and geographically disadvantaged states, and see further, *infra*, Ch. 13.
[193] See *supra*, pp. 114–7.   [194] See Ch. 11.   [195] Ibid.   [196] See *infra*, pp. 160–79.

(d) Common Heritage

Although the term 'common heritage' is frequently used loosely by environmentalists to refer either to all the living and non-living resources of nature or
to the global environment as an ecological entity, for legal purposes the term
is currently confined to the narrow meaning attributed to it in two conventions, namely, the 1979 Moon Treaty and the 1982 UNCLOS, only the first
of which is in force.[197] Though both apply the concept to areas beyond
national jurisdiction, they relate in this respect only to their non-living
resources, to which in the latter treaty a precise and narrow definition is given.
The concept was put forward by Malta to the United Nations General
Assembly as the basis on which a new regime for exploiting the resources of
the sea-bed in the interest of all mankind could be built.[198] It was included
both in a 'Declaration of Principles Governing the Sea-bed and Ocean
Floor'[199] and in Articles 136 and 137 of the 1982 UNCLOS, which pronounce the resources of the deep sea-bed beyond national jurisdiction (the
Area) to be 'the common heritage of mankind', vested in mankind as a whole,
on whose behalf an International Sea-bed Authority (ISBA) established under
the UNCLOS shall act. All activities in the Area must be conducted under
this Authority.

As employed in the Moon Treaty and the 1982 UNCLOS, the concept of
common heritage implies that the resources of these areas cannot be appropriated to the exclusive sovereignty of states but must be conserved and
exploited for the benefit of all, without discrimination. The concept thus
differs from common property in allowing all states to share in the rewards,
even if unable to participate in the actual process of extraction. The ISBA
represents an elaborate form of international management and regulation in
order to control the allocation of exploitation rights and the equitable sharing
of benefits.[200] The establishment of some form of international management
is also envisaged by the Moon Treaty.[201] Both schemes also require the states
concerned to take measures of environmental protection. Article 145 of the
1982 UNCLOS gives the ISBA authority to adopt 'appropriate rules regulations and procedures' to prevent, reduce, and control pollution or 'interference with the ecological balance of the marine environment', and to protect
natural resources, flora and fauna.[202] Article 209 requires states to adopt laws

---

[197] Kiss, 175 *Recueil des cours* (1982), 99; Arnold, 9 *Int. Lawyer* (1975), 1538; Ogley, *Inter-
nationalising the Sea-bed* (Aldershot, 1984); Pardo and Christol, in Macdonald and Johnston,
Structure and Process, 643; Brownlie, 162 *Recueil des cours* (1979), 289–300. On the status of the
Moon, see *infra*, pp. 415–18.

[198] *Note verbale*, 17 Aug. 1967, Permanent Mission of Malta to the UN Sec. General, UN
Doc. A/6095.

[199] UNGA Res. 2749 XXV (1970), adopted 108 to none, with 14 abstentions.

[200] See *infra*, pp. 171–2.   [201] Article 11(5).

[202] See Draft Regulations on Protection and Preservation of the Marine Environment, UN
Doc. LOS/PCN/SCN.3/WP.6/Add. 5 (1990).

and regulations 'no less effective' than the rules approved by the ISBA. Common heritage resources, unlike common property, will thus be subject to regulation by a strong international authority, which, as we shall see in Chapter 4, is in this respect unique among international institutions with environmental responsibilities.

Although in convening the 3rd UNCLOS, the General Assembly stated that it was 'conscious that the problems of ocean space are closely related and need to be considered as a whole',[203] the 1982 UNCLOS neither applied the common heritage regime to the waters above the deep sea-bed, nor to the living resources found anywhere in the oceans. Nor has the concept yet found any further explicit applications. The General Assembly has declined to adopt a Maltese proposal to designate the global climate as the common heritage of mankind, preferring instead to describe it as a matter of 'common concern'.[204] It remains to be seen whether this term will acquire any wider legal significance beyond indicating that all states have a legitimate interest in protecting the atmosphere as a global unity. Similarly, the parties to the Antarctic Treaty system have determined that a comprehensive regime for the protection of that area and its dependent and associated ecosystems should be adopted 'in the interest of mankind as a whole',[205] but they have avoided direct analogy with the moon or deep sea-bed. A case can be made for the proposition that Antarctica nevertheless has many of the features of a common heritage regime, but such a view remains controversial and does not take full account of the complex legal and political status of that continent, nor of the absence of any scheme for sharing resources.[206]

Moreover, there remains the objection that common heritage is still of doubtful legal status following its well-known rejection by the United States and other countries opposed to ratification of the 1982 UNCLOS and the Moon Treaty. Significantly it was not employed in the Ozone Convention.[207] Some conventions do use the term or others such as the 'world heritage of mankind' in their preambles in a hortatory sense.[208] But these are better viewed, like the term 'common concern', as expressions of the common interest of all states in certain forms of ecological protection,[209] and not as

---

[203] UNGA Res. 2750 XXV (1970), adopted by 108 to 7, with 6 abstentions.

[204] UNGA Res. 43/53 (1988). See *infra*, Ch. 10, and Boyle, in Churchill and Freestone (eds.), *International Law and Global Climate Change* (London, 1991), ch. 1.

[205] 1991 Protocol to the Antarctic Treaty on Environmental Protection, Preamble.

[206] See Kiss, 175 *Recueil des cours* (1982), and cf. Charney and Francioni, in Francioni and Scovazzi (eds.), *International Law for Antarctica* (Milan, 1987), 55 and 101. See also 1988 Convention for the Regulation of Antarctic Mineral Resource Activities (not in force), on which see Cook (ed.), *The Future of Antarctica* (Manchester, 1990); Keynan, 58 *NILR* (1991), 173 and *infra*, pp. 173–4.

[207] See further, *infra*, pp. 404–6.

[208] e.g. 1972 Convention for the Protection of World Cultural and Natural Heritage, and see further, *infra*, pp. 448–52 for other examples.

[209] *Supra*, text at nn. 17–20, and see Kiss, 175 *Recueil des cours*; Brunee, 49 *ZAORV* (1989), 791; Kirgis, 84 *AJIL* (1990), 525; and see *infra*, Ch. 4.

attempts to internationalize ownership of resources. Common heritage is important, however, in providing one of the most developed applications of trusteeship or fiduciary relationship in an environmental context,[210] and in that sense it represents a significant precedent whose implications are further explored in the following chapter.

(2) Conservation and Sustainable Development as Emerging Obligations of International Law

How far it can be assumed that international law now imposes on states a general obligation of conservation and sustainable development of natural resources and the natural environment remains an open question. These concepts, and the extent to which they govern the exploitation of living resources, are considered more fully in Chapters 11–13. The *Icelandic Fisheries* case, and the various fisheries treaties considered there, do support the existence of a customary obligation to co-operate in the conservation and sustainable development of the common property resources of the high seas. To these precedents may be added the network of marine pollution treaties and the emergence of a customary obligation to protect and preserve the marine environment, considered in Chapter 7. The provisions of a growing body of global and regional treaties concerned with international water-courses, wildlife conservation, habitat protection, endangered species, specially protected marine areas, and cultural and natural heritage also suggest that conservation and sustainable development have acquired a wider legal significance beyond that implied in the *Icelandic Fisheries* cases.[211]

Some of these agreements, such as the 1972 World Heritage Convention,[212] impose little by way of concrete obligations, however, or deal only with particular aspects of the conservation problem, as in the 1973 Convention on International Trade in Endangered Species, considered in Chapter 12. It may thus be said that it is difficult to treat these treaty regimes, or the limited indications of customary rules derived from case law, as adding up to the systematic endorsement of an obligation of conservation and sustainable development of all natural resources in international law. Moreover, although a reasonably comprehensive pattern of international co-operation now exists for the protection of common areas, such as the high seas or deep sea-bed, and for Antarctica, based respectively on the 1982 UNCLOS and related agreements, and on treaties forming the Antarctic Treaty System, including the

---

[210] Kiss, 175 *Recueil des cours*, and see *infra*, Ch. 4.

[211] See Chs. 6, 7, 11, and 12, and also New Zealand Resources Management Act, 1991, based explicitly on the WCED's concept of sustainable development.

[212] Lyster, *International Wildlife Law* (Cambridge, 1985), ch. 11, and see *Commonwealth of Australia* v. *State of Tasmania* (1983) 46 *ALR* 625, at 697 ff., per Mason J, and cf. Gibbs CJ, at 658–66. See *infra*, Ch. 12.

1991 Protocol to the Antarctic Treaty on Environmental Protection, it cannot necessarily be assumed that comparable obligations apply to areas which fall wholly within the boundaries of national sovereignty, such as tropical forests. This point is implicit in the conclusion of the legal experts of the WCED that

To the extent that this basic obligation [to conserve natural resources and the environment] concerns international or transboundary natural resources or environmental interferences, it already may in many respects be deemed to find substantial support in existing general international law.[213]

A more progressive argument would point to the widespread international endorsement of sustainable development as the central concept of international environmental policy. In Chapter 2 we saw how it has been employed at the Stockholm Conference in 1972, by the WCED, and in the declarations and policy statements of numerous intergovernmental conferences and international organizations. The World Charter for Nature[214] is indicative of this international endorsement of sustainable development as a concept of universal significance. The Charter does not confine itself to the conservation of international or transboundary resources, but calls instead for 'All areas of the earth, both land and sea' to be subject to principles of conservation. 'Special protection' must be given to unique areas, representative ecosystems, and habitats of rare or endangered species; ecosystems and land, atmospheric and marine resources must be managed to achieve 'optimum sustainable productivity' without endangering other ecosystems or species. Living resources must not be used in excess of their capacity for regeneration, and irreversible damage to 'nature' must be avoided. Moreover, even in this non-binding form, sustainable development may nevertheless be part of the 'soft law' governing exploitation of natural resources, as in the case of tropical forests, where an action plan and guidelines for sustainable management have been adopted by the ITTO. It is clear that few states would quarrel with the proposition that development should be sustainable and that all natural resources should in principle be managed in this way. This evidence, coupled with indications of supporting state practice, might be sufficient to crystallize the *opinio juris* into a normative standard of international law, or even into a peremptory norm of international law.[215]

What is lacking, however, is any comparable consensus on the meaning of sustainable development, or how to give it concrete effect in individual cases. As Handl observes, 'Without authoritative third-party decision-making, conflicting claims about the concepts' specific normative implications will abound

---

[213] Munro and Lammers, *Environmental Protection and Sustainable Development*, 44.
[214] *Infra*, Ch. 11 n. 32.
[215] See e.g. *Paramilitary Activities in Nicaragua Case* (Merits), *ICJ Rep. (1986)*, 14, and Handl, 1 *YIEL* (1990), 25. See also New Zealand Resources Management Act, 1991, *supra*, n. 211.

and disputes over application will be exceedingly difficult to resolve.'[216] Similar comments are applicable to the use of 'conservation' as a principle of international law. In these circumstances, states retain substantial discretion in giving effect to the alleged principle, unless specific international action has been agreed. Thus, to return to the example of tropical forests, little of value can be inferred from a broad principle of sustainable development without reference to state practice and the practice of international organizations and lending agencies such as the World Bank.[217]

Draft articles on sustainable development are included in the legal principles adopted by the WCED, and in a draft Charter and Convention on the Environment and Development proposed by the Council of Europe.[218] These instruments do not solve the problem of identifying what constitutes sustainable development in any particular context; they do, however, point to the emerging legal status of sustainable development as a principle of international law, and to the changing status of natural resources and ecosystems, which, as we saw earlier, can in many cases no longer be regarded as property to be freely exploited. The conclusion that international law now requires a standard of sustainable development to be met is not untenable; it simply lacks adequate articulation at present for confident generalizations to be made.[219]

(3) General Principles of International Law Governing Resource Exploitation and Protection of the Environment

(a) Reasonable Use

The principle that common spaces are open for use by all nations entails an obligation not to abuse this right or to interfere unreasonably with the freedoms of others. Article 2 of the 1958 High Seas Convention requires states to act with reasonable regard for the interests of others, and the same principle is reiterated in the 1982 UNCLOS. The latter Convention also provides that states shall fulfil in good faith the obligations assumed under this Convention, and shall exercise the rights, jurisdictions, and freedoms recognized in this Convention in a manner which would not constitute an abuse of right.[220] Article 2 of the 1958 Convention formed the basis for the International Court's judgment in favour of the United Kingdom in the *Icelandic Fisheries* case.[221] The Court referred to the parties' obligations to undertake

---

[216] Handl, 1 *YIEL* (1990).

[217] See e.g. the International Tropical Timber Organization's Guidelines for the Sustainable Management of Natural Tropical Forests, adopted 1990, and the Tropical Forest Action Plan, adopted in 1985. World Bank policy is summarized in *The World Bank and the Environment* (Washington, DC, 1991), 80–92.

[218] WCED, Legal Principles, Articles 2 and 3, in Munro and Lammers, *Environmental Protection and Sustainable Development*; Council of Europe, Draft Charter and Convention, in 1 *YIEL* (1990), 484.

[219] Handl, 1 *YIEL* (1990), 24–28, and see further *infra*, Chs. 11–13.

[220] Article 300.   [221] *Supra*, n. 190.

negotiations in good faith to reach an equitable solution of their differences, and to pay due regard to the interests of other states in the conservation and equitable exploitation of high seas fishing resources. Similarly, in the *Nuclear Tests* cases,[222] Judge De Castro referred to Article 2(2) in the context of alleged high seas pollution emanating from atmospheric nuclear tests. State practice has afforded some support for the view that such tests are permissible in so far as they are reasonable, although more recent declarations by nuclear states and the trend of global and regional treaties now favours a complete prohibition.[223]

There is no judicial authority for the application of a reasonableness test in judging the permissibility of other forms of pollution. But the inference that pollution from any source may be illegal if it unreasonably interferes with fishing or other uses of the oceans is supported by Article 11 of the 1983 Quito Protocol to UNEP's Lima Convention for the Protection of the Marine Environment of the South East Pacific, and by Article 4(6) of the 1986 Noumea Convention for the Protection of the Natural Resources and Environment of the South Pacific Region.[224]

Reasonableness is essentially a basis for resolving competing claims where otherwise lawful activities conflict. It is not as such a principle of substantive environmental protection. While as a last resort it may enable states to argue that pollution or the exploitation of natural resources are illegal if so excessive that the interests of other states are disproportionately affected, it is not a substitute for other, more concrete rules limiting the right of states to pollute or requiring sustainable use of resources.

(b) Abuse of Rights

It has been said that it is not unreasonable to regard 'abuse of rights' as a general principle of international law, but that it is a doctrine which must be used with 'studied restraint'.[225] Some versions of the principle are more relevant to environmental questions than others. The concept can be treated as one which limits the exercise of rights in bad faith, maliciously or arbitrarily.[226] In this form it is already an element in some of the rules examined earlier, including the duty to negotiate and consult in good faith referred to in the *Lac Lanoux* arbitration and the *Icelandic Fisheries* cases. This tells us nothing about the content of legal rights and duties but is essentially a method of interpreting them.[227]

An alternative view treats abuse of rights as simply another way of formu-

---

[222] *Supra*, n. 95.   [223] See Ch. 9.   [224] See Ch. 8.

[225] Brownlie, *Principles of Public International Law* (4th edn., Oxford, 1991), 444–6; Kiss, 7 *Ency. of Pub. Int. L.* (Amsterdam, 1984), 1; Lauterpacht, *The Development of International Law by the International Court* (London, 1958), 164.

[226] Cheng, *General Principles of Law* (London, 1953), 121–36; Kiss, 7 *Ency. of Pub. Int. L.*

[227] Friedman, 57 *AJIL* (1963), 288; Elkind, 9 *Vand. JTL* (1976), 57.

lating a doctrine of reasonableness or a balancing of interests. In this sense it is part at least of the law of the sea, but this again adds nothing to the points made in the previous section. Some authors also regard the *Trail Smelter* arbitration and other formulations of the *sic utere tuo* principle as indicative of an implicit abuse of rights doctrine. Once again, the question is not whether it is correct to do so, although some writers deny that it is, but whether this interpretation adds anything useful to the elaboration of substantive rights and obligations concerning transboundary relations, the prevention of pollution, or the conservation and use of resources.[228] Lauterpacht observed that in the relative absence of concrete rules and prohibitions of international law, abuse of rights offered a general principle from which judicial organs might construct an international tort law in accordance with the needs of interdependent states.[229] But this is to observe the generality of nascent rules of law which have subsequently acquired much greater particularity through codification and elaboration, primarily in treaty form. To the extent that present rules require a balancing of interests, or incorporate limitations of reasonableness, it may remain appropriate to describe this as a limitation on abuse of rights, but it does not affect the force of Ago's conclusion that international illegality is constituted by a failure to fulfil an international obligation, and that 'abuse of rights would be nothing else but failure to comply with a positive rule of international law thus enunciated'.[230] On this view, abuse of rights is not an independent principle, but simply an expression of the limits inherent in the formulation of certain rights and obligations which now form part of international law. Any wider use of the doctrine is likely, as Brownlie observes, to encourage instability and relativity.

(c) Equity and Equitable Utilization

The role of equity in international environmental law, as in general international law, is controversial.[231] Some writers see most environmental problems as requiring 'equitable solutions', in which more concrete rules of law are displaced or interpreted in favour of an *ad hoc* balancing of interests.[232] Used in this general sense equity is little different from concepts of reasonableness or abuse of rights and suffers the same objections of encouraging instability and relativity in the legal system. There is of course nothing to stop states agreeing to settle disputes on an 'equitable' basis, and in some cases of

---

[228] Elkind, 9 *Vand. JTL* (1976); Cheng, *General Principles of Law*, 130; Kiss, 7 *Ency. of Pub. Int. L.*; Handl, 69 *AJIL* (1975), 56–7.

[229] *The Function of Law in the International Community* (London, 1933), 295–306.

[230] II *Yearbook ILC* (1971), pt. 1, 221, paras. 25–31.

[231] See generally, Janis, 7 *Ency. of Pub. Int. L.* (Amsterdam, 1984), 74; Weil, *The Law of Maritime Delimitations* (Cambridge, 1989), 162–7; Goldie, in Utton and Teclaff (eds.), *Transboundary Resources Law* (Boulder, Colo., 1987), 103; Handl, 14 *RBDI* (1978), 40; Schachter, *Sharing the World's Resources.*

[232] See *supra*, p. 99.

air and water pollution they have indeed found it in their interests to do so,[233] but political accommodation should not be confused with determinations of international law.

In some situations, however, rules of law may require resort to equity to resolve disputes. 'Equitable utilization' is generally regarded as the primary rule of customary law governing the use and allocation of international watercourses,[234] and, as we have seen, UNEP's 'principles' concerning other shared natural resources follow the same view. In the *Icelandic Fisheries* cases the ICJ also referred to the need for an equitable allocation of common property fishing stocks,[235] while the ILC's proposals for equitable limitations on the entitlement of states to conduct risky activities within their territory suggests the possibility of more novel applications of the principle.[236]

The 'equitable' utilization of resources entails a balancing of interests and consideration of all relevant factors. What these factors are, and how they should be balanced depends entirely on the context of each case. No useful purpose can be served by attempting generalized definitions of what is essentially an exercise of discretion, whether by judges or other decision-makers. This discretion can be structured, however, and rendered more predictable, by careful analysis of international practice or by explicit recognition of relevant criteria in treaties or other instruments.[237] Moreover, as later chapters will show, the negotiation of equitable entitlements to the exploitation of natural resources can be facilitated by co-operation through intergovernmental institutions.[238]

Apart from its generality, and limited capacity for prescribing predictable outcomes, equitable utilization is sometimes also deficient in addressing environmental problems only from the perspective of those states sharing sovereignty over the resource or engaged in its actual exploitation. It is thus less well suited to accommodating common interests, or the protection of common areas, since these require a wider representation in any process for determining a balance of interests.[239]

4. RELATED ISSUES

(1) Military Activities and the Environment

A number of multilateral conventions have sought to place limitations on the deliberate infliction of environmental damage for military purposes or during

---

[233] See Chs. 6 and 10.   [234] See Ch. 6.   [235] *Supra*, n. 190.   [236] *Supra*, n. 135.
[237] See e.g. the ILC's draft articles on the Non-Navigational Uses of International Watercourses, *infra*, Ch. 6 n. 47, but cf. Brownlie, 162 *Recueil des cours* (1979), 287. Brownlie is too dismissive of equity as a major source of principles for resource allocation. cf. Schachter, *Sharing the World's Resources*, 64–83.
[238] Schachter, *Sharing the World's Resources*, 70, and see *infra*, Chs. 6 and 13.
[239] Boyle, 14 *Marine Policy* (1990), 151, and see *infra*, Chs. 4 and 6.

armed conflict. Some protection is afforded by restraints on methods of warfare and the infliction of unnecessary suffering found in the 1949 Geneva Conventions and in the earlier Hague Conventions, whose provisions were held declaratory of customary law by the Nuremberg Tribunal.[240] More recent agreements make explicit reference to the environment, however. The 1977 Environmental Modification Convention prohibits the hostile use of environmental modification techniques having 'widespread, long-lasting or severe effects'. This Convention is in force and has been ratified by major military powers, although not by Iraq, whose actions in setting fire to Kuwaiti oil wells in 1991 would possibly have been a violation. Violations of the UN Charter will, however, entail responsibility under international law to make reparation, and Security Council Resolution 687 (1991) holds Iraq liable on this ground for 'direct loss, damage, including environmental damage and depletion of natural resources' arising out of its conflict with Kuwait.

Also adopted in 1977, Additional Protocol I to the 1949 Geneva Conventions similarly prohibits methods of warfare intended or expected to cause 'widespread, long-term and severe damage to the natural environment', or to prejudice the health or survival of the civilian population. This terminology was understood to be directed at high-level policy-makers authorizing the use of unconventional weapons such as chemical agents or herbicides, and not at incidental or collateral environmental damage caused by those conducting conventional warfare.[241] The protocol also requires parties to take care to protect the natural environment, and places limits on the circumstances in which 'works or installations containing dangerous forces', including dams and nuclear power plants can be made the object of attack.[242] The latter limitations are also found in Protocol II dealing with non-international armed conflict. These protocols are widely ratified, but not by major Western military powers. During the 1991 conflict with Iraq, a number of nuclear installations, power plants, and water supply systems were attacked by Western airforces, causing serious damage, and casting doubt on the usefulness or general acceptability of the 1977 protocols.[243] Proposals have subsequently been made for the adoption of a fifth Geneva Convention, intended to cover protection of the environment in times of armed conflict.[244] The ILC's draft Code of Offences Against the Peace and Security of Mankind would also treat serious

---

[240] 1899 Hague Convention II with respect to the Laws and Customs of War on Land; 1907 Hague Convention IV respecting the Laws and Customs of War on Land; 1949 Geneva Conventions relating to the Protection of Victims of Armed Conflicts. See also 1972 World Heritage Convention, Article 6.

[241] See Articles 35, 54(2), 55(1), and Aldrich, 26 *VJIL* (1986), 711.

[242] Articles 55(1), 56(1).

[243] See generally Kalshoven, *Constraints on the Waging of War* (Dordrecht, 1987); Aldrich, 26 *VJIL* (1986); id., 85 *AJIL* (1991), 1.

[244] Plant (ed.), *Environmental Protection and the Law of War* (London, 1992).

and intentional harm to the environment as a crime against humanity and allow for individual responsibility.[245]

It should not be assumed, however, that rules of customary international law governing environmental protection do not apply in times of armed conflict, or that further international agreement is necessary to regulate environmentally harmful attacks. In the *Corfu Channel* case,[246] the ICJ referred to 'elementary considerations of humanity' in finding Albania bound to notify approaching warships of a known danger from mines, while, in the *Nicaragua* case,[247] the Court treated restrictions on the threat or use of force as peremptory norms of international law. Moreover, as against states not parties to an international armed conflict, belligerents enjoy no special privileges and remain bound by general rules of international law. Multilateral treaties for the protection of the environment may be affected in times of armed conflict by the doctrine of *rebus sic stantibus*, and must be interpreted according to the intention of the parties, but their continued validity as regards relations between belligerent and non-belligerent states is not otherwise affected.[248] Even between belligerent states, such treaties will not necessarily be suspended. *A fortiori*, if the conflict is not international, treaty rules will in general continue to apply. Few environmental treaties make explicit provision for derogation or suspension in time of war; in the view of one group of writers this supports their conclusion that the general rule is one of non-suspension of such treaties in time of armed conflict.[249]

Most environmental treaties do, however, contain clauses which preclude their application to ships or aircraft entitled to sovereign immunity. Thus, neither the 1969 Intervention Convention nor the 1989 Salvage Convention apply to such vessels, nor do the London or Oslo Dumping Conventions. Some treaties, while denying jurisdiction over foreign vessels entitled to immunity, require their parties to ensure as far as possible that their sovereign vessels act in a manner consistent with the treaty's requirements. Both the 1973 MARPOL Convention, and the marine pollution provisions of the 1982 UNCLOS are in this category.[250] Moreover, although both the 1969 Intervention Convention and the 1969 Convention on Civil Liability for Oil Pollution Damage do not apply to military vessels, several parties to the 1986 Convention on Early Notification of Nuclear Accidents have given notice when nuclear powered military submarines encountered difficulties at sea, although the latter convention is not explicitly applicable to military facilities.[251]

---

[245] See *infra*, pp. 208–10.   [246] *ICJ Rep.* (1949), 4.   [247] Ibid. (1986), 14.

[248] On this and subsequent points, see generally Bothe, Cassese, Kalshoven, Kiss, Salmon, and Simmonds, *Protection of the Environment in Times of Armed Conflict*, European Parliament (1985), section 3.

[249] Ibid. citing Article 19 of the 1954 International Convention for the Prevention of Pollution of the Sea by Oil as one of the few which do provide for suspension.

[250] 1973 MARPOL Convention, Article 3(3); 1982 UNCLOS, Article 236.

[251] See Ch. 9.

Conventions dealing with liability for nuclear accidents are also silent on their application to military facilities, but, like the 1969 Oil Pollution Convention, they relieve the operator or owner of all liability for incidents due to armed conflict, hostilities, civil war, or insurrection.[252]

The law of armed conflict is one of the least sophisticated parts of contemporary international law.[253] It lacks any institutional structure for supervision of compliance, and relies mainly on the good faith of the parties to a conflict for implementation and application. The remote possibility of resort to criminal sanctions *ex post facto* is not a reliable means of ensuring its satisfactory operation. Moreover, although it is clear that international law does not relieve states of their obligations of environmental protection during conflicts, and, as in the case of Iraq, responsibility may be imposed for environmental injury, this does not of itself afford adequate assurance of military restraint. Obligations of prior environmental impact assessment, consultation, and co-operation are inherently difficult to apply in time of war. Certain measures can be taken, however, to ensure that the more precautionary or preventive approach which now characterizes environmental lawmaking is also applied to the military sphere.[254] Chemical and biological weapons, and other forms of warfare can be assessed in advance to determine their likely impact on the environment. A number of treaties already place limitations on chemical warfare and the use of inhumane weapons,[255] and the Environmental Modification Treaty was partly inspired by the use of toxic defoliation agents in Vietnam. Sites of special cultural or ecological significance can be protected from attack or military use, and for this purpose the 1972 World Heritage Convention has some relevance. The control of environmental risks posed by the military use of nuclear power and nuclear weapons remains unsatisfactory, partly because it falls largely outside the existing regulation of civil uses of nuclear energy. This is a topic which could usefully be addressed by NATO or the CSCE in their work on environmental issues.

What does need to be emphasized is the importance of making environmental consequences a serious concern in military decisions. In this respect it is unfortunate that the 1977 Protocols remain controversial. The active role of the UN Security Council during the 1991 Gulf conflict, and its appreciation of the environmental implications, does offer some means of ensuring that pressure for compliance with the rules governing armed conflict is applied to

---

[252] 1960 Paris Convention on Third Party Liability in the Field of Nuclear Energy, Article 9; 1963 Vienna Convention on Civil Liability for Nuclear Damage, Article 4(3), *infra*, Ch. 9.

[253] Greenwood, in Butler (ed.), *Control over Compliance with International Law* (Dordrecht, 1991), 195; Cassese, *International Law in a Divided World* (Oxford, 1986), ch. 10.

[254] See commentary in Plant, *Environmental Protection and the Law of War*, ch. 9.

[255] 1928 Geneva Protocol on Chemical and Bacteriological Warfare; 1980 Geneva Convention on Inhumane Weapons.

the parties involved. Moreover, the Gulf conflict also involved UNEP and IMO in co-ordinating international action to mitigate some of the more serious environmental effects. This is a role for appropriate international institutions which could also usefully be developed. In short, the continued relevance of international law governing protection of the environment, and of environmental institutions, in situations of armed conflict needs to be stressed.

(2) International Trade and the Environment

As we shall see in subsequent chapters, a number of international agreements place restrictions on certain environmentally harmful forms of international trade. The two primary examples are the 1973 Convention on International Trade in Endangered Species and the 1989 Basel Convention for the Control of Transboundary Movements of Hazardous Wastes.[256] Other treaties also limit trade with non-parties as a means of putting pressure on these states to participate in environmental protection regimes, and to ensure that the object and purpose of these agreements is not undermined. The 1987 Montreal Protocol for the Protection of the Ozone Layer limits trade in ozone depleting substances for these reasons, and comparable policies have been adopted at various times by the parties to the 1946 International Convention for the Regulation of Whaling, and the 1972 London and Oslo Dumping Conventions.[257] United States legislation also allows limitations on imports of fish and fish products for the purpose of persuading supplier nations to comply with conservation measures, including the moratorium on whaling adopted by the IWC in 1985, and the US Marine Mammals Protection Act.[258] More commonly, national environmental regulations may require imported goods and commodities to comply with local standards of labelling, packaging, or manufacture, thereby setting standards with which other states' producers must in effect comply.

Trade restrictions of these kinds raise problems of potential conflict with the rules governing free trade established by the General Agreement on Tariffs and Trade, or within free trade areas such as the EEC.[259] In 1991 a GATT dispute settlement panel concluded that the extraterritorial application of US laws restricting tuna imports in order to reduce incidental dolphin catches was a violation of US obligations under the agreement.[260] In its view,

---

[256] Chs. 8 and 12 respectively.

[257] See Chs. 8, 10, and 12.

[258] 22 USC § 1978 (Pelly Amendment) 1971, and 16 USC § 1821 (Packwood Magnusson Amendment) 1979. See *Japanese Whaling Association* v. *American Cetacean Society*, 478 US 221 (1986); Zoller, *Enforcing International Law Through US Legislation* (Dobbs Ferry, NY, 1985); and Caron, 16 *ELQ* (1989), 311.

[259] Handl, 1 *YIEL* (1990), 15; Rehbinder, in Dupuy (ed.), *The Future of International Law of the Environment* (Dordrecht, 1985), 357.

[260] Panel Report on US Restrictions on Imports of Tuna, 30 *ILM* (1991), 1598.

a prohibition of tuna imports from Mexico or from intermediary states could not be justified by the limited exceptions allowed under Article 20 of the GATT. This permits non-discriminatory measures 'necessary to protect human, animal or plant life or health', or 'relating to the conservation of exhaustible natural resources'. The first of these exceptions was construed as covering only the use of sanitary measures to protect health or life within the jurisdiction of the importing country. The second exception was also inapplicable because it did not extend to the extraterritorial application of conservation policies, and because the unpredictable conditions established by US law for foreign fishing could not be regarded as primarily aimed at the conservation of dolphins. Moreover, given the availability of other possible measures to protect high seas resources, including the negotiation of cooperative arrangements with Mexico, the restrictions were found to be unnecessary for this purpose and to operate in an arbitrary manner with regard to Mexican catches. US regulations requiring the use of 'dolphin friendly' labels on tuna products were not considered inconsistent with the GATT, however.

These interpretations are not necessarily conclusive, and are subject to renegotiation of the terms of GATT itself. They do, however, indicate that national trade restrictions adopted on environmental grounds must be carefully defined if they are not to encounter difficulties under GATT. The restrictive interpretation given to Article 20 by the GATT panel may also pose difficulties for the implementation of other international environmental treaties. Expert advice given during negotiation of the Montreal Protocol on Protection of the Ozone Layer was that non-discriminatory trade restrictions under this agreement would be justified on health protection grounds under GATT,[261] and the same may be true of the Basel Convention. But the CITES Convention is intended to create a globally effective conservation regime, not merely one benefiting conservation within the jurisdiction of the importing state, and its compatibility with GATT is less clear following the panel's inerpretation of Article 20. The rules governing incompatible treaties in Article 30 of the Vienna Convention on the Law of Treaties provide *inter alia* for the priority of the later treaty as between states parties to both instruments, or for the application of whichever of the two treaties binds both parties. These rules have been described as 'not entirely satisfactory', and they are in any case only residuary in character, and dependent on interpretation of the relevant instruments.[262]

A policy of unrestricted free trade in all commodities will inevitably conflict in certain areas with environmental protection requirements, particularly where these do not enjoy the support of both importing and exporting

[261] See Ch. 10 n. 120.
[262] For a fuller analysis, see Sinclair, *The Vienna Convention on the Law of Treaties* (2nd edn., Manchester, 1984), 93–8.

countries. It may impede not only the use of trade sanctions by environmentally conscious importing states, as in the US–Mexico tuna dispute, but
also hamper efforts by environmentally conscious developing countries
seeking to ensure sustainable development of natural resources through
export limitation. At present, the tendency is for GATT to operate in favour
of free trade interests in developed states and advocates of unrestrained
development of resources in developing countries. The only satisfactory
answer to this problem may be to introduce into the GATT explicit rules for
environmental protection, such as are now found in EEC law. Although
national environmental measures may involve a breach of Article 30 of the
Treaty of Rome on grounds of disproportionality if they go too far, protection
of the environment is a mandatory requirement of Community law which can
limit the application of Article 30. Thus the ECJ has held in the *Danish
Bottles*[263] case that obstacles to the free movement of goods resulting from
disparities between national laws must be accepted in so far as these laws are
applicable without distinction to domestic and imported items and are necessary to satisfy mandatory environmental requirements of Community law.
Denmark was thus free to require the reuse of drink containers. This is
clearly a much more satisfactory approach than the present terms of GATT.

International trade law need not operate as an impediment to national
measures of environmental protection, provided it is not interpreted or applied
with excessive rigidity. It is this aspect of GATT which requires renegotiation
and clarification.[264]

5. CONCLUSIONS AND ASSESSMENT

This chapter has attempted to draw from the few relevant cases, and general
principles of law and the growing body of treaties, 'soft law' instruments, and
state practice indications of the main principles of international law governing
the protection of the environment. It must be stressed, however, that this
accumulation of precedents does not necessarily reflect the actual practice of
all states in all circumstances. There is a risk of appearing to attribute too
much weight to what remain in many respects developing trends whose legal
status is insecure and not universally established.

Some of the treaties relied on in earlier sections, such as the ECE Convention on Environmental Impact Assessment, are recent, not yet in force, and
have few if any parties. This treaty is also regional, not global in scope, and

---

[263] *Re Disposable Beer Cans* (1989) 1 *CMLR* 619. See Kromarek, 2 *JEL* (1990), 89.

[264] See GATT Secretariat, *International Trade 1990–91* (Geneva, 1992) which reviews the
interaction of trade and the environment. In October 1991 the GATT Council convened a
Working Group on Environmental Measures and International Trade to examine, *inter alia*,
whether existing international environmental agreements conform to GATT.

due account must be taken of the relative paucity of precedents supported by developing states. Like the draft ILC articles also relied on here, treaties of this kind reflect the continued operation of a process of codification and law-making which will be complete only when supported by the evidence of widespread, representative, and consistent state practice normally required for creation of customary international law.[265]

There are treaties, such as the 1982 UNCLOS, some of whose provisions, although not in force, largely meet these conditions, but even here, some of the more novel articles have not yet been acted upon by states, and cannot be regarded as law.[266] Thus it remains important to consider in subsequent chapters how far the general norms identified here codify existing law or have influenced the practice of states. This observation applies with equal force to 'soft law' instruments, such as UNEP's Principles of Conduct Concerning Natural Resources Shared by Two or More States, or its Montreal Guidelines for the Prevention of Pollution from Land-based Sources. Such instruments, although lacking legal force, have nevertheless had an impact on the development of state practice, or have led to the conclusion of further regional or global treaties. They should not be dismissed as being of no legal significance, and to this extent their use by UNEP for lawmaking purposes has been in some cases of some help to the process of progressive development.[267]

Caution is also needed before drawing general conclusions from the limited context of certain precedents, such as fisheries treaties and the *Icelandic Fisheries* case. While the law may be well established in areas such as the conservation of marine living resources, it is still necessary to ask what evidence there is for the application of some of these rules to more novel situations, such as the prevention of global climate change or the conservation of tropical forests.

Some of these considerations go far in explaining why customary international law is of relatively limited utility in providing normative standards for the resolution of evolving environmental problems. As Handl observes, the increasing pace of change in the scientific, economic, and social aspects of the global environmental crisis has placed enormous strain on the capability of the international legal system to keep up.[268] Customary law lacks the capacity to set standards which are precise enough, flexible enough, and sufficiently capable of rapid articulation. The major sources of international environmental lawmaking have thus been multilateral treaties, both regional and global. But here too, such treaties have been able to provide only a general framework. Much of the more important work of developing precise rules has fallen in practice to the institutions and intergovernmental bodies which these

---

[265] See *North Sea Continental Shelf Case, ICJ Rep.* (1969), 16; *Nicaragua Case* (Merits), *ICJ Rep.* (1986), 14 and *supra*, Ch. 2. But see the 1992 Rio Declaration, *infra*, Ch. 14.
[266] See Ch. 7.   [267] See Chs. 6 and 8.   [268] 1 *YIEL* (1990), 4.

environmental treaties have created, and whose operation is examined in the next chapter.

It would be misleading in the extreme to view orthodox customary law-making as an apt description of the process just described. Rather, what has occurred is an accretion of negotiating experience and regulatory techniques during the twenty years since the Stockholm Conference. The most notable feature of environmental treaties over this period is their increasing sophistication, characterized by the greater attention now paid to questions of effective supervision, the position of non-parties, and the problems of amendment and flexibility. The 1989 Basel Convention on the Control of Transboundary Movements of Hazardous Waste, and the 1987 Montreal Protocol for Protection of the Ozone Layer represent the most developed examples of this sort.[269] Within their own sphere, these treaties are far more important than customary law, and the key question is less their contribution to precedent, than their effectiveness in practice in securing their objectives. For this reason subsequent chapters will attempt in appropriate cases not merely to review the content of these treaties, but to assess their operation. In those areas where no such formal structure of regulation and supervision exists, the role of international law is necessarily much weaker. Even where the problem of identifying the rules can be resolved, the remedies and processes then available for securing compliance present their own difficulties, which we shall explore in Chapters 4 and 5.

[269] See Chs. 8 and 10.

4

The Structure of International Environmental Law II: Enforcement, Compliance, and Dispute Settlement

1. INTRODUCTION

The development of rules of international law concerning protection of the environment is of little significance unless accompanied by effective means for ensuring enforcement, compliance, and the settlement of disputes. The more traditional approach to this subject is the familiar one of interstate claims based on the principle of state responsibility, and employing the variety of forms of dispute settlement machinery contemplated in Article 33 of the UN Charter. There are various disadvantages to enforcing international environmental law in this way, particularly if it involves compulsory resort to judicial institutions.[1] These disadvantages include the adverse effect on relations between the states concerned; the complexity, length, and expense of many international proceedings; the technical character of environmental problems and the difficulties of proof which legal proceedings may entail; and the unpredictable outcome of litigation, a consequence of the unsettled character of much of the law on this subject. Perhaps the most significant objection is that the traditional model exemplified by the *Trail Smelter* case is concerned largely with affording reparation or other remedies as a response to violations of international law. Such a system is inherently bilateral and confrontational in character: it assumes that 'injured states' whose rights are affected are the primary actors in seeking compliance with legal standards of environmental protection. Its closest analogy in national legal systems is the law of tort, and adjudication is the method of dispute settlement to which it is most suited.

Claims for transboundary pollution damage are thus the most obvious application for this approach, yet in practice even here the obstacles are such that states have preferred to avoid the law of state responsibility and to rely on

[1] See generally Bilder, 144 *Recueil des cours* (1975), 141; Cooper, 24 *CYIL* (1986), 247; Levin, *Protecting the Environment* (New York, 1977).

fulfil this fiduciary role have proved disappointingly inadequate. In some cases they lack a wide enough remit, or sufficient resources. More fundamentally, they are no more than the expression of their members' willingness or unwillingness to act. In that respect they are no different from the United Nations itself, or from any other political institution. Their basic weakness has tended to be an inability to reach agreement on difficult issues or to ensure the full participation of all the states most closely concerned. Moreover, even where adequate participation is achieved, such bodies are often open to the criticism that their decisions represent only the lowest common denominator of agreement, and result in weak standards of environmental protection. Thus a collective approach may in some cases prove an impediment to stronger action at national level. The International Atomic Energy Agency, whose record is considered in Chapter 9, is perhaps the best example of this phenomenon. The true role of such bodies may thus be closer to legitimation of national policies than to acting as a fiduciary for the interests of the environment.

2. STATE RESPONSIBILITY IN INTERNATIONAL LAW[5]

(1) The Basis of State Responsibility

State responsibility, or international liability as it is sometimes referred to,[6] is the principle by which states may be held accountable in interstate claims under international law. Such claims may be brought before international arbitral tribunals or the International Court of Justice, as in the *Trail Smelter* arbitration, the *Lac Lanoux* arbitration, or the *Nuclear Tests* cases. Alternatively, states may use diplomatic means to press claims and negotiate settlements.

The foundation of responsibility in most cases lies in the breach of obligations undertaken by states or imposed on them by international law.[7] Responsibility in environmental cases will normally arise either because of the

---

[5] Brownlie, *System of the Law of Nations: State Responsibility* (Oxford, 1983); Jiménez de Arechaga, in Sorensen (ed.), *Manual of Public International Law* (London, 1968), 530; id., 159 *Recueil des cours* (1978), 267; Smith, *State Responsibility and the Marine Environment* (Oxford, 1988); Dupuy, *La Responsabilité internationale des états pour les dommages d'origine technologique et industrielle* (Paris, 1976); id., in OECD, *Legal Aspects of Transfrontier Pollution* (Paris, 1977); Spinedi and Simma (eds.), *UN Codification of State Responsibility* (New York, 1987); Francioni and Scovazzi (eds.), *International Responsibility for Environmental Harm* (Dordrecht, 1991), esp. chapter by Mazzeschi; Hardy, 36 *BYIL* (1960), 223; Handl, 74 *AJIL* (1980), 525; ILC, Draft Articles on State Responsibility; pt. 1, II *Yearbook ILC* (1980), pt. 2, 30.

[6] On the various uses of the terms 'responsibility' and 'liability', see Boyle, 39 *ICLQ* (1990), 8. In this chapter the terms are employed interchangeably in so far as public international law is concerned, but the normal use of responsibility is to refer to the obligations of states, and liability to refer to the consequences which ensue from a breach of those obligations.

[7] Article 3, ILC Draft Articles on State Responsibility; Brownlie, *System of the Law of Nations*, 37 f., 60–2.

breach of one or more of the customary obligations referred to in Chapter 3, or because of a breach of treaty. The concept is thus not confined, as is sometimes implied, to affording reparation for environmental harm, but has a potentially wider application in the general enforcement of international obligations concerning the environment.

Only the state's own obligations are in issue here. Private parties or companies are not in general subjects of public international law, although as we shall see in Chapter 5, the practice of channelling environmental liability towards private actors in national law is now a widely developed alternative to the international liability of states in cases of pollution damage. But the problem of attributing private conduct to states will seldom impinge on responsibility in international law for non-performance of the state's own environmental obligations. Even where an activity causing environmental harm is conducted by private parties, as in the *Trail Smelter* case, the issue remains one of the state's duty of control, co-operation, or notification, which cannot be avoided by surrendering the activity itself into private hands.[8] In this chapter, therefore, it is important to remember that we are not concerned with the conduct of individual polluters, fishermen, or multinational enterprises, but with states themselves, and in particular with their obligations of due diligence. The state is in this sense a guarantor of private conduct, but its responsibility is direct, not vicarious.

Some writers have argued, however, that a form of strict or absolute responsibility for environmental harm exists which is not based on any breach of obligation by states, but arises independently through general principles of law, equity, sovereign equality, or good neighbourliness.[9] Sometimes confusingly referred to as 'liability for risk', this theory of non-wrongful liability has been adopted by the International Law Commission as the basis of its topic 'International Liability for Injurious Consequences Arising out of Acts Not Prohibited by International Law'.[10] The underlying thesis for the Commission's work is that an alternative conceptual basis is needed in order to accommodate strict or absolute liability for lawful activities which cause environmental harm without any failure of due diligence, and to allow for the continuation of such harmful but socially useful activities. The cogency of this thesis is doubtful in the view of many writers, who argue that the case law,

---

[8] Handl, 74 *AJIL* (1980); Jiménez de Arechaga, in Sorensen, *Manual of Public International Law*, 560 ff. and cf. ILC Draft Articles 8, 11; Brownlie, *System of the Law of Nations*, 159 ff.; and *Case Concerning US Diplomatic and Consular Staff in Tehran, ICJ Rep.* (1980), 3.

[9] Handl, 16 *NYIL* (1985), 77–8; Goldie, 14 *ICLQ* (1965), 1189; id., 9 *CJTL* (1970), 283; id., 16 *NYIL* (1985), 175; Reuter, 103 *Recueil des cours* (1961), 590–5.

[10] Barboza, *6th Report*, UN Doc. A/CN. 4/428 (1990) with draft articles 1–33 and, *Report of the ILC to the UN Gen. Assembly*, UN Doc. A/45/10 (1990), 242; Boyle, 39 *ICLQ* (1990); Magraw, 80 *AJIL* (1986), 305; Akehurst, 16 *NYIL* (1985), 8; Handl, ibid. 49; Pinto, ibid. 17; Erickson, 51 *ZAORV* (1991), 94. For cogent criticism of the confusion of strict liability with liability for risk see Handl, 13 *CYIL* (1975), 164.

such as *Trail Smelter* and *Corfu Channel*, is based on responsibility for breach of obligation and not on some alternative theory, and that what matters is the content of the relevant rules of international law.[11] Moreover, the point has already been made that the Commission's attempt to avoid prohibition of environmentally harmful activities by distinguishing between liability for lawful activities and responsibility for wrongful ones is fundamentally misconceived. It fails to appreciate that much of the law of state responsibility, including the *Trail Smelter* case, is concerned with lawful activities which have caused harm, and that it is not the activity itself which is prohibited, but the harm which it causes.[12] This is the perspective from which the tribunal in *Trail Smelter* approached the issues: its final order required that the smelter be prevented from causing damage through fumes, and to that end it prescribed a control regime. Nowhere was it suggested that the operation of such industrial plants was prohibited or wrongful.

Thus the reasons advanced by the ILC do not make it necessary to depart, even in an environmental context, from the view that responsibility in international law rests primarily on some breach of obligation, however defined. But it does not follow that states may not as a matter of customary law acknowledge some obligation to make reparation for environmental harm without any failure of due diligence, or that general principles of law may not also support such a conclusion. What matters is not the theoretical basis of responsibility, but the role which state practice, international jurisprudence, and the views of writers attribute to concepts of fault, strict liability, or absolute liability in contemporary international law concerning environmental injury.

(2) Fault and Due Diligence

To describe the law of state responsibility as based on fault is misleading and liable to confuse. Both the *Corfu Channel* case, and the manner in which writers have subsequently interpreted that judgment, illustrate the dangers of trying to make general propositions on this subject. Two points must be borne in mind regarding 'fault' in international law. The term can be used subjectively, requiring intention, recklessness, or negligence on the part of the state or its agents,[13] or it can be used objectively, meaning simply the breach

[11] Brownlie, *System of the Law of Nations*, 50. See also Smith, *State Responsibility*, 40 f., 124 f., and for a particularly good analysis, Mazzeschi, in Francioni and Scovazzi, *International Responsibility*.
[12] See *supra*, pp. 89–102, and see Brownlie, *System of the Law of Nations*, 50; Akehurst, 16 *NYIL* (1985); Boyle, 39 *ICLQ* (1990). For a defence of the ILC's approach cf. Magraw, 80 *AJIL* (1986); Handl, ibid.; and Pinto, ibid.
[13] See the dissent of Judge Krylov, *Corfu Channel Case*, *ICJ Rep.* (1949), 72, requiring *dolus* or *culpa*, and Oppenheim, *International Law*, i (5th edn., London, 1955), 343: 'An act of state injurious to another is nevertheless not an international delinquency if committed neither wilfully and maliciously nor with culpable negligence.'

of an international obligation.[14] Used in the subjective sense, 'fault' is almost never the basis of responsibility in environmental disputes, although it is not inappropriate to use the term to describe the reckless or intentional infliction of avoidable injury in situations such as atmospheric nuclear tests.[15] But the point is that fault of this subjective kind is not normally a necessary condition of responsibility. Jiménez de Arechaga aptly explains this view: 'The decisive consideration is that unless the rule of international law which has been violated specifically envisages malice or culpable negligence, the rules of international law do not contain a general floating requirement of malice or culpable negligence as a condition of responsibility.'[16] Used in the objective sense of breach of obligation, however, 'fault' is simply tautologous, unless the particular obligation itself incorporates subjective elements. Thus, while it is not erroneous to describe the breach of an objective standard of diligent control of harmful activities as amounting to 'fault', it adds nothing to our understanding of the concept of responsibility to do so. Far more significant, as we have seen, is the question how due diligence is to be defined,[17] but what is clear is that no additional requirement of intention, malice, or recklessness on the part of the state is required. References to 'fault' in this context are otiose.

(3) Strict or Absolute Liability for Pollution Damage

Strict liability may have various meanings, both in national and international law. It may simply imply a reversal of the burden of proof in order to place on the defendant state the onus of showing that it was not negligent or otherwise at fault, in which case its diligence or state of mind may remain relevant. Alternatively, strict liability may imply that a failure of due diligence or subjective fault are not required, but that other defences are available. Used in this sense it differs from absolute liability only in the greater range of exculpatory factors which may negative responsibility. This is an important difference, however, which not all writers on the subject observe, and it can be seen most clearly in the conventions on civil liability considered below.[18]

It should not be assumed that even absolute liability necessarily means that no defences will be available. In its draft articles on state responsibility, the

---

[14] Jiménez de Arechaga, in Sorensen, *Manual of Public International Law*, 534–7, and Handl, 13 *CYIL* (1975), 162–7, prefer this interpretation of *Corfu Channel*. Brownlie, *System of the Law of Nations*, 38–48, observes: 'The approach adopted by the majority of the Court fails to correspond with either the *culpa* doctrine or the test of objective responsibility' (p. 47).

[15] See *infra*, pp. 358–60.

[16] In Sorensen, *Manual of Public International Law*, 535. See also Handl, 13 *CYIL* (1975), 164; Brownlie, *System of the Law of Nations*, 44 ff.; Smith, *State Responsibility*, 15–20.

[17] See *supra*, pp. 92–4.

[18] See pp. 292–8, 371–85. See also Goldie, 16 *NYIL* (1985), 175; Smith, *State Responsibility*.

ILC has identified a number of circumstances which may preclude wrongful-ness in international law.[19] These include lawful countermeasures, consent, *force majeure*, distress, necessity, and self-defence. The precise contours of these defences need not be considered here; what they demonstrate is the minimum from which any concept of responsibility must start. Moreover, it seems also generally accepted that no responsibility of any kind will attach to environmental risks of which the state concerned was not and could not have been aware. Knowledge of the risk of harm was an essential condition of Albania's responsibility in the *Corfu Channel* case.[20]

For the reasons explained in the previous section, the question whether states may be held strictly or absolutely liable for environmental harm cannot be answered merely by asking whether fault is a necessary condition of responsibility in international law. Simply to show that *dolus* or *culpa* are not required is not enough: something more is needed.[21] There are two possible bases for a standard of responsibility more onerous than due diligence. The first focuses, as we have seen, on the definition of the particular primary obligation in question. Thus the obligation to control sources of harm represented by Principle 21 of the Stockholm Declaration is capable of interpretation either as an obligation of due diligence or as one of unqualified prevention of harm.[22] Depending on which interpretation is correct, objective responsibility may sustain either responsibility for a failure of due diligence, or a form of strict or absolute liability for breach of obligation. The second approach derives a principle of strict or absolute liability in international law either from its recognition in international jurisprudence and state practice, or by analogy from general principles of national law or civil liability treaties which channel liability to private actors.

(a) The Views of Writers

The argument that there is a relatively straightforward connection between responsibility and the fact of harm is put most strongly by writers such as Goldie and Schneider.[23] They see *Corfu Channel* and *Lac Lanoux* as pointing to the emergence of strict liability as a general principle of international law. Goldie's argument draws on equity as the doctrinal basis of a system of strict liability for states. He treats risk creation as a form of expropriation of the adjacent state's use of its territory and invokes the notion of unjust achievement. The heavy reliance he places on inference from general principles of

[19] Articles 29–33, *supra*, n. 5. See Jagota, 16 *NYIL* (1985), 249.
[20] See *supra*, p. 96.
[21] Jiménez de Arechaga, in Sorensen, *Manual of Public International Law*, 271; Handl, 13 *CYIL* (1975), 163 f., who criticizes Goldie for equating strict liability with the absence of intention or negligence.
[22] See *supra*, pp. 91–5.
[23] Goldie, 14 *ICLQ* (1965) 9; Schneider, *World Public Order of the Environment* (London, 1975), ch. 6. See also Kelson, 13 *Harv. ILJ* (1972), 235 ff.

national law is the most questionable part of this thesis, and his interpretation of the international case law is not widely accepted.

Others, more plausibly, are more cautious. Jenks identifies ultra-hazardous activities as a distinct category for which strict or absolute responsibility is an exceptional principle, justified as a means of shifting the burden of proof and ensuring a more equitable distribution of loss.[24] This view is shared by the rapporteurs of the International Law Commission in the topic 'International Liability'.[25] In defining what constitutes an 'ultra-hazardous activity', most attempts focus more on the seriousness of the potential harm than on the likelihood of the risk occurring. One obvious candidate for this category is the risk posed by nuclear power plants.[26] Beyond that, the boundaries are more questionable and views are divided on whether the category should extend to activities whose effects are only cumulatively harmful, as in the *Trail Smelter* case.[27] An alternative approach to the problem of definition is to apply the category only to cases covered by specific agreement, but the only clear example of such an agreement is the 1972 Space Objects Liability Convention, under which states bear direct and absolute responsibility for damage on earth.[28] Significantly, treaties concerned with nuclear accidents and oil pollution at sea do not follow this example.[29]

Thus it is apparent that a strict or absolute standard of responsibility for environmental harm enjoys some support among writers as an exceptional principle applicable to ultra-hazardous activities, however these are defined. But as a general principle, covering all sources of transboundary harm, it is the alternative thesis, that states are in general responsible for environmental damage only if it results from a want of due diligence, which is more strongly supported by Dupuy, Handl, and others.[30] They see this as the dominant theory supported by state practice. They point to the ambiguity or inconclusive character of much of the jurisprudence, and to its misinterpretation by other writers, and they place more reliance on the evidence of treaty formulations of the obligation to prevent harm and of the responsibility of states. They are sceptical of strict or absolute responsibility as a general principle of law supported by national legal systems, while accepting that in specific cases a

---

[24] 117 *Recueil des cours* (1966), 105. See also Hardy, 36 *BYIL* (1960); Smith, *State Responsibility*, 112–25; Handl, 13 *CYIL* (1975), 68 ff.; and Brownlie, *System of the Law of Nations*, 50.

[25] *Supra*, n. 10.

[26] See Ch. 9.

[27] Jenks, 117 *Recueil des cours* (1966), in favour. The ILC's draft articles on international liability now apply to activities with a low probability of disastrous or considerable injury and to those with a high probability of minor or significant harm, but initially covered only higher than normal risks: see Boyle, 39 *ICLQ* (1990), 7.

[28] Jiménez de Arechaga, in Sorensen, *Manual*, 539, and see *infra*, Ch. 10.

[29] See Chs. 7 and 9.

[30] Jiménez de Arechaga, in Sorensen, *Manual; Smith, State Responsibility*; OECD, *Legal Aspects of Transfrontier Pollution* (Paris, 1977), 386; and Dupuy, ibid. 353; Handl, 74 *AJIL* (1980), 535 ff.

system of liability for exceptionally dangerous activities not founded on a failure of due diligence may be appropriate.

(b) The Case Law

Despite valiant attempts by various writers to invest the limited case law with definitive significance, the only plausible conclusion is that it is inconclusive. The final award in *Trail Smelter* required payment of further compensation if harm occurred notwithstanding Canada's compliance with the regime of control laid down in an order which owes much to a *compromis* instructing the tribunal to effect a permanent solution 'just to all the parties concerned.' This part of the award has nevertheless been variously read in support of a general principle of strict or absolute liability, but the failure of many writers to identify precisely which principle the case supports indicates the difficulty of drawing firm conclusions from it. Since Canada's responsibility for provable damage was accepted by the parties at the outset, the award was not concerned with establishing a standard of responsibility in international law, but only with deciding what compensation was due and what the terms of future operation of the smelter should be.[31] This does not provide a strong affirmation of strict or absolute liability as a general principle. In any event, as Dupuy points out, whatever the case decides, it must be read in the light of subsequent state practice, which in his view favours due diligence in similar circumstances.[32]

The decision of the International Court of Justice in the *Corfu Channel* case has suffered widely varied interpretations, but in reality tells us only that there is a duty to make diligent efforts to warn of known hazards to other states. It permits no definitive conclusions about the role of due diligence in cases of environmental injury, but it is difficult to reconcile the Court's efforts to establish what preventive steps the Albanian authorities could have taken to warn shipping with the view that states are strictly or absolutely responsible.[33] Most of the debate about the role of fault in this case has centred on the choice between subjective and objective definitions referred to earlier, not on the question whether the obligations of states are absolute or qualified by diligent conduct.

For different reasons, the *Nuclear Tests*[34] cases are also unhelpful. Decided by the ICJ in 1974, they deal with a series of deliberate test explosions, not with operational pollution or nuclear accidents. The claimants did not seek

---

[31] Handl, 13 *CYIL* (1975), 167–8; Smith, *State Responsibility*, 113 f.; Rubin, 50 *Oregon LR* (1971), 259.

[32] Dupuy, in Bothe (ed.), *Trends in Environmental Policy and Law* (Gland, 1980), 369, 373.

[33] *ICJ Rep.* (1949), 22–3; cf. Judges Winiarski, at 53–6 and Badawi Pasha, at 65. See Hardy, 36 *BYIL* (1960), 229; Smith, *State Responsibility*, 112 f.; Brownlie, *System of the Law of Nations*, 40–8; Handl, 74 *AJIL* (1980), 165–6.

[34] For a full discussion of these cases, see Ch. 9.

reparation for proven damage, but only a judgment that there should be no further testing, no deposit of nuclear fallout in breach of their territorial sovereignty, and no more interference with high seas freedoms. The Court made no findings on any of these issues but dismissed the case on the ground that it no longer had any object, France having undertaken unilaterally to discontinue further atmospheric tests. Only Judge de Castro made reference to the argument that nuclear testing may involve the breach of a state's obligation not to use its territory for acts contrary to the rights of other states.[35]

Although Principle 21 of the Stockholm Declaration of 1972 now incorporates this obligation,[36] it too is an inconclusive guide to the nature of responsibility for environmental damage, and must be interpreted within the framework of customary rules on which it is based. Reviewing the proceedings of the Preparatory Committee for the Stockholm Conference, Handl concludes that they provide little or no support in favour of any specific theory of liability, let alone a form of liability that is dependent on a link of causation as the only prerequisite.[37]

(c) Treaty Practice

Only exceptionally do treaties adopt a form of responsibility for damage placed directly on states without more.[38] On the contrary, some treaties, such as Articles 139 and 235 of the 1982 UNCLOS, specify that it is only for the nonfulfilment of their international obligations that states are responsible. There are comparable examples dealing with international watercourses and Antarctica.[39] Most treaty obligations to prevent pollution or protect the environment are expressed in terms of diligent control of sources of harm, exemplified by Article 194 of the 1982 UNCLOS,[40] but it is necessary to look at each treaty obligation individually to assess the circumstances in which a state may be held responsible for non-compliance resulting in harm.

Nor have states made any real attempt in their environmental treaties to facilitate the making of international claims as a method of compensating environmental injury. Instead of developing the law they have de-emphasised their own responsibility by adopting civil liability schemes or encouraging equal access to national legal remedies for private parties. This trend is evident in the law of the sea and for nuclear activities, but it also applies to

---

[35] *ICJ Rep.* (1974), 389.

[36] See *supra*, pp. 90–5.

[37] Loc. cit., *supra*, n. 5, at 535–40 and see also Jiménez de Arechaga, 159 *Recueil des cours* (1978), 272; Dupuy, *La Responsabilité*, 355–8.

[38] 1972 Space Objects Liability Convention, *infra*, Ch. 10.

[39] 1961 Treaty Relating to the Co-operative Development of the Water Resources of the Columbia River Basin, Article 18; 1988 Convention for the Regulation of Antarctic Mineral Resource Activities, Article 8.

[40] See *supra*, pp. 91–4.

transboundary air and water pollution.[41] Although a few other treaties contemplate the development of a liability regime, many ignore the issue of compensation for damage altogether, since it tends to be controversial in negotiations. Thus there is little evidence that in their treaty practice states have done anything to endorse or develop a form of state responsibility based on standards of strict or absolute liability.

(d) State Claims

State claims do not in general support any particular standard of responsibility. This point can be observed most clearly in claims concerning nuclear accidents or tests. Only the Cosmos 954 claim[42] brought by Canada explicitly adopts the view that states are absolutely liable for ultra-hazardous activities as a matter of general principle, but this claim was also based on the 1972 Space Objects Liability Convention, which specifically provides for absolute liability, and was settled *ex gratia* by the Soviet Union. In cases of damage caused by pollution of international watercourses, states have preferred to channel claims through national courts, relying on principles of civil liability. The Sandoz accident and other cases of Rhine pollution have been dealt with in this manner, and not by interstate claims.[43] The *Trail Smelter* case remains the only example of a claim for air pollution damage based on state responsibility. If that case were to arise today, it seems more likely that it too would be resolved by transboundary civil actions, once equal access for transboundary claimants in such cases had been assured.[44]

(e) General Principles of Law

The argument that a standard of state responsibility can be inferred by analogy from general principles of law rests on the use of strict liability in national legal systems and in civil liability treaties, particularly those dealing with oil pollution at sea and nuclear accidents.[45] It is true that many legal systems do entertain strict liability in certain cases. The common law principle employed in *Rylands* v. *Fletcher*[46] and in certain nuisance cases is also found in many civil law systems, especially in situations of ultra-hazardous activities.[47]

---

[41] See Chs. 6, 7, 9, 10, and Handl, 74 *AJIL* (1980), 540–3; Pinto, 16 *NYIL* (1985), 28 ff.

[42] Claim for damage caused by Cosmos 954, 18 *ILM* (1979), 902; Schwartz and Berlin, 27 *McGill LJ* (1982), 676 and see *infra*, Ch. 9 for other state claims concerning nuclear accidents.

[43] See Ch. 6.

[44] See Ch. 5.

[45] Barboza, *6th Report*, 9, para. 9; Goldie, 14 *ICLQ* (1965); Kelson, 13 *Harv. ILJ* (1972), and see *infra*, Chs. 7 and 9.

[46] (1868) LR 3 HL 330. See also *The Wagon Mound (No. 2)* [1967] 1 AC 617, per Ld. Reid.

[47] Markesinis, *The German Law of Torts* (Oxford, 1986); Kelson, 13 *Harv. ILJ* (1972); Butler, *Soviet Law* (2nd edn., London, 1988), 192; Lawson and Markesinis, *Tortious Liability for Unintentional Harm in the Common Law and Civil Law*, i (Cambridge, 1981), ch. 4. Recent Legislation in some states specifically applies strict liability to pollution damage: see 1986 Swedish Act concerning Damage to the Environment and 1990 German Environmental Liability

But there are significant differences in the scope of strict liability: in French law it is, for example, an accepted principle of governmental liability, while in England, activities conducted by public bodies under statutory authority are usually excluded from *Rylands* v. *Fletcher*.[48] Moreover the use of strict or absolute liability in civil liability treaties is normally part of a complex scheme of loss distribution whose principles cannot easily be replicated in public international law. These treaties were in any case intended to channel limited liability to the private party responsible for the activity in question: they tell us nothing about state responsibility in international law.[49]

These observations are not necessarily an obstacle to an international court relying on general principles to found a principle of strict liability in international law. As Lord McNair observed in connection with the use of general principles:

The way in which international law borrows from this source is not by means of importing private law institutions lock, stock and barrel, ready-made and fully equipped with a set of rules. It would be difficult to reconcile such a process with the application of general principles of law. In my opinion, the true view of the duty of international tribunals in this matter is to regard any features or terminology which are reminiscent of the rules and institutions of private law as an indication of policy and principles rather than as directly importing these rules and institutions.[50]

Given that the decision is thus one of legal policy, an argument based on general principles cannot be dismissed. But international courts have been cautious in making use of this source of law, mainly because it constitutes a form of judicial lawmaking independent of the will of states. References to national law in the *Trail Smelter* case were carefully controlled by the *compromis* and agreed by the states concerned.[51] Where this is not the case, it seems likely that an international court would hesitate to impose a general principle of strict or absolute liability, however widely evidenced in national law, in the face of the contrary evidence of state claims and treaty formulations referred to earlier. For this reason objective responsibility for breach of an appropriately defined obligation is a firmer foundation for a standard of responsibility not dependent on a failure of due diligence.[52]

Act, on which, see Hoffman, 38 *NILR* (1991), 27, and see also EEC Draft Directive on Civil Liability for Waste, *infra*, Ch. 8 n. 176. This directive is not in force.

[48] *Dunne* v. *NW Gas Board* [1964] 2 QB 605 and cf. Brown and Garner, *French Administrative Law* (3rd edn., London, 1983), 120–5.

[49] See Chs. 7 and 9, and Handl, 92 *RGDIP* (1988), 35 ff.

[50] *South West Africa Case, ICJ Rep.* (1950), 148. See generally, Cheng, *General Principles of Law* (Cambridge, 1987); Friedman, 57 *AJIL* (1963), 279.

[51] See the tribunal's award at 35 *AJIL* (1939), 698 and 714 ff.

[52] Handl, 92 *RGDIP* (1988), argues that objective responsibility is a general principle of law, but seems to equate the concept with strict liability. For reasons explained earlier this misconceives the nature of objective responsibility.

(f) Developing Trends

The arguments for using a standard more demanding than due diligence to shift the burden of unavoidable loss back to the polluting state remain strong, particularly where the source is an ultra-hazardous activity, such as a nuclear power plant. In the absence of reciprocal acceptance of risk, making the victim suffer is not an attractive policy.[53] Nor is due diligence always an easy standard to administer unless clearly accepted international standards defining the content of this duty can be identified. A heavy burden of proof will be placed on the state which has to establish a failure of due diligence. In the case of complex processes, such as nuclear reactors, this will be especially difficult unless liberal inferences of fact are allowed, or the burden of proof is placed on the polluter.[54]

Such considerations underlie the International Law Commission's attempt to develop a new regime of international liability applicable to activities involving the risk of very considerable harm, or a higher than normal risk of less serious harm.[55] The essential feature of this regime is a standard of strict liability for environmental injury, except in cases of armed conflict, natural phenomena of exceptional, irresistible, and inevitable character, or where the harm is caused intentionally by a third party. Resort to civil liability proceedings will also preclude state responsibility for the same harm.[56]

These articles represent more a development of international law than the codification of existing law. Nevertheless the successful articulation of criteria for adopting a general principle of strict liability in environmental cases would be an invaluable contribution to the subject, as uncertainty regarding state responsibility for the Chernobyl accident clearly shows.[57] However, strict liability is not necessarily advantageous if it involves either set limits on reparation or an equitable balance which spreads the loss across polluter and victim states alike.[58] This remains an important objection to the scheme proposed by the ILC. By contrast, the concept of objective responsibility for breach of obligation builds on a clearly established principle of international law and can accommodate a standard of responsibility approaching that of strict liability where necessary. Moreover, the full reparation due in this context avoids the dilution of responsibility inherent in the ILC's regime.

[53] Quentin-Baxter, II *Yearbook ILC* (1981), pt. 1, 113–18; Barboza, ibid. (1986), pt. 1, 160; Handl, 92 *RGDIP* (1988).
[54] cf. *Corfu Channel Case, ICJ Rep.* (1949), 18 where the court did allow certain inferences from the fact of Albania's exclusive territorial control. On proposals for placing the burden of proof on the polluter, see McCaffrey, *Report of the ILC to the UN Gen. Assembly*, 43rd Session, UN Doc. A/43/10 (1988), 68.
[55] *Supra*, n. 10.
[56] 1990 draft articles, *supra*, n. 10.
[57] See Ch. 9.
[58] Handl, 92 *RGDIP* (1988); Boyle, in Francioni and Scovazzi, *International Responsibility*; and see *infra*, pp. 152–3.

(4) Remedies

Where the responsibility of a state is established, an obligation to make appropriate reparation arises. This can entail extensive consequences. The injured state may require the other to:

(i) discontinue the act;

(ii) apply national legal remedies;

(iii) re-establish the situation existing before the act in question, or to the extent that this is impossible, pay corresponding compensation;

(iv) provide guarantees against repetition.[59]

The effect of these requirements was indicated in the *Chorzow Factory* case: 'reparation must, as far as possible, wipe out the consequences of the illegal act and re-establish the situation which would, in all probability, have existed if that act had not been committed.'[60] Additionally, the injured state may enjoy rights of reprisal and suspension of its legal obligations towards the offending state.[61] If it is accepted that a wrongful act is also an international crime, other states will also incur a duty of non-recognition of its legality.[62]

Reparation in the law of state responsibility is not an inflexible concept, however. As Brownlie observes: 'the interaction of substantive law and issues of reparation should be stressed.'[63] The appropriateness of particular forms of reparation, or of other remedies, thus depends on the circumstances of individual cases. In environmental disputes, states will primarily be concerned with preventing anticipated injury in breach of obligation, securing adequate guarantees against repetition, or obtaining compensation for environmental injury. It must also be remembered that restitution of the environment may often be impossible, impracticable, or not economically justifiable.

(a) Preventive Remedies

Although the ICJ has power to make interim orders of protection which are comparable to interlocutory injunctions,[64] the *Nuclear Tests* cases suggest

---

[59] ILC, Draft Articles on State Responsibility, Part 2, II *Yearbook ILC* (1984), pt. 1, 2; *Report of the ILC to the UN Gen. Assembly*, 44th Session, UN Doc. A/44/10 (1989), 188; id., UN Doc. A/45/10 (1990), 179. See generally Mann, *Further Studies in International Law* (Oxford, 1990), ch. 4.

[60] *Chorzow Factory Case (Indemnity) (Merits) PCIJ*, Ser. A, No. 17 (1928), 47–8.

[61] *Naulilaa Case*, 2 *RIAA* (1928), 1012; *Air Services Arbitration*, 54 *ILR* (1978), 304.

[62] *Infra*, n. 94, and see also *Namibia Advisory Opinion, ICJ Rep.* (1971), 16 for other situations in which a duty of non-recognition may arise.

[63] *System of the Law of Nations*, 234. See also Combacu and Alland, 16 *NYIL* (1985), 108, who argue that 'it is above all the consideration of "content" of the primary obligation in its widest meaning, which explains why a certain consequence is attached specifically and *ab initio* to its breach.'

[64] *Nuclear Tests Cases, ICJ Rep.* (1973), 99 and 135 (Interim measures); *Icelandic Fisheries Cases, ICJ Rep.* (1974), 12 and 30; *Case Concerning Diplomatic and Consular Staff in Tehran, ICJ Rep.* (1980), 7; Gray, *Judicial Remedies in International Law* (Oxford, 1987).

that an international tribunal cannot grant injunctions or prohibitory orders restraining violations of international law.[65] This is an obvious weakness in the potential use of international judicial tribunals to deal with cases involving environmental risks to other states. It casts serious doubts on the capacity of the system of state responsibility to secure compliance with environmental obligations, rather than simply to compensate states for the consequences of their breach. Declaratory judgments have, however, been employed by international tribunals in interpreting treaties and affording satisfaction in cases of breach of customary obligations, and some writers have also argued that a declaration may be equivalent to an injunction where it is used as a means of passing judgment on the legality of proposed conduct.[66] A strong dissent by four judges favoured this form of remedy in the *Nuclear Tests* cases, but the majority took a more restrictive view of the Court's power.[67] Their decision suggests that: 'problems which do not involve any direct injury to a particular state but rather affect the international community as a whole cannot be dealt with by means of a bilateral claim for a declaratory judgment.'[68] States seeking to complain of injury to the environment of common areas may thus be confined to diplomatic protest and measures of retorsion, or resort to international supervisory institutions.[69]

(b) Repetition and Future Conduct

The *Trail Smelter* case does indicate that states may be enjoined to take measures to prevent repetition of environmental injury for which they have been held responsible.[70] In that case Canada was ordered to adopt a regime for regulating the future operation of the smelter, including the payment of compensation for any damage which recurred notwithstanding compliance. Although Canada had not right to cause serious injury to the United States, its right to continue to operate the smelter was maintained. Thus, despite admission by Canada of a breach of obligation, a balance of interests between the two parties was achieved through the tribunal's order, and indeed this formed the main object of the arbitration.[71] There is no reason in principle

---

[65] *ICJ Rep.* (1973), 131, per Ignacio Pinto, but cf. *ICJ Rep.* (1974), 389, per de Castro. Gray, *Judicial Remedies*, 65–6, 95, cites the *Tehran Hostages Case* as possible authority for a power to grant injunctions but notes the Court's failure to address the question.

[66] Gray, *Judicial Remedies*, 96–107; Mann, *Further Studies*, 137–8. In the *Paramilitary Activities in Nicaragua Case, ICJ Rep.* (1986), 14, the Court decided that the United States was under a duty to cease and refrain from all acts constituting breaches of its legal obligations towards Nicaragua, but it did not order it to do so.

[67] See *ICJ Rep.* (1974), 253. cf. the refusal of the Court to treat Australia's application as a request for a declaration, at 263, para. 30, with joint dissenting opinion of Judges Waldock, Onyeama, Dillard, Arechaga at 312–17, and see Gray, *Judicial Remedies*, 104–6.

[68] Gray, *Judicial Remedies*, 214.

[69] See *infra*, pp. 160–79.

[70] 35 *AJIL* (1941), 712 ff. Gray, *Judicial Remedies*, 12 emphasizes that the *compromis* expressly empowered the tribunal to prescribe measures.

[71] Rubin, 50 *Oregon LR* (1971); Read, 1 *CYIL* (1963), 213; Boyle, 39 *ICLQ* (1990), 18–19.

why in other situations an international tribunal should not approach the question of responsibility for continuance of environmentally harmful activities in this way, using the remedies at its disposal to achieve a balance of interests. It does not inevitably follow that state responsibility is a system in which 'the winner would take all',[72] and lead to the prohibition of harmful activities. Negotiated settlements of environmental disputes have normally been equally sensitive to the need to achieve an equitable solution, without thereby weakening the underlying rules of international law which structure their negotiations.[73]

(c) Restitution and Compensation

Where environmental harm or injury is suffered by the claimant state, compensation for damage is likely to be the normal remedy sought by way of an international claim. Controversy surrounding restitution in international law makes it 'difficult to state the conditions of its application with any certainty',[74] and there are no examples of its use in an environmental context. Legal restitution, that is an order for the repeal or alteration of some legislative, judicial, or administrative act, may be appropriate where a treaty provision or international standard is not complied with.[75] The *Trail Smelter* award comes close to restitution in this sense in so far as it compels the more diligent regulation of the smelter.

What is mainly in issue, however, is whether harm not quantifiable in terms of damage to property or economic loss is recoverable by way of monetary compensation. This question is significantly dependent on the content of state's primary obligations of environmental protection.[76] To the extent that these do cover the protection of common areas, ecosystems, wildlife, or wilderness areas, reparation should include clean-up costs, damage limitation, and possible re-instatement of the environment. State practice and judicial precedent are too limited in this field to draw confident conclusions, but reparation for such damage occurring to a state's territory is covered by a number of modern liability treaties or provisions,[77] and may possibly be

---

[72] This extreme view of reparation was adopted by Quentin-Baxter, II *Yearbook ILC* (1981), pt. 1, 117. cf. Boyle, 39 *ICLQ* (1990), and *supra*, pp. 94–5.

[73] See e.g. the 1976 Rhine Chlorides Convention, *infra*, Ch. 6.

[74] Brownlie, *System of the Law of Nations*, 222; Gray, *Judicial Remedies*, 12.

[75] *Chorzow Factory Case*, PCIJ, Ser. A, No. 17 (1928); but cf. Gray, *Judicial Remedies*, 13 and 95 f., who cautions that this case turns on interpretation of a treaty and that actual awards of *restitutio in integrum* are rare.

[76] See *supra*, pp. 98–102.

[77] 1984 Protocol to the 1969 Brussels Convention on Civil Liability for Oil Pollution Damage; 1989 International Salvage Convention; 1988 Convention for the Regulation of Antarctic Mineral Resource Activities, Article 8.

inferred in the Cosmos 954 claim.[78] It is also included in the ILC's proposed regime of international liability.[79]

In principle, compensation should fully restore the injured party's position. There is some evidence, however, that the application of a strict or absolute liability principle may entail a limitation of damages. In the Cosmos 954 claim Canada did not recover its full costs of $14 million, but claimed $6 million, and settled for $3 million. In its proposed regime of international liability, the ILC has adopted the position that harm must 'in principle, be fully compensated', but may be reduced if it appears equitable to share certain costs among the states concerned.[80] However, the 1972 Space Objects Liability Convention provides that compensation shall be determined in accordance with 'international law and the principles of justice and equity', but must be sufficient to restore the party on whose behalf the claim is presented 'to the condition which would have existed if the damage had not occurred'.[81] Moreover, the international precedents do not go so far as the civil liability treaties, where specific monetary limits on compensation are an essential part of a complex scheme of loss distribution.[82] Thus it is uncertain how far the measure of reparation in international law is limited and whether this depends on the choice of liability standard.

(d) Breach of Treaty

Apart from an obligation to offer reparation, a breach of treaty may additionally entitle the injured state to retaliate by taking proportionate countermeasures aimed at restoring equality between the parties, or to terminate or suspend the treaty in relation to a party in material breach, as provided for by Article 60 of the Vienna Convention on the Law of Treaties.[83] The application of these responses depends in part on the object and purpose of the treaty concerned, and for that reason may be inappropriate in the case of multilateral co-operation treaties, including those concerned with environmental protection. In such cases resort to international supervisory institutions

---

[78] *Supra*, n. 42, and see generally Gray, *Judicial Remedies*, 88–90. cf. the 1972 Space Objects Liability Convention, and the nuclear liability conventions, *infra*, Ch. 9, which define damage to mean loss of life, personal injury, or loss or damage to property. Schwartz and Berlin, 27 *McGill LJ* (1982), 717 argue that the 1972 Convention does cover clean-up costs by way of mitigation of damage.

[79] *Supra*, n. 10.

[80] 1990 Draft Article 23, *supra*, n. 10.

[81] Article 12.

[82] See Chs. 7 and 9, and see Boyle, in Francioni and Scovazzi, *International Responsibility*.

[83] *Chorzow Factory Case*, PCIJ Ser. A, No. 8/9 (1927), 21; *Namibia Advisory Opinion*, ICJ Rep. (1971), 16; *ICAO Council Case*, ICJ Rep. (1972), 67; *Air Services* arbitration, *supra* n. 61, and see Rosenne, *Breach of Treaty* (Cambridge, 1985); Reuter, *An Introduction to the Law of Treaties* (London, 1989), 150 ff.; Mazzeschi, in Spinedi and Simma, *UN Codification of State Responsibility*, 57; Briggs, 68 *AJIL* (1974), 51.

is a preferable method of ensuring the continued integrity of the treaty regime.[84]

(5) Standing to Bring Claims[85]

Standing to bring international claims is in principle confined to 'injured states'. What this means can be observed in the second phase of the *South West Africa* case.[86] Liberia and Ethopia, although original members of the League of Nations with certain rights under the mandates agreement, were held to have no legal right or interest in South Africa's compliance with its obligations towards the inhabitants of the territory. That was a matter for the League alone and individual members acquired no independent standing to bring violations before the ICJ. This was an unusual case, however, whose unsuccessful outcome is a consequence of a narrow analysis of the legal relationship between the League, its members, and the mandatory power. Although the term 'injured state' has been defined by the ILC in broadly comparable terms, to include one whose legal rights or interests, including those arising under multilateral treaties, are directly or indirectly infringed by the defendant state, this will cause little difficulty in most inter-state environmental disputes. A denial of high seas fishing rights, as in the *Icelandic Fisheries* cases,[87] or high seas pollution affecting coastal interests would clearly fall within the ILC's definition, for example.

More problematical, however, are violations of international law affecting only the global commons, or areas of common concern, such as the ozone layer or global climate. As in the *Nuclear Tests* cases,[88] such violations may not *per se* affect the rights of any individual state, but rather those of the community of states as a whole. The problem of standing in this context is thus particularly concerned with how community rights can be enforced, if at all, by unaffected states through interstate claims, or by some other form of public interest representation.

International law does recognize the possibility that in exceptional situations certain obligations which benefit all states may have to be enforced by third states on behalf of the international community. In the *Barcelona Traction* case[89] the ICJ referred to obligations '*erga omnes*' in respect of which all states would enjoy standing to bring claims, and the normal nationality of claims rules would cease to apply. Certain human rights norms are among those the

---

[84] See *infra*, pp. 162–3.
[85] ILC, Draft Articles on state Responsibility, pt. 2, Article 5, *Report of the ILC to the UN Gen. Assembly*, UN Doc. A/44/10 (1989), 218 and commentary, II *Yearbook ILC* (1985), pt. 2, 25; Gray, *Judicial Remedies*, 211–15; Charney, 10 *Mich. JIL* (1989), 57; Weil, 77 *AJIL* (1983), 430 ff.
[86] *ICJ Rep.* (1966), esp. 20–3; Brownlie, *Principles of Public International Law* (4th edn., Oxford, 1990). 466–73.
[87] *ICJ Rep.* (1974), 3.   [88] Ibid. 253 and 457.   [89] *ICJ Rep.* (1970), 3.

court had in mind,[90] and a number of human rights treaties permit violations to be brought before judicial tribunals by any member state.[91]

The protection of common areas such as the high seas presents a comparable problem to the protection of human rights in that without community standing no means of direct enforcement by other states would exist. The same point applies where states have undertaken to protect their own environment in circumstances where their failure to do so has no impact on the interests of other states or on common areas. In the *Nuclear Tests* cases the ICJ was unsympathetic to the notion of an *actio popularis* allowing high seas freedoms to be enforced as obligations 'erga omnes', and it did not follow its earlier dicta. Nor has it applied the concept in any other case. But, in a somewhat different form, the point has found more favour with the ILC. Article 19 of its draft articles on state responsibility[92] characterizes certain serious breaches of international obligations essential for the protection of fundamental community interests as international crimes. States committing such breaches are not thereby rendered subject to 'criminal' penalties in any sense, and the terminology is misleading and liable to confusion with crimes against international law, committed by individuals.[93] This categorization does have two important consequences, however. First, other states must refrain from recognizing the legality of the situation, or from assisting the state responsible in maintaining it.[94] Secondly, all states will be 'injured states', with standing to seek appropriate remedies.[95]

This concept of criminal responsibility clearly applies only to a limited category of obligations and only to serious breaches of those obligations. In some of its applications, such as the non use of force, or the prevention of genocide, it substantially coincides with the concept of peremptory norms of international law from which no derogation is permitted.[96] As defined by the ILC, however, it also includes obligations for 'the safeguarding and preservation of the human environment such as those prohibiting massive pollution of the atmosphere or of the seas.' This definition is not meant to be exhaus-

---

[90] Ibid. 32, and see *Reservations to the Genocide Convention Advisory Opinion, ICJ Rep.* (1951), 23; *Case Concerning Diplomatic and Consular Staff in Tehran, ICJ Rep.* (1980), 42; *Nuclear Tests Cases, ICJ Rep.* (1974), 303 per Judge Petren, but cf. the critical views of Judge de Castro at 387. See also Riphagen, II *Yearbook ILC* (1980), pt. 1, 119–20, paras. 64 and 65.

[91] See e.g. *Ireland* v. *UK, ECHR*, Ser. A, No. 25 (1978), at 90.

[92] *Supra*, n. 5. See generally Weiler, Cassese, and Spinedi (eds.) *International Crimes of State* (Berlin, 1989); Gilbert, 39 *ICLQ* (1990), 345; Marek, 14 *RBDI* (1978), 460; Brownlie, *System of the Law of Nations*, 32 ff.; Tunkin, *Theory of International Law*, trans. Butler (London, 1974), 396–404; Weil, 77 *AJIL* (1983), 423.

[93] See *infra*, pp. 208–10.

[94] ILC, Draft Articles on State Responsibility, pt. 2, Article 14, II *Yearbook ILC* (1984), pt. 1, 2, and see also *Namibia Advisory Opinion, ICJ Rep.* (1970), 16.

[95] ILC, Draft Article 5, *supra*, n. 85.

[96] Spinedi, in Weiler, *et al.*, *International Crimes of State*, 22; Gaja, ibid. 159 ff.

tive; it might reasonably extend to species or ecosystem destruction, or tropical deforestation with serious atmospheric consequences.

The inclusion of environmental obligations in Article 19 of the ILC's draft has not been favourably received by all states, nor by some writers who have pointed to the absence of any reference to criminal responsibility in environmental treaties.[97] This reasoning is too narrow, however. It overlooks the attempt made in 1977 to bring the natural environment within the protection of obligations of humanitarian conduct by prohibiting ecological warfare intended or likely to cause 'widespread, long-term and severe damage'.[98] Moreover it also fails to take account of the growing number of multilateral treaties concerned with the protection of the global environment and areas of common interest or concern, such as the Ozone Convention, the London Dumping Convention, the Antarctic Mineral Resources Convention, the Convention for the Control of Transboundary Movements of Hazardous Wastes, and the World Heritage Convention. These cannot be dismissed as mere expressions of a principle of good neighbourliness: the collective interest which all parties have in the enforcement of such treaties may enable any of them to seek remedies whether or not they are affected by a violation.[99] The new concept of the 'common concern of mankind', applied by UNGA Resolution 43/53 to the global climate and considered in Chapter 10, carries the same implication.[100]

A more fundamental objection is the uncertainty inherent in the concept of international crimes, and the continuing opposition which the creation of this new category of international responsibility has encountered.[101] Even if the necessity of allowing third states standing to enforce collective or community interests is recognized, it can be supplied more simply by the category of obligations *erga omnes* without embracing the notion of criminality.[102] Thus it

---

[97] Spinedi, ibid. 61–2; Marek, 14 *RBDI* (1978), 477–8.

[98] 1977 Geneva Convention on the Prohibition of Military or Hostile Environmental Modification; Articles 35, 55, 1977 Additional Protocol 1 to the 1949 Geneva Conventions, and see *supra*, pp. 127–31.

[99] ILC, Draft Articles on State Responsibility, pt. 2, Article 5(2)(f); II *Yearbook ILC* (1985), pt. 2, 27, at paras. 23–4. The ILC draft limits this rule to treaties which expressly provide for the protection of collective interests: this seems unduly narrow, but cf. *SS Wimbledon*, PCIJ, Ser. A, No. 1 (1923), 20, and Gray, *Judicial Remedies*, 211 ff. For a more cautious view, see Hutchinson, 59 *BYIL* (1988), 151.

[100] Kirgis, 84 *AJIL* (1990), 525; Boyle, in Churchill and Freestone (eds.), *International Law and Global Climate Change* (Dordrecht, 1991), ch. 1; but cf. Brunee, 49 *ZAORV* (1989), 791.

[101] See Marek, 14 *RBDI* (1978); Gilbert, 39 *ICLQ* (1990); and Brownlie, *System of the Law of Nations*; and the continuing controversy in the ILC: *Report of the ILC to the UN Gen. Assembly* UN Doc. A/44/10 (1989), 194 ff.

[102] The ILC does not seem to regard 'international crimes' and violations of obligations *erga omnes* as synonymous, since its definition of the former refers only to 'serious breaches of obligation'. The categories may of course overlap. See Spinedi, in Weiler, *et al.*, *International Crimes of State*, 136 ff., and Weil, 77 *AJIL* (1983).

cannot be assumed that Article 19 represents international law. Nevertheless, these developments are enough to cast serious doubt on the reasoning employed in the *Nuclear Tests* cases to deny the applicants' standing.

Whether the right to protect community interests is expressed in terms of international crimes, or as a consequence of obligations *erga omnes*, it does not follow that the full range of remedies will be available to third states acting for this purpose.[103] It is, for example, unlikely that individual states will be entitled to demand reparation for material damage to the global environment beyond any clean-up or reinstatement costs which they may incur. The availability of particular remedies will depend on the circumstances of the breach, the suitability of alternative remedies, the extent to which the claimant state's interests are affected, and the nature of the risk to the international community. Account must also be taken of the risk that permitting multiple claimants may render settlement of a dispute more difficult or lead to measures disproportionate to the violation or injury. This may mean that in some cases the protection of community interests will involve no more than the right to make diplomatic protests and apply lawful sanctions, such as a refusal of access to fish stocks or an embargo on trade.[104] It follows that supervision of community standards by intergovernmental commissions will often be a more effective and realistic remedy.

An alternative to interstate proceedings, however, is to allow international organizations with responsibility for protection of the global environment to act in the public interest. Bodies such as the UN General Assembly, ECOSOC and possibly UNEP already have the competence to seek advisory opinions from the ICJ on questions of international law, and the *Western Sahara* case[105] shows how this power can be used even in cases concerned with matters of interstate controversy. To give NGOs the right to request advisory opinions, however, would require a significant revision of the ICJ Statute[106] and would again raise the problem of multiple plaintiffs with competing interests. If some form of public interest litigation is to be allowed before the ICJ, empowering international organizations is for this reason to be preferred.

---

[103] Charney, 10 *Mich. JIL* (1989), and id., in Francioni and Scovazzi, *International Responsibility*; but cf. Abi-Saab, in Weiler *et al.*, *International Crimes of State*, 141.

[104] See generally, Zoller, *Peacetime Unilateral Remedies: An Analysis of Countermeasures* (Dobbs Ferry, NY, 1984); id., *Enforcing International Law through US Legislation* (Dobbs Ferry, NY, 1985); Frowein, 47 *ZAORV* (1987), 67; Caron, 16 *ELQ* (1989), 311.

[105] *ICJ Rep.* (1975), 12. See Merrills, *International Dispute Settlement* (2nd edn., Cambridge, 1991), 122–3.

[106] On the limited standing of individuals and organizations in advisory proceedings, see Brownlie, *Principles of Public International Law*, 580–3.

(6) The Local Remedies Rule[107]

It should briefly be noted here that international claims involving responsibility for injury to aliens, or violation of human rights norms, have been conditional in international judicial and arbitral practice on the prior exhaustion of local remedies, which usually entails resort to the relevant national legal system as a preferred means of redress. Only if justice is effectively denied, or if no redress is available will an international claim then be admissible.

The application of this rule to international claims involving state responsibility for environmental injury is not clearly established. It was not applied in the *Trail Smelter* arbitration because no local remedies were available to the transboundary litigants, but the development of equal access schemes and civil liability treaties which facilitate transboundary proceedings[108] may have altered the picture since then. These can afford adequate and effective remedies for pollution damage suffered by individuals, and insistence on exhaustion of local remedies of this kind would be consistent with a policy emphasizing the direct liability of the polluter for environmentally harmful activities referred to earlier.

Two objections may be made to the application of the rule. First, unlike cases involving injury to aliens, transboundary victims of environmental damage are not voluntarily within the jurisdiction of the respondent state.[109] However, this will not be true where the victim has the choice of suing in the place where the injury occurred, rather than in the respondent state. Secondly, if it is accepted that the rule should apply to injury to individuals or their property, it may still be thought inappropriate to claims involving direct injury to the state's environment, or *a fortiori* in cases concerning the global commons, because these are too far removed from the original justification for the rule and its application could require states to submit themselves to foreign jurisdiction. Thus Amerasinghe concludes that there is significant judicial precedent and state practice supporting the proposition that 'the rule of local remedies does not become relevant where there is a direct injury to a state even though there may also be an infringement of the rights of one of its nationals.'[110]

(7) Conclusions: The Utility of State Responsibility

While potentially effective as a means of resolving environmental disputes, reliance on state responsibility has serious deficiencies. First, cases may be

---

[107] See Amerasinghe, *Local Remedies in International Law* (Cambridge, 1990).

[108] See *infra*, pp. 197–206.

[109] Van Lier, *Acid Rain and International Law* (Alphen aan den Rijn, 1981).

[110] *Local Remedies in International Law*, 113. On 'direct' injury to states' interests, see Brownlie, *System of the Law of Nations*, 236–9. Brownlie notes that the COSMOS 954 claim involved injury 'directly' to state interests.

brought only by states; the provision of diplomatic protection is discretionary and the state entitled to claim is the sole judge of whether it should do so.[111] This decision may be made on grounds unrelated to the environmental issues in the individual case. Especially where the harm is to common spaces, or where states may be reluctant to create precedents affecting their own future conduct, there is less likelihood that a willing plaintiff will appear or press claims to the full. Moreover, the jurisdiction of international tribunals is rarely compulsory;[112] without agreement to resort to third-party settlement, claims can only proceed by negotiation. Whatever method is used, the process will often be slow and expensive, and it gives the individual victim no control over the negotiation of any settlement.

Secondly, since claims may be made only by states with standing, and the remedies available may be limited or inadequate, there is a particular problem in using international claims as a means of protecting the environment of common areas. This leads one writer to conclude that:

in so far as the concept of responsibility to the international community as a whole is a reality, this is through the functioning of international organizations rather than any formal judicial procedure. International organizations provide a partial substitute for the lack of any general action on behalf of the world community and also for the lack of compulsory judicial settlement.[113]

Thirdly, although compensation for the costs of transboundary environmental damage may be recovered through international claims, state responsibility is an inefficient means of allocating these costs. Uncertainty surrounding liability standards, the type of environmental damage which is recoverable, and the role of equitable balancing means that the outcome of any claim remains inherently unpredictable and points to the absence of a fully principled basis for determining who should bear transboundary costs. A due diligence standard will leave the burden of unavoidable harm to lie where it falls, with the innocent victim, but a strict or absolute liability standard, accompanied by limits on the amount of compensation, may also mean that innocent victims will still bear some of the cost even in cases of avoidable injury. No consistent preference emerges from the precedents; rather we are faced with a choice. Transboundary environmental costs can be treated as a shared burden, implying, at its strongest, an obligation of equitable utilization of territory and resources. Alternatively, these costs can be directed back to the state which caused them, emphasizing in full its obligation to control sources of harm and protect the environment.[114]

---

[111] *Barcelona Traction Case, ICJ Rep.* (1970), 4, at paras. 78–9. Claims in respect of injury to individuals must also satisfy the nationality of claims rule: see *Nottebohm Case, ICJ Rep.* (1955), 4.

[112] Statute of the ICJ, Article 36.

[113] Gray, *Judicial Remedies*, 215, and see *infra*, pp. 160–79.

[114] Boyle, in Francioni and Scovazzi, *International Responsibility*. See also Handl, 92 *RGDIP* (1988).

The most important objection to state responsibility, however, is that it is an inadequate model for the enforcement of international standards of environmental protection. Like tort law, it can complement, but does not displace, the need for a system of environmental regulation. It is this failing which explains the emphasis states have placed on the development of treaty regimes of environmental protection and their supervision by international institutions, and the failure to develop or reform the law of state responsibility for environmental harm. Moreover, states have in many cases found equal access and other civil liability schemes a better means of allowing the recovery of transboundary environmental costs. For most forms of transboundary or marine pollution damage civil liability and insurance schemes now represent the primary recourse available to individual claimants.[115] Such remedies also emphasize the responsibility of individual polluters for the protection of the environment. In this respect state responsibility operates too indirectly and may appear to exempt those corporations or officials whose actions, policies, or decisions have lead to harmful consequences. One writer concludes that: 'It is not surprising in such circumstances if states behave badly.'[116]

But it does not follow that state responsibility is of no continuing significance. First, without the more comprehensive codification of environmental standards, and the wider use of supervisory institutions, there may be no other basis for enforcing customary international law in many cases. Secondly, civil liability schemes, although valuable, have their own drawbacks and deficiencies which make it necessary to retain the option of recourse through international claims. This point is particularly clear with regard to major nuclear accidents, such as the Chernobyl disaster.[117] Lastly, institutional supervision, whatever its potential, does not always work as an effective substitute.

3. REGULATION AND SUPERVISION BY INTERNATIONAL INSTITUTIONS

(1) The Role of International Institutions

In Chapter 2 we saw how international institutions such as UNEP, FAO, and IMO have contributed to the development of international environmental policy goals and the codification and further elaboration of international environmental law. In this chapter we consider the role of international institutions, particularly those of an intergovernmental character, as mechanisms which facilitate its implementation and enforcement. The key tasks which such bodies perform in this context are those of information and data

---

[115] See Ch. 5.   [116] Allott, 29 *Harv ILJ* (1988), 1.
[117] See Ch. 9, and Boyle, in Francioni and Scovazzi, *International Responsibility*; Handl, ibid.

collection, receiving reports on treaty implementation by states, facilitating independent monitoring and inspection and acting as a forum for reviewing the performance of states or the negotiation of further measures and regulations.[118] Such bodies may thus acquire law enforcement, lawmaking, and dispute settlement functions. In some cases they are also responsible for the allocation or management of natural resources.

International institutions are useful for law enforcement purposes in so far as they enable states to be held accountable to other member states, exercising a form of collective or community supervision. To the extent that such bodies are open to participation of other interested bodies or NGOs with observer status this accountability may also extend to a wider public, although none of the environmental treaties goes as far as the ILO Convention, under which employers and trade union organizations participate directly in the process of scrutiny.[119] Accountability is exercised mainly by techniques of general supervision or control of states in the performance of their international obligations, or of other agreed standards of conduct. These obligations or standards will usually have a treaty basis, partly because institutional supervision has proved to be a widely acceptable method of treaty enforcement, but the technique is also capable of application to rules of customary law. It is, for example, one method by which the principle of equitable utilization of shared resources can be implemented,[120] or by which preferential or shared rights to common resources such as high seas fisheries can be allocated, as in the *Icelandic Fisheries* case.[121]

Supervision of this kind generally also entails the negotiation and elaboration of detailed rules, standards, or practices, usually as a means of giving effect to the more general provisions of framework treaties. Not only does this form of lawmaking or international regulation facilitate treaty implementation, it also gives treaties a dynamic character and enables the parties to respond to new problems or priorities. The Antarctic Treaty System is a particularly good example of this feature. Through periodic review meetings, the parties have negotiated treaties to regulate the conservation of seals, marine living resources, minerals exploitation, and its environmental impact, and have also agreed measures to protect flora, fauna, and the environment.[122]

---

[118] See Kiss, in Kalshoven, Kuyper, and Lammers (eds.), *Essays on the Development of the International Legal Order* (Alphen aan den Rijn, 1980), 99; Luard, *International Agencies* (London, 1977), ch. 17; Morgenstern, *Legal Problems of International Organisations* (Cambridge, 1986), ch. 3; Skubiszewski, 41 *BYIL* (1965), 198; Kimball, 20 *ODIL* (1989), 147; Brownlie, *Principles of Public International Law*, ch. 27.

[119] See Luard, *International Agencies*, and Morgenstern, *Legal Problems of International Organisations*, 78 ff. and 117, and see also *supra*, Ch. 2. On participation by NGOs, see *infra*, n. 139.

[120] See Ch. 6.

[121] *ICJ Rep.* (1974), 3. See Ch. 13.

[122] See 1959 Antarctic Treaty, Article 9; 1972 Convention for the Conservation of Antarctic Seals; 1980 Convention for the Conservation of Antarctic Marine Living Resources; 1988

Thus the combination of regulatory and supervisory functions in the hands of international institutions is first of importance in making international agreements more effective in their operation. The absence of any provision for institutional supervision or regulation is, by contrast, often a sign that the treaty in question is ineffective and leads to obsolescence. Older treaties in this category, such as the 1940 Western Hemisphere Convention, have for this reason aptly been described as 'sleeping treaties' and their impact on contemporary environmental protection is likely to be limited. As Lyster observes: 'simply by requiring its Parties to meet regularly to review its implementation, a treaty can ensure that it stays at the forefront of its Parties' attention.'[123] Regulation and supervision by international institutions has been identified as part of a general trend away from the solution of problems by strictly judicial means and towards the resolution of conflicts through an equitable balancing of interests and *ad hoc* political compromise.[124] Used in this way international institutions become a forum for dispute settlement and treaty compliance through discussion and negotiation, rather than by adjudication of questions of law or interpretation. Moreover, community pressure and the scrutiny of other states in an intergovernmental forum may often be more effective than other more confrontational methods. The International Whaling Commission and the consultative meeting of the London Dumping Convention afford particularly good examples of this form of conflict resolution.[125]

Secondly, as we have seen, individual states may lack standing to bring international claims relating to the protection of global common areas, such as the high seas. In such cases accountability through international institutions may be the only practical remedy available.[126] This problem can only partly be circumvented by resorting to other methods of enforcing environmental co-operation and protection treaties. Compliance with the MARPOL Convention, the London Dumping Convention, or the CITES Convention, to take three examples, cannot readily be secured by suspension or termination of the treaty in case of material breach, as envisaged by Article 60 of the Vienna Convention on Treaties, since that would primarily harm the international community, not the defaulting state, and would run counter to a policy of

---

Convention for the Regulation of Antarctic Mineral Resource Activities; 1964 Agreed Measures for the Conservation of Antarctic Flora and Fauna; 1990 Comprehensive Measures for the Protection of the Antarctic Environment and Dependent and Associated Ecosystems; 1991 Protocol to the Antarctic Treaty on Environmental Protection; and generally Francioni and Scovazzi (eds.), *International Law for Antarctica* (Milan, 1987).

[123] Lyster, *International Wildlife Law* (Cambridge, 1985), 12.

[124] Gehring, 1 *YIEL* (1990); Simma, in Macdonald and Johnston (eds.) *Structure and Process of International Law* (The Hague, 1983), 485; Rosenne, *Breach of Treaty* (Cambridge, 1985), 39–44.

[125] On the IWC, see Birnie, 29 *NRJ* (1989), 903, and *infra*, Ch. 12, and on the LDC, see *infra*, pp. 320–32.

[126] Kiss, in Kalshoven, *et al.*, *Essays*, and see *supra*, pp. 154–7.

ensuring the widest possible participation in such agreements.[127] Moreover, it is possible for international institutions to give a more flexible interpretation to treaties of this kind and to apply to this process a specialized expertise based on experience and knowledge of the issues concerned, and aimed at securing compliance, rather than adjudicating on breach. Thus it is not surprising that provision for institutional supervision and regulation is now common in environmental treaties. It is certainly a more significant basis for dispute settlement in an environmental context than state responsibility.

(2) Models of International Supervisory Institutions

The use of international institutions for these purposes is not new. It dates back to the Rhine Commission, established in 1815, with power to regulate navigation on the river, and to settle disputes.[128] A more elaborate example of the same phenomenon developed after the First World War with the institution of mandated territories by the League of Nations. These were later succeeded by United Nations trust territories. In each case the Covenant and the Charter respectively prescribed certain basic obligations for the administering state to perform in fulfilling its 'sacred trust' to bring the territories in question to full self-determination.[129] The essence of this trust, like the concept of common heritage later employed by the 1982 UNCLOS, was that its performance required international scrutiny and supervision. But, although disputes concerning these territories could come before the Permanent Court or the International Court of Justice in certain circumstances,[130] judicial settlement was not the primary method for supervising the performance by administering powers of their treaty obligations. Instead, the Mandates Commission of the League, or the Trusteeship Council of the UN, were invested with supervisory powers, consisting principally of a reporting and reviewing function. As Judge Lauterpacht observed, explaining the role of the former body:

The absence of purely legal machinery and the reliance upon the moral authority of the findings and reports of the Mandates Commission were in fact the essential features of the supervision of the mandates system. Public opinion—and the resulting

---

[127] Simma, in Macdonald and Johnston, *Structure and Process in International Law*; and Rosenne, *Breach of Treaty*, pp. 39–44 and see *supra*, n. 83.

[128] Congress of Vienna, Final Act, 1815, Article 32, Annex 16B; Revised Convention on the Navigation of the Rhine, Mannheim, 1868; Convention to Amend the Revised Convention for Rhine Navigation, Strasburg, 1963, and Additional Protocol 1972. See also the 1856 Treaty of Paris which established the first Danube commission. See *supra*, Ch. 2, and Skubiszewski, 41 *BYIL* (1965); Vitanyi, *The International Regime of River Navigation* (Alphen aan den Rijn, 1979), chs. 1–2.

[129] Covenant of the League of Nations, Article 22; UN Charter, ch. 12.

[130] See *South West Africa Case, ICJ Rep.* (1950), 128; *South West Africa Cases, ICJ Rep.* (1962), 319 and (1966), 9; *Namibia Advisory Opinion, ICJ Rep.* (1971), 16.

attitude of the Mandatory Powers—were influenced not so much by the formal resolutions of the Council and the Assembly, as by the reports of the Mandates Commission which was the true organ of supervision.[131]

The Trusteeship Council and the Mandates Commission are important precedents because they represent a model of accountability to the whole international community, made more effective by a structure which facilitated open scrutiny and publicity for states failing to meet their obligations, but reinforced by the ultimate authority of the UN General Assembly, or the League Council before it, to pronounce on the conduct of the mandatory power in case of non-compliance. In this capacity, as the *Namibia Advisory Opinion*[132] confirmed, the General Assembly could terminate the rights of the administering power for material breach of treaty, and itself assume responsibility for administration.

Some of the techniques of political supervision and control employed here have been widely used since 1945, more especially in the field of human rights.[133] A good example is the work of the UN Human Rights Committee, whose members act in a personal capacity. This Committee receives reports from states on their implementation of the 1966 Covenant on Civil and Political Rights, and it may also consider complaints of non-compliance in cases where its competence to do so has been recognized by the state concerned. A somewhat similar procedure is found in the 1985 Convention Against Torture. The European Convention on Human Rights, and the Inter-American Human Rights Convention also employ supervisory commissions, but in both cases the more prominent role is given to judicial supervision, and individuals may be allowed separate standing to press complaints.

These are among the more sophisticated forms of international supervision. No institution, including the UN, has comparable authority in environmental matters, reflecting the more tentative and still recent commitment of states to environmental protection. Nevertheless, a provision for the parties 'to keep under continuous review and evaluation the effective implementation'[134] of their obligations, or some similar wording, is found in most modern environmental treaties, and for this purpose resort to institutional supervision and control has been widely adopted. The 1982 UNCLOS reflects the importance of this development in its articles on preservation of the marine environment, which require states not only to monitor the risks or effects of marine pollution and to assess the potential effects of activities, but also to report on

---

[131] *South West Africa (Voting Procedure)* Case, *ICJ Rep.* (1955), 121.
[132] *Supra*, n. 130.
[133] See generally Cassese, *International Law in a Divided World* (Oxford, 1986), ch. 11; Henkin (ed.), *The International Bill of Rights* (New York, 1981), ch. 14; Robertson and Merrills, *Human Rights in the World* (3rd edn., Manchester, 1989); Trindade, 202 *Recueil des cours* (1987), 9.
[134] 1989 Basel Convention on the Control of Transboundary Movements of Hazardous Wastes, Article 15; *infra*, Ch. 8.

these matters to 'the competent international organizations'.[135] As we have seen, such an obligation is a particularly important means of ensuring that activities affecting common areas like the high seas receive adequate international scrutiny. The 1988 Convention for the Regulation of Antarctic Mineral Resource Activities[136] takes this process one stage further by subjecting all such activities to the prior consent of an international commission and creating in effect a regime of international management. The only other international organization with a comparable power of veto on environmental grounds is the Oslo Dumping Commission, and its role is much more modest.[137]

Two rather more basic models of institutional supervision are found in the majority of treaties dealing with the environment. One consists of regular meetings of the parties, with institutional continuity usually provided by a permanent secretariat. This model is adopted by the 1972 London Dumping Convention (considered in Chapter 8), the UNEP Regional Seas Conventions, the 1959 Antarctic Treaty (although this lacks a permanent secretariat), and the 1973 Convention on International Trade in Endangered Species (considered in Chapter 12). The alternative and perhaps more flexible approach is to establish a formal commission, in which member states are represented. This method is employed by the 1974 Paris Convention on the Prevention of Marine Pollution from Land Based Sources, the 1976 Rhine Pollution Conventions, the 1972 Oslo Dumping Convention, the 1974 Helsinki Convention on the Protection of the Baltic Sea and, as we shall observe in Chapters 12 and 13, it is common in the case of multilateral fisheries or marine living resources treaties, including the 1980 Convention for the Conservation of Antarctic Marine Living Resources and the 1946 International Convention for the Regulation of Whaling.

The International Joint Commission (IJC), established by the US and Canada in the 1909 Boundary Waters Treaty represents a third model, unique among environmental bodies in exercising quasi-judicial functions and having a composition independent of its member governments.[138] It is noteworthy, however, that these states have been reluctant to allow the IJC to perform a truly supervisory role, probably because of its independent structure. In all other cases considered in this work the supervisory body, whether a meeting of the parties or a Commission, is in substance no more than a diplomatic conference of states, and the existence in some of these cases of a separate legal personality does not alter the reality that the membership of these institutions is in no sense independent of the states they represent. Lack of such independence is not necessarily a weakness, however. Because most

---

[135] Articles 204–6. See *infra*. Ch. 8.
[136] Watts, 39 *ICLQ* (1990), 169; Heap, in Cook (ed.), *The Future of Antarctica* (Manchester, 1990).
[137] See *infra*, pp. 328–30.   [138] See Ch. 6.

environmental commissions have a responsibility for the development of regulatory standards and the adoption of further measures, they cannot operate like the Human Rights Committee. These tasks can only be performed by an intergovernmental forum with appropriate negotiating authority.

Not all of these bodies operate with the same openness or publicity as the Trusteeship Council. Nevertheless there is now greater willingness to grant observer status, particularly to environmental NGOs, and these have brought to bear an effective influence because of their freedom from governmental control and their ability to influence public opinion and supranational bodies such as the European Parliament and the Council of Europe. Here too, the fear of adverse publicity can be turned into a weapon for ensuring treaty compliance, and putting pressure on states for stricter standards or better enforcement.[139]

(3) Supervisory Techniques

Effective supervision of the operation and implementation of treaty regimes depends on the availability of adequate information. This can be obtained in several ways.

(a) Reporting

Most treaties require states to make periodic reports on matters affecting the treaty. The extent of this obligation varies, but it will usually cover at least the measures taken by the parties towards implementing their obligations. Information must also usually be provided to enable the parties to assess how effectively the treaty is operating. The 1974 Paris Convention for the Prevention of Marine Pollution from Land-based Sources, for example, calls on the parties to communicate the results of monitoring of levels of marine pollution and on the effectiveness of measures adopted to reduce it.[140] The Basel Convention on the Control of Transboundary Movements of Hazardous Wastes requires an annual report on all aspects of transboundary trade and disposal of such substances, and on 'such other matters as the conference of the Parties shall deem relevant'.[141] Similarly, Article 8 of the 1973 CITES

---

[139] Treaties which allow observer status for environmental NGOs include the 1985 Ozone Convention; the 1946 International Convention for the Regulation of Whaling; the 1972 London Dumping Convention; the 1973 CITES Convention; the 1979 Convention on the Conservation of Migratory Species of Wild Animals; the 1979 Convention on the Conservation of European Wildlife and Natural Habitats; and the 1989 Convention on the Control of Transboundary Movements of Hazardous Wastes. On the role of NGOs, see Tolbert, in Churchill and Freestone (eds.), *International Law and Global Climate Change* (London, 1991), ch. 6; Morgenstern, *Legal Problems of International Organisations*, 86 ff.; Kimball, in Soons (ed.), *Implementation of the Law of the Sea Convention Through International Institutions* (Honolulu, 1989), 139.

[140] Articles 11, 17. See also 1982 UNCLOS, Article 206, which calls for information on environmental impact assessments to be supplied.

[141] Article 13.

Convention provides for the parties to maintain records of trade in listed species and to report on the number and type of permits granted. This information must be made available to the public. In some cases reporting requirements are designed to monitor how well the parties are enforcing a treaty. Thus the 1946 International Convention for the Regulation of Whaling and the 1991 Protocol to the Antarctic Treaty on Environmental Protection oblige the parties to communicate reports submitted by national inspectors concerning infractions, while the 1973 MARPOL Convention calls for reports from national authorities on action taken to deal with reported violations and on incidents involving harmful substances.[142]

This sort of information is meant to enable the parties to review and evaluate the treaty's impact. Where the treaty additionally requires the information to be made public, NGOs and other interested groups are also able to monitor progress. The obvious weakness, however, is that much will depend on the diligence and accuracy of the reporting authorities.

(b) Fact-Finding and Research

International institutions are not, however, confined to a passive role as recipients of information. In many cases the power they enjoy to conduct fact-finding or research provides the essential scientific basis for adopting measures and formulating policies of conservation and pollution control. They may also offer a measure of independent verification of the information supplied by states, a point explicitly recognized in the 1978 Great Lakes Water Quality Agreement.[143] The value of information obtained independently of governments is obvious in the operation of fisheries conservation bodies and other highly contentious situations. Thus it is important that these bodies should not be dependent on government scientists for expertise, but should be able to employ their own experts, or call on international scientific bodies such as the International Council for Exploration of the Seas (ICES) or the Scientific Committee for Antarctic Research (SCAR).[144] The latter possibility is essential if small and modestly resourced institutions are to have access to high quality independent advice. The FAO and a variety of NGOs may also provide useful, though in the latter case not always detached, expertise.

(c) Inspection

The most assertive method of information-gathering and supervision allows international institutions to undertake inspections to verify compliance with

---

[142] See Chs. 7 and 12.   [143] See Ch. 6.
[144] See e.g. 1980 Convention for the Conservation of Antarctic Marine Living Resources; 1946 International Convention for Regulation of Whaling; 1978 Convention on Future Multilateral Co-operation in the North-West Atlantic Fisheries; 1980 Convention on Future Multilateral Co-operation in the North-East Atlantic Fisheries, *infra*, Ch. 13.

international agreements and standards. The strongest examples of inspection by international agencies are found in the arms-control field.[145] Here inspections are usually compulsory and reports are sent to the Security Council. The IAEA's inspection powers with regard to non-proliferation of nuclear weapons conform to this pattern. But the powers of inspection of this agency with regard to the safety of nuclear installations are not compulsory: they may be employed only if requested by states.[146] This is the more usual pattern of environmental treaties, where provision for inspection by international institutions is exceptional. The main examples are all concerned with marine living resources. The International Whaling Commission has power to appoint observers who are carried on board whaling vessels and report back to the Commission. But these observers are nominated by member states willing to participate in the scheme on a mutual basis. In practice this means that observers from whaling nations are appointed to inspect each other's operations.[147] This falls well short of independent compulsory inspection. A few fisheries treaties have somewhat similar provision for mutual inspection, again reporting to the relevant Commission.[148] Only in the Antarctic treaty system have states accepted compulsory inspection as a means of informing the Consultative Meetings of possible violations of applicable treaties.[149] Thus there is clearly room for the wider adoption of institutional inspection as a means of enforcing environmental treaties, although this observation must also take account of the additional provision made by some treaties for national inspection and of the role of NGO's in bringing to light violations.

(4) Standard-Setting and International Regulation

Most environmental treaties provide for the negotiation and adoption through international organizations of further measures, including regulations, standards, and guidelines. In fisheries and wildlife commissions the purpose of these is to establish conservation methods, such as closed seasons or catch

[145] See e.g. 1990 Arms Control and Disarmament Agreement; 1968 Nuclear Non-Proliferation Treaty; UN Security Council Resolution 687 (1991); and Butler (ed.), *Control Over Compliance with International Law* (Dordrecht, 1991), 31.

[146] *Infra*, Ch. 9.

[147] Birnie, 29 *NRJ* (1989); Lyster, *International Wildlife Law*, 31 f. Power to make regulations for methods of inspection was added to Article 5 of the ICRW by a 1956 protocol; no agreement on a scheme for international observers was reached until 1974. See Birnie, *International Regulation of Whaling*, i (Dobbs Ferry, NY, 1985), 199.

[148] 1949 International Convention for North-West Atlantic Fisheries, Protocol on Joint Enforcement; 1978 Convention on Future Multilateral Co-operation in North-West Atlantic Fisheries, Article 18.

[149] The 1959 Antarctic Treaty, Article VII and the 1991 Protocol to the Antarctic Treaty on Environmental Protection, Article 13 provides for national inspectors, but the latter also makes provision for the meeting of the Consultative Parties to appoint observers to act on its behalf. The parties to the 1980 Convention for the Conservation of Antarctic Marine Living Resources have so far failed to agree on an inspection scheme.

limitation practices. In pollution control or environmental protection bodies such measures may be used to set detailed emissions standards, impose technical control requirements, or establish other methods of implementing the duty of due diligence in the regulation of harmful activities.

The form in which such standards or regulations are adopted varies widely. In some cases new treaties may be required. As we have seen, the Antarctic Treaty System has extended its regulatory scope mainly in this way. The 1982 UNCLOS indirectly incorporates by reference treaties on dumping and pollution from ships among the category of internationally agreed rules and standards of pollution control to which it refers.[150] Other treaties provide for the negotiation of protocols to lay down detailed standards. The 1979 Geneva Convention on Long-Range Transboundary Air Pollution and the 1985 Vienna Convention on the Protection of the Ozone Layer are two instruments which have relied on this method.[151] Other treaties also contain technical annexes in which specific standards are set: the 1973 MARPOL Convention regulates various aspects of pollution from ships in this way. More informal methods of rule-making, such as recommendations, resolutions, codes of practice, and guidelines all fall into the category of 'soft law', but they are nevertheless the means by which many pollution or conservation bodies are empowered to take further measures of treaty implementation. The legal status of these instruments was considered in Chapter 1.

Whether formally binding or not, all of these various methods of rule-making have in common that no obligation may be imposed on any state without its consent. Differences do exist in the manner in which this is achieved, but it is one of the more serious problems of international regulation that requirements of unanimity, consensus, or two-thirds majority voting are the typical conditions for adoption of new measures in whatever form, and moreover, that to enter into force, new treaties, protocols, or amendments thereto will normally require positive ratification. This is an often slow process which can be a serious impediment to necessary lawmaking, since, as we saw in Chapter 1, states which fail to ratify will not be found. An alternative approach relies on tacit consent or non-objection to bring amendments to technical annexes into force within a set time-limit. This method of amendment reverses the normal procedure and is now widely used for annexes to treaties such as the MARPOL Convention, the Basel Convention, the CITES Convention, and most fisheries conventions, since it enables schedules of protected species, prohibited substances, or conservation regulations to be changed speedily as circumstances require. But states still remain free to opt out of these amendments if they object in time.

This freedom has seriously limited the ability of a number of commissions to function effectively as regulatory bodies. Fisheries commissions in par-

---

[150] See Chs. 7 and 8.   [151] See Ch. 10.

ticular have had difficulty setting appropriate catch quotas.[152] The International Whaling Commission too has had problems persuading Japan, Norway, and other whaling states to accept amended regulations or moratoria approved by substantial majorities, and resort to the objections procedure has enabled whaling states to delay many conservationist proposals. But the relative ease of amending regulations adopted under this convention 'has proved a most useful and flexible instrument for reflecting changes in attitudes and practice, and thus for resolving issues.'[153] Moreover, diplomatic and economic pressure applied by other states may help to make persistent objectors comply with majority decisions; such pressure was used successfully by the United States to persuade Japan to accept a whaling moratorium adopted by the IWC in 1982.[154] Leverage of this kind may not always be available, however: Chapters 8 and 10 show how difficult it has been to persuade the EEC and the United States to accept stricter standards for land-based sources of marine pollution or air pollution. But the success of the parties to the London Dumping Convention in progressively adopting stricter standards leading towards the ultimate elimination of dumping at sea shows how in the right conditions substantial changes can come about by agreement, as does the decision of the parties to the CITES Convention in 1990 to eliminate international trade in African ivory. Other forms of pressure or persuasion can also be built into some treaty regimes. The Ozone Convention and its protocols employ a trust fund and technology transfer provisions to encourage participation by underdeveloped states, while parties are forbidden to trade with non-parties in ozone depleting substances or their products.[155] Similar restrictions on trade with non-parties have been employed in the Basel Convention for the Control of Transboundary Movements of Hazardous Waste, the CITES Convention, and by the International Whaling Commission.[156] Article 10 of the 1980 Convention for the Conservation of Antarctic Marine Living Resources does not resort to these tactics but instead allows the CCAMLR Commission to put pressure on non-parties whose activities affect implementation of the Convention. This attempt to involve non-parties is a distinctive feature of treaties comprising the Antarctic Treaty System, but it is probably too limited in scope and insufficiently supported by acquiescence to constitute an assertion of jurisdiction or to create an objective regime binding on all states.[157]

---

[152] See Ch. 13.   [153] Birnie, 29 *NRJ* (1989), 913, and see *infra*, Ch. 12.

[154] Lyster, *International Wildlife Law*; Zoller, *Enforcing International Law through US Legislation* (Dobbs Ferry, NY, 1985), 84–97.

[155] See *infra*, pp. 404–8.

[156] Lyster, *International Wildlife Law*, 29 and 256; Birnie, 29 *NRJ* (1989), 918; id., 12 *ELQ* (1985), 675; and *infra*, pp. 332–43.

[157] For an outstanding debate on the controversial status of the Antarctic Treaty System against third states, see papers by Brunner, Charney, and Simma in Francioni and Scovazzi, *International Law for Antarctica*. See also 1982 North Atlantic Salmon Convention, Article 2(3); 1978 Convention for Future Co-operation in North-West Atlantic Fisheries, Article 19.

(5) International Management

Measures of the type considered above may increase the costs of isolated opposition to majority decisions, but they cannot guarantee either participation or adherence to treaty standards by all states. Resort to 'soft-law' techniques only partially resolves this dilemma, since there is no obligation to comply. The more radical alternative is to allow majorities of states to impose regulations on dissenting minorities, but this is at variance with the philosophy of consent of which the international legal order is based. At present, however, only the EEC has moved significantly in this direction by providing in Articles 100A and 130S of the 1986 Single European Act for the possibility of deciding by qualified majority vote binding on all member states what action is to be taken by the Community to protect the environment, including measures to harmonize national laws. The 1987 Montreal Protocol to the Ozone Convention is more radical than earlier precedents in enabling combined majorities of developing and industrialized states to amend standards set by the protocol for production or consumption of controlled substances.[158] These adjustments are automatically binding on all parties, whether or not they voted in favour. Withdrawal from the protocol is then the only option for those to whom the amendment is unacceptable. Clearly, the intention here is to make opposition to majority decisions as difficult and costly as possible.

Also noteworthy are a small number of proposed international institutions which, if they ever come into existence, will perform functions more appropriately described as international resource management. Their responsibilities include protection of the environment of the areas in question, but they differ from other control and supervisory bodies in that the right of individual states to exploit the resource is subordinated to the authority of collective decision-making. These institutions thus possess considerably stronger powers than is normally the case, since exploitation may take place only with their prior consent and subject to rules some of which are established by qualified majorities which bind all participants. The two most prominent examples are the International Sea-bed Authority (ISBA), which will begin to function when the 1982 UNCLOS enters into force, and the Antarctic Mineral Resources Commission, which would have been established under the 1988 Convention for the Regulation of Antarctic Mineral Resource Activities.

(a) The International Sea-bed Authority

The ISBA is concerned only with the exploration for and exploitation of deep sea-bed mineral resources; earlier proposals to extend its authority to include

---

[158] 1987 Montreal Protocol on Substances that Deplete the Ozone Layer, Article 2(9) as amended 1990; *infra*, pp. 406–11.

management of high seas fisheries and protection of the whole marine environment were not pursued.[159] Article 187 of the 1982 UNCLOS states that 'The Authority is the organization through which states Parties shall ... organise and control activities in the [deep sea-bed] Area, particularly with a view to administering the resources of the Area.' No exploitation of those resources may take place outside the control and administration of this body, which is given the duty to adopt appropriate rules, regulations, and procedures for ensuring effective protection of the marine environment, both in relation to pollution and the protection and conservation of natural resources and flora and fauna.[160]

The ISBA comprises several elements, including a political organ, the Assembly, consisting of all member states, and to which other organs of the authority are responsible. Its approval is necessary for the adoption of regulations governing exploitation and exploration of the deep sea-bed, including environmental protection measures, and it also approves arrangements for the equitable sharing of benefits derived from sea-bed activities. The second component is the Council, a small executive body reflecting a balance of geographical, political, and economic groupings, whose functions are, *inter alia*, to establish specific policies, to supervise and co-ordinate the implementation of the convention's provisions on the deep sea-bed, to approve proposed plans for exploration and exploitation, and to make recommendations to the Assembly. For these purposes the Council may rely on an Economic Planning Commission and a Legal and Technical Commission. Thirdly, the authority also controls a body described as 'the Enterprise'. The latter's task is to carry out sea-bed mining activities on its behalf. Finally, 'Sea-bed Disputes Chamber' of the Law of the Sea Tribunal will have competence over disputes concerning sea-bed operations and the ISBA.

This structure, both complex and controversial, was designed as the means of implementing the concept of the common heritage of mankind, which the 1982 UNCLOS applies to deep sea-bed mineral resources. Similar institutional support is also envisaged in the 1979 Moon Treaty as an essential condition for the application of the same concept to the exploitation of mineral resources on the celestial bodies, but the treaty leaves the creation of such a body to later negotiation.[161]

---

[159] 1982 UNCLOS, Articles 156–70. For earlier proposals, see Carroz, 21 *SDLR* (1984), 516–17; Kenya, Draft Articles for the preservation and protection of the marine environment, UN Doc. A/CONF. 62/C3/L. 2 (1974).

[160] Draft Regulations on Protection and Preservation of the Marine Environment From Activities in the Area, UN Doc. LOS/PCN/SCN. 3/WP. 6/Add. 5 (1990), and LOS/PCN/SCN. 3/CRP. 11 (1991), and see *supra*, Ch. 3 n. 202.

[161] Cheng, *CLP* (1980), 213.

(b) The Antarctic Mineral Resources Commission

Although the Antarctic Mineral Resources Convention[162] does not adopt the common heritage principle, and it leaves responsibility for exploitation of mineral resources solely in the hands of states parties, the institutional machinery it envisages has many similarities with the International Sea-bed Authority. Overall political supervision falls in this case to a special meeting of the parties, whose functions are limited to expressing views on applications for exploration and development in Antarctica. Since this body can only give advice, the real decisions are taken by the Commission, which comprises only those states with an interest in minerals exploitation, either because they are Consultative Parties of the Antarctic Treaty,[163] or because they are proposing to conduct some minerals related activity. The Commission's main tasks are to determine where mineral activity may take place, to regulate it, to adopt measures for the protection of the environment and dependent and associated ecosystems, to facilitate environmental impact assessment, and 'to keep under review the conduct of Antarctic mineral resource activities with a view to safeguarding the protection of the Antarctic environment in the interest of all mankind.' It is assisted by a Scientific, Technical and Environmental Advisory Committee. Detailed control of the exploitation of particular areas of the Antarctic opened for mineral activity is performed by a regulatory committee established for each area. As in the case of the ISBA, no exploitation of Antarctic minerals may take place without the approval of these bodies, and environmental and other regulations which are adopted become binding on all states who participate. Securing such approval under the Antarctic Minerals Convention is a particularly burdensome process whose complexity reflects the differing interests of states involved in Antarctica and the controversial character of proposals for minerals exploitation there, due largely to their possible environmental impact.

(c) The Significance of the ISBA and Antarctic Mineral Resources Commission

For reasons partly of political, economic, and ideological opposition, and in the case of Antarctica, because of a growing interest among some states in the idea of a continent preserved from exploitation, or as a 'world park', it is quite possible that neither of these institutions will come into being.[164] Their

---

[162] Articles 18–33; see Watts, 39 *ICLQ* (1990); Oxman, 21 *Inter American LR* (1989), 17.

[163] The Consultative parties to the 1959 treaty are the claimant states, the other original parties, and any other party 'during such time as that Contracting Party demonstrates its interest in Antarctica by conducting substantial scientific research activity there'.

[164] See generally, Oxman, Caron, and Buderi, *Law of the Sea: US Policy Dilemma* (San Francisco, 1983), chs. 6 and 8; Simmonds, *OGTLR* (1987), 191, 246, 306, and ibid. (1988), 42; Beck, *The International Politics of Antarctica* (London, 1986); Francioni and Scovazzi, *International Law for Antarctica*; and see now 1991 Protocol to the Antarctic Treaty on Environmental Protection, Article 25, which places a 50-year moratorium on mineral activities in Antarctica.

bureaucratic complexity is another factor in the probable failure of attempts to internationalize the management of resource exploitation and environmental protection in common areas. Moreover, like the International Atomic Energy Agency,[165] they are open to the serious objection of a conflict of interests. It is questionable how far bodies with a primary responsibility for the development of a resource may at the same time also regulate its environmental impact, but in this respect they share the problems of many national authorities with similarly contradictory functions.

Nevertheless, both institutions represent a model of international trustee-ship whose environmental protection and resource conservation potential is worth noticing. By taking away from states control over resource allocation and regulation of the environment they overcome the two central problems confronting the more limited kind of control and supervisory institutions established under other treaties. Crucially, they substitute an obligation to comply with majority or consensus decisions for an obligation merely to co-operate in reaching such decisions through good faith negotiation. As Wijkman points out, the latter type of voluntary agreement under which international fisheries commissions have typically operated quickly breaks down and has proved economically inefficient in utilizing common property or arresting the 'tragedy of the commons'. He concludes that: 'When many governments share a resource, the management authority must be given power to determine harvesting limitations unilaterally and to enforce the observance of national quotas allocated within this general limit.'[166] If this cannot be achieved, it may be preferable to remove the resource from a common property regime entirely, as has now happened for fish stocks falling within the exclusive economic zone.[167] A similar inability to make international control of the high seas environment fully effective has also resulted in the transfer to coastal states of pollution jurisdiction in this zone.[168] However, as we shall see in Chapters 7 and 13, it is not clear that this policy has been successful.

Moreover, many global environmental problems cannot be handled in this way. The need for effective international management institutions cannot be avoided, for example, in implementing the Vienna Convention for Protection of the Ozone Layer, or for any new treaty aimed at halting global climate change. These problems demand 'an institution with the ability to impose onerous standards and to enforce them effectively',[169] a point explicitly

---

[165] See Ch. 9.

[166] Wijkman, 36 *Int. Org.* (1982), 511; Koers, *International Regulation of Marine Fisheries: A Study of Regional Fisheries Organizations* (London, 1973).

[167] 1982 UNCLOS, Articles 61–70; Carroz, 21 *SDLR* (1984); *infra*, Ch. 11; but cf. Johnston, 22 *ODIL* (1991), 199.

[168] Boyle, 79 *AJIL* (1985), 347; 1982 UNCLOS, Articles 56, 207–12; *infra*, Ch. 7.

[169] Plant, in Churchill and Freestone, (eds.), *International Law and Global Climate Change* (London, 1991), 165.

recognized by the Hague Declaration of 1989 when endorsing the creation of a new institutional authority for combating global warming.[170] Thus, despite the opposition it has encountered, international management may represent a model whose advantages are inescapable if collective interests are to be regulated and protected more effectively in future. It is in this sense that the older models of mandated and trusteeship territories referred to earlier represent useful precedents for such concerted action.

(6) Membership

The potential effectiveness of supervisory or management institutions is significantly affected by their composition. A crucial question is whether the membership is limited to those who benefit from the activity or resource in question, as in the consultative meetings of the Antarctic Treaty system, or whether membership is drawn from a wider category including those who may be adversely affected. Examples of the latter are the London Dumping Convention Consultative Meeting, and the International Whaling Commission. Both of these bodies now contain a preponderance of members opposed respectively to dumping and whaling and this has greatly facilitated gradual progress towards the decision to phase out dumping and impose a moratorium on whaling, despite inconclusive scientific evidence in both cases. These are institutions in which community pressure is arguably at its strongest because of their broadly drawn membership and because they have allowed significant NGO involvement at meetings of the parties: they have substantially answered the question who may speak for the global commons in their respective areas of competence,[171] and can be regarded as bodies which have successfully fulfilled a fiduciary role on behalf to the environment.

Other institutions are less favourably composed, especially at regional level. One of the reasons for the ineffectiveness of fisheries commissions is that their membership is usually drawn exclusively from those states participating in the exploitation of a particular area or stock. As Koers has observed, 'such restrictions on membership may also result in the organization becoming an instrument to further the interests of its members rather than as an instrument to regulate marine fisheries rationally.'[172] Much the same can be said of regional seas bodies including commissions on land-based sources of marine pollution. In the latter case a regional approach is dictated both by geopolitical considerations and the special ecological needs of enclosed or semi-enclosed seas,[173] but it has the effect of leaving environmental protection in the hands

[170] Sands, 30 *Harv. ILJ* (1989), 417.
[171] cf. Schneider, *World Public Order of the Environment* (London, 1979), 89, and see *infra*, Chs. 8 and 12.
[172] Koers, *International Regulation of Marine Fisheries*, 126.
[173] See Ch. 8.

of those whose economic and industrial activities would be most affected by high standards or strict enforcement of pollution controls. What is lacking in these cases is a constituency of outside states able to speak for the environmental interests of a wider community.

A second problem arises where membership and functions are too narrowly defined: the wrong states may address the issues from the wrong perspective. Chapter 6 indicates how this problem affects international watercourse commissions. These bodies are invariably composed of riparian states, yet they are expected to take account of the needs of the marine environment, and thus of coastal states who may be affected by river-borne pollution. A more appropriate solution would be to broaden membership to include coastal states, or at least ensure co-ordination of related treaties by combining the institutional machinery. The Oslo and Paris Commissions, considered in Chapter 8, apply the latter approach to the control of land-based pollution and dumping off North-West Europe. A similar need for co-ordination affects living resource management where the needs of interdependent or associated stocks must be accommodated, and where problems of pollution control may also be relevant. Here the preferable solution, at least in theory, is the ecosystem approach adopted by the Convention on Conservation of Antarctic Marine Living Resources, although it is not clear that this body has in fact operated as intended.[174] Some regional seas treaties also combine responsibility for pollution control and ecosystem protection, as envisaged by Article 194(5) of the 1982 UNCLOS.[175]

In spite of difficulties in their practical operation, there are advantages in a regional approach to some environmental issues.[176] Such arrangements do facilitate policies and rules appropriate to the needs of particular areas. Political consensus may be obtainable at a regional level which could not be achieved globally. Co-operation in enforcement, monitoring, and information exchange may be easier to arrange. These advantages are recognized in a number of treaties, including the 1982 UNCLOS, whose environmental provisions assume the need for appropriate regional and global action. But it is important not to overlook the weaknesses of many regional regimes, or the benefits to be derived from ensuring that such regimes are structured within a framework of minimum global standards, with some oversight and supervision at global level. Chapter 8 shows clearly both the benefits of co-ordinating regional action within a global framework such as the London Dumping

---

[174] Howard, 38 *ICLQ* (1989), 135, and see *infra*, Ch. 11.

[175] 1986 Noumea Convention for the Protection of the Natural Resources and Environment of the South Pacific; 1976 Barcelona Convention for the Protection of the Mediterranean Sea and 1982 Protocol Concerning Specially Protected Areas; 1985 Nairobi Convention for the Protection, Management and Development of the Marine Environment of the East African Region.

[176] Okidi, 4 *ODIL* (1977), 1; Alexander, 71 *AJIL* (1977), 84.

Convention, and the limitations of leaving the problem to regional solutions alone, as in the case of land-based sources of marine pollution.

(7) Dispute Settlement by Intergovernmental Institutions

Intergovernmental institutions exercising regulatory and supervisory functions can provide both formal and informal methods of dispute settlement. Little more need be said regarding the latter; examples given earlier and in subsequent chapters show how far these institutions have succeeded in acting as a forum for discussion and negotiation of agreed solutions to environmental problems. In this sense their importance lies in their ability to avoid resort to formal dispute settlement methods of mediation, conciliation, arbitration, or judicial settlement.[177] In exceptional cases, however, formal dispute settlement may fall within the competence of an international organization dealing with environmental matters. Once again the International Joint Commission is a leading example. Article 10 of the 1909 Boundary Waters Treaty permits it to act as an arbitrator, with the consent of both parties, but for reasons explained in Chapter 6 it has not found favour in this role. More use has been made of its power of conciliation under Article 9 of the treaty, because this places no obligation on the parties to comply with its recommendations. It was asked to conciliate in the early states of the *Trail Smelter* dispute, but without ultimate success. In the early 1980s the IJC also acted as mediator between British Columbia and the City of Seattle in the Skagit River dispute. But the 1987 Montreal Protocol to the Ozone Convention is now a more significant precedent. This is the first environmental treaty under which the parties have adopted a formal non-compliance procedure. An implementation committee reviews complaints concerning implementation of the Montreal Protocol by any party and reports to the meeting of the parties. This body is empowered to decide on measures necessary to ensure full compliance.[178] The existence of this mechanism makes it clear that complaints of non-compliance do fall within the competence of the meeting of parties, and that measures may be adopted to ensure compliance. But, as Gehring observes, even without such a formal procedure, non-compliance cases are likely to be handled in a similar way in other international environmental regimes. The parties will seek to shape consensus on the issue in conflict, and their decisions and interpretations will try to reinforce the stability of the specific legal regime as whole.[179]

Global or regional organizations may also provide good offices, mediation, or conciliation for states involved in environmental disputes. The World Bank mediated a solution to the Indus Rivers dispute, resulting in negotiation of the 1960 Indus Waters Treaty.[180] UNEP may offer its good offices or act as a

---

[177] Cooper, 24 *CYIL* (1986), 308.
[178] UNEP/OZL. Pro. 2/3, Annex III, and see *supra*, pp. 409–10.
[179] 1 *YIEL* (1990), 54.   [180] Cooper, 24 *CYIL* (1986), 285.

mediator or conciliator, since its responsibilities include the power to provide 'at the request of all the parties concerned advisory services for the promotion of co-operation in the field of the environment', and the Executive Director can also bring problems to the attention of the Governing Council for its consideration.[181] The common characteristic of each of these methods of third-party dispute settlement, however, is that the conclusions of the third party are not binding on the parties to the dispute. In this sense they represent merely another means of facilitating negotiation, while leaving the final decision in the hands of the parties.

(8) The Utility of International Supervision

If, as the evidence suggests, international institutions are a necessary component in the development and enforcement of rules and standards of environmental protection, it is then essential to concentrate attention on ensuring that they work effectively. Four features stand out as important in this respect.

First, community pressure will only be applied if the right community of interest is defined. As we have seen, institutions whose membership is too narrowly drawn are more likely to legitimize pollution or the over-exploitation of resources than to tackle them. Secondly, publicity is an essential ingredient if these institutions are to be made responsive to a wider public. That may entail a greater willingness to facilitate NGO participation, and to publish reports and findings. Thirdly, in ensuring compliance with treaty obligations, the institution should have a measure of independence from the states concerned. While for negotiating purposes it clearly cannot function like a human rights institution composed of independent members, environmental monitoring, scientific recommendations, and inspection regimes will not be successful if they are wholly under the control of member states. These functions must be carried out with objectivity and detachment and the institution must therefore be structured in such a way as to facilitate this goal. Lastly, the problem of dissentient minorities must in the end be addressed if environmental protection regimes are to establish common rules and implement collective policies followed by all member states. It is for this reason that the tentative steps taken in the 1987 Montreal Protocol to the Ozone Convention towards majority decision-making are of particular significance, since they do increase the likelihood of more stringent standards being adopted and enforced. This precedent, if already acceptable in this context, could usefully be followed elsewhere.

These prescriptions identify the need for incremental improvements in

---

[181] UNGA Res. 2997 XXVII (1972); Levin, *Protecting the Human Environment* (New York, 1977), 25 f.

existing structures, which themselves represent a pragmatic attempt to find workable answers to difficult problems affecting many states with diverse and competing interests. The record of this system does not justify the conclusion that international environmental law is unenforceable, but neither does it give grounds for satisfaction or complacency. The essential modesty of what has been achieved falls well short of international management of the global environment, and remains heavily dependent on progress by consensus. If this is politically inevitable it is nevertheless worth observing the conclusions of the World Commission on Environment and Development: 'There is a growing need for effective international co-operation to manage ecological and economic interdependence. Yet at the same time, confidence in international organizations is diminishing and support for them is dwindling.'[182] Improving and measuring the performance of international institutions was for this reason a major item on the agenda of the UNCED Conference in 1992. Included among the matters considered prior to the Conference were the facilitation and encouragement of wider participation, especially by developing countries, the provision of better financing arrangements, and improvements in the rule-making and amendment procedures of existing treaty institutions.[183] Moreover, as we shall see in later chapters, environmental disasters such as the sinking of the *Exxon Valdez*, the Gulf War, and the Chernobyl accident have shown the capacity of some existing global institutions such as IMO and IAEA both to provide assistance and to respond with necessary legislative initiatives, despite their relative weakness as supervisory bodies. What must be remembered in any general assessment is the diversity of the institutions under review and of their functions.

4. OTHER METHODS OF DISPUTE SETTLEMENT[184]

(1) International Adjudication

Resort to the International Court of Justice or to binding arbitration has been of limited significance in the development of international environmental law, although the seminal contribution of the small number of arbitral awards and ICJ judgments has been observed in Chapter 3. Adjudication may be relevant, however, as a means of supervising treaty compliance, and in determining applicable rules and principles of general international law.

---

[182] WCED, *Our Common Future* (Oxford, 1987), 9.
[183] See e.g. Sand, *Lessons Learned in Global Environmental Governance* (New York, 1990), 6–20; UNCED, *Research Paper No. 27: Marine Environment and Marine Pollution* (Geneva, 1991).
[184] See generally Merrills, *International Dispute Settlement* (2nd edn. Cambridge, 1991); Cooper, 24 *CYIL* (1986); Levin, *Protecting the Human Environment*.

(a) Adjudication and Treaty Compliance

Adjudication as a means of ensuring treaty compliance is rarely used in instruments concerned with environmental matters. Three European treaties dealing with wildlife conservation, pollution of the Rhine, and land-based sources of marine pollution allow any party to refer disputes concerning their 'interpretation or application' to arbitration,[185] while the 1972 London Dumping Convention provides for such disputes to be referred unilaterally to arbitration or by agreement to the ICJ.[186] The 1958 Geneva Convention on Fisheries and Conservation of Living Resources requires certain conservation disputes to be submitted to a special commission, whose decisions are binding, but subject to review after two years.[187] The treaty is not widely ratified, and the special commission procedure has never been invoked. A few more treaties allow optional acceptance of the compulsory jurisdiction of the ICJ or arbitration in the event of dispute, or include these among the methods parties may agree to use.[188] Many environmental treaties have no dispute settlement clause at all; others require only the use of negotiation, or in a few cases, conciliation.

This pattern is consistent with the view that international adjudication, based on rules of international law, has too many disadvantages in an environmental context to be widely attractive to states as a primary means of dispute settlement. The inclusion of a formal compliance procedure in the 1987 Montreal Protocol to the Ozone Convention[189] emphasizes the importance of collective supervision by the parties in this context, while the protocol's relatively weak dispute settlement clause indicates its secondary role and the continuing opposition of many states to compulsory adjudication.[190]

But it does not follow that resort to judicial machinery is necessarily inconsistent with primary reliance on political and institutional methods of treaty supervision. This can be observed in the *ICAO Council* case,[191] where Article 84 of the Convention on International Civil Aviation gave the ICJ jurisdiction over disputes concerning the 'interpretation or application' of the convention. In rejecting the argument that it was deprived of jurisdiction in a dispute concerning the competence of the ICAO Council, the court observed:

---

[185] 1979 Berne Convention on the Conservation of European Wildlife and Natural Habitats, Article 18; 1976 Convention on the Protection of the Rhine Against Chemicals, Article 15; 1974 Paris Convention for Prevention of Marine Pollution from Land-based Sources, Article 21.

[186] Article 11, as revised 1978.

[187] Articles 9–12. See Ch. 13.

[188] e.g. 1989 Basel Convention on Transboundary Movement of Hazardous Wastes, Article 20; 1980 Convention for the Conservation of Antarctic Marine Living Resources, Article 20; 1979 Geneva Convention on Long-Range Transboundary Air Pollution, Article 13; 1973 CITES Convention, Article 18; 1991 ECE Convention on Environmental Impact Assessment in a Transboundary Context, Article 15.

[189] *Supra*, n. 178.   [190] See *infra*, pp. 409–10.   [191] *ICJ Rep.* (1972), 46.

the appeal to the court contemplated by the Chicago Convention and the Transit Agreement must be regarded as an element of the general regime established in respect of ICAO. In thus providing for judicial recourse by way of appeal to the court against decisions of the Council concerning interpretation and application ... the Chicago treaties gave member states, and through them the Council, the possibility of ensuring a certain measure of supervision by the Court over those decisions. To this extent, these treaties enlist the support of the Court for the good functioning of the organization and therefore the first reassurance for the Council lies in the knowledge that means exist for determining whether a decision as to its own competence is in conformity or not with the provisions of the treaties governing its action.[192]

This judicial review function in respect of matters of treaty interpretation and application is particularly important where international institutions are endowed with significant powers or where such powers are conferred on states. This is why the 1982 UNCLOS makes extensive provision for compulsory judicial settlement of disputes by the proposed Law of the Sea Tribunal, by arbitration, or by the Sea-bed Disputes Chamber. If a stronger model of multilateral decision-making is to be developed in the environmental field, as the Montreal Protocol to the Ozone Convention suggests, then the argument for judicial review becomes stronger and more important, and the 1982 UNCLOS can be seen as a possible precedent in this respect.

(b) Dispute Settlement under the 1982 UNCLOS[193]

Article 286 of the 1982 UNCLOS is a general provision for unilateral reference of disputes concerning interpretation or application of the Convention to the Law of the Sea Tribunal, the ICJ, or an arbitral tribunal constituted under the provisions of the Convention. The court or tribunal chosen will also have jurisdiction to interpret or apply international agreements 'related to the purposes of the Convention' if they so provide. Article 286 is broad is scope. It includes allegations that 'a coastal state has acted in contravention of specified international rules and standards for the protection and preservation of the marine environment which are applicable to the coastal state ...'[194] or, in more general terms, that a flag state has failed to perform its obligations. But, although fisheries disputes are also in general subject to compulsory jurisdiction, there are far-reaching exceptions in this case, which exclude disputes relating to the exercise of sovereign rights over living resources in the EEZ, including the determination of a total allowable catch, harvesting capacity, and the allocation of surpluses.[195] Allegations of a

---

[192] Ibid. para. 26.
[193] 1982 UNCLOS, Articles 279–99 and annex VI; Churchill and Lowe, *The Law of the Sea* (2nd edn., Manchester, 1988), 335 ff., Birnie, in Butler (ed.), *The Law of the Sea and International Shipping* (New York, 1985), 39; Oxman, in Soons (ed.), *Implementation of the Law of the Sea Convention through International Institutions* (Honolulu, 1989), 648.
[194] Article 297(1).
[195] Ibid. (3)(a).

failure by coastal states to ensure proper conservation and management of stocks must, however, be submitted to conciliation,[196] though its outcome is without mandatory effect. Disputes concerning activities in the deep sea-bed area, including the acts of the ISBA or violation of the convention's sea-bed articles or of other regulations by states parties fall within the separate jurisdiction of the sea-bed disputes chamber.[197]

These provisions cannot take effect until the convention comes into force, and they raise certain problems of overlapping authority and fragmentation in the judicial elaboration of the law of the Sea. But they are indicative of the importance of judicial supervision in controlling the exercise of jurisdiction and authority conferred by the Convention on states, particularly coastal states, and on international institutions. It is one of the very few treaties under which environmental disputes will be within the compulsory jurisdiction of international tribunals.

The 1982 UNCLOS is concerned with much wider range of issues, however; it was intended to be a 'package deal' whose provisions would represent a global consensus, from which only limited derogation would be permitted. Compulsory third-party dispute settlement is thus an integral element in a Convention whose integrity and consistent application were among the primary interests of many states involved in its negotiation. Judicial supervision can be seen in this context as an essential means of stabilizing a complex balance of rights and duties, while accommodating inevitable pressure for continued development of the law to fit new circumstances.[198] Few of these considerations apply with the same force to other environmental treaties, which in most cases are less concerned with the allocation and control of power than with facilitating co-operative solutions to common problems. In this context institutional supervision remains in general the more appropriate means of control and development.

(c) The European Court of Justice

The European Community has competence both to adopt environmental regulations and directives, and to conclude treaties on conservation matters and environmental protection.[199] It is party to a number of European pollution treaties, including the 1974 Paris Convention for the Prevention of Pollution from Land-based Sources, the 1979 Geneva Convention on Long-Range Transboundary Air Pollution, and the 1976 Rhine Chemicals and Chlorides Conventions. It has also ratified or signed a number of important global

---

[196] 1982 UNCLOS, Article 297(1)(b).   [197] Articles 186–91.
[198] Oxman, in Soons, *Implementation of the Law of the Sea Convention*, 650.
[199] Article 130R, Single European Act, 1986; Simmonds, 218 *Recueil des cours* (1989), 13; Birnie, in Brown and Churchill (eds.), *The UN Convention on the Law of the Sea: Impact and Implementation* (Honolulu, 1988), 527; Freestone, *JLS Special Issue: Law, Policy and the Environment* (1990), 135, and see further *supra*, Ch. 2.

instruments, including the 1973 CITES Convention, the 1985 Vienna Convention for the Protection of the Ozone Layer and subsequent protocols, and the 1989 Basel Convention for the Control of Transboundary Movement of Hazardous Wastes. The Community also concludes fisheries agreements on behalf of all member states. Most of these are 'mixed agreements' to which both the Community and member states are parties, in so far as they deal with matters not exclusively within the competence of member states alone or of the community alone.

The European Court of Justice is a regional international tribunal with powers of judicial supervision over the enforcement and implementation of such treaties by member states and the Community. Under Articles 169 and 170 of the EC Treaty cases may be brought to the court by the European Commission, or by other member states alleging non-compliance by a member state with its obligations under the EC treaties. This extends to treaties such as those referred to earlier which are concluded by the Community with non-members under the procedure laid down in Article 228(1) and which are therefore also binding on member states. In the case of 'mixed agreements', however, enforcement powers can only be invoked in respect of those provisions which relate to obligations within the Community's sphere of competence. There is also a procedure under Article 175 of the EC Treaty whereby a failure of the Community to act may be reviewed by the Court.[200]

It must be observed that neither Articles 169 nor 170 permit enforcement actions against member states by private individuals or organizations. Nor, it seems, can such persons rely on the Community's failure to act against a member state as the basis for proceedings before the Court under Article 175. At most, individuals or environmental organizations may petition the Commission to take action, but community law makes no wider provision for public interest litigation before the court as such.[201] Nevertheless, the procedures available have allowed the Commission to bring successful actions in a number of environmental cases involving non-compliance with treaties to which the Community is a party.[202] Although member states cannot be compelled to implement the Court's judgments, and have not done so in all cases, both the tradition of adherence to the rule of law in most member states

---

[200] On the enforcement of Community Law, see generally Hartley, *Foundations of European Community Law* (2nd edn., Oxford, 1988), 282 ff.; Collins, *European Community Law in the United Kingdom* (4th edn., London, 1990), 216–26; Brown, *The Court of Justice of the European Communities* (3rd edn., London, 1989); Rehbinder and Stewart, *Environmental Protection Policy* (New York, 1988), ch. 6.

[201] See generally Collins, *European Community Law in the United Kingdom*, 227–8; Schermers and Waelbrook, *Judicial Protection in the European Communities* (4th edn., Deventer, 1987), 286. But see now Cases 6/90 and 9/90, *Francovich and Bonifaci* v. *Italy*, judgment of the ECJ of 19 Nov. 1991 in which the Court held that a Member state is obliged to compensate individuals for *damage suffered* as a result of non-implementation of an EC directive. This may afford individuals a somewhat broader right of action to enforce community law.

[202] *Infra*, Ch. 5 n. 30.

and the political pressure which other members can exert in cases of non-compliance serve to ensure that in most cases the Court's findings are observed.

The EEC system represents the most highly developed form of regional supervision applicable to environmental matters. While it constitutes an important model because of the prominence given to judicial supervision, it should not be assumed that this has universal significance given the rather special relationship on which the Community's extensive system of political and legal integration rests.

(d) Adjudication and Customary Law

States are of course free to resort to adjudication as a means of settling questions of customary international law, or general principles of law, in environmental disputes. We saw in the introduction to this chapter why they have been reluctant to do so. Two points may be developed. The first problem is that the jurisdiction of the ICJ is based on consent: it has no general jurisdiction to hear applications submitted unilaterally save to the extent provided by Article 36(2) of the Statute of the Court, or in other treaties. Secondly, the Court decides cases in accordance with international law.[203] There are limitations on its ability to reform or develop established rules of law, even where states are agreed that change is necessary. Thus in the 1974 *Icelandic Fisheries* case,[204] the Court was able to depart only to some extent from established customary rules, but failed to reach a solution acceptable either to the parties or to the international community as a whole. In these circumstances, negotiation is likely to be a more successful method of law-making. Where the law is less clear, states face substantial uncertainty in submitting the outcome to the Court's jurisdiction, and the Court itself may be unwilling to adjudicate if, as in the *Nuclear Tests*[205] cases, there is no consensus on the rules applicable to the dispute. In a subject where legal rules are still developing, and underlying consensus not yet fully established, the role of adjudication is likely to be limited.

These factors help explain the reluctance of states to resort to judicial machinery, even in situations such as the Chernobyl disaster, or acid rain in Europe and North America. The possibility that a judicial award might establish precedents with unwelcome implications for the plaintiff state is also a significant factor in many environmental disputes, and favours negotiated solutions and resort to multilateral treaties as the most predictable means of balancing the conflicting interests of those concerned. This may change as

---

[203] Article 38, Statute of the ICJ. Note Article 38(2), however.

[204] *ICJ Rep.* (1974), 3. Note also Canada's revision of its acceptance of the compulsory jurisdiction of the ICJ in 1970 to exclude disputes concerning the Arctic Waters Pollution Act. It was most unlikely that the Court could have found in Canada's favour had this legislation been challenged in the ICJ. On this, see further, pp. 278–9.

[205] *ICJ Rep.* (1974), 253; *infra*, Ch. 9.

consensus on some basic rules of environmental protection begins to emerge, however. Moreover, the sporadic acceptance of the ICJ's compulsory jurisdiction does mean that from time to time important issues of environmental significance will continue to come before it, as in the *Nauru* case.[206]

(2) Diplomatic Methods of Settlement

(a) Mediation and Good Offices[207]

These methods of dispute settlement involve the assistance of a third party in facilitating negotiations. The process is voluntary and works only if the parties want to reach agreement. The use of international institutions for these purposes was considered earlier, and a number of environmental treaties allow for the possibility of mediation or good offices.[208] The main virtue of both types of settlement process is that the parties are able to avoid taking adversarial roles, while the third party is not involved in a formal adjudication.

(b) Conciliation and Inquiry[209]

Conciliation and inquiry involve more than facilitating negotiations. In the former a third party may be empowered to indicate possible solutions, which may include findings on matters of law and of fact. Commissions of inquiry will normally deal only with fact-finding. The parties are not obliged to accept the findings or proposed solutions, however.

Conciliation is provided for in the case of fisheries disputes under the 1982 UNCLOS;[210] it is also one of the roles of the US–Canadian International Joint Commission.[211] The compliance procedure adopted under the Montreal Protocol to the Ozone Convention may also correspond to conciliation.[212]

Provision for inquiry is unusual in environmental treaties, despite the issues of fact which frequently arise. But there are many instances of states resorting to scientific inquiry to establish the causes or consequences of environmental pollution.[213] The 1991 ECE Convention on Environmental Impact Assess-

---

[206] See 1 *YIEL* (1990), 271.

[207] Cooper, 24 *CYIL* (1986), 284; Barnes, in Dupuy (ed.), *The Future of International Law of the Environment* (Dordrecht, 1985), 167.

[208] e.g. 1974 Helsinki Convention on the Protection of the Marine Environment of the Baltic Sea Area, and see the 1979 Berne Convention on the Conservation of European Wildlife and Natural Habitats, Article 18(1).

[209] Cooper, 24 *CYIL* (1986), 287, and see Bar-Yaacov, *The Handling of International Disputes By Means of Inquiry* (London, 1974). See 'UN draft Rules for the Conciliation of Disputes between States', 30 *ILM* (1991), 231.

[210] Article 297.

[211] See *supra*, pp. 177–8.

[212] Ibid. See also 1969 International Convention on Intervention on the High Seas in Cases of Oil Pollution Casualties, Article 8.

[213] See e.g. the use of the IJC under Article 9 of the US–Canada Boundary Waters Treaty and *ad hoc* scientific bodies appointed to report on acid rain in North America, in Schmandt, Clarkson, and Roderick, *Acid Rain and Friendly Neighbours* (2nd edn., Durham, NC, 1988).

ment also provides for an inquiry procedure to determine whether a proposed activity is likely to have a significant adverse transboundary impact.[214] A number of European states have proposed the establishment of a similar procedure to be operated by UNEP.[215]

5. CONCLUSIONS

In considering how the international legal system handles the resolution of disputes concerning environmental matters, the diversity of issues needs to be emphasized. Where the problem is one of compliance with agreed standards of global or regional environmental protection, techniques of international supervision and control afford the best forum for a community response appropriate to the protection of common interests. Such techniques will be stronger and more effective if they facilitate openness, informed scrutiny, and resort where necessary to judicial organs by way of review. These techniques should not be seen as an inferior substitute for judicial control, but as a potentially more effective means of exercising a limited form of international trusteeship over the environment. Moreover, effective multilateral supervision also makes unilateral responses less likely and ensures greater consistency and continuity in the development of state practice.

Resort to international judicial machinery remains an alternative means of resolving environmental claims, but its utility should not be exaggerated. International proceedings will rarely be the best way of settling claims for environmental injury affecting other states; in this context greater reliance has rightly been placed on facilitating resort to national legal systems, considered in the next chapter. International adjudication can also provide a form of third-party determination of rights over resources, or over common spaces, but here too, political supervisory institutions will usually prove more attractive to states because of their various advantages, including flexibility, accessibility, and capacity for resolving matters multilaterally without necessarily following existing rules of international law.

The ILC's present work on 'International Liability' remains a missed opportunity to place the subject of state responsibility for environmental damage on a more satisfactory basis. It provides little useful clarification on some of the central issues, including the standard of liability, the availability of remedies, and questions of standing. It is thus doubtful whether the concept of state responsibility will assume greater significance than at present in the resolution of environmental issues, although at bilateral level it may continue to afford a basis for settling some disputes.

[214] Article 3. See also 1974 Nordic Convention for Protection of the Environment, Articles 11–12.
[215] UNCED, Prepcom, UN Doc. A/CONF. 151/PC/L. 29 (1991).

In the next chapter we shall consider alternative approaches to the implementation and enforcement of international environmental law which have begun to change significantly the emphasis of the whole subject. Less reliance is now placed exclusively on the resolution of interstate disputes, or on mechanisms of international supervision. The development of human rights claims to a decent environment, and the economic logic of the 'polluter pays' principle have made resort to individual claims in national law an increasingly attractive means of dealing with domestic or transboundary environmental issues. But the diversity of these issues needs emphasis in this context also. National remedies are not normally alternatives to the system considered in this chapter, but are more often complementary to it, and only in certain respects more useful. The variety of approaches now available for the resolution of environmental disputes does indicate an increasing measure of sophistication in the international legal system, but it cannot yet be concluded that this system functions fully effectively or without significant difficulty.

5

The Structure of International Environmental Law III: The Role of National Law and the Right to a Decent Environment

1. INTRODUCTION

(1) Environmental Rights

The orthodox view that international law is concerned with the rights and obligations of states, whether *inter se*, or within the context of an international community, is open to two objections when applied to the protection of the environment. First, it fails to represent fully the reality of the international legal system as it applies to matters of environmental protection. This can be seen in the role played by NGOs in the operation of international institutions, and it will be further observed with regard to individuals in this chapter. Secondly, there are arguments of principle in favour of a more broadly based system which may accord rights, or in some cases obligations, to individuals, peoples, generations and animals or possibly to the natural environment itself. Claims of this kind are usually intended to effect a reorientation of the relationship between man and the environment, through broader participation in the process of law enforcement, dispute resolution, and environmental guardianship.[1]

The claim that individuals, peoples, generations, animals, or the environment enjoy or should enjoy environmental rights raises the question what is meant in this context by the notion of a 'right'. Such claims do not necessarily entail conferring rights enforceable through legal proceedings. Rather, advocates of environmental rights use this terminology to ascribe value or status to the interests and claims of particular entities.[2] By doing so, they seek to force lawmakers and institutions to take account of those interests, to accord

---

[1] Giagnocavo and Goldstein, 35 *McGill LJ* (1990), 345; Stone, 45 *SCal. LR* (1972), 450; Tribe, 83 *Yale LJ* (1974), 1315; Brown-Weiss, *In Fairness to Future Generations* (Dobbs Ferry, NY, 1989); Crawford (ed.), *The Rights of Peoples* (Oxford, 1988); D'Amato and Chopra, 85 *AJIL* (1991), 21.

[2] Giagnocavo and Goldstein, 35 *McGill LJ* (1990), 356–7.

them some priority which they might not otherwise enjoy and to make them part of the context for interpreting legal rules. The entrenchment of such values as rights within the legal system may extend to the appointment of representatives to speak or act on their behalf, but, as an articulation of values, such rights do not cease to be significant merely because no formal means can be found for their expression.

Critics point out that it is simply unnecessary to construct 'rights' of this kind to deal with problems of value and conflicting social activities.[3] The attempt to do so may lead to the false assumption that social changes are thereby effected. To argue that value should be ascribed to peoples, animals, or the environment, does not tell us what that value should be or how it should be weighed against other values or 'rights'. It may assume, moreover, that such common interests are incapable of protection unless represented independently of other interests, and that legal procedures are the best means for doing so. The argument for environmental rights in this form shares the problems of expressing and implementing claims to economic and social rights in legal form, with the added complication that the claimants may not yet exist, may be non-human, or inanimate.

Thus the main danger of the rights argument is its over-extension. It is not clear that it leads necessarily to any greater protection for the environment than is already available in international law, or that could be made available simply through better regulation. But Stone's argument that giving rights is not the same as introducing more protective rules should be noted. He points out that 'rights' introduce a flexibility and open-endedness that no rule can capture.[4] Where this argument is likely to have most impact is in those cases where the protection of a state's own domestic environment is affected, since in general states have greater freedom under existing law to manage their internal problems as they please. In this context the assertion of a right to a decent environment does become significant.

(2) Individual Rights and Obligations in National Law

The argument for individual rights and by extension those of companies and possibly NGOs, stands apart as perhaps the strongest of these claims. Here, the more pragmatic point is that by addressing the position of individuals and other legally significant entities directly, international law facilitates a more effective approach to the enforcement and implementation of environmental law, primarily through the use of national legal systems. The importance of national law can be observed at three levels, and involves not only the attribution of rights, but also of obligations.

---

[3] Ibid. 361; Emond, 22 *OsHLJ* (1985), 325; Elder, ibid. 285.
[4] Stone, 45 *SCal. LR* (1972), 488.

First, national law is the medium through which states will usually implement their international obligations and regulate the conduct of their own nationals and companies both inside their borders and beyond. In this sense it enables the notion of individual responsibility to become part of the system of enforcement. Moreover, for the purpose of making international regimes more effective, international law may afford states an extended or extraterritorial protective jurisdiction to act against non-nationals, as in the exclusive economic zone, or to treat certain offences as crimes against international law over which all states have jurisdiction.

Secondly, national law may be used as a means of reallocating transboundary environmental costs. In this sense it represents an alternative to reliance on interstate claims, over which its main advantage is that it gives individuals control over the proceedings and places liability directly on the polluter concerned. The role of international law in this context is to ensure that obstacles to transboundary litigation are removed and in certain cases to ensure also that liability standards are harmonized and an effective remedy guaranteed.

Finally, national law may give individuals a means of securing protection from transboundary harm without resort to the intervention of their own government, and may in some cases also allow them to compel governments to abide by their international obligations. This possibility depends on the character of the legal system in question, but it can be facilitated by international recognition of a right to a decent environment or of a right of equal access to transboundary remedies. In this broader sense, individuals and NGOs can be empowered to act as part of the enforcement structure of international environmental law. In general, making national remedies available is consistent with the view that there are significant advantages in avoiding resort to interstate remedies for the resolution of transboundary environmental disputes wherever possible.[5]

2. HUMAN RIGHTS AND INDIVIDUAL REMEDIES

(1) The Right to a Decent Environment

The most far-reaching application of the argument for extending environmental rights is found in the view that international law recognizes a human right to a decent, viable, or healthy environment.[6] At its strongest, the existence

---

[5] Levin, *Protecting the Human Environment* (New York, 1977), 31–8; Sand, in OECD, *Legal Aspects of Transfrontier Pollution* (Paris, 1977), 146; Bilder, 144 *Recueil des cours* (1975), 224; Handl, 1 *YIEL* (1990), 18 ff.

[6] Steiger, *et al.* in Bothe (ed.), *Trends in Environmental Policy and Law* (Geneva, 1980), 1; P. M. Dupuy, in R. J. Dupuy (ed.), *The Right to Health as a Human Right* (Alphen aan den Rijn, 1979), 340; Shelton, 28 *Stanford JIL* (1991), 103; ECOSOC, Commission on Human Rights, *Proposals*

of such a right would legitimize international supervision of the whole range of a state's domestic environmental policies, and not merely of their extra-territorial effects; it might entail allowing individual claimants access to human rights institutions, such as the UN Human Rights Committee or the European Court of Human Rights, and it would also have implications for the rights and remedies to be afforded before national courts. The freedom of states to claim that matters within their borders fell within the reserved domain of domestic jurisdiction would be severely curtailed.

Most writers are, however, sceptical of the view that a right to a decent environment presently forms part of international law in this extended form. Dupuy argues that it is not inherent in the human condition, unlike the right to life, that its character is derived from other economic and social rights, like the right to health, and that it lacks any mechanism for enforcement.[7] Although the World Commission on Environment and Development favoured a fundamental right for all human beings to an environment adequate for health and well-being, it pointed to the absence of treaty provisions and concluded that this right was not yet well established.[8] Others have observed that such an anthropocentric approach may ignore the interests of other species or of the world's ecological balance, and thereby encourage over-exploitation of natural resources to the overall detriment of the environment. Moreover, both the content of the proposed right, and whether it should benefit individuals, or only 'peoples', remain uncertain.[9]

(a) International Recognition of a Right to a Decent Environment

Principle 1 of the 1972 Stockholm Declaration declared that 'man has the fundamental right to freedom, equality and adequate conditions of life in an environment of a quality that permits a life of dignity and well being.' Sohn argues that this formulation can support an individual rights interpretation,[10] but it is significant that no treaty refers explicitly to the right to a decent environment in these terms. When the concept is employed in a similarly autonomous form, as in Article 24 of the African Charter on Human and Peoples' Rights,[11] it appears as a collective right only: 'All peoples shall have

---

for a Study of the Problem of the Environment and its Relation to Human Rights, UN Doc. E/CN.4/Sub.2/1990/12; id., *Human Rights and the Environment, Preliminary Report*, UN Doc. E/CN.4/Sub.2/1991/8; Natural Heritage Institute, *Preliminary Report on Legal and Institutional Aspects of the Relationship between Human Rights and the Environment* (Geneva, 1991).

[7] *Supra*, n. 6. See also Jacobs, 3 *HRR* (1978), 170–3; Alston, 78 *AJIL* (1984), 607, but cf. Sohn, 33 *AULR* (1982), 1.

[8] Munro and Lammers, *Environmental Protection and Sustainable Development* (London, 1986), 39.

[9] Shelton, 28 *Stanford JIL* (1991).

[10] Sohn, 14 *Harv. ILJ* (1973), 455. cf. the 1989 Hague Declaration on the Environment which appears to endorse a collective right to 'viable' environment.

[11] Van Boven, 7 *HRLJ* (1986), 183; Bello, 194 *Recueil des cours* (1985), 9. See also 1989 ILO Convention 169 Concerning Indigenous and Tribal Peoples in Independent Countries.

the right to a general satisfactory environment favourable to their development.' On this view it is independent of other rights, addresses the fundamental question of environmental quality, and is comparable to rights such as self-determination or economic and social rights, whose implementation by states is subject to political supervision by various UN organs, and not by judicial bodies such as the European Court of Human Rights. But the existence of such collective rights has itself been controversial. Although a recent Unesco study argues that collective rights do exist and form an essential basis for the full enjoyment of individual rights, many writers remain opposed to their extension.[12]

The more common view, however, is that no independent right to a decent environment has yet become part of international law, but that environmental rights can be derived from other existing treaty rights, such as life, health, or property. In an individual petition under Article 6(1) of the 1966 UN Covenant on Civil and Political Rights it was argued that the dumping of nuclear wastes in a Canadian town violated the right to life of its inhabitants and future generations.[13] The application was dismissed due to failure to exhaust local remedies. Article 8 of the European Convention on Human Rights, which guarantees respect for private and family life and home, and Article 1 of Protocol 1, which protects possessions and property, have also been relied on unsuccessfully in a case which reached the European Court of Human Rights involving airport noise.[14] Neither case excludes the possibility that a sufficiently serious environmental interference with an individual's quality of life would constitute a violation by the state of an individual's rights under the respective treaties. But, although in *Powell and Rayner* the European Court of Human Rights observed that 'regard must be had to the fair balance that has to be struck between the competing interests of the individual and of the community as a whole', it was clearly reluctant to interfere with the discretion of individual governments in determining where this balance should lie. It is difficult to infer from this judgment the conclusion that either the right to life or to private life offers a useful basis for environmental rights except in cases where public bodies afford individuals little or no protection

---

[12] Unesco, Final Report and Recommendations of an International Meeting of Experts, 1989, 11 *HRLJ* (1990), 441; Van Boven, 7 *HRLJ* (1986); but cf. Brownlie, in Crawford, *The Rights of Peoples*, 1, and other works cited *supra*, n. 7. See generally, Capotorti, in Macdonald and Johnston (eds.), *The Structure and Process of International Law* (Dordrecht, 1983), 977.

[13] UN HRC, Decision No. 67/1980 v. Canada (1990).

[14] *Powell and Rayner* v. *UK*, ECHR, Ser. A, No. 172 (1990). See also *Arrondelle* v. *UK* 5 EHRR (1983) 118 (European Commission on Human Rights). Weber, 12 *HRLJ* (1991), 180 ff., argues that Article 2 of the *ECHR*, which guarantees a right to life, is a better basis for environmental protection than Article 8, and observes that the narrow economic interpretation of Article 1, Protocol 1, in these cases 'has the consequence that environmental effects are only caught by Article 1 of Protocol 1 to the extent that a loss in value of a property exposed to such environmental effects occurs'.

against the most seriously harmful pollution or environmental nuisance.[15]

The right to a healthy environment is more clearly recognized in a number of treaties, however. Article 12 of the 1966 UN Covenant on Economic and Social Rights refers to the right to improvement of environmental and industrial hygiene, while a broader link between health and the environment has found favour with WCED, ECE, WHO, OAS, and the UN General Assembly.[16] Instruments adopted or proposed by these bodies in most cases endorse what appears to be a collective right, to be guaranteed by government action, but with no provision for individual enforcement. A similar approach is found in the majority of those national constitutions which now refer to protection of the environment.[17]

Reference to human rights intruments thus affords no clear conclusions concerning the individual or collective character of the proposed right to a decent environment, or the extent to which it can be derived from other rights. The tentative recognition accorded to the concept in human rights instruments and national constitutions may suggest that it is beneficial, but this conclusion depends on how the problem of anthropocentricity referred to earlier is resolved, and how the content of the right is defined.

(b) Human Rights and Anthropocentricity

WCED's argument is that the right to a healthy environment applies only *vis-à-vis* other humans or states, and thus does not imply an anthropocentric approach. This explanation misses the point that such a right may reinforce the assumption that the environment and its natural resources exist only for human benefit, and have no intrinsic worth in themselves. But, as we shall see in later chapters, it is clear that international law does not disregard the intrinsic value of the environment, including natural ecosystems and species. This much is demonstrated by treaties concerned with Antarctica,[18] the World Heritage Convention, the Berne Convention on the Conservation

---

[15] For successful use of the right to life before Indian courts, see *infra*, n. 24, and see also Weber, 12 *HRLJ* (1991), 181. Some writers attribute a narrower meaning to the right to life, implying some form of intentional homicide: see e.g. Dinstein, in Henkin (ed.), *The International Bill of Rights* (New York, 1981), 115–16.

[16] 1988 Additional Protocol to the Inter-American Convention on Human Rights, Article 11; 1989 European Charter on Environment and Health; 1990 Draft ECE Charter on Environmental Rights and Obligations; WCED, Legal Principles, Article 1; 1989 Convention on the Rights of the Child, Article 24(2)(c). UNGA Resolution 45/94 (1990) 'Recognises that all individuals are entitled to live in an environment adequate for their health and well-being' and calls on governments to enhance efforts in this respect.

[17] China, Article 9; Cuba, Article 27; Czechoslovakia, Article 15; Yemen, Article 16; Ecuador, Article 19; Greece, Article 24; Guyana, Article 36; Honduras, Article 145; India, Article 48A; Iran, Article 50; Korea, Article 35(1); The Netherlands, Article 21; Peru, Article 123; Portugal, Article 66; Spain, Article 45; Thailand, Article 65; Turkey, Article 56; USSR, Article 42; Yugoslavia, Article 87. See generally Steiger, *et al.*, in Bothe, *Trends in Environmental Policy*.

[18] 1959 Antarctic Treaty; 1980 Convention for the Conservation of Antarctic Living Resources; 1991 Protocol to the Antarctic Treaty on Environmental Protection.

of European Wildlife and Natural Habitats, the CITES Convention,[19] and several marine pollution agreements,[20] as well as the World Charter for Nature. In these cases, the interests of the environment or of animals are at present protected primarily by the collective processes of institutional supervision referred to in previous chapters. The addition of a human rights argument can be seen as complementary to this wider protection of the biosphere, reflecting the impossibility of separating the interests of mankind from those of the environment as a whole, or from the claims of future generations, quite apart from the intrinsic merit of a healthy environment as the foundation of human survival.[21] But such an approach will only work to the extent that it de-emphasizes the uniqueness of man's right to the environment and conforms more closely to the characterization of this relationship as a fiduciary one not devoted solely to the attainment of immediate human needs.

The implications of the argument from anthropocentricity are thus essentially structural. They require the integration of human claims to a decent environment within a broader decision-making process, capable also of taking account of the competing interests of future generations, other states and the common interest in common spaces and wildlife preservation. This argument seems to favour the formulation of a collective rather than an individual right to a decent environment, since this most readily facilitates the balancing of such polycentric interests through international co-operation and supervisory institutions. But it also points to the inappropriateness of human rights institutions, with their more limited perspective, for the task of supervision and balancing which this argument would require. Some alternative institutional machinery would be needed, able to take a more holistic view, however difficult this may be to achieve in practice.

(c) Procedural Rights for Protection of the Environment

Perhaps the most plausible interpretation is that the content of the right to a decent environment does not require any particular kind or quality of environment as such, but has instead the character of a procedural right.[22] On this analysis, it is not a collective right but instead becomes instrumental in securing for individuals rights of access to information, to participation in decision-making processes and to administrative and judicial remedies. Its implications are concerned primarily with the rights afforded within national legal systems to challenge actions or decisions detrimental to environmental interests. This procedural interpretation avoids anthropocentricity to the

---

[19] Wildlife treaties are considered in Ch. 12.
[20] 1972 London Dumping Convention; 1984 Protocol to the 1969 Convention on Liability for Oil Pollution Damage; 1989 International Salvage Convention; *infra*, Chs. 7 and 8.
[21] Shelton, 28 *Stanford JIL* (1991).
[22] Ibid. See also UN Doc. E/CN.4/Sub.2/1991/8, *supra*, n. 6.

extent that such rights can be exercised on behalf of the environment or of its non-human components. It also avoids the uncertainty inherent in any attempt to define the right in terms of quality standards.

Principle 23 of the World Charter for Nature, and the draft ECE Charter on Environmental Rights and Obligations reflect this procedural approach to the issue of definition. The ECE Charter is particularly significant, because it is the first international instrument to provide for individual access to a comprehensive range of administrative and judicial proceedings and remedies for the prevention and reinstatement of environmental damage, and participation in decision-making processes.[23] It invites member states to reflect these rights in their national legislation. Some constitutions and national legal systems already do so. Prompted by the Bhopal chemical plant disaster, the Indian Supreme Court has made particular use of new environmental provisions of the Indian Constitution in facilitating public interest litigation against state governments. Its decisions have included the explicit adoption of a right to life approach in cases concerning pollution and environmental harm, and the imposition of a rule of absolute liability for hazardous industrial activities which goes beyond the old common law rule derived from the English case of *Rylands* v. *Fletcher*.[24]

Public interest litigation in other jurisdictions can also be seen as part of the same trend towards enhancing the participation of individuals and NGOs in environmental decision-making. Decisions of courts in the United States, the Netherlands, New Zealand, and Australia have granted *locus standi* in administrative review proceedings to environmental groups and NGOs on a relatively liberal basis, although such groups must usually demonstrate some interest in the issue beyond a mere concern for the environment.[25] Freedom of information legislation may have an important effect in making it possible for individuals and environmental groups to make use of these remedies and to mount campaigns. Access to environmental information is called for in the

---

[23] See also 1991 ECE Convention on Environmental Impact Assessment in a Transboundary Context, Articles 2(6) and 3(8).

[24] *Rural Litigation and Entitlement Kendra* v. *State of Uttar Pradesh*, AIR 1985 SC 652; id., AIR 1987 SC 359; id., AIR 1988 SC 2187; *T. Damodhar Rao* v. *Municipal Corporation of Hyderabad*, AIR 1987 AP 171; *M.C. Mehta* v. *Union of India* (1987), 1 SCC 395; id., (1987), 4 SCC 463; *M.C. Mehta (II)* v. *Union of India* (1988), 1 SCC 471; and see also Environment (Protection) Act 1986 (No. 29), s. 19, and Indian Constitution Article 51A. See generally Abraham and Abraham, 40 *ICLQ*, (1991), 360 ff.; Pathak, 14 *CLB* (1988), 1171; Jaswal, *The Role of the Supreme Court with Regard to the Right to Life and Personal Liberty* (Delhi, 1990), 388.

[25] *Sierra Club* v. *Morton*, 405 US 727 (1972); *Japanese Whaling Association* v. *American Cetacean Society*, 478 US 221 (1986); *Australian Conservation Foundation* v. *Commonwealth of Australia* (1980), 54 ALJR 176; *Environmental Defence Society* v. *South Pacific Aluminium* (No. 3) (1981) 1 NZLR 216; *R.* v. *Secretary of State for the Environment ex parte Rose Theatre Trust Ltd.* [1990] 1 QB 504; *Vereniging Milieudefensie* v. *Hoofdingenieur—Directeur van de Rijkswaterstaat in de Directie Noordzee*, 11 *NYIL* (1980), 318; *Stichting Naturen Milieu* v. *Minister of Transport and Waterways*, ibid. 319; Bentil, *JPEL* (1981), 324; McCaffrey and Lutz, *Environmental Pollution and Individual Rights* (Deventer, 1978).

draft ECE charter and in conventions drafted by the Council of Europe, it has been endorsed by the CSCE, and it is required by EEC directives.[26] Transboundary access to information is also part of the equal access principle.[27]

Such litigation can also serve as a means of making public bodies accountable for their actions under international law. It has enabled environmental groups in the United States to seek review of governmental decisions concerning the CITES Convention and the Whaling Convention.[28] In Australia, the Commonwealth Government has relied on its constitutional power of treaty-making in actions concerning non-compliance by state governments with measures designed to give effect to the World Heritage Convention.[29] The Commission of the European Communities is similarly empowered to bring proceedings against member states for non-compliance with Community directives implementing treaties to which the Community is a party.[30]

(d) The Value of a Human Rights Approach

While it is not yet possible to conclude that international law directly protects the right to a decent environment as such, it is clear that many states have recognized its importance in various forms, at national and international level. This is a desirable development. Adequate protection of the global environment depends on the interplay of international and national measures, and the use of national legal systems by individuals or environmental groups creates additional pressure for compliance by governments with their international obligations. More generally, the existence of individual procedural rights helps shape domestic environmental policy and facilitates the resolution of transboundary conflicts through equal access to the same private law procedures. It gives NGOs an opportunity to bring legal proceedings or to challenge proposed developments on a public interest basis. It would be entirely realistic for international law to encourage these trends.

The attempt to define a decent environment in qualitative terms is less

---

[26] Council of Europe Draft Convention on Damage Resulting from Activities Dangerous to the Environment, 1990, 20 *EPL* (1990), 238, Articles 13–17; ECE Draft Charter on Environmental Rights and Obligations, 1990, Articles 4–13; CSCE, Report on Conclusions and Recommendations of the Meeting on the Protection of the Environment, Sofia, 1989; EC Directives 90/313/EEC and 85/337/EEC. See also UK legislation on access to environmental legislation: Control of Pollution Act, 1974; Water Act, 1989; Environmental Protection Act, 1990, ss. 64–7, and for consideration of access to environmental information under the European Convention on Human Rights, see Weber, 12 *HRLJ* (1991) 182 ff.

[27] See *infra*, pp. 197–201.

[28] *Defenders of Wildlife Inc* v. *Endangered Species Authority*, 659 F. 2d 168 (1981); *Japanese Whaling Association* v. *American Cetacean Society*, 478 US 221 (1986); Gibson, 14 *ELQ* (1987), 485.

[29] *Commonwealth of Australia* v. *State of Tasmania* (1983) 46 ALR 625; *Richardson* v. *Tasmanian Forestry Commission* (1988) 77 ALR 237; *Queensland* v. *The Commonwealth of Australia* (1989), 167 CLR 232; Tsamenyi and Bedding, 2 *JEL* (1990), 117.

[30] 1957 EEC Treaty, Articles 169–71, 228(2); Hartley, *Foundations of European Community Law* (2nd edn., Oxford, 1988), 283, and see *EC* v. *France*, ECJ *Case*, 182/89, 2 Nov. 1990 (violation of CITES Convention).

convincing, and, at most, seems possible only if viewed in the context of other collective economic and social aspirations. The strongest argument in favour of a qualitative interpretation is that other human rights are themselves dependent on adequate environmental quality, and cannot be realized without governmental action to protect the environment. This is doubtless true, but does not overcome the problems of implementation and definition which are the main obstacles to the development of environmental law along such lines.[31]

(2) Equal Access and Non-Discrimination

Equal access and the principle of non-discrimination represent a second and more limited approach to the resolution of international environmental conflicts through individual rights. These principles are designed to accord transboundary claimants the same rights within national legal systems as citizens enjoy, and to ensure that the same standards of legality are applied both to domestic and transboundary environmental harm, or to projects which may entail harmful effects.

(a) OECD Policy

OECD is the only international organization to have elaborated the content of the equal access and non-discrimination principles in detail or to rely on them as an important element in the development of international environmental law. Although its recommendations and decisions in this respect are not as such binding, they do have some influence on the practice of member states. As defined by OECD,[32] the principles have five elements: provision of information concerning projects, and new activities, which may give rise to a significant risk of pollution; access to information held by public authorities and made available to the public; participation in hearings, preliminary enquiries, and the making of objections in respect of proposed decisions by public authorities which could lead directly or indirectly to pollution; recourse to and standing in administrative and judicial procedures, including emergency procedures; equivalent treatment to that afforded in the country of origin in cases of domestic pollution for the purpose of preventing or abating pollution or compensating for the damage it causes. These rights are to be accorded not only to individuals affected by transfrontier pollution but also to foreign non-governmental organizations and public authorities in so far as

---

[31] See ECOSOC, Commission on Human Rights, *Human Rights and the Environment, Preliminary Report*, UN Doc. E/CN.4/Sub.2/1991/8.
[32] OECD Council Recommendations C(74) 224; C(76) 55; C(77) 28; repr. in OECD, *OECD and the Environment* (Paris, 1986). See generally McCaffrey, 1 *EPL* (1975), 1; Smets, 9 *EPL* (1982), 110; Willheim, *AYIL* (1976), 174; OECD, *Legal Aspects of Transfrontier Pollution* (Paris, 1977).

comparable entities possess such rights under the domestic law of the state concerned.

Some form of equal access is now quite widely available in Western Europe and North America.[33] The most comprehensive provision is found in the 1974 Nordic Convention for the Protection of the Environment.[34] This agreement applies to all environmentally harmful activities resulting in discharges which cause any form of environmental nuisance, including air and water pollution or radioactivity. It affords individuals full procedural rights before the courts or administrative authorities of any of the parties to the same extent and on the same terms as a legal entity of the state in which the activities are being carried out.[35] Transboundary nuisances must be equated with those within the state where the activity is located.[36] Supervisory authorities of other states parties also enjoy equal access on comparable terms to institute proceedings or be heard in matters relating to the permissibility of environmentally harmful activities. To enable them to perform this public interest role notification must be given when proposed activities may cause significant nuisance in another contracting state.

Reviewing the operation of this Convention, however, Phillips concludes that it has not removed the political and other considerations which constrain national agencies from according full equality of treatment for neighbouring states, and he points to widespread ignorance of the Convention among these agencies.[37] They have not availed themselves of the provisions for on-site inspection and institutional proceedings before administrative courts in other states, nor has there been consensus about the circumstances in which notification of other parties is necessary. Moreover, although citizen participation in transboundary proceedings is a useful feature, the limited standing afforded in Scandinavian courts has helped to ensure that this possibility has been little used. Thus the practical significance of the Nordic Convention has arguably been much overrated in the earlier literature, despite its evident potential.

No other treaty so fully adopts OECD policy, but a number of agreements, considered below, provide for equal access to civil courts in respect of tort liability and this right may also be available as a matter of national law.[38] Access to administrative proceedings for transboundary claimants has been accorded in France, the Netherlands, and Switzerland, but is not necessarily available in all European countries or elsewhere.[39] The question thus arises

---

[33] OECD Secretariat, Report on Equal Access in OECD Member Countries, in OECD, *Legal Aspects of Transfrontier Pollution*, 54; Pacteau, ibid. 203; Sand, ibid. 146.

[34] Kiss, 20 *AFDI* (1978), 808; Broms, in Flintermann, Kwiatkowska, and Lammers (eds.), *Transboundary Air Pollution* (Dordrecht, 1986), 141; Phillips, ibid. 153.

[35] Article 3.   [36] Article 2.

[37] Phillips, in Flintermann, *et al.*, *Transboundary Air Pollution*.   [38] See *infra*, pp. 201–6.

[39] Munro and Lammers, *Environmental Protection*, 121–2, but see Bothe, in Flinterman, *et al.*, *Transboundary Air Pollution*, 125, and cf. the decision of the Austrian Supreme Administrative Court in *Township of Freilassing* v. *Austria*, noted in OECD, *Legal Aspects*, 149, and see also Rehbinder and Stewart, *Environmental Protection Policy* (New York, 1988), 166–8.

whether the provision of equal access is required by international law, or whether it is simply made available as a matter of national discretion.

(b) Equal Access and Customary International Law

It is possible to argue that transboundary litigants must be afforded equal access and non-discriminatory treatment as part of the general obligation of due diligence in the prevention, reduction, and control of transboundary harm considered in Chapter 3. Nevertheless, the evidence of state practice is insufficient to conclude that in its fullest sense, as defined by OECD, equal access has become part of customary law. Nor does it enjoy the clear endorsement of international policy statements. As we have seen, the Stockholm Declaration on the Human Environment refers generally to man's fundamental right to an environment that permits a life of dignity and well-being, but does not as such provide explicitly for equal access, or non-discrimination. UNEP's 1978 'Principles of Conduct' concerning shared natural resources call on states to 'endeavour' to provide equivalent access, treatment, and remedies for persons in other states adversely affected by environmental damage resulting from the use of shared resources, and there is a comparable provision in its 1985 Montreal Guidelines for the protection of the marine environment from land-based sources. A few treaties concerned with shared watercourses do facilitate equal access in respect of interference with or diversion of the flow of water, but these are the exception, not the general practice.[40] Apart from OECD, the only other bodies whose endorsement equal access has unequivocally secured are the World Commission on Environment and Development and the UN Economic Commission for Europe.[41]

An alternative argument might seek to derive equal access rights from human rights law, relying on the principle of equal protection of the law and non-discrimination found in Article 7 of the Universal Declaration on Human Rights and in Article 26 of the 1966 International Covenant on Civil and Political Rights.[42] This latter provision is not confined to forms of discrimination, such as race or sex, which it specifically mentions, but is open-ended, and therefore in principle also capable of application to transboundary discrimination which lacks legitimate purpose or has disproportionate effects. It

---

[40] e.g. 1909 US–Canada Boundary Waters Treaty, *infra*, Ch. 6. See, also, ILC draft articles on the Law of Non-Navigational Uses of International Watercourses, 1991, Article 32, which prohibits discrimination in granting access to judicial and other procedures in respect of international watercourses, and 1982 ILA Montreal Rules on Water Pollution in an International Drainage Basin, Article 8.

[41] WCED, Legal Principles, Article 20; ECE, 1990 Charter on Environmental Rights and Obligations; 1991 ECE Convention on Environmental Impact Assessment in a Transboundary context, Article 2(6).

[42] See also 1981 African Charter on Human and Peoples' Rights, Articles 2, 3; and generally Bayefsky, 11 *HRLJ* (1990), 1; Ramcharan, in Henkin (ed.), *The International Bill of Rights* (New York, 1981), 246.

might reasonably be asserted that the arbitrary exclusion of transboundary litigants violates this standard of international legality.[43] But some human rights instruments, including the European Convention on Human Rights, do not contain an autonomous non-discrimination clause of this kind,[44] while in general international law, the principle of non-discrimination appears confined to racial, and possibly sexual discrimination.[45] Although WCED included non-discrimination in its proposed legal principles on environmental protection, its legal experts concluded that it was still an 'emerging principle of international law' in this context.[46]

(c) Limitations on the Utility of Equal Access

Equal access suffers several evident disadvantages. First, it guarantees no substantive standard of environmental protection, and no harmonization of legal systems and remedies. It does not compel states to create for their own nationals any of the procedural rights to which it refers. Much will thus depend on such matters as the availability of public participation in environmental impact assessment procedures, on the liberality of rules of standing in administrative proceedings and on the role of public authorities in individual countries. If no relevant rights exist for the state's own citizens, if they are not protected by human rights law or international agreement, or if they are narrowly prescribed, the same limitations will affect transboundary claimants. Thus equal access is mainly useful where the relevant legal systems offer comparable levels of substantive protection, as in Scandinavia, or where common standards are established by agreement, as in the EEC.

A second problem with equal access is that it is primarily a remedy for localized problems in border areas. Its significance declines where the effects are global or continental in character and emanate from generalized sources. It will not help to control ozone depletion, global climate change or long-range transboundary air pollution, or species extinction, and in these situations resort to interstate remedies and regulation will be essential.

Nevertheless, the potential of equal access as a means of resolving some transboundary problems without resort to interstate claims is significant. As Sand has observed: 'Opening local remedies to foreign parties can go a long

---

[43] Bayefsky, 11 *HRLJ* (1990), 8; *South West Africa Case*, *ICJ Rep.* (1966), 306, per Judge Tanaka; Ramcharan, in Henkin, *The International Bill of Rights*, 263. See also EEC Treaty, Article 7.

[44] *ECHR*, Article 14: 'The enjoyment of the rights and freedoms *set forth in this Convention* shall be secured without discrimination . . .'; 1969 American Convention on Human Rights, Article 1, but cf. Article 24.

[45] *Namibia Advisory Opinion*, *ICJ Rep.* (1971), 57; *South West Africa Case*, *ICJ Rep.* (1966), 293–300, per Judge Tanaka; Bayefsky, 11 *HRLJ* (1990), 18–24; 1965 International Convention on the Elimination of All Forms of Racial Discrimination; 1979 Convention on the Elimination of All Forms of Discrimination against Women.

[46] Legal principles, Article 13. The principle has also been adopted by ECE in its Draft Charter on Environmental Rights and Obligations.

way toward de-escalating transboundary disputes to their ordinary neighbour-hood level.'[47] This is especially so in cases where compensation is sought for transboundary harm. In this context equal access forms part of a general trend to rely on civil liability as the primary remedy in preference to the law of state responsibility.[48]

(3) Civil Liability for Environmental Damage in Transboundary Proceedings

(a) Advantages

For the individual victim of transboundary environmental damage, the main advantage of recourse to civil liability proceedings is that this affords a direct and immediate remedy without resort to interstate claims or the complexities of the law of state responsibility. Crucially, any proceedings will be wholly at the plaintiff's discretion.

A second advantage is that recourse to civil liability helps implement the 'polluter pays' principle referred to in Chapter 3. This principle provides an important justification for harmonization of national environmental liability laws, and for affording transboundary access to appropriate remedies. In essence, it favours directing the primary liability for damage away from states under international law, and instead passes transboundary costs directly to the operator or owner of the installation, industry, or activity in question. The extent to which this approach actually results in the ultimate polluter paying the full costs will then depend not on procedural obstacles but on whether liability is strict or dependent on proof of negligence, on whether it is limited in amount and on whether environmental clean-up and reinstatement costs are included.[49]

These advantages are such that international policy and state practice have shown a strong preference for the direct accountability of the polluter in national law as the best means of facilitating recovery of compensation for pollution damage. This can be observed in OECD's principle of equal access,[50] in certain UNEP guidelines,[51] and in several significant treaties, including Article 235(2) of the 1982 UNCLOS and the 1988 Convention

---

[47] Sand, *Lessons Learned in Global Environmental Governance* (New York, 1990), 31, and id., in OECD, *Legal Aspects*, 146.

[48] See Ch. 4.

[49] Boyle, in Francioni and Scovazzi (eds.), *International Responsibility for Environmental Harm* (Dordrecht, 1991), ch. 15, and see *infra* Chs. 7 and 9.

[50] See *infra*, pp. 204–5.

[51] Principles of Conduct in the Conservation and Harmonious Utilization of Natural Resources Shared by Two or More States, 1978, Article 14; Montreal Guidelines for the Protection of the Marine Environment Against Pollution from Land-based Sources, 1985, Article 17; Principles Concerning the Environment Related to Offshore Drilling and Mining within the Limits of National Jurisdiction, 1981, sections 34–42. On the legal status of these, see *supra*, pp. 47–52.

for the Regulation of Antarctic Mineral Resource Activities.[52] The former requires states to ensure that recourse is available within their legal systems for prompt and adequate compensation for marine pollution damage caused by persons under their jurisdiction. The latter requires the operator of any Antarctic mineral undertakings to be held strictly liable for any damage to the environment or ecosystem.[53] Other treaties, including those dealing with oil pollution from ships or with nuclear accidents, establish more complex schemes, considered below.[54] These precedents have influenced negotiations concerning liability for dangerous activities harmful to the environment, and for the carriage of hazardous and noxious substances and wastes.[55] Moreover, as part of his regime of liability for hazardous activities, ILC rapporteur Barboza has proposed that states should be required to give their courts jurisdiction to deal with transboundary claims in accordance with national law without discrimination based on nationality, domicile, or residence.[56]

Principle 22 of the Stockholm Declaration, which called on states to co-operate in the development of international law concerning liability and compensation for environmental damage, did not specify that it should take the form of civil liability, but in practice what has begun to emerge is a dual system, in which civil liability will generally represent the most efficient means of securing redress, save where its disadvantages leave state responsibility as a subsidiary remedy of last resort.

(b) Disadvantages

Without international co-operation and agreement, transboundary civil proceedings encounter several serious obstacles in many jurisdictions. The most important is the rule applied by some legal systems which denies courts jurisdiction over actions concerning foreign land.[57] This rule may bar plaintiffs from bringing proceedings in the courts of the state from which the harm has originated. Its existence explains why the *Trail Smelter* case was referred not to the Canadian courts but to arbitration.[58]

A plaintiff who seeks to avoid this jurisdictional problem by resorting to

---

[52] Article 8.

[53] See also 1982 UNCLOS, Annex III, Article 22 which imposes liability for deep sea-bed mining.

[54] See Chs. 7 and 9.

[55] Council of Europe, Draft Convention on Damage Resulting from Activities Dangerous to the Environment, 20 *EPL* (1990), 238; 1989 ECE Convention on Civil Liability for Damage Caused During Carriage of Dangerous Goods by Road, Rail and Inland Navigation Vessels, and see also *infra*, pp. 297–8 and 340–1.

[56] ILC, Barboza, 6th Report on International Liability, UN Doc. A/CN. 4/428 (1990), Articles 28–30.

[57] See for example, *British South Africa Company* v. *Compania de Moçambique* [1893] AC 602; *Hesperides Hotels Ltd.* v. *Muftizade* [1979] AC 508; and see generally McCaffrey, 3 *CWJIL* (1973), 191; Willheim, *AYIL* (1976), 186, and OECD, *Legal Aspects*, 98–102.

[58] Read, 1 *CYIL* (1963), 222.

courts in his own state, where the damage has occurred, faces other difficulties. These may include a defence of sovereign immunity, if the foreign enterprise is governmental in character. Some states now deny such immunity where the tort is deemed to have taken place within their territory, or where it is not committed 'in the exercise of sovereign authority'.[59] The latter point could be relied on to exclude immunity for most industrial activities on the ground that they are *iure gestionis*, which is the view taken by German courts when the Soviet Union was sued in respect of the Chernobyl disaster.[60] Schreuer notes that a rigid requirement that the tort take place entirely within the territory of the forum would continue to allow immunity in cases of transboundary pollution, but international judicial decisions and state practice generally give territoriality a more extended definition under which it is sufficient if the effects are present in the forum state.[61] In any event, international law does not require states to grant immunity in these circumstances, it merely permits them to do so, and the rules applied by any one jurisdiction should not be given undue weight.

Other problems will relate to the choice of applicable law, the enforcement of any judgment against a foreign defendant, who may have no assets within the jurisdiction of the court, and the possible use of a *forum non conveniens* defence. These difficulties are exacerbated in the case of ships or nuclear installations where the defendant's main or only asset may have been lost in the accident giving rise to proceedings. There is also likely to be difficulty obtaining injunctions relating to activities in the territory of other states.[62]

The plaintiff may thus prefer the foreign forum, if available, in order to be sure of an effective remedy. Much will then depend on how satisfactorily the legal system of that forum deals with polluting activities. If it is unduly favourable to local industry, the transboundary plaintiff may be left with no redress, or with rights of a very limited character only. Thus, determining where to bring the proceedings may be critical to their success.

These are essentially issues of private international law, but they are sufficiently important for the intervention of public international law to have become necessary in order to remove some or all of the obstacles. There are two ways in which this can be done: by requiring adequate provision for equal access, or by securing a harmonization of civil liability laws on an agreed basis. Both techniques have been used to make civil liability more widely available to transboundary plaintiffs, and to guarantee an effective remedy.

[59] See for example, UK State Immunity Act, 1978, ss. 3(3)(c), 5 and generally, Schreuer, *Sovereign Immunity* (Cambridge, 1988), ch. 3.

[60] ILA, Cairo Conference (1992), *Second Report on State Immunity*, 11. Note, however, that the nuclear liability conventions require immunities to be waived; see *infra*, ch. 9.

[61] Schreuer, *Sovereign Immunity*, 61, but cf. *Handelswerkerij Bier* v. *Mines de Potasse d'Alsace*, Case 21/76, II ECJ Rep. (1976), 1735, and *Lotus Case*, PCIJ Ser. A, No. 10 (1927).

[62] McCaffrey, 3 *CWJIL* (1973); Willheim, *AYIL* (1976); and OECD, *Legal Aspects*, ch. 4.

(c) Equal Access and Civil Liability

The positive impact of OECD's principle of equal access[63] is best observed in the provision which now exists in Western Europe for transboundary civil liability. The effect of the 1974 Nordic Convention,[64] and of the Brussels and Lugano Conventions on Civil Jurisdiction and the Enforcement of Judgments[65] is that civil remedies are now available to transboundary claimants throughout Scandinavia, the EEC, and EFTA. In North America, legislation of some US states and Canadian provinces follows the pattern of the 1982 Uniform Transboundary Reciprocal Access Act, a model law drafted by national bar associations.[66] In some cases existing law, particularly in the US, already permits access for foreign claimants.[67] Civil actions have become the accepted method for recovering damages in respect of transboundary air and water pollution in all these jurisdictions. Some bilateral agreements also apply equal access to liability for nuclear accidents, although this is uncommon.[68]

There is less evidence of support for the principle of equal access to civil liability proceedings in other regions. As we have seen, the principle was not referred to in Principle 22 of the Stockholm Declaration, nor is it found in UNEP's regional seas treaties, or in others concerned with dumping and land-based sources of marine pollution.[69] At best, with a few exceptions, UNEP has mostly followed the position taken in the Stockholm Declaration. Moreover, an altogether different approach has been adopted in regional and global treaties dealing with ultrahazardous activities, including oil tankers and nuclear installations.[70] Thus, in so far as Article 235(2) of the 1982 UNCLOS and the ILC's articles on international liability incorporate equal access, they do not yet represent a clear international consensus on the general principle of facilitating equal access, nor do they necessarily rest on widespread state practice in the developing world.

---

[63] See *supra*, pp. 197–81.   [64] *Supra*, n. 34.

[65] See Dashwood, Hacon, and White, *Civil Jurisdiction and Judgments Convention* (Deventer, 1987).

[66] National Conference of Commissioners on Uniform State Law, 1982, implemented by legislation in South Dakota, New Jersey, Colorado, Montana, Wisconsin. See Rosencrantz, 15 *EPL* (1985), 105.

[67] See for example, *Michie* v. *Great Lakes Steel Division*, 495 F. 2d. 213 (1974); Ianni, 11 *CYIL* (1973), 258. See also 1973 US Trans-Alaska Pipeline Authorisation Act, s. 204(c), 43 USC s. 1653 (c)(1) which allows 'any person or entity, public or private, including those resident in Canada', to invoke the Act's liability system.

[68] See Ch. 9.

[69] See for example, 1976 Barcelona Convention for the Protection of the Mediterranean Sea, Article 12; 1982 Convention for the Conservation of the Red Sea, Article 13; 1978 Kuwait Convention for Co-operation on the Protection of the Marine Environment from Pollution, Article 13; 1983 Convention for the Protection and Development of the Marine Environment of the Caribbean, Article 14; 1972 London Dumping Convention, Article 10, but cf. UNEP guidelines, *supra* n. 51, which do contain more detailed provision.

[70] See *infra*, pp. 292–8, and 371–84.

Moreover, equal access is not necessarily the best way to deal with civil liability, unless, as we have seen, the law of the state where the harm originates makes adequate provision, or its choice of law rules allows reference to the law of the place where the injury occurs. The criticism that where this is not the case, equal access may prove more favourable to the polluter can be overcome, however, by giving the plaintiff the choice of venue in which to bring proceedings.[71] The European Court of Justice has interpreted Article 5 of the 1968 Brussels Convention on Jurisdiction and Enforcement of Judgments in this sense in its decision in *Handelswerkerij Bier* v. *Mines de Potasse d'Alsace.*[72] This convention facilitates choice of forum by making judgments obtained in one jurisdiction enforceable in another, but it does not solve the problem of choice of applicable law. The Dutch district court which heard the liability proceedings in the *Handelswerkerij* case tried unsuccessfully to do so by applying international law to determine the liability of the defendants.[73] Alternatively, some legal systems are willing to apply whichever national law is most favourable to the plaintiff in transboundary claims.[74] Neither enforceability of judgments nor choice of law is regulated by OECD's scheme of 'equal access', however.

The choice of venue in the Brussels Convention scheme is also found in the ILC articles on international liability,[75] but it does not at present have many other applications. Only the 1962 Nuclear Ships Convention and the 1977 Convention on Civil Liability for Oil Pollution Damage Resulting from Sea-bed Exploration or Exploitation of Submarine Mineral Resources afford such a choice of venue; neither is in force, and the latter convention is regional only.

Equal access thus offers certain advantages over interstate proceedings as a means of establishing liability, but it provides only a partial answer. The more comprehensive solution is represented by the model found in several civil liability treaties.

(d) Civil Liability Treaties and Ultra-hazardous risks

A group of treaties dealing with nuclear risks and oil pollution has created

[71] Willheim, *AYIL* (1976), 186.

[72] *Supra*, n. 61, and see Rehbinder and Stewart, *Environmental Protection Policy*, 171 ff.

[73] Reported in 11 *NYIL* (1980), 326 and 14 *NYIL* (1984), 471. See Rest, 5 *EPL* (1979), 85. The district court's use of international law was overruled on appeal, on the ground that customary international law was inapplicable to a dispute between private parties, but its judgment awarding damages against the defendants for a tort under Dutch law was upheld: see Court of Appeal decision, reported in 19 *NYIL* (1988), 496. See now, however, EEC Proposed Directive on Civil Liability for Damage Caused by Waste, COM (89) 282, which if adopted will harmonize liability laws and avoid the need to rely on national or international law.

[74] For example, Germany, on which see Rehbinder and Stewart, *Environmental Protection Policy*, 172 ff., and see also *Poro* v. *Houillères du Bassin de Lorraine*, 11 *Neue Juristische Wochenschrift* (1958), 752, noted in OECD, *Legal Aspects*, 148. cf., however, ILC draft Articles on International Liability, *supra*, n. 56, Article 30, which require courts to apply their own national law.

[75] *Supra*, n. 56, Article 29(c).

a special international regime of civil liability for these ultra-hazardous activities.[76] Their main advantage is that they require the parties to adopt a strict liability standard, but they also limit the total liability of the operator or owner concerned. Payment of damages is assured by compulsory insurance and in some cases by additional compensation funds which come either from states operating nuclear installations,[77] or in the case of oil tankers, from the oil industry.[78] These conventions are examined in more detail in Chapters 7 and 9. They are important precedents for the sort of provision necessary to make such risks internationally acceptable, although they raise serious questions about the distribution of loss. None of the schemes follows the 'polluter pays' principle in full. Instead the burden of major losses is distributed partly to the operator, partly to the industry or state concerned, and beyond that it falls on the innocent victim, or must be recovered in interstate claims.[79] It is in these circumstances that state responsibility remains an important subsidiary remedy.

Nevertheless both schemes offer significant advantages. Equal access does not afford the same assurance of compensation, nor does it compel harmonization of liability standards. Civil liability treaties do thus give individual plaintiffs quite significant benefits provided liability limits are realistic and are supported by additional compensation. This, however, is not invariably so.[80]

3. CRIMINAL RESPONSIBILITY

The notion that individuals, and by extension also corporations, bear a responsibility towards the environment is not new. The Stockholm Declaration referred in Principle 1 to man's 'solemn responsibility' to protect and improve it. Subsequent formulations have preferred to emphasize the individual character of this obligation. Thus the World Charter for Nature talks of the duty of 'each person' to act in accordance with its terms.[81] The ECE Charter of Environmental Rights and Obligations states that 'Everyone has the responsibility to protect and conserve the environment for the benefit

---

[76] 1960 Paris Convention on Third Party Liability in the Field of Nuclear Energy; 1963 Vienna Convention on Civil Liability for Nuclear Damage; 1962 Brussels Convention on the Liability of Operators of Nuclear Ships; 1971 Brussels Convention Relating to Civil Liability in the Field of Maritime Carriage of Nuclear Material; 1969 Brussels Convention on Civil Liability for Oil Pollution Damage with 1984 Protocol. See *infra*, Chs. 7 and 9, and Boyle, in Francioni and Scovazzi, *International Responsibility for Environmental Harm.*, 338.

[77] 1963 Convention Supplementary to the Paris Convention, *infra*, Ch. 9.

[78] 1971 International Convention on the Establishment of an International Fund for Compensation for Oil Pollution Damage, *infra*, Ch. 7.

[79] Boyle, in Francioni and Scovazzi, *International Responsibility for Environmental Harm.*

[80] Ibid., and *infra*, Ch. 9.   [81] Principle 24. See *infra*, Ch. 11.

of present and future generations.'[82] Moreover, a number of constitutions, including Article 51A of the Indian Constitution, refer to the individual's duty to protect and improve the natural environment or some similar concept.[83]

None of these instruments creates legally binding obligations for individuals as such. But they do provide a justification for using criminal responsibility as a means of enforcing international environmental law. The importance of criminal responsibility is that it provides added incentive to refrain from harmful conduct by emphasizing its culpable character, and, in many cases, by allowing more stringent enforcement measures or penalties to be imposed.[84] Its use can be observed in the requirements of treaty enforcement in national law, in instances of extraterritorial jurisdiction, and in the concept of environmental crimes against international law.

(1) Enforcement in National Law

The implementation of most environmental treaties will usually require legislative and enforcement measures to be taken by governments. In general these are part of the obligation of due diligence which states are called on to perform. How a state effects the performance of this obligation will depend on what is required by the particular treaty, but in many cases the choice of means is left to the state's discretion.[85] Whether it relies on the criminal law to regulate individual or corporate conduct will then depend on the legal system in question. Other possible options include civil remedies, administrative or fiscal measures, and voluntary restraints.[86] But there are some situations for which states have agreed that conduct is sufficiently objectionable that criminal penalties are required. This is typically the case in treaties covering trade in hazardous and other wastes, marine pollution and trade in or possession of endanged species.[87] Criminal penalties are normally also employed to deal with illegal fishing.

---

[82] Principle 2.

[83] See also Yemen, Article 16; Papua-New Guinea, Article 5; Peru, Article 123; Poland, Article 71; Sri Lanka, Article 28; USSR, Article 67; Vanuatu, Article 7.

[84] See generally Richardson, Ogus, and Burrows, *Policing Pollution* (Oxford, 1982), 15–17.

[85] The distinction between obligations of conduct and obligations of result is relevant here. See in particular II *Yearbook ILC* (1977), pt. 2, 11–30.

[86] For a review of differing national approaches to the enforcement of environmental law, see Zalob, 3 *Hastings ICLR* (1980), 299.

[87] 1989 Basel Convention for the Control of Transboundary Movements of Hazardous Wastes, Article 4(3), 4(4); 1991 Bamako Convention on the Ban of the Import into Africa, etc., of Hazardous Wastes, Article 9(2); 1973 MARPOL Convention, Articles 4(2), 4(4); 1972 London Dumping Convention, Article 6(2); 1974 Paris Convention for the Prevention of Marine Pollution from Land-based Sources, Article 12(1); 1987 Protocol for the Prevention of Pollution of the South Pacific by Dumping, Article 12(2); 1982 UNCLOS, Articles 217(8), 230; 1973 CITES Convention, Article 8(1).

(2) Extra-Territorial Criminal Jurisdiction

Jurisdiction in this context means the capacity of a state under international law to prescribe and enforce laws. It is primarily an attribute of the sovereignty of states over their own territory, or over their own nationals.[88] Jurisdiction based on nationality is not confined to individuals, but applies also to companies, ships, aircraft, and spacecraft. The state retains jurisdiction over its nationals even when they are abroad or on the high seas; it is on this basis that flag states remain responsible for regulating pollution or fishing from ships on the high seas or in the maritime zones of other states.[89] Nationality is also in practice the only accepted basis for regulating persons and activities in Antarctica.[90] Although in principle there is nothing to stop states regulating their nationals when operating in other states, in practice most states will confine such cases of concurrent jurisdiction to serious criminal offences.[91]

In addition to these general principles of jurisdiction in customary law, international law also recognizes certain forms of extraterritorial jurisdiction based on the so-called protective principle. This is particularly important in the law of the sea. It provides the justification for the extension of coastal state jurisdiction within the exclusive economic zone for the purposes of protecting the marine environment and conserving living resources. The content of this jurisdiction is carefully defined by treaty and customary law, and it is not unlimited. Moreover the power to enforce coastal state laws within the EEZ is more restricted than the power to prescribe. These limitations are more fully considered in later chapters.[92] The important point, however, is that this extended jurisdiction enhances the enforcement machinery in these two areas of environmental law. In both cases the main argument in favour of extra-territorial criminal jurisdiction has been the failure or inability of the flag state to police the high seas effectively. A similar argument underlies the possible extension of the concept of universal jurisdiction to cover certain environmental offences.

(3) Universal Jurisdiction and Crimes against International Law

Universal jurisdiction entitles a state to prosecute an offence even in the absence of any connection based on nationality, territory, or the protective

---

[88] See generally Bowett, in McDonald and Johnston, *The Structure and Process of International Law* (Dordrecht, 1983), 555; Brownlie, *Principles of International Law* (4th edn., Oxford, 1990), ch. 14.

[89] See Ch. 7.

[90] Antarctic Treaty, 1959, Article 8; Triggs (ed.), *The Antarctic Treaty Regime* (Cambridge, 1987), 88.

[91] States are not entitled to *enforce* their laws on the territory of another state, however. On the more complex problems of jurisdiction over companies and their subsidiaries, see Bowett, in McDonald and Johnston, *Structure and Process.*

[92] See Chs. 7 and 13.

principle.[93] Piracy is the clearest and least controversial example of this much disputed form of jurisdiction, which rests on the assumption that the crimes in question are contrary to international public order. Thus it is the interest of every state in suppressing such offences which justifies their status as crimes which any state may prosecute.[94] Other possible examples, including war crimes, torture, genocide, and hijacking are more doubtful, either because jurisdiction rests on treaties alone, as in the case of hijacking,[95] or because it is not truly universal, as in the case of genocide.[96] The basis of the ILC's proposed 'Code of Offences Against the Peace and Security of Mankind', and of conventions dealing with torture and hijacking, is that every state in whose territory the alleged perpetrator is present shall either try or extradite.[97] The ILC has also considered the establishment of an international criminal court with jurisdiction to try crimes against international law.[98]

It is the ILC's version of the universality principle with which the concept of port state jurisdiction employed in Article 218 of the 1982 UNCLOS is broadly comparable. The crucial feature of this article is that it gives the state in whose port the vessel is present the right to prosecute for pollution offences committed on the high seas or in the maritime zones of other states, subject to a right of pre-emption by the flag state. But, unlike other applications of the principle, this article represents an extension so far not reflected in state practice.[99] It is also the only application relevant to the enforcement of environmental law.

However, the principle of treating certain categories of environmental offences as crimes against humanity has been included in the ILC's draft Code of Offences. Its 1986 formulation referred to 'any serious breach of an international obligation of essential importance for the safeguarding and pre-servation of the human environment.'[100] A subsequent revision referring to 'any serious and intentional harm to a vital human asset, such as the human environment,' was modified again in 1991 to cover those who wilfully cause or order the causing of 'widespread, long-term and severe damage to the *natural*

---

[93] Bowett, in McDonald and Johnston, *Structure and Process*, 563 ff.

[94] *Lotus Case*, PCIJ, Ser. A, No. 10 (1927), 70. It is of course necessary for states to adopt appropriate national legislation to give effect to their right of prosecution.

[95] 1963 Tokyo Convention on Offences Committed on Board Aircraft; 1970 Hague Convention on Unlawful Seizure of Aircraft; 1971 Montreal Convention for the Suppression of Unlawful Acts Against the Safety of Civil Aviation; 1988 Convention for the Suppression of Unlawful Acts Against the Safety of Maritime Navigation.

[96] 1948 Genocide Convention, Article 6, allows this crime to be prosecuted by the state where the events took place, or by an international penal tribunal. No such tribunal exists: See further, Graefrath, 1 *EJIL* (1990), 67.

[97] *Report of the ILC* (1991), GAOR A/46/10; see also 1985 Torture Convention, Article 5.

[98] See Graefrath, 1 *EJIL* (1990), 67.

[99] See Ch. 7. No comparable attempt has been made to extend jurisdiction over fisheries offences on the high seas.

[100] Article 12(4), II *Yearbook ILC* (1986), pt. 1, 86.

environment'.[101] This vague phraseology leaves much to be desired, including the question whether the harm must violate some treaty or rule of customary law, or whether otherwise lawful development activities might be caught simply because of their intentional character and harmful effects. A preferable approach would limit the category to violations of applicable international rules intended to cause serious harm to the natural environment; a possible example would be the conduct of Iraq in setting fire to Kuwaiti oil wells in 1991.

Nevertheless it is by no means clear that such a rule in whatever form at present part of international law. States have generally been reluctant to allow broad claims of universal jurisdiction and this aspect of the ILC's draft code remains controversial, with some states preferring to confer jurisdiction on an international tribunal, which has yet to be established.[102] Even practice in trying terrorists and drug smugglers rests more on application of the protective or passive personality principles or on agreement with other states.[103] Moreover, although the 1977 Additional Protocol I to the Geneva Conventions includes provisions on protection of the environment in time of armed conflict, which some writers see as representing customary law, it falls short of including these articles in the category whose grave breach constitutes war crimes.[104] The ILC's proposals can thus be regarded only as a tentative step towards broadening the category of crimes against international law. The inclusion of environmental offences may prove a significant development if adopted in practice, however, because of its potential utility in protecting the global commons.[105] Here there is a case for treating very serious and deliberate pollution as equivalent to piracy, since the public interest of all states is affected and effective enforcement may otherwise be lacking. In this respect the argument for universal jurisdiction over individuals mirrors the argument for an *actio popularis* covering 'international crimes' under Article 19 of the ILC's articles on state responsibility, in so far as it enables states to take unilateral action to protect community concerns.[106]

---

[101] Article 14(6), *Report of the ILC* (1989), GAOR A/44/10, 168 f.; Article 26; *Report of the ILC* (1991), GAOR A/46/10. See also draft Article 22(2)(d).

[102] Graefrath, 1 *EJIL* (1990).

[103] *Tel-Oren* v. *Libyan Arab Republic*, 77 *ILR* (1984), 193; *US* v. *Gonzalez*, 776 F. 2d. 931 (1986); and see US–UK Exchange of Letters concerning measures to suppress the Unlawful Importation of Narcotic Drugs, in 21 *ILM* (1982), 439. cf. *US* v. *Yunis*, 30 *ILM* (1991), 403 and Lowenfeld, 83 *AJIL* (1989), 880.

[104] Additional Protocol I Relating to the Victims of International Armed Conflicts, Articles, 35, 55, 56, and 85, and see Cassese, *International Law in a Divided World* (Oxford, 1986), 273–5. See generally *supra*, pp. 127–31.

[105] Niekirk, 93 *SALJ* (1976), 68 offers too broad a basis for treating serious pollution as a crime against international law.

[106] See *supra*, pp. 154–7. See Bilder, 14 *Vand. JTL* (1981), 73 ff., who views this form of universal jurisdiction as an example of 'custodial responsibility' for common areas and community interests.

4. GENERATIONAL RIGHTS

As early as 1946, the International Convention for the Regulation of Whaling recognized the interest of the nations of the world in safeguarding whale stocks 'for future generations'. The same generational perspective underlies references in the 1972 Stockholm Declaration to man's responsibility to protect the environment and the earth's natural resources.[107] The nature of this responsibility to future generations is spelt out more fully in the World Charter for Nature.[108] This calls on states to ensure genetic viability, the maintenance of animal population levels sufficient for their survival, the conservation of representative samples of ecosystems, the management of resources to maintain optimum sustainable productivity and coexistence, including their non-utilization in excess of natural capacity for regeneration, and the avoidance of irreversible environmental damage.

These international declarations indicate the importance now attached in international policy to the protection of the environment for the benefit of future generations. The concept of sustainable development is in many respects itself an expression of the same concern for the interests of the future. So, it has been argued, is the concept of common heritage of mankind.[109] The theory of inter-generational equity has been advanced to explain the optimum basis for the relationship between one generation and the next. This theory, as expounded by Brown-Weiss and in the Goa Guidelines on Inter-generational Equity, requires each generation to use and develop its natural and cultural heritage in such a manner that it can be passed on to future generations in no worse condition than it was received.[110] Central to this idea is the need to conserve options for the future use of resources, including their quality, and that of the natural environment.

Despite its conceptual elegance, the apparent simplicity of the theory of inter-generational equity is deceptive. While accepting the right of present generations to use resources for economic development, it fails to answer the question how we should value the environment for the purpose of determining whether future generations will be worse off.[111] Moreover its concentration

---

[107] Principles 1 and 2. See also 1968 African Convention on the Conservation of Nature and Natural Resources.

[108] See Ch. 11.

[109] Brown-Weiss, in Buergenthal (ed.), *Contemporary Issues in International Law* (Kehl, 1984), 270.

[110] Brown-Weiss, *In Fairness to Future Generations* (Dobbs Ferry, NY, 1989); Goa Guidelines on Inter-generational Equity, 1988, ibid., Appendix A. See also Redgwell, in Churchill and Freestone (eds.), *International Law and Global Climate Change* (London, 1991), ch. 3; D'Amato, 84 *AJIL* (1990), 190; Brown-Weiss, ibid. 198; Gundling, ibid. 207.

[111] Redgwell, in Churchill and Freestone, *International Law and Global Climate Change*; Christenson, 1 *YIEL* (1990), 392. For an economist's analysis of how to value the environment on a sustainable basis, see Pearce, *Blueprint for a Green Economy* (London, 1989).

on relations between one generation and the next does not convincingly answer the equally pressing question of how benefits and burdens should be shared within each generation.[112] Thus, although the content of the theory is well defined, it rests on some questionable assumptions concerning the meaning of economic equity.

Weiss argues that inter-generational equity is already part of the fabric of international law. It is true that the policy which underlies a number of pollution treaties is the avoidance of irreversible harm, as in the Ozone Convention.[113] It is also possible to point to conservation treaties, and conservation obligations in customary law, which require co-operation in the management of stocks and ecosystems for the purpose of maintaining sustainable productivity.[114] Future generations will benefit to the extent that these regimes are successful, but in many cases they have not been, and the record of actual practice casts doubt on the level of commitment to any theory of inter-generational equity. The phasing out of dumping at sea, particularly of radioactive waste, and the adoption of an interim moratorium on whaling do perhaps point to an emerging concern for the interests of future generations,[115] but these examples do not yet justify general conclusions about the creation of generational rights in international law.

But the essential point of the theory, that man has a responsibility for the future, is incontrovertible, however it is expressed. The question then becomes one of implementation.[116] The examples of the London Dumping Convention and International Whaling Commission do show that some international institutions already accommodate the needs of future generations in a balancing of interests. Wider adoption of the precautionary principle, and of policies of sustainable development, will entail more institutions following this lead. Weiss takes this fiduciary model of man's relationship with the environment somewhat further by proposing the creation of a planetary ombudsman, and a commission on the future of the planet. Some of these proposals are also adopted by the WCED.[117] Representation of future generations in legal proceedings before international courts is another possibility, but would require radical changes to the jurisdiction of the ICJ. Some interstate proceedings can already be interpreted in this way, however.[118]

5. ANIMAL RIGHTS AND 'ECO-RIGHTS'

If the rights of peoples and of future generations can be accommodated within a fiduciary model of international environmental law, there is no difficulty

---

[112] Gundling, 84 *AJIL* (1990), 211.
[113] See also Principle 6, Stockholm Declaration, 1972.
[114] See *infra*, pp. 448–52.   [115] See Chs. 8 and 12.   [116] Gundling, 84 *AJIL* (1990).
[117] Munro and Lammers, *Environmental Protection and Sustainable Development* (London, 1987).
[118] *Nauru* v. *Australia ICJ Rep.* (1992), 240.

making similar accommodation for the 'rights' of animals or the environment in general. The question then becomes one of considering whether international law protects animals, ecosystems, and the environment for their intrinisic value, or simply for man's benefit. The international legal system is not necessarily anthropocentric, but in practice it will be if the value of non-human interests is disregarded. On this question, as chapters 11 and 12 make clear, the answer remains uncertain. Older conservation treaties do tend to stress that human use and benefit to mankind are the criteria for international protection.[119] This is true even of some more recent instruments such as the 1968 African Convention on the Conservation of Nature. On the other hand, there is evidence, as we have seen, that international law does recognize the intrinisic value of the natural environment and of animals.[120] The argument that whales, or other species, now enjoy a right to life will be plausible to the extent that international protection of these animals is no longer founded solely on their usefulness to man. At this point, as elsewhere in this chapter, we are clearly in the realms of developing international law.[121]

6. CONCLUSIONS

This chapter points first to the evolving interaction of international and national legal systems in the overall structure of international environmental law. It emphasizes that Principle 1 of the 1972 Stockholm Declaration has not been without legal effects, in the use of transboundary litigation to afford remedies for and against private parties, in the recognition of a constitutional right to a decent environment in several national legal systems, and in tentative progress towards developing international human rights law.

Secondly, it emphasizes the complexity of the balancing process which lies at the heart of any concept of sustainable development, and its translation into the form of legal rights. The claims of man, both now and in future generations, to live in a decent environment capable of sustaining life of acceptable quality, need little justification. Nor, when viewed against the need for biological diversity, unity of ecosystems, and the preservation of options implicit in WCED's formulation of sustainable development, do the claims of animals to international protection appear controversial. The fundamental difficulty lies in reconciling these competing claims, and for the lawyer, identifying the contribution which law can make to the process of achieving an acceptable balance. Implementation remains the major problem affecting such

[119] See for example, 1946 International Convention for the Regulation of Whaling; 1958 Geneva Convention on Fishing and Conservation of the Living Resources of the High Seas; *infra*, Chs. 11–13.

[120] *Supra*, nn. 18–20.

[121] See D'Amato and Chopra, 85 *AJIL* (1991).

claims, and no convincing solution has been afforded either by WCED or by other advocates of inter-generational equity, human rights, and sustainable development. In subsequent chapters we shall see how far, if at all, some of these claims have been realized, and whether they remain, in practice, matters more appropriate for politicians and economists than for lawyers to resolve.

6

Pollution of International Watercourses

1. INTRODUCTION

(1) The Scope of International Watercourse Law

The object of this chapter is to consider how far principles of international law provide for the environmental protection of international watercourses. The term 'international watercourse' is used here primarily as a convenient designation for rivers, lakes, or groundwater sources shared by two or more states. Such watercourses will normally either form or straddle an international boundary, or in the case of rivers, they may flow through a succession of states.[1]

In dealing with shared or transboundary watercourses a second problem of geographical definition arises. How much of the whole watercourse system is it proper to include? The possibilities range from simply that portion which crosses or defines a boundary, to the entire watershed or river basin, with its associated lakes, tributaries, groundwater systems, and connecting waterways wherever they are located. The latter interpretation may result in limitations on the use of a very substantial proportion of a state's internal river systems and their catchment areas,[2] and lead to the imposition of a responsibility on watercourse states to protect their own environment, as well as that of their neighbours. But if the narrower approach is preferred, the efficient environmental management of transboundary flows may be seriously impeded. For this reason the broadest possible geographical scope for the law of international watercourses is to be preferred. As the International Law Association's Commentary notes: 'The drainage basin is an indivisible hydrologic unit which requires comprehensive consideration in order to effect maximum utilization and development of any portion of its waters.'[3] International codification and state practice reflect differing views on this question, however. Modern bilateral and regional treaties have tended to adopt the basin approach, because it is the most efficient means of achieving control of pollution and water utilization.[4] Examples of such arrangements are wide-

---

[1] See Lipper, in Garretson, *et al.* (eds.), *The Law of International Drainage Basins* (New York, 1967), 16; Lammers, *Pollution of International Watercourses* (The Hague, 1984), 17.
[2] Sette-Camara, 186 *Recueil des cours* (1984), 117, 130.
[3] ILA, Helsinki Rules, *Report of the 52nd Conference* (1966), 485; Teclaff, *The River Basin in History and Law* (The Hague, 1967).
[4] Kearney, II *Yearbook ILC* (1976), pt. 1, 184 ff.

spread in Africa[5] and the basin concept is also used in controlling toxic pollution of the Rhine and the Great Lakes.[6] It has been favoured by declarations of international conferences, notably the Stockholm Conference on the Human Environment[7] and the UN Water Conference held at Mar Del Plata in 1977,[8] and it forms the basis of codification undertaken by the Institut de Droit International[9] and of the International Law Association's Helsinki and Montreal Rules.[10] The ILA's definition of an international drainage basin is the most extensive: 'covering a geographical area extending over two or more states determined by the watershed limits of the system of waters, including surface and underground waters, flowing into a common terminus.'[11] Despite the obvious utility of a broadly comprehensive definition of a watercourse, and its clear endorsement in international policy, this remains a relatively recent approach only partially reflected in state practice.

Older treaties are more likely to follow the narrower definition found in the Final Act of the Congress of Vienna, which focused on international rivers separating or traversing the territory of two or more states and declared them open for navigation by all riparians.[12] Although inappropriately narrow for environmental purposes, this definition has remained influential.[13] Moreover, some treaties apply only to boundary waters. The 1909 Boundary Waters Treaty,[14] which still governs watercourse relations over a large part of the

---

[5] Examples include the 1972 Senegal River Basin Treaty, UN Doc. ST/ESA/141, *Treaties Concerning the Utilization of International Watercourses*, 16; 1987 Zambezi River System Agreement, 27 *ILM* (1988), 1109; 1963 Act Regarding Navigation and Economic Co-operation between States of the Niger Basin, Ruster and Simma, *International Protection of the Environment* (New York, 1977), xi. 5629; 1964 Convention and Statute Relating to the Development of the Chad Basin, Ruster and Simma, xi. 5633. See McCaffrey, *Third Report on International Watercourses, etc.*, UN Doc. A/CN.4/406 (1987), 18; Godana, *Africa's Shared Water Resources: Legal and Institutional Aspects of the Nile, Niger and Senegal River Systems* (London, 1985). The concept has also been applied to some rivers in South America: see 1978 Treaty for Amazonian Co-operation, 17 *ILM* (1978), 1045; 1969 Treaty on the River Plate Basin, 875 *UNTS*, No. 12550, on which see Trevers and Day, 30 *NRJ* (1990), 87.

[6] 1976 Convention on the Protection of the Rhine Against Chemical Pollution, 16 *ILM* (1977), 242; 1978 Great Lakes Water Quality Agreement, 30 UST 1383, TIAS 9257 amended 1983, TIAS 10798. See Utton and Teclaff, *Transboundary Resources Law* (Boulder, Colo., 1987), 27 ff.

[7] UNCHE, Action Plan for the Human Environment, UN Doc. A/Conf. 48/14/Rev. 1, Rec. 51.

[8] *Report of the UN Water Conference, Mar Del Plata*, 14–25 Mar. 1977. See generally II *Yearbook ILC* (1986), pt. 1, 325 ff.

[9] 49 *Ann. Inst. DDI* (1961), pt. II, 381; 58 *Ann. Inst. DDI* (1979), pt. II, 197; Salmon, ibid. 193–263.

[10] Helsinki Rules, *supra*, n. 3, and Montreal Rules, ILA *Report of the 60th Conference* (1982), 535 ff.

[11] Helsinki Rules, Article II.

[12] See *Report of the ILC*, II *Yearbook ILC* (1979), pt. 1, 153 f.; Utton and Teclaff, *Transboundary Resources Law*, 2.

[13] See *Territorial Jurisdiction of the International Commission of the River Oder Case*, PCIJ, Ser. A, No. 23 (1929), 27–9; Lammers, *Pollution*, 110–13.

[14] UN, *Legislative Texts and Treaty Provisions*, ST/LEG/SerB/12, 260; repr. 146 *Recueil des cours* (1975), 307. cf. 1960 Netherlands–FRG Frontier Treaty, Ruster and Simma, xi. 5588.

US–Canadian border, excludes tributary waters and rivers flowing across the boundary, although it does apply to transboundary pollution.[15]

Among some states, usually those enjoying an upstream position, there is resistance to the more extensive basin concept as a basis for environmental control.[16] For this reason, the International Law Commission, in its work on the non-navigational uses of international watercourses, has had to avoid reference to drainage basins. As special rapporteur Evensen reported in 1983:

> For several reasons, the concept of 'international drainage basin' met with opposition in the discussions both of the Commission and of the Sixth Committee of the General Assembly. Concern was expressed that 'international drainage basin' might imply a certain doctrinal approach to all watercourses regardless of their special characteristics and regardless of the wide variety of issues of special circumstances of each case. It was likewise feared that the 'basin' concept put too much emphasis on the land areas within the watershed, indicating that the physical land area of a basin might be governed by the rules of international water resources law.[17]

Subsequent draft articles have therefore referred only to 'international watercourses',[18] but have defined the term watercourse broadly, to mean 'a system of surface and underground waters constituting by virtue of their physical relationship a unitary whole and flowing into a common terminus'.[19]

Despite support for the drainage basin concept in modern treaty practice and the work of international codification bodies, the evidence of disagreement in the ILC suggests that it is premature to attribute customary status to this concept as a definition of the geographical scope of international water resources law.[20] With respect to pollution control, however, this conclusion may not greatly matter. As Lammers argues,[21] even where pollution obligations are placed only on a particular portion of an international watercourse, such as the boundary waters, it will still be necessary for states to control pollution of the wider drainage basin to the extent necessary to produce the desired result in boundary areas. In consequence, 'This means that for the question of the legal (in)admissibility of transfrontier water pollution, it makes little sense to distinguish between such concepts as 'international watercourse' or 'waters of an international drainage basin'.[22] Experience with the pollution of US–Canadian boundary waters[23] suggests that this conclusion may be optimistic, however.

[15] cf. Preliminary Article, and Article IV.
[16] Schwebel, II *Yearbook ILC* (1979), pt. 1, 153 ff.; Evensen, ibid. (1984), pt. 1, 104 f.; McCaffrey, ibid. (1986), pt. 1, 101, para. 16.
[17] Ibid. (1983), pt. 1, 167, para. 71.
[18] 1984 Draft Articles, ibid. (1984), pt. 1, 101; 1991 Draft Articles, *Report of the ILC to the Gen. Assembly*, UN Doc. A/46/10 (1991), 161.
[19] 1991 Draft Article 2. See also II *Yearbook ILC* (1986), pt. 2, 62, para. 236, and *Report of the ILC*, 154–60 where objections to the term 'watercourse system' are noted. Under the 1991 draft, a watercourse is 'international' if parts are situated in different states.
[20] Sette-Camara, 186 *Recueil des cours* (1984), 128. Some writers disagree, however. See Lipper, in Garretson, *et al.*, *International Drainage Basins*, 15 ff.
[21] Lammers, *Pollution*, 110–13.   [22] Ibid. 343.   [23] See *infra*, pp. 245–8.

(2) Water Resources: Principles of Allocation

One approach to the admissibility of watercourse pollution is to treat it as an aspect of the allocation of water resources. Before considering specific issues relating to pollution it is therefore necessary to establish the basis on which water resources will be allocated among those states with a claim to their use. Four theories are commonly advanced:[24] territorial sovereignty, territorial integrity, equitable utilization, and common management.

(a) Territorial Sovereignty

One view is that states enjoy absolute sovereignty over water within their territory and are free to do as they please with those waters, including extracting as much as necessary, or altering their quality, regardless of the effect this has on the use or supply of water in downstream or contiguous states. This theory is often known as the Harmon doctrine, after the United States Attorney-General who asserted the absolute right of the United States to divert the Rio Grande.[25] Modern commentators mostly dismiss the doctrine. Apart from its bias in favour of upstream states, it has little support in state practice and does not seem to represent International Law.[26] Even the United States quickly retreated from the full Harmon doctrine in treaties with Mexico[27] and Canada[28] which are more consistent with the principle of

[24] Colliard, in OECD, *Legal Aspects of Transfrontier Pollution* (Paris, 1977), 263; Teclaff and Utton (eds.), *International Environmental Law* (New York, 1974), 155; Lipper, in Garretson, *et al.*, *International Drainage Basins*, 15 ff; Dickstein, 12 *CJTL* (1973), 487; Bourne, 6 *UBCLR* (1971), 115; Cohen, 146 *Recueil des cours* (1975), 227.

[25] 'The fact that the Rio Grande lacks sufficient water to permit its use by the inhabitants of both countries does not entitle Mexico to impose restrictions on the United States which would hamper the development of the latter's territory or deprive its inhabitants of an advantage with which nature had endowed it and which is situated entirely within its territory. To admit such a principle would be completely contrary to the principle that the United States exercises full sovereignty over its national territory', 21 *Ops. Atty. Gen.* (1895), 274, 283.

[26] Teclaff and Utton, *International Environmental Law*, 156; Lipper, in Garretson, *et al.*, *International Drainage Basins*, 23; Lester, 57 *AJIL* (1963), 828, 847; Dickstein, 12 *CJTL* (1973), 490 ff.; Bourne, 3 *CYIL* (1965), 187, 294 ff.

[27] See 1906 Convention between the United States and Mexico concerning the Equitable Distribution of the Waters of the Rio Grande for Irrigation Purposes, 34 *Stat.* 2953; 1944 Treaty between the United States and Mexico Relating to the Utilization of the Waters of the Colorado, Tijuana and Rio Grande Rivers, 3 *UNTS* 314; 1973 Agreement on the Permanent and Definitive Solution of the International Problem of the Salinity of the Colorado River, 12 *ILM* (1973), 1105. See Brownell and Eaton, 69 *AJIL* (1975), 255; Arechaga, 159 *Recueil des cours* (1978), 188 ff. McCaffrey, II *Yearbook ILC* (1986), pt. 1, 105–9, concludes: 'viewed in the context of United States diplomatic and treaty practice, the 'Harmon Doctrine' is not, and probably never has been actually followed by the state that formulated it.'

[28] 1909 Boundary Waters Treaty, *supra*, n. 14; 1961 Treaty Relating to the Co-operative Development of the Water Resources of the Columbia River Basin, 542 *UNTS* 244. McCaffrey, II *Yearbook ILC* (1986), 108, observes that 'the reservation by each party in Article II [of the 1909 Treaty] of "exclusive jurisdiction and control" over successive rivers within its territory is far from being tantamount to an assertion of a right to use waters within its territory with no regard

equitable utilization. There are echoes of the doctrine in a few other trans-boundary river disputes. India at one time asserted 'full freedom ... to draw off such waters as it needed' from the Indus, but here again, the treaty which concluded this dispute is generally regarded as effecting an equitable apportionment of the waters.[29] The Harmon doctrine has never had much currency in Europe because of its fundamental inconsistency with the freedom of navigation which characterized major European rivers after 1815.[30]

(b) Territorial Integrity

Equally questionable is the obverse of the Harmon doctrine, the principle of absolute territorial integrity or riparian rights. This theory would give the lower riparian the right to a full flow of water of natural quality. Interference with the natural flow by the upstream state would thus require the consent of the lower riparian. In this form the doctrine appears devoid of more than limited support in state practice, jurisprudence, or the writings of commentators.[31] It is sometimes confused with the idea that states may acquire servitudes in the use of rivers, and with the principle that states may not use or permit the use of their territory in such a manner as to cause harm to other states.[32] But these are separate principles; neither of them necessarily benefits only downstream or contiguous states, nor can it safely be assumed that they confer rights amounting to absolute territorial integrity.

(c) Equitable Utilization

The most widely endorsed theory treats international watercourses as shared resources, subject to equitable utilization by riparian states.[33] This proposition requires some clarification, however. The view that international watercourses are 'shared resources' was initially adopted by the ILC, and enjoys some

---

whatsoever for resulting damage to the other country.' See generally, Zacklin and Caflisch, *The Legal Regime of International Rivers and Lakes* (The Hague, 1981), ch. 1; Cohen, 146 *Recueil des cours* (1975); Ross, 12 *NRJ* (1972), 242; Arechaga, 159 *Recueil des cours* (1978), 189 ff.

[29] McCaffrey, II *Yearbook ILC* (1986), pt. 1, 109 f. See 1960 Indus Waters Treaty, 419 *UNTS* 125.

[30] Cohen, 146 *Recueil des cours* (1975), ch. 1, contrasts European and N. American experience: transboundary navigation was less important in the latter case. Austria appears to have supported the doctrine, however: Bourne, 3 *CYIL* (1965), 205. On early navigation regimes for the Rhine and the Danube, see *supra*, Ch. 4 n. 128.

[31] Lipper, in Garretson, *et al.*, *International Drainage Basins*, 18; Bourne, 6 *UBCLR* (1971), 119.

[32] Colliard, in OECD, *Legal Aspects*, 265, uses the phrase 'absolute territorial integrity' in this way.

[33] McCaffrey, II *Yearbook ILC* (1986), pt. 1, 110–13; Lipper, in Garretson, *et al.*, *International Drainage Basins*, 41 ff.; Dickstein, 12 *CJTL* (1973), 492 ff.; Bourne, 6 *UBCLR* (1971), 120; Arechaga, 159 Recueil des cours (1978), 192 ff.

support,[34] but the concept itself has encountered significant opposition among states on account of its alleged novelty and uncertain legal implications. Specific reference to 'shared resources' was deleted from ILC draft articles in 1984,[35] in the belief that nothing of substance was thereby lost and that what mattered was the elaboration of obligations and rights attaching to watercourses which are in practice shared.[36] Among these obligations is the principle of equitable utilization.

Equitable utilization rests on a foundation of equality of rights, or shared sovereignty, and is not to be confused with equal division.[37] Instead, it will generally entail a balance of interests which accommodates the needs, and uses of each state. This basic principle enjoys substantial support in judicial decisions, state practice, and international codifications. In the *River Oder* case, the Permanent Court of International Justice had to consider the right of lower riparians to freedom of navigation in Polish waters upstream. Its main finding favoured a community of interest in navigation among all riparian states, based on equality of rights over the whole navigable course of the river.[38] Although confined to navigation, the principle on which this case is based supports a comparable community of interest in other uses of a watercourse.[39] It is implicitly followed in the *Lac Lanoux* arbitration, where the tribunal recognized that, in carrying out diversion works entirely within its own territory, France nevertheless had an obligation to consult Spain, the other riparian, and to safeguard her rights in the watercourse.[40] This does not mean that any use of an international watercourse affecting other states requires their consent, but it does indicate that the sovereignty of a state over rivers within its borders is qualified by a recognition of the equal and correlative rights of other states.

Settlements of river disputes in North America and the Indian Sub-Continent by states which had previously asserted a different position tend to confirm this conclusion.[41] These and other examples of state practice listed in

---

[34] *Report of the Executive Director of UNEP*, UNEP/GC/44, para. 86; *Lac Lanoux* arbitration, 24 *ILR* (1957), 119, which refers to 'sharing of the use of international rivers'; Draft Articles on Int. Watercourses, Article 5, II *Yearbook ILC* (1980), pt. 2, 120–36; Lammers, *Pollution*, 335.

[35] Evensen, II *Yearbook ILC* (1984), pt. 1, 110, para. 48.

[36] McCaffrey, ibid. (1986), pt. 1, 103, para. 74: 'It therefore appears that, while the reformulation of article 6 has resulted in the loss of a new and developing concept [shared natural resources], it has produced greater legal certainty, and, when viewed in connection with other draft articles, has not resulted in the elimination of any fundamental principles from the draft as a whole.'

[37] Lipper, in Garretson, *et al.*, *International Drainage Basins*, 44 f.; Arechaga, 159 *Recueil des cours* (1978), 192; McCaffrey, II *Yearbook ILC* (1986), pt. 1, 103 f.

[38] *Territorial Jurisdiction of the International Commission of the River Oder* Case, *PCIJ*, Ser. A, No. 23 (1929). See also *Diversion of Water from the Meuse* Case, *PCIJ*, Ser. A/B, No. 70 (1937).

[39] Arechaga, 159 *Recueil des cours* (1978), 193 ff.; Lipper, in Garretson, *et al.*, *International Drainage Basins*, 41 ff.; Lammers, *Pollution of International Watercourses*, 507; McCaffrey, II *Yearbook ILC* (1986), pt. 1, 114.

[40] 24 *ILR* (1957), 101; Lester, 57 *AJIL* (1963). See *infra*, pp. 234–41. 2(5).

[41] *Supra*, n. 27–9.

the work of the International Law Commission have persuaded successive rapporteurs to endorse equitable utilization as an established principle of international law.[42] This view has generally been supported by states.[43] Article 5 of the 1991 draft articles thus provides:

1. Watercourse states shall in their respective territories utilise an international watercourse in an equitable and reasonable manner. In particular, an international watercourse shall be used and developed by watercourse states with a view to attaining optimal utilization thereof and benefits therefrom consistent with adequate protection of the international watercourse.[44]

The same principle has also been adopted in other codifications, such as the ILA's Helsinki Rules, which give states a 'reasonable and equitable share in the beneficial uses of the waters'.[45]

What constitutes 'reasonable and equitable' utilization is not capable of precise determination. As in other contexts, whether the delimitation of continental shelves according to equitable principles, or the allocation and regulation of shared fishing stocks, the issue turns on a balancing of relevant factors and must be responsive to the circumstances of individual cases.[46]

In its draft articles, the ILC has identified factors relevant to determining equitable and reasonable utilization.[47] These include:

(a) geographic, hydrographic, hydrological, climatic, ecological, and other factors of a natural character;
(b) the social and economic needs of the watercourse states concerned;
(c) the effects of the use or uses of the watercourse in one watercourse state on other watercourse states;
(d) existing and potential uses of the international watercourse;

---

[42] McCaffrey, II *Yearbook ILC* (1986), pt. 1, 103–5, 110 ff.; Schwebel, ibid. (1982), pt. 1, 75 ff.

[43] *Report of the ILC to the Gen. Assembly* (1987), UN Doc. A/42/10, p. 70; See also Evensen, II *Yearbook ILC* (1984), pt. 1, 110; Schwebel, ibid. (1982), pt. 1, 75. See also Recommendation 51 of the UN Conference on the Human Environment which calls on states to 'consider' when 'appropriate' the principle that 'the net benefits of hydrologic regions common to more than one national jurisdiction are to be shared equitably by the nations affected.'

[44] *Report of the ILC to the Gen. Assembly*, UN Doc. A/46/10 (1991), 161.

[45] 1966 Helsinki Rules, Article IV. The Commentary describes equitable utilization as 'the key principle of international law in this area'. See also Institute of International Law, Salzburg Session, 1961, Resolution on the Utilization of Non-maritime International Waters, Article 3: 'If states are in disagreement over the scope of their rights of utilization, settlement will take place on the basis of equity, taking particular account of their respective needs, as well as of other pertinent circumstances.'

[46] *North Sea Continental Shelf Case, ICJ Rep.* (1969), 50, para. 93. See also *Tunisia–Libya Continental Shelf Case*, ibid. (1982), 18; *Malta–Libya Continental Shelf Case*, ibid. (1985), 13; *Gulf of Maine Case*, ibid. (1984), 246; *Icelandic Fisheries Cases*, ibid. (1974), 3; and 1982 UNCLOS, Articles 69, 70, 87, and *supra*, pp. 126–7.

[47] Draft Article 6, *supra*, n. 44. cf. ILA Helsinki Rules (1966), Article V, and *Report of the African–Asian Legal Consultative Committee*, summarized in II *Yearbook ILC* (1982), pt. 1, 87, paras. 94–8.

(e) conservation, protection, development, and economy of use of the water resources of the watercourse and the costs of measures taken to that effect;

(f) the availability of alternatives, of corresponding value, to a particular planned or existing use.

This list is not meant to be exhaustive; consideration must be given to all the interests likely to be affected by the proposed use of the watercourse.[48] More importantly, a listing of factors says nothing about the priority or weight given to each one, or how conflicts are to be reconciled. These remain matters for judgment in individual cases,[49] and for this reason, uncertainty in application is the main difficulty affecting the principle of reasonable and equitable use. Unlike the delimitation of continental shelves, third-party settlement has not been widely used in river disputes and comparable judicial elaboration is lacking. The better solution given the greater complexity of the balancing process involved and the likelihood that the needs of states may change, is probably some form of common management designed to achieve equitable and optimum use of the watercourse system.[50] Thus the principle of equitable utilization leads naturally to the fourth theory on which the allocation of water resources has been based, that of common management.

(d) Common Management

Common management is the logical combination of the idea that watercourse basins are most efficiently managed as an integrated whole, and the need to find effective institutional machinery to secure equitable utilization and development.[51] It represents a community of interest approach which goes beyond the allocation of equitable rights, however,[52] and opens up the possibility of integrated development and international regulation of the watercourse environment. This important trend has already been referred to in part 1 of this chapter. As we have seen, modern state practice prefers the basin or hydrologic system approach to watercourse management.[53] This is usually accompanied by the creation of international institutions in which all riparian states collaborate in formulating and implementing policies for the development and use of a watercourse. Examples of such arrangements are the Lake

---

[48] Lac Lanoux arbitration, 138 f., 'Account must be taken of all interests, of whatsoever nature, which are liable to be affected by the works undertaken, even if they do not correspond to a right'; see also ILA 1966 Helsinki Rules, Commentary, 488.

[49] Report of the ILC to the Gen. Assembly (1987), 83; ILA, 1966 Helsinki Rules, Commentary, 489.

[50] Schwebel, II Yearbook ILC (1982), pt. 1, 76, para. 70; McCaffrey, ibid. (1986), pt. 1, 132, para. 177.

[51] Schwebel, ibid. (1982), pt. 1, p. 76, para. 70.

[52] Lipper, in Garretson, et al., International Drainage Basins, 38.

[53] Supra, n. 4 and 5.

Chad Basin Commission,[54] the River Niger Commission,[55] the Permanent Joint Technical Commission for Nile Waters,[56] the Zambezi Intergovernmental Monitoring and Co-ordinating Committee,[57] the Intergovernmental Co-ordinating Committee of the River Plate Basin,[58] and the Amazonian Co-operation Council.[59] Such institutions are not confined to basin treaties, however; the Danube Commission[60] and the US–Canadian International Joint Commission[61] are two examples of common management applied to a more limited watercourse area.

These institutions vary in their detailed form and the scope of their responsibilities. Some are not involved in environmental management;[62] in other cases, such as the International Commission for the Protection of the Rhine,[63] or the Moselle Commission,[64] this is their only purpose. As in the case of fisheries or wildlife conservation commissions their success is dependent on the degree of co-operation they can engender.[65]

Common management institutions have become the basis for environmental regulation of a small number of watercourses.[66] Progressive development of this approach has been widely endorsed by international political institutions[67] and adopted by codification bodies. Both the Stockholm Declaration on the Human Environment[68] and the UN Water Conference Mar Del Plata Action

---

[54] Convention and Statute Relating to the Development of the Chad Basin, 1964, *supra*, n. 5.

[55] Act regarding Navigation and Economic Co-operation between the States of the Niger Basin, 1963, *supra*, n. 5.

[56] Agreement Between the UAR and the Republic of the Sudan for the Full Utilization of Nile Waters, 1959, and Protocol Establishing Permanent Joint Technical Committee, 1960, in UN, *Legislative Texts and Treaty Provisions Concerning the Utilization of International Rivers for Purposes Other than Navigation*, UN Doc. ST/LEG/Ser.B/12, 143 ff.

[57] Agreement on the Action Plan for the Environmentally Sound Management of the Common Zambezi River System, *supra*, n. 5. See *infra*, p. 248.

[58] Treaty on the River Plate Basin, 1969, *supra*, n. 5; Treaty on the River Plate and its Maritime Limits, 1973, 13 *ILM* (1973), 251.

[59] Treaty for Amazonian Co-operation, 1978, *supra*, n. 5.

[60] Convention Regarding the Regime of Navigation on the Danube, 1948, 33 *UNTS* 196.

[61] Boundary Waters Treaty, 1909, *supra*, n. 14.

[62] e.g. the 1948 Danube Commission. The Commission has, however, regulated pollution from ships using the Danube: see II *Yearbook ILC* (1974), pt. 2, 351 f. On East European practice, see Bruhacs, 54 *Yearbook of the AAA* (1984), 84, and see now the 1990 Agreement Concerning Co-operation on Management of Water Resources of the Danube Basin, OJ/EEC No. L/90, 20.

[63] *Infra*, pp. 243–5.

[64] 1961 Protocol Concerning the Constitution of an International Commission for the Protection of the Moselle Against Pollution, Ruster and Simma, ii. 5618.

[65] See *supra*, pp. 160–79.

[66] See *infra*, pp. 241–8.

[67] UN Committee on Natural Resources, UN Doc. E/C.7/2 Add. 6, 1–7; Economic Commission for Europe, Committee on Water Problems 1971, UN Doc. E/ECE/Water/9, annex II; Council of Europe Rec. 436 (1965).

[68] 1972 Stockholm Action Plan for the Human Environment, UN Doc. A/Conf. 48/14/Rev. 1, Rec. 51.

Plan[69] in 1977 call on states to establish such commissions where appropriate for co-ordinated development, including environmental protection. This policy is reflected in the draft articles produced by the Institute of International Law[70] and by the ILC. The latter's 1984 draft articles[71] indicate some of the functions these international commissions are intended to serve:

(a) to collect, verify, and disseminate information and data concerning utilization, protection, and conservation of the international watercourse;
(b) to propose and institute investigations and research concerning utilization, protection, and control;
(c) to monitor the international watercourse on a continuous basis;
(d) to recommend to watercourse states measures and procedures necessary for the optimum utilization and the effective protection and control of the watercourse;
(e) to serve as a forum for consultations, negotiations, and other procedures for peaceful settlement entrusted to such commissions by watercourse states;
(f) to propose and operate control and warning systems with regard to pollution, other environmental effects of water uses, natural hazards, or other hazards which may cause damage or harm to the rights or interests of watercourse states.[72]

Although co-operation in joint management institutions is not obligatory, the foregoing declarations recognize that it is a necessary and desirable principle, aptly described by the ILC's rapporteur as a 'principle of progressive international law'.[73] Examples of state practice in the functioning of such institutions are considered further below.[74]

2. OBLIGATIONS TO PROTECT WATERCOURSE ENVIRONMENTS

(1) Pollution and Permissible Uses of Watercourses

River pollution generally originates from industrial effluent, agricultural run-off, or domestic sewage discharge. Apart from specific treaty regimes, there is little contemporary support for the view that such polluting uses are *per se* impermissible.[75] The evidence of state practice is inconsistent, but few

---

[69] *Report of the UN Water Conference, Mar del Plata*, 14–25 Mar. 1977. See also, UN, *Experience in the Development and Management of International River and Lake Basins*, 1981.
[70] 1961 Session, Resolution on Non-Maritime International Waters, Article 9; 1979 Session, Resolution on the Pollution of Rivers and Lakes, Article 7(G).
[71] II *Yearbook ILC* (1984), pt. 1, 112–16.
[72] Ibid. Article 15.   [73] Ibid. 112, para. 59.   [74] See *infra*, pp. 241–8.
[75] Salmon, 58 *Ann. Inst. DDI* (1979), 193–9; Sette Camara, 186 *Recueil des cours* (1984), 117, 163.

modern treaties endorse an absolute prohibition on detrimental alteration of water quality.[76] Instead, the modern trend is to require states to regulate and control river pollution, prohibiting only certain forms of pollutant discharge, and distinguishing between new and existing sources.[77]

Early European practice did frequently prohibit industrial or agricultural pollution harmful to river fisheries or domestic use.[78] Only as the balance of demands on river utilization changed did this strict approach give way to a more varied pattern. For major industrial rivers, such as the Rhine, the later treaties show clearly a greater tolerance of polluting uses.[79]

North American practice followed a similar trend. A prohibition of pollution of boundary waters was not strictly enforced.[80] Despite the explicit priority given to domestic and sanitary uses by the 1909 Boundary Waters Treaty, industrial and agricultural pollution of the Great Lakes became established, until a new regulatory regime was agreed in 1972.[81] Until 1973 the United States maintained that it was not required to deliver to Mexico water of

---

[76] Colliard, in OECD, *Legal Aspects of Transfrontier Pollution*; Lammers, *Pollution of International Watercourses*, 122 ff.; McCaffrey, *4th Report on International Watercourses* (1988), UN Doc. A/CN. 4/412/Add. 1, 1–18. Treaties which do absolutely prohibit pollution include the 1956 Czechoslovakia–USSR Frontier Agreement, Article 14; 1961 Polish–USSR Frontier Treaty, Article 19; 1964 Finland–USSR Agreement Concerning Frontier Watercourses, Article 4. See also 1971 Declaration on Water Resources (Argentina–Uruguay); 1971 Act of Santiago Covering Hydrologic Basins (Argentina–Chile).

[77] See *infra*, pp. 230–2. Few watercourse treaties define the term pollution, however. The 1909 Boundary Waters Treaty and the 1963 Agreement Concerning the International Commission for the Protection of the Rhine Against Pollution use the term but do not define it. Differing definitions are offered by the ILA's 1966 Helsinki Rules, Article 9, the IDI's 1979 Resolution on the Pollution of Rivers and Lakes, Article 1, and the ILC's 1991 Draft Articles, Article 21(1). See also 1978 Great Lakes Water Quality Agreement Article 1(J).

[78] 1869 Convention Between the Grand Duchy of Baden and Switzerland Concerning Fishing in the Rhine, Ruster and Simma, ix. 4695; 1887 Convention Establishing Uniform Provisions on Fishing in the Rhine and its Tributaries, Article 10, ibid. 4730; 1893 Convention Decreeing Uniform Regulations for Fishing in Lake Constance, Article 12, ibid. x. 4759; 1923 Agreement between Italy and Austria Concerning Economic Relations in Border Regions, Article 14, ibid. xi. 5504; 1922 Provisions Relating to the Belgian–German Frontier, Part III, Article 2, ibid. 5495; 1882 Convention between Italy and Switzerland Concerning Fishing in Frontier Waters, ibid. 5413; 1906 Convention between Switzerland and Italy Establishing Uniform Regulations Concerning Fishing in Border Waterways, Article 12, ibid. 5440; for more recent examples, see 1957 Agreement Concerning Fishing in Frontier Waters (Yugoslavia–Hungary), Article 5, ibid. ix. 4572; 1971 Frontier Rivers Agreement (Finland–Sweden), Ch. 1, Articles 3, 4, Ch. 6, Article 1, ibid. x. 5092. See generally Colliard, in OECD, *Legal Aspects of Transfrontier Pollution*.

[79] 1892 Convention between Luxemburg and Prussia Regulating Fisheries in Boundary Waters, para. 11, Ruster and Simma, ix. 4753; 1922 Agreement Relating to Frontier Watercourses, Article 45 (Denmark-Germany), ibid. 5473; 1958 Convention Concerning Fishing in the Waters of the Danube, Article 7, UN, *Legislative Texts*, *supra*, n. 14, 427; 1912 Agreement on the Exploitation of Border Rivers for Industrial Purposes (Spain–Portugal), Ruster and Simma, xi, 5449; 1956 Convention on the Regulation of the Upper Rhine (France–FRG) UN, *Legislative Texts*, 660.

[80] 1909 US–Canada Boundary Waters Treaty, Article IV. See Zacklin and Caflisch, *International Rivers and Lakes*, ch. 1; Bourne, 28 *NILR* (1981), 188; Ross, 12 *NRJ* (1972).

[81] See *infra*, pp. 245–8.

any particular quality from the Colorado River, provided its polluting use of the river for irrigation was reasonable.[82] Nor do treaties elsewhere typically prohibit polluting uses. The 1960 Indus River Treaty limited industrial use and required measures to prevent undue pollution affecting other interests, but the implication that polluting uses are entitled to consideration consistent with equitable utilization is clear.[83]

State practice regarding land-based sources of pollution in general does point to the prohibition of discharges of certain toxic substances, especially if these are persistent or highly radioactive.[84] But so long as no such substances are involved, the main conclusion must be that most polluting or environmentally harmful uses of international rivers are wrongful only if they infringe the rights of other states.[85] States do, however, have a number of claims on the quality of a watercourse. These include the right to equitable utilization, to protection from sources of serious harm, and to procedural rights of information exchange, consultation, and negotiation.[86]

Moreover, these rights must now be set in the context of the emergence of an obligation to regulate and control sources of river pollution, in particular where these contribute to pollution of the marine environment.[87] This approach to pollution control is important because it moves the issue away from exclusive concentration on the rights of riparians and acknowledges the broader international significance of watercourse environments; it places more emphasis on environmental protection, and illustrates in particular how equitable utilization, the most widely accepted principle of watercourse law, is perhaps the least useful for the development of environmental law.

(2) Pollution and Equitable Utilization

From the perspective of equitable utilization, problems of water quality and pollution are contingent on a balance of interests between the riparians involved. Pollution will be impermissible if it deprives other states of their

---

[82] See 1944 Colorado River Treaty, UN, *Legislative Texts*, 236 and cf. 1973 Agreement on Permanent and Definitive Solution of the International Problem of the Salinity of the Colorado River, 12 *ILM* (1973), 1105; Brownell and Eaton, 69 *AJIL* (1975), 255.

[83] Article 4. See *supra*, n. 29.

[84] See Ch. 8.

[85] See generally, Salmon, 58 *Ann. Inst. DDI* (1979), 193–263; Lester, 57 *AJIL* (1963); Dickstein, 12 *CJTL* (1973); Bourne, 6 *UBCLR* (1971); Sette Camara, 186 *Recueil des cours* (1984); Lammers, *Pollution of International Watercourses*; Zacklin and Caflisch, *International Rivers and Lakes*, 331.

[86] Other approaches, such as abuse of rights or good neighbourliness are sometimes referred to in the literature but there is no evidence that these reflect international practice or afford additional bases for resolving pollution disputes: Lester, 57 *AJIL* (1963), 833 ff.; Sette Camara, 186 *Recueil des cours* (1984), 164 ff., and see generally, *supra*, pp. 124–6.

[87] See Ch. 8.

claim to equitable utilization.[88] The strongest view is that this equitable approach takes precedence over other possible principles, notably the obligation to prevent serious harm to other states. Used in this sense, the threshold of wrongful injury will turn not on the seriousness of the injury alone but on its reasonableness judged against other equitable factors. Thus the ILC's rapporteur noted: 'an equitable use by one state could cause "appreciable" or "significant harm" to another state using the same watercourse, yet not entail a legal "injury" or be otherwise wrongful.'[89]

Although this approach may have merit in other contexts, such as the diversion of waters, the evidence for applying it to pollution or environmental injury is not extensive. The *Lac Lanoux* case was not concerned with pollution, except as a possible violation of Spain's rights to share in the watercourse, and it held only that diversion of the waters which caused no such injury to Spain and which was accompanied by a full opportunity for consultation did not require her consent or violate any international obligation.[90] Handl's argument that the case confirms recourse to a balancing of interests as a means of determining responsibility for pollution injury rests on slender inference from Spanish interpretation of the relevant treaty.[91] Indeed, by accepting that 'only a limited amount of damage' might be caused to other states, Spain's argument rather points in the opposite direction.[92] Reliance on *Trail Smelter*[93] to support a balance of interests is similarly unconvincing, because this interpretation confuses responsibility for harm with the availability of injunctive relief.[94] This factor also makes analogous decisions of federal courts questionable precedents on the role of equity in water pollution cases.[95] On the contrary, the US decisions relied on in *Trail Smelter*, and the *Trail Smelter* case itself, insist that states have no right to cause serious injury by pollution, not that they have no right to cause inequitable or unreasonable injury.[96]

---

[88] Handl, 13 *CYIL* (1975), 156; Lipper, in Garretson, *et al.*, *International Drainage Basins*, 45 ff.; Lester, 57 *AJIL* (1963), 840; Dickstein, 12 *CJTL* (1973), 492 ff.; Teclaff and Utton, *International Environmental Law*; *Report of the ILC to the Gen. Assembly* (1987), UN Doc. A/42/10, at 54 ff.

[89] McCaffrey, II *Yearbook ILC* (1986), pt. 1, 133 ff.; see also Schwebel, ibid. (1982), pt. 1, 103, draft Article 8(1): 'The right of a system state to use the water resources of an international watercourse system is limited by the duty not to cause appreciable harm to the interests of another system state, except as may be allowable under a determination for equitable participation for the international watercourse system involved'; and p. 145, draft Article 10(3): 'Consistent with [Articles 6, 7, 8] . . . a system state is under a duty to maintain pollution of shared water resources at levels sufficiently low that no appreciable harm is caused to any system state . . .'. See Handl, 13 *CYIL* (1975), 180.

[90] 24 *ILR* (1957), 101, 111–12, 123–4. See Lester, 57 *AJIL* (1963), 838 ff.

[91] Handl, 13 *CYIL* (1975), 180 f. See also Dickstein, 12 *CJTL* (1973), 494 f. cf. Handl, 26 *NRJ* (1986), 405, 421 f., however.

[92] At 124.

[93] 33 *AJIL* (1939), 184 and 35 *AJIL* (1941), 684.

[94] But cf. Dickstein, 12 *CJTL* (1973), 493 ff.

[95] Lammers, *Pollution of International Watercourses*, 486 ff. See also *infra*, n. 120.

[96] Handl, 26 *NRJ* (1986), 421 f.

Among international codifications, only the International Law Association's Helsinki Rules explicitly require states to prevent pollution injury 'consistent with the principle of equitable utilization'.[97] This provision purports to rely mainly on *Trail Smelter* and other authorities considered here; not surprisingly it has been strongly criticized.[98] In contrast, the International Law Commission has moved away from a similar position initially adopted by rapporteurs Schwebel and McCaffrey.[99] Instead, although its draft articles do recognize that protection and conservation of the watercourse are relevant factors in determining equitable utilization, it has chosen not to make the obligation to prevent serious harm or pollution injury to other states conditional on equitable balancing.[100] Indeed, it has now favoured the opposite view, that: 'A watercourse state's right to utilise an international watercourse in an equitable and reasonable manner finds its limit in the duty of that state not to cause appreciable harm to other watercourse states.'[101]

This appears the more realistic conclusion, consistent with practice in other areas, such as pollution of the marine environment. What it implies is that equitable utilization may be relied on to determine the permissibility of pollution injury falling below the threshold of serious or significant harm, but not to excuse injury above that threshold. Such injury will itself be inequitable.[102]

There remains the possibility that a polluting use not causing serious harm to other states may nevertheless be inequitable. This determination does involve a balance of interests among competing riparians. The sort of factors to be taken into account in carrying out this balancing process were noted earlier.[103] Two points are particularly important to pollution and environmental issues. Where potential uses conflict, such as industrial waste disposal and fishing, no priority can be assumed. Some treaties do establish priorities, but there is no settled practice and each river must be considered individ-

---

[97] loc. cit., *supra*, n. 3, Article 10(1). The Commentary notes, at 499: 'the international duty stated in this Article regarding abatement or the taking of reasonable measures is not an absolute one. This duty, therefore, does not apply to a state whose use of the waters is consistent with the equitable utilization of the drainage basin.' See Handl, 13 *CYIL* (1975), 183 ff.; Bourne, 6 *UBCLR* (1971), 125 ff. See also ILA Montreal Rules on Transfrontier Pollution, 1982, Article 3(1); and cf. ILA Montreal Rules on Water Pollution in an International Drainage Basin, 1982, Article 1, and the 1973 Draft Declaration of the Asian–African Legal Consultative Committee, II *Yearbook ILC* (1974), pt. 2, 338.

[98] Dickstein, 12 *CJTL* (1973), 495 ff.; Handl, 26 *NRJ* (1986), 421 ff.

[99] *Supra*, n. 89. See Handl, 13 *CYIL* (1975), 425 ff. Rapporteur Evensen initiated this change with his draft Article 9, II *Yearbook ILC* (1983), pt. 1, 172.

[100] Draft Articles 5, 7, 21(2), *supra*, n. 44. For the text of Article 21(2), see *infra*, n. 115. cf. also the Resolution of the IDI of 1979 on Pollution of Rivers and Lakes and International Law, Article II, and UNEP's 1978 Principles of Conduct Relating to National Resources Shared by Two or More States, UNEP/IG.12/2, Article 3, *supra*, pp. 114–7.

[101] *Report of the ILC to Gen. Assembly* (1988), UN Doc. A/43/10 at 84. cf. McCaffrey, II *Yearbook ILC* (1986).

[102] Handl, 13 *CYIL* (1975), 421–7; *Report of the ILC to Gen. Assembly* (1988), 83 f.

[103] See *supra*, pp. 219–22.

ually.[104] The ILA's Helsinki Rules reflect this point by providing that no category of user has inherent preference over any others.[105] Thus protection of the river environment and its living resources must compete with other claims. Secondly, there is no automatic preference for established uses. An inflexible rule protecting such uses would in effect allow the creation of servitudes. These have not generally found favour with states.[106] Instead, commentators and the views of codification bodies suggest that an equitable balance of interests may in an appropriately strong case allow for the displacement or limitation of earlier established uses. At most these earlier uses enjoy a weighty claim to qualified preference.[107] European and North America practice referred to earlier seems consistent with this conclusion, which the *Lac Lanoux* case implicitly supports.[108]

Equitable utilization is useful as a means of introducing environmental factors into the allocation of shared watercourse resources, but as a basis for comprehensive environmental protection of those watercourses it is a principle of only modest utility. Not only is it unpredictable in application, through its stress on the individuality of each river and the multiplicity of relevant factors,[109] but it tends to neglect the broader environmental context of rivers as part of a hydrologic cycle affecting the health and quality of the oceans.[110] Moreover, the common regional standards of water quality necessary in that context are less likely to find a place in equitable arrangements balancing only the needs of riparians.[111]

As we have seen, equitable utilization is generally workable on a multilateral basis only if supported by appropriate institutions and co-ordinated policies. Thus, only as part of the trend to common management and international regulation of transboundary watercourses does it have a more convincing role in resolving environmental disputes.[112]

---

[104] See e.g. 1909 Boundary Waters Treaty, *supra*, n. 14, Article VIII (US–Canada); 1960 Indus Waters Treaty, *supra*, n. 29, Articles 3, 4 (India–Pakistan); 1976 Convention on the Protection of the Rhine Against Chemical Pollution, *supra*, n. 6, Article 1.

[105] Article VI. See also Lipper, in Garretson, *et al.*, *International Drainage Basins*, 60 ff.

[106] See Lester, 57 *AJIL* (1963), 834 ff.: 'The concept of international servitudes is thus of negative value, since its characteristics illustrate the irrelevance of municipal law notions of property and permanence to the problem of international river pollution.'

[107] Lipper, in Garretson, *et al.*, *International Drainage Basins*, 50–8; 1966 ILA Helsinki Rules, *supra*, n. 3, Articles V(d), VII, VIII, and commentary at 493.

[108] Bourne, 3 *CYIL* (1965), 187, 234–53.

[109] Lipper, in Garretson, *et al.*, *International Drainage Basins*, 66; Handl, 13 *CYIL* (1975), 189 f.

[110] See Ch. 8.

[111] Boyle, 14 *Marine Policy* (1990), 151; Handl, 13 *CYIL* (1975), 191 f. Note also his observation that in a bilateral context, 'it is entirely conceivable that ecological factors, to the extent they are of actual or potential concern to other riparian states, might after all be insufficiently taken into account or altogether disregarded in a solution that primarily promotes the interests—and at that perhaps those of a socio-economic nature at the cost of ecological ones—of the directly involved states.'

[112] Lester, 57 *AJIL* (1963), 84 f.; Dickstein, 12 *CJTL* (1973), 498 f.; Bourne, 6 *UBCLR* (1971), 136; Teclaff and Utton, *International Environmental Law*.

(3) Customary Obligations to Prevent Harm to Other States

The proposition that states are under a customary obligation to prevent serious harm to others through their use of an international watercourse is not itself controversial. Article 7 of the International Law Commission's draft articles states the general principle,[113] which successive rapporteurs and the Commission have regarded as a codification of established customary law for all forms of damage to other states.[114] The general principle clearly includes pollution or environmental damage, as Article 21(2) goes on to provide:

Watercourse states shall, individual or jointly, prevent, reduce and control pollution of an international watercourse that may cause appreciable harm to other watercourse states or to their environment, including harm to human health or safety, to the use of the waters for any beneficial purpose or to the living resources of the watercourse . . .[115]

This provision is based on Article 194 of the 1982 UNCLOS and other precedents considered in Chapter 3 and is supported by international codifications, and by numerous writers,[116] although the number of watercourse treaties which expressly or implicitly incorporate such an obligation is not large.[117] But the *Trail Smelter* arbitration,[118] the *Lac Lanoux* arbitration,[119] decisions of some national courts,[120] and a number of international declara-

---

[113] *Supra*, n. 44. See also 1978 UNEP Principles of Conduct Relating to Natural Resources Shared by Two or More states, *supra*, n. 100, Article 3, and see generally, *supra*, Ch. 3.

[114] Schwebel, II *Yearbook ILC* (1982), pt. 1, 91, para. 111; Evensen, ibid. (1983) pt. 1, 172; McCaffrey, ibid. (1986), pt. 1, 133; *Report of the ILC to the Gen. Assembly*, UN Doc. A/43/10 (1988), 88 ff.

[115] For commentary, see *Report of the ILC to the Gen. Assembly* (1990), UN Doc. A/45/10 at 159. For earlier versions, see Evensen, *2nd Report*, I *Yearbook ILC* (1984), pt. 1, 118–20, Articles 20–3; Schwebel, *3rd Report*, II *Yearbook* (1982), pt. 1, 144, Article 10; McCaffrey, *Report of the ILC to the Gen. Assembly* (1988), UN Doc. A/43/10, 57, Article 16(2).

[116] Commentary, (1990) UN Doc. A/45/10, 159 ff., and see ILA, 1966 Helsinki Rules, Article X, and commentary, *1966 Report*, 497 f.; Lammers, *Pollution of International Watercourses*, 123, 342; Zacklin and Caflisch, *International Rivers and Lakes*, 336; Salmon, 58 *Ann. Inst. DDI*, 209; Sette-Camara, 186 *Recueil des cours* (1984), 165, and see the survey of opinions by Schwebel, *3rd Report*, II *Yearbook* (1982), 92 ff.

[117] See e.g. 1909 Boundary Waters Treaty (US–Canada), Articles II, IV; 1960 Indus Waters Treaty (India–Pakistan), Article 4; 1922 Agreement Relating to Frontier Watercourses (Germany–Denmark); 1960 Convention on the Protection of Lake Constance Against Pollution; 1950 Treaty Concerning the Regime of the Soviet Hungarian Frontier, Article 17; 1960 Treaty concerning the Course of the Common Frontier (Germany–Netherlands), Article 58; 1976 Convention on the Protection of the Rhine Against Chemical Pollution; 1990 Agreement Concerning Co-operation on Management of Water Resources of the Danube Basin (EEC–Austria), OJ No. L/90/20, Article 3. See also ECE draft Convention on the Protection and Use of Transboundary Watercourses and International Lakes, ENVWA/WP.3/R.19/Rev. 1 (1991).

[118] See Ch. 3.

[119] 24 *ILR* (1957), 101. See text at n. 90.

[120] See *Trail Smelter* arbitration, 35 *AJIL* (1941), 686, 714–17; *Missouri* v. *Illinois*, 200 US 496 (1906); *New York* v. *New Jersey*, 256 US 296 (1921); *North Dakota* v. *Minnesota*, 263 US 365

tions[121] provide further confirmation of the Commission's view that Article 21(2)'s antecedents are well grounded in state practice.[122]

As we saw earlier, however, views differ on whether the obligation not to cause harm represents the limit of equitable utilization of a watercourse, or is itself subject to equitable balancing involving other factors. Thus despite its general acceptability, the status of this obligation as an independent principle remains unsettled.[123] Moreover, it encounters in this context the same difficulties of interpretation as elsewhere, notably that it is uncertain whether the obligation is one of due diligence in preventing harm, or whether the state must meet a stricter standard.[124] Nor is it certain what threshold of harm determines the wrongfulness of any injury to other states.[125] International claims concerning watercourse damage, such as the *Gut Dam* arbitration, do not permit useful inferences on these questions.[126] The work of the ILC has provided some clarification however.

One ILC rapporteur, McCaffrey, has dealt with the choice between a standard of due diligence and more stringent obligations of pollution prevention in international watercourses. Although the latter interpretation is implicit in the view of some members of the Commission who have continued to favour a regime of strict liability for watercourse pollution, the rapporteur could find little or no evidence of state practice recognizing strict liability for damage which was non-accidental or did not result from a dangerous activity.[127] In his view, this indicated that the standard required of the state was generally one of due diligence, implicit in the *Trail Smelter* arbitration and supported by state practice. This standard afforded the appropriate flexibility and allowed for adaption to different situations, including the level of development of the state concerned. Moreover, to minimize any problems of proof,

---

(1923). See Lammers, *Pollution of International Watercourses*, 486. Many commentators are critical or cautious of the use of federal case law in this context: see Handl, 13 *CYIL* (1975), 182 ff.; Rubin, 50 *Oregon LR* (1971), 259, 266 ff.; Lester, 57 *AJIL* (1963), 844–7. The role of equity in these cases is another uncertain factor: see *supra*, n. 95. In *Handelswerkerij Bier* v. *Mines de Potasse d'Alsace* (1979) *Nederlandse Jurisprudentie*, No. 113, 313–20 a Dutch Court, relying on *Trail Smelter*, applied the principle *sic utere tuo*, etc., as a principle of international law in determining the liability of a French undertaking for river pollution damage in the Netherlands, but this was overturned on appeal: see *supra*, Ch. 5 n. 73.

[121] 1971 Act of Asuncion on the Use of International Rivers, Resolution No. 25, para. 2; 1971 Act of Santiago Concerning Hydrologic Basins, para. 4; African–Asian Legal Consultative Committee, Draft Declaration on the Law of International Rivers, 1973, paras. IV, VIII.

[122] *Report of the ILC to the Gen. Assembly* (1988), UN Doc. A/43/10, at 60, para. 148 (draft Article 16(2)).

[123] See *supra*, pp. 226–9.

[124] See Ch. 3.

[125] See Ch. 3.

[126] *Gut Dam* arbitration, *Settlement of Claims* (US–Canada) excerpted in *Report of the Agent of the United States*, 8 *ILM* (1968), 118; *Diversion of Water from the Meuse Case*, PCIJ, Ser. A/B, No. 70 (1937), 16. Both cases were concerned only with interpretation and application of bilateral treaties. See Lammers, *Pollution of International Watercourses*, 504.

[127] *Report of the ILC to the Gen. Assembly* (1988), UN Doc. A/43/10, 64 f.

the rapporteur believed that due diligence should be treated as a defence to be established by the source state, which would presumptively be liable.[128]

McCaffrey's interpretation of the state's primary obligation is not explicit in draft Article 21, but is apparent in Article 23, which requires states to 'take all measures . . . that are necessary' to protect and preserve the marine environment.[129] Most of the more modern treaties support his interpretation, although others which prohibit pollution, or specified forms of pollution may sustain a stricter interpretation.[130] Thus although the context and formulation of individual treaties is important and may lead to a different conclusion, the evidence does tend to favour the rapporteur's interpretation of a general obligation of due diligence in he regulation and control of pollution in international watercourses. Moreover, use of the formula 'prevent, reduce and control' in draft Article 21 was intended to allow for differentiation in measures taken with regard to new or existing sources of pollution, and to that extent also supports the rapporteur's view that there is no absolute obligation of prevention.[131]

In defining the threshold at which this obligation operates the Commission's articles use the term 'appreciable harm' throughout. This term was first adopted by rapporteur Schwebel, who intended it to mean more than perceptible, but less than 'serious' or 'substantial', the two other qualifications often used in this context.[132] The commission itself endorsed the view that there must be harm of some consequence, for example to health, industry, agriculture, or the environment, but that this need not be 'momentous or grave', and it has concluded that 'appreciable' is the preferable term.[133]

Some members have argued that this is too vague a test to incorporate in national law; others believe it sets too low a threshold which might inhibit industrial growth.[134] The rapporteur has defended his choice by pointing to the evidence of acceptance in state practice,[135] and the need for consistency with other ILC topics, notably 'International Liability' where the same issue arises.[136] In his view the term is as objective as possible without specific agreement on scientifically determined thresholds of permissible emissions. The development of more exact international standards, such as those prohibiting toxic emissions, or limiting discharges, will thus tend to amplify the more general criteria.

---

[128] *Report of the ILC to the Gen. Assembly* (1988), UN Doc. A/43/10, 68–9.
[129] See *infra*, pp. 233–4.
[130] See e.g. the Indus, Lake Constance, Danube Basin, Rhine Chemicals Treaties, *supra*, n. 117, and cf. 1909 Boundary Waters Treaty (US–Canada), Article IV, and treaties listed *supra*, n. 78.
[131] *Report of the ILC* (1990), UN Doc. A/45/10, 161, and see *supra*, pp. 91–4.
[132] II *Yearbook ILC* (1982), pt. 1, 98, paras. 130–41. See *supra*, pp. 98–102.
[133] II *Yearbook ILC* (1982), pt. 1, 98, para. 141; *Report of the ILC to the Gen. Assembly* (1988), UN Doc. A/43/10, 85–6.
[134] *Report of the ILC to the Gen. Assembly*, 62, para. 154.
[135] Ibid. 86 f, and see Schwebel *3rd Report*.
[136] Barboza, *4th Report on International Liability* (1988), UN Doc. A/CN4/413, para. 42.

(4) An Obligation to Protect the Environment?

The foregoing discussion reflects the perspective of traditional customary law regarding pollution control obligations. As we have seen, these obligations are of a very general character and their main concern is the protection of other states from harm. The ILC's work point, however, to the emergence of a more comprehensive approach to watercourse pollution which involves an obligation to protect and preserve 'the ecosystems of international water-courses' and a duty to the take all measures necessary to protect and preserve the marine environment against inputs of pollution from rivers.[137] As the ILC report notes, commenting on earlier versions of these articles,

All speakers... expressed support for the inclusion of a general obligation on the protection of the environment of international watercourses and of the marine environment from pollution. This general duty was said to be well grounded in state practice as was evidenced by various international agreements.[138]

Thus the ILC's articles recognize that the international nature of a water-course is no longer solely defined by its transboundary character, but also by its environmental impact on shared resources or common spaces, and that these impacts must be taken into account in preventing watercourse pollution. The beneficiaries of this obligation will not be other riparians alone, but will include states whose maritime zones or interest in the high seas environment is affected. The elaboration of detailed standards of pollution control and prevention and their supervision by international commissions or other collective institutions are recognized as essential features of this approach to environmental protection. Thus the ILC's draft articles define 'pollution' in broad terms, meaning 'any detrimental alteration in the composition or quality of the waters' resulting from human conduct, and they require states to consult with a view to listing substances whose discharge into the watercourse is to be controlled or prohibited.[139] What this suggests is an attempt to integrate the elements of modern practice in common management regimes for international watercourses with regional arrangements for controlling rivers as land-based sources of pollution.[140]

To facilitate this integration, the initial introduction of equitable criteria into the obligation to protect the marine environment has now been removed from the ILC's draft articles, because it did not reflect either the regional seas

---

[137] 1991 Articles 20 and 23, and for commentary, see *Report of the ILC to the Gen. Assembly*, UN Doc. A/45/10 (1990) at 147 and 169. See also draft Article 22 which deals with the introduction of alien or new species detrimental to the ecosystem, and commentary ibid. 167.

[138] *Report of the ILC to the Gen. Assembly* (1988), UN Doc. A/43/10, 70, para. 171. See generally ibid. 55–7, 69–72.

[139] 1991 draft Articles 21(1) and 21(3). cf. draft article 21(2), however, and cf. other definitions referred to *supra*, pp. 98–102.

[140] See *infra*, pp. 316–7.

treaties, or the 1982 UNCLOS, and was undesirable in principle for reasons considered earlier. The article proposed in 1990 now corresponds closely to Article 207 of the 1982 UNCLOS, which deals generally with land-based pollution, and thus it sets no specific standard of conduct beyond an obligation to take measures 'taking into account generally accepted international rules and standards.'[141] The regional seas treaties considered in Chapter 8 do support the underlying implication of the ILC's codification that the basis of pollution control in international rivers is no longer to be found mainly in customary obligations concerning equitable utilization or harm prevention, but in regional regimes employing common standards of environmental protection for river pollution, and in the requirements of international co-operation, but, as we shall see in Chapter 8, there remain problems of co-ordinating the operation of watercourse and regional seas commissions in a manner which achieves the Commission's objective.

(5) Transboundary Environmental Co-operation[142]

(a) Notification, Consultation, and Negotiation in Cases of Environmental Risk

The application to international watercourses of the principle that states are entitled to prior notice, consultation, and negotiation in cases where the proposed use of a shared resource may cause serious injury to their rights or interests is amply supported by international codifications,[143] declarations,[144] case law,[145] and commentators.[146] In this context procedural requirements are particularly important as a means of giving effect to the principle of equitable utilization and for avoiding disputes among riparians over the benefits and burdens of river development.[147]

---

[141] 1991 draft Article 23, and see *infra*, Ch. 8.

[142] See generally Caponera, in Utton and Teclaff, *Transboundary Resources Law*, 1; Godana, *Africa's Shared Water Resources*, chs. 5, 6, 8; Kiss and Lambrechts, 15 *AFDI* (1969), 718.

[143] ILA, Montreal Rules on Water Pollution in an International Drainage Basin, 1982, *supra*, n. 10, Articles 5, 6; Institute of International Law, Resolution on the Utilization of Non-Maritime International Waters, 1961, *supra*, n. 9, Articles 5–8; ILC draft Articles 11–19, *supra*, n. 44, and Commentary in *Report of the ILC to the Gen. Assembly* (1988), UN Doc. A/43/10, 114 ff; ILA, Helsinki Rules on the Uses of the Waters of International Rivers, 1966, *supra*, n. 3, Articles XXIX, XXX. Note, however, that the latter rules only 'recommend' the provision of information, including notice of proposed works and provide that states 'should' resort to negotiation; for comparison with other formulations, see Bourne 10 *CYIL* (1972), 215 f.

[144] e.g. 1933 Montevideo Declaration on the Industrial and Agricultural Use of International Rivers, 28 *AJIL Supp.* (1934), 59–60; Stockholm Conference on the Human Environment, 1972, UN Doc., A/Conf. 48/14, 'Action Plan', Recommendation 51; Council of Europe, Recommendation 436 on Fresh Water Pollution Control, 1965, and 1967 European Water Charter, II *Yearbook ILC* (1974), pt. 2, 341 ff.

[145] *Lac Lanoux* arbitration, 24 *ILR* (1957), 101.

[146] Kirgis, *Prior Consultation in International Law* (Charlottesville, Va., 1983), ch. 2, reviews the state practice in detail. See also Bourne, 22 *UTLJ* (1972), 172; ibid., 10 *CYIL* (1972); Evensen, *1st Report*, II *Yearbook ILC* (1983), pt. 1, 173 ff.; McCaffrey, *3rd Report* (1987), UN Doc. A/CN.4/406, Add. 2, 139 ff.

[147] McCaffrey, *2nd Report*, II *Yearbook ILC* (1986), pt. 1, 139.

These procedural principles are generally regarded as applicable to cases of possible serious injury or appreciable adverse effects.[148] Moreover, although many older treaties are concerned only with works which affect navigation or the flow or course of a river, the same procedural norms have been applied to the adverse effects of river pollution or the risk of serious environmental harm.[149] European treaties expressly requiring prior consultation in such cases include the Convention on the Protection of Lake Constance[150] and the 1974 Nordic Convention on the Protection of the Environment.[151] In other treaties, such as the 1973 Agreement between the US and Mexico,[152] references to consultation in case of possible 'adverse effects' will also cover pollution or environmental harm, unless as in the case of the 1960 Indus Waters Treaty, their terms are too specific to include consultation in such situations.[153] This conclusion is implicitly supported by the ILC's draft articles, which do not distinguish consultation in cases of environmental harm from other possible adverse effects. Furthermore, the growing practice of consultation, through international river commissions, on the establishment of pollution emission standards, toxic discharges, and measures threatening increased pollution points to an implied obligation covering these matters even where there is no treaty requirement to consult.[154] Treaties relating to land-

---

[148] ILC draft articles, 1991, Article 12; 1961 Salzburg Rules, Articles 4, 5; ILA Helsinki Rules, 1966, Article XXIX; Bourne, 22 *UTLJ* (1972), 174–5, and 233 n. 143, and see generally UNEP Principles of Conduct Relating to Natural Resources Shared by Two or More states, 1978, *supra*, n. 100; Kirgis, *Prior Consultation in International Law*, 359.

[149] Kirgis, *Prior Consultation in International Law*, 40 and 86.

[150] 1960 Convention on the Protection of Lake Constance Against Pollution, Article 1(3), UN *Legislative Texts*, UN Doc. ST/LEG/SER.B/12, 438 and see also 1966 Treaty Regulating the Withdrawal of Water from Lake Constance, 620 *UNTS* 198; Kirgis, *Prior Consultation in International Law*, 24 observes: 'These two treaties set up a comprehensive prior consultation system for Lake Constance, without requiring prior consent.' See also 1990 Agreement Concerning Co-operation on Management of Water Resources in the Danube Basin, *supra*, n. 117.

[151] *Supra*, Ch. 5 n. 34.

[152] 1973 US–Mexico Agreement on the Permanent and Definitive Solution to the International Problem of the Salinity of the Colorado River, *supra*, n. 82, Article 6. Kirgis, *Prior Consultation in International Law*, 66, notes: 'Arguably the 1973 agreement represents United States acquiescence in repeated Mexican assertions that the Wellton-Mohawk project violated its rights. One result of that assertion-acquiescence process was the US promise to engage in consultation before embarking on any similar project in the future. Thus it is a particularly significant indication of current normative expectations regarding changes in the water quality of a successive river.' See also the 1960 Netherlands–FRG Frontier Treaty, *supra*, n. 14, Articles 60–2; Kiss and Lambrechts, 726 ff.

[153] *Supra*, n. 29. This treaty requires consultation only in respect of engineering or hydro-electric works causing interference with waters: Kirgis, *Prior Consultation in International Law*, notes: 'the Treaty neither expressly nor by implication requires consultation before new potential pollutants are introduced into the waters', at 44–5.

[154] See e.g. 1964 Statute Relating to Development of the Chad Basin, *supra*, n. 5, Article 5; 1962 Convention Concerning the Protection of the Waters of Lake Geneva Against Pollution, Ruster and Simma, x. 4872, on which see Kiss and Lambrechts, 15 *AFDI* (1969), 732–3; Kirgis, *Prior Consultation in International Law*, 25; the same point applies to the Rhine, Moselle, and Saar

based sources of pollution provide further evidence of the importance of this form of institutional consultation machinery in relation to river pollution.[155]

As in other respects, regional patterns may be significant, and Europe and North America offer the most developed examples of co-operation in matters of notification and consultation. But although practice with regard to environmental risks for international watercourses elsewhere is less extensive, there is no evidence of any substantial departure from the general principles under discussion here.[156] Nor has any distinction been drawn in an environmental context between contiguous and successive rivers or lakes.[157] Only a few states, such as Brazil, have persistently opposed explicit consultation obligations for successive watercourses, and the normative significance of such practice is questionable.[158] But while the general principle is beyond serious argument, its application may pose difficulties in particular cases. One of the most difficult questions remains that of deciding who determines when the circumstances require prior notification and consultation. The principle of good faith imports some limit of reasonableness in unilateral assessments by the proposing state, and in the *Lac Lanoux* arbitration, the tribunal observed:

A state wishing to do that which will affect an international watercourse cannot decide whether another state's interests will be affected; the other state is sole judge of that and has the right to information on the proposals.[159]

Thus the decision is not one for the proposing state alone to take once the possibility of adverse affects is foreseen.[160] The affected state is itself entitled to initiate the process of notification and consultation, if the proposing state does not act.[161]

There is scope for abuse in this formulation, however, which has prompted the ILC to adopt a broader, additional, requirement of consultation wherever

---

Commissions and to the 1909 US–Canada Boundary Waters Treaty (Under Article 9); see Kirgis, ibid. 28, who notes other examples.

   [155] See Ch. 8.

   [156] See e.g. 1964 Agreement Concerning the Niger River Commission, Article 12, 587 *UNTS* 19; 1964 Statute Relating to Develoment of the Chad Basin, Articles 5, 6, *supra*, n. 5; 1968 African Convention on the Conservation of Nature and Natural Resources, Articles 5(2) and 14(3), Ruster and Simma, v. 2037; 1971 Act of Santiago Concerning Hydrologic Basins, II *Yearbook ILC* (1974), pt. 2, 324; 1971 Buenos Aires Declaration on Water Resources, ibid. 324; 1971 Act of Buenos Aires on Hydrologic Basins, ibid. 325; Kirgis, *Prior Consultation in International Law*, 77; Bourne, 22 *UTLJ* (1972).

   [157] Kirgis, *Prior Consultation in International Law*, 26.

   [158] Brazilian opposition to prior consultation requirements is summarized ibid. 72 ff. The 1978 Amazonian Co-operation Treaty, *supra*, n. 5, Article 21, provides for the Amazonian Co-operation Council to consider plans and directives presented by the parties, but it contains no other prior consultation provision.

   [159] *Supra*, n. 145 at 119.

   [160] Kirgis, *Prior Consultation in International Law*, 41 argues: 'Any reasonable doubt must be resolved in favour of notification.'

   [161] See *infra*, nn. 182–4.

there are 'possible effects' of whatever kind, including beneficial ones.[162] This is complemented by its more general provision for co-operation in the exchange of information relating to the state of the watercourse.[163] Although the 1933 Montevideo Declaration[164] is among a few instruments supporting consultation in situations unqualified by reference to possible adverse effects, it is doubtful whether such an extensive obligation represents established law.[165] The most that can be said is that a state must notify and consult wherever a possible conflict of interest exists.

The purpose of prior notification is of course to provide adequate information on which consultation can if necessary take place. An obligation to notify is widely accepted in watercourse treaties and international declarations.[166] It has been treated as customary law by successive rapporteurs of the ILC, whose draft articles provide that notification must be timely, allow a reasonable period for reply, and contain sufficient information for evaluation of the impact of the proposal.[167] The Commission's reports provide substantial evidence of the adoption of these principles in agreements among riparian states, although in certain respects its proposed articles go beyond international practice, for example in stipulating six months as a reasonable maximum period for reply.[168]

Where notification confirms the existence of a conflict of interests, or where affected states request it, consultation and negotiation are required. The *Lac Lanoux* arbitration[169] shows how the process of prior consultation and negotiation has been interpreted by an international tribunal, not only as a treaty stipulation, specific to relations between France and Spain,[170] but more generally as a principle of customary law.[171] The tribunal found that: 'The

---

[162] 1988 draft Article 11; cf. draft Article 12, *supra*, n. 148, and see McCaffrey, 17 *Denver JILP* (1989), 505, 511 f.

[163] Article 10; see *infra*, p. 240.

[164] See *supra*, n. 144.

[165] See Bourne 22 *UTLJ* (1972), 173 ff.; Kirgis, *Prior Consultation in International Law*, 41 n. 146, observes that the *Lac Lanoux* arbitration leaves this question undecided.

[166] See *Report of the ILC to the Gen. Assembly* (1988), UN Doc. A/43/10, 117–24; McCaffrey, *3rd Report*, II *Yearbook ILC* (1987), pt. 1, 28–35, and e.g. 1923 Convention Relating to the Development of Hydraulic Power Affecting More Than One State, 36 *UNTS* 77; 1960 Convention on the Protection of Lake Constance Against Pollution; *supra*, n. 150; 1960 Indus. Waters Treaty, *supra*, n. 29; 1990 Danube Basin Agreement, *supra*, n. 150.

[167] 1991 draft Articles 12, 13, and *Report of the ILC to the Gen. Assembly* (1988), 115–26; 1984 draft articles. 11, 12; Evensen, *2nd Report*, II *Yearbook of the ILC* (1984), pt. 1, 114 and *1st Report*, ibid. (1983), pt. 1, 174–6. See also ILA Helsinki Rules, 1966, Article XXIX, and IDI Salzburg Resolution, 1961, Article 5.

[168] *Report of the ILC to the Gen. Assembly* (1988), 125 ff. Article 15 requires the notified state to respond as early as possible. cf. Evensen, *1st Report*, 175, where six months is proposed only as a reasonable *minimum* period for reply, and Article 3(1) of the 1990 Danube Basin Agreement, *supra*, n. 150 which provides for consultations within 3 months of notification.

[169] *Supra*, n. 145.

[170] 1866 Treaty of Bayonne and Additional Act, 56 *BFSP*, 212 and 226.

[171] *Lac Lanoux* arbitration, *supra*, n. 145, at 129 f. See Bourne, 22 *UTLJ* (1972), 197: 'This

conflicting interests aroused by the industrial use of international rivers must be reconciled by mutual concessions embodied in comprehensive agreements.'[172] Consultation and negotiation in good faith are required, not as a mere formality, but as a genuine attempt to conclude an agreement. Each state is obliged to give a reasonable place to the interests of others in the solution finally adopted, even if negotiations for this purpose are unsuccessful, 'though owing to the intransigence of its partner'.[173] But subject to compliance with these procedural obligations, other states have no veto over the development of a river.[174]

In most respects the International Law Commission's draft articles closely follow the principles laid down in the *Lac Lanoux* arbitration, the *Icelandic Fisheries* case,[175] and the *North Sea Continental Shelf* case[176] concerning the conduct of consultations and negotiations.[177] Where the implementation of planned measures would be inconsistent with the equitable utilization of a watercourse, or would cause appreciable harm to other states, an 'equitable resolution' is called for. Although reliance on equitable solutions in cases of transboundary harm has been criticized earlier,[178] the Commission's conclusion that international law requires states to notify and negotiate as a means of reconciling conflicting rights and interests is clearly consistent with the recognition of equitable utilization as the main basis for allocation of rights and interests in shared water resources.

The ILC articles also indicate some of the consequences of failure to notify or negotiate with affected states. This will first be a breach of obligation and may render the state responsible for harm caused by the omission.[179] Another possible consequence is the loss of any claim to priority,[180] but this is rejected by Bourne as unsupported by authority.[181] As we have seen, the ILC's articles also allow the potentially affected state to request information and negotiation,

---

decision of course was based on the terms of the treaty. Nevertheless, it does intimate that there is a general principle of customary international law requiring states to take the interests of co-basin states into consideration and thus necessarily leads to the obligation to give notice, to consult and to negotiate.' Kirgis, *Prior Consultation in International Law*, 39, views the case as supporting a customary obligation to engage in 'meaningful preliminary negotiations'.

[172] *Supra*, n. 145 at 119.

[173] Ibid. 141, and see 119, 128.

[174] Ibid. 128–38. Some treaties do, however, require prior *consent* of the affected riparians before works can be undertaken: this practice is reviewed by Kirgis, *Prior Consultation in International Law*, 40, who concludes that it is mainly European but does not apply to pollution or environmental harm.

[175] *ICJ Rep.* (1974), 3, paras. 71 and 78.

[176] Ibid. (1969), 3, paras. 85 and 87.

[177] See *Report of the ILC to the Gen. Assembly* (1988), 131–3; Kirgis, *Prior Consultation in International Law*, 362 ff.

[178] See *supra*, pp. 226–9.

[179] Bourne, 22 *UTLJ* (1972).

[180] ILA Helsinki Rules, 1966, Article XXIX(4).

[181] 22 *UTLJ* (1972), 190.

if it has serious reasons for the request.[182] This approach is consistent with the view of the *Lac Lanoux* tribunal that 'if the neighbouring state has not taken the initiative, the other state cannot be denied the right to insist on notification of works or concessions which are the object of a Scheme',[183] and it accords with state practice in several disputed cases.[184]

Failure to respond to notification, or to an offer of consultation, may indicate tacit consent to any proposed works.[185] On the other hand, the ILC's draft provides that although the proposing state may then proceed with its plans, it remains subject to obligations of equitable utilization and the prevention of serious injury.[186] The implication here is that whatever tacit consent arises from a failure to reply or participate in negotiations does not extend to a breach of the proposing state's obligations. This conclusion is more in keeping with the situation following an unsuccessful attempt to negotiate a settlement.[187] But in cases where negotiations fail, the argument for tacit consent of any kind is clearly absent; where they never take place at all this is less apparent, and the ILC leaves unresolved what role tacit consent does then play.

The ILC has also adopted the view that during the period for reply, consultation, and negotiation, good faith requires that implementation of any plans be postponed, but not indefinitely.[188] Prolonging negotiations will itself be inconsistent with good faith, and to counter this possibility, the Commission adopts a six-month limit, or other 'agreed reasonable period' during which to resolve the dispute.[189] State practice undoubtedly favours postponement, but the evidence suggests that this is often much more protracted than the Commission envisages.[190]

---

[182] 1991 draft Article 18, and see *Report of the ILC to the Gen. Assembly* (1988), 134–6. See also 1990 Danube Basin Agreement, *supra*, n. 117, Article 3.

[183] Loc. cit., *supra*, n. 145, at 138.

[184] See e.g. the Sudanese–Egyptian dispute regarding consultation over the Aswan High Dam and the US–Mexico dispute regarding salinity of the Colorado River, noted in Kirgis, *Prior Consultation in International Law*, 43 and 66.

[185] Bourne, 22 *UTLJ* (1972), 181.

[186] *Report of the ILC to the Gen. Assembly* (1988), 129 ff., and 1991 draft Article 16.

[187] *Supra*, text at n. 173.

[188] *Report of the ILC to the Gen. Assembly* (1988), draft Article 14, at 127 ff., and Article 17, at 130 ff.

[189] Ibid. cf. Article 6 of the 1961 IDI Salzburg Resolution which allows for negotiation 'within a reasonable time' and see Bourne, 10 *CYIL* (1972), 231 f.

[190] e.g. the *Lac Lanoux* negotiations, which began in 1917, and the proposal eventually considered by the tribunal was put forward in 1950. The case was referred to arbitration in 1956. Negotiations between Sudan and Egypt over the Aswan Dam took five years: see Garretson, *The Law of International Drainage Basins*, 274 f. Kirgis, *Prior Consultation in International Law*, 73 observes that Brazil's objections to prior consultation may be attributable to the likelihood of delays in its economic development. For examples of treaties which support postponement, see 1964 Chad Basin Statute, and 1960 Convention on the Protection of Lake Constance, Article 1.

(b) Information Exchange and Environmental Impact Assessment

The regular exchange of data and information on the state of the watercourse, and on the impact of present and planned uses can also be regarded as part of a general obligation to co-operate. The ILA's 1966 Helsinki Rules recommend such an exchange, while the ILC's draft articles require it.[191] The ILC's rapporteur has pointed to the large number of agreements, declarations, and resolutions which provide for exchanges of information,[192] such as the 1944 US-Mexico Agreement,[193] the 1960 Indus Waters Treaty,[194] the 1961 Columbia River Treaty,[195] and the 1964 Niger Treaty.[196] Additionally, Article 5 of the ILA's 1982 Montreal Rules on Water Pollution in an International Drainage Basin requires states to exchange information on pollution of basin waters.[197] The practice of river commissions dealing with pollution has facilitated and encouraged such exchanges.[198]

Bourne, reviewing the state practice, concluded that a general obligation to exchange information about watercourses had not yet crystallized into international law,[199] but in view of the ILC's more recent evidence, this may be too cautious. Moreover the importance of regular exchanges of information in fulfilling the obligations of equitable utilization of a shared resource and preventing harm to other states or the environment can be emphasized in support of the ILC's draft articles.[200]

(c) Emergency Co-operation

The general principle that states must notify each other and co-operate in cases of emergency to avert harm to other states applies also to international watercourses. Bourne views it as part of a state's duty of reasonable care in the supervision of its territory;[201] McCaffrey treats it as part of the duty of equitable utilization.[202] Most of the treaties are concerned more with natural disasters, such as floods,[203] but a few such as the 1976 Rhine Chemicals

---

[191] 1966 ILA Helsinki Rules, Article XXIX(1); 1991 ILC Draft Article 9. See also the 1933 Montevideo Declaration, *supra*, n. 144.

[192] *4th Report* (1988), UN Doc. A/CN.4/412, at paras. 15–27; *Report of the ILC to the Gen. Assembly* (1988), 106–14.

[193] *Supra*, n. 152.

[194] *Supra*, n. 153.

[195] UN, *Legislative Texts*, UN Doc. ST/LEG/SER.B/12, 206.

[196] *Supra*, n. 156.

[197] *Supra*, n. 143. See also the 1987 ECE Principles on Co-operation in the Field of Transboundary Waters, Doc. E/ECE.42/L.19, and 1979 IDI Resolution on the Pollution of Rivers and Lakes, Article 7, *supra*, n. 9.

[198] See e.g. 1976 Rhine Chemicals Convention, Articles 2, 8, 12; 1978 Great Lakes Water Quality Agreement, Article IX, *infra*, pp. 245–9.

[199] 22 *UTLJ* (1972), 206.

[200] McCaffrey, *3rd Report*, 1987, paras. 29–38; *4th Report*, 1988, paras. 12–14 and 27.

[201] 22 *UTLJ* (1972), 186 ff.

[202] *4th Report* (1988), para. 27.   [203] Bourne, 22 *UTLJ* (1972), 182.

Convention,[204] require notification to other states and relevant international organizations in cases of accidental discharge of toxic or seriously polluting substances likely to affect other states. Switzerland was criticized by its neighbours in 1986 for its failure to offer timely warning under Article 11 of this agreement when fire at the Sandoz Chemical plant caused toxic pollution of the Rhine.[205] The ILC's draft articles adopt this precedent and provide for notification of incidents resulting in 'pollution or environmental emergency'.[206] Resolutions of the IDI and ILA also support notification to other states where there is the risk of sudden increase in transboundary pollution.[207]

The ILC's draft articles now extend the obligations of a riparian beyond mere notification in cases of a pollution emergency, and require it to take action to prevent, mitigate, or neutralize the danger to other watercourse states.[208] This is in keeping with precedents in other fields, such as the Law of the Sea, and with the obligation of due diligence on which the decision in the *Corfu Channel* case[209] is based, but it is as yet reflected in only a few watercourse treaties such as the 1961 Columbia River Basin Treaty.[210]

3. REGIONAL CO-OPERATION AND ENVIRONMENTAL REGULATION

The management of international watercourses through regional co-operation provides the most comprehensive basis for environmental protection and pollution control. First, the institutional framework of river commissions which usually accompanies such regional schemes offers a forum for notification, consultation, and negotiation to take place, for co-ordinating responses to emergency situations, for data and information on environmental matters and water quality to be collected and disseminated,[211] and for the co-ordination of research. These are important functions for such bodies.

---

[204] Article 11. See also the 1976 Convention on the Protection of the Rhine Against Pollution by Chlorides, Articles 4 and 11; and the 1978 US–Canadian Great Lakes Water Quality Agreement, *supra*, n. 6, Article X(2).

[205] Rest, 30 *GYIL* (1987), 160, 162, 165.

[206] 1991 Draft Article 25(2) and *Report of the ILC to the Gen. Assembly* (1988), para. 180. See also McCaffrey, *4th Report* (1988), para. 27; Evensen, *1st Report* (1983), para. 176.

[207] IDI, 1979, Resolution on the Pollution of Rivers and Lakes, Article 7, *supra*, n. 197; ILA, Montreal Rules on Water Pollution in an International Drainage Basin, Article 5, *60th Conference* (1982), 540.

[208] *Report of the ILC to the Gen. Assembly* (1990), UN Doc. A/45/10, 175, and 1991 Draft Articles 25(3) and (4).

[209] *ICJ Rep.* (1949), 4; *supra*, pp. 108–9.

[210] loc. cit., *supra*, n. 195, Article 18(3), and see 1974 Paris Convention for the Prevention of Marine Pollution from Land-Based Sources, Article 13. See also the 1990 ECE Code of Conduct on Accidental Pollution of Transboundary Inland Waters, E/ECE/1225.

[211] See above, n. 154, and *Report of the ILC to the Gen. Assembly* (1988), 108.

Secondly, international river commissions facilitate adoption, implementation, and periodic review of common environmental standards. Not all river commissions have this role, but the growing number which do is evidence of their significance in controlling watercourse pollution.[212] Moreover these river commissions are complemented by a series of multilateral treaties which establish institutions and standards for the regulation of marine pollution from land-based sources, including national and international rivers.[213] Thus in North-Western Europe, the 1974 Paris Convention has now become the main basis for regional control of river pollution,[214] together with measures adopted by the EEC.[215] From this perspective the relative weakness of international commissions established to protect European rivers such as the Rhine, Moselle, and Saar from pollution is less significant than it might appear,[216] and the chapter on land-based sources of pollution should be read in conjunction with the comments made here.

Individual river commissions differ in their exact functions, in their powers, and in their success at persuading member governments to adopt and implement effective environmental measures. Nevertheless they share certain common characteristics.[217] The most important of these are their inherent flexibility and their dependence on agreement among their members. With some exceptions, they are aptly described as resembling intergovernmental conferences in many respects.[218] Thus their effectiveness is primarily dependent on negotiated solutions to shared pollution problems. These points are well illustrated by consideration of some of the more significant commissions in Europe, North America, and Africa.

[212] See 1964 Finland–USSR Agreement Concerning Frontier Watercourses, 537 *UNTS* 231: 1962 Convention Concerning the Protection of the Waters of Lake Geneva Against Pollution, *supra*, n. 154; 1961 Protocol Establishing an International Commission for the Protection of the Saar Against Pollution, Ruster and Simma, xi. 5613; 1961 Protocol Concerning the Constitution of an International Commission for the Protection of the Moselle Against Pollution, *supra*, n. 64; 1963 Agreement Concerning the International Commission for the Protection of the Rhine Against Pollution, Ruster and Simma, x. 4820; 1976 Rhine Chlorides and Chemicals Conventions, *supra*, n. 204; 1971 Finland–Sweden Frontier Rivers Agreement, II *Yearbook ILC* (1974), pt. 2, 319; 1909 US–Canada Boundary Waters Treaty *supra*, n. 14; 1978 US–Canada Great Lakes Water Quality Agreement, *supra*, n. 6; 1973 Argentina–Uruguay Treaty Concerning the River Plate, *supra*, n. 6; 1964 Statute Relating to the Development of the Chad Basin, *supra*, n. 5; 1987 Agreement on the Action Plan for the Environmentally Sound Management of the Common Zambezi River System, *supra*, n. 5; 1990 Magdeburg Convention on the International Commission for the Protection of the Elbe, OJ/EEC/No. C93 (1991), 12.

[213] See *infra*, pp. 308–14.

[214] Ibid.

[215] *Infra*, n. 226.

[216] For treaties relating to these rivers, see *supra*, n. 212. On their operation, see Lammers, 5 *NYIL* (1974), 59; id., 27 *NILR* (1980), 171; Kaminga, in Zacklin and Caflisch, *International Rivers and Lakes*, 371; Bouchez, in Van Panhuys *et al.*, *International Law in the Netherlands*, i (The Hague, 1978), 215; Lammers, *Pollution of International Watercourses*, 165–96.

[217] See generally, Kiss and Lambrechts, 15 *AFDI* (1969), 718; Godana, *Africa's Shared Water Resources*, ch. 6.

[218] Kiss and Lambrechts, 15 *AFDI* (1969), 728.

(1) The International Commission for Protection of the Rhine

This commission was established in 1950 and reorganized in 1963.[219] Its functions were initially to arrange for research into Rhine pollution, and to make proposals and prepare guidelines for protection of the river from pollution.[220] However, these required the unanimous agreement of the parties.[221] Beyond collaboration through the commission, no other obligations of pollution control were created. Despite serious problems of chemical and salt pollution in the river, Lammers, reviewing the work of the commission in its first twenty years concluded that 'the Rhine Commission had not been able to achieve any result of significance'.[222] Investigations had been carried out, but inability to reach agreement on specific measures had blocked progress.

Not until 1976 was it finally possible to negotiate, through the Commission, framework conventions on chemicals and chlorides pollution. Under the 1976 Rhine Chemicals Convention, the parties are committed to progressive elimination or strict regulation of specified groups of pollutants.[223] Emissions of both categories are controlled by a system of prior authorization by governments, and emission standards for eliminating the more serious pollutants are proposed by the Commission. Standards for other pollutants are determined nationally.[224] The Rhine Commission is also given responsibility for co-ordinating national programmes, receiving reports from governments, evaluating results, and proposing further measures. It thus performs monitoring, regulatory, and supervisory functions in respect of member states' fulfilment of their obligations, but effective implementation continues to depend on further agreement on emission standards and the degree of co-ordination of national measures.[225] The development of EEC emission and water quality standards for most of the Rhine's riparians goes some way towards achieving this.[226]

[219] 1963 Agreement concerning the International Commission for the Protection of the Rhine, *supra*, n. 212. See Lammers, *Pollution of International Watercourses*, 168. The Rhine Protection Commission should not be confused with the General Commission for the Rhine established by the Congress of Vienna in 1815, on which see *supra*, Ch. 4 n. 128.

[220] Article 2.

[221] Article 6.

[222] *Pollution of International Watercourses*, 175.

[223] 1976 Convention on the Protection of the Rhine Against Chemical Pollution, *supra*, n. 86, Article 1, and Annexes I and II; Lammers, *Pollution of International Watercourses*, 187.

[224] cf. Articles 3–5 (Annex 1 substances) and Article 6 (Annex II substances).

[225] Lammers, *Pollution of International Watercourses*, 189–90.

[226] Switzerland is the only non-EEC riparian. Emissions directives are: 73/404/EEC (OJ L347: Detergents); 76/464/EEC (OJ L129: Dangerous substances); 82/176/EEC (OJ L81) and 84/156/EEC (OJ L74: Mercury); 83/513/EEC (OJ L291: Cadmium); 84/491/EEC (OJ L274: Lindane); 86/280/EEC (OJ L181: DDT); 78/176/EEC (OJ L54) and 83/29/EEC (OJ L32: Titanium). Water quality standards are set by directives 75/440/EEC (OJ L194); 80/778/EEC (OJ L229); 78/659/EEC (OJ L222); 76/160/EEC (OJ LJ1); 80/68/EEC (OJ L20). The EEC is a party to the Rhine Chemicals Convention.

The Rhine Chlorides Convention[227] is intended to reduce French chloride discharges into the river, and to prevent any increase in discharges by other parties. After a long delay occasioned by France, the treaty entered into force in 1985. The Rhine Commission's functions under this treaty include receiving national reports, making proposals for further limitations, and monitoring compliance with chloride levels set by the Convention.[228] This treaty sets an unusual precedent in distributing across all riparians, including injured states downstream, the costs of measures taken by France to control chloride pollution.[229] In most watercourse treaties these costs fall on the polluting state. What the Chlorides Convention represents is an attempt to produce an equitable solution of the dispute between France and the Netherlands in which neither side pressed its legal rights to the full.

Both the Rhine treaties provide for compulsory unilateral arbitration[230] as a remedy for breach of obligation by states parties, but no such claims have been made, even when, as in the Sandoz accident, there is evidence of a possible breach of obligation.[231] Instead, damage occurring in downstream states has been the subject of civil actions in national courts or before the European Court of Justice. These cases illustrate the value of European Community law in affording a choice of venue for claims brought directly against polluters in private law, and a preference for local remedies over international claims even for clean-up costs incurred by riparian governments.[232]

The regime for protecting the environment of the Rhine can be criticized mainly for dealing with only two types of pollutant and for the slow pace of progress. As Lammers points out, it has been easier to secure commitments to prevent new or increased pollution than to reduce existing pollution.[233] But the institutional structure now compares favourably with other such bodies and the Chemicals Convention has the significant merit of applying to the Rhine Basin, not just to the Rhine itself. By providing detailed standards for national regulation over most of this basin, the EEC has done some of what remains lacking in many other international river basins. Moreover, in 1987, following the Sandoz accident, the Rhine states were at last persuaded to

[227] 1976 Convention on the Protection of the Rhine Against Pollution by Chlorides, *supra*, n. 204. See Lammers, *Pollution of International Watercourses*, 183 ff.

[228] Articles 2, 3, 6, 9.

[229] Lammers, *Pollution of International Watercourses*, 176 ff.

[230] Chlorides Convention, Article 12(3); Chemicals Convention, Article 15.

[231] D'Oliviera, in Francioni and Scovazzi (eds.), *International Responsibility for Environmental Harm* (Dordrecht, 1991), 429.

[232] *Handelswerkerij Bier* v. *Mines de Potasse d'Alsace*, II ECJ Rep. (1976) 1735, interpreting the 1968 European Convention on the Recognition and Enforcement of Judgments to allow proceedings in the place of injury or in the place of discharge. For Dutch litigation, see *supra*, Ch. 5 n. 73. See also Rest, 5 EPL (1979), 85; id., 30 *GYIL* (1987); Lammers, *Pollution of International Watercourses*, 196–206. On claims brought in the Sandoz accident, see n. 231.

[233] *Pollution of International Watercourses*, 192 f.

adopt a 'Rhine Action Programme' to reduce structural pollution and minimize the risk of further accidents.[234] The objects of this programme, which is supervised by the Rhine Commission and by regular ministerial conferences, include restoration of the living species of the river, the maintenance of its drinking quality and the protection of the water quality of the North Sea. It is likely that its operation will increasingly be co-ordinated with the Paris Commission and the International North Sea Conference.[235] Thus, the Rhine now offers an example of significant progress in the regional management of watercourse pollution and the first to take account of the marine environment.

(2) The US–Canadian International Joint Commission

The International Joint Commission was established by the 1909 Boundary Waters Treaty with jurisdiction over all rivers and lakes along which the US–Canadian border passes.[236] This is not fully a 'basin treaty', since for most purposes 'boundary waters' excludes tributaries or rivers flowing across the boundary,[237] but it does cover the Great Lakes, and transboundary pollution.[238]

Uniquely, and unlike the Rhine Commission, the IJC does not resemble an intergovernmental conference. Rather, it is more like an administrative agency, composed not of representatives of the parties, but of independent experts who function quasi-judicially through public hearings and whose decisions are rendered by majority vote.[239] Its unity, its independence of both governments, and the binding character of its decisions are its most important and unusual characteristics.[240]

The importance of these features is that the Commission's approval is required before either state may permit the use, obstruction, or diversion of waters affecting the natural level or flow.[241] Although for these purposes each state enjoys 'equal and similar rights', it is the Commission's decisions which apportion those rights according to criteria which protect existing uses and give preference to domestic and sanitary purposes, navigation, power, and

---

[234] Rhine Action Programme, adopted by the 8th Ministerial Conference of the Rhine states, 1987. The agreement is not a treaty, however: see Nollkaemper, 5 *IJECL* (1990), 123.

[235] Ibid. 129 ff. On the Paris Commission and the INSC, see below, Ch. 8.

[236] Text in Cohen, 146 *Recueil des cours* (1975), 221; see also Bourne, 28 *NILR* (1981), 188; Schmandt, Clarkson, and Roderick (eds.), *Acid Rain and Friendly Neighbours* (2nd edn., Durham, NC, 1988), ch. 8; Graham, in Zacklin and Caflisch, *International Rivers and Lakes*, 3; Bilder, 70 *Michigan LR* (1972), 469.

[237] Preliminary article.

[238] Article IV, prohibiting pollution, applies to 'waters flowing across the boundary'.

[239] Boundary Waters Treaty, Articles 7, 8, and 12; Cohen, 146 *Recueil des cours*, 257 ff. and 267 ff.

[240] Cohen, 146 *Recueil des cours*, 257; Bilder, 70 *Michigan LR* (1972), 518 ff.

[241] Boundary Waters Treaty, Articles 3, 4.

irrigation in that order.[242] Thus its primary function is to make binding determinations regarding the equitable utilization of the flow of the waters.

But these powers apply only within a narrow field of uses; they do not address questions of water quality and are therefore of limited environmental relevance. The Boundary Waters Treaty does prohibit pollution of boundary waters and waters flowing across the boundary,[243] but the parties have in practice treated this provision as a basis for compromise and balancing of interests, not as an absolute prohibition.[244] Moreover, the Commission's role under the treaty in pollution disputes is essentially one of conciliation and inquiry: it makes findings of fact and recommendations on matters referred to it by either party.[245] These findings and recommendations are not binding, and the terms of reference are carefully controlled by the parties. Thus its independence in investigating pollution matters is strictly limited in scope, and may even hamper its usefulness as a bargaining forum.[246]

Environmental problems have been referred to the Commission however, particularly since 1945, and this has enabled it to fulfil some of the monitoring and policy-formation functions of other more recently established bodies. Its most significant achievement has been a report on the Great Lakes, resulting in the negotiation of two agreements on Great Lakes Water Quality in 1972 and 1978.[247] As an ILC study notes: 'This report and full response by Governments dramatically illustrates the increasingly important role that the Commission is playing in dealing with environmental questions along the Canada–United States boundary.'[248] Generally the Commission has had a record of making politically acceptable recommendations and a good reputation for fact-finding; its flexibility has been a major asset.[249] It has not found favour in its other role as an arbitral body,[250] however, mainly because it lacks appropriate expertise. The *Trail Smelter* and *Gut Dam* arbitrations[251] were conducted by *ad hoc* tribunals; in all other cases direct negotiation has been the parties' preferred method of dispute settlement.[252]

The Great Lakes Water Quality Agreement of 1978 replaced the earlier

---

[242] Boundary Waters Treaty, Article 8; Cohen, 146 *Recueil des cours*, 254–6.
[243] Article IV.
[244] Bilder, 70 *Michigan LR* (1972), 511–17.
[245] Article IX; Cooper, 24 *CYIL* (1986), 247, 285–90, who also notes the Commission's role as a mediator; Bilder, 70 *Michigan LR* (1972), 513 ff. An unratified treaty drafted in 1920 would have given the Commission power to investigate violations of Article IV of its own motion and required parties to take proceedings against the persons responsible: Ruster and Simma, xi. 5704; Bilder, ibid. 490 f.
[246] Bilder, 70 *Michigan LR* (1972), 520 f.
[247] Ibid. 489 ff. Schmandt, Clarkson, and Roderick, *Acid Rain*, 194–7.
[248] II *Yearbook ILC* (1974), pt. 2, 355.
[249] Schmandt, Clarkson, and Roderick, *Acid Rain*, 191–4; Bilder, 70 *Michigan LR* (1972), 520 f.
[250] 1909 Boundary Waters Treaty, Article X.
[251] 8 *ILM* (1969), 118.   [252] Cooper, 24 *CYIL* (1986).

agreement of 1972.[253] Its purpose is to restore and maintain the waters of the Great Lakes basin ecosystem and its geographical coverage is therefore broader than the 1909 treaty.[254] The parties undertake to reduce or eliminate to the maximum extent practicable the discharge of pollutants, to prohibit toxic discharges, and to adopt water quality standards and regulatory measures consistent with minimum quality objectives set out in the treaty.[255] These objectives are kept under review by the parties and the IJC, which makes appropriate recommendations.[256] Further measures involving the treatment of discharges from industrial, agricultural, municipal, and other sources are also specified.[257] The agreement is comprehensive in character, comparable to treaties on land-based sources of marine pollution.[258]

Under it, the IJC acquires additional powers and responsibilities in collecting data, conducting research and investigations, making recommendations, and reporting on the effectiveness of measures taken under the Agreement.[259] For these purposes it uses its own scientific and quality advisory boards.[260] Unusually it also has authority to verify independently the data and information supplied by the parties. Thus it has now acquired most of the characteristic roles of other pollution commissions, save that of acting as a forum for intergovernmental negotiation. The parties are, however, required to consult and review the Commission's periodic reports and consider appropriate action,[261] so it may act as a useful catalyst for negotiation.

Recognition of the need for an ecosystem approach combined with comprehensive environmental policies based on adequate research and monitoring are the most significant features of this agreement.[262] The IJC's role is important in providing the necessary independent review and enabling policy to evolve in an adaptable and informed way. In all of these respects the 1978 Agreement is one of the more advanced watercourse agreements; as already observed, it is perhaps closer in form to treaties aimed at protecting regional seas from land-based pollution. However, it is noteworthy that the parties have not extended this comprehensive approach to other elements of their transboundary watercourse system.[263] North American practice thus falls short of co-operation in taking all reasonable measures to protect the ecosystem of their shared watercourse system,[264] but, in respect at least of the Great Lakes, it offers a strong example of such co-operation.

---

[253] 1978 agreement, *supra*, n. 6. 1972 Agreement, 11 *ILM* (1972), 694. On the 1972 agreement, see Cohen 146 *Recueil des cours*, 278 ff.; Kiss and Lambrechts, 20 *AFDI* (1974) 797. On the 1978 Agreement, see Rasmussen, *Boston CICLJ* (1979), 499.
[254] Article II.   [255] Articles II–V.   [256] Article IV(2).
[257] Article VI.   [258] See *infra*, pp. 304–20.
[259] Article VII.   [260] Article VIII.   [261] Article X.
[262] Schmandt, Clarkson, and Roderick, *Acid Rain and Friendly Neighbours*, 203.
[263] cf. the 1961 Columbia River Basin Treaty, *supra*, n. 195.
[264] cf. ILC draft Article 17, *Report of the ILC to the Gen. Assembly* (1988), 69.

As in Western Europe, equal access to national remedies is the preferred means of affording redress for damage caused by transboundary water pollution. Article 2 of the Boundary Waters Treaty is an early example of equal access for individual litigants in North American practice. US case law and some Canadian provincial statutes do offer some scope for applying this principle to transboundary water pollution, as well as to air pollution, but significant jurisdictional and procedural problems remain.[265] Moreover, the absence in North America of any treaty comparable to the European Convention on the Recognition and Enforcement of Judgments would preclude proceedings in the place of injury comparable to the *Handelswerkerij* litigation.[266]

(3) The Zambezi River System

The Agreement on the Action Plan for the Environmentally Sound Management of the Common Zambezi River System,[267] concluded in 1988, represents the most ambitious approach to environmental protection of a river basin in the developing world. It is untypical of earlier treaties in Africa, whose main concern was river development, but it exemplifies the potential of common management in addressing environmental problems.[268]

The Agreement provides a comprehensive environmental management programme, drawn up with UNEP assistance and based on recommendations of the Stockholm Conference, the Mar Del Plata Action Plan and the Cairo Programme for African Co-operation on the Environment. It forms part of UNEP's programme for environmentally sound management of inland waters,[269] and seeks to deal with water resources and environmental protection in a co-ordinated manner intended to ameliorate existing problems and prevent future conflicts. States are required to take 'all appropriate measures' to implement the policies and objectives established by the plan. An Intergovernmental Monitoring and Co-ordinating Committee provides policy guidance, oversees implementation, and evaluates results. But this body has few real powers; it lacks a regulatory function and has no right to be consulted before states make adverse use of the resource. Like other commissions it cannot compel action, and its success will turn largely on its ability to negotiate detailed measures with individual governments, and in acting as an effective forum for information gathering and environmental assessment. It is too early to tell what level of success this treaty will have in comparison to its European or North American counterparts.

---

[265] *Michie* v. *Great Lakes Steel Division*, 495 F. 2d 213 (1974); Cooper, 24 *CYIL* (1986), 271–81; and see generally, *supra*, pp. 197–206.

[266] *Supra*, n. 230.

[267] Zambezi River System Agreement, 1987, *supra*, n. 5.

[268] Godana, *Africa's Shared Water Resources*, and see *supra*, pp. 222–4.

[269] Rummel-Bulska, 54 *Ybk. of the AAA* (1984), 75.

4. CONCLUSIONS

The law of international watercourses has for most of its history been concerned with the allocation and use of a natural resource of international significance, not with its conservation or environmental protection. The point was made in Chapter 3, however, that requirements of conservation and sustainable development are of increasing importance in regard to these resources, and the evidence of this chapter indicates how far such obligations now affect the management of international water resources.

While it can be asserted with some confidence that states are no longer free to pollute or otherwise destroy the ecology of a shared watercourse to the detriment of their neighbours or of the marine environment, definitive conclusions concerning the law in this area are more difficult to draw. There is first, the major problem of the diversity of watercourse systems and the regional and bilateral arrangements governing their use. From this body of treaty law and state practice only the most general of inferences can usefully be made. With regard to pollution control and environmental protection the difficulties of generalization are exacerbated by the relatively sparse and recent character of the precedents and practice which can be relied on.

Secondly, although the ILC's draft articles, which received their first reading in 1991, do reflect existing international law, they remain in certain major respects controversial, and a number of issues are still unsettled, including their ultimate form, as a framework treaty, or as non-binding guidelines.[270] In particular, the relationship between equitable utilization, which is a right as well as a duty, and the obligation of harm prevention, is a major source of difficulty. This is of less significance for pollution control, where the general obligations of states to control this form of harm are fairly well accepted, than for other uses of a watercourse, where the implications of giving the no-harm principle explicit precedence are more far-reaching.

These difficulties, and other objections to the ILC draft expressed by some governments and writers, should not be exaggerated. It must be stressed that international watercourses are not the subject of a separate and wholly self-contained body of law, but are also governed by rules and principles, and in some cases also by international agreements, of more general significance. As we have seen, the law of the sea may be particularly relevant where pollution affects the marine environment. But it is not simply pollution which is the main problem, but a broader question of ecological protection. Many international and national watercourses are also important habitats for wildlife and migratory species, such as salmon, and these may be seriously affected by the

---

[270] See UN Doc. A/CN.4/L.456 (1990) for comments made by states on this issue, and for discussion of the ILC draft, see papers collected in 3 *CJIEL and P* (1992), 1 ff.

building of dams, or the re-routing of rivers and draining of wetlands. Thus conservation treaties and related rules of international law governing living resources, including fisheries, are of particular importance in this context, and reference should be made to later chapters where these matters are considered.

The importance of viewing an international watercourse not merely as a shared natural resource to be exploited, but as a complete ecosystem whose development has diverse effects of an international character also emphasizes the limited utility of the principle of equitable utilization. Although correctly seen as the main principle of international watercourse law, this principle cannot sustain more than a modest role in allocating riparian rights. It affords an insufficient basis for measures of more comprehensive environmental protection.

Such measures can only usefully be negotiated multilaterally, with their implementation subject at least to intergovernmental supervision and control, as we saw in Chapter 4. In this respect, the development of co-operative regimes for the common management of international watercourses has not yet been sufficiently comprehensive or effective. Environmental protection arrangements in Europe and North America are incomplete, apply only to certain rivers, and have only slowly been implemented. African watercourse treaties are sophisticated in content, but of little practical importance due to their limited implementation. The record of states in the co-operative management of watercourse resources is thus an inadequate one, despite the general international endorsement of this approach in principle.

7

The Law of the Sea and the Regulation of Marine Pollution

1. INTRODUCTION[1]

The high seas are the world's largest expanse of common space, freely used by man for navigation, exploitation of their living resources, extraction of mineral wealth, and as a disposal area for the waste products of industry, domestic life, and war. The emergence of serious environmental problems was evident as early as 1926, when a draft convention on pollution from ships was drawn up at a conference in Washington, but not opened for signature. The pressure of international competition for living resources led to the conclusion of the first multilateral treaties on seals, fisheries, and whaling in the early twentieth century.[2] But it was only after the Second World War that problems of over-exploitation of resources, and the steady increase in the volume and effects of pollution from land and seaborne sources reached an intensity that required concerted international action. The subsequent history and development of fisheries conservation in international law is considered in Chapter 13. Regulation of marine pollution was somewhat slower to develop, reflecting the more limited interest of states in this problem, and the limitations of scientific understanding of oceanic processes.

By the late 1960s, however, awareness of the impact of pollution on coastal environments, on fisheries, and on human populations had become widespread. The *Torrey Canyon* disaster in 1967, involving the contamination of large areas of coastline by oil, exemplified the risk posed by the daily transport of large quantities of toxic and hazardous substances at sea. The discovery that mercury emissions from a factory at Minamata in Japan had poisoned fish and endangered the lives and health of coastal communities showed that the problem was not confined to the operation of ships, but required comprehensive control of all potential pollution sources, including

---

[1] See generally O'Connell, *The International Law of the Sea* (Oxford, 1984), ii, ch. 25; Churchill and Lowe, *The Law of the Sea* (2nd edn., Manchester, 1988), ch. 15; Johnston (ed.), *The Environmental Law of the Sea* (Berlin, 1981).

[2] 1911 Convention for the Preservation and Protection of Fur Seals, 104 *BFSP* 175; 1923 Convention for the Preservation of the Halibut Fishing of the Northern Pacific, 32 *LNTS* 94; 1930 Convention Establishing an International Pacific Salmon Fisheries Commission, 184 *LNTS* 306; 1931 Convention for the Regulation of Whaling, 155 *LNTS* 349. See *infra*, Chs. 12 and 13.

those on land. Since then, scientific studies conducted by GESAMP, and at regional level, have shown a steady increase in pollution of the sea by oil, chemicals, nuclear waste, and the effluent of urban, industrial society.[3] The control, reduction, and elimination of marine pollution have become a major issue in the law of the sea, requiring the creation of a substantial body of new law.

This process of legal development, initially based on *ad hoc* attempts to regulate specific problems, such as pollution from ships or dumping, was given substantial impetus by the 1972 Stockholm Conference on the Human Environment. The Action Plan adopted by the Conference indentified many of the weaknesses of earlier attempts to protect the marine environment, and made certain recommendations which have subsequently formed the basis for further action.[4] In particular, the Conference called on states to accept and implement existing legal instruments for the control of marine pollution, which many had not done, and to ensure that they were complied with by vessels flying their flag or operating in areas under their jurisdiction; it also supported proposals for new conventions on dumping and pollution from ships, which led to the adoption of the 1972 London and Oslo Dumping Conventions and the 1973 MARPOL Convention respectively. The Conference also called for stronger national controls over land-based pollution. Other recommendations dealt with support for research and monitoring programmes at national and international level, using existing international institutions or agencies such as IMO, the IOC, and GESAMP, and with co-ordination and stimulation of international action through UNEP. A set of general principles for the assessment and control of marine pollution was endorsed. These included a definition of 'marine pollution' based on the formulation adopted by GESAMP, and a series of general obligations to protect the marine environment from all sources of pollution, which formed the basis for articles later incorporated in the 1982 UNCLOS, and in UNEP's regional seas treaties.

The 1982 UNCLOS was intended to be a comprehensive restatement of almost all aspects of the Law of the Sea. Its basic objective is to establish

a legal order for the seas and oceans which will facilitate international communication, and will promote the peaceful uses of the seas and oceans, the equitable and efficient utilization of their resources, the conservation of their living resources, and the study, protection and preservation of the marine environment.

The Convention thus attempts for the first time to provide a global framework for the rational exploitation and conservation of the sea's resources and the

---

[3] See Ch. 8 nn. 1, 2, and 28, and see generally Cusine and Grant (eds.), *The Impact of Marine Pollution* (London, 1980); Schachter and Serwer, 65 *AJIL* (1971), 84.

[4] UN Doc. A/CONF.48/14/Rev. 1, Action Plan, Recommendations 86–94, and see also Intergovernmental Working Group on Marine Pollution, UN Doc. A/CONF.48/8, para. 197, repr. as Annex III to the Conference Report. See further Ch. 2, *supra*.

protection of the environment, which can be seen as a system for sustainable development, and as a model for the evolution of international environmental law[5]. Moreover, it gives special recognition in various ways to the interests of developing states, in particular though provision for transfer of science and technology and a partial reallocation of fisheries resources. Other measures intended to benefit developing states are noted later in this chapter and in Chapter 8.

The articles of the 1982 UNCLOS on the marine environment thus represent the culmination of a process of international lawmaking which has effected a number of fundamental changes in the international law of the sea.[6] Of these perhaps the most important is that pollution can no longer be regarded as an implicit freedom of the seas; rather, its diligent control from all sources is now a matter of comprehensive legal obligation affecting the marine environment as a whole, and not simply the interests of other states. A second, less radical alteration is to the balance of power between flag states, more concerned with freedom of navigation and fishing, and coastal states, more concerned with effective regulation and control, although many states fall into both categories and thus faced complex policy choices in negotiating the 1982 UNCLOS. Thirdly, more than any other part of international environmental law, the emphasis in this subject is no longer placed on state responsibility for environmental damage, but instead rests primarily on international regulation and co-operation in the protection of the marine environment. In the structure of this legal regime, flag states, coastal states, port states, and international organizations and commissions each have important roles, powers, and responsibilities, which in certain respects combine to produce one of the more successful examples of international environmental co-operation. This chapter deals only with the main principles of international law governing protection of the marine environment, with particular emphasis on the 1982 UNCLOS and pollution from ships. Pollution from dumping and land-based sources is the subject of Chapter 8, and the conservation of the sea's living resources is dealt with in Chapter 13.

2. CUSTOMARY LAW AND THE 1982 UNCLOS

(1) High Seas Freedoms and Reasonable Use

Protection of the marine environment was not given special importance in the Geneva Conference on the Law of the Sea in 1958, and the Geneva

---

[5] UN Doc. A/44/461 (1989), *Report of the UN Secretary General on the Protection and Preservation of the Marine Environment.*
[6] Boyle, 79 *AJIL* (1985), 347; Schneider, 20 *CJTL* (1981), 243. See also Kwiatkowska, *The 200-Mile EEZ in the New Law of the Sea* (Dordrecht, 1989), ch. 5; McConnell and Gold, 23 *CWRJIL* (1991), 83.

Conventions have little to say on the subject. Articles 24 and 25 of the High Seas Convention do require states to prevent oil pollution from ships, pipelines, and sea-bed operations, and pollution from radioactive substances, but they fall short of acknowledging a more comprehensive duty to prevent marine pollution or protect the marine environment, and offer no definition of the term 'pollution'. The content of even these limited obligations was uncertainly defined, and states were left with much discretion in the choice of measures to take. The articles did refer to 'taking account' of 'existing treaty provisions', a formulation intended to cover the 1954 London Convention for Prevention of Pollution of the Sea by Oil, and to 'any standards and regulations which may be formulated by the competent international organizations', which in this instance meant the IAEA's regulations on the disposal of radioactive waste,[7] but this did not mean that states were obliged either to become parties or to follow the standards set by these international regulations. In practice, the 1958 Conventions seemed to suggest that states enjoyed substantial freedom to pollute the oceans, moderated only by the principle that high seas freedoms must be exercised with reasonable regard for the rights of others. This view was not contradicted by the 1954 London Convention, which did not entirely prohibit discharges of oil from ships at sea, nor by the IAEA's regulations, which permitted the disposal of low-level radioactive waste. The test of reasonableness still remains a useful principle for accommodating lawful but conflicting uses of the sea.[8] But the evidence now points firmly towards the emergence of more specific rules of international law governing the protection of the marine environment, such as the prohibition of radioactive pollution of the seas, referred to in Chapter 8, or the authoritative exposition of the no-harm principle in relation to pollution from ships, considered below.

(2) A Duty to Protect the Marine Environment

The emergence of a more strongly expressed obligation to protect the marine environment is evidenced by Articles 192–5 of the 1982 UNCLOS, by regional treaties, and by other multilateral agreements negotiated progressively since 1954. These include the 1972 London Dumping Convention, the 1973/8 MARPOL Convention, which deals with pollution from ships and supersedes the earlier 1954 Convention, and a variety of regional treaties requiring states to control land-based sources of marine pollution, dumping, and sea-bed operations.[9] The degree of acceptance of these various treaties and the consensus expressed by states in negotiating the environmental

---

[7] See Ch. 8.
[8] See Ch. 3, and generally *Icelandic Fisheries Case*, *ICJ Rep*. (1974), 4.
[9] On regional treaties, see *infra*, pp. 260–3.

provisions of the 1982 UNCLOS suggest that although this agreement is not in force, its articles on the marine environment are supported by a strong measure of *opinio juris* and represent in certain respects an agreed codification of existing principles which have become part of customary law.[10] There is thus nothing essentially novel in the proposition first articulated in Article 192 of the 1982 Convention that 'states have the obligation to protect and preserve the marine environment', although this may not have been the case when the article was first proposed in 1975. Moreover, in according preservation of the environment priority over the sovereign right of states to exploit their natural resources, referred to in Article 193, Article 192 is somewhat more strongly expressed than Principle 21 of the 1972 Stockholm Declaration.

The content of this obligation is elaborated in more detail by Article 194 and subsequent provisions. It is evident from the Convention, first, that its protection extends not only to states and their marine environment, but to the marine environment as a whole, including the high seas. This goes beyond the older customary rule based on the *Trail Smelter* arbitration, and reflects its extension to global common areas contemplated by Principle 21 of the Stockholm Declaration. Moreover, the 'environment' for this purpose includes 'rare and fragile ecosystems as well as the habitat of depleted, threatened or endangered species and other forms of marine life'.[11] The obligation of states is thus not confined to the protection of economic interests, private property or the human use of the sea implied in the Convention's definition of 'pollution'.[12] This conclusion is consistent with the provisions of modern treaties dealing with the wider environmental impact of marine pollution, including the 1984 protocol to the 1969 Convention on Civil Liability for Oil Pollution Damage, the 1989 Salvage Convention, and a number of regional treaties and protocols concerned with specially sensitive ecological areas,[13] although many of these instruments are not yet in force.

Secondly, the 1982 UNCLOS represents an important advance over the earlier Geneva Conventions by formulating the obligation of environmental protection in terms which are comprehensive of all sources of marine pollution.[14] Thus it applies to ships, land-based sources, sea-bed operations, dumping, and atmospheric pollution, and provides a framework for a series of treaties both global and regional on each of these topics. In this respect the comprehensive scope of the 1982 Convention follows the pattern

---

[10] *Supra*, n. 6. On the drafting history of Articles 192–5 see Nordquist (ed.), *United Nations Convention on the Law of the Sea: A Commentary*, iv (Dordrecht, 1991), 36 ff.

[11] Article 194(5).

[12] Article 1(4), *supra*, Ch. 3.

[13] 1985 Nairobi Protocol Concerning Protected Areas and Wild Flora and Fauna in Eastern Africa; 1982 Geneva Protocol Concerning Mediterranean Specially Protected Areas; 1990 Kingston Protocol Concerning Specially Protected Areas and Wildlife of the Wider Caribbean, on which see Freestone, 5 *IJECL* (1990), 362.

[14] Article 194.

established by the 1974 Helsinki Convention for the Protection of the Marine Environment of the Baltic Sea, and subsequently adopted in UNEP's regional seas treaties.

But perhaps its most significant feature is the way the Convention handles the concept of due diligence. As with other treaties it makes reference to the need to take 'all measures necessary' to prevent and control pollution damage to other states, but it moderates this requirement by allowing use of the 'best practicable means at their disposal and in accordance with their capabilities' where the risk is to the marine environment in general, rather than to other states. This wording implies a somewhat greater flexibility and discretion, particularly for developing countries, whose interests received particular attention in the drafting of this part of the Convention.[15] The significance of this point can be seen more clearly in Articles 207 and 212, dealing with the control of land-based and atmospheric sources of pollution, where reference is made to economic capacity, development needs, and 'characteristic regional features'. State practice in regard to these two sources of pollution is examined in Chapters 8 and 10 and confirms the view that the Convention's treatment of both issues largely defers to the priorities set by individual states.

These unhelpful generalities are absent, however, in the provisions dealing with pollution from ships, dumping, and sea-bed operations, and it is here that the Convention does establish some important and concrete principles. The essential point in these cases is that states must give effect to or apply rules and standards to less onerous than 'generally recognised international rules and standards'. Although precise phraseology varies in detail, and not all writers are agreed on the correct interpretation, the importance of Articles 208, 210, and 211 of the Convention seems to be that they have the effect of incorporating by implication the 1972 London Dumping Convention and the 1973/78 MARPOL Convention and quite possibly other treaties, IMO codes, and international guidelines agreed and adopted by a preponderance of maritime states into the primary obligation of states to prevent pollution. If this view is correct, then states which have ratified the 1982 UNCLOS will thus be compelled to adopt the basic standards set *inter alia* by those two treaties, even if they are not parties to them.[16] A more ambitious argument is that non-parties may as a matter of customary law be bound by the basic

---

[15] Nordquist and Park (eds.), *Reports of the US Delegation to the UN Convention 3rd UNCLOS* (Honolulu, 1983), 47–51, 74, and 89; Kindt, 20 *VJIL* (1979), 313; Nordquist iv, 64.

[16] Boyle, 79 *AJIL* (1985). On the variety of meanings attributed to the phrase 'generally accepted', see Vukas, in Soons (ed.), *Implementation of the Law of the Sea Convention Through International Institutions* (Honolulu, 1990), 405; Bernhardt, 20 *VJIL* (1980), 265; Van Reenen, 12 *NYIL* (1981), 3; Vignes, *AFDI* (1979), 712; Timagenis, *International Control of Marine Pollution* (Dobbs Ferry, NY, 1979), 603–7. For the status of other IMO and ILO conventions as 'generally accepted international standards' for the purposes of Article 211 of the 1982 UNCLOS, see Valenzuela, in Soons (ed.), *Implementation of the Law of the Sea Convention Through International Institutions* (Honolulu, 1990), 187.

principles of the Dumping and MARPOL Conventions due to their wide-spread ratification, and the general compliance of non-parties in enforcement measures, as well as their indirect incorporation into the codification brought about by the 1982 UNCLOS.[17] Expressed in different terms, the 1982 Convention is important because it uses these treaties and other internationally agreed standards, such as IAEA guidelines or IMO conventions, to define the detailed content of the customary obligation of due diligence as formulated in Article 194. The generality and uncertainty which limit the usefulness of the 'no-harm principle' in other contexts are thus potentially reduced, although as some writers point out, the lack of clarity in defining precisely which rules must be observed may in practice give states some discretion to pick and choose.

More than any other aspect of the 1982 Convention, these provisions are indicative of an altered sense of priorities in the treatment of marine pollution. It is no longer essentially a matter of high seas freedom moderated by reasonable use, but one of legal obligation to protect the environment. Whereas previously states were to a large degree free to determine for themselves whether and to what extent to control and regulate marine pollution, they will now in most cases be bound to do so on terms laid down by the 1982 Convention and other international instruments. Because of the widespread acceptance of the basic treaties on pollution from ships, and possibly also on dumping, this proposition holds good notwithstanding that the 1982 UNCLOS itself is not in force; the impact of the Convention's articles on the marine environment lies essentially in their expression of principles of customary law, whether those reflected in prior state practice, or subsequently developed.

3. REGIONAL PROTECTION OF THE MARINE ENVIRONMENT[18]

(1) The 1982 UNCLOS and Regional Rules

Although the 1982 Convention, like the law of the sea itself, is primarily concerned with a global system of international law governing all aspects of the use of the oceans, the Convention's express reference at various points

---

[17] See generally *North Sea Continental Shelf Case, ICJ Rep.* (1969), 3; *Paramilitary Activities in Nicaragua Case*, ibid. (1986), 14. As of June 1991, 66 states representing 88% of world shipping tonnage were parties to Annexes I and II of MARPOL; 63 states including all those engaged in dumping at sea were parties to the London Dumping Convention, on which see further, *infra*, Ch. 8.

[18] Johnston, *Regionalisation of the Law of the Sea* (Cambridge, 1978); Yturriaga, 162 *Recueil des cours* (1979), 319; Okidi, *Regional Control of Ocean Pollution* (Alphen aan den Rijn, 1978); Boyle, in Butler (ed.), *The Law of the Sea and International Shipping* (New York, 1985), 315; Boczek, 16 *CWRJIL* (1984), 39; Goncalves, 3 *Marine Policy* (1979), 255; Johnston and Enomoto, in Johnston (ed.), *The Environmental Law of the Sea* (Gland, 1981), 285.

to regional rules, regional programmes, regional co-operation, and so forth does indicate that we are not necessarily dealing with a single legal regime of universal application but with one which allows for significant regional variations. This point is not confined to the articles on protection of the marine environment, but it is particularly significant in that context.

Nowhere does the Convention specify what is meant by 'regional', although the term is clearly something less than 'global'. The best interpretation is that a region is defined by the context in which the issue arises. Article 122 offers one approach in its reference to enclosed or semi-enclosed seas, defined as: 'a gulf, basin or sea surrounded by two or more states and connected to another sea or the ocean by a narrow inlet or consisting entirely or primarily of the territorial seas and exclusive economic zones of two or more coastal states.' A number of treaties concerned with protection of the marine environment are regional in this sense, notably those relating to the Mediterranean, the Baltic, the North Sea, the Red Sea, and Persian Gulf. What makes these areas special is their relative ecological sensitivity and separation from the marine environment of adjacent oceans. They represent in varying degrees 'problem sheds' or areas within which the levels of pollution are relatively or completely independent of discharges elsewhere, and which require regional co-ordination if control measures are to be effective.[19] These considerations are of particular significance in the control of land-based sources of pollution, and as we shall see in the next chapter, the 1982 Convention's articles largely assume that this source will be controlled nationally and regionally, rather than by global rules. This partly accounts for the extreme generality of the Convention's provisions on the subject, although some progress has subsequently been made in strengthening regional action.

A 'region' does not have to be composed on this ecological basis, however. Political considerations, common interests, or geographical proximity are other factors influencing the conclusion of regional treaties.[20] Some of the UNEP regional seas treaties relate to oceanic coastal areas where the only factor connecting participants is their location on a common coastline, rather than any identity of interest or shared ecological problems. The conventions dealing with the Pacific coast of South America, the Atlantic coast of Africa, and the Indian Ocean fall into this category.[21] Others, in the South Pacific, or

---

[19] Okidi, 4 *ODIL* (1971), 1; Schachter and Serwer, 65 *AJIL* (1971), 84.

[20] Alexander, 71 *AJIL* (1977), 84; id., 2 *ODIL* (1974), 151; Hayward, 8 *Marine Policy* (1984), 106.

[21] 1981 Lima Convention for the Protection of the Marine Environment and Coastal Area of the S. E. Pacific; 1981 Abidjan Convention for Co-operation in the Protection and Development of the Marine and Coastal Environment of West and Central Africa; 1985 Nairobi Convention for the Protection, Management, and Development of the Marine and Coastal Environment of East Africa.

the Caribbean, are largely defined by the proximity and shared interests of a number of island states.[22]

Leaving aside their composition, the more important question concerns the role which it is appropriate for regional regulation of the marine environment to play. There are several possible answers to this question. At one level, regional arrangements are simply a means of implementing policies which are necessary in the interests of a specific community of states and which can best be tackled on a regional basis. Co-operation in cases of pollution emergencies, or in the exploitation of fishing stocks are good examples, because the range of states affected is relatively limited. In other cases, such as enclosed or semi-enclosed seas or Arctic waters, physical characteristics may dictate the regional application of more onerous standards of pollution prevention than would suffice for oceanic areas. This factor is the main justification for special regional rules governing the discharge of pollution from ships or the dumping of waste at sea.[23] The need to cater for such special cases is recognized in the 1982 UNCLOS, although it is important to observe that for pollution from ships or dumping the Convention insists that regional rules should be no less effective than more generally accepted international rules, and that regional treaties cannot be taken as an opportunity for falling below those rules. By facilitating some regional flexibility, however, regional arrangements do help accommodate the special needs and varying circumstances of a range of seas with diverse ecological and oceanographic characteristics to a general international law of the sea. A second reason for resort to regional arrangements is that they may facilitate co-operation in monitoring, supervision, and enforcement, as we saw in Chapter 4. This is particularly true in the North Sea, the Baltic, and the Mediterranean, where intergovernmental supervisory institutions have been established; there are other regions, however, where no effective multilateral commissions exist, or where the role played by institutions remains limited to a symbolic presence.[24] A number of UNEP regional seas institutions fall into this category, having never in practice functioned. Lastly, regional treaties can be seen as a means of giving effect to the framework provisions of the 1982 Convention, and as evidence of the implementation and adoption of that Convention's main principles at regional level. Their conformity in most respects with the 1982 UNCLOS is some indication of their legislative function in international law, and of the present

---

[22] 1983 Cartagena Convention for the Protection and Development of the Marine Environment of the Wider Caribbean; 1986 Noumea Convention for the Protection of the Natural Resources and Environment of the South Pacific Region.

[23] 1982 UNCLOS, Articles 211(6); 234; 1972 Oslo Dumping Convention, and see *infra*, Ch. 8.

[24] See Ch. 8.

legal status of the 1982 Convention's provisions on protection of the marine environment.[25]

(2) Regional Seas Agreements

Some twenty treaties can be identified which are 'regional' in the various senses described above and which relate to the protection of the marine environment. These fall into two main groups; first, those concerned with enclosed or semi-enclosed seas in the northern hemisphere where the major problems are those of industrial pollution and land-based activities, and secondly, a group of UNEP-sponsored treaties of less detailed character which establish a broadly uniform pattern of principles for a majority of developing countries in the southern hemisphere. The number of states now involved in these regional seas treaties, and in other UNEP regional seas programmes, is such that they cannot be dismissed as special cases; they represent a substantial body of practice of more general significance for the law of the marine environment as a whole.

(a) The North Sea and North-East Atlantic[26]

This area is not covered by one comprehensive treaty, but by a series of agreements dealing with specific issues. As a result there is significant over-lapping coverage and a particular need for co-ordination among the institutions created to service each treaty. The 1969 Bonn Agreement for Co-operation in Dealing with Pollution of the North Sea by Oil was replaced in 1983 by a revised agreement which deals with pollution emergencies and co-operation. A comparable agreement of 1971 makes similar provision for co-operation among Nordic states.[27] The 1972 Oslo Dumping Convention, amended by subsequent protocols, applies to a wider area which extends to the North-East Atlantic, the North Sea, and the adjacent Arctic seas. Land-based pollution is dealth with by the 1974 Paris Convention, which covers the same area as the Oslo Convention. Both of these treaties share a common secretariat with the Bonn Convention and are due to be replaced by a single comprehensive framework agreement in 1992.[28] Since, as we shall see, the regulation of pollution from ships is best dealt with at the global level, there are no

---

[25] See further Boyle, in Butler, *The Law of the Sea and International Shipping*. Some provisions of regional agreements do pose problems of conformity with the 1982 UNCLOS, however: see for example, 1981 Lima Convention for the Protection of the Marine Environment of the South-East Pacific, Article 1 (area of application).

[26] See generally IJlstra, 3 *IJECL* (1988), 181; Saetevik, *Environmental Co-operation Among North Sea States* (London, 1986); and papers collected in 5 *IJECL* (1990).

[27] 1971 Copenhagen Agreement Concerning Co-operation in Taking Measures Against Pollution of the Sea by Oil. See also 1990 Lisbon Agreement of Co-operation for the Protection of the North-East Atlantic Against Pollution.

[28] See Ch. 8.

regional agreements dealing with this aspect, except in regard to enforcement, for which in the North Sea a common scheme of port inspection exists. In addition to these agreements, the series of International North Sea Conferences (INSC) has defined increasingly stringent political objectives for comprehensive pollution control and reduction in the North Sea. The declarations of these Conferences are not treaties, but the principle of good faith may entail a significant commitment to ensure effective implementation. Moreover, the EEC has become a significant regional institution in adopting measures for protection of the marine environment of the North Sea, the Baltic, and the Mediterranean; its policy has had particular impact on the Paris Commission, mostly of a negative kind.[29]

(b) The Baltic and Mediterranean[30]

The 1974 Helsinki Convention for the Protection of the Marine Environment of the Baltic Area was the first regional seas treaty to adopt a comprehensive approach to marine pollution. It sets particularly stringent standards for dumping at sea, and applies rules modelled on the MARPOL Convention to pollution from ships. It also deals with airborne and land-based sources of pollution. This Convention was an important influence on the formulation of the marine pollution provisions of the 1982 UNCLOS, and of the first of UNEP's regional seas treaties, the 1976 Barcelona Convention for the Protection of the Mediterranean Sea. Like the Helsinki Convention the latter agreement follows the concept of a comprehensive framework model, although in somewhat different form. In this case separate protocols deal with land-based sources of marine pollution, dumping and specially protected areas. The Barcelona Convention is unusual in having to accommodate not only the interests of developed northern hemisphere industrialized economies but also the less developed countries on its southern and eastern shores.

(c) Other UNEP Regional Seas Treaties

UNEP's regional seas programme,[31] initiated in 1974, covers ten areas where regional action plans are operative or under development. Apart from the Mediterranean these include the Kuwait Action Plan Region (covering the Arabian Gulf), the West and Central African Region, the wider Caribbean,

---

[29] On the INSC and EEC, see ibid.

[30] Johnson, 25 *ICLQ* (1976), 1; Boczek, 72 AJIL (1978), 782; Jaenicke, in Park (ed.), *The Law of the Sea in the 1980s* (Honolulu, 1980), 493; Chircop, in Law of the Sea Institute: *Proceedings of 25th Annual Conference* (Malmo, 1991).

[31] See generally Hulm, *A Strategy for the Seas: The Regional Seas Programme, Past and Future*, UNEP (1983); UNEP, *Environmental Law in the UNEP* (Nairobi, 1990); id., *Achievements and Planned Development of UNEP'S Regional Seas Programme* (Nairobi, 1982); IMO/UNEP, *Meeting on Regional Arrangements for Co-operation in Combating Major Incidents of Marine Pollution* (London, 1985); UNEP, *Assessment of UNEP's Achievement in Oceans Programme Element* (Nairobi, 1985); Sand, *Marine Environmental Law in the UNEP* (Dublin, 1988).

the East Asian Seas Region, the South East Pacific, the Red Sea and Gulf of Aden, the South Pacific, Eastern Africa, and the South Asian Seas. Most of these action plans make provision for environmental assessment, management, legislation, and institutional and financial arrangements. They are of particular significance for developing states in facilitating co-operation and the provision of assistance in the management of marine pollution problems in regions where expertise and facilities may be lacking. Most of the regional programmes include arrangements for combating major incidents of marine pollution, and the regional treaties all have protocols on this subject.

Following the pattern established by the Barcelona Convention, most of the regional seas programmes are now supported by framework conventions. These apply in the Persian Gulf, the Red Sea and Gulf of Aden, the East African side of the Indian Ocean, the South Pacific, the Latin American side of the South East Pacific, the Caribbean, and the West African side of the South Atlantic.[32] Their geographical scope includes the territorial sea and exclusive economic zones of the parties. All are comprehensive in their inclusion of sources of marine pollution, but unlike the European treaties, few set detailed regulations or establish special regional standards. Thus the 1983 Quito Protocol remains the only southern hemisphere agreement dealing in detail with land-based sources of pollution within the UNEP programme, while the only protocol on dumping applies to the South Pacific. Specially protected areas of ecological sensitivity are covered by protocols in the East African region, the Caribbean, and the South Pacific. No special regional arrangements for enforcement exist within the UNEP regions, and in so far as reference is made to applicable international standards for pollution from ships these relate to the 1973/8 MARPOL Convention. Most of UNEP's regional treaties reflect the negligible level of international control over landbased and airborne pollution set by the 1982 UNCLOS and considered more fully in Chapters 8 and 10.

The Regional Seas Programme has proved its flexibility as a model for facilitating co-operation, co-ordinating training and technical assistance, enabling new protocols and institutions to be added as necessary, focusing attention on regional pollution problems and their interrelationship, and stimulating research. To this extent, as indicated in Chapter 2, it has been one of UNEP's more successful programmes. An important weakness, however, remains the limited participation of states in some regions and the poor record of ratification and implementation of some of the conventions or their pro-

---

[32] 1976 Barcelona Convention for the Protection of the Mediterranean Sea Against Pollution; 1982 Jeddah Convention for the Conservation of the Red Sea and Gulf of Aden Environment; 1978 Kuwait Convention for Co-operation on the Protection of the Marine Environment from Pollution, and see others listed *supra*, nn. 21 and 22. An East Asian Convention was due for adoption in 1991. See generally Edwards, in Carroll (ed.), *International Environmental Diplomacy* (Cambridge, 1988), 229.

tocols. A more damning criticism is that the programme has demonstrated environmental awareness without providing the means to tackle problems seriously. The lack of adequate financial and technical resources is a serious obstacle to the implementation of much of the regional seas programme. A UNEP report on the West and Central African programme in 1989 noted the shortfall in contributions to the trust fund established to support implementation of that programme and observed the inability of UNEP's environment fund to continue as the major source of financial resources. The inadequacy of national administrations in Africa has further hampered effective implemenation of various protocols and the action plan. Similar problems have affected the Mediterranean and Caribbean programmes.[33]

4. POLLUTION FROM SHIPS[34]

(1) The Nature of the Problem

Pollution from ships is generally of two kinds: operational and accidental. Operational pollution is a function of the manner in which ships operate. Oil tankers, for example, traditionally washed their oil tanks and disposed of oily residues at sea, causing significant volumes of pollution. The objective of international regulation in this context has been to eliminate the need for such discharges, through technical solutions and the provision of shore facilities. The second form of marine pollution, more dramatic but in aggregate less significant, emanates from marine casualties. The sinking of large oil tankers such as the *Torrey Canyon*, the *Amoco Cadiz*, or the *Exxon Valdez* exemplifies the scale and potential severity of such accidents, whose seriousness derives mainly from the volume of oil or other pollutants released in one place. Such accidents harm coastal communities, fisheries, wildlife, and local ecology. In some areas, such as the Arctic or Antarctic, climatic conditions exacerbate both the long-term effects and the difficulty of dealing with this kind of pollution. The purpose of regulation here is to minimize the risk and give coastal states adequate means of protecting themselves and securing compensation.

Neither problem should be exaggerated; as we shall see in Chapter 8, the major sources of marine pollution are on land, not afloat. But, like nuclear installations, oil tankers and other vessels carrying hazardous and noxious cargoes represent a form of ultra-hazardous risk for all coastal states, which it

---

[33] UNEP, *West and Central African Action Plan: Evaluation of its Development and Achievements* (Nairobi, 1989). For earlier more positive assessments, see UNEP, *Assessment of UNEP's Achievements, etc.*, and see generally *supra*, pp. 47–52.

[34] See generally M'Gonigle and Zacher, *Pollution, Politics and International Law* (London, 1979); Abecassis, *Oil Pollution from Ships* (2nd edn., London, 1984); Gold and Johnston, in Clingan (ed.), *Law of the Sea: State Practice in Zones of Special Jurisdiction* (Honolulu, 1982), 157; Wang, 16 *ODIL* (1986), 305; Bernhardt, 20 *VJIL* (1979), 265.

is the object of international law to moderate and control. A dominant theme of the UNCLOS III conference was the failure of the traditional structure of jurisdiction over ships and maritime areas to protect the interests of those coastal states whose proximity to shipping routes made them particularly vulnerable. On the one hand the duty of the flag state to adopt and enforce appropriate regulations was too imperfectly defined and observed. On the other, the power of the coastal state to regulate shipping and activities off its coast was too limited. The 1973 MARPOL Convention and the 1982 UNCLOS address these problems by extending the enforcement powers of coastal and port states, at the expense of the flag state's exclusive authority, and by redefining and strengthening the latter's obligations towards the protection of the marine environment. The result is a relatively complex structure of authority over maritime activities which tries to reconcile the effective enforcement of environmental regulations with the primary concern of maritime states in freedom of navigation.[35]

(2) Jurisdiction to Regulate Vessel Pollution

(a) Flag state Jurisdiction and International Standards

The primary basis for the regulation of ships is the jurisdiction enjoyed by the state in which the vessel is registered or whose flag it is entitled to fly ('the flag state'). These conditions determine the nationality of the ship. Although Article 5 of the 1958 High Seas Covention refers to the need for a genuine link between the state of nationality and the ship, this ambiguous provision has not prevented the emergence of 'flags of convenience', where registration, rather than ownership, management, nationality of the crew, or the ship's operational base, is the only substantial connection. The more convincing proposition is not that international law prohibits flags of convenience, but that once a state has conferred the right to fly its flag, international law requires it to exercise effective jurisdiction and control over the ship in administrative, technical, and social matters. Thus it is the flag state which is responsible for regulating safety at sea and the prevention of collisions, the manning of ships and the competence of their crews, and for setting standards of construction, design, equipment, and seaworthiness.[36] These responsibilities also include taking measures to prevent pollution.

Moreover, in customary law, only the flag state has jurisdiction to enforce

---

[35] Boyle, 79 *AJIL* (1985); Bernhardt, 20 *VJIL* (1979), and see generally Allott, 77 *AJIL* (1983), 1.

[36] 1958 Geneva Convention on the High Seas, Articles 5, 10; 1982 UNCLOS, Articles 91, 94, 211(2); 1954 London Convention for the Prevention of the Oil Pollution from Ships; 1973 MARPOL Convention; 1986 UN Convention on Conditions for Registration of Ships; 1974 Safety of Life at Sea Convention; see generally Churchill and Lowe, *The Law of the Sea*, ch. 13; O'Connell, *The International Law of the Sea*, ii, ch. 20.

regulations applicable to vessels on the high seas. In the *Lotus* case,[37] the Permanent Court of International Justice referred to the principle that no state may exercise any kind of jurisdiction over foreign vessels on the high seas, but by this it meant only that foreign vessels could not be arrested or detained while on the high seas, not that regulations could not be enforced by other states once the ship had voluntarily entered port. As we shall see, this case forms the possible basis for port state jurisdiction over high seas pollution offences referred to in Article 218 of the 1982 UNCLOS. Even when the ship is within the territorial jurisdiction of other states, however, the flag state does not lose its jurisdiction; regardless of where it is operating, a ship must therefore comply with the laws of its own flag.

Customary international law thus gives the flag state ample power to regulate marine pollution from vessels, and other aspects of the operation of ships likely to pose a risk to the environment, such as seaworthiness standards. Moreover, as we have seen, it requires them to do so effectively. Both the content of this duty, and the manner in which it is enforced have been the subject of more specific international agreements, negotiated mainly through IMO, which is usually the 'competent international organization' referred to in this context by the 1982 UNCLOS.

The purpose of these agreements is to provide internationally recognized common standards for flag states and coastal states to follow in regulating the safety of shipping and the protection of the environment. They include the 1966 International Convention on Load Lines, the 1972 Convention on the International Regulations for Preventing Collisions at Sea, and the 1974 Safety of Life at Sea Convention (SOLAS), which are intended to minimize the risk of maritime accidents by regulating navigation, construction, and seaworthiness standards. A 1978 Protocol to the SOLAS Convention makes the use of certain additional safety features mandatory for oil tankers and other large vessels, both for safety of navigation and pollution prevention purposes. ILO Convention No. 147 Concerning Minimum Standards in Merchant Ships and the 1978 IMO Convention on Standards of Training, Certification, and Watchkeeping lay down additional standards for competency, hours of work, and manning of vessels.[38]

Many of these agreements are very widely ratified and adopted by maritime states, and most can be readily amended and updated by IMO. Although in most cases their primary purpose is to ensure better safety standards, they are also an essential means of reducing the threat to the marine environment

---

[37] *PCIJ*, Ser. A, No. 10 (1927), 169.

[38] See generally Juda, 26 *ICLQ* (1977), 558; Blanco-Bazan, in Law of the Sea Institute: *Proceedings of the 25th Annual Conference* (Malmo, 1991); Valenzuela, in Soons, *Implementation*; Churchill and Lowe, *The Law of the Sea*, ch. 13; Osieke, 30 *ICLQ* (1981), 497. On IMO, see *supra*, Ch. 2. In 1991, IMO adopted revised guidelines on Management for the Safe Operation of Ships and for Pollution Prevention, MSC 59/33/Add. 2, Annex 30.

posed by maritime accidents. To that extent they constitute a form of inter-national regulation of the environmental risks of transporting oil and other substances by sea, with IMO acting as the main regulatory and supervisory institution. Two other agreements deal specifically with operational pollution and the reduction of accidents, however: the 1954 London Convention for the Prevention of Pollution of the Sea by Oil, and the 1973 International Convention for the Prevention of Pollution from Ships (MARPOL).

(b) The 1954 London Convention[39]

This Convention marked the first successful attempt at international regula-tion of oil pollution from tankers. It was successively amended until its replacement in 1973 by the new MARPOL Convention, but some forty states remain bound only by the older treaty. Few if any of these are major tanker operators, however.

The 1954 Convention employed several techniques for minimizing opera-tional discharges of oil. It controlled their location, by defining prohibited areas and excluding coastal zones; it controlled the quantity of pollution, by limiting the rate of discharge; it controlled the need for discharges, by setting construction and equipment standards intended to reduce the volume of waste oil, or to separate oil from ballast water, and by calling on governments to provide port discharge facilities. As the convention bagan to influence the construction of tankers, so it was possible to introduce progressively stricter standards, including under a 1969 amendment, the so-called 'load on top system' which enabled tankers to discharge oily residues to land-based reception facilities.

There was nothing inherently defective in this approach to the regulation of operational pollution, and the convention was clearly capable of responding to technical progress. It was not particularly successful, however, for two reasons. First, the enforcement record of flag states was not strong: many had insufficient interest in pursuing enforcement vigorously in areas beyond their territorial jurisdiction and they were in any case confronted with practical problems of collecting evidence and bringing proceedings against ships which rarely entered their ports. Secondly, not all flag states were parties to the convention, nor did the 1958 High Seas Convention, with its requirement only to 'take account' of existing treaty provisions, compel states to apply the London Convention. Some flags of convenience were thus able to avoid the more onerous regulations, which coastal states could do little to enforce. The Stockholm Conference in 1972 identified both failings in its recommenda-tions on marine pollution, which called on states to accept and implement available instruments and to ensure compliance by their flag vessels.[40]

---

[39] O'Connell, *The International Law of the Sea*, ii, 1000; Abecassis, *Oil Pollution from Ships*, ch. 3; M'Gonigle and Zacher, *Pollution, Politics and International Law*, 85 ff.

[40] *Supra*, n. 5, and see generally Lowe, 12 *SDLR* (1975), 624; M'Gonigle and Zacher,

(c) The 1973/1978 MARPOL Convention[41]

This convention, first adopted in 1973, was substantially revised in 1978 to facilitate entry into force. The parties presently comprise over 85 per cent of the gross registered tonnage of the world's merchant fleet. It is thus beyond question that it is now included in the 'generally accepted international rules and standards' prescribed by Article 211 of the 1982 UNCLOS as the minimum content of the flag state's duty to exercise diligent control of its vessels in the prevention of marine pollution.[42] As we have seen, there are strong grounds for treating the MARPOL Convention as a customary standard to be complied with by the vessels of all states, whether or not they have chosen to ratify.

The MARPOL Convention's approach to the regulation of oil pollution is broadly similar to the 1954 Convention in relying mainly on technical measures to limit oil discharges. It also sets new construction standards, however, which are more stringent for new vessels. The discharge of small quantities of oil is still permitted, but only if it takes place *en route*, more than fifty miles from land and not in special areas where virtually all discharges are prohibited.[43] The special areas listed in the convention as regards oil pollution include the Mediterranean, the Black Sea, the Baltic, the Red Sea, and the Persian Gulf—all enclosed or semi-enclosed seas, where, as we saw earlier, more stringent standards are necessary. The Gulf of Aden and the Antarctic have subsequently been added to this list. In general terms, these provisions are meant to take advantage of modern technology and operating methods to eliminate all but minimal levels of oil discharge, to ensure that these have the least impact on coastal states, and to emphasize port discharge for residues which cannot otherwise be disposed of. The regulations can be amended as necessary by IMO or by a conference of the parties.

In other respects, however, the MARPOL Convention differs significantly from the earlier scheme. First, it is no longer confined to oil pollution, but also regulates other types of ship-based pollution, including the bulk carriage of noxious liquids and garbage from ships.[44] It thus provides some evidence of internationally agreed standards of environmentally sound management for the transport of chemicals and hazardous wastes, and may be relevant in determining the obligations of states under the 1989 Basel Convention, considered in Chapter 8.

Pollution, Politics and International Law, ch. 8; Birnie, in Cusine and Grant, *The Impact of Marine Pollution*, 95.

[41] O'Connell, *The International Law of the Sea*, ii, 1003; Abecassis, *Oil Pollution from Ships*, ch. 3; M'Gonigle and Zacher, *Pollution, Politics and International Law*, 107 ff.

[42] *Supra*, n. 16.

[43] Annex 1, regulations 9 and 10.

[44] Annexes II and V. Annexes III and IV deal with harmful substances in packaged form and sewage from ships, but are not yet in force (1991).

Secondly, a much more effective scheme of enforcement and compliance was adopted in response to pressure from coastal states dissatisfied with the observance of the 1954 treaty. This scheme involves the co-operation of coastal states, port states, and flag states in a system of certification, inspection, and reporting whose purposes are to make the operation of defective vessels difficult or impossible and to facilitate the performance by flag states of their primary jurisdiction to prosecute and enforce applicable laws. It is this scheme which has made the MARPOL Convention a major advance on the 1954 treaty and which provides evidence of the impact independent inspection can have in securing compliance with environmental protection treaties.

(d) Certification and Inspection under the MARPOL Convention

The flag state has two main responsibilities in ensuring that its vessels comply with the technical standards set by MARPOL. It must inspect the vessel at periodic intervals, and it must issue an 'international oil pollution prevention certificate'.[45] This certificate provides prima-facie evidence that the ship complies with the requirements of MARPOL: it 'shall be accepted by the other parties and regarded for all purposes covered by the present Convention as having the same validity as a certificate issued by them.'[46] But the Convention does not leave the question of compliance to the flag state alone. A novel provision of MARPOL, subsequently adopted in other IMO Conventions, is that ships required to hold a certificate are subject additionally to inspection by any party in whose ports they are present ('port states').[47]

This form of port state control is not to be confused with the extended port state jurisdiction provided for in Article 218 of the 1982 UNCLOS, since it involves no extraterritorial competence to legislate or enforce treaty-based or customary rules of law beyond the port state's own waters. MARPOL relies instead on the undoubted jurisdiction possessed by states to regulate conditions of entry to or passage through their internal waters, including ports.[48] In this sense the practice, while novel in its application to pollution, is not a departure from existing principles of maritime jurisdiction referred to earlier.

Inspection under Article 5 of the MARPOL Convention may be carried out to confirm possession of a valid certificate, or to determine the condition of the ship, but in the latter case only where there are 'clear grounds' for believing that it does not correspond 'substantially' with the certificate. Where non-compliance is revealed, port states must not allow such ships to sail unless they can do so without presenting an unreasonable threat of harm to

---

[45] Annex I, Regulations 4 and 5.   [46] Article 5(1).

[47] Ibid. (2). IMO Resolutions A.466(XII), A542(13), MEPC. 26(23) and A-(17) provide guidance for port states in implementing port state control.

[48] Churchill and Lowe, *The International Law of the Sea*, ch. 3, but cf. qualifications noted by Valenzuela, in Soons, *Implementation*, 200 ff.

the marine environment. Their most effective sanction is therefore to restrain the vessel in port until it can be repaired to a suitable standard or directed to a repair yard. In less serious cases, the ship must be reported to the flag state for appropriate action or prosecuted for any violation of the port state's own law which arises from non-compliance with the convention.[49] The port state must not unduly delay ships, however.[50]

Port state inspection may also be used to supply evidence of a violation of the Convention's discharge regulations. This facility may be crucial to the enforcement of these regulations. The problem facing the flag state is that without co-operation from port states in furnishing evidence it may be unable to mount successful prosecutions. With this in mind, Article 6 of MARPOL therefore permits inspection by port states for this purpose, and does not limit the power to situations where there are 'clear grounds' for suspicion, as in Article 5. A report must be made to flag states when a discharge violation is indicated, and flag states must then bring proceedings if satisfied that the evidence is sufficient. It is also open to any party, including a coastal state, to request inspection by the port state if there is sufficient evidence that the ship has discharged harmful substances 'in any place'. This would include high seas violations as well as violations in the maritime zones of other states. But, although port states do prosecute pollution violations occurring in their own internal waters or territorial sea, and Article 220(1) of the 1982 UNCLOS confirms their power to do so, neither MARPOL nor customary law confers on them any extraterritorial jurisdiction to prosecute violations which occur elsewhere.[51]

An efficient scheme of port state inspection and control is in many respects a more practical means of deterring sub-standard vessels than flag state enforcement, since such vessels will more often come within the reach of port states. It also reduces the need for coastal states to interfere with passing traffic, while facilitating prosecution of those ships which offend within coastal zones. Moreover it has the merit that it can be applied to the vessels of non-parties to MARPOL as a condition of port entry. Article 5(4) of MARPOL supports this view by requiring port states to ensure that no more favourable treatment is given to the ships of non-parties. State practice indicates that non-parties have generally acquiesced in this application to their vessels of MARPOL standards. Article 211(3) of the 1982 UNCLOS requires port states to give due publicity to port entry conditions, and to communicate them to IMO, but it too assumes their right to determine these conditions for themselves. The conclusion that non-party flag states are effectively bound by MARPOL in this manner further strengthens the earlier argument for

---

[49] Articles 4, 5(3); Churchill and Lowe, *The International Law of the Sea*, 219.
[50] Article 7.
[51] 1982 UNCLOS, Article 220(1), but cf. 1982 UNCLOS, Article, 218, *infra*, however.

treating the convention as indicative of the flag state's obligations in customary law. It does mean that these states have little to gain by staying outside the Convention.[52]

Since the impact of port state inspection will tend to be reflected in traffic patterns, with substandard vessels favouring the more lenient ports, these inspection schemes will not work effectively unless they operate systematically and consistently. Where, as in Western Europe, ports in a variety of jurisdictions are potentially available, co-ordination is essential. Under the Paris Memorandum of Understanding on Port state Control, concluded in 1982, fourteen Western European states now co-operate in a programme of vessel inspection which aims to ensure that each participating administration inspects at least 25 per cent of foreign vessels calling at its ports annually.[53] The cumulative effect is that over 70 per cent of all ships sailing to Western Europe are inspected, not only for compliance with MARPOL standards but also in respect of other IMO conventions and recommendations, including the 1974 SOLAS Convention. The benefits of this programme can be seen in the high degree of compliance, but it also ensures that vessels will not be subjected to repeated inspection at different ports. The United States achieves comparably high levels of inspection, and there are similar schemes in Japan, Canada, and certain other states.

(e) Jurisdiction under the MARPOL Convention

Negotiation of the MARPOL Convention coincided with increasing pressure from coastal states for extension of their pollution control jurisdiction beyond the narrow three-mile territorial sea which then prevailed for most states. It was clear that this controversial question would be an important topic for consideration in the UNCLOS III negotiations. For this reason MARPOL itself relies, like the 1954 Convention, primarily on regulation and prosecution by flag states, but it leaves open the possibility of extending the jurisdiction of coastal and port states by providing in Article 4(2) that 'Any violation of the requirements of the present Convention within the jurisdiction of any party to the Convention *shall* be prohibited and sanctions *shall* be established therefore under the law of that Party.' This can be read as a recognition of the customary rule that coastal states may regulate pollution within their own internal waters and territorial sea, although it arguably goes further by turning a power to regulate into a duty to do so. But Article 9(3) at the same time makes clear that the term 'jurisdiction' in the Convention 'shall be construed in the light of international law in force at the time of application or interpretation of the present Convention.' Thus it must now be read in the

---

[52] See Valenzuela, in Soons, *Implementation*, 205 ff.

[53] 21 *ILM* (1982), 1. See generally the annual reports of the Port State Control Committee, and Valenzuela, in Soons, *Implementation*, 208; Kasoulides, ibid. 422; id. 5 *IJECL* (1990), 180, where weaknesses in the operation of the scheme are pointed out.

light of subsequent developments, including the emergence of coastal state pollution jurisdiction in the exclusive economic zone, considered below. The important point here is simply that MARPOL itself does not prevent the extension of jurisdiction beyond the territorial sea, but neither does it authorize or compel such action.

The convention does try to strengthen flag state enforcement in a number of ways, however. Regardless of where they occur, violations must be prohibited, proceedings must be brought if there is sufficient evidence, and penalties must be adequate in severity. It is not open to the flag state to adopt a more lenient attitude simply because the offence is committed on the high seas or in the waters of some distant state: these are precisely the situations where its duty to act effectively requires emphasis. In order to facilitate flag state prosecution of such offences, all parties are required to report incidents at sea involving harmful substances, and the flag state must then act appropriately when informed of suspected violations.[54] Moreover, as we saw earlier, evidential problems can be overcome if port state inspections identify substandard vessels or discharge violations. Thus MARPOL does go some way towards promoting more effective enforcement by flag states, but it does not entirely remove the practical problems which in many cases have made port state control the more realistic method of ensuring higher levels of compliance.

(f) Assessing the Impact of MARPOL[55]

While the evidence of inspections conducted under various IMO conventions in Western Europe and North America does show high levels of compliance with IMO Conventions, it also indicates that vessels registered in developing countries or flying their flags represent the greatest percentage of deficiencies. The average detention rate for substandard vessels in Paris MOU ports in 1990 was 4.48 per cent, but rates of over 15 per cent were recorded for vessels from Morocco, St Vincent, Honduras, and Malta. This suggests that the impact of IMO Conventions is not consistent in all regions. It cannot be assumed that the problem is simply one of flags of convenience, however, since a number of these, including Liberia, have established good records. Moreover, only 10 per cent of all detentions in MOU ports were of oil tankers; by far the largest category of substandard vessels were the less environmentally significant dry cargo and bulk carriers. What does appear tenable is that due largely to the success of port state control within the northern hemisphere, MARPOL has been substantially more effective than the 1954 London Convention in ensuring that ships operating there meet the

---

[54] Article 4.
[55] *Supra*, n. 53, and see also IMO Docs. MEPC/30/17 (1990); MEPC/26/14 (1988); MEPC/25/12 (1987); MEPC/24/14 (1986); MEPC/23/13 (1985); and Sasamura, in Law of the Sea Institute, *Proceedings of 25th Annual Conference* (Malmo, 1991).

appropriate technical requirements for pollution control and maritime safety.

Illegal discharges can only be controlled if they are reported and if action is then taken, however. In practice this assumes a level of detection by surveillance and monitoring of vessels at sea which is only likely to be attainable by developed coastal states with appropriate resources in aircraft and naval or coastguard patrols. Moreover, the failure of many coastal states to adopt extended enforcement jurisdiction in their EEZ has meant that prosecutions for discharges in waters beyond the territorial sea remain largely the responsibility of flag states. Reports communicated to IMO concerning the application of MARPOL have given no reliable indication of the record of flag state prosecutions, nor of the Convention's success in reducing high seas pollution, since only a minority of mainly developed states have submitted reports as required. These do show extensive referral of violations by port and coastal states, but subsequent flag state action is reported in less than a quarter of such cases between 1985 and 1989. The 1990 Report of the Paris Memorandum noted a substantial improvement in follow-up action by port state authorities within its area, but also observed that differing legal standards for collection and exchange of evidence continue to make successful prosecution of polluters difficult.[56]

The 1990 GESAMP report[57] estimates that 46 per cent of total input of oil to the sea originates from shipping, including accidental spills. It notes a decline in oil spillages at sea up to 1986, due in part to a large reduction in the volume of transported oil, but concludes that the entry into force of MARPOL has also contributed to a major reduction in operational pollution from all types of vessel. This conclusion is shared by a report prepared for IMO by the US National Academy for Sciences in 1990,[58] which found that a total of 568,800 tons of oil entered the sea from ships in 1989, compared to 1.47 million tons in 1981. It concluded that MARPOL had had 'a substantial positive impact'. But of this total only some 114,000 tons entered the sea as a result of accidents; most of the remainder was discharged by tankers during the course of ballasting and tank cleaning or by other types of ship in the form of waste oil. The persistence of these operational discharges does indicate a continuing inadequacy in the provision of port reception facilities, a long-standing problem despite the obligation to provide them placed on port states by the MARPOL Convention,[59] and the efforts of IMO through advice and assistance to ensure compliance. Moreover the report also noted the inadequate enforcement of the convention in some areas, the inadequate

---

[56] Paris Memorandum, *Annual Report* (1990), 20, and see Kasoulides, in Soons, *Implementation*, 432.

[57] GESAMP, *The State of the Marine Environment* (Nairobi, 1990).

[58] 4 *IMO News* (1990), 16. See also Sasamura, in, Law of the Sea Institute, *Proceedings of 25th Annual Conference*.

[59] Annex I, Reg. 12.

training of crews in MARPOL requirements, and the effect of equipment malfunctioning on pollution control. Other reports indicate a more recent increase in the number of pollution incidents, however, and figures for the waters around the United Kingdom in 1989 confirm this trend.[60] Since the GESAMP report was prepared the *Exxon Valdez* and other major maritime disasters have also occurred, indicating continued weaknesses in the construction standards for oil tankers and the proficiency of their crews. Although the average annual accidental oil-spill rate for tankers in the period 1981–9 was only 114,000 tonnes, compared to 390,000 in the period 1974–80, annual figures fluctuate widely and have risen substantially in 1988 and 1989. Quantifying MARPOL's impact is thus not straightforward, and the data do not point to any clear conclusion, except that operational pollution has undoubtedly declined.

(g) Flag State Jurisdiction under the 1982 UNCLOS

The 1982 UNCLOS makes radical changes in the exclusive character of flag state jurisdiction, but leaves intact the central principle of earlier law that the flag state has responsibility for the regulation and control of pollution from its ships. This duty is redefined, however, in terms requiring greater uniformity in the content of regulations. These must now 'at least have the same effect' as the MARPOL Convention, which as we saw earlier represents 'generally accepted international rules and standards' in this context. Since flag states retain a discretion under this wording to set more onerous standards, the effect of Article 211 of UNCLOS is to make MARPOL, and other relevant international standards referred to earlier, an obligatory minimum.

Article 217 reinforces this conclusion by requiring flag states to take measures necessary for the implementation and effective enforcement of international rules and standards. These measures must include the certification and inspection procedures instituted by MARPOL, and must be sufficient to ensure that vessels are prohibited from sailing until they can comply with the relevant regulations. The remaining provisions of Article 217 reiterate the obligation of flag states to investigate violations and bring appropriate proceedings, and to act on the request of other states where a violation is reported. In substance, therefore, a flag state bound by Article 217 is required to do all that the MARPOL Convention already demands. There is thus nothing novel in principle in the treatment of flag state regulation in the 1982 UNCLOS: it fully accords with existing customary and conventional law,[61] although as with other provisions of the convention these articles are part of a broader package deal and are not necessarily applicable in every respect to ships of non-parties.

[60] ACOPS, *Yearbook* (London, 1990), 8.
[61] Boyle, 79 *AJIL* (1985), 363 ff; Popp, *CYIL* (1980), 3; Bernhardt, 20 *VJIL* (1979).

(3) Coastal State Jurisdiction

(a) In the Territorial Sea and Internal Waters

The coastal state's jurisdiction to regulate vessels depends on its sovereignty or sovereign rights over maritime zones contiguous to its coasts. Until recently, these zones have for the most part been of limited extent. In internal waters, such as ports, the coastal state is free to apply national laws and determine conditions of entry for foreign vessels. The United State's Oil Pollution Act of 1990 relies on this power to regulate safety and construction standards for oil tankers that considerably exceed international standards set by IMO conventions. This remains an unusual assertion of pollution jurisdiction, however, whose compatibility with other treaty commitments may be questionable; for most states the interests of comity with other nations and freedom of navigation will usually dictate greater restraint in the unilateral adoption of pollution regulations.[62]

In the territorial sea, the coastal state also enjoys sovereignty, and with it the power to apply national law.[63] The coastal state's right to regulate environmental protection in territorial waters has been assumed or asserted in national legislation, and treaties on such matters as dumping or pollution from ships. This right includes three important powers: the designation of environmentally protected areas,[64] the designation and control of navigation routes for safety purposes,[65] and the prohibition of pollution discharges.[66]

In each of these respects the coastal state enjoys a substantial measure of national discretion: it is for example free to set stricter pollution discharge standards than the international standards required by the MARPOL Convention. But unlike the earlier Territorial Sea Convention of 1958, or the 1973 MARPOL Convention, which are silent on the point, the 1982 UNCLOS excludes from the coastal state's jurisdiction the right to regulate construction, design, equipment, and manning standards for ships, unless giving effect to international rules and standards, which for this purpose

---

[62] See generally Churchill and Lowe, *The Law of the Sea*, ch. 3; O'Connell, *The International Law of the Sea*, ch. 22. For the US Oil Pollution Act, see *infra*, n. 170, and cf. critical analysis by Valenzuela, in Soons, *Implementation*, 212 ff.

[63] Churchill and Lowe, *The Law of the Sea*, ch. 4; O'Connell, *The International Law of the Sea*, chs. 19 and 24.

[64] See protected areas protocols, *supra*, n. 13; for examples of national legislation, see UK Wildlife and Countryside Act, 1981; US Marine Protection, Research and Sanctuaries Act, 1972.

[65] 1982 UNCLOS, Articles 22. This requires states to take into account the recommendations of the competent international organization but does not explicitly require IMO approval. See also 1972 Convention on the International Regulations for Preventing Collisions at Sea; Fitch, 20 *Harv. ILJ* (1979), 127; Gold and Johnston, in Clingan, *Law of the Sea*; *State Practice*, etc, 157; Gold, 14 *JMLC* (1983), 136; Plant, 14 *Marine Policy* (1990), 71; IJlstra, in Soons, *Implementation*, 216. On passage in straits, see 1982 UNCLOS, Article 41.

[66] 1972 London Dumping Convention; 1973 MARPOL Convention, Article 4(2); 1982 UNCLOS, Article 21(1)f.

means primarily the MARPOL Convention, and the 1974 Safety of Life at Sea Convention.[67] The reason for this exclusion is self-evident: if every state set its own standards on these matters ships could not freely navigate in the territorial sea of other states. This would contravene the most important limitation on the coastal state's jurisdiction with regard to any of the above matters: that it must not hamper the right of innocent passage through the territorial sea or suspend the right in straits used for international navigation.[68] This right is enjoyed by the vessels of all nations, and it is an essential safeguard for freedom of maritime navigation. Foreign vessels do not thereby acquire exemption from coastal state laws, but these laws must be in conformity with international law, and must not have the practical effect of denying passage.[69]

What then can a coastal state legitimately do when a foreign vessel is found violating international pollution regulations in the territorial sea, or when it poses a risk of accidental pollution or environmental harm? What the coastal state cannot do is to close its territorial waters to foreign ships in innocent passage, even where their cargo presents a significant environmental risk, as in the case of oil tankers.[70] Passage in these circumstances does not cease to be innocent, and must be afforded without discrimination. At most, the coastal state will be entitled to take certain precautionary measures to minimize the risk: it may, for example, require ships carrying nuclear materials or other inherently dangerous or noxious substances, such as oil or hazardous waste, to carry documentation, observe special precautionary measures established by international agreements such as MARPOL, or confine their passage to specified sea lanes in the interests of safety, the efficiency of traffic, and the protection of the environment.[71]

The application of these principles can be observed in state practice concerning environmentally sensitive areas covered by special areas protocols, or designated by IMO. In such cases the passage of ships may be regulated in order to minimize the risk of adverse environmental effects or serious pollution, but here too, the important point is that while ships may be required

---

[67] 1982 UNCLOS, Article 21(2); Article 211(4). See especially the opposing views of Canada and Bulgaria on this question, 3rd UNCLOS, 6 *Official Records*, 109 and 112.

[68] *Corfu Channel Case, ICJ Rep.* (1949), 1; 1958 Territorial Sea Convention, Articles 14–16; 1982 UNCLOS, Articles 17–19, 24–25; Churchill and Lowe, *The Law of the Sea*, 68, and see generally Ngantcha, *The Right of Innocent Passage and the Evolution of the International Law of the Sea* (London, 1990).

[69] Territorial Sea Convention, Article 17; 1982 UNCLOS, Article 21(4).

[70] 1982 UNCLOS, Article 24(1).

[71] 1982 UNCLOS. Articles 22(2), 23; IMO Res. A578(14), 1985, and see Fitch, 20 *Harv. ILJ* (1979); Gold, 14 *JMLC* (1983); and Plant, 14 *Marine Policy* (1990). See also 1989 Basel Convention on the Control of Transboundary Movements of Hazardous Wastes, Article 4(12) and 1991 Bamako Convention, Article 4(4)(c), *infra*, Ch. 8 n. 152, but see *contra* Haiti, *Note Verbale* of 18 Feb. 1988, in 11 *LOSB* (1988), 13 and Pineschi, in Francioni and Scovazzi (eds.), *International Responsibility for Environmental Harm* (Dordrecht, 1991), 299.

to avoid certain areas, the right of innocent passage is not lost.[72] In 1990, Australia obtained IMO designation of the Great Barrier Reef as a 'particularly sensitive sea area' within an extended territorial sea and imposed compulsory pilotage requirements. The United States has also designated the Florida Keys as an 'area to be avoided' and prohibited the operation of tankers in these waters under the 1972 Marine Protection, Research, and Sanctuaries Act.

Nor does the actual violation of regulations necessarily deprive the vessel of its right of innocent passage. Innocent passage is defined by the 1958 Territorial Sea Convention as passage which is 'not prejudicial to the peace, good order or security' of the coastal state. This vague terminology appeared to allow coastal states ample room for subjective judgments of the question of innocence, and it is arguably not an accurate reflection of the treatment of innocent passage in the *Corfu Channel* case. That decision implied a rather more objective test, and it is this approach which is much more fully reflected in Article 19 of the 1982 UNCLOS. This provision was not intended to change the law, but to clarify it in rather more satisfactory terms, which afford less scope for potentially abusive interference with shipping. The significant point is that only pollution which is 'wilful and serious' and contrary to the Convention will deprive a vessel in passage of its innocent character, which necessarily excludes accidental pollution from having this effect. Moreover, while operational pollution is invariably deliberate, it is less often serious, and may sometimes be justified by weather or distress. Under this formulation, therefore, it will rarely be the case that ships causing operational pollution will cease to be in innocent passage. Only when they do lose this right can their entry into territorial waters be denied, or their right of passage terminated.

Customary law probably does allow the coastal state to arrest ships engaged in illegal pollution or dumping in the territorial sea, however. Both the 1972 London Dumping Convention and the 1973 MARPOL Convention require coastal states to apply and enforce their provisions against all vessels in the territorial sea, and this right is recognized in the 1982 UNCLOS, subject to that Convention's provisions on innocent passage and the existence of clear grounds for suspecting a violation.[73] As we have seen, however, the practical exercise of a right to arrest ships in passage poses serious dangers to navigation, and it is rarely used as a means of enforcing anti-pollution regulations. The preferable solution is to rely on port states for this purpose.

---

[72] 1982 Geneva Protocol Concerning Mediterranean Specially Protected Areas, Article 7(c); 1990 Kingston Protocol Concerning Specially Protected Areas, etc., of the Wider Caribbean, Article 5(2)(c); and see IMO, Working Group on Guidelines for Particularly Sensitive Sea Areas, MEPC 29 and 30 (1990). cf., however, Canada's Arctic Waters Pollution Act, 1972, and 1982 UNCLOS, Article 234, on which see *infra*, text at nn. 80 and 86.

[73] 1972 London Dumping Convention, Article 7; 1973 MARPOL Convention, Article 4(2); 1982 UNCLOS, Article 220(2).

The 1982 UNCLOS does not alter these basic principles of customary law or extend the coastal state's rights in the territorial sea. In this context its purpose is simply to clarify and define the limits of those rights. The territorial sea regime envisaged by the Convention is thus a compromise: it offers coastal states power to control navigation and pollution, while preserving rights of passage and international control of construction, design, equipment, and manning standards.[74] What the Convention does change is the breadth of the territorial sea, which it extends from three to twelve miles, a decision now overwhelmingly approved in state practice. By itself, however, this extension was not enough to satisfy the needs or claims of coastal states. The more important decision, therefore, was to go beyond the territorial sea by giving coastal states pollution control jurisdiction in a new exclusive economic zone created by the 1982 UNCLOS.

(b) Coastal State Prescriptive Jurisdiction in the EEZ

The major innovation of the 1982 UNCLOS provisions on the marine environment is the exclusive economic zone (EEZ), which extends to 200 nautical miles from the territorial sea baseline and confers on coastal states sovereign rights over living and mineral resources, and jurisdiction with regard to the protection and preservation of the marine environment.[75] This zone differs from the extended jurisdiction over fisheries recognized by the ICJ in the *Icelandic Fisheries* case because it gives the coastal state rights to resources which are not merely preferential but potentially exclusive. Although in that sense the Convention's provisions make new law, the consensus behind the adoption of the EEZ was such that it has rapidly been translated into state practice by coastal state claims to exclusive fishing zones and full EEZs. In the *Libya–Malta Continental Shelf* case the ICJ found that: 'the institution of the EEZ with its rule on entitlement by reason of distance is shown by the practice of states to have become part of customary law'.[76] Thus the principle of extended coastal state rights beyond the territorial sea is now part of international law, although the precise claims made in this zone by individual states have varied, in some cases widely.[77] It should be recalled moreover that the EEZ does not arise automatically: it has to be claimed, and, in the case of pollution jurisdiction, legislation will usually be necessary for the coastal state to acquire the necessary competence. Some states have made no EEZ claims; only a small number have in practice extended their jurisdiction

---

[74] Popp, 79 *AJIL* (1985). See, however, M'Gonigle and Zacher, *Pollution, Politics, and International Law*, 244–5 for critical analysis of this part of the 1982 Convention.

[75] 1982 UNCLOS, Article 56. See Orrego-Vicuna, *The Exclusive Economic Zone: Regime and Legal Nature Under International Law* (Cambridge, 1989); Kwiatkowska, *The 200-Mile EEZ*; Attard, *The Exclusive Economic Zone* (Oxford, 1987).

[76] *ICJ Rep.* (1985), 13, at para. 34.

[77] See Burke, 9 *ODIL* (1981), 289; Krueger and Nordquist, 19 *VJIL* (1979), 321; Wolfrum, 18 *NYIL* (1987), 121.

over pollution from ships in the EEZ, or over dumping.[78] Others, such as the United States, which claims an EEZ, and the United Kingdom, which does not, have asserted rights only for certain purposes, including fishing, within the 200-mile zone, but have not legislated to control pollution from shipping beyond the territorial sea.[79]

Some states had already begun to make such claims beyond their territorial waters before the UNCLOS III negotiations began. The earliest example was Canada, whose Arctic Waters Pollution Act of 1970 unilaterally imposed extensive environmental controls over shipping within a 100-mile area off its northern coasts.[80] This legislation not only banned polluting discharges and allowed Canadian authorities to restrict navigation, it also permitted Canada to establish mandatory construction standards for oil tankers seeking to use Arctic waters. Canada's claim was specific to these waters, and was based on their fragile ecology and peculiar navigational hazards, but it met strong opposition from the United States and other nations fearful of the implications for freedom of maritime navigation. The issue was debated during the 1973 MARPOL negotiations, but without agreement.

Faced with the inadequacy of earlier attempts to control pollution from ships, however, a strong lobby at the UNCLOS III conference, led by Canada and Australia and supported by the majority of developing states, sought a general extension of coastal state legislative and enforcement jurisdiction beyond the relatively limited changes wrought by MARPOL.[81] The adoption by the conference of the EEZ involved a compromise between the more extensive claims of these states and the concerns of maritime nations. Once coastal states had abandoned their support for a much broader margin of territorial sea, maritime states were prepared to accept the principle of extended jurisdiction for specific purposes. The central feature of the new EEZ regime is that it preserves for all states high seas freedom of navigation within the zone, rather than the more restrictive territorial sea right of innocent passage, in contrast to earlier 200-mile claims made by a number of

---

[78] States whose EEZ legislation extends to pollution from ships or provides for the adoption of necessary regulations include the USSR, 1984 Edict on the EEZ, Article 19(3); Romania, 1986 Decree of the Council of State Concerning the Establishment of the EEZ, Article 13(b); New Zealand, Territorial Sea and EEZ Act, 1977 s. 27; Indonesia, Act No. 5 of 1983, Articles 8, 11, 16, and see Franckx, 1 *IJECL* (1986), 155. On jurisdiction over dumping, see *infra*, Ch. 8 n. 101.

[79] US Presidential Proclamation on the EEZ, 1983; US Fisheries Conservation and Management Act, 1976; UK, Fishery Limits Act, 1976.

[80] See Johnson and Zacher, *Canadian Foreign Policy and the Law of the Sea* (Vancouver, 1977), ch. 3; Henkin, 65 *AJIL* (1971), 131; Pharand, *The Law of the Sea of the Arctic with Special Reference to Canada* (Ottawa, 1973); Smith, 13 *VJIL* (1976), 609; Bilder, 14 *Vand. JTL* (1981), 141. Canada has since redrawn its territorial sea baselines to extend its jurisdiction over the waters of its northern archipelago, and has also claimed a 200-mile EEZ.

[81] *3rd UNCLOS, Official Records*, ii. 317–20; Nordquist and Park, *Reports of the US Delegation to the 3rd UNCLOS*, 47–51, 74, and 89; M'Gonigle and Zacher, *Pollution, Politics and International Law*, ch. 6; Nordquist, *UN Convention*, iv, 180 ff.

Latin American states.[82] Coastal states acquire responsibility for regulating pollution from sea-bed installations, dumping, and activities within the EEZ, but their regulatory jurisdiction over vessels is limited to the application of international rules for enforcement purposes only.[83]

The effect of this new regime is less radical than some coastal states had sought. That it does no more than permit them to apply MARPOL and other relevant conventions is evident from the wording of article 211(5) of the 1982 UNCLOS, which refers only to coastal state laws 'conforming to and giving effect to generally accepted international rules and standards' for the prevention, reduction, and control of vessel-source pollution.[84] In this context MARPOL and possibly other international standards thus represent the limit of coastal state competence and act as a necessary restraint where there is evident potential for excessive interference with shipping. Thus, coastal states have acquired little real discretion about the kind of pollution legislation they may apply in the EEZ. In particular, as in the territorial sea, they are denied the power to set their own construction, design, equipment, and manning standards for vessels. Even in cases of special circumstances, where more stringent pollution discharge controls are permitted, Article 211(6) of the Convention requires the designation of these areas to be approved by IMO and supported by scientific and technical evidence. This is little more than a re-enactment of the special areas provisions of MARPOL designed for the needs of enclosed or semi-enclosed seas;[85] it does not confer any additional freedom on coastal states to act unilaterally in prohibiting pollution in the EEZ.

The solitary exception to the Convention's preference for the application of internation regulations in the EEZ is found in Article 234. This article was a concession to Canadian and Soviet interests in the protection of the Arctic Ocean. It applies to ice-covered areas within the limits of the EEZ, and allows coastal states a broad discretion, free from IMO supervision, to adopt national standards for pollution control, provided only that these have due regard for navigation and are non-discriminatory. It remains uncertain whether this Article goes as far as Canada's Arctic Waters Pollution Act in authorizing limitations on navigation.[86]

In general, the 1982 UNCLOS can best be seen as serving the interests of maritime states within the EEZ although the extension of jurisdiction does give a wider area of control to coastal states if they choose to use it. In the

---

[82] 1982 UNCLOS, Articles 56(2), 58. On earlier Latin American claims to 200-mile jurisdiction, see Orrego Vicuna, *The EEZ: A Latin American Perspective* (Boulder, Colo., 1984), ch. 2.

[83] Articles 208, 210, 211(5) and (6).

[84] On the meaning of this phrase, see *supra*, n. 16.

[85] See *supra*, pp. 267–8.

[86] McRae and Goundrey, 16 *UBCLR* (1982), 197; Pharand, 7 *Dalhousie LJ* (1983), 315.

exercise of jurisdiction within this area, coastal states must have due regard for the rights and duties of other states, including the right of freedom of navigation. This freedom is largely protected by ensuring uniformity of applicable pollution standards, and by preserving the ability of maritime states to influence the formulation of those standards within IMO. Although the international regulations adopted through that body represent an expression of compromise and common interest among the various groups represented there, there is little doubt that maritime states have tended to predominate;[87] the continued growth of flags of convenience since 1982 makes the identification of this group an increasingly difficult task, however, and it should not be assumed that states with a low registered tonnage, such as the United States, do not have a substantial interest in maritime navigation, or that their influence in IMO can be disregarded. Nevertheless the essential point remains that the Convention's articles on the regulation of vessel pollution by coastal states are primarily important as a basis for enforcement of MARPOL and other international standards, and do not authorize 'creeping jurisdiction' over the high seas.

(c) Enforcement Jurisdiction of Coastal and Port States under UNCLOS

It was eventually accepted during the UNCLOS negotiations that the problem of non-compliance with international regulations could not be remedied by flag state enforcement alone, and that the port state control provisions of MARPOL were not in themselves a sufficient alternative. The main question was whether to allow coastal states full authority to arrest and prosecute vessels for pollution offences within the EEZ, a solution consistent with the extension of their prescriptive jurisdiction, or whether to concentrate instead on the increased use of port state jurisdiction as the main complement to the flag state's authority. The advantage of the former was that it would give those states which suffered most from poor enforcement the opportunity to protect themselves directly, rather than by relying on flag states. The disadvantages were the threat to freedom of navigation, and as in the territorial sea, the practical dangers of interfering with ships at sea. Moreover, coastal state enforcement afforded no remedy for high seas pollution offences outside the EEZ. From this perspective, port state jurisdiction to prosecute violations emerged as the more attractive alternative, since it presented no danger to navigation and afforded better facilities for investigation and the collection of evidence concerning offences, regardless of where they had taken place.[88]

The result, once more, is a compromise between the two extremes. Coastal states are not given full jurisdiction to enforce international regulations against

---

[87] See especially M'Gonigle and Zacher, *Pollution, Politics and International Law*, chs. 3 and 7; Fitch, 20 *Harv. ILJ* (1979).

[88] Lowe, 12 *SDLR* (1975); Bernhardt, 20 *VJTL* (1979); Kasoulides, in Soons, *Implementation*; ILA, *Report of the 56th Conference* (1974), 400–8.

ships in passage in the EEZ. They can do so if the vessel voluntarily enters port,[89] but otherwise their powers in the EEZ itself are graduated according to the likely harm. Only when there is 'clear objective evidence' of a violation of applicable international regulations resulting in a discharge of pollution which causes or threatens to cause 'major damage' to the coastal state are arrest and prosecution permitted, but where the violation has resulted only in a 'substantial discharge' causing or threatening 'significant pollution', the vessel may be inspected for 'matters relating to the violation', that is, in effect, for evidence of the illegal discharge, provided this is justified by the circumstances, including information already given by the ship.[90] The ship may in this case only be detained if necessary to prevent an unreasonable threat of damage to the marine environment.[91] Where none of these conditions exist, the coastal state is confined to seeking information concerning the ship's identity and its next port of call.[92] The port state may then be asked to take appropriate action.

Although these graduated enforcement powers in the EEZ leave coastal states considerable latitude in determining what action is justified in individual cases, and may for that reason lead to uncertainty and inconsistency in their use, they do amount to rather less than the competence enjoyed by coastal states in the territorial sea, and in less serious cases they still leave enforcement to flag states, or as we shall see, to port states. In this form the jurisdiction of coastal states remains a limited one for protective purposes only, but this is consistent with the nature of their rights in the EEZ. In practice, few states have resorted to the exercise of these powers in full and it is doubtful whether in this respect Article 220 of the 1982 UNCLOS has had any significant effect, so far.[93]

In contrast to the limited jurisdiction of coastal states, the more radical development is that Article 218 gives port states express power to investigate and prosecute discharge violations wherever they have taken place. This power covers both high seas offences, and violations within the coastal zones of another state, although in the latter case the port state may only act in response to a request from the state concerned. Apart from this limitation, the port state's jurisdiction under this article is independent, in the sense that no request from the flag state is necessary, but the flag state does enjoy a right of pre-emption, considered below.

---

[89] Article 220(1). This power applies only to violations which have occurred 'within the territorial sea or the exclusive economic zone of *that* state'.

[90] Articles 220(5) and (6).

[91] Article 226(1)(c).

[92] Article 220(3).

[93] For the drafting history of Article 220, see Nordquist, *UN Convention*, iv, 281 ff. For national legislation, see Romania, 1986 Decree Establishing the EEZ, Article 11; USSR, 1984 Edict on the EEZ, Article 15. Kwiatkowska, *The 200-Mile EEZ*, p. 183 notes the failure of some of these laws to incorporate all the conditions envisaged by Article 220.

The obvious advantage of Article 218 is that it may ensure prompt prosecution where the coastal state is unable or incompetent to act, or where the vessel is unlikely to come within the flag state's authority. In effect this article recognizes the inability or ineffectiveness of flag states when dealing with pollution incidents on the high seas, and gives the port state the power to act in the public interest, independently of any effects on its own waters or of any jurisdictional connection based on nationality, territory, or protection. In that sense, Article 218 creates a form of universal jurisdiction, concurrent with that of the flag state, and in some cases, with the coastal state.[94]

It is, however, a novel development in the law of the sea to confer jurisdiction on port states in this way. Although the *Lotus* case did permit Turkey to prosecute a foreign vessel in a Turkish port for an offence which had occurred on the high seas, that decision owed much to the erroneous equation of ships with floating territory, and the court's specific conclusion regarding collisions has since been reversed by treaty.[95] Thus it cannot convincingly be asserted that the exercise of port state jurisdiction contemplated by Article 218 is based on existing customary law, although as we saw in Chapter 4, it goes some way towards supporting the ILC's treatment of pollution offences as crimes against international law in cases of special gravity. But there is no evidence that port states have resorted to this extended method of enforcement; on the contrary, port state practice appears to remain firmly within the more limited regime of control provided for by MARPOL. The better view at present therefore is probably that Article 218 remains *lex ferenda*.[96]

Moreover, although flag states would no longer enjoy exclusive jurisdiction over high seas offences if Article 218 enters into force, the result is not concurrent jurisdiction in the ordinary sense, where either party is entitled to prosecute. Except in cases of major damage to the coastal state, the flag state under the 1982 Convention has in all cases a right of pre-emption,[97] which enables it to insist on taking control of any prosecution. It must continue the proceedings, and it loses the right if it repeatedly disregards its obligation of effective enforcement of international regulations. Nevertheless, in most cases it remains the flag state which will determine whether proceedings by coastal states or port states are to be allowed.

Finally, in exercising any of these enforcement powers, coastal or port states must observe certain safeguards whose purpose is to prevent oppressive

---

[94] See Ch. 5 for further discussion, and see generally Nordquist (ed.), *UN Convention*, iv, 258 ff.

[95] *PCIJ* (1927) Ser. A, No. 10, 169 and cf. 1952 Brussels Convention for the Unification of Certain Rules Relating to Penal Jurisdiction; 1958 High Seas Convention, Article 11; 1982 UNCLOS, Article 97. For criticism of the *Lotus Case*, see II *Yearbook ILC* (1956), 281; Brownlie, *Principles of Public International Law* (4th edn., Oxford, 1990), 301–2.

[96] Kwiatkowska, *The 200-Mile EEZ*, 185.

[97] Article 228. See Kwiatkowska, *The 200-Mile EEZ*, 184; Nordquist, *UN Convention*, iv, 348 ff.

exercise of their authority.[98] In particular they must not act in a discriminatory fashion. Monetary penalties only may be imposed for violations, except in the case of wilful and serious pollution of the territorial sea. There are also special rules safeguarding passage in straits used for international navigation. Military or government-owned vessels in non-commercial service continue to enjoy immunity from the jurisdiction of port and coastal states in all circumstances, although states must ensure that these act in a manner consistent with the Convention's provisions on the environment 'so far as is reasonable and practicable',[99] and should presumably discipline officers responsible for pollution offences, including collisions.

5. POLLUTION INCIDENTS AND EMERGENCIES AT SEA

(1) International Co-operation and Assistance[100]

International co-operation to deal with pollution incidents or emergencies at sea is primarily a matter of prudent self-insterest, but international law does impose certain obligations on states confronted with such risks. Both customary law and Article 198 of the 1982 UNCLOS indicate that once they are aware of imminent or actual pollution of the marine environment, states must give immediate notification to others likely to be affected.[101] This requirement is also reiterated in most regional seas agreements.[102] In addition, regional agreements, and the 1982 UNCLOS require states to co-operate, in accordance with their capabilities, in eliminating the effects of such pollution, in preventing or minimizing the damage, and in developing contingency plans.[103]

---

[98] Articles 223–33; Nordquist, *UN Convention*, iv, 320 ff.

[99] Article 235; 1926 Brussels Convention for the Unification of Rules Concerning the Immunity of State Owned Ships.

[100] See generally Kiss, 23 *GYIL* (1980), 231; Abecassis, *Oil Pollution from Ships*, ch. 7; IMO/UNEP, *Meeting on Regional Arrangements for Co-operation in Combating Major Incidents of Marine Pollution* (London, 1985); de Rouw, in Law of the Sea Institute, *Proceedings of 25th Annual Conference* (Malmo, 1991).

[101] *Supra*, pp. 108–9.

[102] See e.g. 1976 Barcelona Convention, Article 9(2); 1983 Cartagena Convention, Article 11(2); 1978 Kuwait Convention, Article 9(b); 1983 Bonn Agreement for Co-operation in Dealing with Pollution of the North Sea by Oil and Other Harmful Substances, Article 5. See also 1990 International Convention on Oil Pollution Preparedness, Response and Co-operation, Article 5(1).

[103] 1982 UNCLOS, Article 199; 1983 Bonn Agreement; 1971 Copenhagen Agreement Concerning Co-operation in Measures to Deal with Pollution of the Sea by Oil; 1974 Helsinki Convention on the Protection of the Marine Environment of the Baltic Sea Area, Annex VI; 1976 Barcelona Protocol Concerning Co-operation in Combatting Pollution of the Mediterranean Sea in Cases of Emergency; 1978 Kuwait Protocol Concerning Regional Co-operation in Combatting Pollution in Cases of Emergency; 1981 Abidjan Protocol Concerning Co-operation in Combatting Pollution in Cases of Emergency; 1981 Lima Protocol on Regional Co-operation in Combatting Pollution of the S. E. Pacific in Cases of Emergency; 1982 Jeddah Protocol Concerning Regional Co-operation in Combatting Pollution in Cases of Emergency; 1983 Cartagena Protocol Concerning Co-operation in Combatting Oil

Article 7 of the 1990 Convention on Oil Pollution Preparedness, Response, and Co-operation, a global instrument adopted by IMO following the *Exxon Valdez* disaster in Alaska, further commits parties to respond to requests for assistance from states likely to be affected by oil pollution. IMO must be informed of major incidents,[104] and under Article 12, it is given responsibility for co-ordinating and facilitating co-operation on various matters, including the provision on request of technical assistance and advice for states faced with major oil pollution incidents. Parties may also seek IMO's assistance in arranging financial support for response costs.[105] In these respects IMO's role is comparable to that enjoyed by IAEA under the Convention on Assistance in Cases of Nuclear Emergency.[106] Although not in force, the 1990 Convention has provided the basis for IMO co-ordination of technical support and financial assistance for governments dealing with serious marine pollution during the conflict in the Persian Gulf in January 1991.[107] Further co-ordination is provided regionally by centres established with the assistance of IMO and UNEP.[108] In the North Sea, the 1983 Bonn Agreement divides that area into zones for which states are individually or in some cases jointly responsible, but other parties remain obliged to use their best endeavours to provide assistance if requested. Although these agreements generally allocate the costs of co-operative action to the state requesting assistance, or to those which act on their own initiative, this is usually without prejudice to rights to recover these costs from third parties under national or international law.[109]

(2) Controlling Pollution Emergencies

(a) General Obligations

Quite apart from their obligation to co-operate, states may also be required to respond to pollution emergencies individually, in cases where the incident falls within their jurisdiction or control. Failure to do so may then amount to a breach of the state's obligations in customary law to control sources of

---

Spills in the Wider Caribbean Region; 1987 Noumea Protocol Concerning Co-operation in Combating Oil Pollution Emergencies in the South Pacific Region; 1985 Nairobi Protocol Concerning Co-operation in Combating Marine Pollution in Cases of Emergency; 1990 Lisbon Agreement of Co-operation for the Protection of the North-East Atlantic Against Pollution. See also bilateral arrangements between the UK and France, UK and Norway, Denmark and Germany, and Caribbean Island states, listed by IMO, *supra*, n. 100, at para. 2.10. Other bilateral agreements apply between the US and Canada and the US and Mexico.

[104] Article 5(3).

[105] Article 7(2).

[106] See Ch. 9.

[107] UNCED, Prepcom, UN Doc. A/CONF.151/PC/72 (1991).

[108] e.g. the Regional Marine Pollution Emergency Response Centre in Malta, the Marine Emergency Mutual Aid Centre in Bahrain, and the Regional Co-ordination Unit, in Jamaica. See IMO/UNEP, *Regional Meeting, supra*, n. 100.

[109] 1983 Bonn Agreement, Article 9; 1990 Oil Pollution Preparedness, Response, and Co-operation Convention, Annex.

pollution, even if the emergency itself is not attributable to state action or inaction.[110] This assumption is consistent with the 1982 UNCLOS, which requires states to ensure that pollution arising from 'incidents or activities' under their jurisdiction or control does not spread beyond areas where they exercise sovereign rights, or is not transferred to other areas.[111] Moreover, Article 194 specifically mandates measures to prevent accidents and deal with emergencies emanating from all sources of marine pollution. Such detailed requirements are not generally found in regional treaties, however.[112]

The 1990 Convention on Oil Pollution Preparedness, Response, and Co-operation[113] applies these basic principles in more detailed form to oil pollution incidents caused by ships, offshore installations, and port-handling facilities which threaten the marine environment or the coastline or related interests of individual states. The parties must take all appropriate measures to prepare for and respond to such incidents. In particular, a national system capable of responding promptly and effectively must be established, including the designation of a competent national authority and a national contingency plan. Information concerning these arrangements must be provided to other states. Parties are also required to ensure that offshore oil operations within their jurisdiction, and port-handling facilities, are conducted in accordance with emergency procedures approved by the competent national authority. These provisions are somewhat stronger than those generally found in a number of regional or bilateral schemes.[114]

Although the primary responsibility for responding effectively will thus fall in most cases on the relevant coastal states, flag states also have a responsibility for ensuring that their vessels are adequately prepared to deal with emergencies. Article 3 of the 1990 Convention requires the parties to ensure that vessels flying their flag have on board an oil pollution emergency plan in accordance with IMO provisions, which, however, have yet to be adopted. For this purpose the Convention provides that vessels are subject to port state inspection under existing international arrangements referred to earlier. At the time of writing it remains to be seen whether the convention, strongly supported by the United States, will secure more general approval.

(b) Coastal State Powers of Intervention[115]

It is unrealistic to expect flag states themselves to maintain the capacity to respond to accidents involving their vessels wherever they occur, and, apart

---

[110] See e.g. *Corfu Channel Cases, ICJ Rep.* (1949), 3 and *supra*, pp. 108–9.

[111] Articles 194(2), 195.

[112] *Supra*, n. 103. But see 1981 Lima Convention, Articles 3(5) and 6; 1978 Kuwait Convention, Article 9(a); 1976 Barcelona Protocol, Article 9; 1990 Lisbon Agreement.

[113] de Rouw, in Law of the Sea Institute, *Proceedings of 25th Annual Conference.*

[114] 1978 Kuwait Convention, Article 9 and Protocol; 1982 Jeddah Protocol; 1981 Abidjan Protocol; 1981 Lima Protocol; 1976 Barcelona Protocol; 1983 Cartagena Protocol.

[115] Abecassis and Jarashow, *Oil Pollution from Ships* (2nd edn., London, 1985), ch. 6.

from the provisions of Article 3, the 1990 Convention does not attempt to make them do so. The right of coastal states to intervene on the high seas in cases of maritime casualities involving foreign vessels that are likely to cause pollution damage is, therefore, an important safeguard for these states in protecting themselves from the risks posed by oil tankers and other ships carrying toxic or hazardous substances in passage near their shores. Although as we have seen, in principle vessels exercising high seas freedoms are subject only to the jurisdiction of the flag state, an exceptional right of coastal state intervention in international law can be derived from the principle of necessity, or less convincingly, from the right of self-defence.[116] Following doubts raised about British intervention in the *Torrey Canyon* tanker disaster, however, the rights of coastal states were clarified by the 1969 Convention on Intervention on the High Seas in Cases of Oil Pollution Casualties.[117] This convention was extended to other forms of pollution by a 1973 protocol.

There can be little doubt today that a right of intervention beyond the territorial sea has become part of customary law. Apart from the widespread ratification and implementation of the 1969 Convention itself, Article 221 of the 1982 UNCLOS and Article 9 of the 1989 International Convention on Salvage respectively assume the right of coastal states to take measures under customary and conventional international law or under generally recognized principles of international law,[118] despite important differences in the wording of these provisions. The 1969 Convention permits parties to take:

Such measures on the high seas as may be necessary to prevent, mitigate or eliminate grave and imminent danger to their coastline or related interests from pollution or threat of pollution of the sea by oil, following upon a maritime casualty or acts related to such a casualty which may reasonably be expected to result in major harmful consequences.[119]

This article places significant limitations on the coastal state's right of intervention. First, it applies only to cases of maritime casualties, defined as:

---

[116] Brown, 21 *CLP* (1968), 113; Jagota, 16 *NYIL* (1985), 266–74; Abecassis and Jarashow, *Oil Pollution from Ships*, 116 f.

[117] O'Connell, *The International Law of the Sea*, ii, 1006; Abecassis and Jarashow, *Oil Pollution from Ships*, 116, paras. 6–14.

[118] Churchill and Lowe, *The Law of the Sea*, 262; de Rouw, in Law of the Sea Institute, *Proceedings of 25th Annual Conference*. A Soviet proposal to incorporate an explicit right of intervention in the 1982 UNCLOS was not accepted: see UN Doc. A/CONF.62/C.3/L.25, 3rd UNCLOS, 4 *Official Records* (1975), 212. The Soviet delegation interpreted the words 'pursuant to international law, both customary and conventional' in Article 221 as giving states not parties to the 1969 Convention the right to intervene 'within the limits defined by that Convention': 3rd UNCLOS, 9 *Official Records*, 162, para. 52. See also Nordquist, *UN Convention*, iv, 303 ff.

[119] Article 1(1). A British proposal to apply the 1969 Intervention Convention to the territorial sea was rejected by the Brussels Conference: see Abecassis and Jarashow, *Oil Pollution from Ships*, 121 f.

a collision of ships, stranding or other incident of navigation, or other occurrence on board a ship or external to it resulting in material damage or imminent threat of material damage to a ship or cargo.[120]

This definition would not cover operational pollution, however serious, or dumping at sea, even if illegal. Moreover, no measures may be taken against warships or government ships under the convention, although in such cases a defence of necessity might nevertheless be relied upon.

Secondly, the references to 'grave and imminent' danger of pollution resulting in 'major harmful consequences' were intended to establish a high threshold of probability and of harm, so as to avoid the danger of precipitate action by coastal states causing undue interference with shipping beyond the territorial sea.[121] Following the *Amoco Cadiz* accident, however, some states, including France, argued strongly that the wording of 1969 Convention was too restrictive, and that intervention should be permitted at an earlier stage.[122] Although the 1969 Convention remains unchanged, the text of Article 221 of the 1982 UNCLOS was altered during negotiations to omit any reference to 'grave and imminent danger', and it now assumes a right of intervention when there is merely 'actual or threatened damage' which may 'reasonably be expected' to result in 'major harmful consequences' to the coastal state's interests.[123] Under the 1969 Convention these harmful consequences include direct effects on coastal activities such as fishing, tourist attractions, public health, and the well-being of the area concerned, 'including conservation of living marine resources and of wildlife'.[124] This is broad enough to justify action necessary to protect the coastal environment.

Thirdly, the measures which coastal states are entitled to take are not specified by the 1969 Convention, but depend on what is necessary for their protection, and must be proportionate to the risk and nature of the likely damage.[125] In the *Torrey Canyon* disaster military aircraft were used to destroy

---

[120] Article 2(1).

[121] The non-application of the 1969 Convention to the territorial sea has left states free to set more liberal conditions for intervention there: see e.g., UK Prevention of Oil Pollution Act, 1971, ss. 12–16, which allows intervention in the territorial sea if 'urgently needed' to deal with a shipping accident which will or may cause pollution 'on a large scale' in the UK or its waters, or adjacent thereto. S.1. (1980) No. 1093 applies the act in very limited circumstances to non-UK registered vessels beyond the territorial sea, and see Abecassis and Jarashow, *Oil Pollution from Ships*, 122.

[122] See Lucchini, 24 *AFDI* (1978), 721; Nordquist, *UN Convention*, iv, 313.

[123] cf. Article 222, ICNT, and see 3rd UNCLOS, 8 *Official Records*, 152; 10 ibid. 100. Note, however, the view of the Soviet delegation at UNCLOS that the proposed text of Article 221 'should not be held to give the coastal state more extensive rights of intervention in cases of maritime casualty than the rights of intervention it already enjoyed under the terms of the International Convention Relating to Intervention on the Hig Seas', quoted in Nordquist, *UN Convention*, iv, 313. Kwiatkowska, 22 *ODIL* (1991), 173 notes that a right of intervention based on the wording of Article 221 has been adopted by Bulgaria, Romania, Malaysia, New Zealand, and the USSR. See also the UK Prevention of Oil Pollution Act, *supra* n. 121.

[124] Article 2(4).   [125] Article 5.

the vessel and set fire to the oil; such extreme action will rarely now be regarded as necessary or useful and is unlikely in most cases to be justified given present experience in handling shipping casualties. The more appropriate response will usually involve supplying the assistance of tugs and salvage services. The main significance of the right of intervention is thus that it allows coastal authorities to override the ship's master's discretion in seeking salvage assistance, and may enable them to direct damaged vessels away from their shores.

The 1969 Intervention Convention also seeks to limit excessive coastal state action by requiring it to consult and notify the flag state and report measures to IMO.[126] The final right of decision remains with the coastal state, however. Damage caused by measures taken in excess of the convention must be compensated, and disputes are subject to compulsory conciliation and arbitration.[127] There is no evidence of serious disputes arising out of the operation of the convention, or through the exercise of intervention rights by non-parties under customary law.

(c) Notification by Vessels

Coastal states can only intervene effectively if informed of impending disasters in a timely manner, whether by surveillance, by other states, or by the masters of vessels, including those in distress. A number of treaties, including the 1990 Convention on Oil Pollution Preparedness, Response, and Co-operation, provide for states to request or require masters of ships and aircraft to report casulaties and pollution observed at sea;[128] as we saw earlier, there is also provision for states themselves to report known pollution hazards to other states.

But a serious weakness of the 1969 Intervention Convention was its failure to deal with the crucial issue of notification by the master of the vessel involved in the maritime emergency. Subsequent treaties have not been wholly successful in remedying this omission. The MARPOL Convention requires masters of vessels involved in pollution incidents to report without delay, but does not say to whom.[129] The 1982 UNCLOS merely provides that international rules and standards should include those relating to prompt notification to coastal states, but seems to assume that no such rules yet exist.[130] A more satisfactory formulation is found in Article 4 of the Oil

---

[126] Article 3.

[127] Articles 6, 8.

[128] See also 1983 Bonn Agreement. Protocols in UNEP Regional Conventions invariably take the stronger form. See e.g., Barcelona Protocol, Article 8.

[129] Article 8, and Protocol 1. See also IMO Resolutions A. 648(16), 1989 and MEPC. 21(22). The protocol was amended in 1986. The provisions of UNEP Regional Seas Protocols will also apply. In some cases these assume that reports will go to the flag state and be communicated from there: see e.g. Barcelona Protocol, Article 8.

[130] Article 211(7). Protocol 1 of the MARPOL Convention could constitute such 'international rules and standards'.

Pollution Response Convention, under which the flag state is responsible for requiring masters to report without delay to 'the nearest coastal state' any event on their ship involving the discharge or probable discharge of oil. But this Convention does not yet take account of the wide variety of other toxic substances now likely to be involved in maritime accidents and emergencies, although it does cover offshore oil installations.

An alternative and possibly more effective approach would concentrate on the power of coastal states to regulate the provision of information by ships concerning pollution incidents in their EEZ or territorial sea. Coastal state interests are sufficiently strongly involved to justify such action to reinforce flag state control. Article 211(5) of the 1982 UNCLOS may provide the legal basis for coastal state regulation based on Protocol 1 of the MARPOL Convention, although none of the regional agreements appears to adopt this approach.

(d) Salvage

The basis on which most maritime salvage services have traditionally operated is the 'no cure no pay' principle. This provides salvors with no reward for work carried out benefiting the coastal state and reducing the liability of the vessel owner for pollution damage if the vessel itself is lost.[131] Coastal state intervention may exacerbate this problem if it renders salvage of the vessel more difficult. The 1969 Intervention Convention allows coastal states to override the master's discretion in calling for salvage assistance and empowers them, as we have seen, to take necessary measures to protect the coastal environment, but it provides no incentive for salvors themselves to assist in this task. Following measures already taken by Lloyds to revise salvage contracts, a new convention dealing *inter alia* with the environmental aspects of salvage was adopted by IMO in 1989.

The 1989 International Convention on Salvage[132] is mainly concerned with private law matters, and the rights of coastal states to intervene remain unaffected, although Article 11 requires them to take account of the need to ensure the efficient and successful performance of salvage operations, and thus may affect decisions on matters such as access to ports. The convention applies to judicial or arbitral proceedings brought in a state party and which relate to salvage operations, but it also covers salvage operations conducted by or under the control of public authorities.[133] It does not cover warships or government non-commercial ships entitled to immunity, nor does it apply to offshore installations.[134]

There are two main features of the convention. Salvors are entitled to 'special compensation' for salvage operations, in respect of a vessel or its

---

[131] Abecassis, *Oil Pollution from Ships*, ch. 8; Redgwell, 14 *Marine Policy* (1990), 142.
[132] Redgwell, 14 *Marine Policy* (1990); Gold, 20 *JMLC* (1989), 487; Kerr, ibid. 505.
[133] Articles 2, 5.   [134] Articles 3, 4.

cargo, which have prevented or minimized damage to the environment, and they have a duty of care to carry out salvage operations in such a way as to prevent or minimize this damage.[135] Thus the convention does not apply to environmental protection unrelated to the salvage of a vessel or its cargo, but it has the important effects that protection of the environment is regarded as a 'useful result' even if the vessel itself is lost, and also that expenses are recoverable in excess of the limit for salvage of the vessel or cargo alone.[136]

Salvors thus have a continued incentive and obligation to mitigate environmental damage even after the vessel is saved, or after it sinks. The salvor is correspondingly penalized by loss or reduction of his reward if through negligence or misconduct damage to the environment is not averted or minimized.[137] Moreover, consistently with the traditional 'no cure no pay' principle the salvor will remain uncompensated for efforts, however great, which lead to no useful result, whether because the vessel is lost, or because damage to the environment cannot be reduced or averted. This convention is not yet in force.

6. RESPONSIBILITY AND LIABILITY FOR DAMAGE

(1) State Responsibility for Marine Pollution[138]

Article 235(1) of the 1982 UNCLOS affirms the orthodox proposition that 'states are responsible for the fulfilment of their international obligations concerning the protection and preservation of the marine environment' and goes on to add that 'They shall be liable in accordance with international law.' There is no reason to doubt that this responsibility extends to flag states in respect of their vessels, and to coastal states in respect of activities which they permit within their jurisdiction or control.[139] A number of authors have argued that in respect to ultrahazardous activities at sea, such as the operation of large oil tankers, the liability of the flag state is strict, and the same view may be taken regarding offshore oil installations because of the serious risks these pose for other states.[140] As we saw in Chapter 4 the evidence in support of a strict liability thesis is by no means strong. Moreover it has not been

---

[135] Articles 8, 14. 'Damage to the environment' is defined in Article 1(d) to mean 'substantial physical damage to human health or to marine life or resources in coastal or inland waters or areas adjacent thereto caused by pollution, contamination, fire, explosion or similar major incidents.'

[136] cf. Article 13 which limits the reward for salvage of the vessel or property to the salvaged thereof.

[137] Articles 14(5), 18.

[138] See generally Smith, *State Responsibility and the Marine Environment* (Oxford, 1988), and *supra*, Ch. 4.

[139] Smith, *State Responsibility*, chs. 10–12.

[140] See e.g., Smith, ibid. 114–18; 160–3; 210–13; and Handl, 74 *AJIL* (1980), 547, where the state practice and literature are reviewed.

applied by the 1982 UNCLOS to state liability for deep sea-bed operations. Instead, Article 139 of the convention provides only that in respect of damage resulting from deep sea-bed operations, states are liable only for a failure to carry out their responsibilities, and shall not be liable for damage caused by national operators 'if the state party has taken all necessary and appropriate measures to secure effective compliance' with the requirements of the Convention. This clearly points to a due diligence standard of liability for states, although operators themselves are made subject to a strict liability standard in draft regulations proposed by the preparatory commission for the ISBA.[141]

A second reason for doubting academic views on the responsibility of states for damage to the marine environment is that there is almost no state practice from which to draw conclusions. In a few cases, flag states have paid compensation for pollution from oil tankers, and some writers treat this as supporting a principle of strict or absolute liability comparable to the position asserted by Canada in the Cosmos 954 claim.[142] These are exceptional examples, however; in general, pollution from ships has not been the subject of interstate claims, even in cases as serious as the loss of the *Amoco Cadiz*, but has instead been dealt with under national law or civil liability and compensation schemes considered below. The same is true of most oil spills from offshore installations. In one of the most serious of these, the IXTOC I blowout, Mexico refused to accept any responsibility for injury caused in the United States, and the matter was ultimately resolved in civil claims.[143] This is consistent with the approach adopted in UNEP's 'Study of Legal Aspects' of offshore mineral exploration and drilling,[144] and with bilateral and regional arrangements elsewhere.[145] Although in 1986 the parties to the London Dumping Convention called for the development of 'procedures for the assessment of liability in accordance with the principles of international law regarding state responsibility for damage to the environment of other states or to any other area of the environment resulting from dumping',[146] no progress has been made, and the question of state responsibility for dumping remains unresolved, under this convention and under all of the regional agreements.

Thus, although at a theoretical level, it is quite correct to conclude that 'the international legal order currently possesses a perfectly adequate foundation for an equitable and effective regime of state responsibility for marine en-

---

[141] Prepcom Doc. LOS/PCN/SCN.3/WP.6/Add.5, Article 122.

[142] *Supra*, n. 140, and see *supra*, Ch. 4.

[143] IXTOC I Agreement, 22 *ILM* (1983), 580; Smith, *State Responsibility*, 117.

[144] UNEP/GC.9/5/Add.5/App. III (1981).

[145] 1977 International Convention on Civil Liability for Oil Pollution Damage from the Exploration for or Exploitation of Submarine Mineral Resources (No ratifications); 1983 Canada–Denmark Agreement for Co-operation Relating to the Marine Environment, Article 8, 23 *ILM* (1983), 269; 1974 Offshore Pollution Liability Agreement, 13 *ILM* (1974) 1409 (since updated), and see generally Caron, 10 *ELQ* (1983), 641; de Mestral, 20 *Harv. ILJ* (1979), 469.

[146] Resolution LDC 21(9), 1986; Kasoulides, 26 *SDLR* (1989), 497.

vironmental injury,'[147] the failure of states to resort to this foundation is its most conspicuous feature. Alternative approaches based instead on the liability of the polluter, have proved more appealing in practice, and for all of the reasons already observed in Chapter 5, these are probably also preferable in principle.

(2) Civil Liability for Marine Pollution

(a) OECD and the 'polluter pays' Principle[148]

OECD's 'polluter pays' principle was examined in Chapter 3. As we saw there, the principle is primarily intended to ensure that the costs of dealing with pollution are not borne by public authorities but are directed to the polluter. OECD has recommended that this principle should be taken into account in calculating the costs of measures taken to prevent and control oil spills at sea, and that liability for the costs of 'reasonable remedial action' should be assigned to the polluter. The effect of this policy is that liability would not be limited to compensation for direct injury, but would include some part of the capital outlay and running costs of monitoring an oil pollution response capability and of restoring the environment to an acceptable state. These costs can be recovered in a variety of ways: through fines, charges, or civil actions for damages.[149] The preamble to the 1991 Oil Pollution Response Convention describes the 'polluter pays' principle as a 'general principle of international environmental law', but as we have seen in Chapter 3, it has until now been more convincingly viewed as an economic policy, without obligatory force.

(b) Liability for Oil Pollution from Ships

The problems of jurisdiction, choice of law, standard of liability, and enforcement of judgments which typically affect transboundary claims for pollution damage are amplified in the case of ships and can result in protracted and unsatisfactory litigation when maritime accidents cause serious pollution. The *Torrey Canyon* disaster of 1967 showed the need for international agreement on a regime of civil liability for such accidents and prompted IMO to call an international conference in 1969.[150] Resolving the difficulties confronting coastal states in securing adequate compensation was not simply a matter of removing jurisdictional obstacles, harmonizing liability, and ensuring the polluter would pay, however. Rather more important was the

---

[147] Smith, *State Responsibility*, 255.

[148] Recommendation C(81) 32 (Final).

[149] OECD, *Combating Oil Spills* (Paris, 1982), 24, gives examples of national legislation. See also OECD, *Economic Instruments for Environmental Protection* (Paris, 1989).

[150] IMCO, *Official Records of the International Legal Conference on Marine Pollution Damage* (London, 1969), and see Keaton, 21 *CLP* (1968), 94; Brown, ibid. 113.

question how the loss should be distributed, given the long-standing tradition of permitting shipowners to limit their liability in maritime claims and the argument that in the case of oil, the cargo owners might reasonably be expected to share in the burden.

The 1969 Convention on Civil Liability for Oil Pollution Damage, in conjunction with the 1971 Convention on the Establishment Fund for Compensation for Oil Pollution Damage, represent one approach to the establishment of a more satisfactory regime for oil pollution liability.[151] This scheme was partially based on the earlier nuclear liability conventions, which are considered in detail in Chapter 9 and to which reference should be made.[152] But it differs from the earlier scheme in several important respects, and unlike that scheme it has been amended by a 1984 Protocol, which, however, has not yet entered into force, and for reasons considered below, is unlikely at present to do so. In this section attention will focus primarily on the differences between the oil pollution and nuclear liability regions.

The most important difference concerns the allocation of liability and the distribution of compensation costs. The 1969 Convention channels liability not to the operator of the vessel, nor to the cargo owner, but to the shipowner,[153] who alone is responsible for the safe and efficient operation and seaworthiness of the vessel. This liability is strict, rather than absolute, in the sense that although no fault or negligence need be shown, it does not arise where the owner can prove that the loss resulted from war, hostilities, insurrection, civil war, or natural phenomena, such as storms, of an 'exceptional, inevitable and irresistible character', or was wholly caused intentionally by a third party or by the negligence of those responsible for navigations aids.[154]

The owner is, however, entitled in most cases to limit his liability, according to a formula related to the tonnage of the ship, and to an overall total.[155] These limits allowed significantly greater sums to be recovered for oil pollution than for other forms of damage covered by other maritime liability conventions in 1969, but they are now insufficient. One purpose of the 1984 protocol is to ensure that they are substantially increased. As with nuclear accidents, the capacity of the insurance market to bear this liability is a significant factor in determining the overall amount, but another is the share of the total loss to be borne by the shipowner.[156] One calculation indicates that under the 1969 Convention the shipowner's share would represent 47 per cent of total costs of an oil spill, and 68 per cent under the 1984 Protocol.[157] Under the 1969 Convention the owner was not entitled to limit liability if the

---

[151] See Abecassis and Jarashow, *Oil Pollution from Ships*, chs. 10 and 11, on which the following text is based.
[152] See also Ch. 5.   [153] Article 3.
[154] Article 3(2). See also Article 3(3).   [155] Article 5.
[156] Abecassis, and Jarashow, *Oil Pollution from Ships*, 215.   [157] Ibid. 241.

incident occurred as a result of his actual fault; the 1984 Convention re-defines this to cover intentional damage or recklessness.

Beyond this total, the main purpose of the International Oil Pollution Compensation Fund (IOPC Fund) established in 1971 is to provide additional compensation so that within the limits of the Fund's total liability, the victims are fully and adequately compensated.[158] However, unlike the European scheme for nuclear accidents, this compensation does not come from states parties, but is constituted from a levy on oil importers, who are mainly the oil companies whose cargoes the vessels are likely to be carrying.[159] Another important difference is that under the 1971 Fund Convention the shipowner is also entitled to have recourse to the fund in order to relieve a portion of his liability even where the total damage does not exceed the limit under the 1969 Convention.[160] Thus the original overall scheme is one in which the total loss is borne, in effect, jointly by the shipowner and by the cargo owners or oil companies. The provision for relieving the shipowner's liability will be re-moved if the 1984 Protocol enters into force; shipowners will then bear the full costs up to the limit of their total liability, and only for additional losses will the Fund's resources be called on.

But the Fund Convention also has an additional, wider, purpose of pro-viding compensation even where no liability for damage arises under the Liability Convention, or where the shipowner's liability is not met by the compulsory insurance he is required to carry, leaving him financially incapable of meeting his obligations.[161] In these respects the Fund provides a form of security for claimants which governments provide under the nuclear liability conventions. However, the IOPC Fund is exonerated from liability where the pollution damage results from an act of war, hostilities, civil war or insur-rection, or where the oil is discharged from a warship or government-owned ship entitled to immunity, or where the claimant cannot prove that the damage resulted from 'an incident involving one or more ships'.[162] The importance of the last provision is that where the source of the oil is unidentified, no compensation is obtainable. Thus there remain certain situations in which the innocent victim will be without any effective recourse. It should also be observed that parties to the 1969 Liability Convention are not obliged to become parties to the Fund Convention, and that a significant number have not done so.

The one remaining respect in which the oil pollution scheme differs signi-ficantly from the nuclear conventions concerns environmental damage. The 1969 Liability Convention covered 'pollution damage', defined by Article 2 as

---

[158] Article 4(1)(c). The Fund's practice is reviewed by Brown, in Butler, *International Shipping*, 275, and see generally the Fund's *Annual Reports*.
[159] See Article 14, however, and see Abecassis and Jareshow, *Oil Pollution from Ships*, 281.
[160] 1971 Fund Convention, Article 5.
[161] Article 4(1)(a) and (b).   [162] Article 4(2).

'loss or damage caused outside the ship' and occurring on the territorial sea or territory of a contracting party, and it expressly included the costs of preventive measures taken to minimize damage. The IOPC Fund has interpreted the phrase 'pollution damage' to cover costs incurred in clean-up operations at sea and on the beach, preventive measures, additional costs, and a proportion of the fixed costs incurred by public authorities in maintaining a pollution response capability, economic loss suffered by persons who depend directly on earnings from coastal or sea related activities, including fishermen and hoteliers, and damage to property.[163] But as Abecassis observes, 'The Convention's definition of pollution is so vague it is not really a definition at all.'[164] This left interpretation in practice to national legal systems, which as in the case of the *Antonio Gramsci*,[165] might allow also claims for the notional costs of damage to the marine environment. A similar claim was initially allowed by a US court in the case of the *Zoe Colocotroni*,[166] where a value was put on the estimated loss of marine organisms and the cost of replanting a mangrove swamp, although this case was not governed by the 1969 Convention. Compensation was, however, reduced on appeal to 'reasonable' measures of restoration. A more precise definition was needed both to give uniformity to these interpretations and to ensure that some recovery of environmental costs would be available in the courts of all parties to the convention.

The 1984 Protocol is thus an improvement on the 1969 Convention in making clear that compensation for impairment of the environment is recoverable, but the relatively narrow terms in which it does so should be noted.[167] Compensation is limited to 'the costs of reasonable measures of reinstatement actually undertaken or to be undertaken'. This would not be broad enough to cover the loss of marine organisms included in the *Zoe Colocotroni* case, or the notional formula for water pollution damage used by the Soviet court in the *Antonio Gramsci* case, and accords with the view of the IOPC Fund Assembly that pollution damage assessment 'is not to be made on the basis of an abstract quantification of damage calculated in accordance with theoretical models'.[168] The new definition also allows recovery for loss of profit arising out of impairment of the environment, for example in the case of

---

[163] See IOPC Fund, *Annual Report* (1988), 58, and cf. 1969 Liability Convention, Arts 1(6) and 2.

[164] *Oil Pollution from Ships*, 209.

[165] Ibid. 209; Brown, in Butler, *International Shipping*, 282 ff.

[166] *Commonwealth of Puerto Rico* v. *SS Zoe Colocotroni*, 456 F. Suppl. 1327 (1978); 628 F2d 652 (1980); see Abecassis and Jarashow *Oil Pollution from Ships*, 551.

[167] Abecassis and Jarashow, *Oil Pollution from Ships*, 237, 277; Jacobsson and Trotz, 17 *JMLC* (1986), 467.

[168] Brown, in Butler, *International Shipping*, 282 ff. See also the claims made in respect of the *Antonio Gramsci* (No. 2), and the *Patmos*, reported in IOPC Fund, *Annual Report* (1990), 23 and 27. In both cases the Fund rejected claims for unquantified environmental damage. See Maffei, in Francioni and Scovazzi, *International Responsibility for Environmental Harm*, 381.

losses suffered by fishermen or hotel owners, but, as we have seen, such claims had already been allowed by the IOPC Fund. It also includes pollution damage in the coastal state's EEZ, or in an area up to 200 miles from its territorial sea baselines. The Protocol's environmental perspective is clearly preferable to the very limited definition of damage found in the nuclear conventions, but it still stops short of using liability to penalize those whose harm to the environment cannot be reinstated, or quantified in terms of property loss or loss of profits, or which the government concerned does not wish to reinstate. To this extent the true environmental costs of oil transportation by sea continue to be borne by the community as a whole, and not by the polluter.

Although over fifty states have become parties to the 1969 Liability Convention, some significant oil-importing states have declined to do so, including the United States, mainly because the liability limits were thought by Congress to be too low. These would have been substantially raised by the 1984 Protocol. Prompted by the *Exxon Valdez* disaster in Alaska, however, the US Oil Pollution Act of 1990 introduces limits on liability under US law greatly in excess even of the 1984 Protocols, and allows unlimited liability in a wider range of situations, including gross negligence, wilful misconduct, and violation of applicable Federal regulations.[169] This must be seen against the total clean-up costs for the *Exxon Valdez* incident estimated at $2,500 million, but it has the effect of precluding US ratification of the Fund and Liability Convention. In 1991, IMO proposed two new protocols to the 1969 Liability and 1972 Fund Conventions in an attempt to encourage wider participation and entry into force of the 1984 revisions.[170] The new liability protocol sets lower qualifying tonnage limits for entry into force, while the fund protocol lowers the threshold of annual oil imports at which a liability to contribute arises. The latter change is necessary to widen the pool of potential contributors to the IOPC Fund, 76 per cent of whose funds are at present provided by Japan, Italy, the Netherlands, France, the UK, and Spain. The remaining thirty-nine members contributed only 24 per cent of the total in 1990, comparable to the Japanese share. That a relatively small number of states are in practice carrying the main burden of the Fund's operation may well explain their reluctance to ratify the 1984 Protocol. Another possible option is to limit the contribution payable by participating states in order to restore a sense of greater equity to the present scheme.

For ships from states not parties to the 1969 and 1971 Conventions, two

---

[169] The Act also leaves individual US states free to adopt their own higher liability standards. See Ruhl and Jewell, 8 *OGTLR* (1990), 234; eid., 9 *OGTLR* (1990), 304; George and de la Rue, 11 *OGTLR* (1990), 363.

[170] IMO Doc. A 17/5(b)/1/Add. 1 (1991), Annex 6. See Abecassis and Jarashow, *Oil Pollution from Ships*, 297, for a review of the arguments for and against ratification of the earlier protocols.

industry schemes exist to provide additional compensation.[171] TOVALOP applies to tanker owners, CRISTAL provides a fund comparable to the IOPC Fund. It should also be noted that there is nothing in the 1969 or 1984 Conventions to prevent parties or their nationals from having resort to the courts of non-party states where these have jurisdiction over oil spills, as in the *Amoco Cadiz* litigation.[172]

Despite their failure to attain wider international acceptance, the Liability and Fund Conventions have been more successful than the comparable nuclear conventions in establishing a workable scheme of civil liability for ultrahazardous risks. Like the nuclear conventions they are an important precedent for the international regulation of other forms of hazardous activity, and an alternative to reliance on state responsibility for pollution damage. As with those conventions also, limitation of liability and equitable sharing of the costs remain controversial, but it is of course precisely those features which make the Convention broadly acceptable to the shipping industry and enable claims to be promptly met.

(c) Liability for Other Forms of Pollution from Ships

The 1969 Liability Convention and the 1971 Fund Convention deal only with oil pollution from oil tankers; they do not constitute a universal regime for all types of cargo or for all types of ship. In particular, no international liability regime presently covers the maritime carriage of chemicals or hazardous wastes, although a 1971 Convention does apply to the maritime carriage of nuclear material.[173] The 1989 Basel Convention on the Control of Transboundary Movements of Hazardous Wastes provides for the negotiation of a protocol on liability, but draft Articles will not be adopted until the first meeting of the parties.[174] Unsuccessful negotiations were conducted in 1984 at IMO to conclude a convention on liability for 'hazardous and noxious substances'; they recommenced in 1991 with the consideration of a draft convention on the carriage of 'dangerous goods' by sea.[175] The term 'dangerous goods' would cover noxious liquids listed in Appendix II of MARPOL, certain other dangerous liquids, goods subject to the International Maritime Dangerous Goods Code, liquefied gas, and certain explosive substances. The convention is modelled closely on the 1984 Protocols to the Civil Liability Convention and other relevant conventions, but the problem in this case is to find some method of spreading and insuring the loss where ownership of the

---

[171] Abecassis and Jarashow, *Oil Pollution from Ships*, Ch. 12.

[172] In this situation the exclusive jurisdiction conferred on the courts of the place of injury by Article 9 is rendered ineffective. For an account of the *Amoco Cadiz* litigation, see ibid. 555.

[173] See *infra*, pp. 371 ff.

[174] See *infra*, pp. 340–1.

[175] IMO Doc. LEG/CONF.6/3 (1984); IMO Doc. LEG 64/4 and 65/3 (1991); de Bièvre, 17 *JMLC* (1982), 61; Drel, in Law of the Sea Institute, *Proceedings of 25th Annual Conference*; Birnie, ibid.

goods is much more widely distributed than is the case in the oil industry. The 1991 draft proposed to make the shipowner liable up to specified limits, supported by insurance, and to provide an additional compensation scheme funded initially by exporting states and thereafter by the shippers of dangerous goods through the purchase of insurance certificates. The compensation scheme would be administered by an Assembly and a Secretariat, which would operate in a manner similar to the institutions established by the earlier convention. Actions for compensation could be brought only in the courts of the state or states where the damage has occurred, except in cases where the damage is caused outside the territory of any state.

7. CONCLUSIONS

This chapter has demonstrated the extent to which an international legal regime for the control of marine pollution from ships has developed since 1972, and the degree to which it has proved effective. Although in certain respects there remain significant problems in enforcing international pollution regulations at sea, and in controlling the risks of serious accidents, there is evidence that relevant international and regional conventions, most notably the 1973/8 MARPOL Convention, have led to improved protection of the marine environment. There is also, as we shall see from later chapters, some reason to conclude that international regulation of serious environmental risks has proved more successful with regard to ships than for other comparably hazardous undertakings. The regulatory system based on MARPOL and on other conventions such as the 1974 SOLAS has worked effectively under the supervision of IMO, which has shown the flexibility and responsiveness necessary to keep pace with new developments, and has successfully provided a forum in which competing interests can be balanced. Moreover, the system of enforcement employed against delinquent vessels has overcome some of the earlier problems of exclusive reliance on flag state control, although it is clear that further improvements remain necessary.

The 1982 UNCLOS has in many respects codified the existing rules of customary and conventional law and has proved largely uncontroversial in its approach to protection and preservation of the marine environment. An acceptable balance of interests between maritime states and coastal states appears to have been achieved. But it is more doubtful whether the Convention's carefully structured extension of coastal and port state jurisdiction has in reality had much impact on the control and reduction of pollution from ships, although the EEZ regime does have significant implications for dumping at sea and the conservation of living resources. The Convention has also been less satisfactory in dealing with other sources of marine pollution, in particular land-based sources, as the following chapter makes clear. Perhaps the most positive element of Part 12 of the Convention is its elevation of international conventions such as MARPOL to the status of international standards within a global regime applicable potentially to all states. The Convention's impact in this respect will largely have been achieved irrespective of its eventual entry into force, or of the relatively small number of parties.

Widespread ratification of the 1982 UNCLOS is important, however. Until then, as we have seen, certain of its provisions, such as those on port-state jurisdiction, cannot take effect. More importantly, without such ratification, unilateral or regional claims to jurisdiction over shipping or living resources may eventually destroy the overall 'package deal' on which the Convention is based. Until entry into force, the dispute settlement machinery which might otherwise restrain such claims cannot take effect,[176] nor will the international management of deep sea-bed exploitation be possible. Whatever the force of objections to the proposed ISBA might be, it remains necessary to have some provision for regulation and supervision of the environmental conseqences of any deep sea-bed mining.[177] Unilateral claims to undertake such operations are in this sense highly questionable since they fail to address how the marine environment would be protected, and offer no basis for reconciling the interests of the international community as a whole with those of exploiting states. This points to a deeper failure in the 1982 UNCLOS and in the law of the sea in general. While generally successful in coping with specific sources of marine pollution, whether from ships or dumping, it does not in practice meet the aspiration of establishing a 'system for sustainable development' of natural resources. Its failings, both in fisheries management, and in the relationship with land-based pollution, are explored more fully in Chapters 8 and 13. While in many respects the 1982 UNCLOS does represent a useful model for the development of international environmental law, these deficiencies should not be overlooked.

[176] See *supra*, pp. 181–2.   [177] See *supra*, pp. 171–2.

8

The International Control of
Hazardous Waste

1. INTRODUCTION

(1) The Nature of the Problem

The issues considered in this chapter include land-based sources of marine pollution, dumping at sea, and the transport of hazardous wastes for transboundary disposal. Although each of these topics is the subject of discrete legal regimes, what links them thematically is that together they represent different stages in a cycle of international pollution and environmental risks emanating largely from the hazardous wastes generated by industry, agriculture, and domestic effluent. Each stage of this cycle, including air pollution and the use of international watercourses, requires co-ordinated international regulation if the environmental consequences are not simply to be transferred from one medium to another, or from the developed world to the developing world.

Despite the considerable attention devoted since 1954 to the control of oil pollution from ships, in practice this is a relatively minor component of marine pollution. By far the major input into the marine environment comes from land-based sources and airborne depositions with additional contributions from dumping at sea. Sewage, industrial waste, and agricultural run-off are the most common types of pollutant which enter the sea from land, mostly through rivers. Some of the substances these sources generate are directly toxic to marine life and humans or spread disease. Others contribute to eutrophication and oxygen depletion, resulting in loss of marine life. Thus effective pollution control is important not only for the general health of the marine environment but particularly for its impact on the conservation of fish stocks and coastal ecology.[1]

In 1990, the second GESAMP report concluded that marine pollution had worsened since 1982.[2] Sewage disposal and agricultural run-off were identified as the most urgent problems requiring international attention. Eutrophication had been occurring with increasing severity in enclosed waters in

---

[1] Cormack, 16 *Marine Policy* (1992), 5.
[2] Group of Experts on the Scientific Aspects of Marine Pollution (GESAMP), *The State of the Marine Environment*, UNEP (1990). See also *infra*, n. 27.

the Baltic, North Sea, Mediterranean, Northern Adriatic, and in parts of Japan and the US east coast. The effects on coastal ecosystems of pollution and development has become a serious threat to wildlife and fish resources. But existing controls on certain persistent toxins such as DDT and chlorinated hydrocarbons had begun to prove effective in European and American waters. In tropical and sub-tropical areas, however, contamination was thought to be rising.

In general, the report's conclusions do point out the strengths and weaknesses of international regulation of the marine environment. Where there are effective international standards, as in the case of nuclear waste disposal, the problem is less serious. Where particular categories of pollutant, such as sewage, are less well regulated, or where no co-ordinated action has been agreed, as in many third world coastal areas, the problems are of increasing severity. Moreover, the report concluded that for the first time there was some evidence that pollution was no longer confined to coastal waters and enclosed seas, although these remain the most seriously affected areas, and it is here in the oceans' most biologically productive region that international action is most urgent. Regional agreements concerned with enclosed or semi-enclosed seas such as the North Sea, the Baltic, or the Mediterranean, have attempted to co-ordinate measures in these areas, but evidence derived from studies of those seas does not indicate that this action has been notably effective in reversing present levels of overall pollution. Thus existing international regulation can be seen as deficient at two levels: it is ineffective in controlling regional problems, and it fails to address land-based pollution comprehensively or globally, omitting several important sources and regions. Put simply, the existing regional conventions on land-based pollution do not work adequately. Only in respect of dumping at sea has substantial progress in controlling and reducing the problem of marine pollution been achieved.

International trade in hazardous substances, such as chemicals or wastes, creates environmental risks which are international in two senses.[3] First, there is the possibility of accidental harm to transit states or the marine environment. Secondly, importing states are at risk where trade takes place without their knowledge or consent, or where, as in the case of some developing states, they possess inadequate management facilities or limited understanding of the risks involved. Trade in these circumstances may be a consequence of lower standards of regulation or of a willingness to accept for use or disposal substances banned or regulated elsewhere; taking advantage of these lower

[3] UNGAOR, 44th Session, *Report of the Secretary General on Illegal Traffic in Toxic and Dangerous Products and Wastes*, UN Doc. A/44/362 (1989); Sebek, 'International Legal Regulation of Trade in Toxic Waste, its Transport and Disposal', in Postiglione (ed.), *Per un tribunale internazionale del ambiente* (Milan, 1990), 285; Kummer and Rummel-Bulska, *The Basel Convention on the Control of Transboundary Movements of Hazardous Wastes and Their Disposal*, UNEP (Nairobi, 1990); Hackett, 5 *AUJILP* (1990), 291; Bothe, 33 *GYIL* (1990), 422.

standards involves a transfer of environmental costs from manufacturers in developed industrialized economies to the peoples and environment of developing states who may be least able to bear them.

Trade in hazardous wastes will be advantageous, however, if it removes for reprocessing or safe disposal substances which could not be dealt with in an environmentally sound manner in the country of origin, or which would otherwise be disposed of at sea. The bulk of this trade does not involve developing states, and a general policy of eliminating it among industrialized nations would be environmentally and economically inefficient and hamper attempts to reduce marine pollution from dumping or land-based sources. Elimination of trade among developed countries would also put further pressure on developing states in Africa, Latin America, and the Caribbean who are already the main recipients of illegal traffic in toxic waste for disposal. The disappearance of landfill sites in industrialized countries, escalating disposal costs, and the difficulty of obtaining approval for incineration facilities have all contributed to a growing demand for waste disposal in the developing world. It is mainly to counter this problem that international regulation of transboundary movements of hazardous waste has proved necessary.

(2) International Policy

As we shall see, the London Dumping Convention, the Basel Convention on the Control of Transboundary Movements of Hazardous Wastes, and, in somewhat weaker form, the regional agreements on land-based sources of marine pollution share a common philosophy indicative of the trend of contemporary international policy. This policy combines an increasingly strong preference for elimination or disposal at source of toxic, persistent, or bio-accumulative waste wherever possible, with, in other cases, a regime of regulation, monitoring, prior environmental impact assessment, or prior consent designed to minimize the risks of disposal and provide for the protection of other states and the environment of common spaces.[4] Until recently international policy towards the disposal of waste substances of environmental significance has best been summarized as an attempt to balance environmental protection and economic development by regulation, not outright prohibition. But this balance has not fallen equally in all cases. A sensitivity to the needs of industrial development and the economic costs of

---

[4] Stockholm Conference on the Human Environment, 1972, UN Doc. A/CONF.48/1/Rev. 1, Declaration, Principles 6 and 7 and Action Plan, Recommendations 55, 71, 86; World Charter for Nature, UNGA Res. 37/7 (1982), paras. 12 and 21; 1982 UNCLOS, Articles 207, 210; UNEP Cairo Guidelines and Principles for Environmentally Sound Management of Hazardous Wastes, 16 EPL (1986), 31; UNGA Res. 43/212 (1988); 2nd International North Sea Conference, 1987, Declaration, esp. para. 21; 1991 Bamako Convention on the Ban of the Import into Africa and the Control of Transboundary Movement and Management of Hazardous Wastes within Africa, Preamble and Article 4 (hereafter '1991 African Convention').

stricter controls on waste disposal are the most important factors accounting for the refusal of states participating in the UNCLOS III negotiations to countenance a stronger regime for the control of land-based marine pollution, and for the resulting failure of regional and national regulation. The special needs of developing states with regard to industrialization have also been acknowledged in this context, allowing them even greater latitude in the adoption of pollution controls.[5]

A quite different picture is apparent when considering the regulation of dumping at sea and the transboundary transport of hazardous wastes. In general, states have been much more willing to endorse and implement a precautionary approach to the prevention of pollution from these sources. As a result, international regulation has been much stronger and more demanding, and has lead to greater protection for developing countries and agreement on the phasing out of all industrial dumping at sea. The emphasis of international policy in these cases is now increasingly in favour of eliminating the need for waste disposal by adopting clean production technology and processes. There is clearly a rather greater political commitment on the part of the international community to control these practices than has yet become apparent with respect to land-based pollution, although here too, recent policy declarations by European states show movement in the same direction. In 1990, UNEP's Governing Council gave greater emphasis to these trends by urging governments to consider clean production methods as a means of implementing the precautionary principle for all sources of hazardous waste, and it also agreed to consider an integrated approach to pollution control taking account of appropriate economic incentives.[6] Moreover, the development of an international strategy for environmentally sound management of hazardous wastes giving priority to waste reduction was part of the agenda for the 1992 UNCED conference.[7] The same conference also called for international action on toxic chemicals and land-based sources of pollution. These decisions point towards an increasing integration of all elements of international waste management and the control of hazardous substances, and the likelihood that policies adopted in existing treaties will have to change. This has already happened with regard to dumping at sea.

(3) Co-operation and Risk Avoidance

Another significant feature of this topic is the importance attached by policy statements and international conventions to procedural obligations of prior

---

[5] Principles 11, 23, Stockholm Declaration, 1972; 1982 UNCLOS, Articles 194(1), 207.

[6] Decision SS. 11/4 B (1990), 20 EPL (1990), 157. See also London Dumping Convention, 13th Consultative meeting, LDC 13/5 (1990), which considers the development of a long-term strategy for the Convention, and OECD Council Recommendation C(90) 164 on integrated pollution prevention and control, 21 *EPL* (1991), 90.

[7] UNCED, Preparatory Committee, 1990, 20 *EPL* (1990), 161.

environmental impact assessment, monitoring, notification, and consultation with other states and international institutions. Extension of these obligations to include environmental impacts on common spaces is essential in minimizing the risk to these areas, including the marine environment, from all forms of industrial and human activity. This point is recognized in Articles 204, 205, and 206 of the 1982 UNCLOS, which codify treaty provisions on monitoring and prior environmental impact assessment for land-based sources of marine pollution and dumping at sea.[8] In both cases, concern for the common interest of all states in the marine environment leads to greater emphasis on the mediating role of international or regional institutions, such as IMO.

However, it is undoubtedly the transboundary impact of disposal of hazardous waste on land which underlies the unusually strong regime of shared responsibility found in the Basel Convention and regional conventions dealing with this subject. Unlike state practice in the case of nuclear installations, or international watercourses, where the polluting state's freedom of action is limited only by its obligation of notification and consultation, the Basel convention firmly asserts the sovereignty of the receiving state to determine what impacts on its territory it will accept: above all, the principle of prior informed consent on which it is based points to an important shift in environmental policy. No longer can it be assumed that waste disposal is permissible unless shown to be harmful. Instead, the precautionary approach to pollution control now entails a willingness to act in cases of potential harm, even though scientific proof is lacking; in effect it forces the proponent to demonstrate that no significant risk of environmental harm will result, and this places greater limits on the freedom which states have hitherto enjoyed in making use of the oceans or of other states as locations for the disposal of hazardous wastes.[9]

2. LAND-BASED SOURCES OF MARINE POLLUTION[10]

(1) The Customary Background

Although estimated to contribute over 80 per cent of all marine pollution, disposal of hazardous wastes at sea was subject to few restraints under international law until the first regional treaties of the 1970s. At most, in-

[8] See *infra*, pp. 314–6, and pp. 327–9.

[9] Second International North Sea Conference, Declaration; Third International North Sea Conference, Declaration; UNEP, *Report of the Governing Council*, 15th Session (1989), GC Res. 15/27; Paris Commission, Recommendation 89/1 (1989); Oslo Commission, OSCOM 88/1 (1988) and OSCOM 89/1 (1989); 1991 African Convention, Article 4(3)(2); see Gundling, 5 *IJECL* (1990), 23, and *supra*, pp. 95–8.

[10] Burchi, 3 *Ital. YIL* (1977), 115; Rémond-Gouilloud, in Johnston (ed.), *The Environmental Law of the Sea* (Berlin, 1981), 230; Kwiatkowska, 14 *ODIL* (1984), 315; Hickey, 15 *SDLR* (1978), 409; Meng Qing-Nan, *Land-based Marine Pollution* (London, 1987); Boyle 16 *Marine Policy* (1992), p. 201.

ferences could be drawn from precedents that marine pollution causing serious damage to another state would be internationally wrongful, and that polluting activities might in some circumstances require consultation with other states likely to be affected. However, as we saw in Chapter 7, the High Seas Convention of 1958 only required states to regulate oil pollution, to take measures to prevent pollution from the dumping of radioactive waste, and to co-operate in preventing pollution from activities involving radioactive materials or other harmful agents.[11] Article 2 of the same convention also incorporated a general prohibition on abuse of rights, and provided some basis for limiting land-based pollution or dumping which interfered with fishing or other uses of the seas.[12] Some later treaties, including the 1982 UNCLOS, affirm customary obligations to protect the environment of other states and avoid abuse of rights.[13] They all recognize a general obligation to protect the marine environment, and support the conclusion that the diligent control of land-based sources of marine pollution required by Articles 194, 207, and 213 of the 1982 UNCLOS constitutes a rule of customary international law.[14]

(2) The 1982 UNCLOS

This convention does no more than establish a general framework for the regulation of land-based sources of marine pollution, but its articles do

[11] Articles 24 and 25. The ILC commentary indicates that the latter part of Article 25 was drafted with nuclear tests in mind. See II *Yearbook ILC* (1956), 286; United Nations Conference on the Law of the Sea, *Official Records* (1958), iv. 84 ff. and Resolution II, adopted 23 Apr. 1958; ibid. ii. 143.

[12] *Nuclear Tests Cases, ICJ Rep.* (1974), 390, per de Castro; *Icelandic Fisheries Case, ICJ Rep.* (1974), 3, and *supra*, Ch. 3.

[13] 1982 UNCLOS, Articles 87(2), 194(2), 300; 1983 Quito Protocol for the Protection of the South-East Pacific Against Pollution from Land-based Sources, Article 11 (hereafter Quito Protocol); 1986 Noumea Convention for the Protection of the Natural Resources and Environment of the South Pacific Region, Article 4(6) (hereafter Noumea Convention). Other regional treaties are silent on these issues.

[14] 1982 UNCLOS, Articles 192, 194; 1974 Helsinki Convention on the Protection of the Marine Environment of the Baltic Sea, Articles 3, 6 (hereafter Helsinki Convention); 1974 Paris Convention for the Prevention of Marine Pollution from Land-based Sources, Articles 1, 4, 5 (hereafter Paris Convention); 1980 Athens Protocol for the Protection of the Mediterranean Sea Against Pollution from Land-based Sources, Articles 1, 5, 6, 7 (hereafter Athens Protocol); 1981 Abidjan Convention for Co-operation in the Protection and Development of the Marine and Coastal Environment of the West and Central African Region, Articles 4, 7 (hereafter Abidjan Convention); 1982 Jeddah Convention for the Conservation of the Red Sea and Gulf of Aden, Articles 1, 6 (hereafter Jeddah Convention); 1983 Cartagena Convention for the Protection and Development of the Marine Environment of the Wider Caribbean, Articles 4, 7 (hereafter Cartagena Convention); 1985 Nairobi Convention for the Protection, Management, and Development of the Marine and Coastal Environment of the East African Region, Articles 1, 7 (hereafter Nairobi Convention); 1986 Noumea Convention, Articles 5, 7; 1983 Kuwait Convention for the Co-operation on Protection of the Marine Environment from Pollution, Articles 3, 6 (hereafter Kuwait Convention) and see Rémond-Gouilloud, in Johnston, *The Environmental Law of the Sea*, 244; Hickey, 15 *SDLR* (1978), 474 ff.; Burchi, 3 *Ital. YIL* (1977), 141 f.; Kuwabara, *Protection of the Mediterranean Sea Against Pollution from Land-based Sources* (Dublin, 1985), 44.

correspond to the practice of states both regionally and nationally and they can be taken as good evidence of the international law on the subject.[15]

Article 207 requires states to take measures, including the adoption of laws and regulations, to prevent, reduce, and control pollution from land-based sources. Its definition of 'land-based sources' includes 'rivers, estuaries, pipelines and outfall structures', to which regional treaties usually add pollution from coastal establishments, and sometimes also from airborne sources.[16] Sea-bed installations are generally dealt with separately by all of the relevant treaties, including the 1982 UNCLOS, and for that reason are not considered here.[17]

Unlike the Conventions's articles dealing with pollution from ships, dumping, or sea-bed installations, Article 207 does not require adherence to any minimum international standards established by international organizations. States must, however, take account of 'internationally agreed rules, standards and recommended practices and procedures'. National laws must also minimize 'to the fullest extent possible' the release of toxic, harmful, noxious, or persistent substances,[18] but it is for each state to determine what measures to take and whether action should be global, regional, bilateral, or national. It is also for each state to determine which substances require regulation and control; the essential point is that it is not discharges of waste which are the object of this obligation, but only discharges which result in 'pollution' as defined by Article 1(4). As we saw in Chapter 3, this term provides only the most general guidance, and precludes useful generalization. Its effect is to give states a further discretion in their implementation of

[15] See generally Ch. 7.

[16] See for example, 1983 Quito Protocol, Article 2; 1981 Abidjan Convention, Article 7; 1983 Cartagena Convention, Article 7; 1985 Nairobi Convention, Article 7; 1986 Noumea Convention, Article 7; 1974 Nordic Convention for the Protection of the Environment, Article 1; and the 1980 Athens Protocol, Articles 1 and 4. cf., however, the 1974 Paris Convention, Article 3 and the 1974 Helsinki Convention, Article 2, which may sustain a more limited interpretation. A 1986 Protocol extends the Paris Convention to cover airborne pollution, on which see further *infra*, Ch. 10.

[17] See 1982 UNCLOS, Article 208. Treatment of sea-bed installations in regional agreements varies: all UNEP Agreements acknowledge an obligation to control pollution from this source, but the 1974 Helsinki Convention treats them as ships (Article 2(4)), the 1980 Athens Protocol excludes them if used for exploration or exploitation purposes (Article 4(2)); the 1974 Paris Convention expressly applies (Article 3) but the 1983 Quito Protocol does not. See also the 1989 Kuwait Protocol Concerning Marine Pollution Resulting from Exploration and Exploitation of the Continental Shelf; 1973/78 MARPOL Convention, Article 2(4) and Annex 1, Reg. 21; 1981 UNEP Conclusions of a Study of Legal Aspects of the Environment Relating to Offshore Mineral Exploitation and Drilling, UNEP/GC.9/5/Add.5/Annex III, 7 *EPL* (1981), 50; De Mestral, *20 Harv. ILJ* (1979), 469; Rémond-Gouilloud, in Johnston, *The Environmental Law of the Sea*, 245.

[18] Articles 207(1), (5). See also 3rd UNCLOS, *Official Records*, ii (1974), 317, para. 20 (Canada), 328 (China), and cf. Kenyan draft articles A/CONF.62/C.3/42 (1974) and 10 power draft A/CONF.62/C.3/L.6 (1974), ibid. iii. 245, 249. For the drafting history of Article 207, see Nordquist (ed.), *United Nations Convention on the Law of the Sea: A Commentary*, iv (Dordrecht, 1991), 125–34.

Article 207. This partly explains the significant variations in what different regional treaties prohibit or control, despite their identical definition of pollution,[19] and shows how contingent on the circumstances of each sea interpretation of this term proves to be in practice. Thus, one of the objects of regional treaties is to identify which substances will be treated as causing 'pollution' and in what circumstances.[20]

Articles 122 and 123 of the Convention, which deal with enclosed and semi-enclosed seas, merely reaffirm the general position that states must co-operate in measures of environmental protection. They do not alter the conclusion that, with regard to the control of land-based pollution, states have a wide discretion concerning the action they must take. At most, these articles may sustain a stronger obligation to co-operate in negotiating common pollution standards than is implied for oceanic areas by Article 207 alone.[21] Major regional agreements on land-based marine pollution do not deal only with enclosed or semi-enclosed seas, nor do institutional arrangements treat enclosed and semi-enclosed seas differently from other oceanic areas.[22] Thus the evidence does not go so far as to support the view that those enclosed or semi-enclosed seas are 'shared resources' subject to the principle of equitable utilization. Thus, although it provides the convention's only significant legal basis for protecting the marine environment from land-based pollution, Article 207 is drafted in terms which give no specific content to the under-lying obligation of due diligence found in customary law. Like the comparable provision dealing with atmospheric pollution (Article 212), it lacks both the more precise content of the articles concerned with pollution from dumping or from ships, or any comparable means for its direct enforcement.[23]

The reasons for this are that states were generally unwilling to adopt a stronger text during the UNCLOS negotiations. They wished to preserve for themselves as much freedom of action as possible in balancing environmental protection measures against the needs of their own economies, where land-based activities generated much of the most harmful pollution. This concern

---

[19] 1974 Paris Convention, Article 1(1); 1974 Helsinki Convention, Article 2(1); 1976 Barcelona Convention for the Protection of the Mediterranean Sea Against Pollution, Article 2(a); 1983 Quito Protocol, Article III; 1982 Jeddah Convention, Article 1(3); 1985 Nairobi Convention, Article 2(b); 1983 Kuwait Convention, Article 1(a); 1986 Noumea Convention, Article 2(f). The 1983 Cartagena Convention does not define pollution.

[20] cf. Annexes I, II, and III of the 1974 Helsinki Convention with Annex B, Parts I and II of the 1974 Paris Convention; and see *infra*, pp. 308–14.

[21] Boyle, in Butler (ed.), *The Law of the Sea and International Shipping* (New York, 1986), 317 ff.; Jaenicke, in Park (ed.), *Law of the Sea in the 1980s* (Honolulu, 1980), 508–11. cf. *Icelandic Fisheries* Case, *ICJ Rep.* (1974), 3.

[22] See *infra*, pp. 316–7, and cf. UNEP, Principles of Conduct in the Field of the Environment Concerning Natural Resources Shared by Two or More States, *supra*, Ch. 3. The Executive Director of UNEP has referred to enclosed and semi-enclosed seas as examples of shared resources, UNEP Doc. GC/44, (1975), para. 86.

[23] cf. Ch. 7, and *infra*, pp. 330–32, and Ch. 10.

for development priorities is evident in the general provisions of the 1982 UNCLOS.[24] Article 193 refers to the sovereign right of states to exploit their own natural resources pursuant to their environmental policies, and in accordance with their duty to protect the marine environment. Article 194(1) moderates the obligation to protect the environment by reference to the use of 'the best practicable means at their disposal and in accordance with their capabilities'. Moreover, although Article 207(4) refers to the establishment of 'global and regional rules, standards and recommended practices' for the control of land-based pollution, it allows account to be taken of 'characteristic regional features, the economic capacity of developing states and their need for economic development.'[25]

This phraseology leaves little doubt that states did not wish to commit themselves to the same level of international control as is imposed on other sources of marine pollution. The social and economic costs of such measures were seen as unacceptably high, and the preferred solution was thus a weaker level of international regulation, a greater latitude for giving preference to other national priorities, and resort to regional co-operation as the primary level at which international action should occur. The largely hortatory character of this policy is evident in the wording of Articles 207(3) and (4), which provide that states shall 'endeavour' to harmonize their policies at the appropriate regional level and to establish global and regional rules. Article 123 is similarly elusive with regard to enclosed or semi-enclosed seas, requiring states only to 'endeavour' to co-ordinate the implementation of their rights and duties with respect to protection of the marine environment. These formulations are without significant normative content. They tend to demonstrate that as it stands, Article 207 does not require states to take effective measures.

(3) Regional Adoption of Common Standards

As we have seen elsewhere, the main environmental benefit of common standards of pollution prevention is that they ensure a co-ordinated approach in areas of common interest such as enclosed or semi-enclosed seas. In the case of industrial pollution an important further benefit is the economic advantage derived from a reduction in unfair competition. The counter arguments applied to land-based sources of pollution are also important however. Strict regulation of this form of pollution has substantial economic, social, and political implications for industrial economies and developing states alike. Those wishing to protect their freedom to decide for themselves

---

[24] See further, Ch. 7.
[25] See also 1980 Athens Protocol, Article 7(2); 1983 Quito Protocol, Article 6, and 3rd UNCLOS, *Official Records, supra*, n. 18.

how to develop may rely on assertions of national autonomy in the use of territory and permanent sovereignty over natural resources to limit the possibilities for international regulation, oversight, and enforcement, as they have done for nuclear power.[26] Moreover, geographical and ecological considerations point to substantial differences in the absorbtive capacity of different seas. Although land-based pollution affects most coastal areas, shallow, enclosed, or semi-enclosed seas such as the Baltic, North Sea, or Mediterranean are especially sensitive,[27] and need greater protection than open occeanic areas. All of these considerations may point to the doubtful utility of seeking detailed international regulation of land-based sources of pollution, and help explain the relatively weak framework approach adopted by the 1982 UNCLOS and UNEP. Not surprisingly, where they have been willing to co-operate, states have preferred regional or subregional arrangements, believing that these offer greater flexibility in accommodating the economic, geopolitical, and ecological needs of particular seas and their adjacent states and provide a better basis for common standards of regulation. But the main consequence of this regionalization of the problem has been the legitimation of weak standards and weak supervisory institutions. States have simply not addressed the regional problems with the seriousness merited by scientific reports.

(a) UNEP's Regional Seas Programme

As we saw earlier, UNEP's regional seas treaties all require states to endeavour to control land-based pollution. These general provisions are no more specific than Article 207 of the 1982 UNCLOS and merely repeat the duty to 'take measures', but they do offer a framework for the negotiation of regional controls, particularly in developing states. Despite its relative success in mobilizing co-operation on other matters and involving a large number of states, however, the potential of the regional seas programme has not yet been fully realized. Only in the Mediterranean, South East Pacific, and Persian Gulf have protocols on land-based pollution been adopted, although negotiations are likely to result in a further protocol for the Caribbean region. But even among parties to these protocols, there is little evidence of extensive co-ordination and co-operation, or of implementation measures, as we shall see below, and at best it can be said of the regional seas programme as a whole

---

[26] *Island of Palmas* Case, II *RIAA* (1928), 829; UNGA Res. 1803 XVII (1962); UNGA Res. 3281 XXIX (1974); Rémond-Gouilloud, in Johnston, *The Environmental Law of the Sea*, 236, and cf. *infra*, Ch. 9.

[27] On the specific problems of these seas, see UK Dept. of Environment, *Quality Status of the North Sea* (1987); Kuwabara, *Protection of the Mediterranean Sea*, ch. 1; Clark (ed.), *Marine Pollution* (Oxford, 1986), ch. 10; Sibthorp (ed.), *The North Sea: Challenge and Opportunity* (London, 1975), 22 ff.; Helsinki Commission, *First Periodic Assessment of the State of the Marine Environment of the Baltic Sea Area* (Helsinki, 1985).

only that it has exercised some influence on the problem of land-based pollution in some of the areas which it covers.[28]

(b) Major Regional Agreements

The major areas covered by regional agreements on land-based sources of pollution are the North-East Atlantic,[29] the Baltic,[30] and the Mediterranean.[31] Two further protocols cover the Persian Gulf and the South East Pacific.[32] These treaties have the characteristics of other regional supervisory regimes. and are comparable to the Rhine Chemicals Convention or the Great Lakes Water Quality Agreement considered in Chapter 6. In some cases the institution they create is a regional commission such as the Paris and Helsinki Commissions, while in others a meeting of the parties is preferred. Other bodies, such as the International North Sea Conference,[33] the European Community,[34] and the Conference on Security and Co-operation in Europe

---

[28] See UNEP, *Progress Report on the Implementation of and Reactions to the Montreal Guidelines* (1991).

[29] 1974 Paris Convention. For an assessment of this Convention, see Wettestad and Andresen, *The Effectiveness of International Resource Co-operation: Some Preliminary Findings* (Lysaker, 1991), 56–73. See also Saetevik, *Environmental Co-operation among North Sea States* (London, 1986), and other literature cited there. The 1974 Nordic Convention for the Protection of the Environment is also relevant.

[30] 1974 Helsinki Convention on which see Johnson, 25 *ICLQ* (1976), 1; Boczek, 75 *AJIL* (1981), 782; Jaenicke, in Park, *Law of the Sea in the 1980s*, 493; Fitzmaurice, *International Legal Problems of the Environmental Protection of the Baltic* (Dordrecht, 1991). See also 1988 Declaration on the Protection of the Marine Environment of the Baltic Sea Area, adopted by the 9th meeting of the Baltic MEPC, in Ruster and Simma (eds.), *International Protection of the Environment* (2nd series, New York, 1990), ii; 1990 Baltic Sea Declaration of the Baltic Environment Conference, 1 *YIEL* (1990), 423, and for recently adopted recommendations see ibid. 118. See also, 1974 Denmark–Sweden Agreement Concerning Protection of the Sound, 6 *New Directions*, 459, and 1974 Nordic Convention.

[31] 1980 Athens Protocol to the 1976 Barcelona Convention (hereafter 1980 Athens Protocol); Kuwabara, *Protection of the Mediterranean Sea*. Subregional agreements include: 1972 Italy–Yugoslavia Agreement on Co-operation for the Protection of the Waters of the Adriatic, 6 *New Directions*, 456; 1976 Agreement on Protection of Mediterranean Coastal Waters (France–Italy–Monaco), Decree 81–96, *Journal officiel de la république*, 30 (1981), 451; 1979 Agreement of Co-operation on Protection of the Marine Environment of the Ionian Sea and Coastal Zones (Italy–Greece), on which see Kuwabara, *Protection of the Mediterranean Sea*, 74.

[32] 1990 Kuwait Protocol for the Protection of the Marine Environment Against Pollution from Land-based Sources and the 1983 Quito Protocol to the 1981 Lima Convention. Subregional agreements in North America include the 1983 US–Mexico Agreement on Co-operation for the Protection and Improvement of the Environment in the Border Area, Annexes I and II (adopted 1987) and Annex V (adopted 1990); the US also co-operates with Mexico in a 'Gulf of Mexico Programme' and with Canada in a 'Gulf of Maine' programme.

[33] 1st International Conference on the North Sea, Declaration, 1984, 14 *EPL* (1985), 32; 2nd Conference, 1987, 27 *ILM*, 835; 3rd Conference, 1990, IMO Doc. MEPC/29/INF.26; Hayward, 5 *IJECL* (1990), 91; Ehlers, ibid. 3; and on the legal status of conference 'declarations', Mensbrugghe, ibid. 15.

[34] Saetevik, *Environmental Co-operation*, chs. 7 and 9; Nollkaemper, 2 *Legal Issues of European Integration* (1987), 73 f.; Prat, 5 *IJECL* (1990), 101. For Community directives, see *supra*, Ch. 6 n. 226.

have also influenced the work of the Paris Commission and the Barcelona Convention and set the political agenda for future action.

Although all the regional conventions follow the same basic approach to pollution control, there are some significant differences and weaknesses. Substances which are seriously toxic, persistent, or bioaccumulative are allocated to a 'black list', but in most cases these need only be eliminated progressively, following standards and timetables to be agreed by the parties. Only in the Baltic is emission of black-listed substances completely prohibited. Less-harmful emissions are put in a 'grey list' and must be controlled so that their amount and location are compatible with protection of the marine environment. Allocation of substances between black and grey lists varies, and is left deliberately flexible and capable of amendment to allow for the circumstances of different areas and changing conditions.[35] Partly because of its more demanding requirements, the Helsinki Convention places very few substances in the black-listed category. The general black-listing of radioactive waste discharges not permitted by international guidelines is an incomplete prohibition which allows some states to dispose of low-level radioactive waste from land notwithstanding that it can no longer be dumped at sea.[36]

National authorities are solely responsible under these agreements for the adoption of emissions policies and the grant of permits, so co-ordination of their implementation depends partly on adherence to licensing criteria indicated in the treaties, and partly on the success of regional institutions in negotiating common emission and water quality standards.[37] Agreement on such issues has been difficult to reach, since states which object to common standards are not bound by them under any of the regional treaties. Enforcement of agreed standards remains in all cases the responsibility of national authorities; there is no provision for independent inspection, or prior approval of permits by intergovernmental bodies, and no formal non-compliance procedure.

Two examples, the North Sea, and the Mediterranean, indicate the essen-

[35] See PARCOM 7/13/1, Annex 5, 'Classification and Allocation of Substances to Annexes' (1985); Venekens-Capkova, 5 *IJECL* (1990), 150. cf. the use of the same technique in the London Dumping Convention, *infra*, pp. 320–32, and in the Rhine Chemicals Convention, *supra*, Ch. 6.

[36] 1974 Paris Convention, Article 5 and Annex A, Part III and PARCOM 88/5, 'Recommendation on Radioactive Discharges'; Athens Protocol, Articles 5 and Annex I; 1983 Quito Protocol, Article 4, and Annex I; 2nd and 3rd International North Sea Conference Declarations. The 1974 Helsinki Convention simply includes all radioactive materials in the category requiring a permit. On dumping of radioactive waste, see *infra*, pp. 323–4.

[37] 1974 Paris Convention, Articles 4, 16; 1974 Helsinki Convention, Articles 6, 13; 1980 Athens Protocol, Articles 6, 7, 14; 1983 Quito Protocol, Articles 5, 6, 15; 1st North Sea Declaration, part 3(c); 2nd North Sea Declaration, para. XV. For standards set by the Paris Commission and the Barcelona Convention, see *infra*, nn. 38 and 46, and for the Baltic, see Helsinki Commission, *1st Periodic Assessment of the State of the Marine Environment of the Baltic Sea Area* (1980–5). On the competing merits of quality and emission standards, see Boehmer-Christiansen, 5 *IJECL* (1990), 139.

tial point common to all four schemes: that even these relatively developed regimes are only as good as the parties allow them to be. The North Sea states are a relatively cohesive and homogeneous group with a strong political commitment to environmental protection through the International North Sea Conference. The Paris Commission's area of responsibility includes the North Sea and it has secured some agreement on common standards for emission of harmful substances, although states which object to its decisions are not bound by them.[38] EEC directives have harmonized some standards for North Sea member states, but the Community has also been a significant obstacle to adoption of stricter standards sought by non-EEC states.[39] Saetevik's review of the work of the Paris Commission up to 1984 is instructive:

Since in practice the states do as they wish, without being restricted to a certain approach or principles, the evident conclusion is that so far the Paris Commission has not succeeded in establishing a common approach that takes account of both environmental and competition considerations.[40]

It is clear on this evidence that some have been more willing to control pollution that others. Since then, however, the International North Sea Conference's calls for stricter regulation and substantial reductions in pollution have quickened progress in the Paris Commission and have led to the adoption of new measures aimed through better use of technology at reducing the need for polluting emissions.[41] Co-operation within the region has as a result become more effective. But the main contribution of this conference so far lies less in concrete action than in the policies it has endorsed: a precautionary approach to integrated protection of the ecosystem, substantial reduction in inputs of all substances that are toxic, persistent and bioaccumulative, and specific targets for reducing certain major pollutants.[42] Implementing these objectives within the timescale set will require not only co-ordinated national action, but co-operation within the EEC, the Paris Commission, and, for international watercourses, the Rhine Commission and

---

[38] Article 18. Standards set by the Paris Commission are listed in Saetevik, *Environmental Co-operation*, ch. 5 and Freestone and IJlstra, *The North Sea: Basic Legal Documents* (Dordrecht, 1991). For a review of the Paris Convention's effectiveness, see Wettestad and Andresen, *International Resource Co-operation*.

[39] *Supra*, n. 34.

[40] *Environmental Co-operation*, 43. Differences in licensing practices are reviewed in PARCOM, 'Licensing and Monitoring of Discharge Procedures Practised by the Parties' (1986).

[41] Hayward, 5 *IJECL* (1990), 94–6; Wettestad and Andresen, *International Resource Co-operation*, 62, and see PARCOM Recommendations 88/5, 89/2, 90/1, 90/2, and decision 90/4.

[42] See esp. the 2nd and 3rd International North Sea Conference Declarations, but cf. the resolution of the European Parliament criticizing the Declarations in OJ EEC No. C113/223 (1990). For interpretations of the precautionary principle, see *supra*, pp. 95–8. Paris Commission Recommendation 89/1 accepts the principle of precautionary action as defined by the INSC and applies it to the whole Paris Convention area.

Switzerland. Experience to date does illustrate the immense complexity of this task and the problems of implementation at national level which will be encountered.[43]

The Mediterranean region is larger, and shows greater economic, social, and political diversity than the North Sea. Land-based pollution in this area is regulated by the 1980 Athens Protocol to the Barcelona Convention, but explicit recognition of the needs of developing states on the southern and eastern shores of this region has made it more difficult to achieve agreement on common standards.[44] EEC directives apply to pollution emanating from the major industrialized economies of the region, but elsewhere, as Kuwabara's 1984 study shows, the record of implementation of the convention in national law has until recently been poor.[45] In the Genoa declaration of 1985, however, the parties committed themselves to a programme intended to lead to substantial reduction in industrial pollution and waste disposal, the provision of sewage treatment plants, and reductions in air pollution affecting the marine environment. Common measures have subsequently been adopted which set quality standards for bathing and shellfish waters and control emissions from some Annex 1 substances. A meeting of the parties in 1987 approved a programme of further measures intended to ensure the progressive implementation of the protocol by 1995.[46]

In 1990 the Conference on Security and Co-operation in Europe recommended that policies for controlling pollution of the Mediterranean should be guided by the 'polluter pays' principle and the 'precautionary approach', and it urged parties to the Barcelona Convention to strengthen all aspects of its implementation, in particular by encouraging non-polluting methods of production and the reduction of waste generation.[47] Its conclusions recognize the inadequacy of progress made so far in protecting the Mediterranean environment and implementing the Athens protocol. A major problem in the Mediterranean is the need for substantial expenditure on control measures and installations: funding from the EEC, the World Bank, and the European Investment Bank may be a key determinant of progress in implementing the priorities set by the Genoa Declaration.

The regional nature of these treaty regimes, the scope for national discre-

---

[43] De Jong, 5 *IJECL* (1990), 31; Gibson and Churchill, ibid. 47. Wettestad and Andresen, *International Resource Co-operation*, are more optimistic in their assessment of the attitude of Paris Commission states.

[44] Article 7. See generally Kuwabara, *Protection of the Mediterranean Sea*, and for other agreements applicable to the Mediterranean, see *supra*, n. 31.

[45] National legislation up to 1983 is reviewed ibid. ch. 4, and Raftopoulos, *The Mediterranean Action Plan in a Functional Perspective: A Quest for Law and Policy*, UNEP (Athens, 1988). For EEC measures, see *supra*, Ch. 6, n. 226.

[46] For measures adopted under this protocol, see UNEP, *Mediterranean Action Plan Technical Report No. 38* (Athens, 1990).

[47] CSCE/RMP.6, Draft Report of the Meeting on the Mediterranean (1990).

tion in the administration of permits, the recognition of a double standard for developing countries, and the absence in some cases of regional agreement on specific standards sharply differentiate control of land-based pollution from the international regulation of pollution from ships, or from dumping. Apart from the obligation to eliminate a flexible category of more harmful substances, regional agreements provide insufficient evidence of uniformity of practice to constitute an international or global standard, and suggest that the customary obligation to prevent marine pollution from land-based sources has remained essentially general in character, with little objective content. Its implementation remains dependent primarily on national action, regional co-operation, and further agreement. The slow progress of such co-operation indicates the continuing importance of industrial and economic factors in this sphere and the desire of states to balance those considerations against the needs of environmental protection.

(4) Procedural Obligations and Risk Avoidance

Regulation is only part of the answer to the problem of protecting the marine environment from land-based sources of pollution. Two procedural obligations are widely recognized in this context: prior environmental impact assessment, and monitoring of the environmental effects of any discharges.[48] These obligations assume particular importance in those regional seas where no agreement on co-ordinated regulatory standards exists, since in these cases they afford the only mechanism for limiting unilateral decisions which disregard impacts on the quality of the marine environment.

The object of prior assessment is to enable 'appropriate measures' to be taken to prevent or mitigate pollution before it occurs.[49] The view that such assessments are required by customary law for impacts on the marine environment is reinforced by the 1982 UNCLOS and regional agreements. Article 206 of the 1982 Convention provides:

When states have reasonable grounds for believing that planned activities under their jurisdiction or control may cause substantial pollution of or significant and harmful changes to the marine environment, they shall as far as practicable assess the potential

---

[48] 1974 Paris Convention, Article 11; 1976 Barcelona Convention, Article 10 and 1980 Athens Protocol, Articles 8, 13; 1983 Kuwait Convention, Articles 10, 11; 1981 Abidjan Convention, Articles 13, 14; 1983 Cartagena Convention, Articles 12, 13; 1982 Jeddah Convention, Articles 10, 11; 1985 Nairobi Convention, Articles 13, 14; 1986 Noumea Convention, Articles 16, 17; 1981 Lima Convention, Articles 8, 9 and 1983 Quito Protocol, Articles 8, 9; UNEP, Montreal Guidelines, Articles 11, 12. Note that the Paris Convention, the Helsinki Convention, the Barcelona Convention, and the Athens Protocol make no provision for prior impact assessment, but see *infra*, n. 51.
[49] UNEP Montreal Guidelines, Article 12; 1986 Noumea Convention, Article 16(2); 1983 Cartagena Convention, Article 12(2).

effects of such activities on the marine environment and shall communicate reports of the results of such assessments [to the competent international organizations].

Some of the regional treaties refer only to 'major projects',[50] so there is some latitude for judgment in determining when the obligation arises and when 'reasonable grounds' exist. Although the Paris, Helsinki, and Barcelona Conventions do not explicitly mention prior assessment, or include such assessments in licensing criteria, EEC law and the practice of the states concerned make such an express provision unnecessary.[51]

Neither the 1982 UNCLOS, nor UNEP's framework treaties require notification and prior consultation with other states likely to be affected by land-based sources of marine pollution. But such an obligation is recognized by the Paris Convention,[52] the Quito Protocol,[53] the Athens Protocol,[54] and by a few treaties dealing with offshore operations.[55] Such treaties cannot be explained by reference to obligations attending the use of 'shared natural resources', since they are not confined to enclosed or semi-enclosed seas, but illustrate the broader customary principle examined in Chapter 3 which requires notification and prior consultation in cases of transboundary risk.

The more difficult question is how to apply this principle of 'good neighbourliness' to cases where harm to the marine environment of the high seas is foreseen. Without exception, all the treaties call for states to monitor pollution and make reports to other parties through regional institutions.[56] Consistent support for this obligation is reflected in Article 204 of the 1982 UNCLOS. But in contrast to situations where other states are at risk, and regional commissions may recommend solutions to parties in dispute,[57] no prior consultation or dispute settlement is required by any of the treaties where only the marine environment is affected; at most, the reporting procedure enables meetings of the parties to review the effectiveness of measures adopted and

---

[50] 1985 Nairobi Convention, Article 13; 1983 Cartagena Convention, Article 12; 1986 Noumea Convention, Article 16; cf. the 1981 Abidjan Convention, Article 13; the 1983 Kuwait Convention, Article 11; and the 1981 Lima Convention, Article 8, which apply to 'any planned activity'.

[51] Paris Commission, 9th meeting 1987.

[52] Article 9.

[53] Article 12.

[54] Article 12.

[55] 1986 Canada–Denmark Agreement for Co-operation Relating to the Marine Environment, Article 4; 1989 Kuwait Protocol on Marine Pollution from Exploration and Exploitation of the Continental Shelf, Article IV; 1990 Draft Protocol for the Protection of the Mediterranean Sea Against Pollution Resulting from the Exploration and Exploitation of the Continental Shelf and Sea-bed, Articles 24 and 25; 1974 Paris Convention, Articles 3(c) and 9; and see also UNEP GC. 9/5/Add. 5/Article III, Aspects Concerning the Environment Related to Offshore Drilling and Mining Within the limits of National Jurisdiction, 1981, Part E.

[56] See 1982 UNCLOS, Articles 204, 205, and *supra*, n. 48.

[57] 1974 Paris Convention, Article 9; 1983 Quito Protocol, Article 12; 1980 Athens Protocol, Article 12, which allow solutions to be recommended to parties in dispute.

press for remedial action: it does not give them a right to be consulted in advance.[58]

These provisions on prior assessment and monitoring reflect relevant provisions of the 1982 UNCLOS, but they do not compare favourably with the stronger regimes of prior consent or prior assessment and consultation through international organizations now found in the London Dumping Convention, the Basel Convention, or the Antarctic Mineral Resources Convention. They do not reflect more recent endorsement of the 'precautionary principle' but are much closer to the procedures adopted in international watercourse agreements. This tends to confirm the earlier conclusion that controls on all sources of land-based pollution remain relatively under-developed, but generally consistent with customary principles.

(5) Relationship with the Law of International Watercourses

As we saw in Chapter 6, international watercourses are not only a source of transboundary pollution, but a major contributor to marine pollution. The development of regional regimes to regulate watercourse environments has many similarities to those now controlling land-based sources of pollution. Nevertheless there are differences between the two categories, and co-ordination gives rise to certain problems. First, it is doubtful whether the concept of equitable utilization has a role in regulating the marine environment, in contrast to the law of international watercourses.[59] Although the obligation to protect the marine environment is not absolute, and allows a significant balancing of interests at various levels, this is not the same as saying that states need only prevent pollution which is inequitable or unreasonable, nor does it imply that abuse of rights is the conceptual basis for pollution control. None of the treaties, including the 1982 UNCLOS and those dealing with enclosed or semi-enclosed seas, supports reliance on equitable utilization or abuse of rights in this way. Second, equitable utilization is mainly concerned with reconciling the interests of riparians, not those of coastal states or of the international community. A system which looks only at riparian interests in individual rivers will fail to offer a basis for common regional standards of environmental protection focused on the needs of particular regional seas. Moreover, equitable utilization is defective in giving

---

[58] cf. the 1989 Kuwait Protocol, *supra*, n. 26, Article 4, which requires prior impact assessment before the grant of a licence for offshore operations and calls for consultation with all other contracting states through the regional organization. This is aimed at protecting the marine environment as such, not merely other states. On dumping, see *infra*, pp. 320–32.

[59] Boyle, 14 *Marine Policy* (1990), 151. cf. the now discarded ILC draft Article 17(2) on 'International Watercourses', and commentary, *Report of the ILC to the Gen. Assembly*, 43rd Session, (1988) UN Doc. A/43/10, 69–72 and the revised draft Article 25. The latter makes no reference to equitable utilization: see *Report of the ILC to the Gen. Assembly* (1990) UN Doc. A/45/10, 169.

too little weight to environmental considerations among a range of other relevant circumstances.[60] Even when implemented by institutional arrangements, as in the Rhine, these are likely to represent the wrong states with the wrong perspective: that of riparian rights.

For all these reasons, the regional treaties on prevention of marine pollution from land-based sources do offer a more appropriate and efficient approach to the problem of protecting the marine environment. Their institutional structure more readily accommodates a balance of interests between the needs of the source states, and the capacity of the marine environment to absorb polluting inputs, since states with a direct interest in use of the sea will be involved. One method of integrating the protection of international watercourses into this system is to create institutional links between watercourse and regional seas commissions, including representation of landlocked riparians and non-riparian coastal states in the appropriate regional bodies. The role now played by the International North Sea Conference in facilitating Swiss participation, and in persuading the Rhine Commission to adopt protection of the marine environment as an objective, offers an example of this approach.[61] Such links by themselves are insufficient, however; what must be emphasized is that the obligations of all states with regard to land-based pollution should be fully applied to international watercourses. European and Mediterranean practice follows this principle explicitly or implicitly.[62] In these cases primary responsibility for agreed measures remains with the relevant international watercourse commission, but riparians assume a responsibility for protecting the marine environment and a duty in customary law towards coastal states and other users of the adjacent seas.[63]

(6) A Global Treaty for Land-based Sources?

The preference of states for regional agreements to control land-based sources of pollution has meant that no global treaty comparable to the London

---

[60] See *supra*, pp. 219–22, and Kuwabara, *Protection of the Mediterranean Sea*, 34.

[61] Burchi, 3 *Ital. YIL* (1977), 133; Kwiatkowska, 14 *ODIL* (1984), 324 ff.; 9th Ministerial Conference of the International Commission for the Protection of the Rhine, 1988. See Nollkaemper, 5 *IJECL* (1990), 125. Switzerland is not yet a party to the Paris Convention, however.

[62] 1980 Athens Protocol, Article 11(1); 1974 Helsinki Convention, Article 6(7); 1974 Paris Convention, Articles 4(3), 14; 3rd International North Sea Conference, *supra*, n. 33. At its 3rd meeting, the Paris Commission resolved that 'there was no doubt that the scope of the Convention included 'such discharges into watercourses as affect the maritime area' and the setting of limit values for those discharges', PARCOM III/10/1.

[63] Nollkaemper, 5 *IJECL* (1990); Rémond-Gouilloud, in Johnston, *The Environmental Law of the Sea*, 236; ILC Draft Articles on 'International Watercourses', 1990, Article 25 and commentary, *supra*, Ch. 6; *contra* Burchi, 3 *Ital. YIL* (1977) but his conclusion relies too heavily on the erroneous view that conventions on land-based sources do not apply to international watercourses.

Dumping Convention exists. States have been willing only to allow UNEP to draft a non-binding instrument, in the form of its Montreal Guidelines for the Protection of the Marine Environment Against Pollution from Land-based Sources.[64] These are intended to offer a 'checklist' for the development of appropriate bilateral, regional, and multilateral agreements, and national legislation. In this respect they have had some influence on the practice of states.[65] Although based on the main provisions of existing regional treaties, and the 1982 UNCLOS, the guidelines reflect the conclusions put forward earlier regarding the customary obligations of states for the protection of the marine environment. In particular, their provisions on monitoring, prior assessment, and notification of pollution affecting other states or the marine environment are consistent with the evolution of procedural obligations for environmental risk management in customary law. Features not generally found in regional agreements relating to land-based pollution are provisions on liability, equal access, and non-discriminatory treatment. Only the Nordic Convention specifically affords such remedies for land-based pollution at present, but as we saw in Chapter 5, equal access to national remedies is now widely available in Europe and North America, and nothing in the guidelines departs in this respect from existing principles adopted by OECD.

The Montreal Guidelines could thus serve as a foundation for a global framework convention or in ensuring that new regional agreements follow a similar pattern. Such a convention, if negotiated, would operate rather like the London Dumping Convention, facilitating the development of international policy, and making provision for institutional supervision by the international community as a whole. Given the weakness of existing regional institutions, and the relative success of the London Dumping Convention, the evolution of a comparable global regime for land-based sources of marine pollution might help to remedy some of the deficiencies identified earlier. But this will only be true if it leads to higher international minimum standards and better supervision.

The Montreal Guidelines themselves are in no sense 'international standards' for the control of land-based pollution. They do call for the negotiation of internationally agreed rules and standards, and the annexes give guidance on control strategies and the classification of substances. States still remain responsible for the negotiation or adoption of detailed standards, taking account of 'local ecological, geographical and physical characteristics, the economic capacity of states and their need for sustainable development and

---

[64] UNEP/WG.120/3, repr. in 14 *EPL* (1985), 77. See generally Meng Qing-Nan, *Land-based Marine Pollution*.

[65] See UNCED, Preparatory Committee, UN Doc. A/CONF.151/PC/71 (1991), 37–57 for an analysis of replies from 34 governments on action taken to implement the guidelines. The nature of the measures reported by individual states varies widely, however, and in many cases amounts to nothing of substance.

environmental protection and the assimilative capacity of the marine environment.' Although this formulation is more favourable to environmental factors than Article 207, a balance between these and economic factors remains at the heart of the Montreal Guidelines. As we have seen, it is this freedom to discount environmental considerations in favour of other priorities which has rendered the present law and practice regarding land-based pollution of the sea largely ineffective. Without the political will to alter existing priorities, higher standards of pollution control will not flow from a new treaty which merely reflects the present position.

But recognition of the need for 'adequate institutional arrangements' to promote and supervise international rules and standards, and monitor the marine environment is probably the strongest argument in favour of a new global treaty. The absence of such an institution at present means there is no forum for measuring regional performance against a wider international standard and also renders the Montreal Guidelines of little practical value since there is no body to supervise their implementation. Thus it is significant that a resolution of the parties to the London Dumping Convention calls for the UN Conference on Environment and Development to consider:

• the creation of a global mechanism to co-ordinate the protection of the marine environment from all sources;
• a global instrument and new and improved regional agreements to address land-based sources of marine pollution;
• the need to address waste management issues by focusing, *inter alia*, on environmentally acceptable land-based alternatives to disposal of wastes into the ocean;
• the need to pursue the elimination of marine pollution through such activities as the adoption, implementation and enforcement of more stringent national and regional controls and the establishment of such measures as clear production methods and technologies;
• the mechanisms required to provide co-operation, transfer of technology and other assistance to developing countries in order that they can fully participate in the above actions.[66]

This resolution indicates with great clarity the view of a body of states that the present international arrangements for controlling land-based sources of marine pollution are inadequate, and that substantial improvements are needed in existing legal and institutional frameworks at global and regional

---

[66] 13th Consultative Meeting of Contracting Parties to the LDC, London, 1990, IMO/LDC 13/15, Annex 4. See also Resolution LDC 40/13 (1990) and *Report of the Intergovernmental meeting of Experts on Land-based Sources of Marine Pollution*, repr. in UN Doc./A/CONF. 151/ PC/71, at 3; UNEP proposals for a global convention, a non-treaty instrument, or a global convention and action plan, ibid. 10, and UNEP decision SS.11/6 (1990) calling for strengthened institutions, legal and other measures at regional and global level.

levels. Proposals for a more comprehensive approach are now also under consideration as part of a review of a long-term strategy for the London Dumping Convention.[67]

3. DUMPING AT SEA[68]

(1) Development of a Legal Regime

The dumping of hazardous waste at sea is subject to the same general restraints in customary law as the discharge of pollutants from land: a duty to avoid unreasonable interference with other uses of the seas, notably fishing, and a duty to prevent harm to other states or pollution of the marine environment are the most significant. In 1972, the Stockholm Conference called for an international regime to regulate dumping,[69] and the London Dumping Convention was duly concluded in the same year. It has since been supplemented by regional treaties, considered below. These precedents form the basis for saying that Articles 210 and 216 of the 1982 UNCLOS codify customary law in so far as they compel states to regulate and control pollution of the marine environment caused by dumping at sea, and they provide the framework for a legal regime which differs in four significant respects from the one governing land-based sources of pollution.

First, the existence and widespread ratification of the London Dumping Convention applicable to all marine areas outside internal waters means that dumping is the subject of a global regime, not primarily a regional one; regional agreements are of significance only in imposing higher standards in enclosed or semi-enclosed seas. Second, this global regime is based on attainment of international minimum standards by all states, which limits their national discretion and makes no allowance for double standards or economic development.[70] Given its widespread ratification, it is clear that the London Dumping Convention provides these minimum international standards, and that it is to this Convention and its annexes that Article 210 of the 1982 UNCLOS refers.[71] In this respect, the legal regime of dumping is closer to the regulation of pollution from ships than to pollution from land-based sources. Third, the London Dumping Convention also distinguishes between different categories of pollutant, but in this case the dumping of more haz-

---

[67] LDC13/5 (1990).

[68] Churchill and Lowe, *The Law of the Sea* (2nd edn., Manchester, 1988), 268 ff.; Letalik, in *The Environmental Law of the Sea*, Johnston, 217 ff.; Finn, 21 *VJIL* (1981), 621.

[69] Recommendation 86(C), Action Plan for the Human Environment.

[70] 1982 UNCLOS, Article 210(6). For an account of the drafting of Article 210, see Nordquist, *Commentary*, iv, 155–68.

[71] Boyle, 79 *AJIL* (1985), 353 ff.; Letalik, *The Environmental Law of the Sea*, 225; Churchill and Lowe, *The Law of the Sea*, 272.

ardous substances is absolutely prohibited, subject only to limited exceptions catering for warships and emergencies, or if the substances appear as trace contaminants only or would be rapidly rendered harmless.[72] This is a much more stringent regime than is found in most regional controls on land-based pollution. Finally, dumping is subject to supervision by an international forum, the London Dumping Convention Consultative Meeting, in addition to regional bodies.

The LDC Consultative meeting has been notably successful in generating international consensus on the development of policy for dumping at sea. It has facilitated the adoption of increasingly stringent standards, and has enabled a wider community of states not engaged in this activity and a number of NGOs to apply pressure on those who are involved to moderate or abandon practices which pose a risk to the marine environment. This is one of the main reasons why the London Convention is widely regarded as one of the more successful regulatory treaties.

(2) International Policy and the Permissibility of Dumping

Neither the London Convention, nor the 1982 UNCLOS, initially prohibited dumping. Rather, their object was to control it. The dumping of particular substances, such as high level radioactive waste, was prohibited only if hazardous on grounds of toxicity, persistence, bioaccumulation, and the likelihood of significant widespread environmental exposure.[73] This approach did not in general go so far as to insist that dumping of other substances might take place only when no land-based disposal option was available, but the existence of land-based alternatives was a factor to be considered in the grant of a licence.[74]

The major argument against dumping at sea, however, is that it allows a small number of industrialized states acting for their own benefit to impose pollution risks on many others, perhaps extending into future generations.[75] While prior assessment of the risks involved, and of the suitability of sites, is intended to minimize the possibility of future harm, it cannot eliminate scientific uncertainty or risk entirely. The issue is thus not solely a question of the availability of less-harmful alternatives; rather, the acceptability of dumping depends significantly on the degree of risk, if any, which the international community is willing to accept without any countervailing benefit. International declarations have now moved away from the view implicit in

---

[72] Articles 4(1)(a), 5; Annex 1, paras. 8, 9, and Annex 6, adopted 1978.
[73] London Convention, Annex 1; Forster, 16 *EPL* (1986), 9.
[74] Annex III (c)(4); Annex 6; and IAEA, Recommendations Concerning Radioactive Wastes and other Matter, 1978, para. B.1.4., *infra*, n. 86; Mani, 24 *Indian JIL* (1984), 235.
[75] Boehmer-Christiansen, 10 *Marine Policy* (1986), 131; Bewers and Garrett, 11 ibid. (1987), 121 f.

the London Convention that dumping at sea is permissible unless proven harmful; instead there is implicit support for the principle of precautionary action:[76] that dumping should be eliminated unless there are no alternatives and it can be proven harmless, a significant reversal of the burden of proof. This shift in emphasis towards other disposal options is particularly apparent in the moratorium on dumping radioactive waste at sea, in the ending of incineration at sea and in the prohibition or phasing out of industrial dumping in the Baltic, North Sea, and African Waters. Moreover, at their 13th Consultative meeting in 1990, the parties to the London Dumping Convention resolved to phase out all sea dumping of industrial waste by 1995 at the latest, and called for the export of wastes for dumping by non-parties to be prohibited.[77] Thus the proposition that dumping remains in principle a legitimate use of the oceans, notwithstanding the possibility of disposal on land, and the possible risk to other states, is now increasingly questionable in the light of recent state practice and international opposition. In this context it is not inappropriate to draw conclusions concerning the development of customary law from the practice of parties to the London Dumping Convention and the various regional agreements. As we shall see, the LDC parties include nearly all the industrialized nations and a comparable number of developing states. There is no evidence, unusually, of any non-party dumping significant wastes at sea, or asserting a freedom to do so beyond that implied by the 1982 UNCLOS and the various global and regional instruments.

(3) What is 'Dumping'?

Dumping is defined by the London Convention and the 1982 UNCLOS as the 'deliberate disposal of wastes or other matter . . . at sea'.[78] Discharges occurring in the normal operation of ships or platforms do not constitute dumping, nor, *a fortiori*, do accidental spillages. Although not explicit in this definition, incineration of waste at sea has been treated as dumping, and is regulated by the London Convention. No agreement exists on the question whether sub-seabed disposal is covered by the 1972 Convention. One view is that such disposal is permitted, because it does not take place 'at sea' but under it.[79] Less convincingly, it is argued that exclusion of sea-bed disposal is

---

[76] Hey, *The Precautionary Approach and the LDC*, published as LDC 14/4 (1991). The author notes, however, that the proposition depends on the definition given to the principle.

[77] LDC Res. 43/13; UNCED, Prepcom, UN Doc. A/CONF. 151/PC/31 (1991), 4–6.

[78] London Convention, Article 3(1); 1982 UNCLOS, Article 1(5); Helsinki Convention Article 2(3); Barcelona Convention, Article 3; cf. the 1972 Oslo Convention, Article 19: ' "Dumping" means any deliberate disposal of substances and materials *into* the sea . . .'. The disposal of ships and aircraft is also included, and the parties have agreed that the term covers disposal of redundant submarines.

[79] Welsch, 28 *GYIL* (1985), 332. The same argument should apply *a fortiori* to subsea disposal achieved by tunnelling from the shore: see LDC 12/16, para. 6.44, (Sweden), but *contra*, at para. 6.56 (Spain).

an 'absurd or unreasonable' interpretation of a convention whose purpose is to protect the marine environment,[80] and that what matters is not the final resting-place of the material but the location of the act of disposal. Both views oversimplify the issue; the key to interpretation, given the object and purpose of the Convention and taking account of Articles 31–3 of the Vienna Convention on the Law of Treaties, has to be whether sea-bed disposal poses any threat to the marine environment: on this basis the parties to the London Convention do agree that no sea-bed disposal of radioactive waste should take place unless the feasibility of isolation of the wastes is proven, and a suitable regulatory framework is elaborated.[81] Whether or not the Convention applies to sea-bed disposal, customary law still requires all disposal to take place in circumstances which are reasonable and which protect the marine environment from pollution.[82]

(4) Radioactive Waste Dumping[83]

The need to find a safe medium for disposal of radioactive waste material is one of the more intractable problems of nuclear power. Disposal in Antarctica is forbidden by treaty;[84] disposal or reprocessing on land carries risks for the health of present and future generations. One response, adopted by several nuclear states including the UK, US, and Japan has been to dump radioactive waste at sea.

Article 25 of the 1958 High Seas Convention requires states to take measures to prevent pollution of the high seas from dumping of radioactive material, taking into account standards set by the relevant international organization. However, this was not meant to be an outright prohibition,[85] and it was left to IAEA to promulgate standards and internationally acceptable regulations. Following this precedent, the London Convention prohibited the dumping only of 'high-level' radioactive matter, defined by IAEA as unsuitable for this form of disposal, and it required the dumping of low-level

---

[80] Curtis, 14 *ODIL* (1984), 383, relying on GAOR Res. 2749 (XXV) (1970); Welsch, 28 *GYIL* (1985), 331 f.; Mani, 24 *Indian JIL* (1984), 240–3.

[81] LDC 8/10; Article 10 of the Noumea Convention puts the matter beyond doubt by prohibiting sea-bed and subsoil disposal in its area. See, however, LDC 41/13 (1990), and PARCOM Recommendation 91/5. The former treats subsea disposal of radioactive waste accessed from land as falling *outside* the LDC; the latter treats such disposal as falling *within* the Paris Convention.

[82] 1982 UNCLOS, Articles 192, 194; 1958 Geneva Convention on the High Seas, Article 2.

[83] Welsch, 28 *GYIL* (1985); Finn, 21 *VJIL* (1981); Curtis, 14 *ODIL* (1984); Mani, 24 *Indian JIL* (1984). Van Dyke, 12 *Marine Policy* (1988), 82; Boehmer-Christiansen, 10 *Marine Policy* (1986); Bewers and Garrett, 11 ibid. (1987) review the scientific studies.

[84] Antarctic Treaty, 1959, Article 5; Recommendation VIII-12, 8th Antarctic Treaty Consultative Meeting, 1975.

[85] (1956) II *Yearbook ILC*, 286.

waste to be conducted according to IAEA guidelines.[86] Exceptionally, these guidelines have acquired some legal force as an international minimum standard for national regulation,[87] and they establish detailed principles for national authorities to follow which seek to balance suitable disposal methods, radiation protection, and overall cost. Some states regard the IAEA Standards as being unacceptably low, however, and apply their own more stringent rules.

Notwithstanding IAEA approval, and favourable scientific assessments, growing opposition among a majority of London Dumping Convention parties and pressure from NGOs led in 1983 to adoption by the LDC parties of a moratorium on all radioactive dumping at sea, pending further study.[88] This moratorium is voluntary and not as such binding on states, nor would an amendment to the Convention's annexes of regulated substances apply to those states which object.[89] Moreover, some parties such as the United Kingdom have continued to reserve their right to resume dumping of low-level radioactive waste,[90] so it cannot yet be considered that it is globally prohibited.

Regional practice is, however, overwhelmingly opposed to radioactive dumping, particularly in enclosed or semi-enclosed seas.[91] It is prohibited by treaty in the Baltic, in the South and South-East Pacific, and the International North Sea Conference agreed in 1990 that the North Sea was not a suitable venue. Most radioactive waste cannot be dumped in the Mediterranean. Parties to the London Convention must respect these regional arrangements. This evidence does indicate a widespread belief that such seas are unsuitable for radioactive dumping because of the risk involved, and it is evident that a

[86] Annex 1, para. 6; Annex II, para. (d). The IAEA's definition and rcommendations appear in IAEA Doc. INFCIRC/205/Add. 1, (1975) and INFCIRC/205/Add. 1/Rev. 1 (1978); see now IAEA, Safety Series No. 78, *Definition and Recommendations for the Convention on the Prevention of Marine Pollution, etc.* (Vienna, 1986), adopted, 1986, at the 10th Consultative Meeting of the LDC.

[87] See Ch. 9.

[88] LDC Resolution 14(7), 1983 and Resolution LDC 21(9), 1985. See Bewers and Garrett, 11 *Marine Policy* (1987) and Forster, 16 *EPL* (1986), 7. Twenty-five states voted for resolution 21(9), six voted against, and six abstained. At their 13th Consultative meeting in 1990 the parties to the LDC called for the disposal of radioactive wastes into sea-bed repositories to be included in the moratorium.

[89] Article 15(2); LDC 12/16, 12th Consultative Meeting, paras. 6 and 39.

[90] See Boehmer-Christiansen, 10 *Marine Policy* (1986). On 23 May 1989 the following announcement was made in Parliament: 'The Government have decided not to resume sea-disposal of drummed radioactive waste, including waste of military origin. None the less, the Government intend to keep open this option for large items arising from decommissioning operations, although they have taken no decisions about how redundant nuclear submarines will be disposed of.' *Hansard*, HC Debs, vol. 153, col. 464 (1989).

[91] Helsinki Convention, Article 9(1); Noumea Convention, Article 10, which also applies to disposal into the sea-bed and subsoil, (Article 11 also prohibits storage of radioactive wastes or matter in the Convention area); 1989 Protocol for the Protection of the South-East Pacific Against Radioactive Pollution; 3rd International North Sea Conference, para. 32 (The United Kingdom did not accept this provision); Barcelona Convention, Protocol for the Prevention of Pollution by Dumping, Annex 1.

heavy burden of proof will face any state seeking to resume oceanic disposal of this type of waste.

(5) Incineration at Sea

The parties to the London and Oslo Conventions have in practice regulated incineration of waste at sea under the respective conventions.[92] The main advantage of the regulations is that permits may be issued for incineration of certain black-listed substances which it is considered impractical to dispose of or treat on land.

Following the decision of the Second International North Sea Conference to phase out incineration in the North Sea, however, parties to both the London and Oslo Conventions have agreed in principle to reduce the use of incineration with a view to termination in 1994.[93] If implemented, this decision will further strengthen the trend towards land-based methods of disposal.

(6) Licensing and Enforcement: Jurisdiction and Control

The essence of the London Convention and of the regional agreements is that no matter of any kind may be dumped at sea without a prior permit issued by the relevant national authorities.[94] Criteria to be considered include the characteristics of the material to be dumped, the site and method of disposal, possible impacts on amenities, marine life, and uses of the sea, the adequacy of the scientific basis for making this assessment, and availability of land-based alternatives.[95] The final judgment rests with the national licensing authority. Moreover, since the object of the London Convention is to set minimum standards of acceptable national regulation, it is open to licensing authorities to adopt additional criteria, or more stringent regulations, or to prohibit dumping altogether.[96]

Under Article 6 of the London Convention, primary responsibility for

[92] London Convention, Annex 1, para. 10 and Annex II, para. (e), Annex III and LDC Resolutions LDC 32(11) and 33(11); Oslo Convention, 1983 Protocol, Annex IV; Forster, 16 *EPL* (1986), 9; Welsch, 28 *GYIL* (1985), 347–51.

[93] 2nd North Sea Conference, Declaration, para. 24; reaffirmed in the 3rd North Sea Conference Declaration, para. 23; LDC Resolutions 35(11) 1988 and 38(13), 1990; OSCOM Decisions 88/1 (1988), and 90/2 (1990).

[94] London Convention, Article 4; Oslo Convention, Articles 6, 7; Helsinki Convention, Article 9; Barcelona Convention, Protocol on Dumping, Articles 5, 6; Noumea Convention, Protocol on Dumping, Articles 5, 6.

[95] London Convention, Annex III; Oslo Convention, Annex III; Noumea Convention, Protocol on Dumping, Annex III; Barcelona Convention, Protocol on Dumping, Annex III.

[96] London Convention, Articles 4(3), 6(3); 1982 UNCLOS, Articles 210(1), (6), and Commentary, in UN, Office of the Special Representative on the Law of the Sea, *Pollution By Dumping: Legislative History* (New York, 1985), 21.

issuing permits rests with the state where the waste is loaded, regardless of the nationality of the ship or aircraft, or where the dumping is to take place. Vessels of parties to the convention cannot escape this provision by loading in non-party states; in this case the flag state is required to act as a licensing authority.[97] Moreover, since flag states will in all cases retain a concurrent jurisdiction over their vessels,[98] they will have a right independent of the London Convention to regulate dumping notwithstanding the grant of a permit elsewhere.

It is also clear that no dumping may take place within the internal waters or territorial sea of another state without its consent; since no claim to innocent passage will be involved where dumping is under way, the coastal state will necessarily enjoy full jurisdiction over ships engaged in this activity.[99] Article 210(5) of the 1982 UNCLOS extends this principle of prior consent to dumping in the exclusive economic zone and on the continental shelf, in respect of which coastal states now enjoy sovereign rights under customary international law.[100] Coastal states thus have jurisdiction to issue licences, and to regulate or prohibit all dumping within 200 miles of their coast, after due consideration of the matter with other states which may be affected.[101] Thus the main significance of the 1982 Convention with regard to dumping is that it gives coastal states a regulatory jurisdiction that was not expressly provided for in the London Convention, and which, as in the case of flag state regulation, may be invoked notwithstanding the grant of a permit elsewhere. This conclusion is further strengthened by the Basel Convention on the Control of Transboundary Movements of Hazardous Waste which requires prior consent to be obtained from importing states before dumping at sea

[97] London Convention, Article 6(2); Barcelona Convention, Protocol on Dumping, Article 10(2); Noumea Convention, Protocol on Dumping, Article 11(2). The Oslo and Helsinki Conventions refer only to 'the appropriate national authority' without definition.

[98] *The Lotus Case*, PCIJ, Ser. A, No. 10 (1927); 1982 UNCLOS, Article 211(2); London Convention, Article 7(1).

[99] 1982 UNCLOS, Articles 18; 19(2)(h); 210(5) and see *supra*, Ch. 7.

[100] 1982 UNCLOS, Articles 55–7; *Libya–Malta Continental Shelf Case, ICJ Rep.* (1985), 13; *North Sea Continental Shelf Case, ICJ Rep.* (1969), 3.

[101] 1982 UNCLOS, Article 210(5); UN, Office of the Special Representative for the Law of the Sea, *Pollution by Dumping*, 59, para. 95. For the legislative history of Article 210 and extension of coastal state jurisdiction, see ibid. 7–24, and Nordquist, *Commentary*, iv, 166–7. Article 13 LDC provides that nothing in the Convention will prejudice the future extension of coastal state jurisdiction. States whose dumping laws now extend to the EEZ include USSR, 1984 Decree on the EEZ, Article 16; Romania, 1986 Decree No. 142 of the Council of State, Article 13; Indonesia, 1983 Article No. 5 on the EEZ, Article 8; Australia, 1981 Environment Protection (Sea Dumping) Act, ss. 4(1) and 10, with SR 1984 No. 423; Nigeria, 1988 Decree No. 42, Article 1(2); UK, Food and Environment Protection Act, 1985, Part II as amended by Environmental Protection Act, 1990, s. 146 part II (the latter applies the legislation also to the continental shelf); Bulgaria, Act of 8 July 1987 Governing Ocean Space. The 1970 Canadian Arctic Waters Pollution Act applies to dumping within Arctic waters, but Canada's 1988 Environmental Protection Act, s. 66(2) applies only to dumping in the territorial sea and internal waters. Many other countries continue to adhere to the latter position.

within their jurisdiction.[102] Despite its global status, the London Convention is not a complete code for the regulation of dumping; it must be read in conjunction with the jurisdiction conferred on coastal and flag states under other treaties and customary international law.

Jurisdiction to enforce laws relating to dumping follows the same pattern. Article 7 of the London Convention requires each party to take measures with respect to vessels or aircraft registered in its territory or flying its flag, or loading matter which is to be dumped, or believed to be engaged in dumping 'under its jurisdiction'.[103] The latter phrase can now be taken as a reference to dumping inside territorial waters, the territorial sea, exclusive economic zone, or continental shelf, as provided for in Article 216 of the 1982 UNCLOS.[104] Both conventions are imperative in requiring states to enforce laws on dumping.[105]

There is little doubt that these provisions reflect customary law, including the evolution of the exclusive economic zone and extension of coastal state jurisdiction, concurrent with that of the flag state. However, they leave open the question of high seas enforcement; since port state enforcement jurisdiction is confined to cases of actual loading, it will not cover high seas dumping.[106] Beyond the EEZ, or in cases where the coastal state does not claim an EEZ, only the flag state will have jurisdiction to enforce dumping regulations, and as we saw in Chapter 7, this may often be an ineffective remedy. Partly for this reason, proposals have been made to involve IMO in a prior justification procedure similar to the Oslo Convention, or alternatively to subject all dumping to multilateral consultation.[107]

(7) Consultation, Monitoring, and Environmental Assessment

Dumping of hazardous waste at sea, particularly in coastal areas, has obvious implications for adjacent states, or those engaged in high seas fishing. Procedural obligations of good neighbourliness will therefore apply as in any other case of serious transboundary pollution risk. This is recognized by the

---

[102] See *infra*, pp. 336–8 and Oslo Commission Recommendation 88/1 para. 3.

[103] See also Barcelona Convention, Protocol on Dumping, Article 11; Noumea Convention, Protocol on Dumping, Article 12. cf. the Helsinki Convention, Article 9 and the Oslo Convention, Article 15 which do not extend coastal state powers beyond the outer limit of the territorial sea.

[104] Article 216(1)(a); UN, *Pollution By Dumping*, 15–17, 29; London Convention, Article 13; Letalik, in Johnston, *The Environmental Law of the Sea*, 224.

[105] cf. Article 216(2) of the 1982 UNCLOS, however: 'No state shall be obliged by virtue of this article to institute proceedings when another state has already instituted proceedings in accordance with this article.'

[106] 1982 UNCLOS, Article 216(1)(c); London Convention, Article 7(b). cf. 1982 UNCLOS Article 218, which confers port state jurisdiction over high seas pollution discharges from ships, *supra*, Ch. 7.

[107] UNCED, Prepcom, UN Doc. A/CONF.151/PC/31 (1991).

London Convention, which *inter alia* requires consultation with other states likely to be affected by emergency dumping of prohibited waste,[108] and by the 1982 UNCLOS, which requires coastal states to consult others who may be adversely affected by dumping in maritime zones.[109] Moreover, in those cases where dumping of prohibited substances is exceptionally permitted, consultation must take place through IMO, whose recommendations on appropriate procedures must be followed.[110] Although IAEA recommendations do not include multilateral consultation before radioactive waste is dumped, an OECD scheme provides for prior consultation among NEA members proposing to dump in the North Atlantic.[111] Both examples go beyond what is normally required in customary law, or in cases of land-based pollution.

The sum of these provisions falls short of a general obligation to consult other states or international organizations in every case of proposed dumping, but, as we have seen, the object of the London Convention is to avoid or minimize the risk of serious pollution damage affecting other states or users of the sea. This is mainly achieved by requiring prior impact assessment before the issue of a permit, which *inter alia* must take account of the effect of dumping on the uses and resources of the sea, and by the requirement to monitor the condition of the seas, keep records of all dumping and make reports to IMO and other parties.[112] These provisions fully support the view that Articles 204, 205, and 206 of the 1982 UNCLOS codify customary law. As a result, no state is now free to undertake dumping unilaterally without regard for procedures which protect the interests of others or of the international community.

Having followed these procedures, however, the London Convention leaves states free to make their own determination of where and whether to dump: they do not need the permission of any international or regional body, save in those exceptional cases where IMO must be consulted. This is entirely consistent with the general principles of customary law concerning procedural co-operation outlined in Chapter 3. But regional practice now goes further than this. Apart from NEA's multilateral consultation mechanism for radioactive dumping, states wishing to dump in the North Sea must now justify in advance to the Oslo Commission that no harm to the marine environment will

---

[108] Article 5(2) and see also Annex 6, part D, para. 11.

[109] Article 210(5).

[110] London Convention, Article 5(2); Annex 6, Part D, Paras. 11–17. See also Oslo Commission, 'Prior Consultation Procedure for Dumping', 9th Meeting, OSCOM 9/13/1 (1983).

[111] OECD Rec. C(77) 115, 'Multilateral Consultation and Surveillance Mechanism for Dumping of Radioactive Waste', 1977, in *OECD and the Environment* (Paris, 1986), 181. This scheme, and IAEA's guidelines, also provide for the presence of international observers during radioactive dumping to ensure that guidelines are complied with.

[112] London Convention, Articles 4, 5(1), 6; Annex III; Annex VI; IAEA Recommendations Concerning Radioactive Waste, 1978, Part B.

result and that no alternative exists.[113] This not only exemplifies a shift in the burden of proof, but gives the Oslo Commission a role in approving dumping which goes beyond the functions ordinarily performed by other international commissions, including the London Dumping Convention.[114] It is the most significant example of the application of a prior consent regime to waste disposal in common spaces, and may indicate the trend of future developments in the London Dumping Convention.

(8) Regional Treaties

Both the London Dumping Convention and the 1982 UNCLOS accept the possibility of regional arrangements for the control of dumping.[115] The London Convention refers in particular to parties 'with common interests to protect in the marine environment in a given geographical area', and allows them to take account of characteristic regional features. Regional agreements may set higher standards, but must not derogate from the global requirements of the London Convention. At present, regional agreements or protocols apply in the North-East Atlantic and North Sea, the Baltic, the Mediterranean, and the South Pacific, areas which are mostly enclosed or semi-enclosed seas and in which dumping may cause special problems.[116] As we have already seen, some of these treaties do set higher standards than the London Convention, particularly in the prohibition of radioactive waste dumping, or in the prohibition or phasing out of all industrial dumping in the Baltic, North Sea, and African waters.[117] Although dumping is not prohibited under the Oslo Convention, the changes in policy pursued by the Oslo Commission clearly reflect a growing belief among North Sea states that it is no longer an

[113] Decision OSCOM 89/1, Annex II; see also Oslo Commission, 'Prior Notification Procedure for Specific Permits', which is intended to give other states the opportunity to advise on the availability of alternative means of disposing of Annex II substances.

[114] Churchill, 18 *JLS* (1991), 166 observes, however, that the United Kingdom has not fully complied with the prior justification procedure: in some cases licences have been issued without reference to the Commission, in others dumping has taken place in disregard of objections from other states. The UK has, however, undertaken to end industrial waste dumping in the North Sea by 1993. It is now the only state undertaking such dumping there. For a fuller analysis of the overall effectiveness of the Oslo Convention and the phasing out of dumping, see Wettestad and Andresen, *International Resource Co-operation*, 46–56.

[115] London Convention, Article 8; 1982 UNCLOS, Article 210(4).

[116] 1972 Oslo Convention for the Prevention of Marine Pollution by Dumping from Ships and Aircraft, 1983 Protocol on Incineration at Sea, 1989 Protocol Extending the Convention to Internal Waters; 1974 Helsinki Convention; 1976 Barcelona Convention, Protocol for the Prevention of Pollution of the Mediterranean Sea by Dumping from Ships and Aircraft; 1986 Noumea Convention, Protocol for the Prevention of Pollution by Dumping.

[117] Helsinki Convention, Article 9 and Annex V; 2nd International North Sea Conference, Ministerial Declaration, para. 22; Oslo Commission, Decision OSCOM 89/1, Annexes I and II; 1991 African Convention on the Transboundary Movement of Hazardous Waste, Article 4(2).

acceptable risk, and the phasing out of industrial waste dumping will eventually apply to the whole Convention area. With the exception of the UK, North Sea states have already ceased industrial dumping at sea. The Oslo Convention has thus generated substantial regional co-operation and has, in general, been a success. The Oslo Commission has also extended its jurisdiction to include dumping in internal waters.[118] Article 8 of the London Dumping Convention requires parties to respect any additional prohibitions or controls adopted regionally.

In all other respects the regional treaties are modelled closely on the London Convention, including their licensing, enforcement, and supervision arrangements. By adding an additional level of institutional supervision they provide a more immediate focus for ensuring compliance, but it seems clear that unlike the control of land-based pollution of the sea, one of the factors which has made the control of dumping effective is the interplay of global and regional rules and institutions. This does suggest that however strong the case for regional arrangements to cater for special circumstances, these are best located within a clear global framework of minimum standards of sufficient stringency, reinforced by the wider community pressure which a body such as the Consultative Meeting of the parties to the London Convention can provide.

(9) Assessing the London Dumping Convention

As we have seen, the London Dumping Convention is generally regarded as one of the more successful regulatory treaties of the 1970s. Trends in the disposal of industrial waste by dumping at sea show a decrease from 17 million tons in 1979 to 6 million in 1987, with rather smaller reductions in the volume of sewage sludge disposed of in this way. A report prepared by IMO in 1991[119] attributes these reductions to the efforts of contracting parties to find alternative disposal methods, to recycle wastes, and to use cleaner technology, and it concludes that the Convention has provided an effective instrument for the protection of the marine environment. The decisions taken by the parties with regard to incineration, radioactive waste, and industrial waste will strengthen this apparent trend towards reduction and eventual elimination of dumping at sea as a method of hazardous waste disposal. Another measure of the Convention's relative success is the number of regional agreements which now supplement its global provisions.

As we saw in Chapter 4, one of the main reasons for the Convention's evolution in this way has been the range and diversity of parties participating

---

[118] 1989 Protocol on Dumping in Internal Waters. Not in force. On the effectiveness of the Convention, see *supra*, n. 114.
[119] UNCED Prepcom, UN Doc. A/CONF. 151/PC/31 (1991).

in regular consultative meetings. Membership of the Convention has remained for some years at approximately seventy, of which nearly half are European or North American industrialized states. The remainder are mainly developing states in Africa, Latin America, and the Pacific Islands. Only about forty parties regularly participate in consultative meetings, but among these there is again an approximate balance of industrialized and developing states. It cannot be said that the Convention is of interest only to industrialized nations, and indeed even some of these, such as the Scandinavian states, are opposed to dumping as a method of waste disposal. Although membership is thus far from universal, there is no evidence either that the Convention is controlled by pro-dumping states, or that significant dumping is practised by non-parties.

In practice, therefore, the Convention has largely achieved its objective of establishing a global framework for international action, despite the differing views of its members with regard to the acceptability of various forms of dumping. The consultative meetings have been able to exercise some control over compliance with the Convention, despite the absence of a formal non-compliance procedure, and have provided a forum for attempts to resolve disputed issues, such as subsea-bed disposal of radioactive waste. The guidelines, recommendations, and control and notification procedures adopted by the consultative meeting have also assisted the parties in effective implementation of the Convention. Moreover, the involvement of NGOs has been an important feature of its operation, enabling environmental and industry groups to lobby members and provide expert advice for the delegations of several states. Greenpeace and ACOPS have been particularly active and effective in pressing for development of the Convention and in bringing to the attention of parties evidence of violations, such as the alleged dumping of radioactive waste by the USSR disclosed at the Fourteenth Consultative Meeting in 1991.

There remain certain weaknesses in the Convention's operation, however, identified by IMO. These include the criticism that too much reliance is placed on enforcement by national administrations, and the absence of adequate international supervision. Some states have called for the adoption of a prior notification, consultation, or justification procedure to be adopted, comparable to those operating under regional treaties such as the Oslo Convention. The compliance of parties with existing reporting requirements has also not been wholly satisfactory. As we have also seen, the Convention does not take account of the subsequent extension of coastal state jurisdiction in the exclusive economic zone, nor has agreement yet been reached on the question of liability for damage, although this is not a serious problem. Compared to the problems attending the operation of regional institutions responsible for controlling land-based sources of pollution, however, these criticisms are relatively minor. The review of a long-term strategy for the

London Dumping Convention, started by the 13th Consultative meeting in 1990, will consider proposals to integrate the Convention into a comprehensive, global environmental protection and waste management framework, to establish a new convention covering both dumping and land-based sources and based on the precautionary principle, to establish a global mechanism dealing with all aspects of marine pollution, and to improve enforcement.

4. INTERNATIONAL TRADE IN HAZARDOUS SUBSTANCES[120]

(1) The Permissibility of Trade in Hazardous Wastes and Substances

International policy declarations disclose differing views on the permissibility of trade in hazardous waste. Industrialized economies represented in OECD and the EEC have accepted that production of hazardous wastes should be minimized as far as possible, that disposal should take place within member states where consistent with environmentally sound management, that trade should be reduced and should take place on a basis of prior notification and environmentally sound management, but they have not sought to eliminate transboundary disposal entirely.[121] Regional groupings of developing states have, in contrast, condemned all trade involving waste disposal in their territories.[122] Their belief has been that regulation will merely legitimize an unacceptable practice. Among the strongest exponents of this view is the Organization of African Unity, which has declared dumping of nuclear and industrial wastes a crime against the African people, and called on African states not to accept waste from industrialized countries. OAU policy is reflected in the 1991 African Convention on Transboundary Movements of

---

[120] Handl and Lutz, 30 *Harv. ILJ* (1989), 351; Sebek, 'International Legal Regulation of Trade in Toxic Waste'; Kummer and Rummel-Bulska, *The Basel Convention*; Hackett, 5 *AUJILP* (1990).

[121] OECD Decision and Recommendation C(83) 180; Recommendation C(76) 155; Resolution C(85) 100 and appendix; Decision and Recommendation C(86) 64, repr. in *OECD and the Environment* (Paris, 1986); Decision C(88) 90, 28 *ILM* (1989), 257; Resolution C(89) 112; Decision C(90) 178; EEC, Directives 84/631/EEC, 85/469/EEC, 86/279/EEC. These directives will be replaced in 1992 by proposed Council Regulation COM (90) 415 Final, which will give effect to the Basel Convention and the 1989 Lomé IV Convention, *infra*, n. 128. See also 1986 Canada–US Agreement on the Transboundary Movement of Hazardous Waste; 1983 US–Mexico Agreement of Co-operation for the Protection and Improvement of the Environment, Annex III, (1987).

[122] ACP/EEC Joint Assembly, Madrid, 1988; ECOWAS, 11th Summit, Lomé, 1988; Final Document of the First Meeting of States of the Zone of Peace and Co-operation in the South Atlantic, Rio, 1988; Organization of African Unity, Resolution CM/Res. 1153, 28 *ILM* (1989), 567. See Sebek, 'International Legal Regulation of Trade in Toxic Waste'. Developing states which have prohibited waste imports include Haiti, Constitution, Article 258; Ivory Coast, Law on Toxic and Nuclear Waste, 1988, 28 *ILM* (1989), 391; Gambia, Environmental Protection Act, 1988, 29 *ILM* (1990), 208; Nigeria, Decree No. 42, 1988, Article 1; Togo, Environmental Code, 1988; Lebanon, Act No. 64/88 (1988); see also Ghana, declaration on signature of Final Act of Basel Convention.

Hazardous Wastes, which prohibits imports into Africa from non-parties and regulates trade in waste among African states.[123]

UNEP has preferred the policy of seeking effective control through international regulation. Its Cairo Guidelines[124] acknowledge the need to respect international law applicable to protection of the environment, in particular Principle 21 of the Stockholm Declaration, and they form the basis of the first attempt at international regulation, the Basel Convention on the Control of Transboundary Movements of Hazardous Wastes and their Disposal. This treaty is closer to the main elements of OECD policy, but African states did participate in the negotiations, and their proposals on specific points were adopted.[125] With the exception of Nigeria, they have not so far supported the Convention by signature or ratification, however. UNEP's Governing Council and the UN General Assembly have called on all states to ratify the Basel Convention, but without prejudice to regional policies.[126]

In the absence of a wider consensus among exporting and importing states, it cannot be said that a policy of ending all trade in hazardous wastes has prevailed at a global level. What has been achieved is a compromise which places three important and far-reaching restrictions on this trade. First, as the 1991 African Convention indicates, it is clear that states have reserved the sovereign right to ban imports individually or regionally and that this right is recognized in the Basel Convention and by OECD states.[127] Moreover, the fourth Lomé Convention, signed in 1989, commits the EEC to prohibit exports of radioactive and hazardous waste to any African, Caribbean, or Pacific states parties to this Convention, and prohibits those states from importing such waste from the EEC or anywhere else.[128] The Basel Convention further strengthens this right to prohibit trade in waste by providing for import bans to be notified to other parties through the secretariat; no state may then permit transboundary movement of wastes to a party prohibiting their import nor, save by special agreement, is transport for disposal by non-parties permitted.[129]

Secondly, transboundary movement is permitted between parties to the

[123] See 21 *EPL* (1991), 66.

[124] Cairo Guidelines and Principles of Environmentally Sound Management of Hazardous Wastes, 1985, UNEP/WG. 122/3; 16 *EPL* (1986), 5 and 31, approved UNEP/GC. 14/30 (1987).

[125] UNEP, *Proposals and Position of the African states During Negotiations on the Basel Convention* (1989); Dakar Ministerial Conference on Hazardous Wastes, 1989.

[126] UNEP/GC. 15/33, *Report of the Governing Council on its 15th Session* (1989), GAOR 44th Session, UN Doc./A/44/25, 160; UNGA, Res. 44/226 (1989).

[127] Basel Convention, Preamble, and Declaration annexed to the Final Act of the Basel Conference, 1989. See also OECD Decision C(83) 180, Preamble; African Convention, Article 4(1). For a full analysis of the Basel Convention, see Kummer, 41 *ICLQ* (1992), p. 530.

[128] 4th Lomé Convention, 1989, Article 39, and Annexes VIII–X, 29 *ILM* (1990), 783.

[129] Article 4(1), 4(2)(e), 4(5), 7, 11, and 13, and see *infra*, n. 160. See also OECD Decision C(83) 180, Principle 8; Decision C(86) 64, Para. I, and African Convention, Article 4(3)(11).

Basel Convention or within Africa but only in circumstances where the state of export does not have the capacity or facilities to dispose of the wastes in an environmentally sound manner itself, unless intended for recycling. To this end, both Conventions are based on a philosophy of minimizing the generation of hazardous waste and promoting disposal at source. The African Convention follows the same policies, but places additional emphasis on the use of clean production methods 'which avoid or eliminate the generation of hazardous wastes'. In these respects both are more radical than the London Dumping Convention or treaties on land-based sources of pollution. They represent the strongest indication of the growing international emphasis on waste disposal at source and the adoption of a precautionary approach to pollution control.[130]

Lastly, the Basel and African Conventions demonstrate widespread agreement that trade which does take place requires the prior informed consent of transit and import states,[131] that illegal trade must be prevented, that illegally imported waste should be accepted for re-import by the state of origin,[132] and that conditions of management, transport, and ultimate disposal must be compatible with the protection of health, the environment, and the prevention of pollution.[133]

These principles probably already represent customary law, since they are supported in part by state practice, by the sovereign right of states to control activities in their own territory, and by the responsibility of exporting states for activities within their jurisdiction which harm other states or the global environment.[134] By also placing on importing states an obligation of environmentally sound management,[135] the Basel Convention recognizes that they too have a responsibility in international law for the protection of their own environment, peoples, and future generations, and it makes their management of imported waste a matter of legitimate international concern. Uniquely, the

[130] Basel Convention, Preamble and Articles 4(2)(a)(b)(d), 4(5), 4(9); Cairo Guidelines, Principle 2; African Convention, Preamble, and Articles 1(5) and 4(3); OECD Recommendation C(76) 155, Annex, Para. 3; UNGA Res. 43/212 (1988), 19 *EPL* (1989), 29; OECD Decision C(90) 178, and Recommendation C(90) 164.

[131] Basel Convention, Article 6; African Convention, Articles 4, 6, and 7. See also OECD Decision C(86) 64, Para. I; EEC Draft Council Regulation COM (90) 415 Final; UNGA Res. 43/212 (1988), and Oslo Commission Recommendation 88/1.

[132] Basel Convention, Article 9; African Convention, Article 9. See also OECD Decision C(83) 180, Principle 9; UNGA Res. 43/212 (1988) and *infra*, n. 155.

[133] Basel Convention, Preamble and Articles 4(2) (c), (d), (e), (g), 7, 8; African Convention, Article 4. See also OECD Decision C(83) 180.

[134] Handl and Lutz, 30 *Harv. ILJ* (1989), 359–60; UNGA Res. 43/212 (1988); Principle 21, Stockholm Declaration on the Human Environment, 1972; Cairo Guidelines, Principle 2. Thirty-six states declared on signing the Final Act of the Basel Conference that they will not permit any imports and exports of wastes to countries lacking the legal, administrative and technical capacity to manage and dispose of wastes in an environmentally sound manner.

[135] Article 4.

Basel Convention is thus based on a system of environmental responsibility shared among all states involved in each transaction.

Trade in hazardous substances not intended for disposal, such as chemicals, is not regulated by the Basel Convention, although the African Convention does apply where substances have been banned, refused registration, or voluntarily withdrawn in the country of manufacture for health and environmental reasons. With this exception the main constraints are those supplied by customary law and non-binding instruments, such as UNEP's London Guidelines for the Exchange of Information on Chemicals in International Trade.[136] The guidelines provide evidence that here too international law recognizes the shared responsibility of importing and exporting states for the protection of health and the environment, in accordance with Principle 21 of the Stockholm Declaration, and an obligation of good neighbourliness. The main requirements are now similar to the Basel Convention; in particular states must give notice of substances they have banned or severely restricted and must ensure that prior informed consent is obtained for any export. A prior consent procedure is also the basis of FAO's revised Code of Conduct on the Distribution and Use of Pesticides. The International Register of Potentially Toxic Chemicals, a UNEP agency, acts as a repository of information and advice on hazardous chemicals and the implementation of policies for controlling potential hazards and evaluating effects on health and the environment.[137]

(2) The Scope of the Basel Convention

The Basel Convention is concerned only with substances which are disposed of or intended for disposal. Despite the breadth of this definition, in reality it covers only household and hazardous waste.[138] Wastes are hazardous only when listed in the Convention's annexes, or if defined as such by national law, and notified to the Convention's Secretariat.[139] Radioactive wastes are excluded, because they are covered by other arrangements.[140] Unlike the

---

[136] UNEP/GC.15/9/Add.2/Appendix and Supp. 3, as amended by UNEP/GC.15/30 (1989) *Report of the Governing Council on its 15th Session*, GAOR, 44th Session, UN Doc. A/44/25, 156. See also UNGA Res. 44/226 (1989), 20 *EPL* (1990) 37, and 19 *EPL* (1989), 40. OECD Resolution C(71) 73 and Recommendation C(84) 37 establish a prior notification procedure, in *OECD and the Environment* (1986), 90 and 137. Other OECD recommendations cover the management and environmental assessment of chemicals, ibid. 93 ff. EEC Regulation COM (90) 591 (1990) proposes to implement the London Guidelines within the EEC.

[137] UNEP/GC.15/28 (1989), *Report of the Governing Council*, loc. cit. prev. n., at 153.

[138] Articles 1, 2(1), Annexes I and II.

[139] Article 3. cf. the London Guidelines on Chemicals in International Trade, *supra*, n. 137, which do no more than provide for the listing of chemicals banned or restricted by national laws, and the African Convention, Article 2, which is broader than the Basel definition.

[140] IAEA, Regulations for the Safe Transport of Radioactive Material, 1988; Code of Practice for the Management of Radioactive Waste from Nuclear Power Plants, 1985; IAEA Code of

London Dumping Convention, there are no categories of hazardous waste which may not be exported. OECD's definition follows the same pattern, but allows for bilateral or unilateral departure from the basic classification.[141] The Basel Convention acknowledges no such freedom but instead sets an obligatory minimum standard for States.[142]

'Disposal' is also defined in broad terms.[143] It includes landfill, release into watercourses, the sea, or sea-bed, incineration, permanent storage, or recycling. One consequence is that the Basel Convention will apply to waste exported for dumping in coastal state maritime zones, where, as we have seen, Article 210(5) of the 1982 UNCLOS already requires coastal state consent.[144]

(3) The Principle of Prior Informed Consent

Only rarely does international law require prior consent of other states before environmentally harmful activities may be undertaken. As we saw in Chapter 3 the *Lac Lanoux* case expressly rejects such a rule for the use of shared resources, nor does it normally apply to pollution of common spaces. In these cases, prior informed consultation at most is called for.[145]

Unusually, the essence of the system of international control established by the Basel Convention is the need for prior, informed, written consent from transit states and the state of import.[146] Only in the case of transit states which are parties to the Convention can this requirement be waived in favour of tacit acquiescence.[147] As in the *Lac Lanoux* case, information must be supplied which is sufficient to enable the nature and effects on health and the environment of the proposed movement to be assessed.[148]

The requirement of prior consent, as we have seen, is simply an expression of the sovereignty of a state over the use of its territory and resources. It is this which differentiates transboundary disposal of wastes from the use of common spaces or shared resources. Where transit takes place through maritime areas, however, no such basis in territorial sovereignty exists. In the exclusive economic zone, foreign vessels enjoy high seas freedom of navigation.[149] In the territorial sea, although subject to coastal state sovereignty, they have a

---

Practice on the International Transboundary Movement of Radioactive Waste, 1990. IMO's International Maritime Dangerous Goods Code covers transport of radioactive materials in ships. None of these instruments is formally binding. See also EEC Draft Directive COM (90) 328 (Final). The African Convention does cover radioactive waste.

[141] Decision C(88) 90, 28 *ILM* (1989), 257.
[142] Article 1(1).   [143] Article 2(4) and Annex IV.
[144] See *supra*, pp. 326–7. See also Oslo Commission Recommendation 88/1.
[145] See *supra*, pp. 315–6, 327–9, and Ch. 6, but cf. OSCOM 89/1, applying the principle of prior consent to dumping in the North Sea, *supra*, n. 114.
[146] Articles 4(1)(c), 4(2)(f), 6(1), 6(2), 6(10), 7.   [147] Article 6(4).
[148] Articles 4(2)(f), 6(1), Annex V.   [149] 1982 UNCLOS, Article 58.

right of innocent passage.[150] Ships carrying dangerous or noxious substances in the territorial sea may be confined to the use of designated sea lanes and are required to carry documents and observe special precautionary measures established by international agreement, but they do not lose their rights of passage, and may not be discriminated against.[151] Article 4(12) of the Basel Convention appears to leave these navigational rights in the EEZ and territorial sea unaffected. In general, maritime states have interpreted this to mean that prior notice or consent for the passage of vessels carrying hazardous wastes or substances is not required, but not all coastal states accept this view.[152] As with oil tankers, the more convincing conclusion is that the passage of ships carrying dangerous cargoes may be regulated by coastal states according to international standards, but these vessels cannot unilaterally be excluded from exercising their rights of navigation, despite the risk they pose.[153]

There are two ways in which the requirement of prior informed consent is enforced. The first is by making the state of export accept the return of illegal waste, where practicable, or, where the importer is at fault, imposing on the state of import a duty to ensure safe disposal of the waste.[154] There is some evidence that state practice already favours the return of waste, which under the Basel Convention would now be regarded as illegal, to the state of origin, as in the case of the 'Karin B', whose cargo Italy was obliged to accept back.[155] The second method employed by the Basel Convention is to ensure that states punish illegal traffic as a criminal offence.[156] It is possible that this provision might justify an extraterritorial protective jurisdiction over foreign nationals engaged in the illegal export of hazardous waste to a country which

---

[150] 1958 Convention on the Territorial Sea and Contiguous Zone, Articles 1, 14–17; 1982 UNCLOS, Articles 2, 17–21; *Corfu Channel Case, ICJ Rep.* (1949), 3.

[151] 1982 UNCLOS, Articles 22, 23, 24, 25; Convention on the Territorial Sea and Contiguous Zone, Article 16(3). Documentation and special precautionary measures are required by the 1973 MARPOL Convention for oil, noxious liquids, and chemicals in bulk. The Final Act of the Basel Conference, Resolution 5 invites UNEP and IMO to review the existing rules on transport of hazardous wastes by sea. See *infra*, n. 166.

[152] See e.g. the British reservation to the Basel Convention, 39 *ICLQ* (1990), 944, but cf., *contra*, Haiti *Note Verbale* of 18 Feb. 1988, 11 *LOSB* (1988), 13, and see *supra*, Ch. 7, text at n. 71. Article 4(4) (C) of the African Convention recognizes 'the exercise by ships and aircraft of all states of navigation rights and freedoms as provided for in international law and as reflected in relevant international instruments'. Proposed US legislation to implement the Basel Convention, under consideration in 1991, specifies that 'movement through the territorial seas of a country consistent with international navigation rights and freedoms shall not, by itself, imply that such a country is a transit country under this subtitle.'

[153] 1982 UNCLOS, Articles 21(2), 211 and *supra*, Ch. 7, but cf. Pineschi, in Francioni and Scovazzi (eds.), *International Responsibility for Environmental Harm* (Dordrecht, 1991), 299.

[154] Basel Convention, Article 9; African Convention, Article 9.

[155] UK House of Lords, *2nd Report of the Environment Committee on Toxic Waste*, i (1988–9), para. 253; Handl and Lutz, 30 *Harv. ILJ*, 360.

[156] Articles 4(3), 4(4), 9(5). See also African Convention, Article 4(1).

has prohibited its import.[157] This would provide an additional enforcement mechanism where the exporting state's procedures were lax or inadequate. One difficulty with these otherwise salutary enforcement rules is the possibility that they may result in illegal dumping at sea; co-ordination of the Basel Convention and the London Dumping Convention is required if this risk is to be minimized.[158] In this respect the African Convention is considerably stronger: Article 4(2) prohibits all dumping at sea by the parties and within the parties' maritime zones. Another problem is the qualified nature of the duty to re-import: 'impracticability' is a vague and subjective notion which the exporting state itself is left to interpret. Once again the African Convention is stronger: Article 9 compels the exporting state to ensure that illegal waste is taken back within thirty days.

(4) Environmentally Sound Management

The primary obligation imposed by the Basel Convention is to manage the transboundary movement of waste in an environmentally sound manner. As we have seen, this obligation applies to exporting, transit, and importing states alike,[159] and also to trade with non-parties, which may only be conducted under an agreement providing for management no less environmentally sound than is required by the Convention.[160] The crucial point is that states must not permit export or import of waste if they believe that it will not be handled in an environmentally sound manner.[161] Developing states do not escape this responsibility for sound management of imported waste; if they cannot meet it, they must either seek assistance, relying on the Convention's provisions for international co-operation, or prohibit the import.[162] Nor can the exporting state escape its obligations by transferring responsibility to the state of transit or import; wherever the waste is sent the exporting state retains a responsibility for ensuring its proper management at all stages until final disposal, and must permit re-import if necessary.[163]

---

[157] *The Lotus* Case, *PCIJ*, Ser. A, No. 10 (1927), 28.

[158] See Basel Conference, Final Act, 9th Resolution, inviting UNEP and IMO to review the relationship of the Basel Convention and the London Dumping Convention, and Sebek, 'International Legal Regulation of Trade in Toxic Waste'. The phasing out of dumping at sea will resolve this difficulty, however. See *supra*, pp. 321–2.

[159] Article 4.

[160] Articles 4(5) and 7 as qualified by Article 11. See also OECD Decision C(86) 64 and Oslo Commission Recommendation 88/1. These instruments call for the application of no less stringent standards to the disposal of waste exported to non-parties. Res. 42/13 LDC, adopted 1990, calls on parties to the London Dumping Convention to prevent the export of wastes for dumping at sea by non-parties, and for the application of standards compatible with the Basel Convention for trade between parties.

[161] Articles 4(2)(e), (g) and 4(8); African Convention, Article 4(3)(n).

[162] Articles 4(2)(g); 10; Handl and Lutz, 30 *Harv. ILJ*, 363.

[163] Articles 4(10), 8; African Convention, Articles 4(3) (O) and 8.

What is meant by 'environmentally sound management' is defined in the Convention only in general terms: 'taking all practicable steps to ensure that hazardous waste or other wastes are managed in a manner which will protect human health and the environment against the adverse effects which may result from such wastes'.[164] More detailed guidance is given in the 1985 Cairo Guidelines,[165] which include the use of best practicable means, approval of sites and facilities, disposal plans, monitoring, public access to information and contingency planning. Although these guidelines are not obligatory, their adoption by UNEP gives them persuasive force as a basic standard for states to meet in fulfilling their obligations under the Basel Convention. As such they have a legal significance comparable to IAEA guidelines for the disposal of radioactive waste.

International standards for the carriage of dangerous goods also govern some aspects of the transport of hazardous waste.[166] In some cases, such as annexes to the MARPOL Convention, these are already legally binding, but the Basel Convention goes further by requiring that packaging, labelling, and transport should conform to generally accepted rules and standards and take account of internationally recognized practices, whether or not these are otherwise obligatory.[167] This is a strong indication that transport failing to comply with these standards cannot be regarded as meeting the obligation of environmentally sound management.

In substance, this obligation is no more than a reformulation of the standard of due diligence which has generally been employed to describe international obligations for the control of environmentally harmful activities or substances.[168] Like the 1982 UNCLOS, the Basel Convention identifies the detailed content of this standard by reference to other instruments, and allows for further development. In this sense its provisions on environmentally sound management are a framework only, not a complete code in themselves.

(5) Implementation and Supervisory Institutions

Apart from requiring implementation in national law, the Basel Convention's primary method of ensuring effective compliance is through institutional supervision. A conference of the parties is established for this purpose, with power to adopt amendments and protocols, and to undertake any additional

---

[164] Article 2(8); African Convention, Article 1(10).

[165] *Supra*, n. 124.

[166] MARPOL Convention, 1973 and 1978 Protocol, Annexes II and III; IMO International Maritime Dangerous Goods Code, on which see Gold, 10 *Marine Policy* (1986), 185. See also Recommendations of the UN Committee of Experts on the Transport of Dangerous Goods, 1977; European Agreement Concerning the International Carriage of Dangerous Goods By Road, 1957; Convention and Regulation on the International Carriage of Dangerous Goods by Rail, 1985.

[167] Article 4(7)(b); African Convention, Article 4(3) (M).   [168] See Ch. 3.

action required to further the objectives of the Convention.[169] The obligatory provision of information from parties regarding transboundary movements, their effects on health and the environment, and any accidents during transport or disposal[170] gives this Conference a basis on which to review the conduct and policies of states, a point of particular importance if compliance by importing states with their obligation of environmentally sound management is to be effectively monitored. The Basel Convention's provision for international supervision thus follows the typical pattern adopted in many environmental treaties. Nevertheless, although several additional functions are given to a secretariat, including assistance in identifying illegal traffic,[171] the role of this body in verifying alleged breaches of obligation under Article 19 of the Convention is confined to relaying 'all relevant information' to the parties. This allows it only a limited monitoring function which falls well short of some proposals made at the Basel Conference to give the Secretariat stronger compliance powers.[172] Neither the secretariat nor other parties are given any power of independent inspection, an omission which significantly limits the potential effectiveness of the Convention's control and supervision regime. The provision for resort to dispute settlement machinery is also rather weak, and requires the agreement of the parties concerned, but optional acceptance of the compulsory jurisdiction of the ICJ or arbitration is allowed.[173] The institutional provisions of the African Convention are very similar.

(6) State Responsibility and Civil Liability

A major omission from the Basel Convention is the absence of any agreement on principles of liability and compensation for damage resulting from transboundary movements of waste. The Convention does require the parties to co-operate in adopting a protocol on this question, and it recognizes that states are liable in international law for the non-fulfilment of their environmental obligations.[174] Potential recourse to customary principles of state responsibility for environmental damage is a necessary element of any regime of environmental protection, but, as in the case of nuclear damage, it must be combined with an effective scheme of transboundary civil liability if compensation is to be a realistic remedy in cases of illegal traffic where recourse is sought against the exporter. A fully comprehensive protocol will thus have to combine both approaches and accommodate the interests of less developed countries. Negotiations began in 1990 to identify the elements of such a protocol, including an international fund from which compensation payments

---

[169] Article 15.   [170] Article 13.   [171] Article 16.
[172] See Kummer, 41 *ICLQ* (1992), and proposal by Nigeria, UNEP/WG.191/CRP.14.
[173] Article 20, Annex VI.   [174] Article 12, and Preamble.

could be made to claimants bringing legal proceedings in national courts.[175] Regional arrangements also make some provision for civil liability. A European Community draft directive proposes to make the producer, importer, or person with actual control of waste strictly liable for injury to the environment.[176] A 1983 US–Mexico Agreement provides for the exporter to be responsible for restoration of damage caused by transborder shipments of waste.[177] This agreement also recognizes that it is open to importing countries to require insurance cover or indemnity bonding as a condition of any import. The 1991 African Convention requires the parties to impose 'strict, unlimited liability as well as joint and several liability on hazardous waste generators'.[178]

(7) An Assessment of the Basel Convention

The most serious criticisms of the Basel Convention are that it legitimizes a trade which cannot adequately be monitored or controlled, and leaves developing states in the third world vulnerable to unsafe disposal practices.[179] Both arguments assume that the Convention will fail in its objectives. Since it is not yet in force, it is too early to draw such firm conclusions. In its favour is the strength of its control regime. The requirements of prior informed consent and re-import in cases of illegal export are particularly effective devices for protecting importing states, and the obligation of environmentally sound management is one of the most extensive in any international environmental treaty, imposed not only for the benefit of the importing state but for the benefit of the international community as a whole. Moreover, the Convention leaves open the possibility of import bans on a national or regional basis, and provides an effective mechanism for publicizing these or other restrictions. The 1991 African Convention indicates how regional measures to give stronger protection to third world countries remain a viable option under the Basel Convention. This is undoubtedly a more realistic means of safeguarding

---

[175] 2nd Report of the Ad hoc Working Group of Legal and Technical Experts, 1991, UNEP/CHW/WG.1/2/LI and Corr. 1, and see *supra*, Chs. 5 and 9; Handl and Lutz, 30 *Harv. ILJ* (1989), 359. Muchlinski, *The Right to Development and the Industrialisation of Less Developed Countries: The Case of Compensation for Major Industrial Accidents*, Commonwealth Secretariat (London, 1989) offers a valuable critique of the issues from the point of view of less developed countries.

[176] Draft Directive on Civil Liability for Waste Damage COM (89)282 (1989). See also the 1989 ECE Convention on Civil Liability for Damage Caused During Carriage of Dangerous Goods by Road, Rail and Inland Navigation Vessels (not yet in force) and Council of Europe Draft Convention on Damage Resulting from Activities Dangerous to the Environment, *supra*, Ch. 5. For US legislation, see the Comprehensive Environmental Response, Compensation and Liability Act, 1980 which creates a 'superfund' for clean-up costs and imposes strict liability.

[177] 1983 US–Mexico Agreement on Co-operation for the Protection and Improvement of the Environment in the Border Area, Annex III of 1987, 27 *ILM* (1987), 25.

[178] Article 4(3)(b).

[179] See further Handl, in Canadian Council on International Law, *Proceedings of the 18th Annual Conference* (1989), 367.

these countries than a complete international ban on all trade in hazardous waste.[180]

But there do remain aspects of the Basel Convention which require careful consideration if it is to succeed in reducing the risks of unregulated waste disposal. Although some progress has been made in defining in more detail what 'environmentally sound management' consists of, the Convention itself acknowledges that further elaboration of this key concept is required.[181] The Convention's implementation remains dependent on assumptions that importing states, especially developing states, can acquire through international co-operation the expertise and technology required to handle this trade, if they choose to do so, and that exporting states are realistically in a position to assess the capabilities of importers. A regime of shared responsibility may be desirable, but it is not clear that impecunious importing states will necessarily have the strongest interest in protecting themselves, nor that exporting states will in practice do this for them. The obvious risk is that both exporting and importing states may take an essentially subjective view of what constitutes 'environmentally sound management' and of the risks involved in transboundary waste movements. How effective supervision by the Conference of the Parties will be remains to be seen, but the argument that informed public scrutiny is likely to be the most effective way of policing transboundary waste movements is a cogent one.[182] This implies a level of transparency and public access to decision-making which the Basel Convention does very little to require or promote,[183] an omission also made more serious by the absence of any provision for independent inspection.

The Convention does offer a model for regulating other problems of transboundary trade, whether in hazardous chemicals or technologies,[184] and it affords evidence of the development of customary principles which may govern these activities. As we have seen, some of its main principles are already applied by analogy to international trade in chemicals. The Bhopal chemical plant accident indicates some of the legal complexities affecting trade in hazardous technology, however, particularly in questions of liability and the obligations of importing states.[185] It remains uncertain how far states have yet recognized a shared responsibility in this context, or whether the

---

[180] *Proceedings of the 18th Annual Conference* (1989), 371.
[181] Article 4(8).   [182] Handl and Lutz, 30 *Harv. ILJ* (1989), 373.
[183] cf. Article 10(4) and OECD's Decision and Recommendation C(88) 55 Concerning Provision of Information to the Public and Public Participation in Decision Making Processes Related to the Prevention of and Response to Accidents Involving Hazardous Substances, 28 *ILM* (1989), 277; EEC Directive 90/313/EEC on Freedom of Access to Information on the Environment, OJ No. L 158/856.
[184] See Handl and Lutz, *Transferring Hazardous Technologies and Substances: The International Legal Challenge* (The Hague, 1989).
[185] See generally Muchlinski, 50 *MLR* (1987), 545; Anderson, in Butler (ed.), *Control Over Compliance with International Law* (Dordrecht, 1991), 83; Francioni, in Francioni and Scovazzi, *International Responsibility for Environmental Harm*, 275.

operation of multinational corporations can effectively be regulated by international law.[186] Yet it is difficult to resist the conclusion that here too the
principle of prior informed consent, and the assurance of environmentally
sound management, have an important place.

5. CONCLUSIONS

The importance of adequate institutional machinery for supervising implementation of environmental protection treaties and ensuring their continued
development is clearly illustrated in this chapter by the failure of regional
institutions dealing with land-based pollution and the relative success of the
London Dumping Convention. The Basel Convention must achieve a comparable degree of participation from states with diverse interests if it is to be
similarly effective at controlling trade in hazardous waste.

The evidence of state practice and the international conventions considered
here do support the propositions expressed by Articles 192 and 194 of the
1982 UNCLOS that states are obliged by international law to protect the
marine environment by taking diligent measures to prevent, reduce, and
control pollution of common areas. The trend towards phasing out most
forms of dumping, both globally and regionally, suggests that the permissibility of dumping hazardous substances at sea is now increasingly questionable. Moreover, the acceptance, both in state practice and in international
conventions, of the principle of prior informed consent as a condition for the
disposal of hazardous wastes and substances in the territory or maritime zones
of other states supports the view that this has become a requirement of
international law. Growing support for a precautionary approach to protection
of the marine environment is apparent in the development of clean technology
requirements, in the prohibition of certain forms of dumping and land-based
disposal to the marine environment, and in the requirement of prior environmental impact assessment for waste disposal activities affecting other states
and the sea. However, the evidence supports the view expressed in Chapter 3
that it is premature to treat the precautionary principle as a requirement of
international law, or to draw firm conclusions regarding its content.

It must also be concluded that the extreme generality and weakness of the
provisions of the 1982 UNCLOS and of regional conventions in dealing with
land-based sources of pollution has both undermined their effectiveness and
contributed to their failure to give more concrete content to principles of
customary law. While a global convention might lead to improved institutional
supervision of measures to deal with this source of pollution, effective action

---

[186] See Handl and Lutz, 30 *Harv. ILJ* (1989), 357–61; Scovazzi, in Francioni and Scovazzi,
International Responsibility for Environmental Harm, 395; Charney, *Duke LJ* (1983), 748.

requires a level of political commitment and international consensus, supported by necessary economic and technical assistance and co-operation, which has so far been absent. Renewed attempts to deal more successfully with these problems, and to integrate the prevention of land-based marine pollution into a much broader framework of sustainable development of coastal zones and ocean resources were made by UNEP and by the Preparatory Committee for the 1992 UNCED Conference.[187] The reports of these bodies acknowledge that much remains to be done to implement the provisions of existing regional agreements on the protection of the marine environment, while noting the significance of financial obstacles to their effectiveness. What is proposed is a new approach to marine resource management which encompasses pollution control, living resource protection, the impact of climate change, the regulation of dumping, and the role of international institutions at global and regional level, and which no longer assumes that the oceans are an 'infinite sink or receptacle for wastes and an endless supply of free and open access resources'. In particular, the reports stress the need to adopt a precautionary approach, and to harmonize management of coastal areas and exclusive economic zones. It remains to be seen whether this appreciation of the limitations of existing international law and institutional arrangements for the management of the relationship between land-based activities and their impact on the oceans will lead to more radical and effective measures of international and regional co-operation.

---

[187] See UNEP, *Report of the Meeting of Government—Designated Experts*, UNEP (OCA) /WG.14/L.1/Add. 2 (1991); UNCED, *Report of the Sec. Gen. of the Conference on Protection of Oceans, etc.* UN Doc. A/CONF.151/PC/30 (1991); id, UN Doc. A/CONF.151/PC/42 (1991); id., UN Doc. A/CONF.151/PC/69 (1991).

9

Nuclear Energy and the Environment

1. INTRODUCTION: INTERNATIONAL NUCLEAR POLICY

As the Chernobyl reactor accident in 1986 has shown, modern nuclear technology creates unavoidable risks for all states, whether or not they choose to use this form of energy. Every state, and the environment, is potentially affected by the possibility of radioactive contamination, the spread of toxic substances derived from nuclear energy, and the long-term health hazards consequent on exposure to radiation.[1] In catastrophic cases the level of injury to individual states and the global environment may be severe. International Law is capable of moderating these ultrahazardous risks, using techniques of international regulation, transboundary co-operation, and liability for damage, but only to the extent that international policy favours environmental protection over the economic benefits perceived to follow from access to nuclear power and other nuclear activities. Such a preference entails limitations on the freedom of states to conduct hazardous activities within their territory, which, as the example of nuclear energy will show, states have been reluctant to accept.

(1) The Growth of Nuclear Power

In the early days of nuclear energy, it was widely believed that the benefits outweighed the risks, and could be shared by all.[2] The optimistic view was reflected in international policy. The International Atomic Energy Agency was created in 1956 with the object of encouraging and facilitating the spread of nuclear power.[3] Atomic energy, it was assumed, would contribute to 'peace, health and prosperity' throughout the world.[4] The prevalent belief then was

---

[1] See IAEA, *Summary Report on the Post Accident Review Meeting on the Chernobyl Accident* (Vienna, 1986); UKAEA, *The Chernobyl Accident and its Consequences* (London, 1987); NEA/OECD, *The Radiological Impact of the Chernobyl Accident in OECD Countries* (Paris, 1988); *Report of the United Nations Scientific Committee on the Effects of Atomic Radiation*, GAOR 37th Session (New York, 1982), and 41st Session (New York, 1986); *Report of the President's Commission on the Accident at Three Mile Island* (Washington, DC, 1979); IAEA/INFCIRC 383 (1990).

[2] Agreed Declaration on Atomic Energy, Washington, 1945, 1 *UNTS* 123 (US, Canada, UK); UNGA Res. 1(1) (1945); President Eisenhower's 'Atoms for Peace Address', GAOR 8th Session, 470th meeting, paras. 79–126; Szasz, *The Law and Practices of the IAEA* (Vienna, 1970), chs. 1 and 2; McKnight, *Atomic Safeguards* (New York, 1971), ch. 1.

[3] Statute, Articles III(1)–(4), amended (1961) 471 *UNTS* 334; (1970) 24 UST 1637.

[4] IAEA Statute, Article III.

that the health and environmental risks could be managed successfully by governments and the IAEA through co-operation on safety matters.

Successive declarations of international bodies maintained this belief in the dissemination of nuclear energy. In 1977, the UN General Assembly reaffirmed the importance of nuclear energy for economic and social development, and proclaimed the right of all states to use it and to have access to the technology.[5] The success of this early exercise in technology transfer can be measured today in over 400 nuclear power plants operating in twenty-six countries.

(2) The Acceptability of Nuclear Weapons

There were fewer illusions about nuclear weapons. Non-proliferation beyond the five permanent members of the UN Security Council quickly became an international arms-control policy, although not accepted by all.[6] Thus, a second role for the IAEA was to ensure that nuclear power was used for peaceful purposes only.[7] In 1968, the policy of non-proliferation and the powers of the IAEA were strengthened by the Nuclear Non-Proliferation Treaty.[8] Three nuclear powers and a large majority of UN members acknowledged 'the devastation that would be visited upon all mankind by a nuclear war', and agreed further measures intended to prevent the spread of nuclear weapons.[9] Although the treaty reaffirmed the belief that nuclear technology, including weapons technology, had beneficial peaceful applications which should be available to all, the linkage between non-proliferation and the peaceful uses of nuclear power has remained controversial for some states, such as India, and hindered agreement on further nuclear co-operation.[10]

The 1968 treaty did nothing to reduce the arsenals of existing nuclear weapons powers. At first the testing of those arsenals proceeded freely,

---

[5] UNGA Res. 32/50 (1977). See also UNGA Res. 36/78 (1981) and GAOR, 41st Session, 1987, *Report of the Preparatory Committee for the UN Conference for the Promotion of Industrial Co-operation in the Peaceful Uses of Nuclear Energy*.

[6] See Willrich, *International Safeguards and Nuclear Industry* (Baltimore, Md., 1973); Potter, *Nuclear Power and Non-Proliferation*; Quester (ed.), *Nuclear Proliferation* (Madison, Wis., 1971); Willrich (ed.), *Civil Nuclear Power and International Security* (New York, 1968); Lamm, *The Utilization of Nuclear Energy and International Law* (Budapest, 1984); SIPRI, *Safeguards Against Nuclear Proliferation* (Stockholm, 1975).

[7] Statute, Articles II, III. The 1957 Euratom Treaty provides for safeguards against diversion among European member states.

[8] Willrich, *Non-Proliferation Treaty* (Charlottesville, Va., 1968); Fischer, *The Non-Proliferation of Nuclear Weapons* (New York, 1971); SIPRI, *Safeguards Against Nuclear Proliferation*.

[9] A comparable regime for South America was established by the 1967 Tlateloco Treaty for the Prohibition of Nuclear Weapons in Latin America; see Redick, in Quester, *Nuclear Proliferation*, ch. 6.

[10] GAOR, 37th Session, 1983, *Report of the Preparatory Committee for the United Nations Conference for the Promotion of International Co-operation in the Peaceful Uses of Nuclear Energy*; id., 40th Session, 1986.

without objection, even in the South Pacific where it was mainly carried out. In the 1950s the main reservations about these tests concerned disruption of local populations and interference with high seas freedoms.[11] The existence of a threat to health and the environment was recognized, however, by three nuclear powers, in the 1963 treaty which banned nuclear weapons tests in the atmosphere, outer space, and under water.[12] But testing by France and China continued, prompting condemnation at the Stockholm Conference in 1972[13] and at the UN.[14]

Australia and New Zealand failed in their attempt in 1974 to have the ICJ declare further French atmospheric tests illegal.[15] Their experience, reinforced by mounting evidence of the long-term effects of earlier tests in Australia and elsewhere,[16] eventually prompted the creation in 1985 of a South Pacific Nuclear Free Zone.[17] The prohibition among the parties of nuclear tests, or the dumping of radioactive waste at sea, within this zone, indicated the growing strength of regional and international opposition to such activities on environmental grounds.

(3) The Emergence of Environmental Concern

It was the popularity of nuclear power as an answer to the oil crisis of the 1970s which ultimately brought long-term health and environmental consequences to the forefront of international concern. The Stockholm Conference in 1972 had called for a registry of emissions of radioactivity and international co-operation on radioactive waste disposal and reprocessing.[18] It recognized that the latter was a growing problem, caused by the increasing use of nuclear power, but offered no clear policy. Oceanic dumping of nuclear waste was partially banned in 1972 and suspended altogether in 1983 pending further assessment of health and environmental hazards, leaving disposal on land or reprocessing as the only viable options.[19] But nuclear reactor accidents

---

[11] McDougal and Schlei, 64 *Yale LJ* (1955), 648; Margolis, ibid. 629.

[12] 1963 Treaty Banning Nuclear Weapons Tests in the Atmosphere, in Outer Space and Under Water.

[13] A/CONF. 48/14/Rev. 1; Res. 3(1), 4 June 1972.

[14] UNGA Res. 3078 XXVIII (1973). Similar resolutions have been passed annually since 1955.

[15] *Nuclear Tests Cases* (Australia v. France), *ICJ Rep.* (1973), 99 (Interim measures); *ICJ Rep.* (1974), 253 (Jurisdiction); (New Zealand v. France), *ICJ Rep.* (1973), 135 (Interim Measures); *ICJ Rep.* (1974), 457 (Jurisdiction); Prott, 7 *Sydney LR* (1976), 433; Dugard, 16 *VJIL* (1976), 463; New Zealand Ministry of Foreign Affairs, *French Nuclear Testing in the Pacific* (Wellington, 1973); Dupuy, 20 *GYIL* (1977), 375; MacDonald and Hough, ibid. 337; Kos, 14 *VUWLR* (1984), 357; see also *infra*, n. 100.

[16] See *Report of the UN Scientific Committee on the Effects of Atomic Radiation*, 1972, GAOR 27th Session, Suppl. No. 25; id., 1982, GAOR, 37th Session, Suppl. No. 45.

[17] 1985 South Pacific Nuclear Free Zone Treaty; Beeby, 17 *VUWLR* (1987), 33.

[18] A/Conf. 48/14/Rev. 1, Rec. 75, *Action Plan for the Human Environment*.

[19] See *supra*, pp. 323–5. Problems arising from the illegal transboundary movement and disposal of nuclear waste are considered at pp. 335–6.

at Three Mile Island in the United States and Chernobyl in the Soviet Union showed how serious were the risks for health, agriculture, and the environment posed by nuclear power.[20] Spreading contamination over a wide area of Eastern and Western Europe, the accident at Chernobyl in 1986, like the sinking of the *Torrey Canyon*[21] in 1967, revealed the limitations of international policy for containing catastrophic risks, and some of the true costs of nuclear power.

Chernobyl cast doubt on the adequacy of national and international regulation of nuclear facilities. It showed how little agreement existed on questions of liability and state responsibility. It gave new importance to the interest of neighbouring states in the siting of nuclear power plants, the opportunities for consultation on issues of safety, and the right to prompt notification of potentially harmful accidents. It demonstrated too, that the fundamentally benign view of nuclear power adopted in the 1950s now required modification, with new emphasis on stronger international control of safety matters.[22] For the first time, an international body, the Council of Europe, was prepared to describe nuclear energy as 'potentially dangerous', to recommend a moratorium on construction of new facilities, and the closure of those that did not meet international standards.[23] Few states have been willing to go this far; the predominant belief remains that through stronger international cooperation, the risks of nuclear energy can be contained and made environmentally acceptable, thereby reducing reliance on fossil fuels, and helping to counter the fear of global warming.[24]

2. THE INTERNATIONAL REGULATION OF NUCLEAR ENERGY: THE ROLE OF INTERNATIONAL ORGANIZATIONS

Like oil tankers, nuclear installations are potentially hazardous undertakings whose risk to health, safety, and the environment is best met by regulation. Because the consequences of failure to regulate adequately may cause injury or pollution damage to other states and the global environment, international regulation—the setting of common standards, supervised by international institutions—offers the best means of ensuring a generally accepted minimum

---

[20] *Supra*, n. 1.

[21] See Brown, 21 *CLP* (1968), 113; *supra*, Ch. 7.

[22] See IAEA General Conference, Special Session, 1986, IAEA/GC (SPL.1)/4 and GC(SPL.1)/15/Rev. 1, at 25 *ILM* (1986), 1387 ff.; OECD Nuclear Energy Agency, 15th Report, *NEA Activities in 1986*, 29 ff.; European Community, *20th General Report* (1986), paras. 759–62; WCED, *Our Common Future* (Oxford, 1987), 181 ff. See Cameron, *et al.* (eds.), *Nuclear Energy Law After Chernobyl* (London, 1988); Sands, *Chernobyl: Law and Communication* (Cambridge, 1988).

[23] Parliamentary Assembly Rec. 1068 (1988).

[24] Blix, 18 *EPL* (1988), 142.

level of environmental protection. The benefits of this approach accrue to the international community, which gains protection from unilaterally chosen levels of risk, but the burdens fall on national governments, which lose the freedom to determine for themselves the most appropriate balance of safety and development in their own territories.

For oil tankers, the choice of strong international regulation has been made. The minimum duties of flag states in matters of environmental protection are laid down in detail in international conventions, and given additional legal force by the Law of the Sea Convention.[25] A relatively strong scheme of enforcement exists. No similar choice has been made for nuclear installations. Here, instead, national sovereignty, and the consequent freedom to set national standards, by and large prevails.[26] International bodies, including IAEA, OECD, and the EEC do have a responsibility for formulating international standards of health and safety regulation. But although these standards are often adopted into national law,[27] in the case of IAEA and OECD they are not as such binding on states in most instances, as we shall see, and lack the force of treaties like the MARPOL Convention. The result is that international regulation of nuclear energy, if it can be so called, is unsatisfactorily weak. It fails, for reasons explained below, to achieve the assurance of minimum standards of environmental protection[28] comparable to those on which other states are entitled to insist in the case of oil pollution. Without binding international standards, no comparable level of international enforcement is possible either.

(1) IAEA and the Regulation of Nuclear Power

The International Atomic Energy Agency was the product of compromise following failure to agree on US proposals for international management of all nuclear power by an international body.[29] Rather, its main tasks were to encourage and facilitate the development and dissemination of nuclear power,[30] and to ensure through non-proliferation safeguards that it was used

[25] MARPOL Convention, 1973 and 1978; 1982 UNCLOS Article 211, 217, 218, 220; *supra*, Ch. 7.

[26] Barkenbus, 41 *International Organization* (1987), 482, 486; Dickstein, 23 *ICLQ* (1977), 426.

[27] See generally OECD/NEA, *Nuclear Legislation: Regulations Governing Nuclear Installations and Radiation Protection* (Paris, 1972); IAEA, *Experience and Trends in Nuclear Law* (Vienna, 1972); id., *Nuclear Law for a Developing World* (Vienna, 1969); id., *Licensing and Regulatory Control of Nuclear Installations* (Vienna, 1975), 3–10, 131–3; OECD, *International Co-operation in the Field of Radioactive Transfrontier Pollution*, 14 *NLB* (1974), 55; Szasz, *The Law and Practices of the IAEA*, ch. 22.

[28] Barkenbus, 41 *International Organization* (1987), 483, 486; Cameron, *et al.*, *Nuclear Energy Law*, 159 ff., 179 ff.; Handl, 92 *RGDIP* (1988), 5.

[29] Szasz, *The Law and Practices of the IAEA*, ch. 1; Potter, *Nuclear Power and Non Proliferation* (Cambridge, Mass., 1982), ch. 2; McKnight, *Atomic Safeguards*, ch. 1.

[30] Statute, Articles III(1)–(4). In practice the development of the international nuclear industry has relied more heavily on assistance from other states than on the IAEA. See Cavers, 12 *Vand.*

for peaceful purposes only.[31] Setting standards for health and safety in collaboration with other international agencies was very much an incidental or secondary responsibility.[32]

The Chernobyl accident has resulted in a significant alteration of the Agency's priorities. The IAEA provided the main forum for consideration of measures made necessary by the accident and member states endorsed the importance of the Agency's role in safety and radiological protection matters.[33] Among the recommendations of a review group were that the Agency should promote better exchanges of information among states on safety and accident experience, develop additional safety guidelines and enchance its capacity to perform safety evaluations and inspections on request.[34] The Convention on Assistance in cases of Nuclear Emergency also gives it the new task of co-ordinating assistance and responding to requests for help.[35]

Thus, despite its very different objectives in 1956, the Agency now attaches high importance to its nuclear safety role. Rather like IMO after the *Torrey Canyon* disaster, it has acquired a new environmental perspective as perhaps the one positive result of Chernobyl.

(a) Powers over Health and Safety

The Statute requires IAEA to establish 'standards' for protecting health and minimizing danger to life and property.[36] In addition, its Health and Safety document sets out a policy on the inclusion of safety standards in agreements with states.[37] This refers to 'standards, regulations, rules or codes of practice established to protect man and the environment against ionising radiation and to minimise danger to life and property.' 'Standards' may thus take a number of different forms, depending on their function, but all serve the same broad purpose of seeking to prevent harm to the environment and adverse effects on other states.

IAEA standards, regulations, codes of practice, guides, and other related instruments cover such subjects as radiation protection, transport and handling of radioactive materials, and radioactive waste disposal.[38] The Nuclear Safety

---

LR (1958), 68; Szasz, *The Law and Practices of the IAEA*, ch. 2; McKnight, *Atomic Safeguards*, ch. 2.

[31] Statute, Article III(5).

[32] Statue, Article III(6); Szasz, *The Law and Practices of the IAEA*, ch. 22.

[33] IAEA, 30th Conference, Special Session, GC/SPL.1/Res. 1. See also statement of the Group of Seven on the implications of the Chernobyl Accident, 15 *ILM* (1986), 1005. See Handl, 92 *RGDIP* (1988); Blix, 18 *EPL* (1988).

[34] IAEA, *Summary Report on the Post Accident Review Meeting on the Chernobyl Accident* (Vienna, 1986).

[35] See *infra*, pp. 365–7.

[36] Article III(6).

[37] Revised safety standards and measures (1976) INFCIRC/18/Rev. 1.

[38] Basic Safety Standards for Radiation Protection, 1982, 28 *NLB* (1981), 38. These are sponsored jointly by IAEA, WHO, ILO, and OECD and are based on the ICRP's 1977

Standards Programme (NUSS), revised in 1988, sets basic international minimum safety standards and guiding principles for regulating the design, construction, siting, and operation of nuclear power plants.[39] The important point is thus that the Agency has competence over a wide range of safety and health issues relating to all aspects of the use of nuclear energy: what it lacks is the ability to give these standards obligatory force.

(b) The Legal Effect of IAEA Health and Safety Standards

Nothing in the Statute confers any binding force on IAEA standards, or requires member states to comply with them.[40] While, under the statute, the same is true of non-proliferation safeguards, in practice IAEA enjoys much stronger power in that field as a result of the 1968 Non-Proliferation Treaty and regional agreements.[41]

The effect of the NPT treaty is to make obligatory the acceptance of non-proliferation safeguards through bilateral agreements with the Agency, and to allow periodic compulsory Agency inspection for the purpose of verification.[42] Compliance with the overall scheme of non-proliferation safeguards is monitored by the UN General Assembly and Security Council.

No comparable attempt has been made to require universal adherence to health and safety standards.[43] Safeguards agreements and safeguards inspections relate only to non-proliferation; they give IAEA no power over health and safety.[44] Only where the Agency supplies materials, facilities, or services

---

recommendations which seek to limit the incidence of radiation-induced fatal cancers and serious genetic disorders to a level accepted by society and to prevent other harmful disorders: Smith, 30 *IAEA Bulletin* (1988), 42. See also Regulations on Safe Transport for Radioactive Materials, 1984; Principles for Establishing Intervention Levels for the Protection of the Public in the Event of a Nuclear Accident, 1985; Code of Practice for Management of Radioactive Waste from Nuclear Power Plants, 1985; Code of Practice on the International Transboundary Movement of Radioactive Waste, 1990.

[39] IAEA GC(XXXII)/Res/489 approved revised texts of five NUSS codes in 1988. According to the Director-General these establish 'the objectives and basic requirements that must be met to ensure adequate safety in the operation of nuclear power plants', 30 *IAEA Bulletin* (1988), 58.

[40] Szasz, *The Law and Practices of the IAEA*, 679 ff.

[41] *Supra*, nn., 8 and 9. For differences between statutory and NPT Safeguards, see Szasz, in Willrich, *International Safeguards*, ch. 4, and McKnight, *Atomic Safeguards*, chs. 7 and 9. Non-proliferation safeguards must also be accepted when IAEA provides assistance: Statute, Article XII.

[42] Article III, NPT Treaty. The terms of NPT safeguards agreements are set out in IAEA/INFCIRC/153, 1972.

[43] Barkenbus, 41 International Organization (1989); Szasz, *The Law and Practices of the IAEA*, ch. 22; Cameron, *et al.*, *Nuclear Energy Law*, 4 ff.

[44] IAEA/INFCIRC/153, paras. 46, 71–3; Szaza, *The Law and Practices of the IAEA*, 662 f. See e.g. Safeguards Agreement between the Agency, Israel, and the United States, 1975, TIAS 8051 and others listed, Ruster and Simma, *International Protection of the Environment* (hereafter 'Ruster and Simma'), xiii. 6468 ff. IAEA/INFCIRC/153, para. 28 defines the objective of NPT safeguards as 'the timely detection of diversion of significant quantities of nuclear material from peaceful nuclear activities to the manufacture of nuclear weapons or of other explosive devices or for purposes unknown, and deterrence of such diversion by the risk of early detection.'

to states does the statute give it the power to ensure, through project agreements, that acceptable health, safety, and design standards are adopted.[45] In such cases, but only in such cases, does it also have the right to examine the design of equipment and facilities to ensure compatibility with its standards, and the right to send inspectors to verify compliance.[46] If these are not met, further assistance may be terminated and membership of the Agency withdrawn.[47] Considerable latitude is normally allowed, however, provided national practices meet the minimum criterion of offering an 'adequate' means of controlling hazards and ensuring effective compliance.[48]

These powers over safety relate only to materials or facilities supplied by[49] or through[50] IAEA; states cannot be required to place their other facilities or materials under its standards merely because they seek its assistance, although they may do so voluntarily.[51] Where assistance is supplied under bilateral agreement without IAEA involvement, even these limited powers are lost, and the practice in such cases has been to provide only for safety consultations with the supplier state.[52]

In a few cases, other treaties do give IAEA standards greater legal standing. The 1958 High Seas Convention[53] requires states to take account of them in preventing pollution of the seas from dumping of radioactive waste. The 1972 London Dumping Convention[54] allows IAEA to determine what high level waste is unsuitable for dumping at sea, and confirms the duty of states to take account of Agency standards on dumping low-level waste. These are exceptional cases, however.

The process of adoption of IAEA health and safety standards confirms their limited legal status. In many cases they are not approved by the Agency's General Conference, in which member states are represented, but by the Board of Governors.[55] They may thus lack even the evidence of international support which approval by the IMO Assembly confers on non-binding IMO

---

[45] Articles III(6); XI, XII/INFCIRC/18/Rev. 1. The Agency does not in fact receive or supply materials as envisaged in Article IX; it now arranges for others to do so.

[46] Statute, Article XII; Inspectors Doc./IAEA/GC(V)/INF. 39, Annex, paras. 9, 11.

[47] Statute, Article XII. For the effect of material breach in terminating or suspending a treaty, see *Namibia Advisory Opinion, ICJ Rep.* (1971), 16, 121; *ICAO Council Case, ICJ Rep.* (1972), 46, 67; Vienna Convention on the Law of Treaties between States and International Organizations, 1985, Article 60; Vienna Convention on the Law of Treaties, 1968, Article 60.

[48] INFCIRC/18/Rev. 1, paras. 2, 4.

[49] See e.g. agreements listed in Ruster and Simma xii and xxvii.

[50] See e.g. trilateral agreements between IAEA, the US, and Argentina, 1978, 30 UST 1539; Indonesia, 1979, 32 UST 361; Malaysia, 1980, 32 UST 2610.

[51] Statute, Articles III(6), XII A; IAEA/INFCIRC/18/Rev. 1, para. 25.

[52] See e.g. US–Brazil Agreement, 1972, 23 UST 2478; US Thailand Agreement, 1974, TIAS 7850; FRG–Brazil Agreement, 1975, Ruster and Simma, xiii. 6472 ff., and others listed at 6415–29.

[53] Article 25. The regulation of nuclear-powered ships is considered, *infra*, pp. 358, 362.

[54] See *supra*, pp. 323–51.

[55] Szasz, *The Law and Practices of the IAEA*, 669 ff.

recommendations.[56] It is thus difficult to describe them even as 'soft law', or to regard them as representing a standard of 'due diligence' for states to meet. This point is particularly relevant when it comes to defining the content of states' obligations in customary law. But approval of the 1988 NUSS Codes by the General Conference may indicate some appreciation of this weakness, and signify an intention to give them a more authoritative status, although still formally non-binding.[57]

(c) Assessing the Role of IAEA Standards

Despite their non-binding character, IAEA health and safety standards are a significant contribution to controlling the risks of nuclear energy. Governments are consulted during the formulation stage[58] and in some cases drafting is carried out in co-operation with specialist bodies, such as International Committee on Radiological Protection.[59] The Agency's standards thus reflect a large measure of expert and technical consensus, and it is for this reason, and not their legal status, that they have been influential and do serve as important guidelines for most states in regulating their nuclear facilities. They have resulted in an appreciable degree of harmonization.[60]

IAEA member states have also considered the possibility of obligatory international minimum safety standards for reactors, but have not reached agreement.[61] Problems of reconciling many different national standards, of modifying existing installations, and of the financial and administrative costs for some states mean that securing such agreement will not be easy. It would require a surrender of national sovereignty in this field, and assumes that uniform standards for various types of reactor are possible and would enhance overall safety. This assumption is not universally accepted.[62] States have instead affirmed their individual responsibility for ensuring nuclear and radiation safety, security, and environmental compatibility, while acknowledging the central role of the IAEA in encouraging and facilitating co-operation on safety and radiological protection.[63] But it is clear that the opportunity which might

---

[56] 1948 Convention on the International Maritime Consultative Organization, Article 16.

[57] IAEA/GC (XXXII)/Res./489 (1988).

[58] Szasz, *The Law and Practices of the IAEA*, 672 f.; IAEA, *Experience and Trends in Nuclear Law* (Vienna, 1972).

[59] The ICRP is a private association of scientific experts, comparable to ICES or SCAR: see Smith, 30 *IAEA Bulletin* (1988), 42. For IAEA co-operation with other international bodies, see Szasz, *The Law and Practices of the IAEA*, ch. 12.

[60] Dickstein, 23 *ICLQ* (1977), 437; Szasz, *The Law and Practices of the IAEA*, 673, 682 ff.; Cameron, *et al.*, *Nuclear Energy Law*, 4, 159 ff., and see *supra*, n. 27.

[61] IAEA, 30th Conference, Special Session, 1986, 16 *EPL* (1986), 138. The conference called for IAEA to consider the matter further: GC/SPL.1/Res./2. UNGA Res. 41/36 (1986) calls for the highest standards of safety in design and operation of nuclear plants.

[62] See Reyners and Lellouche, in Cameron, *et al.*, *Nuclear Energy Law*, 16 f., 164 f., and 182 f.; Handl, 92 *RGDIP* (1988), 5, 7 ff.

[63] *Supra*, n. 33.

have existed in the early stages of nuclear power for establishing stronger international safety regulation has been missed, and that it may now be too late to move significantly in that direction.

(d) IAEA as an International Inspectorate and Review Body

IAEA has very limited power to act as an international nuclear safety inspectorate. Compulsory inspections are possible only where an assistance agreement is in force, and in practice this power is rarely used.[64] The Agency can, if requested, provide safety advice and a review of safety practices at nuclear power stations, through its OSART programme. Up to 1989 thirty-two such reviews had been carried out,[65] including a review of safety provisions at reactors of the Chernobyl type. Nevertheless, if unsafe practices are found, the Agency can only recommend, not enforce changes. Thus, when it inspected Bulgaria's only reactor in 1991 and found it in very poor condition with various safety-related deficiencies, the Agency was able only to urge the Bulgarian government to take immediate measures, but could not compel closure.

One recommendation made in response to the Chernobyl accident was that states should make greater use of the OSART facility, and that IAEA should enhance its capability for providing this service.[66] Even if the Agency cannot ensure compliance, making safety audits of this kind an international norm would provide a means of distinguishing good from bad safety performers, and bring international pressure to bear on the latter.[67] However, the present arrangements for inspection and oversight remain weak and reflect the prevailing reluctance to accept limitations on state sovereignty over nuclear operations within national borders. While IAEA has shown its usefulness in co-ordinating responses to serious accidents and in acting as a forum for consideration of further measures, its role as an international inspectorate remains only a limited guarantee of nuclear safety: the Agency cannot ensure systematic assessment of the safety of nuclear installations, nor, since there is also no reporting procedure, do member states have any basis on which to review and monitor each other's practices. Without such supervision, there is no means of ensuring that agreed minimum standards are met.[68] At its

---

[64] Szasz, *The Law and Practices of the IAEA*, 696.

[65] IAEA, *Annual Report*, 1989. See Barkenbus, 41 International Organization (1987) 484, 486; Cameron, *et al.*, *Nuclear Energy Law*, 184 ff. OSART stands for Operational Safety Review Team.

[66] IAEA, *Summary Report of the Post Accident Review Meeting on the Chernobyl Accident* (Vienna, 1986).

[67] Barkenbus, 41 *International Organization* (1987), 487 ff.; Council of Europe Parliamentary Rec. 1068 (1988) calls for international inspection and monitoring of all nuclear installations. IAEA/GC(XXXII)/Res/459 invites member states to use OSART on a voluntary basis.

[68] Handl, 92 *RGDIP* (1988), 18. cf. the 1989 Basel Convention on the Control of Transboundary Movements of Hazardous Wastes, Articles 13 and 15, *supra*, pp. 339–40, which offers a much better model of international supervision.

General Conference in 1991, however, further resolutions were adopted advocating measures to reinforce international co-operation, stressing in particular the need 'to consider a more thorough and transparent nuclear safety overview process', and a 'harmonised international approach' to all aspects of nuclear safety. Future improvement in the present position may therefore be a possibility.

(2) Other International Bodies

(a) Euratom

The Euratom Treaty was signed by EEC member states in 1957 for the purpose of creating a nuclear common market.[69] It continues to provide the basis of EEC competence in this field.[70] The treaty's objectives include the application of uniform safety standards to protect the health of workers and the general public against radiation.[71] Other provisions are intended to ensure non-diversion of nuclear materials for military purposes.[72] Safety is thus only one aspect of EEC nuclear responsibilities. Unlike the IAEA Statute, however, the Euratom Treaty requires member states to implement safety directives and to ensure that they are enforced.[73]

Since 1959, Community directives have laid down basic radiation standards for health protection.[74] The object of these is to ensure that Community citizens are protected to internationally agreed levels, and that all exposures are adequately regulated and kept as low as reasonably achievable.[75] Radioactivity levels must be controlled by member states and are monitored by the Community through national reporting.[76] Following the Chernobyl accident the Community temporarily restricted the import of affected foodstuffs,[77] and it has now adopted regulations allowing it to specify permitted levels of radiation contamination in food.[78]

---

[69] 1957 Euratom Treaty, Article 2 and Ch. IX; IAEA, *Nuclear Law for a Developing World* (Vienna, 1969), 39 ff.; Cavers, 12 *Vand. LR* (1958), 31 ff.; Grunwald, in Cameron, *et al.*, *Nuclear Energy Law*, 33.

[70] The 1986 Single European Act, Article 25, confers additional environmental competence on the Community, and requires action relating to the environment to be based on 'The principles that preventive action should be taken, that environmental damage should as a priority be rectified at source and that the polluter should pay'. See Glaesner, 6 *YEL* (1986), 283.

[71] Articles 2(b), 30, 31.

[72] Article 2(e) and Ch. VII.

[73] Articles 33, 38.

[74] Directives 76/579, OJ No. L. 187; 79/343, OJ No. L 83; 80/836, OJ No. L 246; 84/467, OJ No. L265; Rehbinder and Stewart, *Environmental Protection Policy* (New York, 1988), 98 ff.; COM (90) 328 proposes amendments to Directive 80/836 in the case of radioactive waste.

[75] 4th Environmental Action Programme (1986) COM (86) 485, 45.

[76] Articles 35, 36 Euratom Treaty. In 1989, the Commission decided to exercise its power of inspection of environmental radioactivity monitoring facilities under Article 35, Euratom, to ensure their proper functioning and efficiency.

[77] Council Regs. 1707/86 and 3955/87.

[78] Council Reg. 3954/87.

At present these are the only aspects of nuclear health and safety covered by Community Law. Due to opposition from some states, there are no rules setting standards for design, construction, and operation of nuclear installations, or for radioactive emissions into air or water. The Community's 'Seveso' directive, which requires that adequate measures be taken to prevent the risk of major accidents at chemical plants or industrial enterprises, does not apply to nuclear installations and processing facilities.[79]

Faced with a reluctance on the part of some member states to allow the Community to regulate nuclear power more comprehensively, the main protection against nuclear risks which Community law and the Euratom treaty offer other states is the right of the Community to be consulted, or notified in certain circumstances. Article 34 of the treaty obliges states to consult the Commission when they propose to conduct particularly dangerous nuclear experiments in their territories, and to obtain its consent if these are liable to affect other member states. This is stronger than the consultation requirements of customary international law considered below because it gives the Commission a power of veto, and suggests that such experiments will otherwise be unlawful.[80]

Article 37 also requires notification to be given to the Commission when radioactive substances are to be discharged which may contaminate other states, for example by disposal at sea or into rivers. In this case the Commission may only comment on the proposal. Neither article requires that other states be consulted at any stage. In that respect both are weaker than customary requirements. Finally, Community law requires nuclear states to give urgent notice to their neighbours of any accident which involves exposure of the population to radiation and to give information on how to minimize the consequences of the accident or of measures taken to deal with it.[81]

Euratom has the clear advantage over the IAEA that it can give legal force to its safety measures and it benefits from the wider and more explicit consultation requirements in cases of transboundary risk. But the safety measures it has adopted are limited in scope and some of those referred to above were only adopted belatedly in response to the Chernobyl accident, which revealed little co-ordination or agreement among member states. Save for its right of access to radioactivity monitoring facilities under Article 35, the Community has no powers of independent inspection and both the Euratom Treaty and Community law fall well short of creating an obligation for

[79] Directive 82/501, OJ No. L 230, Article 2(1); Rehbinder and Stewart, *Environmental Protection Policy*, 97 ff.; Cameron, *et al.*, *Nuclear Energy Law*, 40 ff.

[80] cf. *infra*, pp. 361–4.

[81] Council Directive 80/836, OJ No. L246 (1980), Article 45(5); Council Directive 87/600. See generally, Cameron, *et al.*, *Nuclear Energy Law*, 40 ff. In ECJ Case 187/87 (1988), *Land Sarre* v. *Minister for Industry, Posts and Telecommunictions*, 1 *CMLR* (1989), 529, the Advocate General determined that Article 37 required notification to be given before *authorization* of any discharge.

member states to submit nuclear installations to independent environmental or safety assessment by the Community.

The Commission does have power to propose further health and safety measures under the Euratom Treaty, covering the possible application of emission standards to nuclear installations, the harmonization of safety criteria, the transport of dangerous materials, and the management of radioactive waste, and it has reviewed the adequacy of the policy of risk prevention through consultation and notification.[82] At present, however, the Euratom Treaty has proved little more effective than the IAEA Statute as a basis for regulating nuclear environmental risks, despite its apparent advantages. It is not a good advertisement for the performance of the European Community in environmental matters.

(b) OECD

OECD has been involved in nuclear safety matters through its Nuclear Energy Agency.[83] The aims of this organization are similar to those of IAEA, without its safeguards role. They include encouraging the adoption of common standards for national nuclear legislation dealing with public health and the prevention of accidents.[84] Standards on such matters as radiation protection and waste management have been developed in collaboration with IAEA and other bodies, but once again there is no power to compel compliance. OECD has also been responsible for initiating a convention on third-party liability, and a multilateral consultation procedure for sea dumping of radioactive waste.[85] The main achievements of the NEA appear to lie in the dissemination of information among states and the harmonization of national policies on a basis of consensus.[86]

(c) ILO

ILO has sponsored a widely supported convention on protecting workers against radiation and it issues various non-binding recommendations on the subject.[87]

[82] EC 20th General Report of the Commission, 1986, paras. 759–62; 21st Report, 1987, para. 692; 4th Environmental Action Programme, loc. cit, supra, n. 75.

[83] See Strohl, in IAEA, Licensing and Regulatory Control of Nuclear Installations (Vienna, 1975), 135; OECD Nuclear Legislation; Cameron, et al., Nuclear Energy Law, 6 ff.; Reyners, 32 European Yearbook (1984), 1.

[84] ENEA Statute, Article 1. Radiation protection norms were issued in 1962, 1968, and 1981.

[85] 1960 Convention on Third Party Liability in the Field of Nuclear Energy, infra, p. 371 ff.; 1977 Multilateral Consultation and Surveillance Mechanism for Sea Dumping of Radioactive Waste, supra, pp. 323–5.

[86] Cameron, et al., Nuclear Energy Law, 7 f.

[87] ILO Convention No. 115, Geneva, 1960. For the work of ILO, WHO, and the International Committee on Radiological Protection, see OECD, Nuclear Legislation, 11 ff. The Inter-American Nuclear Energy Commission and the CMEA are reviewed in IAEA, Nuclear Law for a Developing World (Vienna, 1969).

(3) The Significance of International Regulation

International regulation of the safety of nuclear installations and their potential environmental impact is a weak precedent for the control of other ultrahazardous transboundary environmental risks. It gives minimal assurance of common standards, offers limited international inspection and oversight, and leaves governments largely unfettered discretion to determine their own balance of safety measures and economic interest. Moreover it relies heavily on voluntary compliance. This contrasts sharply with the growing strength of international regulation of other forms of pollution, and fails to match the seriousness of the potential transboundary damage nuclear accidents may cause. As a result, principles of state responsibility or civil liability for nuclear damage remain of greater importance in this context than the emergent principle of international regulation. These principles are supplemented by a growing body of state practice concerning consultation, notification, and assistance in cases of transboundary risk or emergency. It is on these aspects of international co-operation that the burden of protection from nuclear risks presently rests.

3. THE CONTROL OF NUCLEAR RISKS

(1) International Obligations

Despite the limited legal content of IAEA standards, and the absence of any treaty commitment to control the environmental risks of nuclear power, there is ample evidence that states do recognize the existence of an obligation to minimize nuclear risks and to prevent injury to other states, or radioactive pollution of the global environment.[88] Nuclear powered merchant ships[89] and satellites[90] must comply with internationally agreed standards of safety and

---

[88] IAEA/GC(SPL.1)Res./1 (1989); Boyle, 60 *BYIL* (1989), 269 ff.; Kirgis, 66 *AJIL* (1972), 290. In the dispute over nuclear testing in the Pacific, France accepted 'its duty to ensure that every condition was met and every precaution taken to prevent injury to the population and the fauna and flora of the world' (note to New Zealand of 19 Feb. 1973, in *French Nuclear Testing in the Pacific*).

[89] 1974 Safety of Life at Sea Convention, Annex, ch. 8 and Attachment 3. See Haselgrove, in Euratom, *Legal and Administrative Problems of Protection in the Peaceful Uses of Atomic Energy* (Brussels, 1971), 567; Berman and Hydeman, ibid. 586; Forte, in Cusine and Grant (eds.), *The Impact of Marine Pollution* (London, 1980), 247; Boulanger, in IAEA, *Experience and Trends in Nuclear Law* (Vienna, 1972), 115; Strohl, ibid. 121. Boulanger, ibid. 125, reviews bilateral agreements relating to port visits by the *N.S. Otto Hahn* and the *N.S. Savannah*.

[90] Committee on the Peaceful Uses of Outer Space, *Report of the Legal Sub-Committee*, 28th Session, UN Doc. A/AC.105/430, Annex III; 1967 Treaty on Principles Governing the Activities of States in the Exploration and Use of Outer Space, 1972 Convention on International Liability for Damage Caused by Space Objects. See *infra*. Ch. 10.

radiation protection, and the same principle is accepted for the transboundary transport of radioactive substances.[91] Only the military uses of nuclear power fall outside these rules, which show that in contrast to their practice concerning nuclear power plants, states are willing to accept obligatory standards of international regulation for nuclear risks when these occur in common spaces. Thus the problem of defining the content of an obligation of due diligence, posed by the uncertain legal status of IAEA standards, is confined mainly to the operation of nuclear power stations within national borders.

Moreover, as we saw in Chapter 8, the dumping of radioactive waste at sea, or its discharge into the marine environment through land-based or airborne sources is largely prohibited, and in so far as it is permitted on the high seas, dumping must comply with international regulations and the requirements of relevant treaty regimes.[92] Further restrictions on radioactive waste disposal exist in the Antarctic,[93] in the South and South-East Pacific,[94] and in Africa.[95] It was argued in Chapter 3 that what constitutes 'pollution' varies according to context, so these precedents are particularly important in showing that the emission of radioactive substances into the environment of common spaces is presumed to constitute prohibited pollution irrespective of any threshold of material injury or interference with amenities or resources.[96] The only possible exception is that below a certain level of radioactivity some proof of harm may be needed.[97]

With regard to nuclear explosions the same conclusion is indicated by the 1963 Nuclear Test Ban Treaty.[98] This treaty prohibits weapons test explosions in the atmosphere, outer space, at sea, in Antarctica, or in any circumstances where radioactive debris spreads beyond the territory of the testing state. Its effect is that tests must be conducted underground and cause no escape of pollution. Not all nuclear powers are parties to this treaty,

---

[91] 1989 Basel Convention on the Control of Transboundary Movements of Hazardous Wastes, *supra*, p. 332 ff.; IAEA Draft Code of Practice on the International Transboundary Movement of Radioactive Waste, 1990, ibid.; 1980 Convention on the Physical Protection of Nuclear Material. This convention deals only with protection against theft, robbery, or unlawful taking, however.

[92] See *supra*, p. 311, n. 36, pp. 323–4.

[93] 1959 Antarctic Treaty, Article 5; Recommendation VIII-12, 8th Antarctic Treaty Consultative Meeting, 1975.

[94] 1986 Noumea Convention for the Protection of the Natural Resources and Environment of the South Pacific, Article II; 1989 Protocol for the Protection of the South East Pacific Against Radioactive Pollution.

[95] 1991 Bamako Convention, *supra*, pp. 320 ff. See also IAEA/GC(XXXII)/Res./490, which condemns all nuclear waste dumping that endangers the environment or public health.

[96] Kirgis, 66 *AJIL* (1972), and *supra*, pp. 98–102.

[97] e.g. in the case of land-based discharges of low-level radioactive waste, *supra*, p. 311.

[98] *Supra*, n. 12. The treaty had 116 parties in 1988. See also the Tlateloco Treaty, *supra*, n. 9. The 1974 US–USSR Treaty on the Limitation of Underground Nuclear Weapons Tests, and the 1976 US–USSR Treaty on Underground Nuclear Explosions for Peaceful Purposes were ratified in 1990.

however,[99] and its status in customary law has been disputed. In the *Nuclear Tests* case,[100] the ICJ declined to decide whether atmospheric tests carried out by France violated customary international law, but it did hold that France had by its public statements unilaterally committed itself to conduct no more tests of this kind.[101] Subsequent tests have in practice complied with the 1963 Treaty. Regional agreements also prohibit all nuclear weapons testing in the territory of South Pacific nations and in Latin America.[102]

Given the weight of international opposition expressed in these agreements to all forms of deliberate radioactive pollution of common spaces, and the tacit compliance of non-parties with the 1963 Treaty since 1980, the case for a prohibition of nuclear testing founded on customary law, but excluding underground tests, is now strong.[103] This conclusion does not extend beyond deliberate nuclear tests or peaceful explosions, however. It does not mean that accidental radioactive explosions, such as the Chernobyl reactor accident, *per se* represent a violation of international law without showing a failure of due diligence,[104] nor does it imply that the actual use of nuclear weapons is forbidden by international law. Although some writers argue that this is the case, their views are based on the indiscriminate character of nuclear weapons and other humanitarian considerations.[105] Explicit treaty limitations on the conduct of military operations place some constraints on methods of warfare which cause widespread, long-term, and severe damage to the natural environment, but the use of nuclear weapons is prohibited entirely only in Latin

---

[99] France and China are the main nuclear states to remain outside the treaty; Israel, Pakistan, South Africa, and India are also non-parties.

[100] *Supra* n. 15. On the question whether atmospheric testing is illegal, cf. Judges Gros, *ICJ Rep.*, 1974, at 279 ff.; Petren at 305 ff.; de Castro at 389 ff.; Barwick at 427 ff. Note also Judge Barwick's point that 'there is a radical distinction to be made between claims that violation of territorial and decisional sovereignty by the intrusion and deposition of radioactive nuclides . . . is unlawful according to international law, and the claim that the testing of nuclear weapons has become unlawful, according to customary law . . .', at 248. See also Pleadings (1978), i. 500 ff.; ii. 264 ff.

[101] On the legal force of unilateral undertakings in international law, see *Nuclear Tests Cases*, *ICJ Rep.* (1974), 253; *Paramilitary Activities in Nicaragua Case*, *ICJ Rep.* (1986), 14. China announced in 1986 that it did not intend to conduct further atmospheric tests. Its last atmospheric test took place in 1980. See SIPRI, *Yearbook* (Oxford, 1987), 45–52.

[102] South Pacific Nuclear Free Zone Treaty, *supra*, n. 17; Tlateloco Treaty, *supra*, n. 9. The Tlateloco Treaty does permit the use of nuclear energy, including nuclear explosions, for peaceful purposes. The South Pacific Treaty prohibits the possession, acquisition, control, or manufacture of 'any nuclear explosive device'.

[103] Lammers, *Pollution of International Watercourses* (Dordrecht, 1984), 319–27; Kirgis, 66 *AJIL* (1972), 295 f., but cf. Margolis, 64 *Yale LJ* (1955) and McDougal and Schlei, ibid., who support only a standard of reasonableness but disagree about its implications for the permissibility of nuclear tests. cf. Singh and McWhinney, *Nuclear Weapons and Contemporary International Law* (2nd edn., Dordrecht, 1989), 230–3, who conclude that the number of adherents indicates that the 1963 Treaty is now accepted as customary law.

[104] Boyle, 60 *BYIL* (1989), 272–4, 290–6; id., in Butler (ed.), *Perestroika and International Law* (Dordrecht, 1990), 203. See generally *supra*, Ch. 3.

[105] See generally Pogany (ed.), *Nuclear Weapons and International Law* (Aldershot, 1987).

America and the Pacific.[106] The 1977 Additional Protocol also prohibits attacks on nuclear power stations not used in support of military operations.[107]

As we saw in Chapter 3, the *Nuclear Tests* cases[108] raised the question whether the deposit of radioactive particles on the territory of another state, or on the high seas, constitutes serious harm or an interference with high seas freedoms. The peculiar difficulty which radioactive fallout poses is that injury may not be immediate or apparent, and the claimants in the *Nuclear Tests* Cases did not allege that they had suffered actual harm, but based the main part of their claim on a violation of their territorial sovereignty.[109] The development of international standards of radiation exposure, based on evidence of long-term effects, provides an obvious method for establishing an agreed threshold of harm which takes account of the absence of immediate injury.[110] Inconsistent practices among those affected were revealed by the Chernobyl accident, and the work of the ICRP, IAEA, WHO, and FAO has in their respective fields subsequently concentrated on elaborating common guidelines.[111] The EEC has also issued new regulations.[112] Thus it is now easier than it was in 1974 to determine when serious radiation injury or harm has occurred, and this should no longer constitute an obstacle to international claims.

With remarkable consistency, the precedents considered here point to the conclusion that Principle 21 of the Stockholm Declaration, and other authoritative statements of the obligation to control sources of environmental harm are applicable to nuclear risks.[113] States do have an international responsibility based in customary law for the safe conduct of their nuclear activities, notwithstanding that they make take place entirely within their own borders.

(2) Nuclear Installations: Notification and Consultation

The evidence of bilateral agreements among European states confirms that principles of notification and consultation intended to minimize transboundary risks have been applied to planned nuclear installations, although most of

---

[106] 1977 Additional Protocol 1 to the Geneva Red Cross Conventions, Articles 35, 55; 1985 South Pacific Nuclear Free Zone Treaty, *supra*, n. 17; 1967 Tlateloco Treaty, *supra*, n. 9.

[107] 1977 Additional Protocol I, ibid. Article 56. See also the condemnation of Israel's attack on an Iraqi nuclear reactor: UN Security Council, Resolution 487 (1981); IAEA Board of Governors, Resolution S/14532 (1981), in 20 *ILM* (1981), 963, but note the US attack on Iraqi nuclear facilities during the 1991 Kuwait conflict.

[108] *Supra*, n. 15.

[109] Handl, 69 *AJIL* (1975), 50, who concludes that material injury is necessary.

[110] Handl, 92 *RGDIP* (1988), 55; Sands, *Chernobyl*, 15.

[111] Sands, *Chernobyl*, 16 ff., gives full details and see also *supra*, n. 38.

[112] *Supra*, nn. 74 and 78.

[113] *Supra*, Ch. 4, but cf. Sands, *The International Law of Liability for Transboundary Nuclear Pollution* (London, 1989) who views this conclusion as arguable, but not clearly accepted.

these treaties are limited to installations within 30 km. of an international border.[114] All require a full exchange of information on the proposed installation, so that other states may review the decision-making process and data and offer appropriate comments on safety and health protection. In most cases permanent commissions are established to consider matters of joint interest affecting public health,[115] but these bodies have no power to limit the parties' freedom of action. None of the treaties gives neighbouring states a veto, nor suggests that the siting of nuclear installations near borders is impermissible or subject to any equitable balance of interests.[116]

In contrast, port visits by nuclear powered vessels have entailed the prior negotiation of bilateral agreements and are subject to the consent of the port state.[117] Where such vessels are merely in transit through the territorial sea of another state, however, the principle of innocent passage applies, as for all vessels, and no obligation of prior notice or consent appears to arise. Such ships may be required to carry documents and observe special precautionary measures established by the SOLAS Convention, however.[118]

Lastly, both the use of nuclear power sources in outer space, and the conduct of nuclear explosions for peaceful purposes appear to require prior notification to the relevant international organization, and must be preceded by a safety assessment. Information on radioactive fall-out must be communicated, and in the case of unplanned satellite re-entry, sub-orbital states are to be consulted.[119]

These precedents all point first, to the conclusion that states are not debarred by international law from acquiring and using nuclear technology simply because it poses a risk of injury to other states or to the environment,

[114] e.g. 1980 Agreement between Spain and Portugal on Co-operation in Matters Affecting the Safety of Nuclear Installations in the Vicinity of the Frontier, Ruster and Simma, xxvii. 420; 1977 Netherlands–FRG Memorandum on Exchange of Information and Consultation in Border Areas, ibid. 275; 1977 Denmark–FRG Agreement Regulating the Exchange of Information on the Construction of Nuclear Installations along the Border, 17 *ILM* (1978), 274.

[115] e.g. 1966 Belgium–France Convention on Radiological Protection with regard to the Installations of the Ardennes Nuclear Power Station, 988 *UNTS* 288; 1982 Switzerland–FRG Agreement on Mutual Information on Construction and Operation of Nuclear Installations in Border Areas, II *Bundesgesetzblatt* (1983), 734, and agreements listed *supra*, at n. 114 between Spain–Portugal and Netherlands–FRG.

[116] Cameron, *et al.*, *Nuclear Energy Law*, 73 ff.; but cf. Handl, 7 *ELQ* (1978), 1, who argues that affected states are entitled to an equitable solution, i.e. more than consultation and negotiation, but less than a veto. See also *infra* n. 120.

[117] Boulanger, in IAEA, *Experience and Trends*, 125; Haselgrove, ibid. In part the insistence on prior agreement reflects the failure of nuclear ship operators to ratify the 1962 Brussels Convention on the Liability of Operators of Nuclear Ships, *infra*, pp. 371 ff.

[118] 1982 UNCLOS, Articles 17–19, 21–4. See *supra*, Ch. 7, and cf. also the transport of hazardous waste, *supra*, p. 337. Article 5 of the 1985 South Pacific Nuclear Free Zone Treaty, *supra*, n. 17, preserves the rights of innocent passage, archipelagic sea lanes passage, and transit passage for nuclear-armed ships in the South Pacific NFZ.

[119] Committee on Peaceful Uses of Outer Space; Tlateloco Treaty, Article 18, *supra*, n. 9, but cf. Article 34, Euratom Treaty, *supra*, n. 80.

nor are they precluded from siting nuclear installations near borders.[120] Subject only to restraints implied by compliance with the required standards of diligent control and procedural obligations considered above, 'each state is free to act within the limits of its sovereignty',[121] and to act on its own assessment of the risk.

Secondly, leaving aside the exceptional rules applied to nuclear ships, the evidence of state practice examined here is consistent with the view that states must notify and consult their neighbours in cases of serious or appreciable transboundary risk, with a view to ensuring reasonable regard for the rights and legitimate interests of other states.[122] As we saw in Chapter 3, the application of this principle to transboundary risks such as nuclear installations represents a logical extension of the *Lac Lanoux* case.[123] Although in its work on 'International Liability', the ILC requires the negotiation in these cases of an equitable balance of interests,[124] state practice continues to favour the more limited principle indicated here.[125]

The narrowness of this principle as it has been applied in state practice should be observed, however, particularly in its application to nuclear power. The Chernobyl reactor was not in a border area, and states have not consulted in such cases, save, as we shall see, in cases of emergency.[126] In contrast, it is significant that the ILC's articles attempt to extend the principle of consultation to all activities creating appreciable risk wherever located.[127] Moreover, it is questionable whether for nuclear installations transboundary consultation is enough to ensure that neighbouring states and the environment are adequately protected from unilaterally determined nuclear risks. What is lacking in such cases is a principle comparable to that which applies in certain

---

[120] Lenaerts, in Cameron, *et al.*, *Nuclear Energy Law*, 73 ff.; Reuter, 103 *Recueil des cours* (1961), 592. But cf. Handl, 7 *ELQ* (1978), 35, who argues that for activities carrying a risk of catastrophic effects, 'barring a special relationship between risk exposed states such as reciprocity of risk creation, or a sharing of benefits to be derived from the proposed activity, such an activity should be considered impermissible', and Kirgis, 66 *AJIL* (1972), 294, who argues for a reasonableness test.

[121] *ICJ Rep.* (1973), 131, per Judge Ignacio Pinto, and see ibid. 135; *ICJ Rep.* (1974), 253 and 457. Note that the court's 1973 decisions ordered France by way of interim measures to 'avoid nuclear tests causing the deposit of radioactive fallout' on the plaintiffs' territory. cf. also New Zealand's reply to the French note regarding nuclear tests, cited, *supra*, n. 88: 'an activity that is inherently harmful is not made acceptable even by the most stringent precautionary measures', and see ILC, Draft Articles on International Liability for Injurious Consequences Arising Out of Acts Not Prohibited by International Law, UN Doc. A/CN.4/428 (1990).

[122] Lenaerts, in Cameron, *et al.*, *Nuclear Energy Law*, 73–8; cf. Handl, 7 *ELQ* (1978), however.

[123] See *supra*, pp. 106–7.

[124] II *Yearbook ILC* (1983), pt. 1, 223, 'Schematic Outline'; Barboza, 2nd Report, II *Yearbook ILC* (1986), pt. 1, 152 ff., id., 5th Report (1989) UN Doc. A/CN.4/428, Article 17, and see Boyle, 60 *BYIL* (1989), 286.

[125] See *supra*, pp. 104–7.

[126] See *infra*, pp. 364–7.

[127] Draft Article 1, UN Doc. A/CN.4/L.438 (1989). See also 1991 ECE Convention of Environmental Impact Assessment in a Transboundary Context, which applies to nuclear power stations and reactors, *supra*, Ch. 3.

cases of dumping at sea, requiring prior consultation and approval of the relevant international organization.[128] This solution seems preferable to one making nuclear activities dependent on the agreement of neighbouring states, but avoids the excessive unilateralism of the present law.

(3) Co-operatation and Assistance in Cases of Nuclear Emergency
(a) Notification

The existence of a general obligation to notify other states and co-operate in cases where they are at risk from nuclear accidents or incidents is confirmed both by regional practice in Western Europe, and by international conventions. Most of the European treaties contain provisions for the timely supply of information in cases of emergency and require radioactivity monitoring systems to be established to alert governments of the danger.[129] A small number also require co-operation in response to such an emergency. Following the Chernobyl accident, the Soviet Union was criticized for failing to give adequate and timely information to other states likely to be affected by the disaster. Implicit in this criticism was a belief that such notification should reasonably be expected.[130] In addition to the practice of a growing number of states supporting such an obligation, IAEA had developed guidelines on reporting of incidents and information exchange in 1985,[131] but these were non-binding.

[128] See Oslo Commission Decision 89/1, *supra*, pp. 328–9.

[129] Agreement between Spain and Portugal, *supra*, n. 114; Belgium–France Convention, *supra*, n. 115; 1979 Agreement between France and Switzerland Concerning Exchange of Information in Case of Accidents, *Ruster and Simma*, xxvii. 382; 1983, UK–France Exchange of Notes Concerning Exchanges of Information, 60 *UKTS*, Cmnd. 9041; 1978 Agreement between Switzerland and FRG Concerning Radiological Disaster Relief, *Ruster and Simma*, xxvii. 337; 1981 Agreement between France–FRG on Mutual Information in the event of Radiological Incidents, I *Bundesgesetzblatt*, 885; 1983 Agreement between France and Luxemburg on Exchange of Information in Case of Radiological Emergencies, 34 *NLB* (1984), 42. A further series of such agreements have been prompted by the Chernobyl accident: 1987 Agreement between Belgium and the Netherlands on Co-operation in Nuclear Safety, 41 *NLB* (1988), 42; 1987 Norway–Sweden Agreement on Exchange of Information and Early Notification Relating to Nuclear Facilities, 17 *EPL* (1987), 41; 1987 UK–Norway Agreement on Early Notification, Cmnd. 371; 1987 Finland–USSR Agreement on Early Notification of a Nuclear Accident, 1987, 39 *NLB*, 4; 1987 FRG–GDR Radiation Protection Agreement, 1987, 40 *NLB*, 44; 1987 Brazil–Argentina Agreement on Early Notification and Mutual Assistance, 39 *NLB*, 36; 1986 Denmark–Sweden Agreement on Exchange of Information and Early Notification, ibid. 35; 1987 Denmark–Poland Agreement on Exchange of Information, 41 *NLB* (1988), 49, and similar agreements with the FRG, USSR, UK, and Finland. These are all intended to give effect to the provisions of the 1986 IAEA Notification Convention. See also EEC Council Directive 87/600, considered above, at n. 81, and on the application of EEC Law generally, see Cameron, *et al.*, *Nuclear Energy Law*, 49 ff.

[130] Group of Seven, Statement on the Implications of the Chernobyl Nuclear Accident, 25 *ILM* (1986), 1005; IAEA General Conference, Special Session, 1986, IAEA GC (SPL.1)/Res./1.

[131] IAEA/INFCIRC/321, Guidelines on Reportable Events, 1985.

One result of Chernobyl was the opening for signature of a Convention on Early Notification of Nuclear Accidents.[132] This imposes on parties a duty to notify other states likely to be affected by transboundary releases of 'radiological safety significance'. Information on the occurrence and on means of minimizing its radiological consequences must be supplied, to enable other states to take all possible precautionary measures. The Convention specifies in detail what information is to be given, and requires states to respond promptly to requests for further relevant information. It is less clear, however, at what point a release acquires radiological safety significance; this provision deliberately avoids objective definition, and thus leaves substantial discretion to states where incidents occur. The effectiveness of the Convention is also dependent on states possessing a basic radiological monitoring and assessment capability. Unlike bilateral treaties in Europe, the Convention does not require states to acquire this capability; where it is lacking, it is difficult to see how they will be able to respond effectively.[133]

Due to superpower opposition, the Convention does not cover nuclear accidents involving military facilities, such as nuclear submarines, but the Soviet Union gave notice when two such vessels ran into difficulty, and the United Kingdom has undertaken to do so.[134] Since the Convention applies only to 'transboundary releases', it would seem that accidents whose consequences do not extend beyond national borders, or which occur wholly on the high seas are also excluded.[135]

A number of states, including the Soviet Union and the United Kingdom, declared that they would observe the Convention pending ratification, and several agreements apply its provisions bilaterally.[136] Although the Convention is open to criticism for the apparent looseness of its terminology, and the range of excluded occurrences, it does now seem to justify the conclusion that the principle of timely notification of nuclear accidents likely to affect other states is a customary obligation. States also support the same principle int the case of accidents affecting nuclear-powered merchant ships or spacecraft.[137]

(b) Assistance

Assistance in cases of nuclear emergency is also the subject of an IAEA Convention, which allows states to call for international help to protect 'life,

---

[132] See generally Cameron, *et al.*, *Nuclear Energy Law*, 19 ff.; Adede, *The IAEA Notification and Assistance Conventions* (Dordrecht, 1987); Handl, 92 *RGDIP* (1988), 24 ff.

[133] Rosen, *IAEA Bulletin* (1987), 34 f.

[134] 25 *ILM* (1986), 1369; the UK declaration specifically includes voluntary notification of military accidents; others refer to 'all' or 'any' accidents.

[135] Cameron, *et al.*, *Nuclear Energy Law*, 24.

[136] *Supra*, n. 129.

[137] SOLAS Convention, *supra*, n. 89, regulation 12; Committee on Peaceful Uses of Outer Space, Article 5, *supra*, n. 90.

property and the environment' from the effects of radioactive releases.[138] IAEA is given a co-ordinating role, and an obligation to respond to a request by making available appropriate resources. No explicit obligation to render assistance is placed on other states, however, even where an installation within their territory is the cause of harm, nor is there any provision for joint contingency planning comparable to that found in many maritime treaties.

Thus, in general, the Convention facilitates, but does not require a response to, nuclear accidents or emergencies. Its main achievement is to give assisting states and their personnel immunity from legal proceedings brought by the requesting state, and an indemnity for proceedings brought by others. These provisions are open to reservation, however.[139]

Like the small number of bilateral treaties which provide in more general terms for emergency assistance,[140] the IAEA Convention leaves responsibility for making the request and taking or directing appropriate action in its territory with the state which needs help.[141] It creates no duty either to seek assistance, or to control the emergency. A failure to do so may of course incur state responsibility if it results in harm to others, under general principles discussed below. But unlike maritime casualties, where states also have a recognized right of intervention or self-help to protect their own coasts,[142] there is no generally accepted basis in international law for intervention by neighbouring states seeking to avert the consequences of a nuclear catastrophe, such as Chernobyl. Any attempt to take unilateral preventive action within another state, or to render unrequested assistance in these circumstances would in principle appear to be a violation of the source state's sovereignty.[143] At most, necessity might be pleaded in defence of any state undertaking such intervention in circumstances of grave and imminent peril.[144] By leaving the requesting state the decisive role, the IAEA Conven-

---

[138] 1986 Convention on Assistance in the Case of a Nuclear Accident or Radiological Emergency; see also IAEA/INFCIRC/310, Guidelines for Mutual Emergency Assistance Arrangements. Assistance under the Convention was given to Brazil in 1987. See generally Cameron, *et al., Nuclear Energy Law*, 26 ff.; Adede, *The IAEA Notification and Assistance Conventions*.

[139] Articles 8 and 10. Four states have excluded Article 8; two have excluded Article 10.

[140] e.g. 1963 Nordic Mutual Emergency Assistance Agreement in Connection with Radiation Accidents, 525 *UNTS* 76; 1966 Belgium–France Convention, *supra*, n. 115; 1981 Belgium–France Agreement on Mutual Assistance in the Event of Catastrophic and Serious Accident, 34 *NLB* (1984), 42; 1977 France–FRG Agreement on Mutual Assistance in the Event of Catastrophic and Grave Disasters, II *Bundesgesetzblatt* (1980), 33; 1980 FRG–Belgium Agreement on Mutual Emergency Assistance, ibid. (1982), 1006.

[141] Article 3.

[142] 1969 Convention on Intervention in Case of Maritime Casualties; 1982 UNCLOS, Article 221; *supra*, Ch. 7.

[143] cf. the Security Council's condemnation of Israel's attack on an Iraqi Nuclear reactor: UNSC Res. 487 (1981); see also IAEA Board of Governors Resolution S/14532, 20 *ILM* (1981), 963; *Corfu Channel* Case, *ICJ Rep.* (1949), 32–6; *Case Concerning Diplomatic and Consular Staff in Tehran* Case *ICJ Rep.* (1980), 43, but see Bilder, 14 *Vand JTL* (1981).

[144] ILC, Draft Articles on State Responsibility, pt. 1, Article 33, II *Yearbook ILC* (1980), 30.

tion does nothing to disturb this position. Assistance, as provided for in the instruments referred to here is thus sharply different from intervention or self-protection. In short, it is not obligatory, it need not be sought, and it cannot be given without consent.

4. STATE RESPONSIBILITY FOR NUCLEAR DAMAGE AND ENVIRONMENTAL HARM

(1) Strict or Absolute Responsibility

The ultrahazardous character of nuclear installations, in the sense that damage caused by accidents may be widespread, serious, and long-lasting, is, for some writers, the basis for asserting that state responsibility in such cases will be strict or absolute.[145] That position, and its application to nuclear energy, is the major focus of attention in this section, although it is questionable whether the ultra-hazardous category is wide enough to cover all nuclear activities, including those, such as discharge of radioactive waste into the sea, whose effects are cumulatively harmful rather than immediately catastrophic.[146]

The main argument advanced by writers rests on inferences about the responsibility of states drawn from the use of strict liability as a general principle in national legal systems and civil liability treaties concerned with nuclear accidents.[147] The tendency of the treaties, however, is to avoid direct implication of the source state in responsibility for damage and to emphasize the liability in national law of the operator or company which caused the damage.[148] The possibility of state responsibility is not precluded, but the scheme of these civil liability treaties involves states only as guarantors of the operators' strict liability, or in providing additional compensation funds. Moreover, the burden of this residual responsibility is either spread equitably across a group of nuclear states, or left in part to lie where it falls through limitation of liability. In neither case does the polluting state bear responsibility for the whole loss.[149] The extent of its liability is further limited by the narrow definition of nuclear damage.[150]

[145] Jenks, 117 Recueil des cours (1966), 105; Smith, State Responsibility and the Marine Environment (Oxford, 1987), 112–15; Handl, 16 NYIL (1985), 68 ff.; id., 74 AJIL (1980), 525; Hardy, 36 BYIL (1960), 237; Goldie, 16 NYIL (1985), 204 ff.; contra, Brownlie, Principles of International Law (4th edn., Oxford, 1990), 475, and see supra, Ch. 4.

[146] Jenks, 117 Recueil des cours (1966), 122, views Trail Smelter as a case of liability for ultra-hazardous operations. This is much broader than most interpretations. The ILC's draft articles on International Liability now apply to activities with a low probability of disastrous injury and to those with a high probability of minor injury: supra, n. 125.

[147] See esp. Goldie, 14 ICLQ (1965), 1189, and supra, pp. 143–9.

[148] See infra, pp. 371 ff.

[149] Ibid., and cf. the 1972 Convention on International Liability for Damage Caused by Space Objects, supra, n. 90.

[150] See infra, pp. 382–3.

These factors make the nuclear liability Conventions weak precedents for any particular theory or standard of state responsibility for harm; they seem inconsistent with the view that states are absolutely or strictly responsible in international law for damage emanating from their territory even in cases of ultra-hazardous activities.[151] As with national laws employing standards of strict or absolute liability contingent on compulsory insurance and limitation of liability, it is difficult to treat complex schemes of loss distribution as indicating a standard of responsibility for states themselves in the less highly developed circumstances of international law.

A second argument concerning the standard of liability is based, as we saw in Chapter 4, on the concept of objective responsibility for breach of obligation. When applied to accidental injury emanating from nuclear installations, this concept focuses on the conduct of the state in failing to meet its obligation of diligent control, and is distinguishable from fault only in eliminating subjective elements of intention or recklessness. Responsibility in such cases is neither strict nor absolute since it cannot be established by proof of damage alone. But where nuclear damage is the result of some internationally prohibited activity, such as the dumping of radioactive waste at sea, or atmospheric nuclear tests, objective responsibility results not from a failure of due diligence, but simply from the harm caused in deliberate violation of international law. This is much closer to a standard of strict or absolute responsibility, and offers a sounder basis for such concepts than any inferences from national law or civil liability conventions.[152] While the evidence of state practice reviewed below does not unequivocally support this analysis, some of the claims in question predate the present consensus on prohibition of deliberate radioactive pollution, and cannot be taken as a wholly reliable guide to the present law.

(2) State Claims

State claims or settlements involving damage caused by nuclear activities provide little support for any one standard of responsibility. Rather, they demonstrate the lack of international consensus on this point. In 1955 the United States paid compensation to Japanese fishermen injured by one of its nuclear tests, but disclaimed any admission of legal responsibility.[153] Japan

---

[151] Miatello, in Spinedi and Simma (eds.), *UN Codification of State Responsibility* (New York, 1987), 306 ff.; Handl, 92 *RGDIP* (1988), 35 ff. *Contra*, Smith, *State Responsibility*, 114 ff., and Kelson, 13 *Harv. ILJ* (1972), 197. Poor ratification of all but the Paris Convention is another factor lessening the significance of these conventions: see *infra*, pp. 383–5.

[152] On objective responsibility, see Ch. 4. On the prohibition of deliberate pollution, see *supra*, pp. 358–61.

[153] Settlement of Japanese Claims for Personal and Property Damage Resulting fom Nuclear Tests in Marshall Islands (1955) 1 *UST* 1, *TIAS* 3160, 4 Whiteman, *Digest* 553; Margolis, 64 *Yale LJ* (1955), 629; McDougal and Schlei, ibid., 648.

and New Zealand reserved the right in diplomatic protests to hold the United States and France responsible for any loss or damage inflicted by further tests in the Pacific,[154] but made no claims. Canada asserted in 1979 that the standard of absolute responsibility for space objects, including those using nuclear power and causing the deposit of radioactive material, had become a general principle of international law, and it relied on this in a successful claim for compensation from the Soviet Union following the crash of Cosmos 954. But this claim was supported by the 1972 Space Objects Liability Convention, to which both states were party;[155] the very different approach of the nuclear liability conventions undermines the relevance of this precedent in other cases of accidental harm.

Responses to the Chernobyl disaster provide the most telling evidence of state practice so far. This accident caused widespread harm to agricultural produce and livestock in Europe and affected wildlife, in some cases severely.[156] Clean-up costs were incurred and compensation was paid by several governments to their own citizens for produce which was destroyed as a precautionary measure, or which was rendered unusable. Evidence of long-term health risks has yet to emerge, but these could be serious.[157]

Despite this provable loss, no claims were made against the Soviet Union by any affected state, although the possibility was considered by some governments.[158] Uncertainty over the basis for such a claim, reluctance to establish a precedent with possible future implications for states which themselves operate nuclear power plants, and the absence of any appropriate treaty binding on the Soviet Union are the main reasons for this silence.[159] It is also unclear whether liability would extend to damage to the environment, or to the costs of precautionary measures taken by governments. The Soviet Union made no voluntary offer of compensation, and questioned the necessity of precautionary measures taken by its neighbours, maintaining that they suffered little or no damage.[160] The failure to demand, or to offer compensation in this case shows the difficulty of reconciling doctrinal support for any standard of strict or absolute responsibility with the evidence of state practice,

---

[154] 4 Whiteman, *Digest* 585 f.; *Nuclear Tests* Cases, ICJ Pleadings (1978), ii. 22–30; Australian notes on the subject made no reference to compensation, but did assert that the tests should be terminated: ibid. i. 22 ff.

[155] Claim for Damage Caused by Cosmos 954, 18 *ILM* (1979), 902; 1972 Convention on International Liability for Damage Caused by Space Objects, *supra*, n. 90. The USSR denied the applicability of the 1972 Convention to the damage which had occurred.

[156] *Supra*, n. 1.

[157] NRPB, *A Preliminary Assessment of the Chernobyl Reactor Accident on the Population of the European Community* (1987) gives an estimate of 1,000 deaths in the EEC. See also UKAEA, *The Chernobyl Accident and its Consequences* (London, 1987), section 7.

[158] West Germany, Sweden, and the UK reserved their position.

[159] Sands, *Chernobyl*, 27.

[160] Proposed Programme for Establishing an International Regime for the Safe Development of Nuclear Energy, 1986, repr. ibid. 227.

limited as it is. It points to the conclusion that responsibility for a failure of due diligence, that is for causing avoidable loss only, provides a more convincing interpretation of the actual practice of states and the present state of customary law in cases of accidental environmental damage.[161]

(3) Reforming the Law of State Responsibility for Nuclear Injury[162]

The desirability of international agreement on appropriate principles of responsibility for interstate claims concerning nuclear accidents was acknowledged by the Soviet Union following Chernobyl.[163] The ILC's articles on 'International Liability' have attracted attention in IAEA as a possible model for a new treaty based on the strict liability of the source state.[164] These articles limit reparation to an 'equitable' level, however. Another possibility is to rely on a reformed system of civil liability conventions, hoping that these will attract more support from states. But limited liability is also an essential feature of these conventions; unless public funds are made more widely available to support claims, recourse to state responsibility will remain necessary in the more serious accidents if affected states are to be fully compensated.[165] Moreover, civil liability schemes do not apply to military nuclear accidents. The two systems of public and private liability are thus better seen as complementary, not as alternatives. The more convincing proposals for reform incorporate elements from both systems: strict liability applied to the source state, coupled with the standard of full reparation which is at present the main advantage of reliance on state responsibility.[166]

However, it is difficult to conclude that state responsibility at present affords a sufficiently principled basis for the settlement of international claims arising out of accidental nuclear damage. Without further agreement on the conditions and extent of its application, and on how the burden of reparation should be allocated among public and private actors, and between beneficiaries and victims, it is unlikely to supply answers which are either clear or predictable in this context. In 1990 IAEA established a Standing Committee on Liability for Nuclear Damage to consider this problem. A majority of states participating agreed on the need for a comprehensive regime of international liability for nuclear damage to complement the existing civil liability regime.

---

[161] See supra, pp. 141–9, but cf. Handl, 92 RGDIP (1988), 47–55.

[162] See generally pp. 158–60.

[163] USSR Proposed Programme, supra, n. 160.

[164] See IAEA/Gov./INF/509 and Politi, in Francioni and Scovazzi (eds.) International Responsibility for Environmental Harm (Dordrecht, 1991), 473. See also Sands, The International Law for Liability for Transboundary Nuclear Pollution.

[165] See infra, pp. 371 ff.

[166] Handl, 92 RGDIP (1988), 41 ff.; Sands, The International Law of Liability for Transboundary Nuclear Pollution; Juste, in Francioni and Scovazzi, International Responsibility for Environmental Harm, 207; and Boyle, ibid. 363.

Proposals were also made to include military activities and weapons tests, and to prescribe obligations for states to prevent and minimize nuclear damage.[167]

5. CIVIL LIABILITY FOR NUCLEAR DAMAGE

Civil liability proceedings are the preferred method employed by the majority of nuclear states for reallocating the costs of transboundary nuclear accidents. In a few cases, bilateral arrangements simply apply the principle of equal access and non-discrimination to nuclear risks, and a number of national legal systems may also facilitate transboundary proceedings.[168]

But the limited utility of equal access has persuaded most nuclear states to adopt a more sophisticated model. This is offered by four international conventions which create a special regime of civil liability.[169] The Paris Convention of 1960,[170] drafted by the OECD, applies to nuclear incidents within Western European member states. The Vienna Convention of 1963[171] offers a comparable scheme for global participation, while two more treaties deal with nuclear ships[172] and maritime carriage of nuclear materials.[173] Of these only the Paris Convention has attracted significant support among nuclear states.[174]

[167] Standing Committee on Liability for Nuclear Damage, 1st Session, SCNL/1/INF 1 (1990); 2nd Session, SCNL/2/INF 2 (1990).

[168] 1974 Nordic Convention on the Protection of the Environment, Article 1; 1976 Nuclear Liability Rules (US–Canada); 1986 Agreement on Third Party Liability in the Nuclear Field (Switzerland–FRG). Soviet Civil Law allows for strict liability in cases of damage caused by sources of 'heightened danger': see Butler, *Soviet Law* (2nd edn., London, 1988), 192 and Hardy, 36 *BYIL* (1960), 235, but offers no facility for equal access by foreign plaintiffs. On equal access generally, see *supra*, pp. 197–201.

[169] See generally, Miatello, in Spinedi and Simma (eds.), *United Nations Codification of State Responsibility* (New York, 1987), 287; IAEA, *Nuclear Law for a Developing World*, 109–82; Hardy, 36 *BYIL* (1960); Cigoj, 14 *ICLQ* (1965), 809; Reyners, in IAEA, *Licensing and Regulatory Control of Nuclear Installations*, 243; OECD, Ad Hoc Group on Transfrontier Pollution, 20 *NLB* (1977), 50; IAEA, *Experience and Trends in Nuclear Law*, 69 ff.; Arrangio Ruiz, 107 *Recueil des cours* (1962), 575 ff.; Fornassier, 10 *AFDI* (1964), 303; Cameron, *et al.*, *Nuclear Energy Law*.

[170] Amended by 1964 Additional Protocol. See IAEA, *International Conventions on Civil Liability for Nuclear Damage* (Vienna, 1976), 22. See also the 1963 Brussels Convention Supplementary to the Paris Convention. Both Conventions were amended by Protocols adopted 16 Nov. 1982. See Berman and Hydeman, 55 *AJIL* (1961), 966; Arrangio-Ruiz, 107 *Recueil des cours*, 582 ff., and explanatory memorandum, 8 *European Yearbook* (1960), 225.

[171] See IAEA, *Civil Liability for Nuclear Damage, Official Records* (Vienna, 1964).

[172] 1962 Brussels Convention on the Liability of Operators of Nuclear Ships; Hardy, 12 *ICLQ* (1963), 778; Konz, 57 *AJIL* (1963), 100; Szasz, 2 *JMLC* (1970), 541; Colliard, 8 *AFDI* (1962), 41; Cigoj, 14 *ICLQ* (1965). The Convention has 6 parties and is not in force. None of the states which license nuclear ships is a party.

[173] 1971 Brussels Convention Relating to Civil Liability in the Field of Maritime Carriage of Nuclear Material, IAEA, *International Conventions on Civil Liability*, 55; Strohl, in IAEA, *Experience and Trends in Nuclear Law*, 89. Eleven parties, in force.

[174] The Vienna Convention had 14 parties in January 1992, of which Argentina, Hungary, Poland, and Yugoslavia possessed nuclear installations. The United States, USSR, Japan, and Canada were not parties. The Paris Convention had 14 parties, all of which were nuclear states.

All four treaties seek to harmonize important aspects of liability for nuclear accidents and incidents in national laws, without requiring complete uniformity in every respect. They create a common scheme for loss distribution among the victims, focusing liability on the operator of a nuclear installation, and based on the principle of absolute or strict liability. These two aspects distinguish the scheme from the principle of equal access to national remedies adopted by OECD, and make it more beneficial to litigants, who are given the assurance of equitable compensation on proof of cause. At the same time, the scheme is also intended to give the nuclear industry protection from unlimited, unpredictable liability involving multiple actions against suppliers, builders, designers, carriers, operators, and states as potential defendants.[175]

The nuclear liability conventions thus reflect on the one hand an early recognition of the need for a stronger, more equitable system of loss distribution, appropriate to the serious risks of nuclear accidents, and on the other a desire to encourage the infant nuclear industry. Both points again distinguish nuclear pollution from transboundary air or water pollution, where equal access has remained the limit of state practice in civil liability matters.[176] While this special nuclear regime does not go so far as the Convention on Liability for Damage Caused by Space Objects[177], in that liability is not placed directly on the state, the influence of the nuclear example can be seen in later treaties dealing with liability for oil pollution.[178]

(1) The Scheme of the Conventions

Although there are variations, the overall scheme of the four conventions is based on the same five elements:

(i) Liability is absolute. No proof of fault or negligence is required as a condition of liability. Certain exceptions such as war, natural disaster, or negligence of the victim may be allowed.[179]

(ii) Liability is channelled exclusively to the operator of the nuclear installation or ship, and all other potential defendants are protected.[180] In

---

[175] Preamble to the Paris Convention, IAEA, *Conference on Civil Liability*, 66 f.; Berman and Hydeman, 55 *AJIL* (1961); Konz, 57 *AJIL* (1963), 105; Cameron, *et al.*, *Nuclear Energy Law*, 98 f.

[176] See Ch. 4.

[177] *Supra*, n. 90.

[178] 1969 International Convention on Civil Liability for Oil Pollution Damage with 1984 Protocol; *supra*, Ch. 7.

[179] Vienna Convention, Article IV; Paris Convention Articles. 3, 9; Brussels Convention on Nuclear Ships, Articles II, VIII.

[180] Vienna Convention, Article II; Paris Convention, Article 3; Brussels Convention on Nuclear Ships, Article II. The Convention Relating to Maritime Carriage, Article I, channels liability to operators who would be liable under the Paris or Vienna Conventions, or under national laws which are at least as favourable to those suffering damage.

certain cases a carrier or handler of nuclear material may be treated as an operator, however.[181]

(iii) Limitations may be placed on the total amount and duration of liability.[182]

(iv) Payment up to the prescribed limit of liability is supported by compulsory insurance or security held by the operator, and guaranteed by the state of installation or registry.[183] Additional public funds are provided under a Convention Supplementary to the Paris Convention,[184] but not under the remaining three conventions.

(v) Rules determine which state or states have jurisdiction over claims, and all other recourse to civil proceedings elsewhere is precluded.[185]

This scheme draws partly on the example of early national nuclear legislation, notably the United States Price-Anderson Act of 1957.[186] In most cases, the treaties leave states considerable discretion to modify their basic elements, however. National laws may thus adopt different limitation periods or insurance and liability ceilings; they may extend the definition of nuclear damage, or choose not to relieve operators of liability in cases of grave natural disaster.[187] Some states have used this power to set much higher liability ceilings; a few, such as the Federal Republic of Germany, have now opted for unlimited liability in certain circumstances.[188]

Although fewer variations are allowed under the Brussels Convention on Nuclear Ships, none of the treaties requires complete uniformity of implementation. Rather, as the IAEA commentary on the Vienna Convention explains, the principal objectives are to enumerate minimum international standards which will be flexible and adaptable to a variety of legal, social, and economic systems, while also designating which state will have exclusive legislative and jurisdictional competence.[189]

---

[181] Vienna Convention, Article II(2); Paris Convention, Article 4(d).

[182] Vienna Convention, Articles V, VI, Paris Convention, Articles 7, 8; Brussels Convention on Nuclear Ships, Articles III, V.

[183] Vienna Convention, Article VIII; Brussels Convention on Nuclear Ships, Article III; Paris Convention, Article 10. Payment of sums due under the latter convention is guaranteed under the 1963 Supplementary Convention.

[184] 1963 Convention Supplementary to the Paris Convention, with Additional Protocols of 1964 and 1982, *supra*, n. 170.

[185] Vienna Convention, Article XI; Paris Convention, Article 13; Brussels Convention on Nuclear Ships, Article X.

[186] Atomic Energy Damages Act 1957, 42 USC 2011–284, as amended. See Cameron, *et al.*, *Nuclear Energy Law*, chs. 9, 10; and Tomain, *Nuclear Power Transformation* (Bloomington, Ind., 1987), chs. 1 and 8. The Act imposes a liability ceiling, requires compulsory insurance, and provides for Federal indemnity payments; it does not make operators exclusively liable, however, and it leaves the standard of liability to be settled by each state, but see *infra*, n. 200.

[187] Vienna Convention, Article IV(3)(b); Paris Convention, Article 9. Germany and Austria reserved the right to exclude Article 9 in its entirety, thus making liability absolute; this is effected in the FRG by the Atomic Energy Act of 1985.

[188] See *infra*, n. 223.   [189] IAEA, *Conference on Civil Liability*, 67.

The Conventions cover most, but not all potential sources of nuclear damage. The Paris and Vienna Conventions apply to 'nuclear installations', a term broadly defined to include reactors, reprocessing, manufacturing, and storage facilities, where nuclear fuel, nuclear material, and radioactive products or waste are used or produced.[190] They also apply to the transport of nuclear material or the handling of nuclear waste.[191] The Brussels Convention covers nuclear powered ships, their fuel and incidental waste, but not the carriage of nuclear material by sea.[192] This latter is subject to other conventional regimes.[193] Most uses and by-products of civil nuclear power will thus fall under one or other of these headings, and only nuclear tests, nuclear weapons, and peaceful nuclear explosions are excluded.

(2) Why Absolute Liability?

The combination of absolute liability with a ceiling on damages, supported by insurance and state indemnity, makes civil liability for nuclear risks unusual. An OECD study notes that these elements are found in national laws and are not new, but

The originality of the system of nuclear liability lies rather in the fact that for the first time these various notions have been systematically applied to a whole industry and have been broadly accepted internationally.[194]

In these conventions the choice of strict or absolute liability was justified on several grounds: it would relieve courts of the difficulty of setting appropriate standards of reasonable care, and plaintiffs of the difficulty of proving breach of those standards, in a relatively new, complex, and highly technical industrial process; the risk of very serious and widespread damage, despite its low probability, placed nuclear power in the ultra-hazardous category; it would be unjust and inappropriate to make plaintiffs shoulder a heavy burden of proof in respect of such an industry whose risks are only acceptable because of its social utility as a source of energy.[195] Thus the arguments are broadly comparable to those used in the case of the state responsibility.

Whether liability is described as absolute or merely strict, is a matter of

---

[190] Vienna Convention, Article I: Paris Convention, Article 1.
[191] Vienna Convention, Article II; Paris Convention, Article 4.
[192] Article XIII.
[193] i.e. the Paris or Vienna Conventions, or other conventions governing maritime cargoes, to the extent that these are not displaced in favour of the Paris and Vienna Conventions by the Convention on Maritime Carriage of Nuclear Material, 1972. See Strohl, in IAEA, *Experience and Trends in Nuclear Law* (Vienna, 1972), 89.
[194] OECD Environment Committee, *Compensation for Nuclear Damage*, 20 *NLB* (1977), 50.
[195] *Conference on Civil Liability*, 76; Cigoj, 14 *ICLQ* (1965), 831 ff.; OECD Environment Committee, *Compensation for Nuclear Damage*, 52. See generally, Goldie, 14 *ICLQ* (1965); Kelson, 13 *Harv. ILJ* (1972), 151; Jenks, 117 *Recueil des cours* (1966).

degree.[196] The more exculpating factors are recognized, such as grave natural disasters or war, the less appropriate it becomes to use the term absolute. Liability is then strict in the limited sense that fault or negligence are not required; in effect the burden of proof is moved to the defendant. On this spectrum, the nuclear liability conventions fall some way between liability for space objects, where few exonerations are allowed,[197] and those dealing with oil pollution, where liability is strict rather than absolute.[198]

The imposition of strict or absolute liability for nuclear incidents is supported by a substantial body of national legislation, including some states which are not parties to the conventions themselves.[199] There are significant exceptions however, including the Soviet Union, which had no specific legislation on the subject.[200] Reference to national tort laws or civil codes may also supply evidence of a general principle of strict or absolute liability for dangerous or unusual activities, but such principles do not invariably cover nuclear installations.[201] One important benefit of the nuclear conventions is thus to clarify and harmonize the standard of liability.

(3) The Channelling of Liability

The channelling of all liability to the operator of nuclear installations or nuclear ships has the advantages of simplifying the plaintiff's choice of defendant and establishing a clear line of responsibility,[202] since one who is

---

[196] Goldie, 14 *ICLQ* (1965), 1215; and id., 16 *NYIL* (1985), 317. Some writers use these terms interchangeably, however, while others prefer to substitute the term 'responsibility for risk': See e.g. Arechaga, 159 *Recueil des cours* (1978), 271 ff. These authors are, however, discussing primarily the responsibility of states in international law, not civil liability.

[197] Goldie, 14 *ICLQ* (1965), 1215, regards both as properly examples of absolute liability. Exceptions allowed in the nuclear conventions include accidents caused by war, hostilities, civil disorder, or grave international disaster. Insurance cover is also unlikely to be available in these cases.

[198] See *supra*, pp. 292–8.

[199] See NEA, *Nuclear Legislation: Third Party Liability* (Paris, 1976). Non-parties with strict liability laws include Canada, Nuclear Liability Act, 1970; Japan, Acts. No. 147 and 148 of 1961, Act No. 53 of 1971; Brazil, Act No. 6453, 1977, 21 *NLB* (1978) (Suppl.), 3; Switzerland, Act on Third Party Liability, 1983, 32 *NLB* (1983) (Suppl.), 3.

[200] On Soviet Law, see *supra*, n. 168. US Federal Law, 42 USC 2210, does not specifically impose strict liability but allows for a waiver of defences and of questions of negligence, contributory negligence, and assumption of risk in indemnity cases. In *Duke Power Co.* v. *Environmental Study Group*, 438 US 59 (1978) this was held to establish the right to compensation without proof of fault. In cases not covered by Federal Law, strict liability is a matter for state law: see *Silkwood* v. *Kerr McGee Corp.*, 464 US 238 (1984); Stason, 12 *Vanderbilt LR* (1958), 93.

[201] Goldie, 14 *ICLQ* (1965), 1247; Kelson, 13 *Harv. ILJ* (1972); Hardy, 36 *BYIL* (1960). It is doubtful whether in the UK publicly operated nuclear installations would at common law be subject to strict liability, either under *Rylands* v. *Fletcher* (1868), LR 3 HL 330 (see *Dunne* v. *NW Gas Board* [1964] 2 QB 806) or nuisance (see *Allen* v. *Gulf Oil* [1981] 1 All ER 353), but liability for nuclear installations is now based on the Nuclear Installations Act 1965.

[202] *Conference on Civil Liability*, 72; Hardy, 36 *BYIL* (1960), 247 ff.; Cigoj, 14 *ICLQ* (1965), 822 ff.

not an operator may not be held liable for incidents falling within the terms of the conventions.[203] The possibility of transferring liability to a carrier of nuclear material[204] or a handler of radioactive waste[205] does not materially diminish this concentration of liability, although it provides for an alternative and more extended definition of the term 'operator', and recognizes that there may be a need for special treatment in such cases.[206] Several operators may also be held jointly and severally liable for the same nuclear incident,[207] and the conventions provide rules for determining when liability for materials in transport passes from one operator to another, and when operators become or cease to be liable for material imported or exported.[208]

The choice of the operator as the focus of liability, rather than any other potential defendant, is based on the assumption that the operator of an installation or a ship is usually in the best position to exercise effective responsibility for it, and to secure adequate insurance.[209] This assumption is not universally shared; German, Greek, and Austrian reservations to the Paris Convention allow for persons other than the operator to be held additionally liable.[210] The main argument for this is that it strengthens the incentive for all concerned, including manufacturers and suppliers, to behave responsibly.

To some extent the nuclear conventions accept this point, by allowing the operator a right of recourse against those who cause nuclear damage intentionally.[211] This is a narrow exception, however, which still leaves the operator solely responsible for the negligence or carelessness of others,[212] unless broader indemnities can be voluntarily negotiated. For most European states, this arrangement has proved acceptable, since operators will be ade-

---

[203] Vienna Convention, Article IV(5): Paris Convention Article 6(b); Brussels Convention on Nuclear Ships, Article II(2).

[204] Vienna Convention, Article II(2); Paris Convention Article 4(d).

[205] Vienna Convention, Article II(2): there is no comparable provision in the Paris Convention. See also Brussels Convention on Nuclear Ships, Article II(4).

[206] Vienna Convention, Article II(1); Paris Convention, Article 4; Hardy, 36 BYIL (1960), 247 f.; Conference on Civil Liability, 74.

[207] Vienna Convention, Article II(3), (4); Paris Convention, Article 5(d); Brussels Convention on Nuclear Ships, Article VII; Conference on Civil Liability, 75.

[208] Vienna Convention, Article II(1); Paris Convention, Articles 4(a), (b); Conference on Civil Liability, 73.

[209] Hardy, 36 BYIL (1960), 247; Cigoj, 14 ICLQ (1965), 823; Konz, 57 AJIL (1963), 105; Strohl, in IAEA, Experience and Trends in Nuclear Law, 89. But cf. the 1969 Convention on Civil Liability for Oil Pollution Damage, supra, pp. 292–8, which places liability on the owner of the ship, rather than the operator. However, this Convention allows a right of recourse against operators or others who cause damage intentionally or recklessly.

[210] Legislation in Austria and Germany has, however, remained within the terms of the Paris Convention on this point. For the position in the United States, see Cameron, et al., Nuclear Energy Law, ch. 9.

[211] Vienna Convention, Article X; Paris Convention Article 6(f); Brussels Convention on Nuclear Ships, Article II(6).

[212] cf. the broader right of recourse allowed under the 1969 Convention on Civil Liability for Oil Pollution Damage, supra, n. 209.

quately protected by insurance. The criticism that denying wider recourse dilutes the incentive for others to behave responsibly[213] can be met in two ways; states are free to employ criminal law or civil penalties,[214] and the efficient control of construction and operational standards for nuclear installations is arguably a sufficient safety policy.[215]

It is important to note that it makes no difference that the operator of a nuclear installation or ship will in many cases be a state, or state entity. The civil liability conventions ensure that states or their organs are precluded from invoking jurisdictional immunities, except in relation to the execution of judgments.[216] Thus, apart from this exception, states sued under the Conventions in their own courts will be subject to the same liability, and enjoy the same defences, as other categories of defendants.

(4) Insurance and Limitation of Liability

The scale of potential damage a nuclear accident could cause is likely to be well beyond the capacity of individual operators of nuclear installations to bear.[217] Ensuring adequate insurance cover or some other form of security is therefore essential if victims are to have an assurance of compensation. The conventions require operators to hold liability insurance or other financial security, on terms specified by national authorities, unless the operator is itself a state.[218] Regardless of the operator's financial solvency, funds should thus be available in the event of an accident.

The assurance of compensation funding is further strengthened by placing an obligation on states to ensure that claims up to liability limits are met.[219] If insurance funds prove insufficient for this purpose, the state must step in and provide them. This is a unique feature of the nuclear conventions; it indicates an acknowledgement of the residual responsibility of states to compensate for

---

[213] Pelzer, 12 *NLB* (1973), 46.

[214] *Conference on Civil Liability*, 83; this argument has been the focus of debate in the United States: see Cameron, *et al.*, *Nuclear Energy Law*, 146 f.

[215] OECD, Environment Committee, *Compensation for Nuclear Damage*, 20 *NLB* (1977), 76.

[216] Vienna Convention, Article XIV; Paris Convention, Article 13(e); Brussels Convention on Nuclear Ships, Article X(3). The exclusion of jurisdictional immunities was opposed by Soviet bloc representatives at the Vienna Conference, and the inclusion of this provision is one reason for their failure to sign the Convention.

[217] The Three Mile Island accident is thought to have cost US $1 billion; $52 million was paid out by insurers: Cameron, *et al.*, *Nuclear Energy Law*, 151 ff. Estimates of the possible cost of a core meltdown in the United States reach $15 billion: US GAO report, *Nuclear News*, Sept. 1986. The Chernobyl accident may have caused damage in the USSR totalling $3 billion, including $1.2 billion in compensation payments: Shapar and Reyners, *The Nuclear Third Party Liability Regime in Western Europe: The Test of Chernobyl*, OECD, (Paris, 1987).

[218] Vienna Convention, Article VII; Paris Convention, Article 10; Brussels Convention on Nuclear Ships, Article III.

[219] *Supra*, n. 183.

damage caused by nuclear activities, where the operator is unable to do so, or is itself a state.[220]

Limitation of the amount of liability is intended primarily to make insurance easier to obtain. Without it, insurers might be reluctant to cover such potentially enormous risks, or to do so fully.[221] In return for this guarantee of compensation for plaintiffs, it also protects the industry itself from a burden of ruinous liability.[222] Since much will depend on the views of individual insurance markets, and their ability to pool risks internationally, the conventions set only minimum limits and allow states to fix higher ones, or to have no limit at all.[223]

The scheme adopted in the conventions is not intended to guarantee compensation for all harm in all cases, for by permitting limitation of liability it necessarily envisages wider distribution of some of the loss among the public at large. The important question is whether these liability limits are adequate and strike the right balance between compensation and industry protection. The evidence suggests that the Vienna Convention in particular does not, and that it is unduly favourable to the nuclear industry. The Paris Convention, in contrast, provides arguably a more satisfactory balance by including governments in the provision of a broader compensation scheme.

The most obvious problem with the Vienna Convention is the disparity between minimum levels of liability[224] and the more recent estimates of the cost of a catastrophic nuclear accident.[225] A large proportion of the loss caused by such an accident would fall on the public and on other states under this Convention if it were implemented at the minimum level of liability. Since only two nuclear states are presently party to the convention, this may be academic, but it is one reason why the promotion of wider ratification may be an inadequate response to the Chernobyl accident.

The limit set by the Brussels Convention on Nuclear Ships[226] is much higher than the level of insurance believed to be obtainable in 1962; the

---

[220] See Miatello, in Spinedi and Simma, *United Nations Codification*, 297–9, 302–5. There is no comparable arrangement under the 1969 Convention on Civil Liability for Oil Pollution Damage.

[221] *Conference on Civil Liability*, 78; Hardy, 36 *BYIL* (1960), 240 ff.; Cameron, *et al.*, *Nuclear Energy Law*, 109.

[222] *Conference on Civil Liability* 78.

[223] Vienna Convention, Article V; Paris Convention, Article 7; *Conference on Civil Liability*, 78. Note that the Brussels Convention on Nuclear Ships, Article III, sets a single obligatory limit, following the practice of maritime liability conventions. The Federal German Atomic Energy Act, 1985, is the first to abolish liability ceilings in a Paris Convention state, although for internal claims only. See Pfaffelhuber and Kuchuk, 25 *NLB* (1980), 70. Switzerland and Japan, who are not parties, also have unlimited liability. See Shapar and Reyners, *Nuclear Third Party Liability*, for comparative tables of national liability limits, and Deprimoz, 32 *NLB* (1983), 33.

[224] Article V provides for US $5 million at 1963 values, worth approximately $58 million in 1988.

[225] See *supra* n. 217.

[226] Article III, 1,500 million gold francs.

intention of states supporting this position was that in practice licensing states would have to provide the necessary additional compensation funds.[227] For this reason, the figure is also higher than the one adopted for large oil tankers in 1969, but unlike that scheme, the nuclear ships scheme is not supported by any additional compensation from industry sources.[228]

Although the Paris Convention liability limits are also low[229] compared to the probable cost of a serious accident, this Convention is supported by a strong system of state funded compensation at a level greatly above the convention's minimum limits.[230] The European scheme thus spreads the burden of compensation more broadly than the Vienna Convention; far from making the polluter and the victims bear the whole loss, it distributes this loss equitably in cases of serious accidents across the community of Western European states as a whole.

The scale of this redistribution can be seen in the figures. Beyond the operator's basic liability of 5 million SDRs a further 170 million SDRs are drawn from the contracting party in whose territory the nuclear installation is situated and an additional 125 million from all other contracting parties.[231] This scheme thus offers far greater potential for meeting the real cost of a serious nuclear accident. It also enables individual states to transfer to the operator a substantially increased share of the risk in cases where there is fault,[232] and has contributed to a general trend towards higher and more uniform liability ceilings in Europe, or to their abolition altogether.[233]

Thus, although all the nuclear conventions focus liability on the operator as the source of the damage or pollution, the Brussels Supplementary Convention clearly recognizes that this approach is insufficient, and unlike the other

---

[227] Konz, 57 *AJIL* (1963), 102 f.

[228] See the International Convention on Civil Liability for Oil Pollution Damage, Article V, which sets a limit of 210 million gold francs; the 1971 International Convention on the Establishment of an International Fund for Compensation for Oil Pollution Damage, and voluntary schemes such as TOVALOP or CRISTAL provide additional sources of compensation from oil industry funds: *supra*, pp. 294–7.

[229] Article 7 establishes a normal level of 15 million SDRs. It leaves states the choice of setting higher or lower limits, taking account of the availability of insurance, but in no case lower than 5 million SDRs. 15 million SDRs is equivalent to approximately US$20 million at 1990 values.

[230] 1963 Brussels Supplementary Convention on Third Party Liability in the Field of Nuclear Energy, 1041 *UNTS* 358, as amended by a Protocol of 1982. See Lagorce, in IAEA, *Nuclear Law for a Developing World* (Vienna, 1969), 143; Fornasier, 8 *AFDI* (1962), 762.

[231] 1982 Protocol. The contribution made by other contracting states is calculated according to GNP and thermal power of installed nuclear reactors under Article 12. 100 million SDRs is worth approximately US$139 million at 1990 values.

[232] Article 5(b). 'Fault' in this context is ambiguous. The 1985 Federal German Atomic Energy Act, s. 37 defines it as causing damage 'wilfully or by gross negligence'. The 1969 International Convention on Civil Liability for Oil Pollution Damage, as amended in 1984, denies the shipowner the right to limit his liability where he caused the damage 'recklessly' or 'with intent'. This suggests that 'fault' in Article 5 does not cover simple negligence.

[233] OECD, *International Co-operation in the Field of Radioactive Transfrontier Pollution*, 14 *NLB* (1974), 55.

conventions it involves states in meeting substantial losses in excess of the operator's capacity to pay or cover through insurance. It cannot be said that any of the nuclear conventions fully implements the 'polluter pays' principle, or recognizes the unlimited and unconditional responsibility of states within whose borders nuclear accidents occur: what they do recognize, if imperfectly, is that the scale of possible damage has to be widely and equitably borne if nuclear power is to be internationally acceptable. This conclusion further weakens the already tenuous case for treating any of these agreements as evidence for the strict or absolute liability of the source state in international law for the full measure of any damage its nuclear activities may cause.

(5) Bringing Claims under the Conventions

The nuclear conventions simplify the jurisdictional issues which would otherwise arise under national law in bringing transboundary civil actions. First, they determine which state has jurisdiction over claims against operators or their insurers. In the case of nuclear installations, the location of the nuclear incident causing the damage, or exceptionally, of the installation itself, is the deciding factor.[234] The object of this extended definition, and the reason jurisdiction does not simply follow the location of the installation, is to cater for incidents caused by material in transit.

Cases of multiple jurisdiction are to be dealt with by agreement of the parties under the Vienna Convention,[235] or by a tribunal under the Paris Convention.[236] This tribunal would decide which court was 'most closely related to the case in question'. In the case of ships, both the licensing state and the state or states where the damage occurs have jurisdiction.[237]

Secondly, judgments given by courts competent in accordance with the conventions must be recognized and enforced in other member states, with certain limited exceptions which do not allow reconsideration of the merits of the case.[238] This facility is now of limited practical importance within most of Western Europe, since judgments will normally be recognized under EEC treaties,[239] but elsewhere it is an important further guarantee of access to compensation funds in transboundary cases.

Actions brought pursuant to all these conventions must commence within the appropriate limitation period, which in each case is ten years from the date of the nuclear incident, unless national law provides differently.[240] The period

---

[234] Vienna Convention, Article XI; Paris Convention Article 13.
[235] Article XI(3).   [236] Article 13(c).   [237] Article X.
[238] Vienna Convention, Article XII; Paris Convention, Article 13(d); Brussels Convention on Nuclear Ships, Article XI(4).
[239] 1968 and 1978 Conventions on Civil Jurisdiction and the Enforcement of Judgments.
[240] Vienna Convention, Article VI; Paris Convention, Article 8; Brussels Convention, Article V.

may be extended, or reduced, but in the latter case it must then be computed from the date on which the plaintiff knew or should have known of the damage and the identity of the operator liable. Since it is characteristic of nuclear radiation that its effects on human health may not become apparent for many years after the event, a limitation period as short as ten years may leave victims to bear their own loss; not surprisingly, several states have now adopted periods of up to thirty years.[241]

(6) Non-Party Claims

None of the conventions categorically extends the benefit of its provisions to claimants who suffer damage in the territory of a non-contracting state, or to incidents which arise there. The Paris Convention gives parties the discretion to do so, but it is otherwise expressly inapplicable.[242] No consistent practice has been followed by contracting parties on this point, but several do allow non-party claims to be made.[243] A similar provision was deleted from the Vienna Convention after opposition to the notion that non-parties might benefit.[244] Both conventions provide jurisdictional rules for incidents occurring outside the territory of a party,[245] but these provisions are intended to resolve conflicts, not to extend the application of either instrument.

The Brussels Convention on Nuclear Ships applies to nuclear damage caused by an incident anywhere involving a nuclear ship of a contracting party,[246] but it is silent on the question whether this is intended to benefit a non-party. Following the normal principles of treaty law, it seems unlikely that either the Vienna or Brussels Nuclear Ships Conventions have created rights for non-party claimants.[247]

The major argument against allowing non-party claims is that with limited insurance funds to call on, adding more claimants will reduce the share available for those in contracting states, without reciprocal benefits. The Paris Convention necessarily accepts this result if its benefits are extended to non-

---

[241] FRG, Atomic Energy Act 1985, s. 32; UK, Nuclear Installations Act, 1965; Switzerland, Act on Third Party Liability, 1983.

[242] Article 3.

[243] Germany, Atomic Energy Act 1985, s. 24(4); Denmark, Compensation for Nuclear Damage Act, 1974, s. 5(1); Finland, Nuclear Liability Act 1972, s. 4; Netherlands, Act on Liability for Damage Caused by Nuclear Incidents, s. 26(1); Sweden, Nuclear Liability Act s. 3; UK, Nuclear Installations Act, 1965, ss. 7, 12.

[244] *Conference on Civil Liability for Nuclear Damage*, Committee of the Whole, 183 f.; Plenary, 121 ff.

[245] Vienna Convention, Article XI(2); Paris Convention Article 13(b).

[246] Article XIII. A recommendation of the Steering Committee of the Paris Convention, made 25 Apr. 1968, states that the Paris Convention is applicable to nuclear incidents on the high seas and to damage occurring on the high seas.

[247] Vienna Convention on the Law of Treaties, 1969, Article 36; *Free Zones of Upper Saxony and the District of Gex Case*, PCIJ, Ser. A/B, No. 46 (1932).

parties, but such claimants are denied recourse to additional public funds provided under the 1963 Supplementary Convention.[248] Extension may be advantageous however; it permits operators to limit their liability to non-party claimants and it may facilitate transport of nuclear materials across non-party territories.[249] In effect it would create an equal access regime for those injured in non-party states, and for that reason extension would be consistent with OECD policy.[250]

None of these provisions is helpful in the case of accidents like Chernobyl, since the issue there involves the liability of a non-party operator rather than extension of benefits to non-party claimants. Non-party operators cannot be held liable under any of the conventions, and jurisdiction will in such cases be determined by ordinary rules of national law, with all the difficulties referred to earlier. Participation in the conventions by nuclear states—the source of potential defendants—is for this reason the best way of gauging international acceptance of the civil liability regime. That is what makes the Vienna Convention a particularly weak precedent, since so few nuclear states are parties to it.

(7) Nuclear Damage and the Environment

A common feature of the nuclear conventions is their relatively narrow definition of 'damage'. Like the *Trail Smelter* case their focus is on loss of life, personal injury, or loss or damage to property.[251] The Brussels and Vienna Conventions do allow parties to extend this definition, but the legislation of OECD states closely follows the provisions of the Paris Convention.[252] What is clearly missing is agreement on a broader environmental or ecological perspective.

Thus the kind of ecological damage to wildlife inflicted by the Chernobyl accident, or the harm to the marine environment which a nuclear incident at sea might produce does not easily fall within the conventions' terms. Here again the 1969 Convention on Civil Liability for Oil Pollution Damage, as amended in 1984, offers a better model which provides for the costs of prevention measures taken to minimise damage and for reasonable measures of reinstatement of the environment.[253]

---

[248] Article 2(a). Article 15 permits states to conclude agreements with non-parties for payment out of public funds, however.

[249] *Conference on Civil Liability*, 184, para. 55.

[250] See OECD recommendations on equal access to national remedies and non-discrimination, *supra*, n. 288. See also Switzerland–FRG Agreement on Third Party Liability in the Nuclear Field, 39 *NLB* (1968), 51.

[251] Vienna Convention, Article 1(1)(K); Paris Convention, Article 3(a); Brussels Convention on Nuclear Ships, Article 1(7); Noltz, *NLB* (1987), 87, and see *supra*, pp. 98–102.

[252] See OECD, *Nuclear Legislation: Third Party Liability* (Paris, 1976).

[253] Article 1(6). See Jacobsson and Trotz, 17 *JMLC* (1986), 467. cf. the 1988 Convention for
16 Regulation of Antarctic Mineral Resource Activities, Article 1(15), and text, *supra*, pp. 98–102.

The nuclear conventions need a more realistic approach to environmental damage if the true costs of nuclear incidents are to be borne by the nuclear industry. Such additional environmental costs might be recoverable against states in international law, however, following the outcome of the Canadian claim for clean-up costs arising out of the Cosmos 954 crash.[254] If this is correct, it confirms that even in cases governed by one of the civil liability conventions, state responsibility for nuclear damage still has a role to play because of the limited reparation allowed by the conventions themselves.

(8) An Assessment of the Nuclear Conventions

Despite its novelty and sophistication, the most significant feature of the common scheme in these conventions is its lack of widespread international support. International willingness to agree to new conventions on notification and assistance following the Chernobyl accident has not been matched by any comparable interest in ratifying earlier liability conventions. This has prompted IAEA to consider ways of encouraging greater participation. One measure already taken is the adoption of a joint protocol to prevent conflicts of law arising from the simultaneous application of the Paris and Vienna Conventions.[255] Another possibility is to reform the Vienna Convention.[256]

At present, the Western European states which are parties to the Paris Convention represent the only significant grouping of nuclear states to have accepted an international agreement on civil liability. This is important since Western Europe has the world's greatest concentration of nuclear facilities and the highest likelihood of transboundary consequences arising from nuclear incidents.[257] But the spread of nuclear power world-wide, and the continental implications of major accidents, such as Chernobyl, makes the failure of the three global conventions to attract support a serious lacuna in the regulation of nuclear power. Of the fourteen parties to the Vienna Convention, only four possess nuclear facilities. Neither the United States nor the USSR chose to ratify. Although the Brussels Convention on Nuclear Ships has six parties, it is not yet in force, because no state licensing such ships has

---

[254] See supra, n. 149.

[255] IAEA Doc. N5/TC/643. It is hoped this Protocol will permit more states to ratify the Vienna Convention, including those who are at present party to the Paris Convention. See Busekist, 43 NLB (1989), 10, and Cameron, et al., Nuclear Energy Law, 112 ff. Hungary, Poland, Chile, and Mexico ratified the Vienna Convention in 1989 or 1990. Ten States including Chile, Denmark, Egypt and Poland had also ratified the 1988 Protocol by January 1992.

[256] In 1990, IAEA established a Standing Committee on Liability for Nuclear Damage with the task of reviewing problems relating to the Vienna Convention and making proposals for a review conference: see supra, n. 167.

[257] Approximately 120 of the world's 400 nuclear reactors are located in the 14 Paris Convention states.

become a party.[258] The Convention on Maritime Carriage of Nuclear Material is in force, and has eleven parties, but these represent only a small proportion of world shipping tonnage. Overwhelmingly, those who operate nuclear installations or nuclear ships have failed to accept the international implications of making civil liability for nuclear damage easier to establish.

In the event of an accident causing damage, claimants in most countries will thus be forced to resort either to ordinary transboundary civil proceedings, or to invoke state responsibility. Yet as we have seen, there are serious obstacles to the former, and much uncertainty over the content of the latter. Even if all four conventions were widely supported, they remain open to criticism in important respects. The narrowness of their environmental focus, the inadequacy of liability limits under the Vienna Convention, the limitation period, the range of exceptions, and the possible dilution of a sense of responsibility on the part of operators of installations are the main points where reform may be desirable.[259] For these reasons, as Handl observes, it is unlikely that the need for responsibility under public international law will ever be wholly superseded by the private law conventions.[260]

More fundamentally, OECD's Nuclear Energy Agency has pointed out that the use of unlimited liability and longer limitation periods by some states, notably West Germany, calls in question the basis of the scheme shared by all four conventions.[261] This may be desirable. Now that the nuclear industry is well established and its risks better understood, it is harder to justify the exceptional level of state support and protection it presently enjoys in matters of civil liability.[262]

Despite these criticisms, the positive features of the four conventions as a model for other areas of environmental interest should be noted. They make individual access to legal remedies much easier than for any other form of transboundary environmental harm, and they eliminate or minimize difficult issues of proof and liability standards. They offer a scheme which ensures the availability of compensation funds regardless of the solvency of the defendant. The Paris Convention, benefiting from the supplementary provision of public funds, is particularly strong in this respect, and it sets an example which other liability conventions could usefully emulate. They also offer a precedent for treating ultra-hazardous but socially desirable activities as risks which require exceptional provision for wider loss distribution, based only in part on the absolute or strict liability of the source of risk. However, lack of general

---

[258] Article XXIV (1). Nuclear ships have been registered in the US, West Germany, USSR, and Japan.

[259] OECD, *Compensation for Nuclear Damage*, 20 *NLB* (1977), 50; Shapar and Reyners, *Nuclear Third Party Liability*; Reyners, in IAEA, *Licensing and Regulatory Control of Nuclear Installations*, 243.

[260] 92 *RGDIP* (1988), 42.

[261] OECD, Nuclear Energy Agency, 15th Activity Report, 1986.

[262] See *supra*, n. 260, and Pfaffelhuber and Kuchuk, 25 *NLB* (1980).

international support considerably weakens the value of that precedent as a basis for drawing inferences about the content of customary international law.[263]

6. CONCLUSIONS

This chapter has dealt with an activity which poses serious risks for the health of populations and the environment of other states and common areas. The lack of binding international standards or of a strong system of international inspection, monitoring, and supervision are the main weaknesses affecting the international regulation of nuclear energy, which in these respects compares unfavourably with more recently developed legal regimes for the management of other hazardous or environmentally harmful activities. Despite its undoubted influence on state practice, the ability of IAEA to ensure the safety of nuclear power rests on a very insecure basis and should not be exaggerated. What is required in this respect is a much stronger scheme of inspection and monitoring of compliance with IAEA minimum safety standards.

Moreover, established legal principles are inadequate for the protection of other states or the global environment. The customary obligation to co-operate with neighbouring states in the management of transboundary nuclear risks is firmly established and entails notification and negotiation aimed at limiting the risk posed by planned activities in border areas, environmental impact assessment, and timely notification of accidents or environmental hazards. But the evidence does not show that activities involving significant transboundary risk are prohibited by international law, nor does it indicate that they may only take place on equitable terms agreed with states likely to be affected. This leaves such states excessively vulnerable to unilateral decisions over which they have little control. A preferable approach would be to apply the precautionary principle by involving the IAEA in approving the safe operation and siting of nuclear installations, especially if near international borders. The Oslo Dumping Commission's prior justification procedure might provide a useful model for such a procedure.

Uncertainty surrounding the content and character of the obligation to prevent serious harm to the environment in this context also diminishes the cogency of state responsibility for the consequences of nuclear activities. Both the standard of conduct required of states in controlling such activities and the standard of responsibility for environmental damage caused by nuclear accidents require clarification by means of an international agreement, accompanied by appropriate supervisory machinery. At present neither the law of state responsibility, nor the complementary system of conventions harmon-

---

[263] See *supra*, pp. 367–8.

izing principles of civil liability, provides a satisfactory basis for allocating the costs of transboundary nuclear damage. Failure to establish the strict or absolute responsibility of the 'source' state in cases of nuclear accidents may leave a heavy burden of loss to fall on 'victim' states and their citizens, while the civil liability conventions provide at best an equitable sharing of the loss which falls well short of the 'polluter pays' approach more commonly supported by international policy declarations. Moreover, even if the sharing of costs through mutual contributions to a compensation fund makes sense among the geographically contiguous group of Western European nuclear states, or similarly in Eastern Europe, it is difficult to see how the principle could be extended satisfactorily to other nuclear states who do not share the risk of accidents in the same way, such as Argentina and Japan. Nor does this kind of mutual compensation fund address the problems of non-nuclear states. This suggests that state responsibility, despite its drawbacks, remains an essential element in the present legal regime for nuclear risks. But it also poses the question why states which cannot or will not make satisfactory arrangements for compensating their non-nuclear neighbours in the event of serious accident should be allowed the freedom to pursue nuclear activities. To assert the right of all states to have access to nuclear technology is, in the context of the present legal regime, most unwise.

10

Protecting the Atmosphere and Outer Space

1. INTRODUCTION

(1) Air Pollution as a Transboundary Problem

The main sources of significant transboundary air pollution are today the sulphur dioxide (SO_2) and nitrogen oxides (NO_x) produced by the combustion of fossil fuels for power generation and industrial use, to which must be added the increasing volume of vehicle exhaust emissions since the 1960s. Both SO_2 and NO_x are emitted naturally into the atmosphere, for example from volcanoes, but these represent only a small proportion of the global total.[1]

Once in the atmosphere, the distribution and deposition of these substances is a function of prevailing winds and weather patterns. Scientific observations and monitoring have shown that sulphur and nitrogen compounds are dispersed atmospherically over thousands of miles. The work of the Programme for Monitoring and Evaluation of Long-Range Transmission of Air Pollutants in Europe (EMEP) has succeeded in quantifying the depositions in each country that can be attributed to emissions in any other, and has shown that in Europe the problem is not simply a bilateral one between adjacent states, but a regional one, in which most states contribute their own share of pollution, but some emerge as substantial net importers.[2] Moreover, research conducted by GESAMP and in the North Sea and Great Lakes has shown that land-based air pollution of the marine environment is also significant, and in the case of metals and nutrients more so than for inputs from rivers, particularly to the open oceans.[3]

---

[1] See generally UN ECE, *Air Pollution Studies*, Nos. 1–6 (1984–9); US National Academy of Sciences, *Atmosphere-Biosphere Interactions: Towards a Better Understanding of the Ecological Consequences of Fossil Fuel Combustion* (1981); id., *Acid Deposition: Atmospheric Processes in Eastern North America* (1983); US Congress, Office of Technology Assessment, *Acid Rain and Transported Air Pollutants: Implications for Public Policy* (1984); UK House of Commons, *4th Report of the Environment Committee: Acid Rain* (1983–4); Stockholm Conference on the Acidification of the Environment, *Report from the Expert Meetings*, 9 EPL (1982), 73 and 100.

[2] Sand, in Helm (ed.), *Energy: Production, Consumption and Consequences* (Washington, DC, 1990), 247.

[3] GESAMP, *The State of the Marine Environment* (Nairobi, 1990), 36; 2nd International Conference on the Protection of the North Sea, *Quality Status of the North Sea* (1987);

Sulphur and nitrogen can be deposited in dry form, or as acid rain, although in both cases the ultimate effect is comparable. Dry deposition is more likely to remain a localized problem, however, Greater transboundary effects are generated by reactions of sulphur, nitrogen, and other substances with water vapour in the atmosphere, where they form acidic compounds, deposited as acid rain, or create other pollutants such as ozone gas (O_3). Sunlight, moisture, temperature and the level of concentration of particles are important factors in this complex chemical process, whose effects are also influenced by climate and location.[4]

Acid deposition has been blamed for increased acidity of soil, lakes, and rivers and for other effects in Europe and North America including reduced crop growth, death or degradation of forests, and the disappearance of fish and wildlife. It appears to accelerate the decomposition of building materials, poses health risks, and increases the release of toxic metals, either directly, or through leaching from soil or corrosion of plumbing. These effects are increasingly well documented in UN and nationally sponsored research programmes.[5] Ozone pollution of the lower atmosphere is thought also to harm crops and forests, either alone, or in combination with acid rain.[6]

(2) Degradation of the Global Atmosphere

Earlier concentration on the transboundary or regional impact of air pollution has given way to the realization that the threat to the atmosphere is now global in scale. During the 1980s evidence emerged linking the release of chlorofluorocarbons (CFCs), halons, and other chlorine-based substances with the gradual destruction of the ozone layer. This layer, located in the stratosphere but still well within the earth's atmosphere, is important because it filters sunlight and protects the earth from ultraviolet radiation. Loss of this atmospheric shield would have serious implications for human health, agriculture, and fisheries productivity over a long period, and could leave future generations a legacy of irreversible harm.[7] Moreover the CFCs which are one of the causes of ozone depletion are also a significant contributor to global atmospheric warming (the so-called 'greenhouse effect'), leading

International Joint Commission, 6th and 7th *Annual Reports on Great Lakes Water Quality* (Ottawa, 1974–80); US NRC and Royal Society of Canada, *The Great Lakes Water Quality Agreement: An Evolving Instrument for Ecosystem Management* (1985).

[4] UN/ECE, *supra*, n. 1; 1982 Stockholm Conference, ibid.

[5] UN/ECE, ibid.; UK House of Commons, *4th Report*, ibid.

[6] UN/ECE, *Air Pollution Study* (No. 3).

[7] WMO, *Atmospheric Ozone 1985* (Geneva, 1986); EPA, *An Assessment of the Risks of Stratospheric Modification* (Washington, DC, 1987); Benedick, *Ozone Diplomacy* (Cambridge, Mass., 1991), ch. 2.

to global climate change, with potentially world-wide effects on sea levels, forests, agriculture, natural ecosystems, and population distribution.[8]

The major risk of global climate change is thought to come from CO_2 emissions and other atmospheric gases including CFCs, methane, and nitrogen oxides. Carbon dioxide is the most significant of these in volume, although not necessarily in its effects; this gas derives from fossil fuel combustion, and like acid rain it is thus inexorably linked with patterns of energy consumption in the developed industrialized world. But there may also be other factors contributing to global climate change, including deforestation in developing countries such as Brazil, emission of methane gas from agricultural sources, and the presence of water vapour. The effects of global climate change would be felt world-wide, but not necessarily with the same impact everywhere. Some countries might benefit from a change to more temperate climates; others, such as low-lying Pacific islands, might disappear altogether.

The likelihood of global climate change, and its causes, remain a subject of dispute among scientists and governments. The Intergovernmental Panel on Climate Change (IPCC), established by UNEP and WMO to review the scientific evidence and make recommendations, reported in June 1990 that emissions resulting from human activities are substantially increasing the atmospheric concentrations of greenhouse gases and, if unchecked, will result in an average additional warming of the Earth's surface greater than any experienced in the previous 10,000 years. Carbon dioxide was estimated to be responsible for half of this enhanced effect. Levels of CO_2, nitrous oxides, and CFCs would adjust only slowly to reduced emissions, but continued emissions at present rates would result in increased concentrations for centuries ahead. In addition, the report predicted an average sea level rise due to thermal expansion and melting of ice of up to 65 cm by the year 2100, with the probability of reduced precipitation in Southern Europe and central North America due to temperature increases. But the report also conceded that there are many uncertainties in the timing, magnitude, and regional patterns of climate change, due to the complexity of the subject and the need for further research. Moreover, although mean average temperatures have risen over the previous 100 years, it is also possible that this could be due largely to natural variations, sunspots, and the influence of oceanic processes on the carbon cycle. Unequivocal evidence of the enhanced greenhouse effect was not yet available, the report concluded.[9]

---

[8] UNEP/WMO, Intergovernmental Panel on Climate Change, *Scientific Assessment of Climate Change* (1990); id., *Potential Impacts of Climate Change* (1990).

[9] Id., *Scientific Assessment* (1990); Biogeochemical Ocean Flux Study, *Oceans and the Global Carbon Cycle* (1989). For a review of the scientific uncertainty and its implications for policy, see White, *Proc. of the ASIL* (1990), 346.

(3) The Legal Status of the Atmosphere[10]

The atmosphere is not a distinct category in international law. Because it consists of a fluctuating and dynamic airmass, it cannot be equated with airspace, which, above land, is simply a spatial dimension subject to the sovereignty of the subjacent states.[11] But this overlap with territorial sovereignty also means that it cannot be treated as an area of common property beyond the jurisdiction of any state, comparable in this sense to the high seas.[12] The alternative possibility of regarding it as a shared resource is relevant in situations of bilateral or regional transboundary air pollution, affecting other states or adjacent regional seas. The Executive Director of UNEP has referred to 'airsheds' as examples of shared natural resources,[13] and this status is consistent with regional approaches to the control and regulation of transboundary air pollution adopted in the 1979 Geneva Convention on Long-Range Transboundary Air Pollution, and in regional seas agreements limiting air pollution of the marine environment of the North Sea, the Baltic, and the Mediterranean.[14]

The shared resources concept is of less use, however, in relation to global atmospheric issues such as ozone depletion or climate change. What is needed here is a legal concept which recognizes the unity of the global atmosphere and the common interest of all states in its protection. The traditional category of common property, is, as we have seen, an inadequate one for this purpose. The same objection applies to the use of 'common heritage' in this context, with the additional difficulty that this concept has so far been applied only to mineral resources of the deep sea-bed and outer space and that its legal status remains controversial following rejection by the United States and a number of other countries opposed to the implications of the term.[15] The atmosphere is clearly not outer space, despite the difficulty of defining the boundaries of that area. Moreover, Article 135 of the 1982 UNCLOS provides that the status of the sea-bed does not affect superjacent airspace, and thus offers no support for any wider use of the common heritage concept. Significantly, it was not employed in the 1985 Vienna Convention for the Protection of the Ozone Layer.[16]

That convention defines the 'ozone layer' as 'the layer of atmospheric ozone above the planetary boundary layer'.[17] This does not mean that the ozone layer is either legally or physically part of outer space. It remains part of the

---

[10] Boyle, in Churchill and Freestone, *International Law and Global Climate Change* (Dordrecht, 1991), ch. 1.

[11] 1944 Chicago Convention on International Civil Aviation, 15 *UNTS* 295.

[12] 1958 Geneva Convention on the High Seas, Articles 1–2; 1982 UNCLOS, Articles 87, 89.

[13] *Report of the Executive Director*, UNEP/GC/44 (1975), para. 86; *supra*, pp. 114–7.

[14] See *infra*, pp. 397–402, and p. 404, and see Handl, 26 *NRJ* (1986), 405.

[15] See *supra*, pp. 120–2.   [16] See *infra*, pp. 404–6.   [17] Article 1(1).

atmosphere, and falls partly into areas of common property, and partly into areas of national sovereignty. One purpose of the convention's definition is to indicate that it is concerned with stratospheric ozone,[18] and not with low-level ozone, which, as we have seen, is an air pollutant. More importantly, however, the definition treats the whole stratospheric ozone layer as a global unity, without reference to legal concepts of sovereignty, shared resources, or common property. It points to the emergence of a new status for the global atmosphere, which makes it appropriate to view the ozone layer as part of a common resource or common interest, regardless of who enjoys sovereignty over the airspace which it occupies.[19]

The same conclusion can also be drawn from UN General Assembly resolution 43/53 which declares that global climate change is 'the common concern of mankind'.[20] This phraseology was the outcome of a political compromise over Malta's initial proposal to treat the global climate as the common heritage of mankind. It has subsequently been followed in the Noordwijk Declaration of the Conference on Atmospheric Pollution and Climate Change,[21] and by UNEP.[22] What it suggests is that the global climate should have a status comparable to the ozone layer, and that the totality of the global atmosphere can now properly be regarded as the 'common concern of mankind'. By approaching the issues from this global perspective, the General Assembly has recognized both the artificiality of territorial boundaries in this context, and the inadequacy of treating global climate change in the same way as transboundary air pollution, for which regional or bilateral solutions remain more appropriate.

As we have seen in Chapter 4, the status of 'common concern' is primarily significant in indicating the common legal interest of all states in protecting the global atmosphere, whether directly injured or not, and in enforcing rules concerning its protection.[23] It should be emphasized, however, that this conclusion may as a matter of law be premature; while international law does recognize common interests, it is not clear that a General Assembly resolution alone is sufficient to confer this status. A more important indication, at least for the ozone layer, is that the 1985 Ozone Convention unquestionably does so.[24]

---

[18] The stratosphere begins between 5 and 10 miles from the earth's surface and reaches a height of approximately 30 miles. Powered aircraft typically operate to heights of 12 miles, and exceptionally to about 20 miles.

[19] International Meeting of Legal and Policy Experts, 1989, Ottawa, Canada, 19 *EPL* (1989), 78.

[20] Boyle, in Churchill and Freestone, *Global Climate Change*.

[21] 19 *EPL* (1989), 229.

[22] UNEP/GC 15/36 (1989).

[23] But cf. Brunée, 49 *ZAORV* (1989), 791, and Kirgis, 84 *AJIL* (1990), 585. See further *supra*, pp. 154–7.

[24] Boyle, in Churchill and Freestone, *Global Climate Change*, and see *infra*, pp. 404–5.

(4) International Policy and the Regulation of the Atmosphere

The foregoing considerations indicate something of the legal and scientific complexity surrounding the protection of the atmosphere and its various components. No single approach or legal regime is likely to be appropriate or possible. Moreover, the control of transboundary air pollution, ozone depletion, and climate change poses difficult choices for many states in matters of economic and industrial policy. The problems of adjustment in the use of energy, and in the consumption of CFCs and other ozone-depleting substances are substantial for industrialized nations, but they are also fundamental to the development aspirations and priorities of developing states.[25]

For these reasons, attempts to negotiate international controls have made relatively slow progress, and for many states the preferable policy, at least initially, has been to delay action pending clear scientific evidence and proof of harm. This explains the emphasis in the recommendations of the 1972 Stockholm Conference on the need for monitoring programmes and more scientific research into the problems.[26] The same pattern has been repeated with regard to long-range transboundary air pollution, ozone depletion, and now climate change. Only gradually have states been persuaded of the need for a precautionary approach to the risk of irreversible atmospheric harm. Although reinforced by a growing body of scientific evidence, a precautionary approach can be seen in the negotiations for the 1985 Ozone Convention and its later protocols and amendments.[27] A comparable consensus on the need for precautionary action to deal with the risk of climate change remains lacking, however, despite growing support in conference declarations.[28]

A second reason for the slow pace of international negotiations has been the need to ensure global participation for any regime to deal with ozone depletion or global climate change. Fundamental questions of economic equity between developed and developing states are raised by these problems, both of which are substantially the result of policies pursued by the former. Yet without constraints on the pursuit of comparable policies by the latter, no control strategy will work. Thus the Ozone Convention affords a good example of factors relevant in securing an equitable balance of interests reconciling the economic concerns of developing countries with controls sought by developed states.[29] To these considerations must also be added the competing claims of future generations to inter-generational equity.[30]

---

[25] See esp. Benedick, *Ozone Diplomacy* (Cambridge, Mass., 1991).
[26] Recommendations 70, 71, 73, 77, 79, 81, and 83, UN Doc. A/CONF/48/14/Rev. 1 (1972).
[27] Freestone, in Churchill and Freestone, *Global Climate Change*, ch. 2, and see *infra*, pp. 404 ff.
[28] Ibid., and see 1990 Bergen Declaration, *supra*, pp. 97–8.
[29] Benedick, *Ozone Diplomacy*; Handl, 1 *EJIL* (1990), 250.
[30] Redgwell, in Churchill and Freestone, *Global Climate Change*, ch. 3; Brown Weiss, *In Fairness to Future Generations* (New York, 1989), 345.

A third important consideration in evaluating legal developments relevant to the protection of the atmosphere is the realization that transboundary air pollution, ozone depletion, and climate change are interrelated problems, whose solution goes to the heart of a policy of sustainable development. This is recognized in the declaration of the 1990 Bergen Conference on Sustainable Development,[31] which supports a range of measures to promote energy efficiency, energy conservation, and the use of environmentally sound and renewable energy sources in order to reduce emissions of greenhouse gases. It should not be assumed that the most appropriate or effective means of implementing these policies are necessarily to be afforded by international law or international regulation.[32] Rather, law is one element in a broader strategy, whose success may, however, depend at least in part on the willingness of states to commit themselves to and to implement effective measures of atmospheric protection. In practice, as we shall see, their record in this respect is in some ways as poor as it is for land-based sources of marine pollution.

2. TRANSBOUNDARY AIR POLLUTION[33]

(1) Customary Law and General Principles

As we saw in Chapter 3, the *Trail Smelter* arbitration held that: 'no state has the right to use or permit the use of its territory in such a manner as to cause injury by fumes in or to the territory of another or the properties or persons therein, when the case is of serious consequence and the injury is established by clear and convincing evidence.'[34] The arbitral tribunal was established in order to determine whether smoke emissions from a Canadian smelter located seven miles from the US border had caused damage in the state of Washington, and if so, what compensation should be paid and what measures should be taken to prevent future damage. The evidential questions were resolved by scientific inquiry, and in its final award, the tribunal laid down a regime restricting the operation of the smelter.

Despite criticism of the tribunal for the limited range of national and international sources on which it relied in determining rules of international

---

[31] 20 *EPL* (1990), 100. See also 1989 Declaration of the Hague, 19 *EPL* (1989), 78; Noordwijk Declaration, *supra*, n. 21; UNEP/GC/15/36 (1989), and 1989 Cairo Compact, 20 *EPL* (1990), 59.

[32] But cf. the International Meeting of Legal and Policy Experts, *supra*, n. 19.

[33] Wetstone and Rosencranz, *Acid Rain in Europe and North America* (Washington, DC, 1983); Flinterman, Kwiatkowska, and Lammers (eds.), *Transboundary Air Pollution* (Dordrecht, 1986); Van Lier, *Acid Rain and International Law* (Toronto, 1981); Schmandt, Clarkson, and Roderick (eds.), *Acid Rain and Friendly Neighbours* (Durham, NC, 1988); Pallemaerts, *Hague YIL* (1988), 189.

[34] 35 *AJIL* (1941), 716; *supra*, pp. 89 ff.

law, there is no reason to doubt that states remain responsible in international law for harm caused in breach of obligation by transboundary air pollution.[35] Moreover, although the *Trail Smelter* case concerned a single known source of pollution with transboundary effects in close proximity, the rule as enunciated by the tribunal is in principle also applicable to more generalized long-range forms of air pollution. Modern monitoring and sampling techniques have made it possible, as we have seen, to calculate with reasonable accuracy the amounts of transboundary pollution emanating from individual countries and to identify the areas where the pollution is deposited.[36] If this is so, then furnishing the necessary proof, even to the 'clear and convincing' standard demanded by the tribunal in the *Trail Smelter* case, need no longer be a potential obstacle to the attribution of responsibility for long-range transboundary air pollution.[37] Nor, as argued in Chapter 3, is there a strong case for treating the rule as one which applies only to unreasonable or inequitable harm to other states; it imposes responsibility for any injury which meets the required threshold of seriousness or significance and which results from a breach of obligation by the source state.[38]

As in other contexts, however, a rule of this generality, applicable only in interstate claims, has proved to be of limited utility. In practice, states have preferred to facilitate redress for transboundary injury through equal access to civil remedies. The *Trail Smelter* arbitration remains the only international adjudication on the subject of air pollution.[39] Moreover, a rule intended mainly to compensate for serious harm is less suitable for determining the content of obligations of diligent control and prevention of air pollution. For this purpose more detailed standards are required to implement a fully preventive approach.[40] These can only be created through negotiation and international co-operation. Some standards of this kind do now exist, in the SO_2 and NO_x protocols to the 1979 Geneva Convention for the Control of Long-Range Transboundary Air Pollution, and under treaties or protocols concerned with land-based sources of pollution.[41] But these are regional framework agreements, with a limited number of parties, not all of whom have accepted or implemented the standards in question. Thus, unlike the 1973 MARPOL Convention, it is less convincing to argue that any of the regional air pollution treaties or their related protocols represent an international

---

[35] See Ch. 4.
[36] Sand, in Helm, *Energy*; Handl, 26 *NRJ* (1986), 440–7; Wetstone and Rosencranz, *Acid Rain*, 159.
[37] Handl, 26 *NRJ* (1986), and see Kirgis, 66 *AJIL* (1972), 294, who doubts whether this standard of proof would today be required in cases of long-range transboundary air pollution.
[38] See *supra*, p. 99, and see Handl, 26 *NRJ* (1986).
[39] But see also the *Nuclear Tests* Cases, *supra*, Ch. 9.
[40] Boyle, in Churchill and Freestone, *Global Climate Change*, and see generally, *supra*, Ch. 3.
[41] See *infra*, pp. 397 ff.

standard of due diligence in customary law.[42] Moreover, whereas the 1982 UNCLOS supports the view that states are required to apply 'international rules and standards' for preventing pollution from ships, in the case of air pollution it leaves states free to set their own national standards, merely requiring them to 'take account' of any international rules and standards in doing so.[43] Customary law remains at a very high level of generality when formulated in this way. Another possibility, however, is to resort to the argument that in the absence of agreed international standards, use of the 'best available technology' or 'best practicable means' represent the minimum definition of a state's obligation to control transboundary air pollution in customary law.[44]

State practice in bilateral air pollution disputes involving the United States, Canada, Norway, Sweden, the United Kingdom, Germany, and France does not suggest that the basic customary rule is without impact.[45] On the other hand, it does not appear to have provided a solution to regional problems of air pollution or acid rain either in North America or Europe.[46] Although those states who are net importers of pollution, such as the Nordic countries or Canada, have from time to time invoked Principle 21 of the Stockholm Declaration, or *Trail Smelter*,[47] the preferred approach of all parties has been to negotiate agreed emissions standards with polluting states, and to seek international regulation on a basis which takes account of the interests of both sides, while leaving aside the question of compensation for long-term damage previously inflicted. The 1979 Geneva Convention on Long-Range Transboundary Air Pollution[48] does therefore suggest that in practice equitable considerations have played an important part in resolving questions concerning the legality of transboundary air pollution, although it remains correct to observe that 'it will be customary international legal principles and rules which will principally shape the parties' respective starting positions and guide states in their negotiations.'[49] Customary international law is not unimportant in the control of air pollution; effective solutions to the problem can only be provided by co-operative regimes of international regulation, however.

---

[42] cf. *supra*, pp. 254–7.

[43] cf. Articles 211 (pollution from ships) with Articles 207 and 212 (land-based and airborne pollution), and *supra*, Chs. 7 and 8.

[44] Handl, 26 *NRJ* (1986), 464, and see *supra*, pp. 92–4.

[45] Handl, ibid., 423, 447–9, and see in particular his account of the *Poplar River* dispute, ibid. See also Bothe, in Flinterman, Kwiatkowska, and Lammers, *Transboundary Air Pollution*, 121 f.

[46] See in particular Wetstone and Rosencranz, *Acid Rain*, and Schmandt, Clarkson, and Roderick, *Acid Rain*.

[47] *Supra*, n. 45.

[48] *Infra*, pp. 397 ff.

[49] Handl, 26 *NRJ* (1986), 467. But cf. Gundling, *Proc. of the ASIL* (1989), 72.

(2) Equal Access, Non-discrimination, and the 'polluter pays' Principle[50]

(a) OECD Policy

OECD was the first international organization to develop an extensive strategy for dealing with transboundary air pollution. It established a European monitoring programme in 1972, and issued recommendations on measurement and control techniques for various forms of air pollution, including the reduction of sulphur dioxide and air pollution from fossil fuels.[51] OECD's policy consisted of encouraging the co-ordination of national control measures, the application of the 'polluter pays' principle to the allocation of pollution costs and the extension of transboundary remedies through equal access and non-discrimination. Its approach has had some influence in Western Europe, and it is particularly important in North America, where interstate agreement on the regulation of transboundary air pollution has been difficult to reach. The major attraction of OECD policy for governments has been the freedom it leaves them to determine their own priorities for pollution control; this freedom has been somewhat reduced as protocols to the 1979 Geneva Convention have been adopted, and by measures taken by the EEC.

(b) European Practice on Equal Access

European practice concerning equal access to transboundary remedies, considered in Chapter 5, is equally applicable to air pollution. Transboundary tort actions for damages are, however, limited by the practical problem of identifying the specific polluter, which is unlikely to be possible except in cases of localized injury. Equal access is thus of little help in dealing with long-range air pollution or acid rain from multiple sources in Europe.[52]

(c) North American Practice on Equal Access[53]

Canada and the United States have accepted that international law requires them to refrain from causing serious injury by air pollution.[54] Since the *Trail Smelter* case, however, individual complainants have been left to pursue private law remedies in transboundary cases. A few state and provincial legislatures in areas affected by air pollution have legislated to facilitate

[50] See Chs. 3 and 5.

[51] *OECD and the Environment* (Paris, 1986), 196–9; and ibid., Recommendations C(74) 16 (1974); C(74) 219; C(85) 101 (1985); Van Lier, *Acid Rain*, 163–72; Wetstone and Rosencranz, *Acid Rain*, 134–40.

[52] Bothe, in Flinterman, Kwiatkowska, and Lammers, *Transboundary Air Pollution*, 126; Kiss (ed.), *The Protection of the Environment and International Law* (Leiden, 1975), 150. On the application of the 1974 Nordic Convention For Protection of the Environment to air pollution, see Phillips, in Flinterman, Kwiatkowska, and Lammers, *Transboundary Air Pollution*, 159–62, and *supra*, pp. 197–201.

[53] See esp. Schmandt, Clarkson, and Roderick, *Acid Rain*, ch. 9.

[54] See Handl, in Flinterman, Kwiatkowska, and Lammers, *Transboundary Air Pollution*, 35.

equal access suits, encouraged by the Transboundary Reciprocal Access Act adopted by national bar associations as a model law.[55] As in Europe, however, individual tort actions are limited by the need to identify specific polluters, although this problem can be eased by the willingness of courts to impose joint liability on multiple tortfeasors, as in *Michie* v. *Great Lakes Steel Division*.[56]

To a limited extent Canadian and US legislation also accepts OECD's non-discrimination standard. Section 115 of the US Clean Air Act,[57] adopted in 1977, permits the administrator of the US Environmental Protection Agency to direct US state governments to take stronger air pollution abatement measures where an 'international agency' or the Secretary of State believes that pollution emanating from these states is endangering health and welfare in a foreign country. This provision was invoked by the EPA in 1980 on the basis of a report of the International Joint Commission concerning air pollution of the Great Lakes. Litigation showed, however, that action under the Act was discretionary and that the EPA could not subsequently be compelled to order abatement measures.[58] Canadian legislation is intended to provide reciprocal protection for the United States.[59] Unlike the Nordic Convention, however,[60] neither state makes provision for reciprocal access by administrative agencies to regulatory or licensing procedures, and the discretionary nature of the legislation means that it is not a reliable mechanism for ensuring that Canadian interests receive equal, or any, consideration in the control of US air pollution. Moreover, US legislation has not been designed to deal with long-range air pollution, but has concentrated instead on controlling local effects on public health and welfare.[61]

(3) The 1979 Geneva Convention on Long-Range Transboundary Air Pollution[62]

(a) The 1979 Framework Convention

Regional co-operation in the control of transboundary air pollution is strongest in Europe, where the problem of acid rain is the most severe. Since 1975, the Conference on Security and Co–operation in Europe has provided the necessary political momentum for the adoption of a European policy on the control of air pollution, and specific measures have been negotiated through

---

[55] See *supra*, pp. 204–5.
[56] 495 F. 2d. 213 (1974); Ianni, 11 *CYIL* (1973), 258.
[57] 42 USC 7415. See Schmandt, Clarkson, and Roderick, *Acid Rain*, 226 f.
[58] *Thomas* v. *New York* 802 F. 2d. 1443 (1986), reversing 613 F. Suppl. 1472 (1985).
[59] Clean Air Act (1980).
[60] *Supra*, p. 198.
[61] Wetstone and Rosencranz, *Acid Rain*, 97–122, but cf. McMahon, in Carroll (ed.), *International Environmental Diplomacy* (Cambridge, 1988), 155.
[62] Gundling, in Flinterman, Kwiatkowska, and Lammers, *Transboundary Air Pollution*, 19; Rosencranz, 75 *AJIL* (1981), 975; Fraenkel, 30 *Harv. ILJ* (1989), 447.

the UN Economic Commission for Europe.[63] This led to the establishment in 1976 of EMEP, the main European monitoring programme, and then in 1979 to the adoption of the Geneva Convention on Long-Range Transboundary Air Pollution.

This Convention remains the only major regional agreement devoted to the regulation and control of transboundary air pollution. It enables the parties to treat the European air mass as a shared resource and the problem as one requiring co-ordination of pollution control measures and common emission standards. In this sense it is comparable to the 1974 Paris Convention on Land-based Sources of Marine Pollution or to some of the more advanced international watercourse agreements.[64] Its purpose is thus to prevent, reduce, and control transboundary air pollution, both from new and existing sources, and it contains no provision on liability for air pollution damage, whether under international law or through civil proceedings.

The treaty came into force in 1983, and now has over thirty northern hemisphere parties in Western and Eastern Europe including the USSR and all the major polluter states. Canada and the United States have also ratified. It is weaker than the states who are net importers of pollutants would have liked, but only through compromise of essential interests on both sides could such widespread adherence by both groups have been achieved.[65]

'Long-range transboundary air pollution', to which it applies, is defined as pollution having effects at such a distance that 'it is not generally possible to distinguish the contributions of individual emission sources or groups of sources.'[66] Thus it is not aimed at *Trail Smelter* type cases, but at regional problems of acid rain and other widely dispersed pollutants. Nor is it confined to effects harmful to health or property. A much broader definition of 'pollution' is used, comparable to those found in marine pollution treaties, and which includes harm to living resources, ecosystems, interference with amenities, and legitimate uses of the environment.[67] Amelioration of a wide range of potential environmental harm is thus the treaty's basic objective.

No concrete commitments to specific reductions in air pollution are contained in the treaty itself. Instead, the parties have committed themselves only to broad principles and objectives for pollution control policy, in language often so weak that one commentary describes the treaty as no more than a 'symbolic victory' intended to reassure both the polluters and the victims.[68]

---

[63] Conference on Security and Co-operation in Europe, Helsinki Final Act, 1975, 14 *ILM* (1975), 1307–9. See Chossudovsky, *East–West Diplomacy for Environment in the United Nations* (New York, 1990), and *supra*, Ch. 2 nn. 116–18.

[64] See Chs. 6 and 8.

[65] Wetstone and Rosencranz, *Acid Rain*, 140–4.

[66] Article 1(b).

[67] Article 1(a). See *supra*, pp. 98–102.

[68] Wetstone and Rosencranz, *Acid Rain*, 145; Gundling, in Flinterman, Kwiatkowska, and Lammers, *Transboundary Air Pollution*, 21–3.

Thus there is only an obligation to 'endeavour to limit' and 'as far as possible, gradually reduce and prevent' air pollution.[69] To achieve this, parties undertake to develop the best policies, strategies, and control measures, but these must be compatible with 'balanced development', and the use of 'best available technology' which is 'economically feasible'.[70] A great deal of latitude is thus left to individual states to determine what level of effort they will put into pollution control and what cost they are willing to pay in overall economic development. For major polluters such as the United Kingdom and West Germany, this elastic obligation was the major condition for their acceptance of the treaty in 1979, and it has since enabled the United States to continue to cause serious pollution in Canada without violating the Convention.

The Geneva Convention also contains provisions on notification and consultation in cases of significant risk of transboundary pollution. These are only loosely comparable to the customary rule requiring consultation regarding shared resources or environmental risk.[71] Only 'major' changes in policy or industrial development likely to cause 'significant' changes in long-range air pollution must be notified to other states.[72] Otherwise, consultations need only be held at the request of parties 'actually affected by or exposed to a significant risk of long-range transboundary air pollution'.[73] However, the 1991 ECE Convention on Environmental Impact Assessment in a Transboundary Context will provide a stronger regime of assessment and consultation covering proposals to operate refineries, power stations, smelters, and other large-scale 'combustion installations' when it enters into force.[74] This convention requires the party initiating a proposed activity to take the initiative in providing notification to those likely to be affected, a position much closer to more recent treaty and ILC formulations than is found in the 1979 Geneva Convention.[75]

Despite its evident weaknesses, the Geneva Convention's main value is that it provides a framework for co-operation and for the development of further measures of pollution control. Articles 3, 4, 5, and 8 commit the parties to exchange information, conduct research, and consult on policies, strategies, and measures for combating and reducing air pollution. The convention is thus both a basis for continuing study of the problem, and for taking further co-ordinated action to deal with it. In this sense the weakness of its obligations is deceptive. Given adequate consensus among the parties,

---

[69] Article 2.

[70] Article 6. This article is directed 'in particular' at new or rebuilt installations.

[71] *Supra*, pp. 102–7.

[72] Article 8(b), Rosencranz, 75 *AJIL* (1981), 977 argues that 'few if any cases are likely to arise to trigger this article' because the threshold is so high.

[73] Article 5.

[74] *Supra*, pp. 105–6. See also 1991 US–Canada Air Quality Agreement, *infra*, n. 97.

[75] cf. *supra*, pp. 234–40.

stronger and more effective measures are possible within this framework. For this reason the creation of convention institutions is, as in other treaty regimes, of particular importance.

(b) The Convention's Institutions

These comprise an executive body, composed of environment advisers to ECE governments, which meets annually, and a secretariat provided by the ECE.[76] The executive body's main task is to keep under review the implementation of the convention, for which purpose it has instituted periodic reviews of the effectiveness of national policies.[77] In this respect the information it receives from the parties as required by Article 8, and from EMEP, is particularly important because it provides data on emissions of a wide range of substances and their distribution,[78] and enables the parties to use the results in determining what further measures are needed. Although the executive body has few powers, and there is no provision for compulsory dispute settlement, its success is best measured by the two protocols which have been negotiated setting specific targets for reduction of SO_2 and NO_x emissions.

(c) Protocols

The SO_2 protocol entered into force in 1987.[79] It requires the parties to reduce emissions or their transboundary fluxes by 30 per cent by 1993. Some countries, including Germany, have unilaterally adopted a higher target. The three major producers of SO_2 pollution, the US, UK, and Poland, have refused to ratify the protocol, however, arguing that their contribution to acid rain damage has not been established, or that the timetable is too strict.[80] The UK has, however, promised to make reductions by the year 2000, and EEC directives will also make stricter standards necessary.[81] Annual sulphur emissions must be reported to the executive body so that compliance can be monitored.[82] At its seventh meeting in 1989, the executive body decided to interpret the protocol as requiring that reduced emissions levels should be maintained or further reduced after 1993, and initiated preparation of a revised protocol with a more sophisticated 'critical loads' approach to future emissions control. The present protocol can be criticized for its somewhat arbitrary results, and its indifference to local variations in SO_2 pollution levels and effects.[83] Nevertheless, it is an indication that despite the 'soft' wording of

---

[76] Articles 10, 11.

[77] Executive Body, 4th Session, 1986, 17 *EPL* (1986), 3.

[78] See Article 9.

[79] Fraenkel, 30 *Harv. ILJ* (1989), 470; Protocol on the Reduction of Sulphur Emissions or their Transboundary Fluxes, 27 *ILM* (1988), 707.

[80] Rosencranz, in Carroll (ed.), *International Environmental Diplomacy* (Cambridge, 1988), 173.

[81] e.g. Council Directive 88/609, and see *infra*, n. 88.

[82] Articles 4, 5.

[83] Fraenkel, 30 *Harv. ILJ* (1989), 470.

the 1979 Geneva Convention, specific commitments can be developed within its terms.

The NO_x protocol was concluded in 1988, after prolonged and difficult negotiations, and it requires parties to stabilize their NO_x emissions or their transboundary fluxes at 1987 levels by 1994.[84] By allowing states to specify an earlier base year for emissions levels, however, some, such as the United States, may actually be able to increase their emissions. The protocol covers both major stationary sources, such as power plants, and vehicle emissions. Its approach to the co-ordination of national measures is more sophisticated than the SO_2 protocol, however, and requires the use of best available technology for national emissions standards, and the eventual negotiation of internationally accepted 'critical loads' for NO_x pollution to come into effect after 1996. This approach is likely to be more suited to regional environmental protection than the flat-rate emissions reductions of the SO_2 protocol, but whether it works in practice will depend on the ability of the parties to reach agreement on the necessary control measures.[85] In 1991, the draft of a third protocol, intended to deal with low-level ozone, was also under discussion.[86]

(d) Implementation and Assessment

Critics of the 1979 Geneva Convention have pointed out the weakness of its provisions and the latitude which it accords states.[87] The difficulty of securing political consensus on specific measures is evident in the compromises and delay which have affected negotiation of the SO_2 and NO_x protocols, and in the failure of some states to ratify them. But these protocols have facilitated legislation by the EEC and some of the parties.[88] Moreover, in their reports to the executive body, the parties have concurred in viewing the convention's impact on air pollution control and air quality management as a positive one, which has resulted in national and international action to improve the environment, to reduce pollution emissions, and to develop control technologies. However, Sand points out that any explanation of the reduction in emissions which has undoubtedly occurred must take account of evidence that these are largely due to reduced economic activity rather than to the effects of control measures.[89] Nor is it clear that the protocols' objectives are nearly

---

[84] 18 *EPL* (1988), 52 and 228; Fraenkel, 30 *Harv. ILJ* (1989), 472; note that 12 countries have made commitments to reduce emissions by more than is required under the Protocol.

[85] Fraenkel; cf. Gundling, *Proc. ASIL* (1989), 72. See *Report of the 8th Session of the Executive Body*, UN Doc. ECE/EB.AIR/24 (1990).

[86] UN Doc. ECE/EB.AIR/WG.4/R.12.

[87] Pallemaerts, *Hague YIL* (1988).

[88] EEC Council Directives 88/609; 88/76; 88/436; 89/458. For UK practice, see Environment Protection Act, 1990; Boyle, 39 *ICLQ* (1990), 940; Churchill, *JLS* (Special Issue, 1990), 162–8.

[89] In Helm, *Energy.* cf. *National Strategies and Policies for Air Pollution Abatement*, UN Doc. ECE/EB.AIR/14, 37.

ambitious enough if they are to be effective in reversing the loss of forests and other effects of acid rain. Nevertheless, one detailed study concludes that the Convention has been a 'qualified' success, due particularly to policy changes within the EEC and to a generally increased public awareness of the issues.[90]

(4) North American Practice

Whereas in Europe there is growing consensus on the adoption of emission controls on a wider range of air pollutants, and on the need for international co-operation to tackle air pollution, this is less so in North America.[91] The International Joint Commission, established by the 1909 US–Canadian Boundary Waters Treaty, has on several occasions been asked to investigate and make recommendations on matters of transboundary air pollution.[92] Its earliest involvement was in the opening stages of the *Trail Smelter* dispute, where in 1931 it recommended payment of $350,000 for damage inflicted in the United States. Later references to the IJC have mainly concerned local air pollution in the Michigan/Ontario border area. Its recommendations on these references are not binding, however. Moreover, the 1909 Boundary Waters Treaty does not prohibit air pollution or require the parties to control it; it merely provides machinery by which transboundary disputes may be adjusted, if the parties choose to use it. Successful use of the IJC to resolve the US–Canadian acid rain controversy would first require agreement on principles and objectives to be applied in the dispute, however.[93]

IJC research was the first to identify air pollution as a serious contaminant of the Great Lakes. In the 1978 Great Lakes Water Quality Agreement,[94] the two states agreed to a programme for identifying airborne pollutants of the waters. Where the atmospheric contribution is shown to be significant, they will also consult on appropriate remedial measures. This is a much weaker commitment than comparable provisions of the Baltic or Paris treaties on land-based sources of marine pollution in Europe.[95] Not only is it limited to the Great Lakes, it places no obligation on the parties and leaves the choice of measures entirely to negotiation and individual discretion.

Both Canada and the US are also parties to the 1979 Geneva Convention on Long Range Transboundary Air Pollution. In 1980, they signed a memorandum of intent to initiate negotiation of a bilateral agreement on trans-

---

[90] Wettestad and Andresen, *The Effectiveness of International Resource Co-operation: Some Preliminary Findings* (Lysaker, 1991), 74–88; cf. Gundling, *Proc. ASIL* (1989), 74, however. For consideration of the development of future strategies and policies, see *Report of the 8th Session of the Executive Body*.

[91] Schmandt, Clarkson, and Roderick, *Acid Rain*; Wetstone and Rosencranz, *Acid Rain*, 141–88; Johnston and Finkle, 17 *Vand. JTL* (1981), 787.

[92] Schmandt, Clarkson, and Roderick, *Acid Rain*, ch. 8.

[93] On the IJC, see generally, *supra*, pp. 245–7.

[94] Ibid.   [95] *Supra*, pp. 304–20.

boundary air pollution.[96] As an interim measure they agreed to develop domestic air pollution control policies and promote vigorous enforcement of existing laws in a manner responsive to the problems of transboundary air pollution. After a period of US opposition to the adoption of further controls on SO_2 and NO_x emissions, an agreement was concluded in 1991 committing the parties to establish specific objectives for emissions' limitations or reductions of air pollutants and to adopt the necessary measures,[97] including reductions in NO_x and SO_2 emissions. Other provisions of the agreement require each party to assess the transboundary air pollution impact of activities within their respective jurisdictions, and to notify, consult, and take measures to mitigate the potential risk. An air quality committee is established to review progress in the implementation of the agreement; its reports are to be available for public comment through the International Joint Commission, the parties must consult to review them, and any recommendations the committee may make. The parties also agreed to consider using the IJC for effective implementation of the 1991 agreement, and to refer disputes to it if these cannot be resolved by negotiation, in accordance with Articles 9 or 10 of the 1909 Boundary Waters Treaty. Thus substantial progress has now been made in securing the basis for an equitable resolution of the long-standing acid rain dispute between the United States and Canada on terms which address both the need for specific emissions reductions and for institutional supervision of their obligations in respect of their shared airmass.

As regards Mexico, the United States has also made some commitments, albeit of a more limited kind. An agreement of 1983 to co-operate in solving border environmental problems has two annexes dealing with air pollution.[98] The first sets specific sulphur emission limits for new smelters, and requires that existing units be effectively controlled in accordance with local law. The second reaffirms Principle 21 of the 1972 Stockholm Declaration on the Human Environment and commits the parties to establish a monitoring scheme for transboundary urban air pollution, to identify major stationary sources, and to explore ways of harmonizing air pollution control standards. The object of both agreements is mainly to control Mexican pollution to US standards; they afford no evidence of serious intention to treat the airmass as a shared resource requiring strong measures of protection.[99]

---

[96] 20 *ILM* (1980), 690.

[97] 1991 Agreement Between the Government of the United States and the Government of Canada on Air Quality. For an account of the earlier stages of this dispute, see Carroll, *International Environmental Diplomacy*, 141–88, and Williams, *Proc. ASIL* (1989), 75.

[98] 1983 Agreement on Co-operation for the Protection and Improvement of the Environment in the Border Area, 1987 Annex IV, Agreement Regarding Transboundary Air Pollution Caused by Copper Smelters, 26 *ILM* (1987), 33; 1990 Annex V Agreement Regarding International Transport of Urban Air Pollution, 30 *ILM* (1991), 678.

[99] See Applegate and Bath, in Flinterman, Kwiatkowska, and Lammers, *Transboundary Air Pollution*, 95–114, and eid, 22 *NRJ* (1982), 1147–74.

(5) Air Pollution of the Marine Environment

Article 212 of the 1982 UNCLOS requires states to adopt laws and regulations to prevent, reduce, and control atmospheric pollution of the marine environment. Like the comparable Article 207 on land-based sources of pollution it sets no specific standards and merely requires states to take account of internationally agreed rules, which they need only endeavour to establish. Like similar articles in most of the UNEP's regional seas treaties, this reflects the minimal level of international control of this form of marine pollution emanating from activities on land.[100] None of the UNEP treaties has resulted in any significant action on a regional basis, except in the Mediterranean, where the 1980 Athens Protocol on land-based sources of pollution applies to air pollution 'but only under conditions to be defined in an additional annex'. No such annex has been agreed. The only significant regional agreements which attempt to control atmospheric pollution of the sea from land-based sources are the 1974 Paris Convention and the 1974 Helsinki Convention, which apply respectively to the North Sea and North-West Atlantic, and the Baltic. The International North Sea Conference has also made recommendations concerning reduction of airborne pollution of the North Sea. Atmospheric pollution caused by incineration of waste at sea is regulated by the 1972 London Dumping Convention and the 1972 Oslo Dumping Convention. These treaties and state practice are considered more fully in Chapter 8.

3. PROTECTING THE GLOBAL ATMOSPHERE

(1) Ozone Depletion

(a) The 1985 Vienna Convention for the Protection of the Ozone Layer[101]

UNEP initiated negotiation of a treaty to protect the ozone layer in 1981.[102] As with the 1979 Convention on Long-Range Transboundary Air Pollution, the interests of several groups had to be reconciled. These included developing countries, such as India, China, and Brazil, which were primarily concerned that restraints on the use of ozone-depleting substances might inhibit their

---

[100] See generally pp. 308–14.

[101] Rummel-Bulska, in Flinterman, Kwiatkowska, and Lammers, *Transboundary Air Pollution*, 281; Williams, ibid., 267; Kindt and Menefee, 24 *TILJ* (1989), 261; Benedick, *Ozone Diplomacy* (Cambridge, Mass., 1991); Engelmann, 8 *EPL* (1982), 49; Heimsoeth, 10 *EPL* (1983), 34; Churchill, in Churchill and Freestone, *Global Climate Change*, 152–6; Lawrence, 2 *JEL* (1990), 17; Brunée, *Acid Rain and Ozone Layer Depletion* (Dobbs Ferry, NY, 1988), 225–54.

[102] For text and commentary on successive drafts, see Ad Hoc Working Group on the Ozone Convention UNEP/WG.69/8; UNEP/WG.78/2; UNEP/WG.78/4; UNEP/WG.78/10; UNEP/WG.94/3; UNEP/WG.94/4 and Adds. 1 and 2; UNEP/WG.94/8; UNEP/WG.94/11.

industrial development, or that alternative technologies might not be available to them. The United States, which had earlier acted unilaterally to reduce domestic production and consumption of CFCs, did not wish to remain at a disadvantage while others went on using them, and its position was strongly in favour of an international control regime. The EEC represented the largest group of producers and was reluctant to commit itself to measures that might prove costly to implement. Moreover, some EEC states resisted controls on the grounds that harmful effects had not been proven, and that the risk remained long term and speculative. Unlike air pollution, however, no regime would be likely to work unless it was global, since the impact of ozone-depleting substances is the same wherever or however they originate, and would affect all states. Thus, as many parties as possible would have to be persuaded to join and there would have to be strong disincentives to deter relocation of CFC production to non-parties.[103]

Again following the pattern of the 1979 Geneva Convention on Long-Range Transboundary Air Pollution, the Vienna Convention for the Protection of the Ozone Layer adopted in 1985 makes reference in its preamble to Principle 21 of the 1972 Stockholm Declaration on the Human Environment, but imposes few concrete obligations. The weakness of its provisions indicates compromise between demands for more research and a commitment to firm action. Parties are to take 'appropriate measures', including the adoption of legislation and administrative controls, to protect human health and the environment 'against adverse effects resulting or likely to result from human activities which modify or are likely to modify the ozone layer.'[104] The nature of these measures is not defined, but the parties must co-operate in harmonizing policies and in formulating 'agreed measures, procedures and standards for the implementation of this Convention.' Nor does the convention specify any particular substances to which these measures must relate; it merely lists in an annex substances 'thought' to have the potential to modify the ozone layer.

The only measures which the convention itself actually requires the parties to take concern assessment of the causes and effects of ozone depletion, the transmission of information, and the exchange of information and technology.[105] These provisions lay the basis for ensuring adequate monitoring and research, and for making substitute technologies and substances available to all, including developing countries. But Article 4, which deals with the acquisition of alternative technology, was most unsatisfactory from the perspective of developing countries, since it merely required states to co-

---

[103] Ad Hoc Working Group, 2nd Session, 1982, 10 *EPL* (1983), 34; UNEP Working Group on CFCs, 16 *EPL* (1986), 139.
[104] Article 2.
[105] Articles 2(2)(a), 4, 5.

operate, in accordance with their own laws, regulations, and practices, in the development and transfer of technology and knowledge. This is significantly weaker than transfer of technology provisions in the 1982 UNCLOS,[106] and essentially leaves the matter to each state's discretion. Article 4 proved inadequate to satisfy the concerns of developing states that CFC substitutes might not be available to them, or would be prohibitively expensive, and the issue was reopened in later negotiations.

Institutions created by the convention comprise a regular conference of the parties and a secretariat. Like the Executive Body of the 1979 Geneva Convention on Long-Range Transboundary Air Pollution, the conference of the parties reviews implementation of the convention, receiving for that purpose reports from the parties and establishing the necessary programmes and policies. It is responsible for adopting new protocols and annexes, and for amending the convention.

Thus the 1985 Convention is largely an empty framework, requiring further action by the parties, who proved unable in 1985 to agree on proposals for more specific control measures.[107] Nevertheless, it is an important precedent with wider significance in environmental law. First, it is explicitly concerned with protection of the global environment, and defines adverse effects to mean: 'changes in the physical environment or biota, including changes in climate, which have significant deleterious effects on human health or on the composition, resilience and productivity of natural and managed ecosystems, or on materials useful to mankind.'[108] This definition both recognizes the impact of ozone depletion on climate change, and adopts an ecosystem approach in terms which suggest that the natural environment has a significance independent of its immediate utility to man. Neither 'conservation' nor 'pollution' are appropriate terms in describing the scope of this convention.[109]

Secondly, the Ozone Convention is one of the first to perceive the need for preventive action in advance of firm proof of actual harm, and in that sense it is indicative of the emergence of a more 'precautionary' approach than had been typical for earlier pollution conventions, including the 1979 Geneva Convention on Long-Range Transboundary Air Pollution.[110]

(b) The 1987 Montreal Protocol

The 1987 Montreal Protocol on Substances that Deplete the Ozone Layer,[111] revised in 1990, represents a much more significant agreement than the convention itself. First, it sets firm targets for reducing and eventually eliminating

---

[106] cf. 1982 UNCLOS, Article 144 and Annex III, Article 5.
[107] UNEP, Ad Hoc Working Group on the Ozone Convention, UNEP/WG.94/9.
[108] Article 1(2).
[109] Supra, pp. 98–102.
[110] Preamble; and see Benedick, Ozone Diplomacy, 45, and supra, pp. 95–8.

consumption and production of a range of ozone-depleting substances. These were supported particularly strongly by the United States, which referred to the need to err on the side of caution and to recall the well-being of future generations, and by the Executive Director of UNEP, whose efforts ensured that a consensus emerged among the scientific experts on predicting the rate of ozone depletion and the regulatory measures needed to protect health and the environment. Following scientific evidence that the standards adopted in 1987 would not be effective in reducing ozone depletion, however, additional substances were included by the amendments adopted in 1990 and the timetable for complete elimination was revised and brought forward to the year 2000.[112] These changes were made possible by the development of new technology and alternative substances, although in some cases these substitutes may still have an ozone-depleting potential, and their use is not without problems. Limited allowance is made for increases in production of ozone-depleting substances to meet domestic needs until 2000, and to facilitate industrial rationalization. Control of both consumption and production was necessary in order to protect the interests of producers and importers by deterring price inflation or over-production in the interim period until the eventual phase-out of these gases.[113]

Secondly, acknowledging the inequity of equal treatment for all, and the very small contribution to ozone depletion made by developing states, the protocol makes special provision for their needs. It was essential to encourage participation by these states, given their potential for increased production of CFCs, and the likelihood that this would simply nullify the actions of developed states. Although the 1987 protocol would have allowed them a possibly substantial increase in production and consumption for domestic needs,[114] this option did not prove sufficiently attractive to prompt India and China to ratify the protocol, and would in any case have reduced its effectiveness. The accelerated timetable set for eventual phase-out by the 1990 revision required a different approach to the position of developing states. Although some allowance is still made in the revised Article 5 for delayed compliance with the control measures by this group, the protocol now adopts new financial and technical incentives to encourage such states to switch as quickly as possible to alternative substances and technologies.[115] Article 10 establishes a fund

[111] Ad Hoc Working Group of Legal and Technical Experts, First Session, UNEP/WG.151/L.4 (1986); id., Second Session, UNEP/WG.167/2 (1987); id., Third Session, UNEP/WG.172/2 (1987). See Benedick, *Ozone Diplomacy*, and UNEP, *Handbook for the Montreal Protocol on Substances that Deplete the Ozone Layer* (Nairobi, 1991), which also gives agreed definitions of various terms.

[112] Amendment and Adjustments to the Montreal Protocol, London, 1990, repr. in Churchill and Freestone, *Global Climate Change*, 224; Benedick, *Ozone Diplomacy*, 139–47, 163–79.

[113] Explanatory Note by the Executive Director of UNEP, Montreal, 1987.

[114] Article 5. See Rosencranz and Scott, 20 *EPL* (1990), 201.

[115] Benedick, *Ozone Diplomacy*, 148–62, 183–98.

financed by those parties to the convention which are not taking advantage of the dispensation allowed for developing countries in Article 5.[116] Its purpose is to facilitate technical co-operation and technology transfer so that developing states do not have to rely on Article 5 to protect their interests but are enabled to comply fully with the protocol's control measures. The revised protocol also requires each party to take 'every practicable step' to ensure that substitutes and technology are expeditiously transferred under 'fair and most favourable conditions' to developing states.[117] Although this provision by no means overcomes the reluctance of chemical companies in the developed world to transfer technology,[118] and does not compel them to do so, the obligation of developing countries to comply with the protocol's control measures 'will depend upon' the effective implementation of these provisions on financial co-operation and transfer of technology. Moreover, if these provisions do not work effectively, developing states may refer the matter to a meeting of the parties, which must decide on appropriate action. Put shortly, developing states are given the power to put pressure on developed states to ensure that they have the necessary means to meet the protocol's target for elimination of ozone-depleting substances. This is one of a number of innovative measures adopted in the 1990 revision to ensure compliance and effective implementation.

Thirdly, the protocol attempts to deal with the problem of non-parties by banning trade in controlled substances with these states.[119] This ban will eventually extend to products containing such substances. The parties must also discourage the export of CFC production technology. During the 1987 negotiations the question of compatibility of this article with the General Agreement on Tariffs and Trade was raised.[120] Since the measures proposed were neither arbitrary nor unjustifiable, and did not discriminate against non-parties as such, but could only be applied against those not following the protocol's control measures, it was concluded that Article 4 would be in accordance with Article 20(b) of the GATT concerning protection of human, animal, or plant life or health, although the final judgment in the event of a bilateral dispute would rest with the contracting parties to GATT. There were already precedents for controls on trade with non-parties in the 1973

---

[116] See Annex IV, Appendix II and IV and World Bank documents in 30 *ILM* (1991), 1735–77. UNCED, Prepcom, UN Doc. A/CONF. 151/PC/58 (1991), 5–7 reviews the working of these funds. This fund will be administered by the World Bank, UNEP, and UNDP. The World Bank's Global Environmental Facility will also be made available, on which see *supra*, Ch. 2 n. 38 and pp. 62–3; Decision II/88, 2nd Meeting of the Parties, UNEP/OzL. Pro.2/3 (1990); Lawrence, 2 *JEL* (1990).

[117] Article 10A.

[118] Rosencranz and Scott, 20 *EPL* (1990). Lawrence, 2 *JEL* (1990), concludes that reluctance to transfer CFC substitute technology is based primarily on financial rather than legal considerations.

[119] Article 4, as revised 1990.

[120] Ad Hoc Working Group, 2nd Session, 22; id., 3rd Session, 18.

CITES Convention, and under resolutions of the parties to the 1972 London Dumping Convention and the 1946 International Convention for the Regulation of Whaling.[121]

(c) Supervision and Compliance Machinery

The institutional provisions of the 1987 protocol merit special note, since they are the key to its flexible development and enforcement.[122] The powers enjoyed by the meeting of the parties to this protocol are in two senses unusual, if not unique, among environmental treaties. First, provided efforts to reach a consensus have been exhausted, certain decisions may be taken by a two-thirds majority which will bind all parties to the protocol, including those who voted against the decision.[123] To maintain the equitable balance between developed and developing states these decisions must be supported by separate majorities of both groups. In this way further adjustments and reductions in the production and consumption of controlled substances may be adopted and will enter into force within six months. The same rule applies to decisions concerning the financial mechanism and under Article 5. Objecting states retain the option of withdrawing from the protocol on one year's notice.[124] Other amendments to the protocol, including the addition of new controlled substances, must be made in accordance with Article 9 of the Ozone Convention, and will be effective only in respect of parties who ratify or accept them.

Secondly, and again unusually, the protocol provides for the negotiation of a formal non-compliance procedure.[125] An interim procedure was agreed in 1990 which any party may invoke unilaterally.[126] An 'implementation committee' hears complaints and submissions from the parties concerned, 'with a view to securing an amicable resolution on the basis of respect for the provisions of the protocol'. The committee reports to a meeting of the parties, which may 'decide upon and call for steps to bring about full compliance.' In addition, as we have seen, the meeting of the parties will also decide on appropriate action when developing states are unable to implement the protocol through the failure of developed states to provide finance or technology.[127] It remains unclear, however, whether parties are bound to comply with any of these decisions.

Article 11 of the Ozone Convention provides for optional acceptance of compulsory arbitration or judicial settlement in the event of a dispute between

---

[121] *Supra*, pp. 131–3.   [122] See *supra*, pp. 166–79.   [123] Article 2(9), as revised 1990.
[124] Article 19, but see 1990 revision.   [125] Article 8.
[126] Decision II/5 and Annex III, UNEP OzL.Pro.2/3 (1990), and see Gehring, 1 *YIEL* (1990), 50–4. For negotiations on the final form this mechanism will take, see Ad Hoc Working Group, 2nd meeting, UNEP/OzL. Pro/WG.3/2/2 (1991) and OzL. Pro/WG.3/3/2 (1991).
[127] Article 5, 1987 Protocol, as revised 1990.

the parties. Alternatively it requires them to negotiate a solution, with the possibility of resort to good offices or mediation. This is not a strong dispute-settlement clause, and the addition of the multilateral non-compliance procedure does emphasize the importance of collective control and supervision by the meeting of the parties as a means of securing implementation of the protocol through multilateral negotiation rather than adjudication.[128]

In other respects the meeting of the parties performs roles comparable to those provided for in other recent environmental treaties, including reviewing implementation of the protocol and making adjustments or amendments. Article 7 of the protocol was revised in 1990 and requires the parties to provide statistical information on production, imports, and exports of controlled substances to the secretariat so that the performance of the parties can be accurately monitored.

(d) Assessing the Montreal Protocol

One measure of the protocol's success is that it had some fifty parties by March 1990, including the USSR, United Kingdom, Germany, United States, and the EEC. Moreover, following the 1990 revisions China and India expressed their intention to ratify and a number of African and Latin American states were already parties. Thus, some progress has been made in securing the necessary level of global adherence for the protocol to work.

Secondly, the protocol has undoubtedly generated support among industrialized states. In some cases additional national measures to secure an early phase-out of CFCs have been agreed. A statement by a group of thirteen industrialized countries during the 1990 negotiations declared their firm determination to 'take all appropriate measures to phase out the production and consumption of all fully halogenated chlorofluorocarbons controlled by the Montreal Protocol... as soon as possible but not later than 1997.'[129] Measures to implement the protocol have been adopted by the United States in the Clean Air Act of 1990[130] and by the EEC.[131] Canada has reported a fall in consumption of controlled substances of 19 per cent; production and consumption in the UK have fallen by 30 per cent and 50 per cent

---

[128] Gehring, 1 YIEL (1990), and see supra, pp. 166–79.

[129] Statement by Governments of Australia, Austria, Belgium, Canada, Denmark, FRG, Finland, Lichtenstein, Netherlands, New Zealand, Norway, Sweden, Switzerland. See also the Resolution by the governments and the European Communities at the Second Meeting of the Parties to the Montreal Protocol, in Benedick, Ozone Diplomacy, 262; the Bergen Declaration on Sustainable Development, 20 EPL (1990), 84; the 1989 Helsinki Declaration on the Protection of the Ozone Layer, 19 EPL (1989), 137.

[130] 20 EPL (1990), 95.

[131] Council Regulations No. 3322/88 and 594/91. See also draft directive COM (91) 220, OJ No. C 192/17, 23.7.91. For UK practice, see Boyle, 39 ICLQ (1990), 942; Churchill, JLS (Special Issue, 1990), 157–62.

respectively, and production of CFCs in West Germany has fallen by 15 per cent.[132]

Thirdly, whereas scientific assessments showed that in its original 1987 form the Montreal Protocol would not have halted an accelerating level of chlorine loading in the stratosphere, the 1990 revisions are predicted to result in a gradually diminishing level after the year 2000.[133] But it will be at least 2040 before the figure returns to 1985 levels, and there will continue to be a significant increase until 2000. Other problems may also affect the success of the protocol,[134] including subsequent evidence of a faster rate of ozone depletion than expected, and of the significant contribution made by air-craft exhaust emissions which are not controlled by the protocol. Moreover, although the protocol has encouraged resort to substitute substances and technologies, as we have seen it is not certain that some of these are not themselves ozone depleting. The use of HCFCs, listed as 'transitional substances' under the 1990 amendments of the Montreal Protocol will for this reason have to be moderate and temporary if the protocol's targets are to be met. Difficulties in matters of technology transfer and intellectual property rights may hamper the attempt to protect the position of developing countries, despite the existence of international funding for their benefit. Lastly, the effective operation of the protocol's compliance procedure is dependent on the reporting of information under Article 7; problems in this respect have required the special attention of a UNEP working group, and remain unresolved.[135] Nevertheless, the Ozone Convention and the Montreal Protocol have created one of the most elaborate and sophisticated models of inter-national control and supervision for environmental purposes; it is this model which may have the most influence on the negotiation of any convention to protect the atmosphere from global climate change.

(2) Global Climate Change[136]

(a) Customary Law[137]

The argument that the 'no harm' principle considered in Chapter 3 applies to the protection of the global atmosphere is not difficult to make. Principle 21 of the Stockholm Declaration on the Human Environment already forms the basis for the 1979 Geneva Convention on Long-Range Transboundary Air Pollution, the 1985 Vienna Convention for the Protection of the Ozone Layer,

---

[132] UNEP/OzL. Pro/WG.2/1/4 (1990), 3.

[133] See table in Benedick, *Ozone Diplomacy*, 177.

[134] Rosencranz and Scott, 20 *EPL* (1990); UNCED, Prepcom, UN Doc. A/CONF.151/PC/58 (1991).

[135] *Supra*, n. 132.

[136] See Churchill and Freestone, *Global Climate Change*; Taylor, 20 *VUWLR* (1990), 45; Nanda, 30 *Harv. ILJ* (1989), 375.

[137] Boyle, in Churchill and Freestone, *Global Climate Change*, 4.

and Articles 192 and 194 of the 1982 UNCLOS, which, as we have seen, requires states to protect and preserve the marine environment from pollution, including atmospheric discharges. Although the global atmosphere is not an area 'beyond the limits of national jurisdiction', and thus does not quite fit the precise terms of Principle 21,[138] it should by analogy fall within the protection afforded by international law to common areas such as the high seas. This conclusion is implicit in the Ozone Convention and in UNGA Resolution 43/53.[139]

Moreover, international claims concerning the conduct of atmospheric nuclear tests provide some precedent for the inference that, like the high seas, the global atmosphere must be used with reasonable regard for the rights of other states, including the protection of their environment and human health. As we have seen in Chapter 9, such tests are now arguably unreasonable and contrary to customary international law.[140] This conclusion may be specific to the discharge of radioactivity, however, and it cannot be assumed that discharges of greenhouse gases or ozone-depleting substances are necessarily unlawful or subject to similar limitations of reasonableness. But the 1977 Convention on the Prohibition of Military or Other Hostile Use of Environmental Modification Techniques does indicate that many states regard the hostile modification of the atmosphere as contrary to international law[141]. UNEP Principles concerning weather modification for peaceful purposes recommend that states should co-operate in informing, notifying, and consulting international organizations and other states in cases of proposed weather modification activities, and that these should only be carried out after an assessment of their environmental consequences and in a manner 'designed to ensure that they do not cause damage to the environment of other states or of areas beyond the limits of national jurisdiction.'[142]

Customary international law, and the responsibility of states for the performance of their customary obligations may therefore provide some legal restraint on the production of greenhouse gases or on the conduct of other activities likely to result in global climate change. But as in the case of acid rain, it is not easy to extrapolate from this conclusion precise standards for the diligent conduct of states. Treaties which might give clarity and content to the customary rule remain incomplete. Reference may be made to the protocols of the 1979 Geneva Convention on Long-Range Transboundary Air Pollution, and to the Montreal Protocol to the Ozone Convention. But there is no agreement on the control of other atmospheric gases such as CO_2 or methane,

---

[138] *Supra*, pp. 390–1.
[139] Ibid. See also UNGA Resolution 44/207 (1989), para. 4, and UNEP Principles of Co-operation in Weather Modification (1980).
[140] *Supra*, pp. 358–61.
[141] *Supra*, pp. 127–31.
[142] UNEP Principles of Co-operation in Weather Modification (1980).

nor does it follow that standards adopted under the above conventions can be generalized into customary law.[143]

Numerous international declarations have called for various measures to reduce the generation of CO_2, and individual governments have in some cases committed themselves to stabilize or reduce emissions over a variety of time scales,[144] but these are negotiating positions, or lack the consistency and consensus necessary to constitute new rules of custom. Moreover, it is clear that some states remain opposed to specific action on CO_2 emissions. The extent to which customary law can usefully be employed to compel states to give priority to preventing global climate change or to the adoption and application of international standards thus remains highly questionable. Only the adoption of a 'precautionary principle' as a legal principle might alter this conclusion if it required states to refrain from increasing or continuing with their present emission levels until they had demonstrated that no harm would ensue.[145] Without dismissing the relevance of customary law as a basis for negotiation, it seems clear that, as in the case of ozone depletion, a global framework treaty is needed to provide for the negotiation of detailed commitments and international supervision.[146]

(b) The Development of a Global Climate Change Convention

The elements of a climate-change convention have been considered by a meeting of experts in Ottawa in 1989[147] and by the Intergovernmental Panel on Climate Change.[148] A draft text was composed from these elements in preparation for the UNCED conference in 1992.[149] The 1989 Ottawa proposals treat the atmosphere as a 'common resource of vital interest to mankind', and declare that states have an obligation to protect and preserve the atmosphere, and must take all appropriate measures to control, reduce, or

---

[143] See Churchill, in Churchill and Freestone, *Global Climate Change*, ch. 9.

[144] 1989 Declaration of the Hague, 28 *ILM* (1989), 1308; EC Council Resolution 89/C183/ 03 on the Greenhouse Effect, 28 *ILM* (1989), 1306; 1989 Noordwijk Declaration on Atmospheric Pollution and Climate Change, 19 *EPL* (1989), 229; World Conference on Preparing for Climate Change, Cairo Compact, 20 *EPL* (1990), 59; Ministerial Declaration, Second World Climate Conference, Geneva, 1990, 1 *YIEL* (1990), 473; Tokyo Conference on the Global Environment, 20 *EPL* (1990), 60; African Conference on Global Warming and Climate Change, Nairobi, 1990, 20 *EPL* (1990), 234. Countries which have stated their intention to stabilize or reduce CO_2 emissions include Japan, Germany, the UK, Canada, France, Italy, Australia, the Netherlands, Belgium, the Nordic states, New Zealand, and Switzerland. The EFTA states and the EEC have also agreed to do so.

[145] See Freestone, in Churchill and Freestone, *Global Climate Change*, Ch. 2, and *supra*, pp. 95-8.

[146] See UNEP, Governing Council Resolution 15/36 (1989); UNGA Res. 44/207 (1989), and conference declarations, *supra*, n. 144.

[147] *Supra*, n. 19.

[148] IPCC, *Report of Working Group III on Response Strategies* (1990).

[149] Barrett, in Churchill and Freestone, *Global Climate Change*, ch. 11.

prevent 'atmospheric interference'. The remaining provisions are comparable to those found in the 1985 Ozone Convention and in more recent pollution treaties, and cover matters such as environmental impact assessment, consultation, and exchange of information. Further protocols would be necessary in order to implement this very general proposal for a framework convention. The IPCC proposal is similar, but places greater emphasis on institutional issues, following the example of the Montreal Protocol. A number of states have supported the view that strong institutional machinery is necessary to combat global climate change, including dispute settlement procedures.[150] The IPCC makes reference to global climate change as the 'common concern of mankind', but 'without prejudice to the sovereignty of states over the airspace superadjacent to their territory', and it refers also to the concept of sustainable development and the needs of future generations. It envisages an obligation to adopt 'appropriate' measures to mitigate the adverse effects of climate change, recognizing the 'responsibility of all countries to make efforts at the national, regional and global levels to limit or reduce greenhouse gas emissions and prevent activities which could adversely affect climate',[151] but also acknowledging the predominant role of industrialized countries in bringing about climate change.

A rather weak climate change convention was adopted at the UNCED conference.[152] The experience of the Ozone Convention suggests that questions of economic development, the interests of developing states and future generations, the provision of financial incentives, technical assistance, and technology transfer are equally important in this context. The development of institutions capable of regulating the global atmosphere, and of ensuring effective compliance and implementation will, as in most of the examples considered in this book, be a key element in the operation of this agreement, which must also enjoy global support and participation.

But the range of issues involved in controlling climate change and its possible effects is significantly broader and more complex than faced the negotiators of the Ozone Convention. Matters such as deforestation, the protection of natural habitats and ecosystems, sea-level rise, development assistance, and sovereignty over natural resources are also important elements of the problem.[153] Increasingly, the sectoral approach which has traditionally predominated in the international regulation of the environment is no longer

---

[150] Declaration of the Hague, *supra*, n. 144.

[151] Grubb, 66 *Int. Affairs* (1990), 67 reviews the possible measures which may be needed to reduce greenhouse emissions. See also Churchill, in Churchill and Freestone, *Global Climate Change*, ch. 9.

[152] UNGA Res. 45/212 (1990) established a negotiating process for a framework convention on climate change, co-ordinated by UNEP and WMO. Reports of the 1st, 2nd, and 3rd Sessions of the Intergovernmental Negotiating Committee are found in UN Doc. A/AC.237/6, 9, and L.9 (1991).

[153] See further, Churchill and Freestone, *Global Climate Change*.

appropriate as the interconnected and global character of the issues becomes apparent. Pollution control and the conservation of resources are both involved, within the broader context of a search for sustainable development. The political and economic complexity of tackling global climate change also has implications for the structure of decision-making within the UN and its specialized organs, including UNEP. This has prompted proposals for giving explicit authority over environmental matters to the Security Council or the Trusteeship Council, for giving UNEP greater status, and for institutionaliz-ing the IPCC.[154] What may become more apparent is a trend, already evident in the Montreal Protocol, to move away from the present system of decentralized decision-making which has characterized the development of international environmental law, and to stress the interdependent and conditional nature of national sovereignty over natural resources, economic development, and environmental policy.

4. OUTER SPACE

Like the high seas, the law of outer space is based on principles of equal access and freedom of exploitation and use by all states.[155] UN resolutions adopted unanimously,[156] and the 1967 Outer Space Treaty, now widely ratified, reflect agreement on a body of general rules governing activities in outer space. Although the lawmaking effect of these instruments is debatable,[157] it seems likely that their environmental provisions are a good guide to states' obligations in space.[158] They reflect customary law relat-ing to other common areas, notably the high seas, and draw on principles now generally confirmed by the Stockholm Declaration on the Human Environment, such as responsibility for harm, although the opportunities for consistent state practice remain few.

Under the 1967 Outer Space Treaty, states must conduct their activities in space with due regard to the interests of others; they must avoid harmful contamination of space or celestial bodies, and take appropriate measures to

---

[154] See Plant, ibid., ch. 10. UNEP Governing Council Resolution SS.II/3/B (1990) calls for the continuation of the IPCC as a joint panel of UNEP and WMO to provide scientific support for a convention on climate change.

[155] Article 1, 1967 Treaty on Principles Governing the Activities of States in the Exploration and Use of Outer Space, including the Moon and other Celestial Bodies; UNGA Res. 1962 XVIII (1963); Fawcett, *International Law and the Uses of Outer Space* (Manchester, 1968), ch. 2; Lay and Taubenfeld, *The Law Relating to the Activities of Man in Space* (1970), ch. 4.

[156] UNGA Res. 1962 XVIII (1963); UNGA Res. 1721 XVI (1961).

[157] Cheng, *International Law Teaching and Practice* (London, 1982), 237; Fawcett, *Outer Space*, 15–16; Lay and Taubenfeld, *Activities of Man in Space*, 84–6.

[158] Christol, *The Modern International Law of Outer Space* (New York, 1982), ch. 4; Lay and Taubenfeld, *Activities of Man in Space*, 189–91; Sand, 21 *ICLQ* (1972), 45.

avoid adverse changes in the environment of the Earth by extraterrestrial matter.[159] Article 9 also requires consultations to be held in advance of any activity or experiment where harmful interference may be caused to the activities of other parties.[160] This was not intended to give other states a veto, but it should entitle them to have their views considered in good faith.[161] Interestingly, this provision goes beyond any explicit treaty requirement affecting the uses of the high seas.[162] As defined here, however, consultation is not meant to protect the environment of Earth or outer space as such; it is directed solely at protecting the interests of states in exploration and use of space.[163]

States are also responsible under the 1967 Treaty for all national activities in outer space and liable for damage caused by objects launched into space.[164] A later treaty[165] and state practice[166] confirm that liability for damage caused on Earth by space objects is direct and absolute; no fault or lack of diligence on the part of the launching or procuring states is necessary.[167] The responsibility of states for their other activities in space is narrower. They are required to ensure conformity with the treaty by means of authorization and continuing supervision of national space activities, whether private or public, a formulation which suggests a standard of due diligence only.[168]

While space objects are thus treated as 'extra hazardous', recoverable damage is defined by the 1972 treaty in terms similar to the *Trail Smelter* case, covering only loss of life, health, personal injury, or damage to property.[169]

---

[159] Article 9; UNGA Res. 1962 XVIII, para. 6.

[160] See also UNGA Res. 1962 XVIII, para. 6. This provision was prompted by the failure of the US to consult other states prior to the West Ford project, in which copper dipoles were distributed in earth orbit. See Lay and Taubenfeld, *Activities of Man in Space*, 189.

[161] Lay and Taubenfeld, *Activities of Man in Space*, 191.

[162] But in the *Icelandic Fisheries Case*, ICJ Reps. (1974), 29, Article 2 of the 1958 High Seas Convention was found to imply a duty to negotiate in good faith over conflicting uses of the high seas.

[163] cf. the broader obligation in Article 9 to avoid adverse changes or contamination in the Earth or space environment. No consultation is required here.

[164] Articles 6 and 7; UNGA Res. 1962 XVIII, paras. 5 and 8. Under Article 7 states retain ownership, jurisdiction, and control over objects and jurisdiction and control over personnel launched into space. Space objects must also be registered with the UN under the 1975 Convention on Registration of Objects Launched into Outer Space. This is mainly to avoid danger of collision, but it also assists identification of space debris causing damage on earth.

[165] 1972 Convention on International Liability for Damage Caused by Space Objects, Article 2. See Christol, *Modern International Law of Outer Space*, ch. 3; Matte, *Aerospace Law* (Toronto, 1977), 153–74; Foster, 10 *CYIL* (1972), 136.

[166] Cosmos 954 Claim, 18 *ILM* (1979), 899, on which see *supra*, pp. 147, 153.

[167] Under Article 3, however, liability for damage to outer space objects requires fault by the state, or persons for whom it is responsible; Article 6 exonerates the launching state where damage results from the act or omission of a claimant state.

[168] 1967 Outer Space Convention, Article 6. cf. Article 139, LOSC imposing similar responsibility for activities on the deep sea-bed, and see *supra*, p. 146.

[169] Article 1.

It is questionable how far harm to the environment of Earth or space is included here.[170] Canada successfully claimed the cost of removing hazardous radioactive debris from her territory when Cosmos 954 crashed, asserting that the deposit of such potentially harmful material constituted 'damage to property' under Article I of the 1972 Space Objects Liability Convention, although reliance was placed also on Article 7 of the Outer Space Treaty and on general principles of international law.[171] Thus, at least in circumstances requiring action to prevent further harm, environmental clean-up and reinstatement costs may be recovered.[172] In addition, introduction of extra-terrestrial matter adversely changing the Earth's environment, contrary to Article 9 of the Outer Space Treaty, would incur responsibility for the sort of general harm to the environment now included in Principle 21 of the 1972 Stockholm Declaration. But the 1972 treaty does not apply to environmental damage above the surface of the Earth, or on celestial bodies.[173] This restriction is not found in Article 7 of the Outer Space Treaty, but indicates that in space or elsewhere, obligations of a regulatory character tend to be defined more broadly in their protective scope than those whose primary purpose is to compensate for damage.

In contrast to earlier instruments, a treaty regulating exploitation of the Moon and other celestial bodies, and declaring them to be the common heritage of mankind, has not secured universal support.[174] No space state is a party, and this treaty cannot be regarded in its entirety as clearly accepted law. But on environmental matters it confirms the principles stated earlier, and simply applies them specifically to the Moon.[175] In this sense it reinforces the obligation of states to protect the environment of space and the celestial bodies, and to avoid interference with the Earth's environment, a point of some importance if there is ever exploitation of the resources of the Moon. It confirms the consistent inclusion of environmental responsibilities in the common heritage concept,[176] even though that concept may otherwise have a

---

[170] cf. *supra*, pp. 98–101.

[171] *Supra*, n. 166. The Soviet Union agreed to pay $3 million in 'full and final' settlement. See Brownlie, *State Responsibility*, 97; Foster, 10 *CYIL* (1972), and *supra*, p. 153.

[172] Christol, *Modern International Law of Outer Space*, 96–7; Haanappel, 6 *J. Space L* (1978), 148. cf. the 1984 Protocol to the Convention on Civil Liability for Oil Pollution Damage, 1969, which allows recovery of the costs of environmental clean-up and reinstatement from oil pollution at sea, *supra*, Ch. 7.

[173] Article 2; Foster, 10 *CYIL* (1972), 184. For a full discussion of what may be recovered under the 1972 Convention, see Christol, *Modern International Law of Outer Space*, ch. 3, and Matte, *Aerospace Law*, 153 f.

[174] 1979 Agreement Concerning the Activities of States on the Moon and Other Celestial Bodies. See Cheng, 33 *CLP* (1980), 213; Christol, *Modern International Law of Outer Space*, ch. 7. But see UNGA Resolution on International Co-operation in the Peaceful Uses of Outer Space, 1990.

[175] Articles 7 and 14.

[176] cf. Articles 142, 145, LOSC, and see *supra*, pp. 120–2.

meaning of its own in each context in which it has so far been employed.[177]

As was the case with the Ozone Convention, these treaties on outer space are mainly remarkable for their willingness to anticipate forms of environmental harm from activities whose effects are still highly speculative. Once again, they show that in regulating the environment, states have gone well beyond the requirements of 'clear and convincing' proof of 'serious damage' set by *Trail Smelter*.[178]

5. CONCLUSIONS

This chapter has illustrated several points of more general significance. First, that customary international law remains important in providing a framework for the negotiation of solutions to problems of global and regional atmospheric protection, despite its relative generality. Secondly, that progress has been made in refining the operation of international regulatory and supervisory regimes, of which the institutional machinery established by the 1985 Ozone Convention and the Montreal Protocol are now among the most significant examples. Thirdly, that substantial problems of global and regional economic equity remain to be addressed if the necessary action to prevent atmospheric interference is to be undertaken by a sufficiently large number of relevant states. Failure to settle this issue effectively is likely to ensure the failure of attempts to prevent global climate change. This observation only serves to emphasize that the use of legal controls and the machinery of international justice cannot of itself ensure the attainment of environmental goals endorsed by international policy-makers, given the substantial changes in energy policy, industrial activity, and technology which are needed, and the economic implications this may have for developed and developing states. It is thus not surprising that the various treaties on protection of the atmosphere examined here represent perhaps the most significant resort to equity in international environmental law and diplomacy.

---

[177] See Christol, *Modern International Law of Outer Space*, 324, and *supra*, Ch. 3.
[178] *Supra*, p. 97

11

Principles and Problems of Conservation and Sustainable Use of Living Resources

1. INTRODUCTION

(1) Differences between Living and Non-Living, Marine and Terrestrial Resources

The commonly used term 'natural resources' comprehends both living and non-living resources; the former are distinguished from the latter by the fact that they are renewable if conserved and destructible if not. Their conservation, moreover, requires inclusion of plants, animals, micro-organisms, and the non-living elements of the environment on which they depend.[1] Preservation of their habitat and of related species is thus an important part of their conservation. In this chapter the principles of international law relating to the protection and conservation of living resources will be identified. Chapter 12 will then address land-based living resources and Chapter 13 marine resources, though clearly some problems and methods of regulation are common to both. This applies in particular to common threats to endangered species, such as trade, draining of wetlands, and capture during regular migrations, or to species of special global concern that are regarded as part of the world's natural heritage. Marine mammals are for this reason mainly dealt with in Chapter 12 together with other mammals. In both chapters attention will be focused particularly on the problems and emergent principles of conservation and management of migratory and endangered species, as they are the ones whose preservation particularly requires international co-operation and development of international law.

There are, however, also important differences in the problems affecting terrestrial and marine living resources. As we saw in Chapter 3, the latter will more often constitute common property or shared resources, and, though subject to over-exploitation, are at least in principle regulated in international law by obligations of conservation and equitable utilization. The former will generally remain within the territory of the state or states where they are found, and their international regulation is accordingly more difficult, requiring as it does limitations on the permanent sovereignty of states over their own natural resources, and resort to concepts such as common interest, common concern, or common heritage to justify such interference, or to

[1] De Klemm, 29 *NRJ* (1989), 932–78; ibid., 9 *EPL* (1982), 117.

the language of animal rights. Moreover, although some forms of animals and plants reproduce prolifically and can thus recover quickly from over-exploitation, as can most species of fish mammals reproduce more slowly, and are thus more susceptible to extinction resulting from over-exploitation, habitat destruction, and other adverse environmental factors, such as pollution, than are fish. Both animals and plants on land are also generally more easily accessible to plunder. On the other hand, terrestrial species are more often domesticated, while only a few marine species are tamed, mainly in zoos. Terrestrial species are also more likely to be valued for their own sake, for example elephants, eagles, and many other large mammals and birds, whereas in the seas such value is placed mainly on cetaceans and pinnipeds.

The threats to wildlife arise from a wide variety of sources. Various species have been captured throughout the centuries not only for food, but for their skins, feathers, and other products used or traded by man, for display in zoos, for scientific research, as pets, and for medicinal, cultural, religious, and artistic purposes, amongst others. Such activities, if excessive, are now seen not only as threats to the existence of individual species or habitats but also to the biodiversity represented by such species, which provides, *inter alia*, a gene pool of immense present and future value to humankind as well as having value for its own sake.

International law has, until recently, tended to adopt an *ad hoc* approach to wildlife protection, related to identification of 'endangered species', that is, species or discrete populations thereof, that are threatened with extinction. In contrast, the law concerning conservation of fisheries has been dominated by their exploitation and has thus concentrated on the need to maintain productivity and to allocate rights of access to these resources, even in the case of marine mammals, though public perspectives and thus the law in relation to their preservation are changing.

(2) Early Concepts and Approaches

Law can serve a number of functions in relation to living resources: it can be distributive, determining who is to have ownership or access to the resources; conservatory, preserving the resources as such, or at least doing so at levels that can sustain exploitation; or proscriptive, prohibiting, for conservatory, ethical, or moral reasons, any exploitation of the resource whatsoever.

Although there have been national laws protecting terrestrial and marine living resources since comparatively early times, the perception that species require conservation under an international legal regime is of comparatively recent origin. It was not until over-exploitation of living resources, especially those hunted by two or more states, began to lead to failures of stocks or herds of particular species so severe that they might be in danger of extinction that serious interest was taken in the need to develop legal obligations and principles for their protection and conservation on a sustainable basis. Birds, salmon, and whales were amongst the first species to excite such interest, originally at the national level. Whales, for example, were regulated *ad hoc* by one or two states from 1597 onwards; national control of the taking of such migratory species was recognized not to be sufficient to conserve them since it could not be enforced on foreign territory or on foreign vessels outside national jurisdiction.[2] The first relevant treaty was the 1885 Convention for the Uniform Regulation of Fishing in the Rhine.[3] But by then the exploitation of such species had in many cases been taking place for hundreds of years, without any control and the theoretical basis of the first legal regimes to be developed necessarily had to take account of this fact.[4] Living species were not treated very differently from other resources, such as minerals, and indeed to this day are frequently included within the general description of 'natural resources', though as sustainable living creatures they—especially those that migrate—are very different from static non-renewable minerals such as oil, gas, and metallic ores. As a result both living and non-living resources have long been regarded as being as 'mineable' as minerals.[5]

Since throughout history mankind has sought to exploit the wealth that such resources bring, the law has primarily been concerned with the problems of allocation of rights over them. The first approaches to this problem were simplistic; as territorial states had sovereignty over their territory, they were assumed to have exclusive rights to all the natural resources found therein and this was extended to the territorial sea and airspace, whether or not the resources were living and migratory. Thus, once they were found in areas subject to sovereignty no other state could have access to them or play a role in their management without the express consent of the territorial sovereign. Natural resources found in areas beyond national jurisdiction, for example, on the high seas or the sea-bed below it or in the airspace above it and indeed the air itself were regarded as common property resources and a doctrine of freedom of access for all states was applied to these areas.

It was only following increasing evidence of the serious adverse effects of over-exploitation of certain species, particularly at sea, that development of more sophisticated legal regimes began, mainly, but not exclusively, in the second half of this century. Until the late nineteenth century scientists had taken little interest in marine biology and it was not until 1902 when the

---

[2] Birnie, *International Regulation of Whaling* (Dobbs Ferry, NY, 1985), i, 102–4, gives examples of whaling regulations.

[3] *Ruster and Simma*, xxv, 200.

[4] Johnston, *The International Law of Fisheries: A Framework for Policy Oriented Enquiries* (New Haven, Conn., 1965), 157–252.

[5] Holt, 9 *Marine Policy* (1985), 192–213.

International Council for the Exploration of the Sea (ICES)[6] was formed, following proposals first made at the International Geographic Congress of 1895, that international efforts were made to co-ordinate, on the basis of an informal 'Gentlemen's Agreement', scientific research on fisheries and to plan, collect, and evaluate data on an international basis.[7] Even today, it is often the research of scientists in a few countries that initiates conservatory legal developments. But as scientific knowledge has grown so too have the perceived dimensions of the legal problems of conservation.

Legal developments have also been influenced by the changing perceptions of philosophers and moralists in relation to living creatures. Early philosophers, such as Plato, made no attempt to distinguish individual animals or accord them rights. They viewed their special attributes as representative of the whole species; it was not considered that the taking of individuals from that species damaged the species as a whole.[8] This belief was reinforced by the view that, unlike humans, animals could not be subject to duties.[9] Even when science and philosophy combined in the Middle Ages in the doctrine of 'natural philosophy' each discipline continued to embrace the generalized concept of 'species' rather than concentrating on individual specimens.

These concepts were underpinned by the Roman law doctrine that animals *ferae naturae* did not belong to any person and could, therefore, be captured by anyone when found in international areas, such as the high seas and the airspace above them. Species which could not be corralled and domesticated, such as fish, marine mammals, and birds outside national territory, were thus regarded as common property resources.[10] These perceptions are now beginning to change, however. Renewed attention is being paid to the concept of animal rights and the common property doctrine is being overlaid with new concepts of 'common heritage', 'common inheritance', 'common interest', and 'common concern'.

(3) Development of New Concepts

(a) Animal Rights

In national law states at first simply regarded animals as either useful or vicious[11] and thus protected only the economic value of wildlife as a source of

---

[6] Went, *Seventy Years Agrowing: A History of the International Council for the Exploration of the Sea 1920–1972* (Charlotteslund, 1972).

[7] Vamplew, *Salvesens of Leith* (Edinburgh, 1975), 140, 148.

[8] Clark, *The Moral Status of Animals* (Oxford, 1977), 64–5; he provides a bibliography of relevant works.

[9] Linzey, *Animal Rights* (London, 1976); Morris, 12 *Jnl. of Legal Education* (1964–5), 185 ff.; Singer and Regan (eds.), *Animal Rights and Legal Obligations* (New York, 1976); Tribe, 83 *Yale LJ* (1976), 1315 ff.

[10] See *Supra*, pp. 117–9; Fulton, *The Sovereignty of the Seas* (Edinburgh, 1911), pp. v–vii; Grotius, *The Freedom of the Sea or the Right Which Belongs to the Dutch to Take Part in the East India Trade*, trans. Magoffin and Scott (New York, 1916).

[11] Linder, 12 *Harv. ELR* (1988), 157–200.

food and clothing, limiting the hunting of certain species to maintain their population levels for these purposes or encouraging the killing of animals thought harmful to humans and their activities. Later wildlife law responded to protect the value placed on hunting and fishing as recreational activities. It is only fairly recently that public concern has developed for protection of animals and for their welfare, as species valuable for their own sake, with special emphasis on endangered species, habitats, and rational management.[12] Legal writers, following the first preoccupations of environmental activists in the Western Hemisphere, have been concerned initially with protection of a few species, for example, whales, polar bears, porpoises, dolphins, sea otters, bald eagles, condors, and the snail darter—in isolation from land-use regulation.[13] A major problem of this topic, presented in this context, is that it is highly complex, involving a wide variety of subjects and issues as well as different jurisdictions and disciplines. It is thus difficult, at both national and international levels, to identify a discrete body of law protecting animals.

It is important, at this stage, to distinguish the different objectives of animal rights advocates, who consider that all species should be protected for ethical and humanitarian reasons, however adverse their effect on humans or on populations or individuals of other species, and of environmentalists, who urge that particular species should be protected for ecological reasons, that is, as part of an ecosystem, which includes the animals, plants, and micro-organisms together with the non-living components of their environment. This difference in views is reflected in the progress of both national and international law and the number and nature of the instruments adopted. It is not possible, for reasons of space, here to examine in detail the legal arguments of the animal rights group (these are considered further in Chapter 5), although there is a growing literature on this aspect[14] and drafts of an international Declaration of Animal Rights[15] as well as of a Convention[16] have been under

---

[12] Ibid. 157–8; see also Bean, *The Evolution of National Wildlife Law* (2nd edn., Washington, DC, 1983), and works cited in Coggins and Smith, 6 *Environmental Law* (1976), 583; Coggins and Patti, 4 *Harv. ELR* (1980), 164.

[13] Coggins and Patti, 4 *Harv. ELR* (1980), 181.

[14] See Linder, 12 *Harv. ELR* (1988), 175 ff.; Regan, *The Case for Animal Rights* (New York, 1983); Singer, *Practical Ethics* (New York, 1979); McIntyre (ed.), *Mind in the Waters* (New York, 1974); Tribe, 83 *Yale LJ* (1974), 1315; Reed, 12 *Idaho LR* (1976), 153; Sagoff, 84 *Yale LJ* (1974), 33; Allen, 28 *NY Law School LR* (1983), 377–429; Stone, 45 *SCal. LR* (1972), 450; Winters, 21 *SDLR* (1984), 911–40; Hersovice, *Second Nature: The Animal Rights Controversy* (Toronto, 1985), 42–55.

[15] Universal Declaration of the Rights of Animals, proclaimed on 15 Oct. 1978 by the International League of Animal Rights. Its Preamble recognizes that 'all animals have rights'; Article 1 provides that 'All animals are born with an equal claim on life and the same rights to existence'; Article 2 that 'Man as an animal species shall not arrogate to himself the rights to exterminate or inhumanly exploit other animals'; Article 3 that 'All Animals have the right to the attention, care and protection of man'; texts in Allen, 28 *NY Law School LR* (1983), 414–15 n. 259. Several members of the Council of Europe had relevant laws by the 1970s, Taylor, 1 *Animal Reg. Stud.* (1977), 73; the United States has extensive legislation, Allen, op. cit. 422–5.

[16] Progress on this is reported *passim* in the Newsletter of the International Committee for a Convention for the Protection of Animals.

consideration from some years at the non-governmental level. This draft declaration is without legal status but has served to focus attention on gaps in the law by laying down in detail the issues relating to animal protection. So far, however, the international community has not developed a legislative response to the questions whether killing animals is wrong or whether all or only some animals are to be regarded as sharing sufficient human characteristics to have individual rights attributed to them and to be legally protected from so-called 'speciesism', as humans are protected from racism. It has, rather, followed the environmentalist view. To date, it is only at the regional level, through the Council of Europe, that a series of European conventions has been concluded protecting animals from suffering, namely, the 1968 Convention for the Protection of Animals During International Transport, the 1976 Convention for the Protection of Animals kept for Farming Purposes, the 1979 Convention for the Protection of Animals used for Slaughter, the 1986 Convention for the Protection of Vertebrate Animals used for Experimental and other Scientific Purposes, and the 1987 Convention for the Protection of Pet Animals.[17]

(b) Common Heritage and Related Concepts

The underlying concepts of common property and related concepts, their development and the problems to which they give rise have been outlined in Chapter 3. New concepts such as 'common heritage' and 'common concern', while of growing importance, are as yet included only in hortatory preambles to wildlife conventions and the growing number of codes, declarations, and strategies for conservation, as illustrated in Chapter 12. Thus common property remains a basic concept of international wildlife law, even though, when coupled with the principle of free access, it leads to over-exploitation and decline of species if hunting expands unchecked. The doctrine of permanent sovereignty over natural resources may also encourage over-exploitation in the absence of clearly established international conservatory obligations. It is thus vital to conservation of living resources both to develop new legal principles and to conclude bilateral, regional, or global regulatory agreements which define 'conservation' and prescribe appropriate measures, as there is no accepted international definition of this term. Before examining the attempts to define or at least give meaning to 'conservation', in such agreements, it is necessary to identify the strategies and mechanisms for implementation laid down in various declarations of international policy.

---

[17] Council of Europe Treaty Series, Numbers 65 (with Additional Protocol, No. 103, of 1979), 87, 102, 123, and 125 respectively; see also Pavan, *A European Cultural Revolution: The Council of Europe's Charter on Invertebrates*, Council of Europe (Strasburg, 1986).

(4) Management Factors and Principles of Living Resource Conservation and Protection

It is now at least clear that the development of law taking account of the international aspects of the problem of conservation of wildlife must be based on recognition of the following factors, *inter alia*: that many species and some of the threats to them migrate across national frontiers; both migratory and non-migratory species need to be protected from the over-exploitation that results from trade in those (or their products) that are regarded as especially valuable internationally; and that it is necessary to protect the whole environment supporting the life-cycle of the species concerned.[18]

Furthermore, experience derived from the first attempts to conserve such species has established three preconditions to ensure the effectiveness of international conventions for this purpose: first, exploitation, when permitted, must be conducted on a rational basis, that is, with conscious, reasonable, objectives, taking account of scientific advice; secondly the species must be regulated as a biological unit, that is, through its whole range; and thirdly, all the relevant ecological factors that affect the conservation of a species and its habitat must be considered.

Achievement of the international controls necessary to secure these aims requires that states co-operate on the widest possible basis in subjecting national sovereignty to the necessary co-ordinated international obligations. The evolution of the regime concerning marine living resources, in particular (see Chapter 13), indicates that merely to allocate migratory living species to national control, or to accord them common property or *res nullius* status in international areas, does not provide an effective solution; both international obligations and international institutions must be established. The first wildlife protection treaty, the 1885 Convention for the Uniform Regulation of Fishing in the Rhine,[19] was followed by the early examples of international commissions referred to in Chapters 12 and 13, but these have now been supplemented by wider international instruments protecting not only marine species but flora and fauna under threat at global or regional levels. Many international agencies have extended their activities to embrace these purposes, ranging from the European Community and the Council of Europe, through the UN's Economic Commission for Europe (ECE) to the World Bank, Unesco, FAO, IUCN, and UNEP, as indicated in this chapter and in Chapter 2, but the necessary global coverage remains far from complete, as illustrated in Chapters 12 and 13.

---

[18] De Klemm, 29 *NRJ* (1989), *passim.*
[19] *Supra*, 421, n. 3.

(5) Institutional Requirements of an Effective Living Resource Regime

Assuming that conservation and management principles can be agreed, the basic legal requirements for the institution of an effective conservation and management regime are: establishment of the source of jurisdiction over the resource; obligations to conduct scientific research and take account of scientific advice; prescription of regulations; establishment of permanent international institutions to provide a forum for discussion, evaluation, co-ordination, and adoption of required measures, *inter alia*; enforcement mechanisms; and dispute settlement arrangements.[20] Chapters 12 and 13 address these issues and trace the emergence of the legal regimes for marine and other living resources, but it is important, before examining these, to identify the global and regional strategies and principles which have recently emerged to guide their development, in order both to evaluate the extent to which new concepts and principles have influenced their conclusion and the extent to which such concepts and principles have become accepted as part of customary international law.

2. THE UN AND THE DEVELOPMENT OF AN INTERNATIONAL REGIME FOR PROTECTION OF LIVING RESOURCES

It cannot be said that prior to the UN's 1972 Stockholm Conference on the Human Environment (UNCHE) any principles concerning conservation of wildlife had clearly emerged in international customary law. The Declaration adopted by this conference, however, identified a number of relevant and important principles which have since been elaborated upon in other sets of principles, guidelines, and standards and have formed the basis of many treaties.

(1) Declaration of the United Nations Conference on the Human Environment (UNCHE) 1972[21]

Several principles important to wildlife conservation were laid down in the UNCHE Declaration (see Chapter 2). They include those safeguarding natural resources, which include fauna, as well as air, water, and land, for the

---

[20] De Klemm, in Johnston (ed.), *The Environmental Law of the Sea* (Berlin, 1981), 85–90. But note that Miles, in reviewing Cushing, *The Provident Sea* (Cambridge, 1988), criticizes a purely science-based approach to management and emphasizes the extent to which political considerations interfere with it and must be provided for, 15 *Marine Policy* (1991), 278. See generally, *supra*, pp. 160–79.

[21] Report of UN Conference on the Human Environment, Stockholm, 5–16 June 1972, UN Doc. A/CONF. 48 114/Rev. 1, on which see *supra*, Ch. 2.

benefit of present and future generations (Principle 2); requiring maintenance of renewable resources (Principle 3); and identifying man's special responsibility to safeguard the heritage of wildlife and its habitat and to improve it (Principle 4). Principles 21 and 22 also are potentially relevant to living resources. The former recognizes states' rights to exploit their own resources pursuant to their own environmental policies, subject to ensuring that their activities do not cause environmental damage. The latter requires states to co-operate in developing the law regarding liability and compensation for such damage, which could include harm to species that cross or reside within the borders of neighbouring states and to their habitats, but the implications of responsibility for damage to migrating species require further development. The principles that relate to development are also relevant but do not strike any clear balance between development and conservation. Thus although endangered or threatened wildlife must be specially protected as a component of development policies, states are free to achieve these goals in their own ways.

A wildlife regime, based on the UNCHE principles, thus should protect fauna and the elements (air, water, land, flora) surrounding them, which at least implies a habitat protection approach, but fauna are none the less re-garded as 'resources' and not accorded any value in their own right. Principle 1, proclaiming man's right to adequate conditions of life in an environment of a quality that permits a life of dignity and well-being can hardly be said to comprehend the rights of animals or other forms of non-human life, since it emphasizes the possibility of continued exploitation, requiring only that the future sustainability of such resources be protected. The concept that wildlife is a form of community 'heritage' to be preserved for future generations remains inchoate in Principle 1, which merely iterates the proposition that man 'bears a solemn responsibility to protect and improve the environment for present and future generations' giving no guidance on the implications of this for wildlife. Principle 2, requiring safeguarding of natural resources for future generations, also does not advance matters as it relates this goal to 'planning or management' only.

(2) UNEP Principles of Conduct in the Field of the Environment for the Guidance of States in the Conservation and Harmonious Utilization of Natural Resources Shared by Two or More States 1978[22]

Though, as we saw in Chapter 3, these principles are generally discussed in the context of mineral and water resources and pollution, they can also apply

---

[22] UNEP/IG, 12/28, Feb. 1978. See also *supra*, pp. 47–52, and pp. 114–7. It should be noted that the Experts Group on Environmental Law of the World Commission on Environment and Development prefers the term 'transboundary natural resources' to 'internationally shared' natural resources, which gives rise to the difficulties associated with claims to sovereignty; Munro and Lammers, *Environmental Protection and Sustainable Development* (London, 1987), 8, 37.

to protection of migratory species by requiring co-operation in conservation and use,[23] conclusion of agreements, use of existing organizations, creation of new ones, environmental assessment, joint research, exchange of information, and notification and consultation on the basis of good faith and good neighbourliness. They too stress the need to develop the law of state responsibility and have to be applied in a way that enhances development, based on the concept of equitable utilization.

The legal status of these principles was discussed in Chapter 1; at best they contribute to the 'soft law' approach. However, the analysis of the provisions of the major wildlife conventions provided in Chapter 12 indicates that these principles are to a remarkable degree reflected in these treaties, and although some have not been acted upon, most have. As we saw in Chapter 6, they do in certain important respects reflect existing customary law.

3. CONSERVATION STRATEGIES

The innovations introduced in conventions for conservation of both marine and land-based flora and fauna are based on or reflect the environmental strategies and concepts referred to in Chapter 2. Three of these are of special importance in wildlife conservation and must be taken into account in formulating the objectives of the conservation regime. These are the World Conservation Strategy (WCS)[24] (recently revised to take fuller account of the concept of sustainable development); the World Charter for Nature (WCN);[25] and the recommendations of the World Commission on Environment and Development (WCED)[26] as supplemented by the 'Global Perspective to the Year 2000 and Beyond'.[27] All these develop the UNCHE and UNEP principles.

(1) World Conservation Strategy 1980

The WCS identifies the priorities and actions at the national, regional, and international levels required to achieve maintenance of essential ecological

---

[23] Principle 1.

[24] *World Conservation Strategy*, prepared by the International Union for Conservation of Nature and Natural Resources (IUCN) with the advice, co-operation, and financial assistance of the United Nations Environment Programme (UNEP) and the World Wildlife Fund (WWF) in collaboration with the Food and Agriculture Organization of the United Nations (FAO) and the United Nations Educational, Scientific, and Cultural Organization, (Unesco) (1980). See also the same organization's new programme *Caring for The Earth: A Strategy for Sustainable Living* (Gland, 1991).

[25] *Infra*, n. 32.

[26] *Our Common Future*, World Commission on Environment and Development (Oxford, 1987).

[27] UN Doc. A/C 2/42/L. 80, 'The Environment Perspective to the Year 2,000 and Beyond', text in 18 *EPL* (1988), 37–8.

processes and life-support systems, preserve genetic diversity, and ensure sustainable utilization of species and ecosystems. It stresses that living resource conservation is not a limited sector but a process that must be considered in all the sectors covered in the strategy; that conservation must thus be integrated with development, which itself must be planned in a more environmentally rational way; that the capacity to ensure conservation must be enhanced, *inter alia*, by developing better and more co-ordinated organization, more effective legislation, and the means to enforce it.

The World Conservation Strategy has recently been supplemented by a programme for 'Caring for the Earth', which defines itself as a 'strategy for sustainable living'. This addresses the problems of integrating conservation and development; it does not address solely conservation issues but takes a broader perspective, acknowledging that action is required on many fronts and that the solution to problems of extinction of species requires solution simultaneously of the problems of environmental degradation. New problems such as climate change and destruction of the ozone layer are covered, as well as the WCED's recommendations on sustainable development. It attempts, *inter alia*, to outline what sustainable development entails in ecological, social, cultural, and economic terms and identifies and sets targets for action. These include the development of environmental law, which the programme perceives as an essential tool for achieving sustainability and strengthening international agreements for the conservation of life-support systems and biological diversity.

The WCS defined 'conservation' in general as 'the management of human use of the biosphere so that it may yield the greatest sustainable benefit to present generations while maintaining its potential to meet the needs and aspirations of future generations.' It thus includes both preservation and maintenance, sustainable use, restoration, and enhancement of natural resources. 'Living resource conservation' is said to be concered with plants, animals, and micro-organisms and such non-living resource elements of the environment as they depend on.

The WCS expressly recognizes the threat posed to species by trade, especially in animals and their products taken from the wild in developing countries, often illegally, and by the effects on them of recreation and tourism. The symbolic, ritualistic, and cultural importance of wildlife to many people is also acknowledged.[28] The destruction of forests and over-grazing of lands for commercial and subsistence purposes and the effect of this on species are emphasized.

Ten priority requirements for the maintenance of ecological processes and life-support systems, preserving genetic diversity[29] and sustaining use of living

---

[28] See *supra*, n. 24.

[29] Ibid. '6. Priority requirements: genetic diversity'.

resources are identified, *inter alia.*[30] They include determining productive capacities of exploited species and ecosystems and ensuring that utilization does not exceed these; setting conservation management objectives for use of species and ecosystems; ensuring access does not exceed the resources' capacity to sustain exploitation; reducing excessive yields to sustainable levels; reducing incidental take as much as possible; equipping subsistence communities to use resources sustainably; maintaining habitats of species; regulating international trade in wild plants and animals; regulating stocking of grazing lands so that the long-term productivity of plants and animals can be maintained; co-ordinating national protected area programmes with international ones.

Securing most of these objectives requires legal action. The WCS thus identifies ways of improving legislation and organization,[31] stressing the need for cross-sectoral organization. It makes proposals for training of officials; inclusion of conservation obligations in constitutions, as appropriate; enactment of laws to protect both use of resources and their ecology; regulating habitat removal and introduction of exotic species; environmental impact assessment; citizen participation in land-use policy formulation; and refining concepts of damage to include long-term environmental damage to individuals and communities through depletion of species or destruction or degradation of ecosystems. The WCS also urges that special attention be given to enforcement, which should be built into the design of legislation by ensuring that it is ecologically, economically, and socially feasible. It proposes that compensation for relief of social hardship resulting from measures should be provided. It recommends that new organizations, structured so as to enable management of resources on a comprehensive, ecosystem basis, rather than on a sectoral basis as at present, should be established for marine resources, with permanent mechanisms for joint consultation among all bodies.

Finally the WCS proposes that the global commons, in which term it includes Antarctica, the oceans, the atmosphere, and climate, should be given special protection; species confined in the open ocean should be regarded as the common resource of humanity; species migrating into that area from national jurisdiction should be regarded as shared resources. Special provision should be made for both and new mechanisms created as required.

The WCS is a purely strategic document; unlike the WCN, discussed below, it has no pretensions to laying down the law, but it does give a clear indication of the essential issues for the development of international law to protect wildlife.

---

[30] WCS, '7. Priority requirements: sustainable utilization'.
[31] Ibid. '11: Improving the capacity to manage: legislation and organization'.

(2) World Charter for Nature (WCN)[32]

In developing a legal regime for wildlife account has also to be taken of the WCN's acceptance that mankind is responsible for all species, and of its provisions for fulfilling this responsibility. It requires, *inter alia*, that 'Nature shall be respected and its essential processes not impaired' (Article 1), that 'The genetic viability on the earth shall not be compromised; the population levels of all life forms, wild and domesticated, must be at least sufficient for their survival, and to this end necessary habitats shall be safeguarded' (Article 2).

So far as implementation proposals are concerned, the WCN offers nothing more than general admonitions and though its general principles are expressed in mandatory terms ('shall' is used throughout rather than 'should'), they are expressed also in very general terms. A French commentator regrets 'son apparence pseudojuridique' adding that 'Il est à craindre que pour avoir vouler proposer du 'droit doux' le législateur ne propose plus ici de droit de tout... pourquoi alors ce masque? Si cette pseudo-règle peut, on espère, servir la cause de la nature, elle ne peut que contribuer a discréditer celle du droit.'[33]

The legal status of the Charter must be assessed by the same tests as other UN resolutions (see Chapter 2). Despite the expression of contrary views,[34] it is difficult to argue that in relation to conservation of resources it has any binding legal status; indeed its drafters accepted that 'by its very nature, the Charter could not have any binding force, nor have any regime of sanctions attached to it'.[35] The use of 'shall' was purely declaratory.[36] None the less, it has been suggested that it should 'be regarded as an instrument having a special character, a declaration of principles after the fashion of such General

---

[32] See Consideration and Adoption of the Revised Draft World Charter for Nature: Report of the Secretary-General, 37/UN GAOR (Agenda Item 21), UN Doc. A/398 (1982); UNGA Res. 37/7, 28 Oct. 1982, repr. in 23 *ILM* (1983), 455–60; 111 states voted for this resolution, 1 against (US), and 18 abstained (Algeria, Argentina, Bolivia, Brazil, Chile, Colombia, Dominican Republic, Ecuador, Ghana, Guyana, Lebanon, Mexico, Paraguay, Peru, Philippines, Surinam, Trinidad and Tobago, Venezuela). See also Burhenne and Irwin, *The World Charter for Nature: A Background Paper* (Berlin, 1983); International Council for Environmental Law, *Commentary on the World Charter for Nature*, IUCN Environmental Law Centre (Bonn, 1986).

[33] Rémond–Gouilloud, 2 *Rev. jurid. de l'env.* (1982), 120–4.

[34] Wood, 12 *ELQ* (1985), 981.

[35] Report of the Ad Hoc Group Meeting on the Draft World Charter for Nature held at Nairobi, 24–7 Aug. 1981, 36 UN GAOR, Annex (Agenda Item 23) at 7, UN Doc. A/539 (1981).

[36] Wood, 12 *ELQ* (1985), 982–4. See also views of Kiss and Singh on the significance of the word 'shall', 14 *EPL* (1985), 37–70; cf. Caldwell, *International Environmental Policy* (2nd edn., Durham, 1990), 90–3, and 'Note on the Use of the Word "Shall"', in Nordquist (ed.), *United Nations Convention on the Law of the Sea: A Commentary* (London, 1991), iv, pp. xli–xlii.

Assembly Resolutions as the Universal Declaration of Human Rights . . .'[37] and the WCN does have some moral and political force, as its restatement in subsequent strategies evidences. Its attempt to set the equilibrium between the use of nature and its conservation accords with current goals of sustainable development and its provisions are now more likely to be influential in international policy-making.

In addition to the principles referred to, the WCN prescribes certain 'Functions'. Article 10 requires 'wise use', namely, states must not use resources beyond their natural capacity for regeneration, and Article 11 requires that activities which might impact on nature must be controlled, using 'best available technologies'. Unique areas must be specially protected, as must representative samples of ecosystems and habitats of rare or endangered species. Ecosystems and organisms used by man are to be managed to sustain optimum productivity without endangering coexisting ecosystems or species. Natural resources must not be wasted but can be used, as long as this does not come close to exceeding their regenerative capacity. Attention must be paid also to ensuring that activities within a state's jurisdiction or control do not cause damage to natural systems in other states or in areas beyond national jurisdiction and that nature in the latter area is safeguarded. Activities causing irreversible damage must be avoided and their likely risks to nature must be examined beforehand; environmental impact assessment must be undertaken; agriculture, grazing, and forest practices must be adapted to the natural characteristics and constraints of given areas.

Article 22 formulates the obligations as those of states, providing that 'Taking fully into account the sovereignty of states over their natural resources, each state shall give effect to the provisions of the present Charter through its competent organs and in co-operation with other states.' However, in Article 23 all *persons* must have the opportunity to participate in formulating decisions directly concerning their environment and must be provided with access to means of redress if it is damaged. Moreover, in Article 24, the WCN states the obligations involved as personal ones, affirming that each *person* has a duty to act in accordance with the provisions of the present Charter and must 'strive to ensure' that its objectives are met.

The Charter was clearly intended by the majority adopting it in the UN to be a contribution to the creation of new binding international law on conservation and, if systematically applied and elaborated, the rules it sets out are capable of being transformed into customary international law and are thus likely to be reflected in future trends. Article 14 requires that its principles be reflected 'in the law and practice of each state, as well as at the international level'.

---

[37] Jackson, 12 *Ambio* (1983), 133; ICEL *Commentary*.

(3) The Report of the World Commission on Environment and Development 1987 (WCED)[38]

The Brundtland Report, which the General Assembly transmitted to all governments and organs, organizations, and programmes of the UN system, inviting them to take account of its analysis and recommendations in determining their policies and programmes,[39] reinforces the UNEP, WCS, and WCN proposals and principles and strongly promotes the aims of sustainable development. It concludes that preservation of soil, water, and of the nurseries and breeding grounds of species cannot be divorced from conserving individual species within natural ecosystems, which contributes to the predominant goals of sustainable development. It identifies the role in this process of various international organizations, such as FAO, UNEP, IUCN, and Unesco, and the need for norms and procedures to be established.

The report lays special stress on the protection of biological diversity. It draws particular attention to Unesco's establishment of biosphere reserves as 'biotic provinces' and calls for a new species convention to be concluded to protect 'universal resources'. It postulates collective responsibility for species as a 'common heritage', which status, it suggests, requires that other states provide financial help for their conservation within national boundaries through establishment of a trust fund to which the states benefiting most from resource exploitation would contribute the most, though an equitable share of the benefits of development of the resources would be attributed to the 'possessor' nations. An environmental role for the World Bank in undertaking environmental impact assessment of its development projects is conceived, with particular attention being accorded to habitat preservation and life support systems. This is already in accordance with the practice of the World Bank as indicated in Chapter 2.

The WCED Report was accompanied by a Report of an Experts Group on Environmental Law. This Group's mandate was to report on legal principles for environmental protection and sustainable development and to make proposals for accelerating the development of relevant international law. The group approved 22 articles stating legal principles which have been referred to throughout this work.[40] All are expressed in mandatory terms, that is, using the word 'shall'.[41] Relevant principles for our purpose include the 'General Principles, Rights and Responsibilities', referred to in Principles 1–7, such as

---

[38] *Our Common Future* (Oxford, 1987).

[39] Un Doc. A/C. 2/42/L 81.

[40] Published separately as Munro and Lammers, *Environmental Protection and Sustainable Development*; see also 18 *EPL* (1988), 36–7. *Our Common Future*, 348–351 summarizes the principles. For a full account, see Munro and Lammers, *Environmental Protection and Sustainable Development*.

[41] For the significance of this usage, see Wood, 12 *ELQ* (1985), and works cited *supra*, n. 36.

the fundamental human right to an adequate environment; inter-generational equity; maintenance of ecosystems and biological diversity and absence of optimum sustainable yield of living resources; establishment of adequate environmental standards and monitoring thereof; prior environmental assessment; prior notification of activities with adverse effects; equal access to court proceedings; ensuring that conservation is an integral part of planning and implementation of development processes and recognizing an obligation to co-operate in good faith in implementing all these rights and obligations.

Twelve others (Principles 9–20) are grouped as 'Principles, Rights and Obligations Concerning Transboundary Natural Resources and Environmental Interferences'. In order to obviate arguments about national sovereignty, these require states to use transboundary natural resources (the Group preferred this term to 'shared natural resources') in a reasonable manner; prevent and abate harmful interferences; take precautionary measures to limit risk and to establish strict liability for harm done; apply, as a minimum, the same standards for environmental conduct and impacts concerning such resources as are applied domestically; co-operate in good faith to achieve optimal use and prevention or abatement of interference with such resources; provide prior notification and assessment of activities having significant transboundary effects and engage in prior consultation with concerned states; co-operate in monitoring, scientific research and standard-setting; develop contingency plans for emerging situations and provide equal access and treatment in administrative and judicial proceedings to all affected or likely to be so.

The two remaining principles relate to state responsibility, requiring states to cease activities breaching international obligations regarding the environment and to provide compensation for harm, and the requirement that states settle environmental disputes by peaceful means. Though these principles are most often discussed and used, as in this work, in relation to use of transboundary water resources, and all forms of pollution, they are all applicable to interference with and harm to living resources and the environment, as we saw in Chapter 4.

In addition to its full report substantiating the proposed principles which, it should be emphasized, is based on trends and precedents drawn from international practice, the Group presented the basic principles, in summary, as 'Elements for a Draft Convention on Environmental Protection and Sustainable Development'.[42] This conforms to the WCED's own recommendation that the UN General Assembly should prepare a Universal Declaration leading later to a Convention on this topic, and IUCN's 'Caring for the Earth' programme, which calls for adoption of a universal covenant on

---

[42] Munro and Lammers, *Environmental Protection and Sustainable Development*, 25–33.

sustainability, a challenge that the General Assembly has met by convening the UNCED, which did not adopt any such conventions.

At the same time that it recommended the WCED Report to governments and UN bodies to take account of in their policies and programmes, the UNGA adopted the 'Environment Perspective to the Year 2000 and Beyond', prepared by a UNEP intergovernmental group 'as a broad framework to guide national action and international co-operation on policies and programmes aimed at achieving environmentally sound development' and specifically as a guide to the preparation of system-wide medium-term programmes of the UN. The 'perspective' addresses development issues and the need for environmentally sound development but includes the need to take note of cross-sectoral impacts and co-ordination, and responsibility for damage, and acknowledges that renewable resources can have sustainable yields only if system-wide effects of exploitation are taken into account. The Environment Perspective declares that safeguarding species is a *moral obligation* of humankind, and urges peaceful settlement of environmental disputes.

There is a considerable similarity and overlap in the principles laid down in the strategies outlined in this section. Only the WCED Legal Experts formulate the principles in specifically legal form, based on analysis of considerable supporting evidence in the form of existing practice and consultations. The repetition of the strategic principles has had significant effect in drawing attention to them but does not in itself confer legal status on them. To ascertain the latter we must evaluate the extent to which the conventions and practice outlined in Chapters 12 and 13 are based upon them.

4. MEANING OF 'CONSERVATION'

(1) Conservation

Since Chapters 12 and 13 are primarily concerned with identifying principles and rules of international law relating to the protection and 'conservation' of living resources, and since the principles and strategies so far adopted frequently use this term, we must now address the problems of definition that immediately arise. What is the meaning or meanings of 'conservation' and of 'living resources' and what is their content? We have outlined the nature of the problems that arise and the requirements, viewed from the scientific and environmentalist standpoint, that have to be met to achieve conservation and the other factors that influence the development of an acceptable protective regime. It is remarkable that few strategies define this term and that the few that do so offer only very general definitions, as we noted in the Introduction to Chapter 1.

One of the first treaties to use the word 'conservation' in its title was the 1958 Geneva Convention on Fishing and the Conservation of the Living

Resources of the High Seas, although others, such as the 1971 Bonn Convention on Conservation of Migratory Species of Wild Animals (CMSWA) and the 1980 Convention on Conservation of Antarctic Marine Living Resources (CCAMLR) (see Chapters 12 and 13) now also do so. Few conventions attempt specifically to define the term, however; most approach it obliquely, defining, for example 'conservation status', as in the CMSWA, or leaving its meaning to be implied from the nature of the measures presented to achieve the aims of conservation expressed in the preamble or substantive articles.

Conservation has in the past not become an issue until the level of threat to a species either endangers its survival or threatens seriously to deplete it or a particular stock.[43] The idea of conserving species for their own value and not simply as resources exploitable by man is of comparatively recent origin. Thus it is not surprising that the sole specific definition of the term in the substantive articles of a treaty, so far as can be ascertained, states that:

As employed in this Convention the expression 'conservation' of the living resources of the high seas means the aggregate of the measures rendering possible the optimum sustainable yield for these resources so as to secure a maximum supply of food and other marine products.[44]

It adds that 'conservation programmes should be formulated with a view to securing in the first place a supply of food for human consumption'. Although the definition is confined by its terms to the purposes of a Convention which has never been widely ratified,[45] it remains in force and the definition, although superseded by more recent values, is still accepted by many states. It is notable, however, that the 1982 UNCLOS does not offer any definition of conservation, despite providing in various articles for 'conservation of marine living resources'[46] although it does lay down in Article 61 certain objectives of conservation and management qualified by various factors.

The ordinary meaning of conservation and to 'conserve' namely, 'to keep in safety or from harm, decay or loss; to preserve in being; to keep alive' or now, more usually, 'to preserve in its existing state from destruction or change'[47] suggest that a higher standard of care is necessary to fulfil conservatory objectives than is actually required by existing conventions. These allow qualification of that objective by economic, social, and developmental re-

---

[42] Munro and Lammers, *Environmental Protection and Sustainable Development*, 25–33.

[43] Hey, *The Regime for the Exploitation of Transboundary Marine Fisheries Resources* (Dordrecht, 1989), 77.

[44] 1958 Geneva Convention on Fishing and the Conservation of the Living Resources of the High Seas, Article 2.

[45] By 1981 only 46 states had become party to it including the UK, USSR, United States, Spain, and France but not Iceland, Japan, Korea, or China (PRC).

[46] e.g. in its Preamble, para. 4; Articles 21(1)(d); 56(1)(a); 61; 78(i); 117, 118, 119(1); 123(a); 277(a).

[47] *Shorter Oxford English Dictionary* (3rd edn, Oxford, 1944), 404.

quirements despite the fact that threats to both marine and terrestrial resources are, since the UNCHE, much more widely perceived. Until the Stockholm Conference, overexploitation was seen (except by a few ecologists) as the only problem. Ecologists' arguments that destruction of habitat by man, pollution, and introduction of alien species which prey on and may eventually replace existing species are now widely accepted as equally serious threats, if not more so.[48] Thus, the IUCN's World Conservation Strategy (WCS), the purpose of which was to draw attention to the urgent need for the conservation of the world's land and marine ecosystems as an integral part of economic and social development, sees conservation as maintenance of life support systems, preservation of genetic diversity, and sustainable utilization of species and ecosystems. It should be noted that the WCS does not suggest that species should not be used but leaves it to be determined what form and level of use meets these conservatory requirements. As we have seen, the strategy has now been supplemented to take more account of the developmental implications of environmental measures within the context of sustainable development.

(2) Maximum Sustainable Yield and Other Management Concepts

To achieve these conservatory objectives the concept of maintaining 'maximum sustainable yield' of living resources is that most widely relied on, at least as a starting-point. It was defined for and refined at the 1955 Rome Technical Conference that preceded the first UN Conference on the Law of the Sea (UNCLOS I) held in Geneva 1958, which adopted the Convention on Fishing and the Conservation of the Living Resources of the Sea.[49] But, as De Klemm has observed, it is paradoxical that the concept became quasi-institutionalized by international law (being found in most fisheries and related conventions in its original or modified form) at a time when scientists were increasingly questioning its applicability to a large number of practical situations.[50] The problem now, therefore, is to redefine the legal content of conservation and secure the necessary changes in fisheries and other relevant living resource conventions. In the MSY concept 'the maximum sustainable yield is the greatest harvest that can be taken from a self-regenerating stock of animals year after year while still maintaining the average size of the stock.'[51] It aims at maintaining the productivity of the oceans by permitting fishermen to take only that number of fish from a stock that is replaced by the annual

---

[48] De Klemm, in Johnston, *Environmental Law of the Sea*, 172–92 and 78–9.

[49] UN International Technical Conference on the Conservation of the Living Resources of the Sea, Technical Papers and Reports, FAO, Rome, 1955. See also Johnston, *International Law of Fisheries*, 50, 59, 76, 100, 337, 344–5, 411–15, 439.

[50] De Klemm, in Johnston, *Environmental Law of the Sea*, 118.

[51] Holt and Talbot (ed.), 'The Conservation of Wild Living Resources', Report of Workshops held at Airlie House, Va., Feb. and Apr. 1975 (unpub.), 30.

rate of new recruits (young fish of harvestable size) entering the stock. Thus MSY is the greatest harvest that can be taken from a self-regenerating stock of animals year after year while still maintaining a constant average size of the stock and is obtained when both fishing mortality and recruitment to the stock are maximised at the same time.

It is not as easy as was thought in the 1950s for population dynamicists confidently and with accuracy to calculate MSY; generally scientific advice consists of a range between a minimum and maximum figure. But this is not the only weakness of the approach. Even in 1958 some scientists challenged the assumption that MSY could be calculated solely on the basis of biological criteria, since these required too high a fishing intensity and would be un-economic. They proposed the objective of 'eumetric fishing'—a state of optimum fishing—within which economic interests could be balanced, with regulation of the fishery being based equally on biological, economic, and social factors and the benefits to producers being accompanied by assured supplies of fish. This would require that an optimum yield (OY) be set, and that it be lower than MSY.[52] MSY as originally expressed is no longer acceptable as a conservation objective because it fails to take account not only of economic objectives but of the ecological relationships of species with each other and with their habitat, of the limits of the given area's biomass and of factors disturbing the environment, such as pollution, habitat loss, disease, current and temperature changes, failures in the food chain of the oceans from disease and other causes. Similar considerations arise in relation to conservation of forms of living resources other than the marine.

Suggested alternative conservation strategies now include maintaining an optimum population (OP), or optimum sustainable population (OSP), or optimum levels thereof (OL), or optimum (or maximum) economic yield (OEY/MEY), or the more complex optimum ecological resource management (OERM).[53]

One of the closest approaches to a broader environmental/ecosystem approach is found in the 1980 Convention on Conservation of Antarctic Marine Living Resources (CCAMLR),[54] the preamble to which recognizes the need to protect the integrity of the ecosystem of the seas surrounding

[52] See Scarff, 6 *ELQ* (1977), 387–400; Johnston, *International Law of Fisheries*, 49–51.

[53] These theories were particularly discussed in relation to the conservation of whales. A useful summary is given in the Draft Report of a Consultation on Marine Mammals held at Bergen, Norway, in 1977; see the Food and Agriculture Organization Advisory Committee on Marine Resources Research Working Party on Marine Mammals, FAO ACMRR/WP/MM, at ss. 9–10; The report of the consultation was published as *Mammals in the Sea*, i–iv, FAO Fisheries Series No. 5, 1978–80. See also Holt and Carlson, *Implementation of a Revised Management Procedure for Commercial Whaling*, International Fund for Animal Welfare (Crowborough, 1991).

[54] Lyster, *International Wildlife Law* (Cambridge, 1985), ch. 9; Vignes, in Francioni and Scovazzi (eds.), *International Law for Antarctica* (Milan, 1987), 341.

Antarctica and to increase knowledge of its component parts. The substantive articles extend its scope to *all* marine living resources in the area within the *whole* Antarctic ecosystem (that is, that lying within the Antarctic convergence, a natural, not a man-made boundary) defined as 'the complex of relationships of Antarctic marine living resources with each other and with their physical environment';[55] they make it clear that birds are included within these resources. 'Rational use'[56] of species is allowed but harvesting must be based on ecological principles with the aim of avoiding reduction of a population to levels below those which ensure its stable recruitment; the stock level is to be maintained close to that which ensures the greatest net annual recruitment. This avoids reference to the criticized criteria of MSY, MEY, OP, etc. The problem of determining this level still remains, however, and progress on conservation under CCAMLR has been slow, even though the Commission and Scientific Committee established by it meets annually;[57] in practice national fishery interests take precedence over the ecosystem approach. Practice under the US Marine Mammal Protection Act 1972,[58] which pioneered this approach, has also evidenced this difficulty. The linking of 'conservation' and 'rational use' in CCAMLR exacerbates the difficulties of following scientific advice, even when available.

The IUCN General Assembly had, in 1976, adopted 'Principles replacing maximum sustainable yield as a basis for management of wild life resources.'[59] These principles required that ecosystems should be maintained in such a state that both consumptive and non-consumptive values can be realized on a continuing basis, ensuring maintenance of both present and future options and minimizing the risk of irreversible change or long-term adverse effects; that management decisions should include a safety factor to allow for limitations of knowledge and imperfections of management; that measures to conserve one resource should not be wasteful of another; that monitoring, analyses, and assessment should precede planned use and accompany actual use of a resource, and the results should be made available promptly for critical public review. It is very useful to bear these optimal objectives in mind

---

[55] Article 1.

[56] Article 2.

[57] Howard, 39 *ICLQ* (1989), 104–49. See esp. 112–15, on the ecosystem approach. He concludes, at 149, that the parties' primary interest is pursuit of national interests in developing fisheries, especially for krill, and controlling scientific research and that conservation remains secondary. He fears that unless there is a change of direction there is little hope that the convention will be successful despite its excellent principles and mechanisms. See also Brown, 10 *Envtl. Consvn.* (1983), 187; Auburn, *Antarctic Law and Politics* (London and Canberra, 1982), 215 ff.; Mitchell and Sandbrook, *The Management of the Southern Oceans* (London, 1980), 49. See also the 1991 Protocol to the Antarctic Treaty on Environmental Protection.

[58] US Pub. L. 92522, 4972, as amended.

[59] IUCN Resolution No. 8, 12th General Assembly of IUCN, 1976. The principles had been developed by an IUCN Workshop on Wild Living Resources, held at Airlie House, Va., in 1974, op. cit., *supra,,* n. 51.

when evaluating the regimes for conservation of wildlife that have been established in recent decades, especially the relevant provisions of the UNCLOS 1982. Such approaches require multi-species management—a highly complex operation—but, as we shall see, many regimes relate to single species and despite the value of an ecosystem approach it is extremely difficult to model it. Moreover it is now being put forward for purposes not envisaged by environmentalists when they first advocated it, namely to justify culling of whales and seals to maintain fish populations (see Chapters 12 and 13). Thus it has many critics[60] and the law can do no more than require it in general terms. Furthermore, it is clear that any concept of conservation must now take account of such closely related issues as climate change, preservation of biological diversity, land-use management, and protection of the oceans from pollution.

It is not, in these circumstances, so surprising that most legal instruments, policy statements, and strategies avoid too rigid a definition of 'conservation' and the Legal Experts Group of WCED preferred a definition in general terms only. For its purposes, the term is used to mean:

the management of human use of a natural resource or the environment in such a manner that it may yield the greatest sustainable benefit to present generations while maintaining its potential to meet the needs and aspirations of future generations. It embraces the preservation, maintenance, sustainable utilization, restoration, and enhancement of a natural resource or the environment.[61]

The WCED gave no indication of the specific measures actually required to achieve this objective.

5. EMERGENCE OF COMPLEX NEW PROBLEMS

The WCS, the WCN, and, expecially, the WCED, have highlighted the growing concern for conserving biodiversity, that is, biological diversity—the variety of life in all its forms.[62] WCED's proposals for a Biodiversity Action Plan, an International Biodiversity Decade, and the conclusion of a convention have introduced a new, complex, and controversial dimension into wildlife conservation. This would require preservation of ecosystem diversity, species diversity, and genetic diversity.[63] Preservation of species diversity is necessary because habitats and species are being destroyed at a greater rate

---

[60] e.g. Gulland, 11 *Marine Policy* (1987), 259–72. He considers that a comprehensive multi-species approach would make a complex situation even more complex.

[61] Legal Experts Group report, in Munro and Lammers, *Environmental Protection and Sustainable Development*, 9 n.

[62] *Supra*, nn. 24, 26, and 32.

[63] Interview with Dr W. Burhenne on biological diversity convention, 3 Ramsar (Apr. 1987), 7.

than ever before in history. As there will never be time to adopt universally an individual species approach to preservation, it is suggested that the aim should be to retain ecosystem diversity, whilst focusing efforts to preserve as a minimum individuals or groups of seven kinds of species, namely: domesticated animals *and* their wild relatives; harvested species; totemic species which have significant socio-cultural, spiritual, or emotional value for people; scientifically important species; candidate species for captive breeding; wideranging species; indicator species, that is, species that indicate the effectiveness of ecosystem maintenance and are valuable for monitoring and evaluating this.

It is, however, important also to preserve genetic variation within species in order for them to adapt and survive and because variability is also the basic material for domestication, plant and animal breeding, and biotechnology. Gene pools representing the range of genetic variations within both the domestic species and their wild relatives should also be preserved. Although some of the conventions discussed in Chapter 12 (for example, the World Heritage, the Ramsar, and the Bonn Conventions) go some way to providing means of achieving this aim, they cover only a small number of ecosystems, species, and ranges of genetic diversity and a comprehensive international convention to conserve biological diversity is now regarded by many as essential. Drafts of such a convention have been considered by the IUCN, UNEP, and various governments and NGOs with a view to adoption at the 1992 UNCED[64] but given the economic complexity of the issues involved, there have been many difficulties in securing agreement on a text (see Chapter 12).

Similar problems, again because of the diversity and complexity of the issues involved, have beset negotiations to develop a convention to control factors contributing to global climate change, which could have considerable effect on habitat protection and the survival of a wide range of species. It suffices here to note that it too will be considered at the 1992 UNCED and that drafts are under negotiation.

The IUCN has continued to draw attention to the alleged weaknesses of both national and international law in relation to achievement of the various principles and purposes articulated in this chapter, in particular to the gaps in the system, duplication of provisions, conflicts in uses and purposes, and inadequate means of enforcement. It has supported the proposal made by the WCED that both an international Declaration and a Convention setting out the principles on Sustainable Development should be adopted and has prepared a draft Covenant on Global Environmental Conservation and the Sustainable Use of Natural Resources for submission to the 1992 World

---

[64] See UNEP GC 15/34 (1989) and SS II/5 (1990).

Conference on Environment and Development.[65] In the absence of such a comprehensive convention, however, living resources, their habitats, and ecosystems are protected on a piecemeal basis only by a series of unrelated conventions, principles, and guidelines; this falls short of the all-embracing approach to conservation proposed by WCS, the WCED, its Legal Experts Group and in the other principles and strategies evaluated in this chapter.

Although it is fair to say that the cumulative measures concluded to protect wildlife represent an *ad hoc* and pragmatic response to the problems involved, none the less an examination of the most important texts does reveal that the problems of implementing the strategies adopted at the more comprehensive international level are gradually being addressed, as we shall see in Chapters 12 and 13. The problems raised in this chapter are discussed there in more depth, with specific reference to the solutions adopted in relevant conventions.

---

[65] See *Report of the Chairman of the Commission on Environmental Policy, Law and Administration to the 18th Session of the General Assembly* (Mar. 1989–Mar. 1990) published in the IUCN *Triennial* Report 1988–90, 81; update for the period Mar. 1990–Nov. 1990, at 3. IUCN General Assembly Resolution 17.22 initiated this draft. UNCED did not adopt conventions on either topic.

12

The Emerging Regime for Conservation of Migratory and Endangered Land-based Species

1. INTRODUCTION

As pointed out in the introduction to Chapter 11, there are differences between land-based and marine species that merit addressing the problems of their conservation in separate chapters, despite several common problems. In so far as these problems are common they have mainly been addressed in comprehensive conservation treaties. Though applying largely to land-based species, these often list some threatened marine species in their annexes, and require comparable forms of protection, whether against harmful effects of trade, or because their habitat is threatened or because of their unique values. We pointed out in that Chapter that unlike marine species, terrestrially based species fall wholly under the sovereignty of the state within whose land frontiers or airspace they are found, even if migratory, and that their regulation, for purposes of conservation and sustainable use, necessitates that state's co-operation and limitations on unfettered claims of sovereignty or sovereign rights. We also emphasized that there are far more terrestrially based mammals, and that they are, with few exceptions, more accessible and vulnerable to capture, over-exploitation, habitat destruction, and the effects of industrialization than those inhabiting the oceans. These threats are increasing as human population expands and the need for animals and their products as food or sources of income accelerates and the means of capturing them become more sophisticated.

Resolution of the problems affecting wildlife conservation has mainly been achieved through the conclusion of international conventions at the global, regional, and subregional level depending on the extent of the areas which threatened species inhabit or through which they migrate.[1] The principles and strategies outlined in Chapters 2 and 11 have had a considerable influence on the development of treaty law in this field.

---

[1] De Klemm, 29 *NRJ* (1989), 932–78; id., 9 *EPL* (1982), 117–28.

2. IMPLEMENTATION OF PRINCIPLES AND STRATEGIES
THROUGH CONSERVATION TREATIES

A wide variety of treaties implementing the principles and strategies referred to in Chapter 11 now exists at the global, regional, and bilateral levels. No convention protects *all* wildlife globally. Some treaties protect a single species, such as polar bears[2] or vicuna,[3] or a group of species, such as whales,[4] migratory birds,[5] Antarctic[6] and North Atlantic seals[7] from excessive exploitation. Others adopt a regional approach to conservation, for example, in the Western Hemisphere (North and South America);[8] Africa,[9] Europe,[10] South-East Asia,[11] the South Pacific,[12] and Antarctica.[13] Many of the newer of these treaties do not now confine themselves to regulating hunting, as did the earlier ones, but provide also for habitat protection. The importance of protecting natural ecosystems as such has begun to be more widely perceived. There are also many bilateral treaties, especially for protection of birds and seals,[14] which reflect these trends.

---

[2] 1973 Agreement on the Conservation of Polar Bears; Lyster, *International Wildlife Law* (Cambridge, 1984), 55–61; Fikkan, 10 *Int. Challenges* (2-1990), 32–8.

[3] 1979 Andean Convention for the Conservation and Management of Vicuna, Burhenne, 979: 94; see also 1969 Convention for the Conservation of the Vicuna, id., 969: 61; Lyster, *International Wildlife Law*, 88–96.

[4] 1966 International Convention for the Regulation of Whaling 1946; Birnie, *The International Regulation of Whaling*, 2 vols. (Dobbs Ferry, NY, 1985); Lyster, *International Wildlife Law*, 17–38.

[5] There have been several regional treaties: 1903 Convention for the Protection of Birds Useful to Agriculture, 51 *UNTS*, 221; 1950 International Convention for the Protection of Birds, 638 *UNTS*, 185; 1970 Benelux Convention on the Hunting and Protection of Birds, 847 *UNTS*, 235 (as amended 1977); Lyster, *International Wildlife Law*, 62–87; De Klemm, 9 *EPL* (1982), 117.

[6] 1972 Convention for the Conservation of Antarctic Seals; see Lyster, *International Wildlife Law*, 39–54.

[7] 1957 Agreement on Measures to Regulate Sealing and to protect Seal Stocks in the North-eastern Part of the Atlantic Ocean (Norway–USSR), 309 *UNTS*, 289; 1971 Agreement between Canada and Norway on Sealing and Conservation of Seal Stocks in the North-West Atlantic, UN Leg. Ser. B/16, 655; Lyster, *International Wildlife Law*, 39–54.

[8] 1940 Convention on Nature Protection and Wildlife Preservation in the Western Hemisphere; Lyster, *International Wildlife Law*, 97–111.

[9] 1968 African Convention on the Conservation of Nature and Natural Resources, administered by the Organization of African Unity. This superseded the 1933 London Convention relative to the Preservation of Fauna and Flora in their Natural State, 172 *UNTS*, 241; Lyster, *International Wildlife Law*, 112–28; also 62–87.

[10] 1979 Convention on the Conservation of European Wildlife and Natural Habitats (Berne Convention); Lyster, *International Wildlife Law*, 129–55.

[11] 1985 ASEAN Agreement on the Conservation of Nature and Natural Resources.

[12] 1976 Apia Convention on Conservation of Nature in the South Pacific.

[13] Agreed Measures for the Conservation of Antarctic Fauna and Flora, 1964, Cmnd. 2822, Misc. 23 (1965); 1980 Convention on the Conservation of Antarctic Marine Living Resources; see also Lyster, *International Wildlife Law*, 48–51, 156–82.

[14] e.g. 1916 US–UK Convention for the Protection of Migratory Birds, 12 *TIAS*, 375; 1936

In addition to the species-specific treaties, there are a number of treaties introducing innovatory protective techniques and approaches. Four, referred to by Lyster as 'the Big Four', are of particular significance and importance to the regime for protection of wildlife, namely the 1971 Convention on Wetlands of International Importance, (Ramsar Convention);[15] the 1972 Convention for the Protection of the World Cultural and Natural Heritage (World Heritage Convention);[16] the 1973 Convention on International Trade in Endangered Species of Wild Fauna and Flora (CITES),[17] the 1979 Convention on the Conservation of Migratory Species of Wild Animals (Bonn Convention).[18]

Also worthy of special mention is the Convention for Conservation of Antarctic Marine Living Resources (CCAMLR),[19] referred to in Chapters 11 and 13, since its definition of marine living resources includes birds and it adopts a holistic ecological approach to conservation whereby the effects of exploitation of one species on all other species and on the marine ecosystem as a whole must be taken into account in taking measures.

A number of the above conventions fulfil the strategic principles examined in Chapter 11 in various ways and to various degrees. An overview of the instruments indicates that to attract the wide range of ratifications necessary for them to succeed as vehicles for the conservation of wildlife, agreements must allow for fair and rational use and exploitation and also permit economic development. To achieve these aims they must provide on a co-operative basis for equitable utilization of so-called 'shared' or 'transboundary' (see Chapter 11) species, as indicated in the relevant UNEP Principles.

Effective conservation of living resources requires that the protection of species in general and of endangered ones in particular be ensured on a sustainable basis. This necessitates regulation on a flexible basis to ensure, *inter alia*, that: species can be added to conventions, as they become threatened; habitats and ecosystems are preserved; introduction of exotic species is controlled; reserved areas are set aside; and that trade in endangered species and their products is limited.

US–Mexico Convention for the Protection of Migratory Birds and Game Mammals, 178 *LNTS*, 309, supplemented by Agreement of 1972, 837 *UNTS*, 125. For a full list of relevant bilateral treaties, see Bernhardt (ed.), 9 *Ency. of Pub. Int. L.* (Heidelberg, 1986), 409–14.

[15] Amended by Protocol concluded in Paris, 3 Dec. 1982, 22 *ILM* (1983), 698; administered by IUCN in co-operation with the International Waterfowl Research Bureau; Lyster, *International Wildlife Law*, 183–207; Navid, 29 *NRJ* (1989), 1001.

[16] Administered by Unesco in co-operation with IUCN and the International Council of Monuments and Sites; Lyster, *International Wildlife Law*, 208–38. See Meyer 2 *Earth LJ* (1976) 45 for background.

[17] Amended 1979, 1983. Lyster, *International Wildlife Law*, 239–77.

[18] Ibid. 278–304.

[19] Ibid. 156–82, and see *infra*, n. 33.

(1) Species Protected by Conventions

(a) Particular Species or Groups: Global Conventions

There are a number of conventions that aim to protect a species or group of species on a global basis. They include the 1946 International Convention for Regulation of Whaling (ICRW), which covers the taking of the so-called 'whales' (but not, in terms, all cetaceans as such), in all waters where whaling takes place, and the 1979 Bonn Convention on Conservation of Migratory Species of Wild Animals, which includes in that term 'the entire population or any geographically separate part of the populations of any species or lower taxon of wild animals, a significant proportion of whose members cyclically and predictably cross one or more national jurisdictional boundaries' (Article 1(1)(a)). The particular species protected within the group at any given time are listed on an amendable schedule in the case of the ICRW, and on an amendable Appendix in the case of the Bonn Convention. Treaties relating exclusively to birds and seals are all regional or bilateral but polar bears and vicuna are protected by specific treaties.

(b) Regional Conventions

Most regional conventions cover a variety of species. The Preamble to the 1940 Western Hemisphere Convention expresses the intention of the American Republics to protect 'representatives of all species and genera of their native flora and fauna, including migratory birds, in sufficient numbers and over areas extensive enough to assure them from becoming extinct through any agency within man's control.' These are then listed in an amendable Annex. The 1968 African Convention, which is in process of revision, ensures in Article VII, the 'conservation, wise use and development of faunal resources' which are listed in an Annex. The 1979 Berne Convention on the Conservation of European Wildlife aims, in Article 1, to conserve those wild fauna in Europe which are listed in amendable appendices (though the Convention is not limited to members of the Council of Europe but is also open to non-members that participated in its elaboration, the EEC, and any other states invited to sign). The 1980 CCAMLR extends to all Antarctic marine living resources, including birds (Article 1). The parties to the 1985 ASEAN Agreement aim at 'ensuring the survival and promoting the conservation of all species under their jurisdiction and control' (Article 3) but only endangered species are listed in an Appendix. The 1950 International Convention for Protection of Birds states that 'all birds should in principle be protected', and that endangered and migratory species require special protection. The 1970 Benelux Convention on the Hunting and Protection of Birds covers game birds and such others as are listed (about sixteen species) but most bird conventions, though covering many species, are bilateral. Article 5(1) of

UNEP's 1986 Convention for the Protection of the Natural Resources and Environment of the South Pacific Region requires parties to ensure 'sound environmental management and development of natural resources' in the Convention area, namely, the 200-mile zones of twenty-three states and territories of the South Pacific states listed.

There are also international conventions protecting single species in specific regions, for example, the 1973 Agreement on the Conservation of Polar Bears, the 1972 Convention for the Conservation of Antarctic Seals, the 1974 Convention for the Conservation and Management of the Vicuna.

(2) Problems of Definition of 'Conservation'

The lack of any clear definition of 'conservation' was observed in Chapter 11; although the purpose of all the conventions referred to above is 'conservation' none defines the term. The discrepancies between the 'ecosystem' definition given by IUCN in the WCS, the sustainable use and development meaning attributed to the term by the WCED Legal Experts Group, and that provided in the 1958 High Seas Convention, based on optimum sustainable yield modified by the need to secure in the first place a supply of food for human consumption, explains why the conventions evade this problem and resort to specification of measures to be taken, expressing their conservatory aims only in general terms. The 1946 Whaling Convention preamble states the desire of its Contracting Governments to 'ensure proper and effective conservation' *and* to achieve 'the optimum level of stocks' but Article V then provides for regulation of 'conservation, development and optimum utilization'. The factors to be taken into account in adopting regulations refer to scientific findings as only one factor amongst others to be taken into account in their adoption; another factor is 'the interests of the consumers of whale products and the whaling industry'.

The 1982 UNCLOS adopts a similar approach in Article 61, requiring the coastal state, 'taking into account the best scientific evidence available to it', to prevent over-exploitation by adopting 'proper conservation and management measures' aimed at achieving the MSY as qualified by both environmental and economic factors and stressing in Article 62 the promotion of optimum utilization of the living resources. The 1979 Bonn Convention, however, requires parties to conserve migratory species and take action to this end, paying special attention to 'species the *conservation status* of which is un-favourable'.[20] It then defines not 'conservation' but 'conservation status', which it postulates as 'the sum of the influences acting on the migratory species that may affect its long-term distribution and abundance' and lists the factors to take into account in determining this. The interpretations of 'wise

---

[20] Bonn Convention, Article I, 1(b) and (c).

use' in the 1971 Ramsar Convention which are outlined later in this chapter are also of relevance. The WCED's Group of Legal Experts, as noted in Chapter 11, favours a definition based on 'optimum sustainable yield' (OSY) in order to achieve and maintain sustainable utilization, since 'sustainable yield' does not allow for error, lack of data or other uncertainties, or interdependence of exploited species and other species or ecosystems. If both predator and prey are taken, MSY cannot be upheld. To be successful as a conservation model, MSY must be based on reliable scientific advice and the data on which this is to be based must also be reliable. But not only are data often non-existent or insufficient but scientific theories used to interpret them often themselves prove inadequate and the advice given is either imprecise or offers wide ranges of allowable catch. Advice may also be compromised by the economic, social, and political needs of those exploiting a species or its habitat.[21] As knowledge advances, moreover, the management theories become more complex and uncertain. The interim cessation of catching prescribed by the IWC in 1982 resulted from the inability of its Scientific Committee to provide the advice necessary to operate its New (now Revised) Management Procedures. Thus whale catching could resume if the scientific data, etc. improve.[22] None the less, as Chapter 13 especially illustrates, MSY remains the predominant conservation concept. Because of these difficulties environmental NGOs are beginning to use 'preservation' or 'protection' as the favoured goal, rather than 'conservation'. The tension between 'conservation' and sustainable economic development is expressed in the 1968 African Convention which noted that 'the interrelationship between conservation and socio-economic development implies both that conservation is necessary to ensure sustainability of development, and that socio-economic development is necessary for the achievement of conservations on a lasting basis'.

(3) Problems Concerning the Nature and Legal Status of the International Community's Interest in Living Resources

The issue here is whether living resources *per se* have any international legal status. While there is no doubt that the international community has an interest in protection of certain species, the extent and nature of this community interest is difficult to determine at present. Whilst it cannot be said that the substantive provisions of the conventions treat living resources as 'common heritage' or give effect to inter-generational rights as conceived by

---

[21] Andresen and Ostreng (eds.), *International Resource Management: The Role of Science and Politics* (Oslo, 1990), 17–23; Fløistad, 10 *Int. Challenges* (2-1990), 12–16; Andresen, ibid. (4-1990), 29–35; id., 13 *Marine Policy* (1989), 99–118; Indreeide, 10 *Int. Challenges* (4-1990), 36–44; Wettestad, ibid. 12–21; Fløistad, ibid. 22–8 (on the role of ICES).
[22] Andresen, 10 *Int. Challenges* (4-1990), 29–35; 13 *Marine Policy* (1989), 99–118, and see *infra*, Ch. 13.

Brown-Weiss,[23] and included in the environmental strategies considered in Chapter 11, some conventions do recognize in their Preambles the moral force of this concept and treat living resources as, at the least, matters of community interest. Unlike later fisheries conventions, even in 1946 the Preamble to the Whaling convention recognized 'the *interest* of the nations of the world in safeguarding for future generations the great natural resources represented by the whale stocks';[24] the 1968 African Convention regarded soil, water, and faunal resources as constituting 'a capital of vital importance for mankind'; the 1985 ASEAN Agreement's preamble recognizes 'the importance of natural resources for present and future generations'; the 1971 Ramsar Convention, more weakly acknowledges 'the interdependence of man and his environment'. Moreover, the 1972 World Heritage Convention declares that 'parts [*sic*] of the natural heritage are of outstanding interest and therefore need to be preserved as part of the world heritage of mankind as a whole'. The Preamble to the 1973 CITES refers, however, to wild fauna and flora as 'an irreplaceable part of the natural systems of the earth which must be protected for *this and future generations to come*'.[25]

The concept of common heritage as the basis of a new international regime for the exploitation of the deep sea-bed was first proposed in 1967 (see Chapter 3) but though it must undoubtedly have influenced discussion in other forums, the form it took in the 1982 UNCLOS is not reflected in living resources conventions. The 1972 World Heritage Convention comes closest to that concept, without establishing comparable machinery for its manifestation. Its Preamble declares that 'deterioration or disappearance of any item of the cultural or natural heritage constitutes a harmful impoverishment of the *heritage of all nations of the world*';[26] that Unesco's constitution requires it to spread knowledge by assessing conservation of the world's heritage and recommending the necessary international conventions; that existing conventions, etc. show the importance of 'safeguarding this unique and irreplaceable *property to whatever people it may belong*',[27] parts of which of outstanding interest need to be preserved 'as part of the *world heritage of mankind as a whole*'.[28] The Unesco General Conference expressed the view, evidenced in the Preamble, that new conventional provisions were necessary to establish an effective system of *collective* protection. The protective responsibility is placed initially on states but Article 6, whilst respecting state sovereignty also recognizes that the cultural and natural heritage constitutes 'a *world*' heritage for whose protection *it is the duty of the international community as a whole to*

---

[23] Brown-Weiss, *In Fairness to Future Generations: International Law, Common Patrimony and Inter-generational Equity* (1989); id., 11 *ELQ* (1984), 495–576; id., Gundling, and D'Amato, 84 *AJIL* (1990), 190–212; see also the examples cited by Munro and Lammers, *Environmental Protection and Sustainable Development*, 42–5, and see *supra*, Ch. 5.

[24] Emphasis added.   [25] Emphasis added.   [26] Emphasis added.
[27] Emphasis added.   [28] Emphasis added.

co-operate'.[29] An intergovernmental World Heritage Committee (WHC) is established by Article 8 to maintain a World Heritage List of properties submitted for inclusion by states and to lay down the criteria for this (Article 11). It is assisted by a secretariat provided by Unesco but no independent International Heritage Authority is established to regulate activities in relation to this heritage, in contrast to the International Sea-bed Authority created by the 1982 UNCLOS.

Though the Preamble to the 1973 CITES Convention acknowledges that wild flora and fauna must be protected for '*future generations to come*',[30] it adds that 'people and states are and should be the best protectors of their own wild fauna and flora'. Whilst noting that in addition 'international co-operation is essential for protection against over-exploitation through international trade', it also does not establish any international management body; only a Management and a Scientific Authority are to be established in each state party (Article IX), backed by a secretariat and biennial Conference of the Parties.

The 1979 Bonn Convention's Preamble is the most positive in stating international community and inter-generational rights. It recognizes that 'wild animals are an irreplaceable part of the earth's natural system which must be conserved for the good of mankind' and that 'each generation of man *holds* the resources of the earth for future generations and has an *obligation* to ensure that this legacy is conserved and, when utilized, is used wisely'.[31] This is the clearest articulation yet in a convention in force of the Brown-Weiss doctrine. This convention is not well ratified—it has only thirty-seven parties at present who have not been active in implementing it—and this preamble too goes on to stress that *states* are the protectors of the species within national boundaries, although conservation and effective management of migratory species require the concerted action of all states within whose boundaries they spend part of their life-cycle. It specifically refers to Recommendation 32 of the UNCHE Action Plan[32] but again no international authority is established; only a small secretariat (Article IX), a Scientific Council (Article VIII), and a triennial Conference of the Parties (Article VII). Finally, it should be noted that the Ramsar Convention's Regina Conference in 1987 refined the interpretation of 'wise use' as employed in that convention to include 'human use of a wetland so that it may yield the greatest continuous benefit to present generations whilst maintaining its potential to meet the needs and aspirations of future generations'.

The preambular articulation of international community interest or inter-generational interest in protection of living resources is generally coupled not with the institution of international management bodies but with expression of the duty of states' parties to co-operate and the establishment of machinery

---

[29] Emphasis added.   [30] Emphasis added.   [31] Emphasis added.
[32] Report of United Nations Conference on the Human Environment 1972, 12.

through which they can do so. This is evidenced in all the conventions cited so far. Of particular interest in this respect also are the regional conventions, even those not identifying 'common interest' as such. The preamble to the 1979 Berne Convention merely expresses the need for 'unity'. It states as an aim of the Council of Europe, the achievement of greater unity among its members and its wish to co-operate with other states on nature conservation. It notes the need for governments to consider conservation for migratory species in particular and to establish international co-operation. Reference is made to the widespread requests for common action made by international bodies, especially the UNCHE and the Council of Europe's own Consultative Assembly. However, no international authority is established; action is left to each Contracting Party, though it institutes a Standing Committee of all the Parties and secretariat functions are fulfilled by the Council of Europe itself. Another regional convention, the 1980 CCAMLR, which adopts an ecosystem approach to conservation of Antarctic marine life, refers in its Preamble to the need for international co-operation and to the 'prime responsibilities of the Antarctic Treaty Consultative Parties for Antarctic environmental protection'. It recognizes the need to establish machinery for co-ordinating measures and studies, institutes a small Secretariat (Article XVII), and a Commission of the Parties which is accorded international personality (Article VIII) and which, inter alia, formulates conservation measures (Article IX) advised by a Scientific Committee of Commission Members. In practice, however, it has not been able to adopt many co-operative measures, having been unable to achieve the consensus among its parties required by its decision-making processes (Article XII) and objection procedures (Article IX).[33]

The African Convention provides no new international machinery for co-operation in disbursement of 'mankind's capital' of living resources. The OAU, acting as its secretariat, has not been active in this respect. The ASEAN Agreement expresses the desire to take both individual and joint conservatory actions, recognizes that international co-operation is essential to attain many of these goals and that the conclusion of the ASEAN Agreement is an essential means of achieving these purposes. Even so, no *supra*national authority is established. To date, however, little action has been taken under the African and ASEAN Agreements and even the long-standing Western Hemisphere (OAS) Convention has been relatively inactive in adopting co-operative conservation measures.

Though co-operation is difficult to achieve in relation to conservation of shared living resources in general, it is to some extent manifested in allocation of rights to exploit fisheries, especially on a regional basis, but this is not

---

[33] Howard, 38 *ICLQ* (1989), 135; Lyster, *International Wildlife Law*; Wettestad and Andresen, *The Effectiveness of International Resource Co-operation: Some Preliminary Findings* (Lysaker, 1991), 28.

proving a successful form of conservation as Chapter 13 evidences. Conventions for conservation of marine living resources do not refer to fish as a natural heritage or to the rights of future generations but even the early fisheries conventions did acknowledge that the stocks they desired to conserve were of 'common concern' to the parties, for example, the Preamble to the 1959 North-East Atlantic Fisheries Convention. Following Canada's adoption of a 200-nautical-mile. Exclusive Fishery Zone, the 1978 Convention on Future Multilateral Co-operation in the North-West Atlantic Fisheries, however, cautiously expresses the desire to promote conservation and optimum utilization, within a framework appropriate to the new regime of extended coastal state jurisdiction, and as its title indicates, it recognizes that accordingly international co-operation and consultation with respect to fisheries in its area must be encouraged. Both conventions, as do other fisheries agreements, establish machinery for co-operation (see Chapter 13).

(4) Co-operation through Bi-lateral Agreements

Though states parties to the 1979 Bonn Convention have failed to negotiate any of the required Range State Agreements between or among themselves to protect listed species, there exist a large number of bilateral co-operative agreements on conservation of nature.[34] A few of these recognize, in terms similar to the multilateral conventions, the international value of the resources

---

[34] See Agreement between Peru and Brazil for the conservation of Flora and Fauna of the Amazon Territories 1975, promoting information exchange and 'in the spirit of co-operation', curtailing import of banned native products; Convenio sobre Protección de Bosques y Fauna e Integración de Parques Frontierizos, La Paz, 1976, introducing co-operative programmes; Agreement between the United States and Mexico on Co-operation to Improve the Management of Arid Lands and Semi-Arid Lands 1979, which requires co-operation, *inter alia*, in management and utilization of flora and fauna, followed in 1978 by an Agreement on Environmental Co-operation (effected by exchange of notes, 14 and 19 June 1978), superseded in 1983 by an Agreement on Co-operation for the Protection of the Environment in the Border Area; L'Accord entre France et Sénégal relatif à leur coopération en matière de protection de la nature et de l'environnment 1985; Memorandum on Implementation of the Agreement between the United States and the USSR on Co-operation in the Field of Environmental Protection, which includes conservation of rare and endangered species of animals and plants, general wildlife conservation and management (which facilitated the Polar Bears Agreement 1973)—both the UK in 1974 and France in 1975 concluded similar accords with the USSR; Agreement between United States and Japan on Co-operation in the Field of Environmental Protection 1975; Exchange of Letters between United States and EEC on Methods for co-operation between them, 1 July 1974, EC SEC (74) 2518 final; the EC has exchanged similar letters with other non-member states such as Switzerland (12 Dec. 1975 SEC (75) 4081), Canada (6 Nov. 1975 SEC (75) 2132 Final), and Austria (28 Apr. 1978); Memorandum of Understanding on Environmental Protection Between the US Environmental Protection Agency and the Federal Ministry of Housing and Environment of Nigeria, Lagos, 22 Sept. 1980, which asserts that co-operation on this 'is an appropriate and important corollary to the two nations economic and technical co-operation' and is to be promoted on the basis of equality, reciprocity, and mutual benefit (Article II), including for preservation of nature. Copies of these agreements are on file at the IUCN Centre for Environmental Law (CEL), Bonn, Federal Republic of Germany (FRG).

concerned. The 1988 US–Canadian Agreement on the Conservation of the Porcupine Caribou Herd recognizes that it is 'a unique and irreplaceable natural resource of great value which each generation should maintain and make use of so as to conserve them for future generations'.[35] It also recognizes the traditional harvesting rights of the indigenous peoples though it acknowledges the need to establish co-operative bilateral mechanisms to co-ordinate the Parties' conservatory activities. It adds, however, that this should not alter domestic authorities' powers regarding management and should be implemented by existing rather than new management structures. The 1985 Agreement between Finland and the USSR on Co-operation in the Field of Environmental Protection states that it was concluded 'on the basis of the friendly neighbourly relations that prevail between the two countries' and expressed the parties' desire to further 'through co-operative work' measures for results in this field since 'economic and social development which heeds the requirements of future generations' requires that the environment be thus protected,[36] as does the Helsinki Final Act of the Conference on Security and Co-operation in Europe 1975.[37]

It is clear from this résumé of the relevant provisions of the leading conservation agreements at international, regional, and bilateral level, that international conservation law as yet neither recognizes that living resources in general or migratory species in particular are a 'common heritage' in the UNCLOS sense nor inter-generational rights as such. There are no provisions corresponding to the establishment by US law of wildlife as a public trust[38] nor has any wildlife body corresponding to the international authority established by the UNCLOS 1982 been instituted. Terrestrial wildlife remains the property of the state within whose boundaries it resides, albeit temporarily; in international areas it is regarded as a common property resource akin to fisheries. But increasingly it is recognized that co-operation between states in conservation regimes is vital to the survival of migratory species. The treaties and agreements evidence such a degree of specific acceptance of the need for such co-operation that both conservation (though undefined) and co-operation can, it is submitted, now be regarded as duties established as part of customary law by state practice. The increasing reference to conservation of species and habitat as community concerns, whatever form of expression is used, enhances the emergence of these duties even in relation to living resources located within areas of national jurisdiction. There is some, but less extensive evidence, on the basis of the growing number of bilateral and regional agreements, that the principle of good neighbourliness is also recognized and that it requires co-operation, notification, and consultation on matters affecting conservation. This conclusion is supported also by the

---

[35] On file IUCN CEL, Bonn.   [36] Ibid.   [37] See Ch. 2.
[38] Nanda, 4 *Millenium* (1975), 101–11, esp. 107–9.

variety of political and administrative bodies established for developing co-operative regulatory measures at national and international levels—regular Conferences of the Parties, Scientific Committee or Councils; Management Authorities, Standing Committees, Commissions, Secretariats.[39] Every agreement has either established such a body, or required designation of the appropriate national agencies, or use of existing international organizations, such as the OAU, OAS, Unesco, the Council of Europe, IUCN, UNEP, or a combination of these.

(5) Co-operative and Conservatory Techniques

It is important also to consider the variety of techniques available under the conventions for development of co-operative measures. Many of these tech-niques can only work on the basis of co-operation, reciprocity, and mutual trust, for example, permit systems; establishment of protected areas; listings of endangered species; joint inspection or enforcement schemes; exchange of scientific data and other information.

(a) Listing, Permit Systems, and Other Techniques

The main technique used in the conventions is to list species, sites, etc. requiring regulation in annexes, appendices, or simply 'lists'. Generally this is combined with a system of permits; each state party being required to enact the necessary legislation. In conjunction with the provision of a regular forum within which the parties can meet, discuss, inform, and negotiate—whether it be an *ad hoc* commission established by the convention, regular conference of the parties, or use of an existing international organization—this institutes the flexible system necessary to fine-tune the requisite conservatory measures to both internationally agreed scientific advice and political support, taking account of the economic and social as well as the environmental effects of the measures and of their impact on development. As an ultimate safeguard of national interests most species conventions, though allowing regulations to be adopted by various forms of majority vote, also include an objections pro-cedure, as under the ICRW (Article V), whereby if states formally object to a new measure within a specified period, they are not bound by it. Alternatively, some conventions provide that if states do not notify any objection they are bound (sometimes referred to as the 'tacit amendment' procedure), which makes introduction of changes somewhat easier than the formal objection procedure.

The ICRW provides a prime but unusual example of the listing, licensing,

---

[39] For numerous examples involving conservation of marine species in developing countries, see Kwiatkowska, 14 *Marine Policy* (1990), 385–420; she identifies at 419–20, 'The Basic Institutional Coverage of the Indian Ocean Region'.

and permit system, which it is appropriate to consider here as the ICRW provides for a fully international regime. It includes, as an integral part of the Convention, a Schedule of regulations, which the IWC can add to or amend annually.[40] Catches can be regulated by setting quotas, done since 1974 under so-called 'New Management Procedures' (NMP, revised at the 43rd IWC Meeting in 1991 and thus now referred to as the RMP), whereby stocks are assessed in relation to their proximity or otherwise to maximum sustainable yield, with due allowance being made for environmental factors affecting this calculation. As quotas could be set at zero, if advisable, all taking of exploited species can be totally prohibited by issuing no permits. This was done in 1982 on an interim basis. Regulations must be based on 'scientific findings' (Article V); the IWC's Scientific Committee has now adopted a cautious policy to achieve this, based on the view that the available scientific information and population theory is so uncertain that catch quotas could not safely be set for any species, though states such as Iceland, Japan, and Norway do not agree and contend that certain stocks and species could still be taken without risk. IWC policy provides an example of the application in a wildlife context of the precautionary principle more familiar in the pollution context (see Ch. 3). Regulations are open to a prolonged objections procedure under Article 3, but this is used much less than in the past because of conservationist pressure from NGOs and non-whaling states. Objecting states have often been compelled to withdraw their objections under pressure, including the use of unilateral economic sanctions,[41] though the compatibility of such sanctions with the General Agreement on Tariffs and Trade (GATT) has been questioned (see Ch. 3).

In the early period of the Commission, when its members were predominantly whaling or former whaling states, quotas tended, as a result of political compromise or use of objection procedures, to be set higher than the MSY proposed by the Scientific Committee, with disastrous results for major stocks. Now the position is reversed but, as a result, the few states that were still catching the larger whales initially increased their issue of so-called 'scientific permits' in order to maintain their whaling vessels in operation pending the possible future lifting of the interim moratorium. This is a legitimate, if undesirable, procedure since it evades the full effect of the zero quotas, because the issue of permits for scientific research is left by Article III of the ICRW to the discretion of the government concerned. The prior consent of the Commission is not required, although the Commission has now instituted procedures enabling it to comment on the need for such research, taking account of the views of the Scientific Committee. A few

---

[40] See generally Birnie, *International Regulation of Whaling*; Tønnessen and Johnson, *The History of Modern Whaling* (London 1982); Scarff, 6 *ELQ* (1977), 326–638.

[41] Gambell, 20 *Mammal Rev.* (1990), 31–43; Birnie, 29 *NRJ* (1989), 903; Zoller, *Enforcing International Law Through US Legislation* (Dobbs Ferry, NY, 1985), 84–97.

states—Japan, Iceland, Norway—none the less initially ignored the Commission's criticism of their research programmes and continued to issue permits, but only Iceland has persisted in this practice. Meanwhile, these states have pressed for the required review of the status of stocks and have provided data, which they consider justifies the reissuing of permits to take a limited quota of minke whales in 1992.[42]

The IWC has confined its use of the Schedule to regulation of the taking of the twelve large whales that were originally the targets of the whaling industry and it has not regulated (with minor exceptions) the small cetaceans. The three-quarter majority vote necessary to amend the Schedule for this purpose has never been obtainable. Thus attempts have been made to protect at least some of these species by listing them on the appendices of other, more recent conservatory conventions, such as the Bonn, Berne, and CITES agreements and by using, as appropriate, the techniques available within the European Community for the adopting of binding Directives and Regulations.

The Whaling Convention provides a particularly interesting example of the use of techniques, which were essentially those common in fishery commissions established between 1930 and 1976 and were aimed at maintaining an exploitative industry, to achieve a purely conservatory objective. In the course of time and in the light of changing opinions about whaling, it has also passed several non-binding conservatory resolutions (which require only a simple majority for their adoption). These, *inter alia*, ban transfer of vessels, equipment, and know-how to non-member states; prohibit trading in whales and whale products (the EC has implemented this by adopting a regulation banning their import into its member states);[43] call for humane killing; and require collection of data on small cetaceans.[44] The Schedule itself was also used to permit, exceptionally, the taking of bowhead whales (otherwise protected from taking) by Alaskan Eskimos in pursuance of their cultural and subsistence rights as native peoples, but only if using their traditional, simple means of killing the whales and for such purposes.

Other conservatory techniques of interest include those laid down in the recently terminated 1957 North Pacific (Behring Sea) Fur Seal Convention (as amended),[45] which introduced the 'abstention principle'. It prohibited pelagic sealing (also with exceptions for native peoples) and established a Commission to recommend conservatory measures for the taking of the seals on land, on the basis of co-ordinated scientific research. Under it, only the

---

[42] See Chairman's Report of the Forty-Second and Forty-Third Meetings of the IWC, 1990 and 1991 respectively.

[43] Council Regulation No. 348/81, Article 1; OJ. EEC. No. L. 39 (12 Feb. 1981), 1 as corrected in OJ No. L. 132 (19 May 1981), 30.

[44] For texts of these and related resolutions, see Birnie, *International Regulation of Whaling*, ii. 775–97.

[45] Lyster, *International Wildlife Law*, 40–9; see also *infra*, Ch. 13.

USSR and United States were permitted to continue sealing and in return undertook each to deliver 15 per cent of the sealskins taken by them to Canada and Japan. This is perhaps the only direct and practical evidence of full application of the UNEP principles of equitable utilization and distribution to be found in such conventions, though it has been argued that in the final analysis even the duties of prior information and consultation have their origin in the concept of equitable utilization.[46] It has, however, remained a unique model, not followed in relation to terrestrial species; even the Convention on Conservation of Antarctic Seals 1972,[47] concluded after the UNCHE, has a more orthodox approach: measures to be taken are listed in an Annex, and are limited to establishing catch quotas, designating areas, gear, etc, implemented through a permit system that must be enacted by each state party.

The 1968 African Convention[48] also lists natural resources in Annexes according to the degree of protection required—those threatened with extinction are banned from hunting except if required in the national interest or for scientific purposes, the others can be listed only under special authority. These provisions can be applied to unlisted species to preserve particular national fauna. Measures taken must be scientifically based and reconciled with customary rights. Parties must also provide conservation education and include conservation and management of natural resources in their development plans.

The Bonn Convention also provides for listing of threatened species in Appendices according to the degree of threat.[49] Under the Bonn Convention the need for conservatory measures depends on whether a species has a favourable or unfavourable 'conservation status', namely, the sum of the influences acting on it that may affect its long-term distribution and abundance (Article 1(1)(c)). Species are listed, on the basis of reliable scientific evidence, in one of two Appendices according to their degree of endangerment. Parties that are Range States of that species, that is, states exercising jurisdiction over any part of the range of a migratory species that is listed as having an unfavourable conservation status, or whose flag vessels take it beyond national jurisdictional limits, must conclude international AGREEMENTS [sic] to conserve them (Article 2). No agreements have yet been concluded though several are contemplated and the number of parties to this convention is small, namely, thirty-seven which is unfortunate since the ultimate effectiveness of its methods depends on wide participation and state practice in conclusion of AGREEMENTS.

[46] Handl, 14 *RBDI* (1978–9), 61; and cf. *supra*, pp. 114–9, pp. 126–7.

[47] Lyster, *International Wildlife Law*, 112–28.

[48] See ibid. 278–304; also De Klemm, 29 *NRJ* (1989), 935–78; Lyster, 29 *NRJ* (1989), 979–1000.

[49] See Lyster, *International Wildlife Law*, 129–55.

The Berne Convention also lists endangered species in two appendices according to the degree of threat (Article 7) and requires parties to take such measures as closed seasons, prohibition of taking (as required), and prohibition of indiscriminate means of capture, though exceptions can be permitted. Parties are also required to take appropriate measures to conserve the habitat of species listed on the appendices. There are special provisions for migratory species. Its Standing Committee of member states of the Council of Europe can make recommendations on these matters. The listing system is also used to protect wetlands (as defined therein) in the Ramsar Convention.[50] Each party must designate suitable wetlands in its territory for inclusion in a List of Wetlands of International Importance (Article 2), maintained by a Bureau established under the Convention. The choice is made on the basis of their international significance in terms of ecology, botany, zoology, limnology, or hydrology. The wetlands remain subject to national sovereignty but parties must promote their conservation in conformity with the international obligations laid down in the convention. Conferences must be held, and now meet regularly as necessary, which can give advice on, amongst other things, conservation, wise use, and management. The obligations are imprecise, expressed in general terms only. In 1987 many improvements were introduced to make the Convention more relevant to developing countries. There is less emphasis on wetland and water-fowl protection as such, more on their value to people also and on wise use.

The World Heritage Convention 1972[51] also accepts that cultural and natural heritage, even though of world significance, remains primarily the property of the state in which it is located (Article 2) but that those areas listed with the approval of the World Heritage Committee (WHC, composed of fifteen of the states parties) established under the convention constitute a world heritage for whose protection it is the duty of the international community as a whole to co-operate (Articles 6 and 11). The WHC thus lists those areas it considers of outstanding universal value in terms of criteria established by it.

Finally, mention must be made of the system underlying the 1973 CITES,[52] one of the most effective and, therefore, important conventions, whereby species whose survival is threatened by international trade therein or in specimens thereof or which may become so unless trade is regulated, are listed on Appendices, which can be amended at the biennial conferences of its parties. Export and import of those threatened with extinction (listed on Appendix 1) requires prior issue and presentation of an export and import permit; these are issued only if certain conditions are met (Article III). Re-

---

[50] See Lyster, *International Wildlife Law*, 183–207.
[51] See ibid. 208–38; Hales, 4 *Parks* (1980), 1–3.
[52] See Lyster, *International Wildlife Law*, 239–77; Fayre, *Convention on Trade in Endangered Species* (Dordrecht, 1990), *passim*.

export similarly requires a prior permit. The advice of both the national Scientific and Management Authorities, established under the Convention, must be sought on questions such as whether export will be detrimental to the species' survival, whether or not the specimen was obtained in breach of state laws, that the method of shipment minimizes risk of injury, damage to health and cruel treatment, etc. The export–import permit system is the crux of this convention but exemptions are permitted, for example, if the specimen was acquired before the convention applied, or the specimens are household effects (subject to various exceptions). Trade with states not party to the convention is permitted only if 'comparable documentation' to that required by CITES is issued by the state concerned. This provides an incentive to join the convention since, as CITES membership expands (it now has 110 parties), there are fewer non-parties with which other non-parties can trade. There is much for the small Secretariat established under the CITES to do since, *inter alia*, it can invite the parties' attention to any matter 'pertaining to the aims of the Convention' (Article XII (2)(e)) and can communicate to the parties concerned relevant information about species and specimens in transit and the status of relevant permits.

(b) Protection of Habitat

The strategies outlined in earlier sections of this chapter stress the need to conserve species' habitats as an integral part of their effective conservation. Fishery conventions generally ignore this aspect, although, even in 1957, the Behring Sea Fur Seals Convention required research on the relationship between fur seals and other marine resources and on whether fur seals had adverse effects on other resources exploited by parties, and the more recent North-East and North-West Atlantic Fisheries Conventions require scientific advice on ecological and environmental factors to be obtained. But several of the major wildlife conventions, many of which list some marine mammals, now specifically provide for habitat protection. Amongst these is the 1968 African Convention, which provides for creation of 'special reserves' set aside for conservation of wildlife and protection of its habitat (Article III) where killing and human settlement is controlled, and also for 'partial reserves' or 'sanctuaries' set aside to protect particularly threatened animal or plant species (especially those listed) and the biotypes necessary for their survival. It also requires maintenance and extension of existing conservation areas and possible creation of new ones to protect representative ecosystems and those peculiar to a territory. Parties must establish protective zones round these areas for control of detrimental activities (Article X).

The 1971 Ramsar Convention is concerned with protecting 'the fundamental ecological functions of wetlands as regulators of water regimes and as habitats supporting a characteristic flora and fauna, especially waterfowl'. The 1972 World Heritage Convention defines 'natural heritage' to include 'areas which constitute the habitat of threatened species of animals of outstanding universal value from the point of view of science or conservation' (Article 2). The 1979 Bonn Convention defines habitat as 'any area in the range of a migratory species which contains suitable living conditions for that species'. Range States of the Appendix I species must try to conserve and restore habitats important to removing these species from danger of extinction (Article III (4)(a)) and AGREEMENTS concluded by Range States must provide for conervation and restoration of habitats important in maintaining a favourable conservation status (Article V(5)(e)). The 1979 Berne Convention's stated titular and preambular aims include conservation of natural habitats, as also do its general provisions. This is a major purpose of the convention. Several articles lay down obligations on parties to promote policies, enact legislation, and take other measures for this purpose (Articles 3, 4, and 12). The 1940 Western Hemisphere Convention's aim is also to protect representatives of species in their natural habitat.

Despite these provisions in major conventions, however, the record of states parties in implementing habitat protection measures is generally considered to be less good than that in implementation of permit systems. States often limit habitat protection to national parks or nature reserves (see below) or do not extend it to certain species. State practice and response to pressure from NGOs in this respect varies as the different fates of certain loggerhead turtle nesting sites in Greece and Turkey reveal; in the former case, a tourist development threatening such sites was stopped; in the latter it was not, though both states concerned are party to the Berne Convention.[53]

(c) Creation of Nature Reserves, Marine Parks, and Protected Areas[54]

There are many problems, both practical and legal, involved in administering such reserves, especially if such parks cross frontier zones. Since species protected in parks on one side of the border may be killed if they migrate across the frontier, co-operative bilateral agreements are essential, based on the principle of good neighbourliness.

In addition to the special reserves and game reserves established by the African Convention, the Western Hemisphere Convention encourages establishment of national parks, national reserves, nature monuments, and strict

[53] Lyster, 'Protection of Wildlife from the Point of View of the North', Paper given at Dartmouth College Colloquium on International Governance, Hanover, United States, 17–19 June 1991; unpublished.
[54] 'Looking at Biosphere Reserves—A 1983 Perspective', 19 *Nature and Resources* (1983), Unesco, Paris; Lambrechts, 4 *Rev. jurid. de l'env.* (1980), 357–72; Dupuy, ibid. 374–8; de Saussay, ibid.; id., *Principles, Criteria and Guidelines for the Establishment of Mediterranean Marine and Coastal Protected Areas*, IUCN (Gland, 1981); World National Parks Congress, Bali 1982, 11 *AMBIO* (5) (1982) and 12 *AMBIO* (1983) (3/4); Declaration of the World National Parks Congress, 10 *EPL* (1983), 62–8; Conservation Foundation Letter (1984), 1–8. De Saussay, 32 *UNASYLVA* (1980), 16–22, gives specific examples of these and of joint commissions.

wilderness reserves, all of which it defines and for which it proposes various protective measures. The Whaling Convention provides for fixing of closed waters, including designation of sanctuary areas (Article V(i)(c)); the Indian Ocean has been so designated and the Seychelles has created such an area. The Ramsar Convention requires establishment of nature reserves on wetlands; many World Heritage listed sites are or have become national parks and sanctuaries; Unesco has also encouraged creation and listing of biosphere reserves.[55]

UNEP has added Protocols on Specially Protected Areas to its Mediterranean and Caribbean Regional Seas Conventions.[56] The Protocol to the Barcelona Convention requires, in Article 3, that such areas be established

to safeguard in particular (a) sites of biological and ecological value; the genetic diversity, as well as satisfactory population levels, of species, and their breeding grounds and habitats; representative types of ecosystems as well as ecological processes; (b) sites of particular importance because of their scientific, aesthetic, historical, archaeological, cultural or educational interest.

It is thus the most ambitious of all instruments in this respect. The parties are required to develop standards for selecting, establishing, managing, and notifying information on such protected areas. The aim is to have a series of interlinked areas throughout the Mediterranean but the obligations are expressed subjectively in 'soft terms': parties are required only 'to the extent possible' to establish such areas and to 'endeavour to undertake the action necessary' in order to protect and, as appropriate, restore them 'as rapidly as possible'. The possible scope of the subject-matter of the measures is, however, spelt out in Article 7 and is quite broad. A potentially controversial issue is the regulation of passage, stopping, and anchoring of ships within these areas; conflicts could develop if the rules concerning innocent passage and rights established under IMO and other relevant conventions are not observed. However, both these Protocols and the 1986 Noumea Convention for the Protection of the Natural Resources and Environment of the South Pacific Region do, for the first time, bring together in one instrument, outside the 1982 UNCLOS itself, the regulation of all sources of pollution and the conservation of living resources. This is now seen to be the approach required for effective conservation on an ecological basis and is commended as such in the various strategies laid down internationally for this purpose.

The ASEAN Convention, in Article 13, requires its parties to establish 'terrestrial, freshwater, coastal or marine protection areas' to safeguard

---

[55] Unesco, *Conventions and Recommendations of Unesco concerning Protection of the Cultural Heritage* (Paris, 1980).

[56] Text of Protocol Concerning Mediterranean Specially Protected Areas, 1982, in Sand, *Marine Environment Law* (Tycooly, 1988), 37–44; text of Protocol to Cartagena Convention concerning Specially Protected Areas and Wildlife, 1990, in 19 *EPL* (1989), 224–8.

essential ecological processes, representative samples of ecosystems, natural habitat (especially of rare or endangered species), gene pools, and reference sources for research, *inter alia*, thus being one of the first conventions to provide for preservation of biological diversity. Several states have enacted national legislation establishing marine parks,[57] but whether or not they have done so in pursuit of the conventions or strategies is difficult to determine. Undoubtedly these are having some effect.

(d) Provision of Financial Assistance

Both the taking of necessary conservation measures and the non-exploitation of wildlife can have adverse economic consequences, especially serious for developing states. To achieve sustainable development on a global basis, and especially to preserve biological diversity, it has been suggested that compensation should be available in such circumstances.

Only one convention originally established a Fund to help achieve its purposes, namely, the World Heritage Convention, Articles 15–18 of which establish the World Heritage Fund for the Protection of the World Cultural and Natural Heritage of Outstanding Universal Value, as a trust fund in accordance with Unesco's financial regulations. The monies are drawn from five sources: compulsory and voluntary contributions of states parties; contributions, gifts, or bequests made by other states, Unesco, and other UN bodies and intergovernmental organizations; public or private bodies and individuals; interest accruing on the Fund; benefit events for the Fund; other authorized sources drawn up by the World Heritage Committee (WHC). The World Heritage Convention requires states to contribute to the trust fund on a basis related to their contributions to Unesco; thus the richer states are expected to pay most. States can choose whether to pay biennially one per cent of their Unesco contribution or pay regularly (at least biennially) a contribution that should not be less than this. There is, of course, nothing to stop parties and non-parties voluntarily contributing more than these amounts or assisting in other forms of fund-raising. The funds can be used only for purposes defined by the WHC in Articles 19–26. Operational guidelines have been promulgated which categorize assistance as preparatory, emergency, or training and technical co-operation, and lay down priorities. Formal agreements are concluded between the committee and party concerned.

In the 1980s a Wetlands Conservation Fund, currently amounting to US$100,000, was established under the Ramsar Convention to facilitate participation by developing states, whose involvement was seen to be in-

---

[57] De Saussay, *Principles, Criteria and Guidelines for the Establishment of Mediterranean Marine and Coastal Protected Areas*; Salm and Clark, *Marine and Coastal Protected Areas: A Guide for Planners and Managers*, IUCN (1983); see, for legislative and institutional support, 35–52, esp. 44–8 on international aspects.

creasingly crucial to that convention's success.[58] It is hoped to increase the amount shortly to US$100 million. Contributions derive mainly from the industrialized states parties and will be used to promote wetland conservation in developing states.

Funds are also available for a variety of purposes within the European Community[59] and now that the EC has, by the Single Act of 1986, placed its environmental policy on a clearer and firmer basis (see Chapter 2), these are increasingly likely to be used for environmental protection. A Protocol has also recently been added to the 1985 Ozone Convention (see Chapter 10) establishing funds to assist poor states to reduce chlorofluorocarbon emissions, which incidentally will help protect species and habitats from the adverse effects of ozone depletion. Finally, the World Bank's new Global Environmental Facility (GEF), referred to in Chapter 2, has been established specifically to aid developing countries relieve pressures on global ecosystems, including preserving biological diversity and natural habitats.

In the wildlife field in general, however, provision of financial assistance is a neglected area of international environmental law. Clearly more states would be prepared to join in conservation conventions and enact the necessary controls if they could be compensated for the economic costs of taking the required restrictive measures. The WCED's proposal for increased UNEP funding is being acted upon but its proposal of an international trust fund for this purpose merits further consideration, its proposal for involvement of the World Bank having borne fruit.[60] Professor Brown-Weiss has also proposed establishment of trust funds to protect the interest of future generations, but in the context of pollution clean-up, not of species restoration.[61] Many other writers have canvassed proposals for taxes and other sources of revenue to provide funds for compensation of the costs of environmental protection.[62] The argument has been succinctly put by the President of Tanzania as follows: 'That Tanzania has a rich wildlife resource is an accident of geography. It belongs to all mankind. The international community should therefore contribute to its survival.'[63]

Glennon argues that certain resources should be regarded as global environmental resources (for example, tropical rain forests; the elephant); all states would have then a right to expect the state of their location to protect

---

[58] Proceedings of the Fourth Meetings of the conference of the Contracting Parties (Ramsar Bureau 1990), 141.

[59] See European Commission, *Financial Aids for the Environment Available from the European Community* (Brussels, 1989).

[60] See WCED Report, 322 concerning provision of UNEP funds and 340–2 concerning global funding proposals, and see generally World Bank, *The World Bank and the Environment* (Washington, DC, 1991).

[61] Brown-Weiss, *In Fairness to Future Generations*, 579.

[62] See works cited by Glennon, 84 *AJIL* (1990), 28 n. 233.

[63] Ibid. 28 and n. 232.

them; correspondingly, the other states would have a duty to share the burden of preserving these resources.[64] He categorizes these as *custodial* (the state of location's duty to preserve the resource) and *support* obligations (the duty of other states to contribute to the preservatory conduct of the custodial state), which could involve both compensation for any resulting loss of export income or paying the enforcement costs of stopping poaching of elephants, etc., or both.

This financial support could either be organized multilaterally through establishment of international funds or unilaterally through so-called 'debt swap' or 'debt for nature' agreements whereby lenders to developing countries forego some or all of the debt repayment in return for the taking by the borrower state of environmentally protective measures, as has already been arranged in some cases.[65] In some cases NGOs have taken over the debt in return for similar commitments.[66] These approaches are gaining support, will be discussed at UNCED, and may be included in any UNCED Declaration.

3. SIGNIFICANCE AND EFFECTIVENESS OF THE REGIME FOR CONSERVATION OF WILDLIFE: CASE STUDIES OF THE MAJOR GLOBAL CONVENTIONS

It is virtually impossible to assess the effectiveness of the regime from a cross-sectoral perspective, for example, to evaluate the effect on conservation of one species of all the measures that have been—or might be—applied to it under the full range of conventions. It is somewhat easier to evaluate the relative effectiveness of the techniques provided under particular conventions, although even here it is not possible to give an overview of all state practice in implementation of a convention; some global conventions are poorly ratified (such as the Bonn Convention) and this *per se* reduces their effectiveness. Glennon, in his recent article assessing the effectiveness of international law for conserving the elephant, concentrates entirely on criticizing the provisions and operation of CITES, which he finds defective, and makes little attempt to identify the relevance and potential of conventions such as the Bonn Convention or World Heritage Convention, to which he makes only cursory reference.[67]

It has always to be borne in mind that a whole range of concepts, principles, and measures, specific and non-specific, can be invoked to protect living

---

[64] Glennon, 84 *AJIL* (1990), 28.
[65] For examples, see ibid. 36, including nn. 293–300; see also letter from Mrs Thatcher (then UK Prime Minister) to Dr Holdgate, Director-General, IUCN, responding positively to such proposals, 20 *IUCN Bull.* 46 (1989), 24.
[66] Glennon, 84 *AJIL* (1990), 36.
[67] Ibid. *passim.*

resources. Some are undoubtedly more effective than others. It is now twenty years since the adoption of the UNCHE Declaration, Recommendations, and Action Plan, which greatly accelerated the conclusion of wildlife conventions in pursuance of their principles, which themselves have been kept in the forefront of international action to preserve endangered species by the numerous strategies adopted since. There is thus now considerable state practice under the major conventions. This has accrued in the form of resolutions, amendments to the relevant appendices, and states' acceptance or rejection of these, making it possible at least to review this aspect. Reviewing relevant national laws implementing these is too vast a task for a work of the present kind. Lyster's seminal work *International Wildlife Law*, however, outlines progress up to 1984 under twenty-seven treaties and refers to many others. In this section, we shall confine our review to those treaties that Lyster designates as the 'big four', which are the centrepiece of wildlife law and which were listed at the outset of this Chapter—the Ramsar, World Heritage, CITES, and Bonn Conventions—since these have and will continue to have, by virtue of their relevance to the objectives of conservation strategies outlined in this chapter, the most influential effect on the development of the international law of conservation of living resources.

(1) The Ramsar Convention on Wetlands of International Importance 1971[68]

This was both the first wildlife convention, the ICRW apart, to aim at global participation and the first to be concerned, at that level, solely with protection of habitat. The general nature of its provisions gives rise to problems of interpretation and weakness of obligations. It is not clear, for example, whether parties have an obligation to promote conservation of listed sites in all states parties or only of their own sites. There are, unusually in relation to the other three conventions, no amendment procedures. Parties have to resort to interpretative recommendations in lieu of these, and have done so in practice. It permits sustainable 'wise use' of sites recorded on a list maintained by its Bureau, but it neither forbids nor regulates the taking of species for any purpose. However, any use must not affect the ecological characteristics of wetland. The Bureau, originally provided by IUCN on an interim basis has, since 1988, been established as an independent office headed by a Secretary General;[69] this has greatly strengthened its role.

[68] Lyster, *International Wildlife Law*, 183–207; Ramsar, The Quarterly Newsletter of the Convention on Wetlands of International Importance Especially as Wildfowl Habitat, Nos. 1 (1987) onwards; Navid, 29 *NRJ* (1989), 1001–16; 20 *IUCN Bull.* 4–6 (1989): Special Report: Wetlands.

[69] Ramsar Convention, Report of the Third Meeting of the Conference of the Contracting Parties, Regina, Canada 1987, 27 May–5 June, Resolution on Secretariat Matters, 1–2. Secretariat established by amendments adopted at an Extraordinary Conference of the Contracting Parties, held at Regina, Saskatchewan, Canada, 28 May–3 June 1987; see Report of this

Despite the fact that it has a relatively small number of predominantly European parties, that it is underfunded and has a small Bureau compared to the other major conventions, the parties have been able to use its provisions and machinery to promote the convention's objectives. By April 1992, 549 wetlands in sixty-five countries (over twenty of them developing) had been placed on its list.[70] Most parties have exceeded its minimum requirements; the UK, for example, had listed thirty-one sites at that date and many others regularly add sites to the list, though both distribution and size of areas covered requires enlargement for conservation purposes. For example, as most parties are European states, only the Western Palaearctic flyway of wildfowl is comprehensively covered at present.

At the first Ramsar Convention meeting, in Cagliari in 1980, detailed criteria for listing of sites were adopted and recommended to the parties. Notably, though the convention's requirement of 'wise use' of wetlands is not defined, this conference recommended that this term 'involves maintenance of their ecological character, as a basis not only for conservation, but for sustainable development'.[71] This was later thought to be too technical a definition, not readily understandable to a broad audience. Though the goal of 'wise use' might differ between states it was considered that there was no fundamental difference between them in the ways through which this goal could be achieved. Thus the Regina Conference in 1987 redefined 'wise use' of wetlands as 'their sustainable utilization for the benefit of human kind in a way compatible with the maintenance of the natural properties of the ecosystem'.[72] This conference also established a Working Group on Criteria and Wise Use and defined 'sustainable utilization' as 'human use of a wetland so that it may yield the greatest continuous benefit to present generations whilst maintaining its potential to meet the needs and aspirations of future generations', for purposes of fulfilling the requirement of Article 3 of the Ramsar Convention that parties supply the Bureau with information on 'wise use'. Finally, it defined 'natural properties of the ecosystem' as 'those physical, biological or chemical components, such as soil, water, plants, animals and nutrients and the interactions between them' [sic].

Some sites are already protected under national law before listing; listing then becomes a means of raising their profile and securing national action when they are threatened;[73] other states list sites not yet protected. State

---

conference and texts, 3. The Convention will maintain its own independent offices both at IUCN, Gland, Switzerland and at the International Waterfowl Research Bureau, UK.

[70] Directory of Wetlands of International Importance; Ramsar, Canada Conference 1987, prepared by IUCN Monitoring Centre, Cambridge, UK (1987) and updates provided by IUCN.

[71] Cagliari Conference, Recommendation 1–4; see also Recommendation 3.3 of the Regina Conference 1987 which upgraded these criteria.

[72] Report of Third Meeting of the Conference of the Contracting Parties, Rec. C. 3.3. (Rev.).

[73] For example, public protest at UK government proposals to blow up an oil tanker off a listed

practice varies in interpreting the Convention, which is unspecific on this point. Most sites at the time of listing are already within nature reserves; some become so after listing but only a few states take measures restricting activities *outside* these areas to protect them from harm. Moreover, although Article 4(1) of the Convention only requires parties to 'promote' the conservation of the sites and establish nature reserves and wardens therefor, parties must inform the Bureau of changes in the sites' ecology, thus enabling evaluation by the Conference of the Parties. Though few parties have provided this information, parties have reported many instances of substantial enhancement of conservation measures taken to avoid disturbance of listed sites.[74] Action has been taken also on the requirement that parties encourage research and exchange of data and relevant publications and promote training of personnel, which should encourage participation and enhance compliance of developing states, but the absence originally of any Fund established by the convention to provide financial assistance limited participation by developing states. Parties were recommended to provide this[75] and as indicated in Section 5(b)(d) have now done so. There was a notable difference in the number of states party to the Ramsar Convention compared to the World Heritage Convention, when the latter but not former had a Fund. An interesting further development concerning financial incentives was the offer by an NGO to provide funding for operation of the new Monitoring Procedures, if Contracting Parties matched this contribution.[76]

Several parties, though not required so to do, have enacted legislation requiring environmental impact assessment of development projects that might affect the listed sites[77] and the Second Conference of the parties held at Groningen in 1984, recommended for priority consideration seven of the Thirty Action Points set out in a Framework Document for Implementation of the Convention.[78]

The lack of amendment procedures is a serious defect in a wildlife conservation convention since it inhibits the flexibility in adapting the convention to changed perceptions and needs that is now considered vital to successful conservation. Protocols have been adopted to bring about substantial changes but expensive extraordinary conferences have to be convened for this purpose

site in Suffolk, resulted in its being towed 20 miles out to sea for this purpose; Lyster *International Wildlife Law*, 190.

[74] Ibid. 192–3.

[75] A Recommendation to the Multilateral and Bilateral Development Assistance Agencies concerning Wetlands urging them to use their influence to promote 'wise use' of wetlands was adopted at the Regina Conference in 1987; Rec. C.3.4. (Rev.).

[76] Ibid. 17.

[77] Lyster, *International Wildlife Law*, 199, cites as examples extant in 1984 relevant Canadian and Japanese laws, planned legislation in the Federal Republic of Germany and the Netherlands and a proposed EC Directive, and see further *supra*, pp. 104–7.

[78] Report of Proceedings of the Second Conference of the Contracting Parties, Groningen, Netherlands, 7–12 May 1984.

and not all parties to the main convention necessarily become parties to the Protocols.[79] The problems in this respect are similar to those besetting the Whaling Convention. However, the Third Meeting of the Parties did establish a Standing Committee to carry out various duties between and during Conferences. This has approved a Monitoring Procedure to give the Bureau a role when reports of changes in the ecological character of wetlands are received.[80]

Despite the growing activity under this convention, national reports submitted by Contracting Parties reveal many persistent problems.[81] However, the strengthening, by recent Conferences of the Parties, of its administrative procedures, the establishment of a permanent Secretariat, a Standing Committee, a financial regime of contributions based on the UN scale and the increases in authority accorded to the Conference will all enhance the effectiveness of this innovative convention, as also will recent moves towards increasing co-operation between its Bureau and those of other conventions, especially that of the Bonn Convention.[82]

(2) World Heritage Convention 1972[83]

The World Heritage Convention, which had 116 parties by 1991, including many developing states, has one important characteristic in common with the Ramsar Convention: it works on the basis of maintaining a list of World Heritage sites. By 1991 there were 358 sites listed in over sixty states, eighty-four of which were outstanding areas of natural heritage. The IUCN conducted the original review of natural sites, though the sites are nominated by the state party in whose territory they are located; and it retains a role under the Operational Guidelines in evaluating the natural heritage nominations, which are submitted to it by the Secretariat. A precise procedure has been laid down; a small Bureau of members of the World Heritage Committee overviews proposals on the basis of 'Operational Guidelines' and distributes its recommendations to all states parties; thus listing takes time.[84] Though the World Heritage Fund provides an incentive for developing states to list sites, not all states whose participation is vital to global conservation of outstanding natural sites are parties to this convention; non-parties include both developing and developed states.

---

[79] See e.g. Protocol to Amend the Convention on Wetlands of International Importance especially as Waterfowl Habitat, adopted by an Extraordinary Conference of the Parties held in Paris, 2 Dec. 1982; 22 *ILM* (1983), 698–702.

[80] Report of Third Meeting of 1987.

[81] Review of National Reports submitted by Contracting Parties and Review of Implementation of the Convention since the Second Meeting in Groningen, Netherlands in May 1984, Rec. C.3.6 (Rev.); Proceedings of Regina Conference, 1987, 185–250.

[82] Navid, 29 *NRJ* (1989) *passim*; for specific examples of co-operation, see 1014–15.

[83] Lyster, *International Wildlife Law*, 208–38.

[84] Hales, 4 *Parks* (1980), 1–3.

The guidelines laid down for listing natural sites, referred to earlier, narrow the choice to physical areas of outstanding universal value. The convention is thus useful to conservation of wildlife only in protecting certain habitats (mostly in national parks); a species itself, however extraordinary, cannot be listed, in contrast to the Bonn Convention or CITES. One of these guidelines enables a site to be listed if it provides an important habitat for a threatened species of universal value even if the area has no other outstanding features; namely, if it contains the most important and significant natural habitats where threatened species of animals and plants of outstanding universal value from the point of view of science or conservation still survive.[85] The site has to fulfil 'conditions of integrity', which ensure that it is large enough to comprehend the essential components of the support system it represents and is sustainable. Listing is subject to the decision of the World Heritage Committee consisting of twenty-one states. Thus, though sites must be selected on their own merits, considerations of balance with cultural sites and cost of and availability of funds for protection are likely to have some influence and political difficulties can intervene if title to the territory concerned is disputed.

A List of 'World Heritage in Danger' is also maintained; the sites must be threatened by 'serious and specific danger' (Article 11(4)); the guidelines require that this be 'proven and specific', for example, there is a threat of a serious decline in the population of an endangered species, or the site is under 'major threats which could have deleterious effects on its inherent characteristics', such as a development plan. Threats must be of a kind that are removable by human action.

The obligations concerning conservation are spelt out in Articles 4 and 5 of the Convention. Parties must do all they can to ensure identification, protection, and transmission of the natural heritage to future generations, using to the utmost their own resources and, when appropriate and obtainable, international financial, scientific, and technical aid and co-operation. They must adopt protective policies, set up management services for conservation, carry out relevant research to remove threats, take other appropriate measures, and institute training. The High Court of Australia held in the case of *Commonwealth of Australia* v. *The State of Tasmania*[86] in 1983 (with the Chief Justice dissenting) that these provisions imposed a legal duty on Australia, a party to the World Heritage Convention, to protect its listed wilderness parks in Tasmania, despite the generality of the expressions used in these articles and the degree of discretion left to states concerning the precise measure to be taken; Australia must act in good faith to do all it could to achieve the objectives of these articles. As no other such cases have arisen it is impossible to say whether other states' courts would hold likewise. These obligations, under the Convention, extend also to non-listed sites that are 'natural heri-

---

[85] Guideline (iv).   [86] 46 ALR (1983), 625.

tage' within the convention's definitions and situated in the territory of the state party concerned. In certain circumstances, properties that have so deteriorated as to lose the characteristics qualifying them for inclusion in the List of threatened sites may be removed from the List.

Finally, states parties must educate their populations to appreciate and enjoy the sites and submit, through the Committee, biennial reports to the General Conference of Unesco on the relevant legislative and administrative measures taken by them. Protection of sites thus becomes a matter of national pride; there is considerable evidence that this is so, but this can also attract visits and cause environmental degradation, requiring further protective measures.

The World Heritage Convention both overlaps and goes beyond Ramsar's scope in relation to conserving habitats, in that it lays more stringent and specific obligations on its parties to take conservation measures and its provisions for financial assistance have provided the model for Ramsar and other conventions which have subsequently followed suit. For sites listed, it provides real protection but the limitations on listing prevent it from being the major instrument of habitat protection.

(3) The Convention on the Conservation of Migratory Species of Wild Animals, 1979 (Bonn Convention)[87]

This Convention, which has only thirty-seven parties, has many problems. It conserves habitat, *inter alia*, as well as aiming to protect species as such during their migrations, in fulfilment of Recommendation 32 of the UNCHE Action Plan. Two meetings of its parties have been held since its entry into force in 1983.[88] Its small secretariat, provided initially by UNEP, is located in Bonn but its under-funding, because of failure of many parties to pay their contributions and expenses (only a third are developed states though they include the EC), has severely limited its staffing, convening of meetings of its Standing Committee, and scope for action.

For those migratory species which during their life-cycle range across national boundaries their conservation requires concerted action by all states that exercise jurisdiction over any part of the range of a particular species. The Bonn convention provides a framework within which these states can co-operate in undertaking scientific research, restoring habitats, and re-

---

[87] Lyster, *International Wildlife Law*, 278–304; id., 29 *NRJ* (1989), 979–1000; Osterwoldt, ibid. 1017–49; Johnson, in Soons (ed.), *Implementation of the Law of the Sea Convention Through International Institutions* (Honolulu, 1990), 363.

[88] See Proceedings of the First Meeting of the Conference of the Parties, Bonn, Federal Republic of Germany, 21–6 Oct. 1985, vols. i and ii (Secretariat of the Convention, Bonn, 1985); Proceedings of the Second Meeting of the Conference of the Parties, Geneva, 11–14 Oct. 1988. The Convention was concluded in Bonn on 12 June 1979; it entered into force on 1 Nov. 1983 and by 1991 had 36 states parties.

moving impediments to the migration of species listed in Appendix I (which covers migratory species that are endangered, that is in danger of extinction throughout all or a significant portion of their range). It also provides for the conclusion of formal conservation 'AGREEMENTS', rendered thus to distinguish them from the other type of agreement referred to in the Convention, which is explained below. These AGREEMENTS are to be concluded among range states of particular migratory species listed on the Convention's Appendix II as having 'unfavourable conservation status' and requiring an international agreement for their conservation and management, or as having a conservation status that would significantly benefit from international co-operation achieved by international agreement. There is thus a considerable difference in the method of protecting species adopted under these two appendices: mandatory obligations are laid down for Appendix I species, whereas AGREEMENTS are required for Appendix II species. The taking of Appendix I species must be prohibited by range state parties, though exceptions, governed by criteria laid down in the convention, can be made.

Species, including marine species, may, however, be listed on both Appendix I and Appendix II, even if they are already within the scope of other relevant treaties, including fishery or marine mammal treaties. For example, the blue, humpback, right, and bowhead whales and the Mediterranean monk seal are listed on Appendix I, along with various terrestrial mammals, and Appendix II now includes white whales and certain populations of common, grey, and monk seals and the sea cow (dugong). The Second Conference of the parties added harbour porpoises, bottlenose, common, risso's, white-beaked and white-sided dolphins, and the long-finned pilot whale but no AGREEMENTS have been concluded for any of these species.

As indicated earlier two kinds of agreement are provided for—referred to as AGREEMENTS and agreements—both of which should cover the whole range and be open to all Range States whether or not parties to the convention. The form of AGREEMENT for Appendix II species to which reference has already been made, must provide for conservation, restoration of habitats important to favourable conservation status (as necessary and feasible), and protection from disturbance of that habitat, including, *inter alia*, introduction or control of exotic species detrimental to it. If required, the AGREEMENT should institute appropriate machinery to execute its aims, monitor its effectiveness, and prepare the necessary reports to the Conference of the Parties. Cognizance is taken of the Bonn Convention's overlap with the International Convention for the Regulation of Whaling; thus AGREEMENTS relating to cetaceans should, at the least, prohibit any taking that is not allowed under other agreements and should provide for accession by non-range states. Article XX(2) of the Bonn Convention provides also that its provisions will not affect the rights and obligations of any Party under any existing treaty; there are at least thirteen treaties that impinge or could impinge on rights concerning marine species alone.[89] If parties to these conventions are simultaneously parties to the Bonn Convention and plan to conclude AGREEMENTS thereunder, it will thus be necessary for them to establish whether any of these other conventions provides for the adoption of stricter regional measures, and to take these fully into account.

The second kind of agreement arises under Article IV(4) of the convention. This article encourages parties to conclude an agreement for any population or any geographically separate part of the population of any species of the lower taxon of wild animals, members of which periodically cross one or more jurisdictional boundaries. These broad terms allow inclusion of species not listed in Appendix II or even falling within the definition of 'migratory' given in the convention. The aim is to promote agreements protecting species that would benefit from international co-operation but whose circumstances either do not fulfil the criteria listed on Appendix II or have not yet led to such listing.

Many of the Convention's terms are ambiguous, including the definition of 'migratory species' in Article 1 to mean, *inter alia* species that 'cyclically and predictably' cross boundaries. For the sake of clarification, the Second Conference of the Parties adopted guidelines for application of the term 'migratory species', indicating that 'cyclically' relates to a cycle of any nature, such as astronomical (circadian, annual, etc.), life, or climatic cycles, and of any frequency, and that 'predictably' implies that a phenomenon can be expected to recur in a given set of circumstances, though not necessarily regularly in time. This removes some of the ambiguity inherent in the original definition; progress on these definitional problems may encourage wider participation in the Convention, though practical application by conclusion of AGREEMENTS would be the best clarifier of its many inadequacies in this respect. No such AGREEMENTS have, however, been concluded to date despite much preparatory work on drafts. Not even an informal agreement, permitted for populations that cross boundaries only periodically, has been concluded, though the Second Conference of the Parties stressed the desirability of concluding both formal and informal agreements and resolved that informal agreements should provide for accession by all Range States whether or not they are parties to the convention. The Second Conference of the Parties also decided to give priority to a review of the status of small cetaceans, including fresh water species, as a basis for proposals for further additions to Appendix II. A Working Group has been established to conduct this over a period of three years. This would fill a gap in the International Whaling Convention's listing of small cetaceans, only two species of which are subject to any form of protection under its Schedule, though information is collected on some of these species that are the object of directed fisheries.[90]

---

[89] They are listed in Johnson, in Soons, *Implementation*.
[90] Schedule to International Whaling Convention.

Definitions of 'Range' and 'Range States' are also given. A list of Range States is maintained by the Secretariat; parties inform it concerning to which of the migratory species listed in the Appendices they consider themselves to be in the relation of Range State; this includes submitting information on vessels registered under their flag engaged in taking these species outside national jurisdictional limits and plans for such activities.

Despite the potential of the Bonn Convention for provision of comprehensive protection of endangered migratory species, this potential is currently far from realization since neither of the techniques it provides—listing or conclusion of agreements—has been fully or effectively put to use. Moreover, the success of the Bonn Convention techniques depends not only on the existence and use of these techniques but on participation in the convention by all states that are Range States of threatened species, which in practice means that near universal membership is required. The Bonn Convention has a small number of parties, but only about half of these have attended the triennial Conference of the Parties to date. Neither the United States nor Canada is party to the Convention; they argue that existing conservation measures or those planned in their countries would not be benefited by the Bonn Convention.[91] Many species are already covered by bilateral agreements listed earlier in this chapter. This, coupled with the facts that not all threatened migratory species have been listed (only a representative sample of forty species was originally listed in Appendix I and only a few more have been added by the conferences), adds to its current ineffectiveness. Listing becomes a matter of political compromise between the interests of conservationists and of exploiters of the species concerned. Following the identification at the first Conference of the Parties in 1985 of certain species requiring AGREEMENTS, attempts have been made to secure such AGREEMENTS for the white stork, European species of bats, Western Palaearctic ducks and geese, and North and Baltic Sea populations of harbour porpoise and bottlenose dolphins; they have all resulted in prolonged negotiation and failure to conclude a single AGREEMENT to date, though drafts have been prepared. Moreover, non-ratification of the Convention by any of the Range States of some of the species originally listed on Appendix I, such as the cahow, the bald ibis, and the kouprey means that the Convention's provisions for their protection is rendered nugatory. These failures have rendered the Bonn Agreement impotent for the time being; as one commentator puts it, it remains a 'sleeping treaty'.[92]

Another impediment to the conclusion of AGREEMENTS is that other international organizations or treaty bodies have interests in the protection of the species discussed, for example, the European Community and the Inter-

---

[91] Osterwoldt, 29 *NRJ* (1989), 1028. Threatened species in these countries are mainly migratory birds covered by the 1916 Convention between the US and Great Britain for the Protection of Migratory Birds.

[92] Lyster, *International Wildlife Law*, 301.

national Whaling Commission. There is both considerable overlap and considerable diffusion of responsibility among relevant conventions, concerning particular aspects or techniques of conservation, for example, between the Ramsar and Berne Conventions and *ad hoc* Conventions on particular species such as whales, seals, birds and turtles, polar bears, and vicuna. There is clearly a need to improve co-ordination and co-operation between these conventions on the grounds of both efficiency and the need for a more holistic approach. We shall return to this point in our conclusions.

The Bonn Convention's broadly drafted terms, none the less open up many advantageous new approaches to conservation of *all* migratory species, including fin fish and shell fish.[93] Its definition of such species allows geographically separate populations to be considered independently. Several such groups have been listed on Appendix I. States with unendangered, well-managed populations can thus still allow some exploitation of species endangered in other states; vice versa, the latter states can protect populations of species not endangered elsewhere. Even a relatively sedentary species can be listed if a significant proportion of its number migrate. Its Scientific Council has been able to offer advice to member states on these matters, but they are not bound to accept this since Article VIII states that the role of that Council is merely to 'provide advice on scientific matters'. It is the Conference of the Parties that determines the Scientific Council's functions, which may only include 'making *recommendations*'[94] on species to be included in the Appendices, together with an indication of their range and on the specific measures to be included in the AGREEMENTS.

It appears that some states parties have been inhibited from concluding AGREEMENTS because they considered that these are a form of treaty, requiring, in some states, parliamentary or other official approval for adoption— a complex problem in federal states—which might have to be sought annually as AGREEMENTS proliferate.[95] The Second Conference of the Parties has agreed that a less formal agreement, such as a Memorandum of Understanding, could appropriately be concluded between governmental administrations, as a preliminary to a more formal agreement.[96]

Although the framework of the Bonn Convention covers all species, it has not worked well so far for the reasons identified. Its limited listing of

---

[93] Id., 29 *NRJ* (1989), 979–1,000. See also Osterwoldt, ibid. 1017.

[94] Article VII(5); emphasis added.

[95] As an example of the internal domestic legislative and other problems inhibiting conclusion of Agreements, see Osterwoldt, 29 *NRJ* (1989), 1035–48, who cites the difficulties attendant on the attempts of Germany, Denmark, and the Netherlands, which had different perceptions as to what constitutes 'taking' of seals under the Bonn Convention, to conclude an agreement for the conservation of the harbour seals in the Wadden Sea.

[96] Lyster, 29 *NRJ* (1989), 992–3; see Aust, 35 *ICLQ* (1986), 787–812, for the theory and practice of such informal agreements; an outstanding example of their value is the Paris Memorandum of Understanding on Port state Control referred to *supra*, Ch. 7.

migratory species and lack of AGREEMENTS means that there are still many gaps in the coverage of such species by international agreements. The Bonn Convention's potential for covering whole flyways and other migratory routes has not been put into effect; its aims have so far been thwarted. It is difficult to argue on the basis of practice under this convention that any customary obligation to conclude agreements on conservation of migratory species has emerged; practice outside the convention, however, does offer evidence of a trend in this direction.

(4) The Convention on Trade in Endangered Species 1973 (CITES)[97]

Unlike the Bonn Convention, CITES has a large number of parties, 113 at the time of writing. Unfortunately, however, though unique and remarkable in many ways, CITES is not designed to protect and conserve migratory or other species in their habitats or to protect them from threats to their existence, such as pollution, over-exploitation, or by-catches. Its sole aim is to control or prevent international commercial trade in endangered species or their products, but as it covers not only species of animals but also of plants, it indirectly does play a role in preserving component parts of the habitat of some species. The number of many species is declining not only because of loss of habitat but also because of increased exploitation and a major contributory factor to this is trade, an especially serious threat since the growth of modern transport facilities by sea, air, and land have facilitated the shipping of live animals and plants and their products all over the world. This trade is very lucrative; millions of live animals and birds are transported to meet the demands of the pet trade; ornamental plants are in great damand; and furskins, shells, leather, timber, and, until recently, ivory and artefacts made from these products are all also traded in on a large scale. The technique of controlling import and export of such species and products is, as remarked earlier in this chapter, included also in some regional and other conventions; the innovatory aspect of CITES is that it has established this technique on a global scale. It consists of regulating by means of a permit system international trade in species that are listed in its three Appendices. Such trade, with some exceptions, is forbidden for species listed in Appendix I, that is, those threatened with extinction.[98] Trade is permitted, subject to control, in species listed in Appendix II, that is, those not yet threatened with extinction but which may become so if trade in them is not controlled and monitored in order to avoid utilization incompatible with their survival; so that threatened

---

[97] Lyster, International Wildlife Law, 239; id., 29 *NRJ* (1989), 979; De Klemm, ibid. 953.

[98] Included in this list are all apes, lemurs, the giant panda, many South American monkeys, great whales, cheetahs, leopards, tigers, Asian and African elephants, all rhinoceroses, many birds of prey, cranes, pheasants, all sea turtles, some crocodiles and lizards, giant salamanders and some mussels, orchids, and cacti.

species are not traded under the pretext that they are species of similar appearance, some non-threatened species are included in this Appendix.[99] International trade is permitted only if there is proper documentation issued by the exporting state. Parties that have stricter legislation, that is, restricting export of species not listed in Appendix I or II, can list these species on Appendix III, whereupon other parties also must regulate trade in them.

The basis of the convention, and the main reason for its effectiveness, is that it has an elaborate but workable operational system in which a national export/import permit system is combined with a national institutional system. Each party has to establish at least one Management Authority and Scientific Authority, which are responsible for checking that the required conditions for issue of permits (laid down respectively in Articles III, IV, and V for each Appendix) have been fulfilled and for granting the permit only if they have been complied with. CITES lays down conditions for export, re-export, and import permits, as required. Article III prohibits the export of specimens of Appendix I species without the prior grant and submission of an export permit. An export permit is issued only if the Management Authority is satisfied not only that the species has been legally obtained but that, if they are to be exported alive, conditions for their transportation conform to the standards laid down in the convention; and only if the Scientific Authority is satisfied that export will not be detrimental to the species' survival. Each transhipment requires an individual permit. Re-export of Appendix I species is banned unless a re-export certificate is issued for which similar pre-requisites apply. An export permit cannot be issued for Appendix I species unless an import permit has already been issued; this latter is not a pre-requisite for export of Appendix II species, however. It is the requirement of an import permit that represents the most effective enforcement technique[100] and, in the case of live specimens, that the intended recipient has the necessary equipment to accommodate and care for it. The further requirement that the relevant Management Authority must also be satisfied that the specimen will be used primarily for non-commercial purposes effectively limits trade among parties to specimens used only for scientific and educational purposes, or, in certain circumstances, to hunting trophies, subject to modifications introduced at the Gaborone Conference in favour of small, exceptional quotas of specimens of species otherwise prohibited from import.[101] Import permits are not required for Appendix II species. A large trade in many of these, therefore, takes place, which has been a matter of concern to the Conference

---

[99] Included in this list are primates, cats, otters, whales, dolphins and porpoises, birds of prey, tortoises, crocodiles and orchids, fur seals, the black stork, birds of paradise, the coelacanth, some snails, birdwing butterflies, and black corals.

[100] In 1986, the UK Nature Conservatory Council (the UK Scientific Authority) advised on about 20,000 permits; Warren, *UK Envl. Law Assoc. Newsletter* (1989), 10.

[101] Lyster, *International Wildlife Law*, 248–9.

of the Parties. It accordingly has made recommendations to ensure that such trade conforms to the CITES requirement that export will not be in such quantities as to be detrimental to the species survival.[102] Each state party is then responsible through exercise of its customs controls, *inter alia*, for ensuring that listed species and specimens imported and exported are covered by the appropriate permits. The effective CITES Secretariat in Switzerland is responsible for monitoring the operation of the treaty and encouraging and facilitating the exchange of information and liaison between member states, other authorities, and organizations. The parties themselves, at their biennial meetings, review the working of the CITES and discuss possible changes to the Appendices—including removal of particular species from the List.

The role of NGOs is crucial to the success of CITES. Data for purposes of monitoring trade are collected by the NGO Wildlife Trade Monitoring Unit (WTMU) located in the UK. It receives governmental information and also information from the IUCN/WWF TRAFFIC (Trade Records Analysis of Flora and Fauna in Commerce) offices in various states. This, backed by information supplied by other NGOs, enables the CITES Secretariat to identify problems and take counter measures, if controls are, or are about to be evaded. Annual reports from member states back up this process. As information accrues, the effectiveness of CITES is correspondingly enhanced. None the less, interpretative problems remain, *inter alia*, as do those of identifying plants and animals in the customs posts, especially as Article II(2)(b) allows so-called 'look alike' species to be added to Appendix II, even if not threatened, to enable effective enforcement; these are 'specimens' of species, defined in Article I(b)(i) as an animal or plant, whether alive or dead, including (for Appendix I and II species) 'any readily recognizable part or derivative thereof'. Such parts include ivory, horns, and skins but, as the term 'readily recognizable' is not defined in CITES, it is left to each state to compile its own list or deal with this problem *ad hoc* since it is essential to effective enforcement that customs officials should be enabled to identify such items. There has been controversy among CITES parties at their Conferences concerning whether or not 'a minimum list' should be produced or whether that would operate as a 'maximum list' leaving items not accepted by some states as falling within the definition, such as turtle soup, to be freely traded outwith CITES controls.

The Conferences of the Parties have, however, dealt with some of the interpretational and operational problems arising. For example, the first meeting at Berne (1976) laid down criteria for the listing and de-listing of species on the Appendices[103] which, under Article XV(1)(b), requires a two-thirds majority of the parties present and voting, and proposed controversial

---

[102] Ibid. 251.
[103] Proceedings of the First Meeting of the Conference of the Parties, Conf. 1.2, 33.

listing of species have been dealt with *ad hoc* at subsequent meetings. The meetings have dealt with a wide variety of questions. *Inter alia*, the San José Second Conference, held in 1978, recommended detailed restriction on import of hunting trophies.[104] The Third Conference held at New Delhi in 1982, recommended that parties, to the extent possible, follow a standard, conference-approved model permit and use special security paper or serially numbered adhesive security stamps.[105] The Fourth Conference held at Gaborone in 1983, recommended identification of species subject to 'significant' international trade in relation to which there was insufficient scientific information on their ability to survive such an amount of trade.[106] The Fifth Conference held at Buenos Aires in 1985, agreed that 'primarily commercial purposes' covered 'all uses whose non-commercial aspects do not clearly predominate' (it being for the importer to establish this) and that 'commercial' included any such transaction even if not wholly commercial.[107] The Sixth conference held at Ottawa in 1986 recommended various measures concerning shipment of live animals in order to ensure their safe handling and welfare in transit and on arrival.[108] At the Seventh Conference held at Berne in 1987, the parties agreed to place the African elephant on Appendix I,[109] thus prohibiting all trade in it, since when trade has declined dramatically. There has been pressure from states such as Namibia, Tanzania, Uganda, and Zambia (whose elephant herds, under good management have recovered from the effects of over-exploitation) to be allowed to carry out limited culls and sell the resulting products in order to generate income for further conservation measures, but this was resisted at the Eighth Conference of the parties held in Kyoto in 1992, since it is impossible to distinguish ivory so obtained and ivory from illegally poached specimens. None the less, some scientists are critical of this decision on the grounds that it neither encourages nor rewards wise conservation and local respect for the law which necessarily, in their view, includes culling as herds recover. They argue that skins at least could be traded.

Opinions are, however divided concerning the effectiveness of CITES in protecting wildlife. Some, like Lyster, consider that real progress has been made under it[110] and especially commend its administrative system that enables the Secretariat to receive and circulate information vital to detection of movement of illegal specimens, and its wide ratification. As Lyster says, at least there is no likelihood of CITES, like the Bonn Convention, becoming

---

[104] Proceedings of the Second Meeting of the Conference of the Parties, Conf. 2.11, 48.

[105] Proceedings of the Third Meeting of the Conference of the Parties, Confs. 3.6 and 3.7, 46–52.

[106] Proceedings of the Fourth Meeting of the Conference of the Parties, Conf. 4.7, 49–50.

[107] Proceedings of the Fifth Meeting of the Conference of the Parties, Doc. 5.10.

[108] Proceedings of the Sixth Meeting, Doc. 6.19; Resolution 6.2.4.

[109] Warren, *UK Envl. Law Assoc. Newsletter* (1989), 11.

[110] Lyster, *International Wildlife Law*, 276–7. Fayre, Convention on Trade in Endangered Species.

a 'sleeping treaty'. Others, however, consider that it has limited practical success and may even have promoted over-exploitative trade.[111] Critics point to over-zealous listing of specimens not seriously endangered, to CITES' weakness in allowing major exemptions, which provide loopholes for illegal trade, and to the practical difficulties of enforcement, which enable large numbers of species listed on all Appendices to escape detection since enforcement is left to individual states parties, whose domestic wildlife laws, scrutiny, and controls vary greatly in their scope and stringency of enforcement. Customs officials may be neither able nor willing to distinguish between exempted and illegal specimens or to identify the 'parts and derivative' from the bulk of trade.

Though an international identification manual would be invaluable, and some states provide this, conference recommendations urging the Secretariat to produce one at the international level have produced only a slow response because of the practical difficulties involved. The Secretariat has, however, arranged enforcement seminars for customs officers and Interpol; facilitated co-operation between them; offered training to Management Authorities; and maintains a collection of slides depicting forged documents.[112] The permission of trade with non-parties is another problem. TRAFFIC is part of a network co-operating with the IUCN in monitoring international trade in wildlife and plants. It reports on the data gathered and provides analyses of wildlife trade statistics. Publicizing this trade in itself provides one of the most effective controls on it.[113] Though CITES Article VII requires that its parties impose penalties for illegal trade, and it approves confiscation and return to the exporting state if specimens are so traded or possessed, these provisions are useless if evasion is relatively easy and are ineffective as a deterrent unless used and unless penalties are internationally harmonized and set at a sufficiently high level. The EC, which is not a party to CITES, has implemented it and has the capacity to require such harmonization among its member states.[114] On the other hand, after 1992, when the EC will have only one outer boundary for customs purposes, fewer transit checks will be available than hitherto. An NGO report on illegal trade in elephant products suggests that the drafters of CITES did not understand how the international trade in wildlife products worked, the measures available under domestic law and its terminology and interpretation.[115]

---

[111] Shonfield, 15 *CWILJ* (1985), 111 and 127–58.
[112] Information provided by Messrs J. Berney and T. Huxley at interviews conducted on 19 Oct. 1987; some parties now provide technical assistance funds for these purposes.
[113] The information is published in the Traffic Newsletter.
[114] EC Regulation (Council Reg. (EEC) N. 3626/82 (as subsequently amended) OJ L384 (i)).
[115] The Environmental Investigation Agency (EIA), an NGO, publicizes details of illegal trade in specimens; see *A System of Extinction: The African Elephant Disaster*, EIA (London, 1989). See also Interpretation and Implementation of the Convention: Review of Alleged Infractions, Report on Sixth Meeting of the Conference of the Parties, Ottawa, Canada, 1987, CITES Doc. 6.19.

Critics point also to the non-binding nature of conference resolutions and the fundamental weakness of the reservations system, which, since it exempts parties formally entering objections to a listing from being bound by it, in effect puts such parties in a position equivalent to non-parties with whom trade is permitted. Reservations can be lodged, on adhering to the convention, to listings on Appendices I and II or within 90 days of their adoption by the Conference, and subsequently at any time in written form, without specification of reasons,[116] a procedure that gives rise to many uncertainties concerning the status and interpretation of the resultant obligations.[117] Exhortations by the Conferences that parties should refrain from use of these procedures has little effect. Compilation by the Secretariat of lists of non-parties whose scientific assessment of whether proposed trade 'substantially conforms' to CITES requirements are found by it not to meet the required standards for issue of permits has been more effective, according to these commentators.

Despite these weaknesses, on balance it is generally agreed that they are not insurmountable; parties have the power to resolve the textual ambiguities and to use enforcement powers effectively, if so minded. Amendment procedures are also available, both for the CITES substantive articles and its Appendices. Even critics concede that CITES provides 'a highly practical mechanism incorporating a structure designed to deal with a complex international situation'[118] which attempts to balance legitimate trade interests in renewable resources with the need to protect endangered species.[119] There is, however, considerable scope for revision.[120] It has been suggested that a limit should be placed on the number of reservations a party may enter; that their duration should be limited and that all reservations should be periodically reviewed.[121] For reasons of political expediency, to maximize participation and protect national interests, most wildlife conventions permit reservations, just as some national legislation permits exceptions to be made for the taking of species otherwise protected.[122]

---

[116] Steward, 14 *Cornell ILJ* (1981), 424–55.

[117] Steward gives practical examples of these problems, ibid. 434–55.

[118] Shonfield, 15 *CWILJ* (1985), 127.

[119] Steward, 14 *Cornell ILJ* (1981), 429; Blanco-Castillo, 'An Analysis of the 1973 Convention on International Trade in Endangered Species of Wild Flora and Fauna, M. Phil. thesis (Univ. of Nottingham, 1988), 302–7.

[120] See Shonfield, 15 *CWILJ* (1985), and Steward, 14 *Cornell ILJ* (1981), *passim*.

[121] Steward, 14 *Cornell ILJ* (1981), *passim*.

[122] e.g. the United States Endangered Species Act (ESA) 1973, PL 93–205, 28 Dec. 1973, 87 Stat. 884, which has been subjected to criticism on this account, though otherwise regarded as a pioneering model in this field; see Campbell, 24 *Environment* 5 (June, 1982), 6–42. There are both similarities and differences, however, between the ESA and CITES.

4. THE REGIONAL APPROACH

The major regional conventions—the 1968 African Convention for Conservation of Nature; the 1940 Western Hemisphere Convention; the 1985 ASEAN Convention; and the 1979 Berne Convention on Conservation of European Wildlife and Natural Habitats—have already been referred to in this chapter, as also has the role of the European Community in this sphere (see Chapter 2) and will not be further elaborated upon. It suffices to say here that the first three have fallen within Lyster's category of 'sleeping treaties' to date, though they have, as illustrated, introduced some innovatory conservation techniques at the regional level. Clearly, regional bodies, though important, cannot protect highly migratory species that migrate globally or traverse the waters or territories of several regions or frontiers that border two or more regions. There is a need for overarching global conventions to protect such species and for co-ordination between the institutions and measures established to administer and operate the regional conventions. A regional approach, though valuable within the region, is not sufficient to solve the problems addressed by the global conventions discussed above, although in so far as species reside in particular regional areas for part of their life-cycle, they can be effectively protected by local measures as long as they are at least as effective as those required under the global conventions.

5. CO-ORDINATION OF CONVENTIONS AND ORGANS

The strategies and principles outlined earlier in this chapter and in Chapter 11 point to the need for better co-ordination and co-operation between bodies concerned in conservation and harmonization of measures both in pursuit of 'holism', to the extent that this is feasible, and of sustainable development. A major purpose of UNCED is to review the UN system with these goals in mind. When a particular species is protected under more than one convention, especially if the conventions address only one aspect of the needs of conservation, for example, hunting, habitat, or trade, it is essential that co-ordination of the measures and organs of the relevant treaties be established. The general problems of co-ordination of activities of international bodies concerned in the same issues have been discussed in Chapter 2. Conservation of marine mammals provides a good example of this. In this respect, the Bonn Convention Secretariat maintains close and regular contact with, and exchanges information with, that of the International Whaling Commission and with the Bureau of the Ramsar Convention and ensures that they are aware of such of its activities as are relevant to these conventions. These bodies also co-operate on the small cetacean issue, holding joint review meetings, as appropriate, with UNEP, IUCN, and FAO within the framework of the Marine Mammal Action Plan.[123]

On a wider basis, initiatives have been taken by both IUCN and UNEP to further co-ordinate and reduce overlap by convening meetings of concerned secretariats. IUCN has convened a meeting, instigated by the Ecosystem Conservation Group (consisting of FAO, UNEP, and Unesco), to which the secretariats of the Bonn, Berne, CITES, Ramsar, and World Heritage and Whaling Conventions were invited, to consider the possibilities of co-operation and it has been suggested that the secretariats of the various conventions might be able to relocate their secretariats within the new IUCN headquarters in Switzerland.[124]

In the context of preparations for UNCED and in particular for a convention on biological diversity (see below), which will require a wide range of co-ordinated actions, UNEP has convened meetings of representatives of governments, international organizations, and relevant convention secretariats, *inter alia*, to rationalize actions under these conventions and to maximize individual and collective potential and effectiveness in this field. These meetings have acted as a catalyst for organizing further participation in each other's meetings on the part of all the concerned bodies.

UNEP has also taken initiatives in organizing a Planning and Co-ordinating Meeting of bodies involved in the Marine Mammal Action plan, including not only concerned UN organizations but ICSU (International Council of Scientific Unions), the IOC (International Oceanographic Commission), the IATTC (Inter-American Tuna Commission), the CCAMLR (Convention on Conservation of Antarctic Mammal Living Resources), and NGOs such as Greenpeace and the International Federation for Animal Welfare.[125] The Council of Europe, as the Secretariat of the Berne Convention, has taken a similar initiative in relation to conservation of the Mediterranean Monk Seal.[126] Although the European Community recently decided to establish a European Environment Agency (EEA) to provide a European environment and observation network and to co-ordinate relevant activities, the EEA is not endowed with any powers to co-ordinate conventions or measures or other work of related agencies.[127] It is arguable, however, that this tentative functional approach, whilst welcome, is merely an attempt to avoid or postpone the need for conclusion of a co-ordinating convention which will require more

---

[123] Marine Mammals: Global Plan of Action, UNEP Regional Seas Reports and Studies, No. 55, prepared in co-operation with FAO, UNEP (Nairobi 1985). Johnson, in Soons *Implementation*, 363.

[124] By Holdgate, Director-General, IUCN, *Ramsar Journal*, 3 (Apr. 1989), 1.

[125] Johnson, in Soons, *Implementation*.

[126] Ibid.

[127] Council Regulation (EEC) No. 1210/90, of 7 May 1990. OJ No. L. 120/1, 11 May 1990.

active melding of measures found in diverse conventions in relation to protection of particular species, whether whales or elephants or sea turtles. As this section and Chapter 2 evidence, the international community is now beginning to address this problem. The UNCED's conclusions could thus be of great importance to future effective conservation of living resources.

6. FUTURE CONVENTIONS

At the time of writing, further conventions and instruments affecting conservation of wildlife, either directly or indirectly, are in process of development. These are conventions on biological diversity, on climate change, and global protection of nature; it was intended that drafts of these be presented for adoption by the 1992 World Conference on Environment and Development. At the time of writing it seems likely that the complexity of the issues involved in all these conventions will result in agreement on little more than 'framework' conventions, if that, and that action on global protection of nature will be confined to Declaration of an 'Earth Charter'.

(1) Proposed Convention on Biological Diversity

'Biological diversity' is a comprehensive term encompassing the entire variety of nature—all species of plants, animals, and micro-organisms as well as the ecosystems of which they are part, including both the number and frequency of ecosystems, of species, and of genes in a given assemblage.[128] It is generally considered from three aspects—genetic diversity, species diversity, and ecological diversity. Genetic diversity comprehends variability within a species, measured by variation in genes within a particular variety, subspecies, or breed; species diversity relates to the range of terrestrial living organisms; ecological diversity concerns the variety of habitats, biotic communities, and ecological processes found in the biosphere and the great variety within ecosystems in terms of difference in habitat and ecological processes.[129]

Conservation of biological diversity is regarded as one of the most urgent issues of our time, essential for sustainable development and functioning of the biosphere and thus for human survival itself. Though vast numbers of species valuable for many beneficial purposes remain undiscovered, especially in tropical areas, huge numbers are also becoming extinct at an unknown and unprecedented rate through human activity, mainly through habitat destruction, much of which is irreversible. There is a need to preserve the

---

[128] Interview with Dr W. E. Burhenne on biological diversity convention, *Ramsar Journal*, 3 (Apr. 1989), 7.
[129] Ibid.

widest possible pool of wild genes since all cultivated plants and domestic animals originate from wild species; representative samples of these should be preserved as a basis for continued genetic choice and improvement. Maintenance and development of agriculture, forestry, and fisheries depend on this but achieving this goal will necessitate, *inter alia*, proliferation of well-managed protected areas.[130]

The UN, the IUCN, and numerous NGOs have decided that there is an urgent need to develop an international treaty for these purposes, as well as national legislation. The International Undertaking on Plant Genetic Resources,[131] the IUCN World Conservation Strategy, the UN's World Charter for Nature, Unesco's Action Plan for Biosphere Reserves, and the UN's Tropical Forest Action Plan (TFAP), referred to throughout this work, all address this problem and many other UN bodies, such as FAO, UNDP, and the IBRD, are also concerned.

Biotechnology, that is, the application of biological systems and organisms to scientific, industrial, agricultural, and environmental processes, although it has the potential to alleviate global problems, such as disease and hunger, and offers many environmental benefits to agriculture, health, and industry, also presents environmental and developmental problems. On the one hand the technology is developed mostly in industrialized countries by private companies and is generally protected by patents; on the other hand the main sources of materials are found in developing countries, which now see biotechnology as a direct means of using their great genetic diversity for sustainable development but consider that they should be financially compensated for such use by foreign states. Many international bodies are involved in various aspects of these problems.

The global and regional conservation conventions discussed earlier in this chapter, such as the Ramsar and Bonn Conventions and CITES, impinge on various issues of biological diversity, but do so sectorally, addressing specific problems; they do not deal with biological diversity as such. For this, a more comprehensive approach is required, establishing general obligations to conserve biological diversity as such within one framework since it would be impossible to renegotiate or amalgamate all these conventions. IUCN, UNEP, and other concerned bodies are involved in drafting such a treaty. The draft addresses establishment of a network of protected areas and a mechanism for determining the priority actions at the international level by setting programmes and goals rather than prescribing the means of achieving them.[132] It is also considered that a funding mechanism should be provided under the

---

[130] Ibid.

[131] Adopted by Resolution 8/83 of the Twenty-second Session of the FAO Conference, Rome, 5–23 Nov. 1983.

[132] *Ramsar Journal*, 3, 7.

convention to enable execution of the programme; it could perhaps be constituted by levying contributions on the use of so-called 'biomaterials'. Activities conducted under existing relevant conventions might be given priority in allocation of funds.[133] In explanatory notes accompanying its proposed draft, IUCN states that it is founded on two fundamental principles—those of the responsibility of states, as guardians of biological diversity for the benefit of present and future generations, and of solidarity between states for the conservation of that heritage.[134]

However, the problems involved are both highly complex and highly controversial, as is revealed in the reports of various UNEP *ad hoc* Working Groups of Experts who prepared 'a legal instrument on biological diversity of the planet'.[135] Some consider that biotechnology must be included, but there is disagreement, *inter alia*, on its definition, on the technology transfer aspects, and on whether its risks should be reflected in the text, and many new elements were suggested for inclusion. Though there is general agreement on most of the items covered in the original IUCN draft, including funding, the UNEP Working Group (WG) on Legal and Technical Aspects concluded that certain issues should be relegated to separate protocols and should aim to incorporate concrete and action-oriented measures for conservation and sustainable utilization of biological diversity.

In discussing the fundamental principles to be cited and included in the elements of a convention, the following principles, *inter alia*, were suggested for inclusion by the WG: the preventive/precautionary approach; that those who damage or destroy must rehabilitate; an element of the 'polluter pays' principle; a requirement of conservation of national biological diversity; and that owners should be duly remunerated. However, it was also suggested that the elements should not be considered as fundamental principles and though it was agreed that the 'heritage of mankind' concept should not be reflected because of its legal implications, it was also agreed that the concept of the 'common concern (or "common responsibility") of humankind' should be introduced into the fundamental principles, though some opposed its inclusion in the substantive draft convention. Equitable sharing of benefits and of the conservation costs of biological diversity is another favoured principle; also that the states benefiting most should pay the most.

---

[133] Ibid.

[134] Explanatory Notes to Draft Articles Prepared by IUCN for inclusion in a Proposed Convention on the Conservation of Biological Diversity and for the Establishment of a Fund for that Purpose (unpub.); obtainable from IUCN Environmental Law Centre, Bonn.

[135] See Reports of the Ad Hoc Working Group of Legal and Technical Experts on Biological Diversity on the work of its First and Second Sessions respectively, UNEP/Bio. Div/WG 2/1/4 of 28 Nov. 1990, First Session, Nairobi, 19–23 Nov. 1990; UNEP/Bio. Div. 2/3, 23 Feb. 1990, Second Session, Geneva, 19–23 Feb. 1990; Final Report of the Sub-Working Group on Biotechnology, UNEP/Bio. Div/SWGB. 1/5/Rev. 1, 28 Nov. 1990.

Problems also arose concerning measures for *in-situ* and *ex-situ* conservation of biological diversity, and their relative importance, and whether 'obligations' should be expressed or some weaker term used. Transfer of technology and access to biotechnology, infringement of sovereignty and property rights were other controversial aspects. It is noteworthy, however, that the text, unusually, does define *in situ* conservation, namely, 'conservation of ecosystems and natural habitats and the maintenance and recovery of viable populations of species in their natural surroundings . . .'

Given the wide divergence of views, it is not surprising that the convention adopted at UNCED is only a very general framework, or that even this was opposed by the United States.

(2) Proposed Convention on the Atmosphere (Climate Change)

It is necessary in the context of this chapter only to remark that, if climate change occurs and if, as a result, sea levels rise, the effect on many species of birds, fish, animals, and plants will be catastrophic if inundation of beaches and wetlands by salt water destroys fresh water habitat and vegetation.[136] Rising temperatures would also affect other habitats of land-based species. It is, therefore, now generally considered advisable to adopt a framework convention which would enable measures to be taken and protocols to be added, should such a situation arise.[137] Elements of such a convention were developed by WMO and UNEP,[138] using the conclusions of the UNEP/WMO Intergovernmental Panel on Climate Change (IPCC) submitted to the Second World Climate Conference in 1990 and other mechanisms accepted by governments.[139] During 1992 negotiations secured agreement on the adoption of another rather weak framework convention in time for the UNCED.[140]

---

[136] See Ince, *The Rising Seas, passim*, esp. 36–57; and Churchill and Freestone (eds.), *International Law and Global Climate Change* (London, 1991).

[137] See Protection of Global Climate for Present and Future Generations of Mankind, UNGA Resolution 44/207, 15 Mar. 1990; Second World Climate Conference, Final Conference Statement, 7 Nov. 1990; text, etc. in 20 *EPL* (1990), 220–33.

[138] In accordance with UNEP Governing Council decision 15/36 (1989), WMO Executive Council resolution 4 (1989) and General Assembly Resolutions 43/53 (1988), and 44/207 and 44/228 (1989).

[139] Barrett, in Churchill and Freestone (eds.), *International Law and Global Climate Change* (London, 1991), 183–200, and see *supra*, pp. 413–5.

[140] UNCED, *Summary of the Current State of Preparations for the United Nations Conference on Environment and Development* to be held in Rio de Janeiro, Brazil, in June 1992, issued by UNCED, 5 Oct. 1991, para. 3(i). See generally, *supra*, Ch. 10.

(3) Future Global Convention for Protection of Nature

During preparations for the UNCED, it was initially proposed that an 'Earth Charter' to ensure the future viability and integrity of the Earth as a 'hospitable home' for human and other forms of life be drawn up.[141] In the event, only a declaration of general principles, the Rio Declaration, was adopted. It remains to be seen whether this will eventually be followed by a global convention.

7. CONCLUSIONS

It has been argued by Glennon that 'It is now possible to conclude that customary international law requires states to take appropriate steps to protect endangered species.'[142] This conclusion is said to be based on state practice, which evidences that 'like highly codified humanitarian law norms that have come to bind even states that are not parties to the instruments promulgating them, wildlife norms also have become binding on non-parties as customary law.'[143] Further, he contends that customary norms are also created by conventions when such agreements are intended for adherence by states generally and are in fact widely accepted.[144] Finally, it has been suggested that they are created by 'general principles of law recognized by civilized nations'[145] and that, for example, because CITES is widely implemented in domestic law, the general principles embodied in states' domestic laws on endangered species may be relied upon as another source of customary law.[146] Further support is alleged to be given to this view by the relevant Resolutions of the General Assembly and international conferences, which have been referred to throughout this work.

The survey of strategies, principles, conventions implementing them, and state practice conducted in this chapter indicates that more cautious conclusions should be drawn than those indicated by Glennon. As we saw in Chapter 1, customary law can emerge from conventions and bind states that have not ratified them only if the provisions in issue are of a fundamentally norm-creating character, both generalizable and applied in state practice with the sense of obligation necessary to establish custom.[147] Even enactment of legislation, let alone mere adoption of treaties, is not conclusive evidence of this obligation; it is necessary to ascertain whether the norm or treaty embodying it is applied and enforced and whether or not the state against

---

[141] Ibid.   [142] Glennon, 84 *AJIL* (1990), 30.   [143] Ibid.
[144] Ibid.   [145] Ibid. 31.   [146] Ibid.
[147] *North Sea Continental Shelf Cases, ICJ Rep.* 1969, at 41–2, para. 41; and *supra*, Ch. 1.

whom it is applied persistently objects. It is extremely difficult to establish practice on these aspects and it has been possible only to review a few known examples in this chapter. The numerous cases of evasion of CITES reported by TRAFFIC show that enforcement of wildlife conventions, even by states parties, is often poor. The limited implementation of many conventions, especially the regional ones, and the fact that many states still exploit most species, does not suggest that protection of endangered species is a requirement of customary law, however desirable it is that it should be. Even the cessation of whale-catching was achieved only through adoption of regulations by states party to the ICRW, setting quotas at zero on an interim basis for a limited period. The ban is currently being reviewed and there is strong pressure to resume whaling on the basis of sustainable development.

What does seem to be emerging from state practice in this field—the adoption of the series of conservation strategies; declarations of principles; the conventions concluded at global, regional, multilateral, and bilateral levels and practice in relation to these—is the creation of a framework within which conservatory, economic, and social goals can be balanced and achieved within the widely accepted but generalized policy of sustainable development, as developed by WCED and UNCED. The relevant strategies (WCS, WCN, WCED, GPY 2000) have no legal content—except in so far as in some respects they incorporate existing rules or norms of customary international law—but set goals, many of which have been achieved through legal processes. These goals include those laid down in the WCN, such as control of adverse impacts, avoidance of damage, protection of unique areas and habitats; in the WCS, such as maintenance of ecological processes, preserving, maintaining, using, restoring, and enhancing resources, minimizing threats to trade, conditioning access, helping poorer countries to sustain development; and in the WCED report, such as preserving biodiversity, co-ordinating activities of organizations, establishing trust funds, controlling access to enable sustainable levels of exploitation, helping poorer countries to sustain development, and improving enforcement. Many of these goals overlap and there is thus much repetition, which serves to draw attention to the issues concerning effective conservation. But adoption of all these goals, except the last, does not take place on a global basis, or wholly through legal developments; progress is made partly through legal measures, partly through public acknowledgement of the moral values of many 'principles' that are evidenced in the reiteration of the principles. It is important in this context to separate goal-setting provisions from legal-norm-creating ones, and to recall that enunciating provisions of any kind does not *per se* make them legally binding as *lex lata*; rather it elevates them to 'soft law' or 'law-in-the-making' *lex ferenda* status. There is none the less now much evidence of adoption of relevant controls *ad hoc* through conventions at various levels, for example, on hunting and taking of particular species; for establishment of parks and

reserved areas; maintaining optimum sustainable yields; improving enforcement systems by instituting permit systems backed by penalties, monitoring and
data collection. There is widespread evidence that most states do accept that it
is their duty to co-operate in protection of living resources but not that they
have to participate in existing conventions for this purpose; to act in good
faith; to arrange some form of equitable use of shared living resources; to act
as good neighbours at the regional level, as required by the UNEP Principles
on Shared Natural Resources.

It is, however, difficult to go further than that; if it can be said that there
is a recognition of a duty to conserve resources its content is unclear—
definitions of conservation are broadly based and differ widely, as we saw in
Chapter 3. Similarly some form of common international interest in certain
endangered species is evident but the different terminology used to express
this and lack of institutional support make it clear that no internationalization
of such living resources has yet occurred. While 'rights of future generations'
are acknowledged in a moral sense they remain inchoate and to some extent
incoherent (see Chapter 5). What is increasingly recognized is the need for
regulation based on treaties to protect wildlife and for widespread participation, implementation, and enforcement of these. Such treaties do enable
specific measures of conservation to be identified and prescribed in a variety
of contexts, as we have seen. Yet it should be recalled that one of the most
widely ratified, CITES, deals only with threats represented by trade, not with
habitat disturbance, over-exploitation, or the problems of migration, and that
wildlife conventions in general are poorly related to or co-ordinated with those
dealing with the activities and sources of pollution most threatening to wildlife. The legal regime established by the existing network of global and
regional conventions is thus far from comprehensive, universal, or effective in
scope or operation. Equitable principles, as indicated in UNEP's Principles
on Shared Natural Resources, are also applicable but have not provided a
solution to the problems of sustainable utilization of living resources. Even in
the case of high seas fisheries, as we shall see in Chapter 13, their impact has
not progressed beyond the provision of commissions for allocation of access to
certain stocks on the basis of political bargaining. In most cases this has
singularly failed to conserve stocks at a level permitting sustainable use.

13
Conservation of Marine Living Resources

1. INTRODUCTION

Although, as we saw in Chapter 11, there are important differences between terrestrial and marine-based living resources, the management factors, principles, and strategies outlined there are equally applicable to fisheries and to the various species of marine mammals. Because of their special characteristics—which render them vulnerable to over-exploitation and other threats—these species are included in most of the more comprehensive conventions discussed in Chapter 12. But, as pointed out in Chapter 11, fisheries, unlike terrestrial species, are not subject to the exclusive sovereignty of one state—except when they are located in internal waters or territorial seas—and generally migrate through a variety of jurisdictional zones in which foreign-flag vessels have certain rights. Fish also have a much quicker recovery rate after depletion than do mammals.

Treaties that apply to conservation of migratory species in general or to trade in endangered species comprehend only such marine species of fish and mammals as are listed in their appendices, as indicated in the previous chapter, but many other marine species are increasingly susceptible to the threat of over-exploitation. Their conservation has, however, mainly been related to controlling access to fisheries and limiting catch. The rise in catches has been phenomenal: in 1938 the world fish catch was 15 million tonnes (m.t.); by 1958 it had risen to 28 m.t.; by 1978 to 64 m.t.; by 1986 to 80 m.t. It is expected that by the year 2000 it may reach 100 m.t., at which point it is likely to level off. The reasons for this increase include rising populations, mostly located on coasts, the increase in the number of independent states, many wishing to enter or expand the fishing industry, but, above all, the enormous advances made in technological means of spotting, fishing, and processing fish.[1] From use of rod and line and small and simple sailing boats operating close-inshore using sisal nets and taking fish mainly for human consumption locally, developed sections of the industry have progressed to the

[1] For a full account, see Gulland, 3 *Marine Policy* (1977), 179–89; *Review of the State of World Fishery Resources*, FAO COFI/91/Inf. 4, Mar. 1991 and Opening Statement by Director-General, FAO IOE. COFI/91/Inf. 3, Apr. 1991; Strategy for Fisheries Management and Development, FAO World Fisheries Conference, Rome, 1984; see also Cushing, *The Provident Sea* (Cambridge, 1988) for a full account of the development of commercial fishing fleets and measures to sustain fish stocks; Juda, 22 *ODIL* (1991), 1–32.

use of sonar, satellites, spotter planes, and helicopters to locate fish shoals and to use of factory/freezer, steam-operated vessels, which can store and process fish on board and thus stay at sea for months at a time, operating in large fleets. These may use beam and otter trawls or fine filament nylon pelagic driftnets, a form of gear used in the open ocean, suspended in the water by floats like a curtain.[2] Such nets can measure as much as 30 miles across and as they are neither permeable nor biodegradable and are often lost irrecoverably at sea, they can float for months or years through the oceans trapping as 'incidental catch', a variety of species, including seals and dolphins. Birds also become trapped when they swim into driftnets while feeding on fish underwater. Even fish targeted in driftnets may die incidentally after becoming entangled in the net. Nets may also be abandoned to escape arrest, when fishermen are observed fishing illegally with them in restricted or prohibited areas. Nets so lost or abandoned may fish on in this ghostly fashion twenty-four hours a day for months. Even after normal use such nets frequently have to be replaced. As they are not biodegradable this presents problems of waste disposal.

In so-called 'industrial fishing', fish are not taken for human consumption but are processed into meal for use as cattle or poultry feed or as fertilizer; it matters little what species are taken or of what size. The effect on certain species has been devastating; not only are they taken in much larger amounts but frequently the species on which the large fish and some marine mammals predate are also removed, which aggravates the decline, since the biomass of a given area can only support a fixed quantity of fish life. Fish processing in industrial fisheries and aquaculture also present waste disposal problems.

The economic waste involved in all these effects increases the capital cost of the fishery and leads in turn to more intensive catching efforts to offset it. There is concern also that the modern techniques have been included in technology transfers to developing countries and that many of the fisheries in which fine-filament nets are used are not subject to any form of international regulation.

Regimes for conservation of fisheries thus now have to address not only control of directed fisheries, but incidental catch of other species in the course of such fisheries and the floating driftnet problems. Other special considerations are the need to distinguish in such regimes fish that are highly migratory, such as salmon and tuna, which may pass through the various jurisdictional areas (internal waters, territorial sea, EEZ, high seas) of several different

---

[2] For details of the nature of this problem and the large number of species intentionally and inadvertently killed in this way, see Johnston, 21 *ODIL* (1990), 1–39; Burke, 20 *ODIL* (1989), 237–40; Report of the Expert Consultation on Large-Scale Pelagic Driftnet Fishing; Rome, 2–6 Apr. 1990; FAO Fisheries Report No. 4349 (esp. at 20, legal aspects); Large-Scale Pelagic Driftnet Fishing, FAO Doc. COFI/91/5, Jan. 1991 and ibid. Suppl. 1, Apr. 1991; Wright and Doulman, 15 *Marine Policy* (1991), 303–37.

states, and amongst such species to distinguish marine mammals, such as cetaceans, dolphins and seals, which are larger and warm blooded, reproduce slowly and give birth to live progeny which require nursing, and are thus more vulnerable to capture and need special protection of various kinds, in various seasons and places.[3]

Finally, it is important in evaluating the regime for conservation of fisheries and new proposals for this purpose to examine control techniques that have already been tried but failed to achieve the desired result.

2. JURISDICTION OVER FISHERIES: CONCEPTS AND LIMITS

The solution to fisheries problems has been made difficult by the evolution since early times of legal concepts and doctrines of the law of the sea attuned to the outdated interests of the seventeenth century (outlined in Chapter 11), which have had a disastrous effect on many marine species. The law has always adapted to fulfil its role of reconciling the conflicting interests of the international community[4], but these, of course, change as states' demands on the oceans change. Grotius, for example, sought to establish the *inclusive* interest of the whole community, as the interest then predominantly beneficial, in propounding the 'free seas'/'common property' approach to high seas resources, based on the impossibility, as then perceived, of either occupying those areas[5] or of exhausting their fish resources, though he accepted that if a great many people hunt on land or fish in a river the species are easily exhausted and control becomes expedient.[6] Others, however, sought to extend *exclusive* rights over the seas and its resources, as did King James I and VI in 1609 over the British and Irish Seas.[7] The first fisheries agreements dealt with problems arising from assertion of exclusive coastal control,[8] and the need for the states concerned to prohibit or control trawling within this limit.

The law's task was, however, from an early date recognized to be that of protecting and balancing the inclusive and exclusive *common* interests of all states in using and benefiting from the sea 'while rejecting all egocentric assertions of special interests in contravention of general community interest'.[9]

---

[3] Burke, 14 *ODIL* (1984), 273–314.

[4] Bowett, *The Law of the Sea* (Manchester, 1967), 1.

[5] Grotius, *Mare Liberum* (1609); trans. Magoffin, in Scott (ed.), *The Freedom of the Seas* (London, 1916), 28.

[6] Ibid. 1, 43, 57.

[7] Fulton, *The Sovereignty of the Sea* (Edinburgh, 1911), 150; see also Selden, *Mare Clausum* (1635), as cited ibid. 366–72.

[8] e.g. that establishing a Mixed Claims Commission for the North-East Atlantic, UN ST/ LEG/SER.B/6, 1957, 738–41, and the North Sea Fisheries (Overfishing) Convention 1882, ibid. 695.

[9] McDougal and Burke, *The Public Order of the Oceans* (New Haven, Conn., 1962), 1.

Following a change of policy in Britain later in the seventeenth century,[10] the inclusive interest in fisheries predominated for the next three hundred years until it became widely apparent that it was no longer in the general community interest. Thus states first sought to maximize the area of the high seas and minimize the breadth of the territorial sea,[11] widely accepted until the 1960s to be three n.m., though from time to time a few states sought to assert exclusive rights to coastal fisheries in zones extended solely for this purpose. Given the prevailing doctrine, they generally claimed a wider territorial sea of up to twelve n.m., or sought to reserve to themselves fishing or sealing in a particular coastal area. Such actions were, however, always protested against.

Objection by Britain to Russia's attempt to extend by ukase its jurisdiction over foreign vessels sealing within 100 miles of its coast indirectly led in 1893 to the seminal *Behring Sea Fur Seals Arbitration*,[12] after Russia ceded Alaska to the United States. Faced with continued decline in seals because of over-exploitation on the high seas, despite its enactment of national laws to conserve the seals and their pupping grounds, which lay within US territorial jurisdiction, the United States arrested British (Canadian) vessels taking the seals on the high seas, arguing that it had a right of protection and property in the fur seals frequenting the Pribilof Islands even when found outside the US three-mile limit. The United States contended that this right was based upon the established practice of common and civil law, the practice of nations, upon the laws of natural history, and upon the common interests of mankind, in view of the fact that the fur seals were bred within its territory, were protected there by the United States and were a valuable resource and source of income for its people. The United States regarded itself as the trustee of the herd for the benefit of mankind. Britain (for Canada), which had protested the Russian ukase, argued that it had full right to hunt the seals on the high seas; the seals were either *res communis* or *res nullius* in status, not the private property of the United States. The United States countered that the high seas were 'free only for innocent and inoffensive use, not injurious to the just interests of any nation which borders upon it',[13] and also that the seals had an *animus revertendi*, returning cyclically to US territory, and were thus to be equated to domesticated animals which could be the subject of property rights.[14]

The arbitral tribunal found against the US arguments. It held that as Britain had protested the Russian ukase, Russia had neither held nor exercised

---

[10] Fulton, *The Sovereignty of the Sea*, 352 ff.

[11] For the history of this period, see ibid.; Churchill and Lowe, *The Law of the Sea* (2nd edn., Manchester, 1988); O'Connell, in Shearer (ed.), *The International Law of the Sea*, 2 vols. (Oxford 1982), 1–28.

[12] 1 Moore *Int. Arbitration Awards* (1898), 755–61; Johnston, *International Law of Fisheries: A Framework for Policy Oriented Enquiries* (New Haven, Conn., 1965), 205–12; McDougal and Burke, *The Public Order of the Oceans*, 942–50; Fulton, *The Sovereignty of the Sea*, 581–5.

[13] 1 Moore *Int. arbitration Awards* (1898), 811.

[14] Ibid. 812, 839, 883–4.

exclusive rights in the Behring Sea areas beyond national jurisdiction. Thus the United States has not acquired such rights from Russia and had no property rights in the seals and no right to protect them beyond the three-mile limit. Freedom of the high seas was held to be the prevailing doctrine.

The importance of this decision to the development of the law concerning conservation of fisheries cannot be overstressed since it laid the foundations of the two pillars on which subsequent developments were founded for the next 100 years. First, it confirmed that the law was based on high seas freedom of fishing and that no distinction was to be made in this respect between fisheries and marine mammals despite the very different characteristics of the latter, which the tribunal had examined; secondly, it recognized the need for conservation to prevent over-exploitation and decline of a hunted species, but, because of the former finding, it made this dependent on the express acceptance of regulation by participants in the fishery.

The two parties in this case having, however, asked the tribunal, if it found against the US, to recommend the conservatory international regulations required, the tribunal thus laid these down. Its nine-point plan for conservation provides a model for fishery commissions to this day: a prohibited zone; a closed season in a defined area of the high seas, with specific exceptions in favour of indigenous peoples as long as they hunted for traditional purposes, using traditional methods; a limitation on the type of vessels used; a licensing system to be operated by the governments concerned; use of a special flag while sealing; the keeping of catch records; exchange of data collected; governmental responsibility for selection of suitable crews; the provisions to continue for five years or until abandoned by agreement. Moreover the tribunal went on to recommend that these regulations be enacted into apposite and uniform national laws in *both* states and that national measures be adopted to ensure their enforcement. Thus the priority of national measures of enforcement, rather than international means, also was established. Finally, a three-year ban on all sealing was recommended, the foundation of the moratorium approach to conservation of marine mammals.

The measures recommended were not conservatory in the modern sense of being based on scientific findings, theories of optimum yield or population, and catch quotas, but were influenced by the adoption in 1882 of the pioneering North Sea Overfishing Convention, the first of its kind. It had introduced several progressive measures to establish order among states fishing in that area by harmonizing the registration and numbering of vessels, prescribing the use of certain kinds of gear, the salvage of derelict gear, and the supervision of these matters by national protection cruisers. Attempts to follow this up by convening a conference to discuss the scientific aspects of fisheries problems eventually led to the establishment of ICES (International Council for the Exploration of the Sea), a co-operative group of scientists drawn from North Atlantic states (See Chapter 2).

Thus, although it perpetuated the high seas freedom of fishing and hence made conservation more difficult, especially in relation to enforcement, the tribunal strongly supported the need for restraint in exploitation, clearly indicated the requisite measures, and recognized that freedom was not absolute but had to be regulated to take reasonable account of the interests of other states.

The decision, however, failed in the short term to have the desired conservatory effect as the tribunal's findings could be addressed to only two of the four states engaged in hunting the Behring Sea fur seals; Russia and Japan were not involved in the case. Thus the US and Canadian vessels owners re-registered their vessels under Japanese and other flags to evade the US and Canadian laws enacting the regulations. Naturally, the decline in seal stocks in that area continued until it was eventually realized by all the participants that only conclusion of an international regulatory treaty among all states involved in the fishery could save them. This cycle of events has been repeated in almost all exploited fisheries as the following sections illustrate.

3. THE DEVELOPMENT OF INTERNATIONAL FISHERIES REGIMES

(1) Fishery Conventions Before the First World War

Before the First World War, only one convention had been directly addressed to and concluded on conservation of fisheries, namely, the 1911 Convention on the Behring Sea Fur Seals. Its origins were of great significance to the development of international law in this field. In 1911, Japan and Russia agreed to subscribe to the regulatory system adopted by the United States and Britain as prescribed by the Behring Sea Fur Seal tribunal. The four states adopted the Convention for the Preservation and Protection of Fur Seals,[15] based on the recommendations of the arbitral tribunal. It was successful in restoring the seal stocks until denounced by Japan in 1940 on the grounds that augmented stocks were allegedly damaging fisheries that were commercially important to Japan. Arguments of this nature are prevalent in fisheries commissions to this day.

The 1911 Convention was replaced in 1942 by a Provisional Fur Seal Treaty[16] concluded only between Canada and the United States. It banned pelagic sealing and introduced the innovatory 'abstention principle'. The seals were to be caught only by the state within whose jurisdiction they were found but as compensation, 20 per cent of the seals taken by the United States were

---

[15]   104 *BFSP* (1911), 175.   [16]   156 *UNTS* 363.

to be given to Canada and *vice versa*; since seals did not migrate into Canadian waters this meant that Canada would in effect be unable to harvest seals from this stock. The United States was exclusively to regulate the seals within its jurisdiction but on the high seas the regulations were enforceable by officers appointed by either state. Offenders could be arrested but had then to be handed over to their national state, under the exclusive jurisdiction of which they remained. Proceedings could be instituted and penalties imposed only by that state, thus preserving this important aspect of the freedom of the seas, despite the acceptance of regulation of the freedom of fishing. This convention (which was revised and regularly renewed until recently, when it was discontinued)[17] remains a unique model so far as the abstention principle is concerned, though the mutual enforcement system was followed by a few later conventions, for example, under Protocols to the 1959 North-East Atlantic Fisheries Convention (NEAFC)[18] and 1949 International Convention for North-West Atlantic Fisheries (ICNAF).[19]

(2) Development of Conservatory Conventions and Commissions, 1920–1945

It is essential to an understanding of the development of the law for conservation of living resources to examine the problems faced in attempting to achieve the necessary regulation since these problems have never been satisfactorily resolved and remain acute in the 1990s, exacerbated by use of modern technology for both ships and gear,[20] and the solutions adopted have currently been called into question. The earliest conventions provided for only three of the five basic legal requirements (namely, jurisdiction, regulation, enforcement) that were stated in the Introduction to Chapter 11 to be the prerequisites of effective conservation. They did not provide for scientific research or establish permanent institutions. The problems leading to the conclusion of the 1882 Overfishing Convention, however, had convinced the states concerned of the need to co-ordinate measures and research on a continuous basis. The founding of ICES in 1902 and the resultant informal co-ordination of scientific advice on North Atlantic fisheries eventually led to provision by ICES of regular scientific advice to the North-East (NEAF) and

---

[17] An Interim Convention on North Pacific Fur Seals was concluded in 1957, 314 *UNTS* 105, in which Japan and the USSR participated; it was amended and extended in 1963, 494 *UNTS* 303; 1969, 719 *UNTS* 313; and again in 1976, 1980, 1984, 1988, but is now discontinued.

[18] 1959 North-East Atlantic Fisheries Convention, 486 *UNTS* 158; 1967 Convention on Conduct of Fishing Operations in the North Atlantic, 1 *ND* 468–75; Carroz and Roche, 6 *CYIL* (1968), 61–90; see Burke, Legatski, and Woodhead, *National and International Law Enforcement in the Ocean* (Seattle, 1975), 12–18.

[19] 1949 International Convention for the North-West Atlantic Fisheries, 157 *UNTS* 157; for further details, see *supra*, n. 18.

[20] See e.g. Driscoll and McKellar, in Mason (ed.), *The Effective Management of Resources* (London, 1979), 126; Cushing, 3 *Marine Policy* (1977), 230–8.

North-West (ICNAF) Atlantic Fisheries Commissions (established in 1959 and 1949 respectively).

The first convention to provide, in addition to the above prerequisites, both for submission of regular scientific advice and for a permanent commission, was the 1923 International Pacific Halibut Convention,[21] concluded between Canada and the United States. It is, therefore, regarded as the first true example of effective regulation of states' exclusive national rights to conserve stocks. Its purpose was to rebuild stocks in international areas and it introduced a uniform system of statistics on the basis of which the complex problems of controlling catch rates could be studied, taking account of the subtle biological relationships of the area as a whole. It instituted the first Fisheries Commission composed of three Commissioners from each party, and provided it with its own independent research staff with power to initiate recommendations. The Commission's powers were later extended to enable it to alter the date of the closed season, divide the waters of the area, limit catches, license vessels, fix their departure dates, collect statistics, fix the type of gear used, close grounds populated mainly by immature halibut, and to instigate scientific investigations.[22] Its powers were further extended by a third Convention in 1937,[23] which allowed it to control the incidental catch of halibut in other fisheries of its parties and to ban the departure of vessels to areas where vessels already *en route* could take the Total Allowable Catch (TAC). Notably, the Commission set the TAC at a level *below* the additions accruing to stocks from growth and recruitment. Unfortunately, growth in catching power soon necessitated drastic reductions in seasons; a new treaty in 1953[24] tried to solve this problem by adding powers to plan fishing effort more evenly through the year by dividing the season.

Another effective *ad hoc* early convention was the 1930 International Convention for the Protection and Preservation and Extension of the Sockeye Salmon Fishery of the Fraser River System[25] (subsequently amended and extended to pink eye salmon[26]) which provided for co-operation between Canada and the United States to improve the stocks originating in that river.

(3) Fishery Conventions and Commissions after 1945

(a) Main Characteristics

By the end of the Second World War very few fisheries commissions had been established; however, in addition to those already noted, a considerable number of fisheries conventions were concluded in the period between 1945 and the first United Nations Conference on the Law of the Sea (UNCLOS I)

---

[21] 32 *LNTS* 93.   [22] 121 *LNTS* 45.   [23] 159 *LNTS* 209.
[24] 222 *UNTS* 78.   [25] 184 *LNTS* 305.
[26] 1956 Pink Eye Salmon Protocol, 290 *UNTS* 103.

in 1958.[27] Most established a commission. The establishment of fisheries commissions, utilizing international law in its constitutional role, and the gradual enlargement of their powers was a seminal development. There is a symbiotic relationship between the development of the law of conservation and the development of scientific knowledge. Though the former necessarily lags behind the latter for political, economic, and social reasons, it cannot progress without an appropriate scientific basis; it must respond both to new scientific data and new scientific theories and take account also of economic, social, and political factors. Commissions provide the forum in which the necessary discussions and negotiations can take place. They are not simply administrative bodies supervising implementation of conservatory regulations (though they can and some do fulfil this role) but act also as a complex, dynamic annual diplomatic conferences in which the political bargaining that leads to the compromises that achieve the consensus on which regulations must be based can be arrived at. They face many problems, however, in finding means of reducing catch to levels that can sustain exploitation on a continuing basis.

Commissions usually (depending on the terms of the convention) meet annually. Conventions now typically provide for voting by Commissioners and differentiate between votes required to amend the substantive articles of the convention (a rare occurrence), which generally requires unanimity, and those required annually to amend regulations concerning catch, gear used, etc. The latter are now usually not included in the main convention but relegated to an Appendix or Annex, which forms an integral part of the convention but is amendable by a two-thirds or three-quarters majority. This system provides a flexible means of adapting the convention to changing scientific advice and other values. Other migratory species conventions (see Chapter 12) have followed this model but as they are primarily concerned with terrestrial species, unlike the fisheries conventions, have not had to make major revisions in order to adapt to the changing jurisdictional zones in the sea.

(b) The Role of FAO

The conventions adopted in this period have been concluded *ad hoc*, outside any global legal framework for fisheries; although suggestions have been made

---

[27] These included: Convention for the Establishment of an Inter-American Tropical Tuna Commission 1949, 99 *UNTS* 4; International Convention for the High Seas Fisheries of the North-West Pacific 1952, 136 *UNTS* 46; Convention Concerning the High Seas Fisheries of the North-West Pacific Ocean 1956, 53 *AJIL* (1956), 763; Permanent Commission for the South Pacific 1954, 201 *UNTS* 374; Agreement between Norway and the USSR on Measures in the North-Eastern Part of the Atlantic Ocean 1957, 309 *UNTS* 43; Convention Concerning Fishing in the Black Sea 1959, 377 *UNTS* 203. For details, see Johnston, *International Law of Fisheries*; Knight (ed.), *The Future of International Fisheries Management* (St Paul, Minn., 1975); Koers, *The International Regulation of Marine Fisheries* (West Byfleet, 1973); for more up-to-date information, see Hey, *The Regime for the Exploitation of Transboundary Marine Fishery Resources* (Dordrecht, 1989), 133–274.

for the establishment of a World Fisheries Organization nothing has come of them.[28] The institution of the UN Food and Agriculture Organization (FAO) in 1945 provided a possible means of monitoring and co-ordinating the activities of *ad hoc* commissions. Article XIV of the FAO treaty provides for the FAO Conference to approve arrangements placing other public international organizations dealing with questions relating to food and agriculture under the general authority of the Organization on such terms as may be agreed with the competent authorities of the organization concerned. This role for FAO has never been fully developed in the fisheries field although the FAO Council and Conference regularly receive reports on the progress of the commissions and FAO sends observers to meetings of those at which it has observer status.

FAO's role in relation to fisheries (see Chapter 2) derives from Article 1(2) of its Constitution,[29] which requires it 'to promote and where appropriate to recommend national and international action with respect to the conservation of natural resources and the adoption of improved methods of agricultural production'; Article XVI, which includes in 'agriculture', fisheries and marine products, and Article IV which empowers FAO, by a two-thirds majority, to submit conventions on these subjects to its members. FAO contented itself, faced with the disparate national interests of its members—which include developed and developing states, coastal, artisanal and distant water-fishing states—initially with a modest advisory and monitoring role, the assembling of data and legislation and provision of assistance in drafting the last. It issues reports on fisheries problems and on national legislation and provides technical assistance and advice, including legal advice, to the developing countries which make up the majority of its membership. It has eschewed any attempt at a global or regional managerial role. It has, however, where no fisheries commissions exist, established, on the instructions of its Conference or Council, nine regional fisheries bodies with responsibility for data collection, scientific research, training, and development (including of aquaculture). It has also established a Committee on Fisheries (COFI) and various committees of fisheries experts, appointed by the Director General in their personal capacity to advise him. It is notable also that the International Whaling Commission, which the United States had at the outset thought should be incorporated into FAO, when the opportunity arose under its convention to consider this, voted against such a move.

Its developing state members now expect it to concentrate its efforts on advising and assisting them to develop the fisheries in their 200-mile Ex-

---

[28] e.g. Koers, *The International Regulation of Marine Fisheries*, 307–24 and Appendix I at 331–9 (draft text of Convention for the Establishment of a World Marine Fisheries Organisation).

[29] For the FAO constitution, see Peaslee (ed.), *International Organizations* (The Hague, 1961), i. 664. For discussion of FAO's role, see Johnston, *International Law of Fisheries*, and *supra*, ch. 2.

clusive Economic (EEZs) or Fisheries Zones (EFZs), to help them draft appropriate management plans and legislation for these purposes and to ameliorate world food problems. The agricultural and forestry problems have tended to overshadow fisheries problems, and the emergence of problems of desertification, deforestation, climate change, and preservation of biological diversity add to their dominance. Thus extension and development of coastal fisheries rather than conservation was the main goal in the 1970s and 1980s, although awareness of the need for effective conservation and enforcement has grown and FAO also promotes effective management of world fishery resources, stresses the frailty of estimates of MSY, the closeness of most world fishing resources to maximum catch limits, and the manifestation of signs of biological degradation and economic waste. Recently, following the development of the UN's and other strategies for sustainable development and calls for a more holistic and ecological approach to environmental pre-servation and protection, referred to in Chapters. 2 and 11, a major thrust of FAO's present and proposed programmes has become the monitoring and prevention of environmental degradation and the promotion of sustainable and environmentally sound development.[30] Such considerations have become important in the light of growing evidence of the risk posed to environmental quality, biological diversity, and sustainability of aquatic resources by the growth of industrial, urban, and agricultural pollution, demographic and urban growth and unwise practices at sea, in coastal areas, in inland fisheries, and in aquaculture, problems which cannot be solved in the fisheries sector but require co-operation both with other concerned bodies and among states. FAO's role in relation to this is dealt with in more detail at the end of this chapter.

(c) Range of Techniques

Before the UNCLOS III, FAO had concentrated more on promoting means of co-operation between fishing states and coastal states; the General Fisheries Council for the Mediterranean was a focus of this approach. Now FAO is more concerned to assist coastal states to form associations amongst themselves, to the exclusion of distant water fishing states, both to increase their bargaining powers in relation to terms of access for the latter to fisheries in their EEZs and to enhance conservation. The South Pacific Forum Fisheries Agency, the new arrangements being developed under the auspices of the Organization of Eastern Caribbean states and plans for West African subregional fisheries commissions reflect this trend, which will be discussed further later.

---

[30] See Opening statement by the Director-General of FAO, op. cit. n. 1, at 2; FAO, *Review of the State of World Fishery Resources* (1991), op. cit. n. 1; and *Progress in Implementing the 1984 World Fisheries Conference's Programme of Action*, FAO Doc., COFI/91/9, Dec. 1990.

Fisheries treaties in the period before the 1958 UNCLOS I were, as out-lined earlier, more concerned with establishing national limits and allocating access than with conservation as such; in so far as they had a conservatory effect it derived incidentally from the regulation of access. They offered a variety of approaches—some were species specific (halibut, salmon, fur seals); some area specific (Behring Sea; North-East or West Atlantic; Pacific) or regional (North Sea); some combined all characteristics. The existing models also provided for and offered choices in relation to various important issues. First, in the setting of Total Allowable Catch (TAC), for example, for halibut, salmon, fur seals, whales; mixed species. Secondly, in membership of com-missions: some had closed membership; some were open; some open to all states in an area; some had specialized Committees for scientific, technical, financial, or scientific matters, which could be established by the Commission or other organs so empowered. In some, voting required concurrence of at least 2 of the 3 commissioners appointed by each party; some had only one commissioner per party; some required unanimity; some required a qualified majority for certain amendments, but allowed others to be adopted by simple majority. Thirdly, though regulatory powers were wide in scope—controlling catching; gear; areas; seasons, etc.—none limited entry or effort (except the Fur Seal Convention which provided for the abstention principle). Some provided techniques for persuading non-members to join, such as prohibiting transfer of vessels to them or trading with them in the fish or products regulated. Fourthly, though enforcement was mainly left to national means, that is, to coastal states in the territorial sea and on the high seas to the flag state, no convention provided for international enforcement (including arrest and prosecution) though some (NEAFC, ICNAF) subsequently instituted limited international surveillance based on mutual inspection. Under this system, vessels of one party would inspect suspected offending vessels of the other(s) on the high seas but could only report offences to the flag state; they could not arrest them. No independent observers or inspectors were carried on board vessels. Finally, though scientific research was required by some conventions to be carried out, some left its execution to national means (IPFSC; ICNAF); some established in-house scientists (IPHC; IPSFC); the NEAFC and ICNAF used the ICES, establishing a special liaison committee for this purpose, with ICES and government scientists on their country's delegations to these commissions meeting together, separately from the com-mission meetings.

Despite these protective treaty provisions many fisheries continued to decline[31] partly because of the inadequacies of scientific knowledge and management theory; partly because such advice as scientists gave was not followed; partly because there was no attempt to limit effort and little attempt

---

[31] Johnston, 21 *ODIL* (1990), *passim.*

to limit the number of vessels having access, and partly because of the lack of fully international inspection and enforcement. Most of these weaknesses derived from the underlying common property/free access doctrine (see Chapters 3 and 11).[32] The decline in some species was so grave that in 1958, when the United Nations convened its first Conference on the Law of the Sea (UNCLOS I), it had seriously and urgently to try to redress these problems, its predecessor, the League of Nations, having failed to do so in 1930.

4. IMPACT ON CONSERVATION OF INTERNATIONAL CONFERENCES ON THE LAW OF THE SEA

(1) Failure of the League of Nations' Efforts to Develop Fisheries Law

Reports from the ICES on the decline of certain fisheries, recommending the measures that should be taken internationally including, in the case of the whales, ensuring uniformity of national legislation, had been submitted to the League of Nations in the 1920s to assist its preparations for a conference to promote the rational exploitation of the seas' resources[33] and consider the possibility of a convention. A committee of scientific, legal, and industrial experts was appointed by the League to consider this. The League Conference on the Law of the Sea, convened in 1930, failed to agree on a draft convention though one rapporteur (Sr. Suarez) had advocated a 'new jurisprudence' to prevent extinction of species useful to man, based on uniform regulations relating to the whole of the waters over the continental shelf. Current regulations, in his view, disregarded biological aspects and disturbed the 'biological solidarity of the oceans', leading to destruction of other species. This biological–geographical solidarity should find its counterpart in legal solidarity in international law.[34] As species frequently migrated from regulated to unregulated areas, existing *ad hoc* agreements were a palliative not a cure for decline, in his view. Fish were internationalists, ignorant of jurisdictional frontiers, said Suarez—'the sea for them is a single realm'. His views are only now becoming prevalent in the FAO's COFI.

Suarez recommended: enunciation of international principles for rational and uniform control of all exploitation of aquatic fauna; creation of reserved zones, in which exploitation would be rotated, with closed periods and fixed ages for killing; effective methods of supervising execution of measures; the convening of a comprehensive conference to discuss all aspects of fisheries.

---

[32] For case studies giving the reasons for this failure, see Koers, in Lay, Nordquist, and Churchill (eds.), *III ND* (1973), 19–35; and Driscoll and McKellar, in Mason, *The Effective Management of Resources.*

[33] For details of this period, see Leonard, 35 *AJIL* (1941), 90–113; see also Rosenne (ed.), *League of Nations Committee of Experts for the Progressive Codification of International Law 1925–1928*, 2 vols. (1972); esp. Annex Report of Sub-Committee on the Exploitation of the Products of the Sea (ii. 231–41).

[34] Rosenne, *League of Nations*, 232–5.

However, though a fully *res communis* approach was advocated by some states even in 1930, more favoured total freedom[35] and Suarez's proposals were not acted upon until 1956 when FAO convened the necessary comprehensive conference in preparation for the First UN Conference on the Law of the Sea.

None the less, the Institute of International Law in 1937 concluded that a 'state would be failing in its international obligations if it neglected to take all proper measures to prevent practices which, in the light of scientific experience, are manifestly contrary to the conservation and the rational protection of the wealth of the sea'.[36] No action was taken on this conclusion as the Second World War intervened.

(2) The Regime Established under the UNCLOS 1 in 1958

In 1950, the General Assembly instructed the International Law Commission (ILC), to prepare draft articles and conventions on the law of the sea. The ILC submitted four draft conventions;[37] first, on the Territorial Sea (TSC), recognizing the sovereignty of coastal states over that belt and therefore over the taking of the living resources found therein; secondly, on the High Seas (HSC), codifying the freedom of the high seas and their common property status,[38] but subject to such rules as were laid down by international law and the added constraint that these freedoms must be 'exercised with reasonable regard to the interests of other states in their exercise of the freedom of the high seas'; thirdly, on Fishing and Conservation of the Living Resources of the High Seas (hereafter referred to as the Conservation Convention), which, whilst it accepted that all states have the right for their nationals to fish on the high seas, recognized that the right was subject to their treaty obligations; the interests and rights of other states provided for in this convention and its provisions on conservation of the living resources therein. Finally, it submitted a Convention on the Continental Shelf (CSC), which allotted to the coastal states sovereign rights over the shelf for purposes of exploring and exploiting the 'natural resources' of that shelf, as defined in the convention.[39] The

---

[35] Suarez's report was circulated to governments for comment; for the relevant questionnaire and replies, see questionnaire No. 7: Products of the Sea Analysis of Replies, ibid. 172, and 22 *AJIL* (1928), Sp. Suppl., 34–8.

[36] Colombos, *The International Law of the Sea* (6th edn., London, 1967), 425, citing 41 *Ann. Inst. DDI* (1953), 268–71.

[37] For detailed analysis of the relevance of these to the conservation of marine living resources, see esp. Johnston, *International Law of Fisheries*; Bowett, *The Law of the Sea*; for the text, see Brownlie, *Basic Documents in International Law* (3rd edn., Oxford 1984), 85–203.

[38] The High Seas Convention, Article 2, states: 'The high seas being open to all nations, no state may validly purport to subject any part of them to its sovereignty' and adds that the freedom of the high seas includes both freedom of navigation and freedom of fishing, *inter alia*.

[39] The Continental Shelf Convention, Article 1, defines the shelf in terms of the depth (up to 200 metres) of waters over the sea-bed and subsoil adjacent to the territorial seas or, beyond that,

convention defined these resources to include 'living organisms, belonging to the sedentary species', further defined as 'organisms which at the harvestable stage, either are immobile on or under the sea-bed or are unable to move except in constant physical contact with the bottom'.[40] This provision, with its ambiguous definition expressed in unscientific terms, was the first treaty provision to segregate the regime for such species from that for free swimming species. It has given rise to problems; for example, conflicts have arisen concerning whether or not lobsters and certain kinds of crabs are sedentary species but adoption of Exclusive Economic Zones has solved these.[41] No specific obligation to conserve 'sedentary species' was laid down in the 1958 convention.

For our purposes, it is noteworthy that of these four conventions (all of which were adopted, entered into and remain in force) only the Conservation Convention imposes any obligation to conserve marine living resources (see Chapters 3 and 11), and its definition of the term is expressed solely in terms of Optimum Sustainable Yield (OSY), unmodified by specific ecological or environmental factors, general economic considerations, or the needs of developing countries, and is directed solely at maximizing the supply of food and other marine products for all states. The TSC does subject the coastal state's sovereignty to the constraints of 'international law'[42] but in 1958 these were negligible at the global level as far as conservation was concerned; existing regulatory agreements (the 1946 Whaling Convention apart) applied only to the high seas. As the CSC removed from the high seas regime the sedentary species of the shelf although the waters above the shelf retained their high seas character,[43] it negated any ecological approach, as also did the fact that each convention was distinct from the others; they were not co-ordinated in any way. Although the CSC did not require its parties to conserve the shelf resources, it did prescribe that exploration and exploitation of the shelf 'must not result in any unjustifiable interference with navigation *fishing or the conservation of the living resources of the sea*, nor result in any interference with fundamental oceanographic or other scientific research'[44] and thereby recognized the need to preserve existing conservation regimes and retain the option of further development of these. However, although it is ambiguous and open-ended in its terminology, it seems likely that its parties were (and are) more concerned with minimizing the impact of offshore installations on high seas fisheries than on sedentary species.

---

to where the depth of the waters above admits the exploitation of the natural resources, and it includes similar areas around islands. See also Article 2(1).

[40] Ibid. Article 2(4).
[41] Azzam, 13 *ICLQ* (1964), 145; Fidell, *Int. Lawyer* (1976), 13; Goldie, 63 *AJIL* (1969), 86.
[42] Territorial Sea Convention, Article 1(2).
[43] Continental Shelf Convention, Article 4.
[44] Ibid. Article 5(1); emphasis added.

The failure of the Conservation Convention to institute an effective conservatory regime has, therefore, particularly serious implications. First, it did not address the problem on a species-specific basis; marine mammals and certain especially sought-after highly migratory species were not distinguished from fish nor given any form of special protection despite the many special characteristics rendering them especially vulnerable to over-exploitation. Secondly, the system established was weak. Because the areas covered were the high seas, subject to the freedom of fishing, only the flag states of the vessels fishing had jurisdiction over their activities, unless the consent of the flag states could be obtained to an international enforcement scheme. The Convention, therefore, though it required states whose nationals fished on the high seas to adopt conservation measures,[45] could do no more than recognize the 'special interest'[46] of a coastal state in maintaining 'the productivity' of the living resources of its adjacent high seas,[47] and when two or more states fished in such an area, could require only that, on the request of any of them, they should 'enter into negotiations with a view to' prescribing conservation measures for their nationals by agreement.[48]

The Convention was limited also in its protection of coastal states interests in maintenance of adjacent high seas stocks. It entitled the coastal state to take part in any system of research and regulation established for conservation purposes, whether or not its nationals fished there, and required that fishing states must, on that coastal state's request, 'enter into negotiations with a view to prescribing by agreement' the necessary conservation measures. The fishing states concerned were prohibited from enforcing in such areas conservation measures opposed to the coastal state's own measures but, again, were only required to enter into negotiations leading to agreed measures. Coastal states could adopt unilateral conservation measures to maintain productivity of the resources in adjacent high seas areas if negotiations with other states concerned failed speedily to lead to agreement, as long as the measures were urgently necessary in the light of existing knowledge, based on appropriate 'scientific findings', and non-discriminatory in form or fact among foreign fishermen.[49]

The problem remained, however, that coastal states had no means of enforcing their national measures on foreign vessels on the high seas and the success of the proposed regime depended on widespread ratification of the Convention by distant water fishing states; their willingness to enter into conservatory agreements; their willingness to adopt and enforce effective conservatory regulations and to resist the demands of their industry to maintain existing catch levels.

In effect, the whole system rested on conclusion of a further large number

---

[45] Conservation Convention, Article 3(1).   [46] Ibid. Article 6.
[47] Ibid. Article 3.   [48] Ibid. Article 4.   [49] Ibid. Article 7.

of international agreements establishing regulations and mechanisms similar to those concluded before 1958. In the event, several major distant water fishing states (for example, Japan, the USSR) never became party to this Convention and even its parties never activated its procedures for resolving the disputes that occurred.[50] The existing and subsequently established fisheries commissions[51] were, for a variety of reasons, generally unsuccessful in conserving stocks at existing levels. Scientific findings were modified for political and economic reasons; enforcement was poor and international inspection both rare and limited to reporting offenders to the flag states without follow-up; dispute settlement procedures, if the conventions provided for them at all, were seldom activated; developing countries involved in particular fisheries, as in the tuna fisheries, considered that their food and developmental needs entitled them to higher catches and that developed states should bear the brunt of any cuts in catch required for conservation.[52] The latter mostly regarded the Convention as a moral code that they preferred not to violate but which they were none the less prepared to ignore in certain circumstances, in the view of many.

Though the Conservation Convention had in its Preamble stressed that the nature of the problems involved in conservation was such that they essentially required international co-operation through the concerted action of *all* states concerned, this was rarely forthcoming. Nor was there any attempt in this period to relate conservation to reduction of pollution or protection of the habitat of species. The wider ecosystem approach was entirely lacking. The UNCLOS II, held in 1960, which failed to reach any agreement, similarly did not tackle the wider conservation problems. It addressed the question of regulating fisheries solely in the context of extending coastal states' control over them by fixing territorial sea and fishery limits on the basis of establishing a six-n.m. territorial sea with a six-n.m. fishery zone beyond. A European Fishery Convention, concluded among North Sea and North Atlantic states in 1964,[53] after the UNCLOS II failure, was concerned with building on this proposal by establishing a formula for fishing limits; its primary aim was not conservation but limitation of foreign access to coastal fisheries though it did extend the scope of the coastal states' regulatory powers by providing for an

---

[50] Conservation Convention, Articles 9–12.

[51] These included, in addition to those already referred to in n. 27, the 1959 Convention Concerning Fishing in the Black Sea; 1965 Agreement between Japan and Korea Concerning Fisheries; 1967 International Convention for the Conservation of Atlantic Tunas; 1969 Convention for the Conservation of the Living Resources of the South-East Atlantic; 1971 Agreement Between Canada and Norway on Sealing and the Conservation of the Seal Stocks in the North-West Atlantic.

[52] For case studies of some of the problems encountered by particular commissions, see Driscoll and McKellar, in Mason, *The Effective Management of Resources*; Cushing, 1 *Marine Policy* (1977), 270–8; Joseph, ibid., 275–88.

[53] 581 *UNTS* 57; text in Churchill, Lay, and Nordquist (eds.), *I ND*, 41–8. For discussion, see Bowett, *The Law of the Sea*.

exclusive six-n.m. fishing limit with a further six-n.m. belt beyond which access was controlled by the coastal state. The ICJ took cognizance of this regional convention, adopting in effect a twelve-n.m. fisheries limit, in arriving at its conclusions in the *Icelandic Fisheries* case (see below).

Major changes in the legal regime thus began to be demanded. Some states had already taken unilateral action to reduce the living resources of the sea as well as of the sea-bed to national jurisdiction in the form of exclusive 200-mile maritime zones or 'patrimonial seas',[54] though their motives were more exploitative than conservatory, and such claims were protested.[55] The Declaration of Principles adopted by the UN Conference on the Human Environment (UNCHE) included principles relevant to living resources (see Chapter 2), which drew attention to the need for conservation; and finally the preparations for and negotiations at the Third United Nations Conference on the Law of the Sea, leading to the adoption of the UNCLOS 1982, revolutionized the international law of fisheries so far as its jurisdictional aspects are concerned. It remains, therefore, to consider to what extent this revolution has changed these and other aspects and introduced more effective conservation.[56]

(3) Conservatory Principles in the UNCHE Declaration 1972; UNEP and Other UN Principles

(a) UNCHE Declaration

Relevant principles (see Chapter 2) include Principle 2, safeguarding natural resources for future generations, and Principle 4 on wise management of wildlife and its habitat within the development planning context, both of which are expressed in very general terms; and Principle 21 stressing states' sovereign rights to exploit their resources under their own environmental policies, subject to their responsibility to ensure that they do not damage other states' environments or that of areas beyond national jurisdiction, and Principle 22 requiring development of the law regarding liability and compensation for pollution and 'other environmental damage', which could include fisheries.[57]

A number of the UNCHE Recommendations are also relevant.[58] These include those urging co-operation among UN agencies and developing

---

[54] A good account of this development is given in Hollick, 71 *AJIL* (1977), 494–9.

[55] For the effect of such protest, see Ch. 1.

[56] See Miles (ed.), *Management of World Fisheries: Implications of Extended Fisheries Jurisdiction* (Seattle, 1989).

[57] Halter and Thomas, 10 *ELQ* (1982–3), 5–35.

[58] Recommendations 32, 33, 38, 46, 47, 49, 50, and 99 are especially relevant. See Birnie, *International Regulation of Whaling*, i (1985) who lists the relevant recommendations at 876–8. See also Report on the United Nations Conference on the Human Environment, Stockholm, 5–16 June 1972, UN Doc. A/CONF. 48/14/Rev. 1., 16–17.

countries in wildlife management and training; protection of areas representing ecosystems of international significance; support by governments and FAO for developing guidelines, etc. for international fishing organizations; promotion of international research on the side effects of national resource-use activities; better and wider data collection and analysis; ensuring full governmental co-operation in strengthening existing international and regional machinery for development and management of fisheries and their related environmental aspects and establishing these in regions where they do not exist. Recommendations concerning control of marine pollution are also indirectly relevant to conservation, but it is clear that all these recommendations set strategic goals and do not constitute legal requirements.

(b) UNEP's Principles on Shared Natural Resources

UNEP's Draft Principles on Utilization and Conservation of Natural Resources Shared by Two or More States (see Chapter 2) are applicable to migratory fisheries that cross boundaries; Principles 1–12 are particularly relevant. Their conservatory aims cover prescription of use of certain kinds of gear and habitat destruction, etc. that have serious effects on fisheries. They stress co-operation and equitable utilization, (see Chapter 3), but couple this with preservation of states' sovereign rights to resources and offer no guidance on determining what is an equitable use of fisheries. They do, however, encourage conclusion of binding bilateral or multilateral regulatory agreements establishing institutional structures (Principle 2). States have now entered into many bilateral fishery agreements[59] and, as illustrated in this chapter, established many fishery commissions and though not all stocks exploited by two or more states are covered, most of those adversely affected by over-exploitation are, though sometimes not all states involved in the fishery concerned are parties to the relevant convention.[60] It is through state practice in these agreements and commissions that equitable solutions are arrived at. The UNEP principles like the UNCHE ones, accept states' rights to pursue their own environmental policies, subject to the duty to avoid damage to the environment of other states or of international areas (Principle 3) but expand somewhat on this duty since states are required to avoid such effects when the use *might* cause environmental damage that could have repercussion on a sharing state's use of the resource, threaten the resources' conservation, or endanger the health of its population (over-exploitation of fisheries could lead to all three effects) but the Principles accept the limitation in this respect of the practical capabilities of states.

No criteria are provided for determining the 'significant' effect on fisheries

---

[59] Carroz and Savini, 3 *Marine Policy* (1979), 79–98 illustrate the extent to which states used this means to implement relevant provisions of the UNCLOS before its entry into force.

[60] e.g. the Whaling Convention and the two tuna Conventions (ICCAT and IATTC).

that would invoke the need for environmental impact assessment (Principle 4), though this gap is now filled partly by UNEP's Guidelines (see Chapter 2) and the 1991 UN Convention on Environmental Impact Assessment in a Transboundary Context.[61] The need for exchange of information, consultation, and the giving of advance notification of plans to exploit shared resources (Principles 5 and 6) are well effected through fisheries agreements, as is the need, based on the customary principle of good faith and good neighbourliness (Principle 7) to co-operate to find a solution. Fisheries agreements follow Principle 8 in providing for conduct of joint scientific studies and assessment to provide data for resolution of environmental problems. It is unlikely that disasters or emergencies arising from fisheries will arise that would invoke Principle 9's duty to inform others, but they could do so, perhaps in the case of fish disease or pollution threats to habitat. Both FAO and fishery commissions, as advocated in Principle 10, have been used to clarify problems arising from conservation and use of fisheries. There are, despite the non-use of the Conservation Convention's arbitration procedures, a few examples of application of Principle 11's requirement of peaceful settlement of disputes concerning fisheries in the referral of some fisheries disputes to arbitration, to the ICJ, or to the European Court of Justice[62] and in the various negotiated settlements. Principle 14 urging provision of access to national courts and remedies and Principle 12 concerning state responsibility for damage, which are discussed in Chapters 5 and 4 respectively, are also applicable in general terms but these principles have not been well developed in relation to over-exploitation of shared fisheries.

These UNEP principles provide the only existing global framework for fisheries exploitation, apart from the 1958 Conservation Convention, the scope of which, as we have seen, is limited and does not deal with most of the matters addressed in the UNEP Principles, and the UNCLOS 1982, which, though not in force, is having a considerable impact on state practice—both in respect of domestic laws and through fisheries agreements and commissions. The hortatory and 'soft law' nature of the UNEP Principles has been emphasized, however, in Chapters 1 and 2. Thus, in so far as the precise obligations of states in relation to fisheries are concerned we must look to customary law, which as we have seen has protected the rights and freedoms of states to exploit these resources, a right qualified only in general terms of 'reasonableness' (as codified in the High Seas Convention, Article 2) or 'due regard' (Article 87(2) UNCLOS) when exploitation takes place on the high seas, and to the specific provisions of the numerous fisheries conventions at the bilateral, regional, subregional, and international levels, applicable either

---

[61] See pp. 105–6.
[62] e.g. *Kramer et al.*, Joined Cases, ECJ Nos. 3/76, 4/76, and 6/76, *ECR* (1976), 1279; *Commission* v. *UK*, ECJ No. 804/79. *ECR* (1981), 1045; *R.* v. *MAFF ex parte Agegate Ltd.* [1991] I All ER. 6; *R* v. *MAFF ex parte Jaderow Ltd.*, [1991] I All ER. 41 (ECJ).

on the high seas, in EEZs or EFZs, in the territorial sea or combinations thereof.

The Charter of Economic Rights and Duties of states, however, for the reasons outlined in Chapter 3, is also relevant to the evolution of a duty to co-operate in exploitation of shared natural resources 'on the basis of a system of information and prior consultation in order to achieve the optimum use of such resources without causing damage to the legitimate interests of others' (Article 3). Its legal status is discussed in Chapter 1; it also falls within the 'soft' rather than the 'hard' law category. The work of the International Law Commission in relation to shared watercourses, analysed in Chapter 6, is also relevant to establishment of a duty to co-operate in relation to shared resources, to have regard to the rights of others and to ensure equitable exploitation that does not harm these rights. The wildlife conventions discussed in Chapter 12 also provide evidence that such a duty to co-operate in these circumstances is increasingly widely accepted by states.

(4) Events Leading to the Third UN Conference on the Law of the Sea (UNCLOS III) 1973–1982: Impact on the UNCLOS 1982 Fisheries Regime

(a) The 'Common Heritage' Concept

Though the origins of the UNCLOS III lay in Malta's request to the UN General Assembly that the resources of the sea-bed and ocean floor beyond national jurisdiction should be used for the benefit of all mankind and be declared 'the common heritage of mankind',[63] Malta did not suggest that the resources of the waters above should be so regarded nor did the Declaration of Principles Governing the Exploitation of the Sea-bed, adopted unanimously by the General Assembly in 1970[64] relate to fisheries in the waters above. Malta's subsequent proposal for a treaty establishing an international agency for this purpose limited it to assuming jurisdiction 'as a trustee for all countries'. A single body was proposed in Malta's draft ocean space treaty[65] to regulate activities relating only to the deep sea-bed. However, since ocean space is a single ecological system and since its uses are interlinked, the new international order should in Malta's view reflect a total and comprehensive approach to the marine environment and to the international regulation of its problems. The UN had already instigated a study of the resources of the sea (including living resources) and the techniques for their exploitation, to identify resources capable of economic exploitation, especially for the benefit of developing states.[66]

---

[63] Note verbale, 17 Aug. 1967 from Permanent Mission of Malta to the UN to the Secretary General, UN. Doc. A/6095; see also Ogley, Whose Common Heritage?: Creating a Law for the Sea-bed (Guildford, 1975), 17–25.

[64] UNGA Res. 2749 (XXV), of 17 Dec. 1970.

[65] Draft Ocean Space Treaty: Working Paper submitted by Malta; AC 138/53, 5.

[66] ECOSOC Res. 112 (XL), 7 Mar. 1967.

The Sea-bed Committee,[67] established by the UN to consider the questions raised by Malta, which met several times between 1967 and 1973, was soon given a broad mandate to discuss and make recommendations upon the wider law of the sea issues, including fisheries. Its activities led the General Assembly in 1970 to convene in 1973 a Third Conference on the Law of the Sea not only to consider the question of a sea-bed regime but also to review, *inter alia*, the subject-matter of the 1958 Geneva Conventions, including the High Seas and the Conservation Conventions. The relevant resolution instructed the conference to deal with a broad range of related issues including fishing and conservation of the sea's living resources, and comprehending the preferential rights to fisheries of coastal states. Shortly after the UNCLOS III opened in 1973, the ICJ delivered a judgment of great significance to these issues purporting to provide for the resolution of the conflict of interests between coastal and distant water fishing states and the need for conservation.

(b) Historic Rights and Preferential Rights of Coastal States: Accommodation of Interests in Fishery Conservation

The 1958 Conservation Convention had recognized only the 'interest' of the coastal state in conservation of fisheries in waters beyond but adjacent to its territorial sea, the limit of which the Territorial Sea Convention and the UNCLOS II had failed to fix. Zones beyond that limit in which coastal states could assert exclusive or preferential rights to fisheries were not universally recognized, whether for conservatory or exploitative purposes. The High Seas Convention had codified 'reasonable' freedom without specific reference to conservation, although thus perhaps providing a limitation on the basis of which conservatory regimes could be developed. The few Latin American states that had from 1947 onwards declared 200-n.m. Maritime Zones in which, *inter alia*, they asserted so-called 'sovereignty' over living resources did not, however, renounce these and following the failure of the UNCLOS I and II to deal with these problems, their practice was gradually followed by other states[68] for a variety of reasons, including the failure of many international fishing commissions to preserve or restore stocks to MSY and thus maintain catch levels. The reasons for this failure were identified earlier in this chapter.

Iceland was one of the states which at UNCLOS I and II opposed the establishment of the six-plus-six-n.m. formula for extension of coastal state control over fisheries and it did not participate in the 1964 European Fisheries Agreement. Its declaration of a 12-mile territorial sea provoked the first dispute with the UK, whose fishermen it excluded from these limits but this

---

[67] Committee on the Peaceful Uses of the Sea-bed and Ocean Floor Beyond National Jurisdiction (PUSOF).

[68] Brown, in Lay, Churchill, and Nordquist (eds.), *III ND*, 157–92.

was settled by negotiation. The extension of its fishery limit to fifty n.m. by Iceland in 1972, however, provoked the Anglo-Icelandic and the Anglo-German fisheries disputes, which were submitted by the UK and West Germany to the International Court of Justice.[69] The Court was asked to decide the legality of Iceland's extension of its fisheries jurisdiction, the continuing rights of the UK and the Federal Republic of Germany to fish in the area, and to pronounce on any requirements for co-operation in adopting conservation measures. The need for co-operation between states in exploitation of natural resources that traverse boundaries had arisen incidentally in two other cases since the *Behring Sea Fur Seals* arbitration, namely the *Lac Lanoux* arbitration,[70] and the *North Sea Continental Shelf* case.[71] These decisions were not referred to by the ICJ in the *Icelandic Fisheries* cases. In the former case, the tribunal, though not finding that use of a river by one state necessitated conclusion of a prior agreement with all the riparian states, remarked that international practice evidenced the belief that states should strive to do so and there existed an obligation to accept in good faith all overtures that could with good will and broad balancing of interests provide states with the best conditions for this. In this case the court found that the upper riparian state had already discharged its duty of diligence in relation to the rights and interests of the lower riparian states. Had this not been so it seems likely that a co-operation agreement would have been required.[72] In the *North Sea* case the Court observed that agreements for joint exploitation were particularly appropriate to preserving the unity of a transboundary mineral deposit though it did not expand on the co-operative aspects or require this.

In the *Icelandic Fisheries* cases the Court found, after surveying existing relevant fisheries conventions and state practice, that Iceland had preferential rights to fisheries beyond its territorial sea (although it did not fix any spatial limit for these) but found also that the UK and Germany retained rights to fish these, based on long-standing historic practice. The Court held, however, that the parties' respective rights were not absolute; both had to take account of and accommodate the rights of the other, in particular:

both states have an obligation to take full account of each other's rights and of any fishery conservation measures the necessity of which is shown to exist in those waters. It is one of the advances of maritime international law, resulting from the intensification of fishing, that the former laissez-faire treatment of the living resources of the

---

[69] *Icelandic Fisheries Cases (UK v. Iceland)* (Merits), *ICJ Rep.* (1974), 3; *(Federal Republic of Germany v. Iceland)* (Merits), ibid. 175. For a full discussion of these, see Churchill, 24 *ICLQ* (1975), 82–105.

[70] *Lac Lanoux* arbitration, 24 *ILR* (1957), 101. See Chs. 3 and 6.

[71] *ICJ Rep.* (1969), 1; for examples, of agreements on joint development arrangement in this respect and a model agreement, see Fox (ed.), *Joint Development of Offshore Oil and Gas*, i and ii (London, 1989 and 1990 respectively).

[72] Hey, *The Regime for the Exploitation*, 33.

high seas has been replaced by a recognition of a duty to have due regard to the rights of other states and the *needs of conservation* for the benefit of all. Consequently, both Parties have the obligation to keep under review the fishery resources in the disputed waters and *to examine together*, in the light of scientific and other available information *the measures required for conservation* and development of *equitable* exploitation of these resources.[73]

As in the *North Sea Continental Shelf* case, the parties were held to be under an obligation to negotiate in good faith; in this case to accommodate their rights and interests, balance and regulate equitably catch limitation, etc., and take full account of each others rights and of fishery conservation measures in discharge of their duty to exercise due diligence, for which purpose they must co-operate by examining the problem together and negotiating.[74]

Much later, in the *Gulf of Maine* case,[75] a Chamber of the ICJ, having delimited a single maritime boundary between the continental shelves and the 200-mile exclusive fisheries/economic zones of the United States and Canada respectively in the George's Bank area of the Gulf, which in fact cut across both fisheries and mineral resource deposits, held that co-operation in relation to developing these resources had become 'all the more necessary' as a result of this decision. It considered also that any adverse effects resulting to fisheries from this bisection would not be sufficiently serious to be taken into account in choosing this line and that any difficulties could be resolved (by co-operation) between the parties, which had good relations. No reference was made to the relevant UNEP Principles.

These cases, it has been suggested by Hey,[76] indicate that co-operation is necessary when natural resources are shared across boundaries or in international areas, in order to discharge the duty of due diligence that arises when rights of this kind of more than one state are involved. They must for this purpose have due regard to other states' rights; provide for management of the resource for the benefit of all interested states; examine jointly the measures necessary for conservation and development of the fishery and arrange for equitable exploitation. Only then will true 'optimum utilization' be achieved, which, in Hey's view, means the best form of use in the context of the interests of all participants. She submits that this qualification of sovereignty and sovereign rights has changed the role of these concepts and shifted the burden of proof; they no longer form the basis of a state's entitlement to exploit parts of shared resources that fall within their territory

---

[73] *Icelandic Fisheries Cases (UK v. Iceland)*, para. 72, p. 31 and *(FRG v. Iceland)*, para. 64, p. 200, emphasis added.

[74] Ibid. paras. 73–5, pp. 31–3 and paras. 64–7, pp. 200–1.

[75] *Gulf of Maine Care (Canada/United States of America), ICJ Rep* (1984), 246.

[76] Hey, *The Regime for the Exploitation*, 34–5; she considers that the ICJ would have been more forthright in the *North Sea* and *Gulf of Maine Cases* if the issue had not been secondary to the primary purpose of establishing the principles of boundary delimitation.

(a concept forming the basis of the UN Declaration on Permanent Sovereignty and the UNEP Principles) but rather the basis on which a state can claim part of the benefits derivable from these resources when located within their territory or jurisdiction. She disagrees with the conclusion of Schewbel, when special rapporteur for the ILC on international watercourses, that the duty to co-operate in such cases is an exception to the concept of permanent sovereignty over natural resources embodied in General Assembly resolutions (see Chapters 3 and 6). Hers is certainly a more attractive view to take from the conservatory standpoint. It remains to ascertain to what extent it is supported in the 1982 UNCLOS.

(5) Concurrent Developments outside the Third UNCLOS Impacting on Conservation of Living Resources

(a) Conservation Treaties

During the period of gestation of the UNCLOS 1982, a new approach was developing outside the Law of the Sea designed to protect living species from various threats by concluding a series of *ad hoc* treaties. New obligations emerged requiring that endangered living resources be conserved for their own value, rather than as species or products for human consumption (see Chapter 11). These treaties, as indicated at the beginning of this Chapter, cover some marine living resources. They include the 1973 Convention on International Trade in Endangered Species (CITES)[77] on whose Annexes are listed some of the marine species endangered by trade in them or their products, including, *inter alia*, all cetaceans and some other marine mammals, such as certain seals; the 1979 Convention on the Conservation of Migratory Species of Wild Animals,[78] on whose Appendices are listed certain species of whales and seals, the dugong and some porpoises and under which AGREEMENTS have been prepared, though not yet adopted, on some small cetaceans and one seal population; the regional 1979 Berne Convention on Conservation of European Wildlife and Natural Habitats,[79] which has also listed a few marine species, and the 1980 Convention on Conservation of Antarctic Marine Living Resources (CCAMLR)[80] that aims at conservation of the whole ecosystem sustaining the living resources of the waters within Antarctic convergence. As these (other than the CCAMLR) are primarily concerned with non-marine living resources, though applicable to marine resources, they are analysed in more detail in Chapter 12. It suffices to note here that, though their more ecological approach is reflected in the UNCLOS 1982 only in very general terms—it has little directly to say about habitat protection and nothing about trade in species—they are now part of an overall

---

[77] See *supra*, pp. 475–80.   [78] See *supra*, pp. 470–5.
[79] See Ch. 12.   [80] *Supra*, p. 445 and Ch. 11.

strategy for preserving marine species that are endangered by the various kinds of threats.

(b) World Conservation Strategy 1980 (WCS)[81]

As outlined in Chapters 1 and 2, faced with the difficulties of securing sufficient support in the expanded international community to conclude treaties on various emergent problems, especially in the field of environment and development, states are increasingly resorting to such 'soft law' devices as setting goals or strategies for achieving these, which are discussed also in Chapter 11. These strategies all require and propose various developments in the law concerning conservation. The WCS recognizes that living resources can be utilized and sets out the basic requirements for conserving all living resources in order to sustain development. This requires that both social and ecological factors be taken into account, as well as the ability of the resource base to sustain exploitation, and that the advantages and disadvantages of alternative actions and approaches be evaluated. It defines conservation but in general terms that are more useful as a goal than as a management tool[82] and requires development of international law in similarly general terms (see Chapter 11).

The WCS makes numerous recommendations, including for the 'global commons', within which area it includes conservation of the great whales. For the whales it recommends a total moratorium on capture until both the consequences for the ecosystem of removing large segments of their population and the stock's capacity to restore itself can be estimated. It stresses in general the ecological approach, the need for regional approaches based on the ecological units of a region and the need to respect and apply UNEP's Principles for Shared Natural Resources.

(c) World Charter for Nature (WCN) 1982[83]

This too is outlined in Chapter 11. It lays down very general principles requiring that nature be respected and its essential processes preserved. These include that ecosystems and marine resources must be managed to sustain optimum productivity without endangering the integrity of the other species and their ecosystems with which they coexist, that conservation of nature in international areas is required, and also co-operation to these ends. The 'Earth Charter' which it was proposed should be adopted by the UN Conference on Environment and Development (UNCED) held in 1992, which may have refined these, was not adopted.

---

[81] World Conservation Strategy (as revised) obtainable from IUCN, Gland, Switzerland; prepared by IUCN with the advice and support of UNEP and WWF (World Wide Fund for Nature); see now as 'Caring for the Earth: A Strategy for Sustainable Living'.

[82] Ibid. Item 1.

[83] UNGA Res. 37/7, of 9 Nov. 1982, 23 ILM (1983), 455–60.

(d) World Commission on Environment and Development (WCED) 1986

The report and recommendations of this body are also considered in Chapter 11, including its advocacy of sustainable development of resources. Its Experts Group on Environmental Law, in arriving at recommendations on legal principles concerning conservation for present and future generations, maintenance of ecosystems, related ecological processes, biological diversity and sustainability, co-operation and protection of transboundary natural resources, examined fisheries treaties *inter alia*.[84]

5. THE 1982 UNITED NATIONS CONVENTION ON THE LAW OF THE SEA[85]

(1) General Approach

As the General Assembly, in its Resolution convening the UNCLOS III, had instructed it to produce a single treaty dealing with over 100 Law of the Sea issues, of which fisheries and scientific research represented only a few items, and as it was decided that the convention should be adopted by consensus if possible, the convention was negotiated and adopted as a 'package deal'. States had to reach compromises on some issues to secure agreement on others of particular concern to them. Fisheries articles could not be voted on separately from those relating to the territorial sea, high seas, and continental shelf, as they were at UNCLOS I in relation to the Conservation Convention. At UNCLOS III the compromises were often achieved by and expressed in the use of ambiguous language or by leaving difficult issues, such as precise formulae for allocation of fish catches or calculation of MSY, to be determined by subsequent agreement or at the discretion of coastal states, subject to considerations laid down in the UNCLOS.

The Convention incorporates the *Icelandic Fisheries* case only in part. After accepting in Part V the new concept of the 200 n.m. Exclusive Economic Zone and dealing with general issues, it adopts a partial-species approach to fisheries: different species are subject to different jurisdictional regimes. Despite the co-ordinated ecosystem strategies referred to in the previous section, the 1982 UNCLOS does not provide any mechanism for co-ordinating either existing fisheries commissions or the relationship between fisheries

---

[84] Munro and Lammers (eds.), *Environmental Protection and Sustainable Development* (London, 1987). See List of International Agreements and other Instruments at 133–43.

[85] For a succinct analysis of the provisions of this Convention, see Churchill and Lowe, *The Law of the Sea, passim*, esp. 223–40. See also Balasubramanian, 5 *Marine Policy* (1981), 313–21; 6 *Marine Policy* (1982), 27–42; and Copes, 5 *Marine Policy* (1981), 217–29, for the impact on conservation of fisheries. Both stress the extent of the consensus arrived at on the relevant provisions and their status as customary law.

conservation and the new conservatory conventions in general. Nor does it deal effectively or in detail with the crucial problem of common stocks, that is, stocks that migrate between or among zones, though it does address it in general terms. It does not clearly endorse an ecosystem or habitat preservation approach though its main article on conservation (Article 61) goes some way towards this and Article 94(5) is relevant to certain endangered species' habitats. Finally, it does not provide any mechanisms for considering or clearly identifying the close inter-relationship of the fisheries (Parts V and VII) and pollution prevention (Part XII) provisions of the Convention, though as the Convention was arrived at and is generally regarded as a 'package deal' the relationship is inherent and the title of Part XII—'Protection and Preservation of the Marine Environment' (rather than 'prevention of pollution') is aimed at emphasizing this.[86]

(2) Jurisdictional Limits and Competences for Conservation of Marine Living Resources[87]

On one aspect of fisheries problems—the attribution of the right to exercise jurisdiction for laying down, applying, and enforcing the corresponding law and concomitant general obligations concerning exploitation of living resources—the 1982 UNCLOS has been successful. Identification of the source of this authority is an important step forward in developing the law of conservation of marine species although it does not, of course, in itself impose any obligation to conserve. In so far as the jurisdictional competence is subjected to the requirements of the UNCLOS and other rules of international law (for example, fisheries and related conservatory conventions), however, both the obligation and, to some extent, its specific content can be identified.

It must be recalled, however, that the UNCLOS is not in force, and we have to look, therefore, to the consensus on these provisions at the UNCLOS III and to subsequent state practice to ascertain the extent to which they now represent customary international law. The relevant provisions relate to the following issues:

(a) Territorial Sea (TS)

The 1982 UNCLOS establishes a twelve-mile limit for the territorial sea, over which the coastal state has sovereignty, subject to any requirements of

---

[86] Nordquist (ed.), *United Nations Convention on the Law of the Sea: A Commentary* (Dordrecht, 1991), iv. 9–12; the commentator suggests that 'preserve' means to conserve the natural resources and retain the quality of the marine environment over the long term (at 11–12).

[87] For a more detailed discussion of these see de Klemm, 4 *EPL* (1978), 2–17; Burke, 14 *ODIL* (1984), 273–314; Appelbaum, in Soons (ed.), *Implementation of the Law of the Sea Convention through International Institutions* (Honolulu, 1989), 282–318.

the UNCLOS and other rules of international law, for example, any conservatory fisheries conventions to which that state is party, which by their terms apply within that area. The Whaling Convention and relevant regulations and directives issued under the Treaty of Rome, by virtue of which the EC's Common Fisheries Policy was established, are among the few that do so. Foreign fishing vessels in innocent passage through the area, as under the 1958 Territorial Sea Convention (TSC), must refrain from engaging in fishing activities.[88] The coastal state can adopt laws and regulations, corresponding to the UNCLOS and other international rules, to prevent infringement of its fishery laws and regulations (and also to preserve the environment, prevent pollution, and control marine scientific research).[89] In international straits also it can prohibit vessels in transit passage from fishing and require their gear to be stowed.[90]

(b) Contiguous Zone

The twelve-n.m. CZ beyond the TS limit constituted by the TSC has been preserved but in amended form. It now extends to twenty-four n.m. without reference to the legal status of its waters (stated in the TSC to be High Seas and therefore open to freedom of fishing) since these now fall within the EEZ (see EEZ below).[91] The coastal state is accorded the right to exercise control only for limited purposes to prevent infringement of specific laws (which do not include fisheries) in its territorial sea. The omission of any reference to fisheries law enforcement in the CZ has caused some confusion in interpretation and application of the corresponding provisions in the 1958 TSC. Some states have included it in their national laws and some national court decisions have assumed that the CZ covers fisheries by analogy, as it does not specifically exclude them,[92] but as the CZ is now part of the EEZ, conservation and enforcement therein is subject to the powers conferred under Part V of the UNCLOS, that is, the EEZ articles.

(c) Archipelagic Waters[93]

Archipelagic states, as defined in the UNCLOS, can draw straight baselines joining the outermost points of their outer islands and reefs. Within the area enclosed the waters are regarded as subject to the sovereignty of the archipelagic state with a status akin to that of the territorial sea since

---

[88] Territorial Sea Convention (TSC), Articles 1, 2, and esp. 14(5); UNCLOS Article 19(2)(i).
[89] TSC, Article 14(5); UNCLOS Article 21(1)(e).
[90] UNCLOS, Article 42(1)(c). The TSC applies similar rules to 'innocent passage' through international Straits in Article 14(5).
[91] TSC, Article 24(1) and (2); UNCLOS, Article 33(1) and (2).
[92] For discussion of this problem, see Churchill and Lowe, *The Law of the Sea*, 112–19. For discussion of the case of *US* v. *Fishing Vessel Taiyo Maru No. 28*, 395 F. Suppl. 413 (1976), see Ciobanu, 70 *AJIL* (1976), 549–53.
[93] UNCLOS, Part IV, Articles 46–53.

the state's exercise of jurisdiction is subject to the UNCLOS provisions on archipelagos and on the right of innocent passage. As the baselines enclosing the archipelago now form the baselines of the territorial sea, the continental shelf and the Exclusive Economic Zone, archipelagic states now control vast areas of fisheries. Article 51, however, requires them to respect existing agreements with other states, which will include those on fisheries and to recognize in certain areas of their waters the traditional fishing rights of immediately adjacent neighbouring states, which can be regulated by bilateral agreements. Though no specific reference is made to conservation this could be required under the relevant agreements. The archipelagic state has the same powers to prohibit fishing and scientific research by vessels in passage through any archipelagic sea lanes it may designate, as have coastal states over transit passage through international straits.[94] The conservation of fisheries in the EEZ of archipelagic states is, of course, subject of the requirements of Article 61 of the UNCLOS.

(d) Continental Shelf

The 1982 UNCLOS, like the 1958 Continental Shelf Convention (CSC), includes marine living 'organisms belonging to sedentary species' within its definition of the 'natural resources' of the shelf over which the coastal state exercises sovereign rights of exploitation,[95] and defines them as 'organisms which at the harvestable stage, either are immobile on or under the sea-bed or are unable to move except in constant physical contact with the sea-bed or subsoil'.[96] This unscientific and ambiguous definition caused some conflicts after the entry into force of the CSC concerning which shelf resources were thus effectively removed from the freedom of fishing.[97] The UNCLOS obviates this problem by making no reference to the precise status of these waters (it simply states that the shelf rights do not affect their status)[98] leaving it to be implied from Part VII on the High Seas, Article 86, that as the waters above the continental shelf are not included in the areas to which Part VII is specifically applied, they thus have, to the extent that they fall within the regime of the 200-mile EEZ, the status of the waters of that zone, which is generally regarded as being *sui generis* (neither high seas nor territorial sea but subject to the special provisions of the convention). As the coastal state now has wide powers to take conservatory measures (taking account of the interdependence of species, etc.) and to control pollution and scientific research in the EEZ (see below), this should improve conservation of sedentary species—even though Article 56(3) subjects the EEZ rights relating to the sea-bed and

---

[94] UNCLOS, Article 54.
[95] CSC, Articles 1, 2(1), (2), and (4); UNCLOS, Article 77.
[96] CSC, Article 2(4); UNCLOS, Article 77(4).
[97] CSC, Article 4; see also *supra*, n. 41.
[98] UNCLOS Article 78(1).

subsoil to the provisions of Part VI concerning the continental shelf, which make no reference to any obligation to conserve its sedentary species—since most sedentary species will be found within the 200-mile limit.

The UNCLOS provides a more precise definition of the outer limit of the continental shelf than did the CSC, which defined it in terms of depth (200 metres) and exploitability of the sea-bed and subsoil beyond the territorial sea. The UNCLOS, like the CSC, recognizes that the continental shelf comprises the sea-bed and subsoil of the areas beyond the territorial sea but adds that it extends throughout the natural prolongation of the coastal states' land territory to the outer edge of the continental margin (it provides a formula for determining this)[99] *or* to a distance of 200-n.m. from the territorial sea baselines when the margin does not extend that far. A distance criterion and a formula for identifying the outer limit, which is set on the margin, replace the open-ended exploitability test of the CSC. If a continental shelf is naturally prolonged beyond 200 n.m. the waters above the sedentary species will not fall under the protective provisions of the EEZ beyond that limit, but as few known or exploited sedentary species are found in this area this is not significant. Moreover, although the shelf resources will be under the exclusive control of the coastal state, this area is removed from freedom of fishing, from the need to promote optimum utilization of fisheries, and from the EEZ's requirements and criteria for granting to other states access to any surplus thereof.[100] However, whereas the CSC required that activities throughout the shelf must not cause any 'unjustifiable interference'[101] to navigation, fishing, scientific research, or 'conservation of the living resources of the sea', the corresponding UNCLOS provision is much less specific regarding conservation, merely requiring that the exercise of the rights of the coastal state over the shelf 'must not infringe or result in any unjustifiable interference with navigation and *other rights and freedoms of other states as provided for in this Convention*'.[102]

(e) Exclusive Economic Zone

In establishing as an Exclusive Economic Zone, subject to coastal state control, an area not exceeding 200-n.m. from the baselines of the territorial sea,[103] the UNCLOS potentially does much to improve the opportunity to apply and enforce any regimes necessary to conserve living resources in that

---

[99] UNCLOS Article 78(1), para. 4.

[100] UNCLOS Article 62(1), (2), and (3). For a detailed comparison and analysis of the relationship of the continental shelf and the EEZ, see Attard, *The Exclusive Economic Zone in International Law* (Oxford, 1987); Kwiatkowska, *The Exclusive Economic Zone* (Dordrecht, 1989); for analysis of the EEZ regime concerning living resources, see Attard, op. cit. 146–91, Kwiatkowska, op. cit. 45–103.

[101] CSC Article 5(1).

[102] UNCLOS, Article 78(2), emphasis added.

[103] UNCLOS, Articles 55–7.

zone since, by removing the area from the scope of application of the doctrine of freedom of fishing[104] that still pertains on the high seas, it removes one of the main causes of the over-fishing to which, as illustrated earlier, that doctrine made a major contribution. But much depends on whether coastal states make effective use of this opportunity to conserve fisheries on a sustainable basis. As several of the coastal states most advantaged by the extensive nature of their EEZ are developing states in Africa, Asia, and Latin America, and small Pacific and Caribbean island states, it may be somewhat difficult for them to do so. The cost of collecting the necessary data, evaluating it, maintaining surveillance over the zone and actively enforcing conservatory laws is the greater the larger the area and, coupled with the historic doctrine of 'hot pursuit' of offending vessels (codified in UNCLOS, Article 111) requires availability of or access to modern equipment (including vessels, aircraft, and satellites) and highly trained personnel. Very few states have scientific research vessels; all these are developed states. This problem, however, can be solved by flag states of distant water vessels applying stricter sanctions[105] and by regional co-operation, by pooling resources, and by provision of technical assistance and advice by international organizations, such as FAO, UNEP, regional commissions, and by other states or groupings thereof, for example, the European Community. FAO has taken major initiatives in these respects and has laid down plans to 1993[106] and beyond.

Even developed states apparently are not succeeding in effectively managing and conserving fisheries in their EEZs or EFZs, whether the zone falls wholly within their exclusive jurisdiction, as in the United States and Canada,[107] or, in the European Community, is subject to terms of equal access for other members of a regional body,[108] which itself lays down the conservation policy.

The UNCLOS accords to the coastal state within its EEZ 'sovereign rights for the purpose of exploring, exploiting, *conserving and managing* the natural

[104] UNCLOS, Article 86, omits reference to the EEZ from application of its provisions relating to the high seas. For discussion of the legal status of the EEZ, see Attard, *The Exclusive Economic Zone in International Law*; Kwiatkowska, *The Exclusive Economic Zone*; Orrego Vicuna (ed.), *The Exclusive Economic Zone* (Boulder, Colo., 1984), 1–121; Phillips, 26 *ICLQ* (1977), 585–618.

[105] Doulman, 11 *Marine Policy* (1987), 25–8.

[106] See, *The Work of FAO in Fisheries during 1992–93*, FAO Doc. COFI/91/12, Feb. 1991; *Fisheries Research Needs of Developing Countries (Progress Report)*, FAO Doc. COFI/91/7, Feb. 1991; *Progress in Implementing the 1984 FAO World Fisheries Conference's Strategy for Fisheries Management and Development*, FAO Doc. COFI/91/2, Jan. 1991.

[107] See Weld, 20 *ODIL* (1989), 285–95; McHugh, 21 *ODIL* (1990), 255–61; Miller, Hooker, and Fricke, ibid. 263–87; Sutinen, Reeser, and Gauvin, ibid. 335–72.

[108] Driscoll and McKellar, in Mason, *The Effective Management of Resources*; Churchill, *Fisheries in the European Community: Sustainable Development or Sustained Mismanagement?*, Law of the Sea Institute, *Proceedugs of 25th Annual Conference* (Malmo, 1991) (publication forthcoming); Report on Joint Conference of UK Parliamentary Maritime Group and The Greenwich Forum held on 26 November 1990: *Managing the EC Fisheries: Past Experience and Lessons for the Future*; Garrod and Whitmarsh, 15 *Marine Policy* (1991), 289–96.

resources, whether living or non-living, of the water superjacent to the sea-bed and its subsoil',[109] as well as over other economic activities. It accords to them also jurisdiction, as provided for in the Convention, with regard to establishment and use of artificial islands, installations, and structures (which could be established for fisheries purpose and often attract fish in any event), marine scientific research and protection and preservation of the marine environment, and other rights accorded under the Convention.[110] In exercising these rights coastal states must have 'due regard' to the rights and duties of other states and their acts must be compatible with the UNCLOS. It is clear that in the EEZ there is neither freedom of fishing nor unfettered freedom of scientific research.[111] Although the UNCLOS endeavours to offset the latter by specific provisions in Part XIII requiring coastal states not to refuse consent for research 'in normal circumstances', it exempts from this research directed at exploitation of resources. As scientific data are vital to knowledge of a fishery and its competent conservation and management, which is required by Article 61, this is a potentially harmful restriction.

The coastal state must determine the total allowable catch (TAC) of living resources of fisheries,[112] and its own capacity to harvest this. Only if it cannot itself take the whole TAC, must it, through agreements and subject to the UNCLOS detailed prescriptions of its regulatory powers, give others access to the surplus.[113] Factors to take into account in allocating this include the significance of those resources to the coastal state's economy and its other national interests[114]—which could include preserving other non-consumptive values of those resources, for example, recreational, historic, scientific, aesthetic.

Conservatory obligations laid down in the 1982 UNCLOS, qualifying the sovereign rights to exploit the EEZ's living resources, are expressed in general terms in Article 61 but create complex obligations. In determining the TAC the coastal state must, taking account of the best scientific advice available to it (no criteria are provided for evaluating this), ensure 'through proper conservation and management measures' that the living resources of the EEZ are maintained and not threatened by over-exploitation.[115] It must co-operate with 'competent' (unspecified) international organizations, whether sub-regional, regional, or global. This conservatory aim, however, is offset by the need to promote 'optimum utilization' and to select measures which will maintain or restore populations—of harvested species only—at levels which can produce MSY (now, as indicated in Chapter 11, a somewhat discredited concept) but only as qualified by 'relevant environmental *and* economic factors.'[116] Optimum utilization, however, does not require full utilization; the

---

[109] UNCLOS, Article 56(1)(a), emphasis added.   [110] Ibid. (b)–(c).
[111] Ibid. Articles 58 and 87.   [112] Ibid. Article 61(1).   [113] Ibid. Article 62(2).
[114] Ibid. (3).   [115] Ibid. Article 61(2).   [116] Ibid. (3), emphasis added.

coastal state is not tied to any specific level and could hold back on full exploitation in the interests of conservation; whether it has a right only to conserve the fisheries is doubtful, except as regards marine mammals, specifically allowed for in Article 65, or under agreements. Other states cannot insist on access to a surplus in such circumstances; the declaration of a TAC is, not, under Article 297(3)(a) and (b), subject to the UNCLOS compulsory dispute settlement procedures, although the coastal state's manifest failure to ensure, by proper conservation and management, that the zone's living resources are not endangered, must be submitted to conciliation procedures established under the UNCLOS. A non-exhaustive list of the factors to be taken into account includes the economic needs of coastal fishing communities, special needs of developing states, fishing patterns, the interdependence of stocks, and any 'generally recommended international minimum standards whether subregional, regional or global.'[117] Curiously, it is only in *formulating* the measures, not in *designing* them that the coastal state must 'take into consideration' such ecological factors as 'effects on species associated with or dependent upon harvested species' with a view to maintaining or restoring these populations 'above levels at which their reproduction may become seriously threatened'.[118] The coastal state and all states participating in the fishery must regularly contribute and exchange a wide range of scientific information and data relevant to conservation through 'competent international organizations' at all levels.

Clearly, all the above provisions provide a better approach to conservation than did the 1958 Conservation Convention but the short-term national interests of some states may well tempt them to give more weight to the economic than the environmental considerations. In any event the factors to take into consideration are complex and difficult to assess with certainty, and collection of the necessary data requires a good deal of expensive effort— which may tax the abilities and will of states with economic problems. States, despite the fact that the common property status of fisheries has not been changed, since fish still migrate, may tend to regard the resources of the EEZ as their 'national property" (the sovereign right to catch or to license others to catch fish is a form of property right but does not confer a right of ownership to specific fish in the sea)[119] and resist application of international regulation within it. That this is so is evidenced by the regulatory structure of the reconstituted North-East Atlantic Fisheries Organization (NEAFO) and the new North-West Atlantic Fisheries Organization (NAFO) that have replaced the old NEAF and ICNAF Commissions following the adoption of EFZs and

[117] Ibid.

[118] UNCLOS, Article 61(4).

[119] For a discussion of a private property approach to regulations, see Mcloney and Pearse, 36 *J. of Fisheries Research Board of Canada* (1979), 859–66, and Neher, Arnason, and Mollett (eds.), *Rights-Based Fishing* (Dordrecht, 1989).

EEZs in the respective areas by their states parties. The sub-areas into which these conventions divide their areas of application now include 'Regulatory' and 'Non-Regulatory' areas, the latter being within the EEZs of one or more of states parties. Binding regulations adopted by the Commissions apply only in the high seas area; the Commission can make only non-binding recommendations to the coastal states concerning species within their EEZs and only on the latter's initiatives. The NEAFO is left largely with a co-ordinating and harmonizing role in relation to measures adopted for Regulatory and non-Regulatory areas; it has no management powers in relation to common stocks. The role of many commissions has been much reduced by the advent of EEZs and EFZs and those affected have revised their conventions on a pragmatic basis similar to the above.

Whilst it is clear that a large number of states has accepted and enacted the new rights and jurisdictional limits and even, in a few cases, rolled back extended territorial sea claims,[120] some are still content to claim only Exclusive Fishing Zones (EFZ) and it appears that most are not generally enacting the detailed obligations laid down in the UNCLOS EEZ provisions, including the conservatory limitations.[121] To the extent that they do so, however, they can now implement and enforce on foreign vessels national laws adopted according to the Convention covering: licensing; levying fees (or compensation in kind); determining species caught and fixing quotas; regulating seasons and areas of fishing, the gear used, types and numbers of vessels fishing, and the age and size of fish caught; requiring information from vessels on catch, effort, and position; requiring that research be conducted and prescribing its means and content; placing observers on board; landing the catch in specified ports of the coastal state; requiring training of local personnel and transfer of technology, including enhancing the coastal states' ability to conduct fisheries research. This provides all coastal states, but especially developing states, with a powerful array of techniques for ensuring conservation and these have been widely enacted and deployed.[122] There appears to be still much to be done to improve management and enforcement within EEZs, however. It has been reported that the pioneering US Fisheries Conservation and Management Act (FCMA) is not working well,[123] but some commentators consider that there is still room for optimism—foreign fishing has been reduced or eliminated; machinery established to manage fisheries; some success has been achieved in rebuilding stocks and the system

---

[120] The Bulletin on the Law of the Sea, UN Office of Ocean Affairs, UN, New York, Nos. 1–16, gives details of current claims and includes many current examples of relevant national laws, etc; see also *FAO Legislative Series*, 21 (1989), (Rev. 3) (Rome, 1990).

[121] For evaluation of state practice, see Juda, 18 *ODIL* (1987), 305–31; Wolfrum, 18 *NYIL* (1987), 121–44; Smith, *Exclusive Economic Zone Claims: An Analysis and Primary Documents* (Dordrecht, 1986).

[122] See *supra*, FAO Leg. Ser. No. 21 (Rev. 3); and n. 108.

[123] McHugh, 21 *ODIL* (1990), *passim*, esp. 260.

works better than any previously tried.[124] There is scope for improvement of enforcement by concentrating efforts on areas with high levels of non-compliance, improving the Fishery Management Plans required by the FCMA; addressing the post-harvesting stages of fisheries management; increasing severity of sanction; ensuring that enforcement authorities are consulted early in the formulation of management measures, and using more non-coercive factors of compliance including social pressure, self-interest, inducement, and obligation.[125]

An unusual aspect of the widespread enactment of 200-mile EEZs and EFZs is the effect within the European Community where the existence of EC Regulations implementing a Common Fisheries Policy (CFP) for community states immediately subjected these areas of extended maritime jurisdiction to a doctrine of equal conditions of access for all member states. The Community as such now sets and allocates the TAC and promulgates the relevant conservatory measures. It also represents its member states in the new NEAF Commission, North-West Atlantic Fisheries Organization, etc. casting a single Community vote; individual EC member states are no longer parties to the relevant fisheries conventions.[126] The community regime does not appear to have been any more effective than its predecessor, the NEAFC's. TACs have been set too high for political reasons; conservation measures have been inadequate and poorly enforced and too many fish, especially juvenile fish, have been discarded at sea under an enforcement regime requiring this to discourage catching of undersized fish.[127]

(f) The High Seas

Since many fish migrate between EEZs and the high seas and many species of marine mammals in particular may spend a considerable part of their lives there during their major migrations between their feeding and breeding grounds, the UNCLOS, in its Part VII relating to the High Seas, though recognizing that all states have the right for their nationals to engage in fishing on the high seas (a state not a private right) subjects this right to existing treaty obligations and the rights and interests of coastal states in conserving stocks that migrate between EEZs (or EFZs) and the high seas, as set out in Articles 63(2) and 64–7 and other specific provisions set out in that Part.[128]

---

[124] Miller, Hooker, and Fricke, 21 *ODIL* (1990), *passim*, esp. 286.

[125] Sutinec, Reiser, and Gauvin, *passim*, esp. 364–6.

[126] For a full account of the CFP of the European Community and its legal basis, see Churchill, *EEC Fisheries Law* (Dordrecht, 1987) and id. *Fisheries in the European Community*.

[127] Churchill, *Fisheries in the European Community*; Symes, 'North Sea Fisheries: Trends and Management Issues', in Freestone and IJlstra (eds.), *The North Sea: Perspectives on Regional Co-operation* (London, 1990), 271–87.

[128] UNCLOS, Part VII, Sec. 2, Article 116; see also Article 87 which codifies freedom of fishing on the high seas but 'subject to the conditions laid down in section 2'; Article 119(3) requires that conservation measures do not discriminate in form or in fact against fishermen of any state on the high seas.

These clearly lay down the duty of states to take, or to co-operate with other states in taking, the measures for their nationals that may be necessary to conserve that area's living resources.[129]

About 400 species are found outside 200-mile zones—fifty of cephalopods, forty of sharks, 230 of other species of fish, and sixty of marine mammals; catching in EEZs has put pressure on these stocks and integrated management in both areas is required.[130] Part VII spells out the duty to co-operate, requiring that states co-operate in the conservation and management of these resources and that states exploiting the same resources or different ones in the same area 'enter into negotiations with a view to taking the measures necessary for the conservation' of these resources. This somewhat imprecise formulation of the duty, which is open to interpretation, reflects the terminology used in the 1958 Conservation Convention. States are required also to co-operate in establishing regional and subregional fisheries organizations for this purpose but only 'as appropriate'.[131] However, Article 119 does specify the factors that states must take into consideration in determining the TAC and other conservation measures for the high seas, in terms that are somewhat similar to Article 61 (though unlike that article, it does not clearly require states to establish a TAC).

These articles do not require in terms, as does Article 61, that the states 'ensure through proper conservation and management measures that the maintenance of living resources is not endangered by over-exploitation'; the concept of management based on MSY qualified by both economic and environmental factors is, however, retained along with reference to consideration of interdependence of stocks, effects on associated species, and any 'generally recommended international minimum standards'. Finally, Article 65, concerning the management and conservation of marine mammals, which is discussed later in this chapter, is applied by Article 120 to conservation of marine mammals on the high seas.

It is clearly important for conservation of fisheries that, to the extent that states claim sovereign rights over fisheries in 200-mile EEZs or EFZs as laid down in the UNCLOS, or on the high seas, they at the same time implement in good faith a conservatory and management regime based on the principles and considerations set out in Article 61. It is apparent from the compendia of national fisheries legislation produced to date by the FAO[132] and the UN[133] and various individual analyses of state practice,[134] that states

[129] UNCLOS, Article 117.
[130] Fishing News International (FNI) (Aug. 1991), 30–1.
[131] UNCLOS, Article 118.
[132] op. cit. supra, n. 120.
[133] Ibid.
[134] e.g. Juda, 18 ODIL (1987); Smith, Exclusive Economic Zone Claims; and Wolfrum, 18 NYIL (1987); see also Hey, The Regime for the Exploitation; Kwiatkowska, The Exclusive Economic Zone,

are not doing so in any uniform fashion. That is not to say that in their administrative practice they do not heed these conservatory requirements, but that they do not obligate themselves to do so in their relevant national legislation partly because of the difficulties encountered in interpreting these provisions. Almost 100 states have now asserted sovereign rights over fisheries up to 200 miles from their coastline.[135] Since the 1970s about eighty of these have sought advice from FAO, either on the drafting of their new legislation, or the management and development of their fisheries or both.[136] Whilst FAO cannot, as a UN specialized agency, take any particular view on the interpretation of ambiguous provisions in the UNCLOS, it can advise on the choices facing its member states (about fifty of which have ratified the UNCLOS and almost all of which have signed it) concerning both interpretation and the complex problems of enactment and implementation of these provisions. This it has done, encouraging multidisciplinary studies, introduction of legal and administrative measures, reviewing existing agreements, evaluating the enforcement problems, and submitting, on request, reports and draft laws. In this process there has been a move away from the old-style conservation statute, as exemplified in UK fisheries laws,[137] based on highly specific prohibitions of the various fishing techniques, etc., outlined earlier in this chapter, towards a more general enunciation of objectives and the means of achieving them, an approach hitherto more familiar in civil than common law systems. This leaves details to be worked out in the light of subsequent experience but results in a diversity of solutions which makes evaluation of state practice difficult.

The general approach, however, remains a sectoral rather than the holistic one advocated in the conservation strategies since this allows for more precise and clear allocation of administrative and management responsibility than the holistic approach. Thus regulation of pollution sources and mineral exploitation is left to other enactments and sectors rather than added to old or modern fisheries conventions and laws enacting them, though the FAO Director-General's recent report to the FAO Committee on Fisheries indicates more awareness of the need to interrelate these issues.[138] UNEP on the other hand has begun to move in the 'holistic' direction, adding, for example, Protocols on Specially Protected Areas to its Barcelona[139] and Cartagena

---

45–93, esp. 45–6; 91–3; Attard, *The Exclusive Economic Zone in International Law*, 146–91, and esp. 152–6.

[135] FAO, op. cit. *supra*, 120, at 2.

[136] Information supplied by Dr W. Edeson, Development Law Service, FAO, Rome, 18 Mar. 1991.

[137] For a résumé of these, see *The Law of Scotland: Stair Memorial Encyclopedia* (London, 1990), xi, paras. 1–240.

[138] Opening Statement to COFI by Director-General of FAO, op. cit. *supra*, n. 1, at 2.

[139] Protocol Concerning Mediterranean Specially Protected Areas, concluded in Geneva, 3 Apr. 1982.

Conventions,[140] which could include fisheries conservation measures, since parties are required to conserve areas of special value, protect threatened or endangered species of flora and fauna and so to manage the latter as to prevent dangers or threats to their existence. UNEP has, in conjunction with concerned regional bodies, prepared a Convention for the Protection of the Natural Resources and Environment of the South Pacific Region (SPREP),[141] whose general obligations include 'environmental management and development of natural resources', albeit its major articles relate to pollution from various sources.

It is important, given the multiplicity of factors affecting fishery conservation, that flexibility be maintained in national legislation and that it be constantly revised. Current practice in this respect is of some interest. Most developing states inherited their legislation from the former colonial powers; thus it was based on the pre-1982 UNCLOS regime and is regarded by them and by FAO as inappropriate to extended coastal state management powers. Fisheries legislation, especially if drafted under FAO auspices, now typically provides for development of a Fisheries Management and Development Plan related to a specific management area and to exploited fisheries only. The United States Marine Mammal Protection Act 1972[142] and the Fishery Conservation and Management Act 1976[143] provided models for this, although more recent examples in developing country practice are simpler.[144] Rather than enacting the specific international obligations (a familiar practice in common law) reference is made to the fact that the state's exercise of its discretion in conservatory measures will be exercised 'according to international law' or 'taking account of existing international obligations'. Most laws remain silent concerning terms of access for foreign fishermen, not because no access will be given, but because of the political sensitivity of this issue and the need to retain flexibility in fisheries management. Thus, legislation commonly either allows in general terms for direct licensing of foreign fishermen or subjects this to conclusion of bilateral access agreements, or offers both alternatives. Rather than defining a 'foreign vessel' for this purpose, legislation now generally defines with some care a 'local fishing vessel'; vessels not conforming to these criteria *ipso facto* become foreign vessels.

[140] Protocol Concerning Specially Protected Areas and Wildlife in the Wider Caribbean Region, concluded Cartagena, 18 Jan. 1990.
[141] Adopted in Noumea in 1986. The first meeting of its Contracting Parties took place in July 1991. Problems arose concerning the desire of the SPREP to obtain autonomy from the South Pacific Commission under whose auspices it was established and whose Secretariat it shared. A new treaty may thus be sought; see *Ocean Policy News* (July 1991), 6.
[142] 16 USC, ss. 1361–2, 137–84, 1401–7 (Suppl. III) 1974; Pub. Law 92–522 (revised several times since its adoption in 1972).
[143] 16 USC. ss. 1801, *et seq.* (Suppl. 1977).
[144] See examples in FAO, op. cit. *supra*, n. 120.

Finally, it should be noted that the UNCLOS enforcement provisions, which prohibit imprisonment as a penalty for violation of fisheries laws[145] are not universally enacted, though conversely some states have abolished this penalty for foreign fishermen whilst retaining it for their own nationals. The Joint Enforcement Schemes instituted under the protocols to the former North-East (NEAFC) and North-West Atlantic (ICNAF) Fisheries Conventions, referred to earlier in this chapter, have not yet been replicated under the more recent regional conventions but the possibility is being considered both for the South Pacific and for the Caribbean.[146] The schemes, if any, are likely to remain limited, as in the past, to mutual inspection rights with offenders merely being reported to their flag states since problems remain concerning acceptability of evidence obtained in one state's jurisdiction for use in the courts of another in the absence of relevant bilateral or multilateral agreement (see Chapter 4).

(g) Common Stocks[147]

A problem that still arises, however, is how to conserve common stocks that traverse the EEZ and high seas/EEZ boundaries. No harmonized standards for conservation of such stocks on the high seas are laid down in the UNCLOS nor are they required to be applied in EEZs. Since fish continue to migrate, whatever the treaty provisions regulating their conservation, the problem of stocks that occur within the EEZs of two or more coastal states, or both within the EEZ and in the area beyond it, must be addressed since their effective conservation requires international co-operation between harvesting and coastal states to regulate them throughout their entire range, that regulations be based on scientific findings, and that this requires the harmonization of such findings. As we saw in Chapter 12, the 1979 Convention on Conservation of Migratory Species of Wild Animals recognizes this. UNCLOS obliges concerned coastal states and states fishing stocks beyond EEZs to 'seek to agree on the measures necessary to co-ordinate and ensure the conservation and development' of such stocks but allows them to do this either 'directly' (that is, bi- or multilaterally) *or* through appropriate regional or subregional organizations;[148] in other words, they are not *required* to use the latter processes. These requirements apply only in the EEZ, not the territorial sea, the relevant articles on which do not require conservation. Stocks could thus migrate from conservation to non-conservation zones and considerable

---

[145] UNCLOS, Article 73 at paras. 2 and 3.

[146] *OPN*, Nov. 1991, 1 states that a collective surveillance and enforcement scheme is being developed by the SPFFA.

[147] For an exhaustive account of this problem and its solution, see Hey, *The Regime for the Exploitation*, 53–118, inc. Annexes I A-H, II A-B, 131–92.

[148] UNCLOS, Article 63; for a critique of these provisions, see De Klemm, 29 *NRJ* (1989), 932–78; id. in Johnston (ed.), *The Environmental Law of the Sea* (Berlin, 1981), 71–192.

discrepancies in management could arise if stocks migrate through all three jurisdictional areas. Exploitation of a high seas stock might not adversely affect it in that area but could become a problem if the same stock is exploited in the EEZ or territorial sea or both and this is not dealt with as a linked problem. Chile, noting the UNCLOS weaknesses in relation to straddling stocks, has proposed that a treaty governing their harvesting and conservation should be concluded.[149]

(3) The Species Specific Approach

It was proposed at the UNCLOS that special regimes should be laid down for certain species that migrate in various ways. The origins of this approach lie more in allocation of access and jurisdictional rights than conservation but the provisions, of course, also allocate control for this purpose. The UNCLOS specifically addresses the following five categories of species.

(a) Highly Migratory Species (HMS)[150]

These are listed in Annex I of the UNCLOS and include various species of tuna, marlin, sail-fish, swordfish, dolphin, shark, and cetacea. The Annex is, however, neither comprehensive (it does not include squid or krill, for example) nor amendable. Although there is a separate article protecting marine mammals, cetaceans were left on Annex I also because small cetaceans are caught incidentally in the monofilament nylon nets used by the tuna industry and it falls within the ambit of ICCAT and the ITTC to deal with this problem.

In addition to the other EEZ requirements, Article 64 requires coastal and other states fishing in a region for the HMS to co-operate directly or through 'appropriate' international organizations 'with a view' to ensuring *and* promoting optimum utilization—thus giving this aim priority over conservation. Unlike marine mammals (under Article 65) HMS are not removed from this requirement. The requirement applies throughout the region, within *and* beyond the EEZ. If no organization exists, the states involved must co-operate to establish one and participate in it. Difficulties could arise if no agreement is concluded for high seas areas (as is required under Article 63(2) for stocks within the EEZ) and concerning how far the wide discretion accorded to coastal states under Articles 61 and 62 undermines the aims of this article. The alternative of direct co-operation means that some HMS may not be

---

[149] *OPN* (Dec. 1989), 2. For Chile's proposal to UNCED, see 19 *LOSB* (1991), 42–4.

[150] For a comprehensive analysis of the relevant principles and finer points of these provisions, see Burke, 14 *ODIL* (1984), 273–314; id., 'Impacts of the UN Convention on the Law of the Sea on Tuna Regulation', *FAO Legislative Study No. 26*, 1982; Castilla and Orrego-Vicuna, 9 *Ocean Management* (1984), 21–33; Weld, 20 *ODIL* (1989), 285–95.

conserved throughout their entire range.[151] There is no clear obligation to establish an organization where one does not exist, or if existing organizations have not proved successful in getting all states involved to participate.[152] The problem of by-catches of dolphins, etc. is not directly addressed; the use of driftnets has, however, become such a serious problem that it has recently been the subject of a GA resolution[153] and a regional convention.[154]

The weaknesses of this article stem from the US wish to remove HMS as far as possible from coastal state control in the EEZ and subject their management to international regulation to ensure that coastal state rights in respect of HMS could be exercised in the same way as over other coastal species. The coastal state thus cannot exercise its right to make decisions until it has discharged its duty to co-operate with other states in promoting conservation and use. The concerned developing coastal states, however, wanted to protect their prior sovereign rights to tuna, etc. as EEZ resources and had been seeking in the tuna commissions higher quotas for 'Resource Adjacent Nations' (RANs). Article 67 tries to accommodate both views. This approach does not seem to be working so far as current state practice is concerned.[155] Following the establishment in 1987 of the South Pacific Forum Fisheries Agency (SPFFA),[156] under the auspices of FAO, it introduced a licensing system for the catching, *inter alia*, of tuna in the Convention area, which comprises the 200-mile zones of participating states and entities, the high seas areas enclosed by these, and certain other specified areas in the Pacific Ocean, which may be added by any party. The United States has paid a considerable sum to the Commission in return for access to a fixed quota of tuna.[157]

As it has, however, proved impossible to persuade all coastal states in whose EEZs relevant tuna stocks are located to participate in the Commissions, the position in customary law thus is now uncertain. Most tuna fishing states, including Japan (the largest), regard HMS as included within the living

---

[151] For the effects of failure to co-operate and the manner of co-operation, see Burke, 14 *ODIL* (1984), 283–93.

[152] Joseph, 1 *Marine Policy* (1977), 275; Joseph and Greenough, *International Management of Tuna, Porpoises and Billfish* (Seattle, 1979).

[153] UNGA Res. 44/225 of 22 Dec. 1989 in which it expressed its concern relating to the problems raised by this practice and asked interested members of the international community to review the scientific data and adopt certain measures for subsequent developments; see Large-scale Pelagic Driftnet Fishing, FAO Doc. COFI/91/5, Jan. 1991 and Report of the Expert Consultation on Large-scale Pelagic Driftnet Fishing, FAO Doc. COFI/91/Inf. 9, Feb. 1991.

[154] Wellington Convention for the Prohibition of Fishing with Long Driftnets in the South Pacific, 1989; see FAO Doc. COFI/91/5, Suppl. I, Apr. 1991, 4.

[155] Burke, 14 *ODIL* (1984), 150.

[156] See Swan, in Soons, *Implementation* 318–43, for details of the practice of the SPFFA; see also Tsamenyi, 10 *Marine Policy* (1986), 29–41, who points out the need to retain ambiguity concerning the issue of sovereignty over HMS in order to secure an agreement (31–6, 41).

[157] *OPN* (Apr. 1987), 1–2.

resources subject to their sovereign rights in the EEZ or EFZ but the US formally continues to insist that customary law excludes coastal states from asserting sovereign rights over tuna. The US Fishery Conservation and Management Act of 1976 and the Reagan Proclamation of an EEZ[158] excluded tuna from US fishery jurisdiction though at the same time asserting rights over all other HMS. The United States bases its position on: the fact that tuna do not reside in EEZs and thus cannot be effectively managed by the coastal state; on Article 64 of UNCLOS; on state practice and on the long-standing nature of its position.[159] The Convention at least represents an improvement on this situation in requiring co-operation in conservation and management since national legislation generally does not evidence this obligation and Indian Ocean coastal and fishing states are now considering giving effect to it by adopting an agreement to establish an Indian Ocean Tuna Commission to control increasing fishing of tuna stocks in that region.[160]

The UNEP Noumea Convention for the South Pacific has been referred to earlier in the context of bringing together within one 'umbrella' framework the protection of natural resources *and* of the marine environment from pollution. It also addresses the problem of high seas enclaves, so-called 'donut holes', which are wholly surrounded by the EEZs of one or more states (as in the Behring Sea where the surrounding states are currently endeavouring to negotiate a co-operation agreement rather than extending their jurisdiction to cover the whole area[161]) but over which the coastal states have no control. These present another conservatory problem concerning HMS, which is not provided for in the UNCLOS.[162] Overall the South Pacific solutions provide a better solution than those currently operative in the Atlantic Ocean,[163] though problems of enforcement remain for adjacent developing states whose zones now cover vast areas.[164]

(b) Marine Mammals[165]

These include the twelve species of so-called great whales, many of which were previously hunted to near extinction; small cetaceans; dolphins; porpoises;

---

[158] 22 *ILM* (1983), 461–9.

[159] Weld, 20 *ODIL* (1989), 294; he advocates elimination of the existing exclusion of tuna from US jurisdictional control under the Magnusson FCMA; but cf. Hilborn and Sibert, 12 *Marine Policy* (1988), 31–9 who consider that some stocks may be considered 'resident' and not require international management though international co-operation on data analysis is required.

[160] Report of Eighteenth Session of the Committee on Fisheries, Rome (1989), FAO Doc. COFI/91/Inf. 7, Feb. 1991, 89, Paris 111–15

[161] See *OPN* (Aug. 1991), 3; also *FNI* (Sept. 1991), 3; negotiations proved difficult, with the USSR favouring a moratorium on all 'donut-hole' fisheries and the United States initially rejecting it but agreement seems likely.

[162] See Burke, 14 *ODIL* (1984), 294; negotiations have, however, now begun to establish a new forum to manage fishing in this area, *OPN* (Aug. 1991), 3.

[163] See Weld, 20 *ODIL* (1989).

[164] See Swan, in Soons, *Implementation*; Tsamenyi, 10 *Marine Policy* (1986); Doulman, 11 *Marine Policy* (1987); Moore, in *Essays in Memory of Jean Carroz*, FAO (Rome, 1987), 159.

[165] See Birnie, *International Regulation of Whaling*, 2 vols. (Dobbs Ferry, NY, 1985); i, ch. 1,

pinnipeds (seals); sirenians; and marine otters. Article 65, headed 'Marine Mammals', is *not* it should be noted confined to Annex I, which relates to Article 64(1) (HMS). These species are, thus, for the first time, fully protected in a UN Convention, since Article 65 is extended by Article 120 to the high seas. It states that:

Nothing in this Convention restricts the right of a coastal state or international organization, as appropriate, to prohibit, limit or regulate the exploitation of marine mammals more strictly than provided for in this Part. States shall co-operate with a view to the conservation of marine mammals and in the case of cetaceans shall in particular work through the appropriate international organizations for their conservation, management and study.

This removes marine mammals from the full application of Part V in that optimum utilization is not required. States can prohibit all taking unilaterally (many now do so)[166] or through international organizations. But the article does not in terms require states to join any particular international body; merely, for cetaceans, to 'work through' *the* 'appropriate body'. In the view of environmentalists the International Whaling Commission (IWC) (see Chapter 12) is the only appropriate body; Canada, however, took the view that the form of co-operation offered in NAFO (providing non-regulatory areas in the EEZ) was the most appropriate, at least for small cetaceans.[167] Article 65 is confusing in its reference to organizations in the plural; its drafters had in mind the use of tuna commissions to control the incidental catch of dolphins and small cetaceans, as well as the IWC for the conservation of the large cetaceans. The Canadian view is that the obligation to 'work through' is fulfilled if the organization is merely consulted or its scientific advice sought and that the state concerned can determine which organization is appropriate. As small cetaceans within the NAFO area are found mainly in the Canadian EEZ, it would be for Canada to manage them; consultation with NAFO would be voluntary and on Canada's initiative. Several states with small cetaceans in their EEZs have in the IWC consistently voted against any extension of its regulatory role to small cetaceans either as a group or (with minor exceptions) *ad hoc*.[168] Some of these actively seek revision of the ICRW, to bring it into line with the NAFO approach to EEZs. Attempts to conclude 'Range State Agreements' for certain species of small cetaceans

for a detailed account of these, and ibid. *passim* for all aspects of the legal problems involved in conservation of marine mammals. See also id., *Legal Measures for the Conservation of Marine Mammals*, IUCN Environmental Policy and Law Paper, 19 (1982); Scarff, 6 *ELQ* (1977), 323–571; Tønnessen and Johnston, *The History of Modern Whaling* (London, 1982).

[166] For examples, see Marashi, Compendium of National Legislation on the Conservation of Marine Mammals, i, FAO/UNEP Project No. 0502-78/02, FAO, Rome (1986).

[167] Written Statements by the delegation of Canada, 2 Apr. 1980, UNCLOS Doc A/Conf. 62/WS/4.

[168] As recorded in the Annual Reports of the International Whaling Commission; see also Birnie, *International Regulation of Whaling*, and id., 5 *Marine Policy* (1981), 277–80.

in some areas under the 1979 Convention on Migratory Species outside the ICRW have similarly been blocked to date although efforts continue. Some consider that the ICRW can be interpreted to cover conservation of threatened small cetaceans if added to its Schedule; others suggest that a new global convention on small cetaceans should be negotiated but it is unlikely that all present members of the IWC would adhere to such a convention which would thus be divisive and less than fully effective.[169]

It can be argued also that Article 65 applies in the territorial sea (though UNCLOS is not specific on this point), since it states 'nothing in the Convention'[170] restricts...; not 'nothing in this Part' and the Whaling Convention applies to whaling in the territorial sea. Since marine mammals, especially the large cetaceans because of their many special characteristics, require careful management through their entire range to conserve them effectively, it is desirable to adopt the interpretation that best fulfils this aim, consonant with the interpretative rules of the Vienna Convention on the Law of Treaties.[171] The ambiguous language used in the UNCLOS was a compromise designed to allay the fears of Latin American and other states that its application to all cetaceans in the EEZ would be obligatory, whilst meeting US interest in securing legitimation of the higher standards adopted in their Marine Mammal Protection Act.

Article 65 is in any case incomplete in its conservatory aspects since it omits any reference to international enforcement requirements; this is left, as for fisheries, to flag and coastal states.[172] An International Observer Scheme was instituted under the ICRW (as amended), based on mutual exchange of observers under bilateral or multilateral agreements between IWC member states but this is now ineffective because of the moratorium on commercial whaling currently adopted by the IWC. A further weakness of Article 65 is that it does not address the problems of habitat disturbance, harassment, and pollution, though marine mammals are particularly susceptible to these threats, nor does it remove them from the possible prohibition of scientific

---

[169] Birnie, 29 *NRJ* (1989), 903–34.

[170] Emphasis added.

[171] These are laid down in Article 31; for text, see Brownlie, *Basic Documents in International Law* (3rd edn., Oxford, 1984), 349–86.

[172] The problems this gives rise to are discussed in Rosati, 14 *CWILJ* (1984), 114–47; he proposes at 147 n. 157 a mutual enforcement permit system in EEZs. The United States has used economic sanctions instituted by amendment of national fishery laws, which provide for prohibition of access to fisheries in the US EEZ, and banning of imports of fish and other products from states that undermine conservation conventions, including the Whaling Convention, to which the US is a party (ibid. 136–8). However, a panel of the General Agreement on Tariffs and Trade (GATT) recently found a US ban on import of Mexican tuna products in 1990 was in violation of the GATT. See *supra*, pp. 131–4. Nevertheless, trade restrictions are approved in the 1973 CITES, the 1990 Protocol Concerning Special Areas and Wildlife for the Wider Caribbean Region and the 1989 Wellington Convention for the Prohibition of Fishing with Long Driftnets in the South Pacific, *inter alia*.

research directed at their characteristics within the EEZ and territorial sea.[173] Although IWC member states are required to provide data, to co-operate in doing so and to base regulations on scientific findings, given the disparities in facilities available to different member states, the scientific advice available thus may not be the best.

As Article 65 has by no means solved the problems of effectively protecting marine mammals, and the IWC has many weaknesses, though global in scope,[174] we must look also to the other relevant conventions, discussed in Chapter 12, which address a wide variety of aspects of the conservatory problem; states have not fully exploited the potential of these. The preservation of the great whales has thus presented and continues to present one of the most difficult and well-publicized challenges to the development of environmental law, since some IWC member states such as Norway, Iceland, and Japan retain an interest in resuming whaling and are currently pressing for allocation of quotas for the taking at least of minke whales, while others seek to maintain the current prohibition on commercial whaling indefinitely.[175] The issue is no longer entirely one of the interpretation of 'conservation' in Article V of the ICRW, or the weight to be accorded to it in relation to 'utilization' of whales, but whether the law should identify and protect certain unique species for other values (see Chapters 5 and 11) and, therefore, prohibit exploitation.

(c) Anadromous and Catadromous Species

These species also are removed from the other provisions of Part V, thus optimum utilization is not required. Anadromous species are those spawned inland, in freshwater rivers, but which spend the major part of their lives at sea, passing through the territorial sea and EEZ to the high seas, before returning to die in the rivers in which they originated. Conservatory measures adopted by the state of origin are rendered useless if the species are over-exploited on the high seas, as happened in particular in the case of North Atlantic Salmon.[176] Salmon are the most commercially valuable of anadromous species. Salmon originating in Canada, Norway, and Scotland and other states bordering the Atlantic, migrate to feeding grounds in the Davis Strait off Greenland and off the Faroe Islands where they intermingle before they

---

[173] Articles 56 and 238–57, taken together, could have this effect.

[174] Birnie, *International Regulation of Whaling*, 635–60; see also *supra*, Ch. 12.

[175] See Chairman's Report of the 43rd Meeting, 27–31 May 1991, IWC, Oct. 1991, International Whaling Commission.

[176] For accounts of this problem, see Windsor, 'A New Treaty to Manage Salmon in the North Atlantic', unpub. paper given by the Secretary of the North Atlantic Salmon Conservation Organization at the Greenwich Forum Conference, Edinburgh, 1–4 Apr. 1984; Little, 28 *Jnl. of Law Soc. of Scotland* (1983), 223–6; for the problems concerning salmon in the North Pacific and revision of the International North Pacific Fisheries Commission, see Miles, in *Essays in Memory of Jean Carroz*.

return to their country of origin. Danish fishermen, having discovered their location, began to take them in the 1970s in increasingly large numbers so that the number of individual salmon returning to the rivers decreased sharply affecting tourism and its by-products and local fishing rights and trade.

The UNCLOS provides that the state in whose rivers the stocks originate has the primary interest in and responsibility for these stocks[177] but, in return for prior rights to exploit them, it must ensure their conservation by establishing appropriate regulatory measures for this purpose and for determining access to these stocks landward of the outer boundary of its EEZ.[178] They are only allowed to be exploited on the high seas in exceptional circumstances.[179] TAC's *can* be set by the state of origin in consultation with other interested states (though it is not required to reach agreement with them)[180] but it is not obliged to set a TAC (or determine its own harvesting capacity), though it retains the discretion to adopt other measures that ensure conservation.

If the banning of fishing on the high seas causes economic dislocation in other states,[181] the state of origin must consult with them in determining the necessary conservation measures, which must have due regard to the needs and conservation requirements of the state of origin. Enforcement (which must respect high-seas freedoms) must be agreed among the state of origin and the others concerned. The state of origin must also co-operate with other states fishing the species, not only on the high seas, but in all areas where fishing has taken place;[182] states fishing the stocks, which have invested in renewal of the stocks in co-operation with the state of origin, by concluding arrangements which give special consideration to these in harvesting the stock;[183] and states through whose EEZ the stocks migrate.

It is not clear whether such coastal states can exercise jurisdiction over stocks not originating in their territory and which they have never fished.[184] The article thus establishes a special discrete conservatory regime, apart from others in Part V; conservation is the aim here, with the secondary interests of other states balanced by co-operation through consultation.

Most fisheries conventions exclude application to salmon and generally, therefore, we have to look for conclusion of specific new conventions and evidence of state practice in relation to this provision of the 1982 UNCLOS to evaluate its status. It is clear that these provisions are entering into state practice as actions under several new treaties or existing treaties illustrate, in particular the innovatory 1982 Reykjavik Convention for the Conservation of

---

[177] UNCLOS, Article 66(1); Article 116(b) also subjects freedom of fishing on the high seas to the rights and interests of coastal states 'as provided in the Convention', i.e. including in Article 66.

[178] Ibid. Article 66(2).　　[179] Ibid. (3)(a).　　[180] Ibid. (2).

[181] Ibid. (3)(a).　　[182] Ibid. (3)(b).　　[183] Ibid. (3)(c).

[184] Hey, *The Regime for the Exploitation*, 64.

Salmon in the North Atlantic Ocean (NASCO).[185] Its Preamble acknowledges the developments in the UNCLOS and specifically provides for acquisition, analysis, and dissemination of scientific information pertaining to the sea salmon stocks, and the conservation, restoration, enhancement, and rational management of these stocks through international co-operation (Article 3(2)). The treaty divides the North Atlantic into three areas, each with its own Regional Commission (Article 3(3)(b)), which provides the forum for consultation and co-operation between the members (Article 4), who can propose regulatory measures and make recommendations to the Council (Article 3(3)(a)) concerning the undertaking of scientific research. The Council must seek the best available information, including ICES' advice. The Commissions must take account of various complex environmental and economic factors, including: efforts of states of origin to implement and enforce measures for conservation, restoration, enhancement, and rational management of stocks in their rivers and waters; the extent to which salmon stocks feed in the area of jurisdiction of each party; the relative effects of harvesting salmon at different stages in their migratory routes; the contribution of parties other than the states of origin to the conservation of salmon which migrate into their areas of jurisdiction, so limiting their catches; the interests of the communities which are particularly dependent on salmon fishery (Article 9).

The first meeting of NASCO was the first time the countries involved in exploiting this species throughout its migration had met together to discuss a problem that essentially had existed for 800 years. The meeting defined the scientific questions, put these to ICES, issued regulatory measures (TACs), discussed the relative rights of originating and 'grazing' (intercepting) states, exchanged information on their laws and established a small secretariat. As its secretary has remarked 'It opens up a new Chapter in the long and distinguished legal history of the salmon'.[186] Recently, however, problems

---

[185] Text in EEC, OJ. 1982, L.. 378, 25; Cmnd. 8830 (1983); the original parties were Canada, EEC, Denmark (for Faroe Islands and Greenland), Finland, Iceland, Norway, Sweden, United States. For further discussion, see Churchill, *EEC Fisheries Law*, 189; Windsor 'A New Treaty'. See also 1985 Treaty Concerning Pacific Salmon between Canada and the United States described in Hey, *The Regime for the Exploitation*, Annex VB, 263. Yanagida, 81 *AJIL* (1987), 577–91, draws attention to the practical difficulties of operating the complex devolved solutions this treaty provides. These involve decision-making and management by four states, one province, and many American Indian and other tribes as well as the application of equitable principles for catch distribution under a treaty which recognizes the special interest of the country of origin in conservation of stocks and provides incentives for it to maintain, conserve, and enhance habitats. A protocol amending the International Convention for the High Seas Fisheries of the North Pacific Ocean, between Japan, Canada, United States 30 *TIAS* 9242 and 205 *UNTS* 80 has now been discontinued, but creation of a new forum which will include the USSR is currently under way. See *OPN* (Aug. 1991), 3.

[186] Windsor, 'A New Treaty', 8. The Annual Reports of NASCO are obtainable from its Secretary.

appear to have been arising in relation to uncontrolled fishing by non-parties on the high seas, impairing NASCO's initial success.

Catadromous species are the opposite of the above; they are spawned at sea and spend the major part of their lives in rivers and lakes. The species of main commercial interest are eels on which coastal industries are based in several states. Article 67 provides that coastal states in whose waters these species spend the major part of their life-cycle are responsible for their conservation and management;[187] they have the primary interest. Exploitation is permitted only to landward of the outer limit of the EEZ. Exploitation in the EEZ is subject to the provisions of Article 67 and those relating to the EEZ.[188] When migrating through another state's EEZ, they are to be regulated both by the state in whose waters they spend the major part of their life-cycle and the state through whose waters they migrate, which must conclude agreements providing for rational management, taking account of the special interest of the former state.[189]

As with anadromous species, Article 116 subjects the freedom of fishing in the high seas to the rights and interests of the coastal states under Article 67, *inter alia*. The 'home' state must ensure conservation *and* optimum utilization of the species (as is required under Articles 61 and 62 for other fish). It must implement the EEZ regime by conserving the species, determining the TAC and its own harvesting capacity, and concluding agreements with third states if a surplus is declared. This is not a different, distinct regime, as is that for anadromous stocks. However, the required co-operative agreements are different from those required for common stocks under Article 63, under which states are on an equal footing; here the 'home' state interest prevails. As exploitation beyond the EEZ is banned, no agreements will need to be concluded for these stocks. As no particular manner of co-operation is prescribed states can act bilaterally or through international organizations.

6. CONCLUSIONS

Despite the major changes and developments in the legal regime for conservation of marine living resources at the international, regional, and national levels, outlined in this chapter, the new perceptions of the aims and objectives of this regime, and general acceptance of the obligation to conserve marine species and stocks thereof, as well as the promulgation of strategies and conventions for achieving these, considered in this chapter and Chapters 11 and 12, doubts remain concerning the effectiveness of the new regime. In particular, the holistic or ecological approach coupled with the proposals by some for multispecies management, does not seem to have been widely

---

[187] UNCLOS, Article 67(1).   [188] Ibid. (2).   [189] Ibid. (2).

adopted in state practice, even by the developed states, including the European Community, which should be better equipped than most states with funds, institutions, and technical and scientific expertise to organize this. Even where it has been included in the substantive treaty articles, as in the CCAMLR, it is difficult to interpret and not successfully applied in practice,[190] as is the term 'conservation' itself.

The 'soft' terminology of the strategies, the removal with the advent of EEZs and EFZs, of over 40 per cent of the seas from international control, the consequently increased power of coastal states and diminution in the role of international commissions in developing and enforcing international conservatory measures, do not necessarily provide sufficiently sharp tools for achievement of the regime's purposes. The world fish catch is rising steadily, as pointed out at the beginning of this chapter; it is expected to rise by a further 20 million tonnes in about a decade. Thus in fourteen years it will rise by an amount exceeding the total world catch before the First World War. On the other hand, a recent study has revealed that developing states themselves have not greatly increased their catches and the earlier pattern of domination of fisheries by twenty major fishing states has been retained, despite the widespread adoption of EEZs and EFZs. Developing states have apparently preferred to garner income from licence fees and other benefits levied on foreign vessels, but are now thus facing major enforcement problems.[191]

Even developed states are finding it difficult to direct fishing effort to the species most able to sustain it and to restrict increases where the stocks can no longer sustain the rising or even previous catch levels, since complex social, economic, and political pressures are involved despite general acceptance of Part V of the UNCLOS and its requirements of conservation and maintenance of optimum sustainable yield. It was recently reported that unless four out of every ten fishing boats in the European Community are scrapped there will soon be no cod, haddock, or other species left to fish in the North Sea, no herring or sprats in the Baltic, and very few fish in other European Community waters either.[192] In the North Sea an independent expert group reported that mortality rates were too high for over 90 per cent of main species caught; they were four times higher than the maximum which would allow a sustainable yield of these species. Only a drastic reduction of 40 per cent of fishing effort would save them.[193] Without reduction in effort of the EC fleets there is a danger that they might try to recoup their losses in international waters where 25 per cent of the Community catch is now made,

---

[190] Howard, 38 *ICLQ* (1985), 114, 135, 140–5. See also *FNI* (Aug. 1991), 8–11.

[191] Juda, 18 *ODIL* (1987), 17–18; cf. also Ponte Corvo, 12 *Marine Policy* (1988), 361–72.

[192] *The Times*, 24 Jan. 1991, 14.

[193] McElroy draws similar conclusions concerning reduction of purse seine vessels in the Java Seas, 15 *Marine Policy* (1991), 271; but note that Spanish fishing vessel owners dispute the North Sea conclusions; see *FNI* Vigo 91 Suppl., Sept. 1991, 2.

since the Community is the world's largest fish importer and there has been a marked shift in dietary preferences therein from meat to fish. Any fleet reductions would have to be accompanied by increased surveillance and enforcement; satellites and integrated computer-vessel location networks are now available for this purpose. The sophisticated quota system introduced by the EC for its multispecies catches requires grading of fish caught by species and size; a computer system can now be used for this, which also improves enforcement[194] but this further highlights the problems experienced by developing countries in enforcing catch restrictions in their EEZs.

It seems likely that there will be growing pressure also on developing states to increase their catches, not only for local consumption, to solve food problems, but also for export purposes, to increase national income and support development. In these circumstances, the strategy of sustainable development advocated especially by the WCED, which is to be addressed by the UNCED, is of particular importance. Developing states, however, generally do not have sophisticated enforcement methods available to them and, unlike in the EC, there are no social funds available for restructuring their industries if they allow their own fleets or access by foreign fleets to exceed the OSY.

In all these circumstances, the more purely conservation-directed treaties discussed in Chapter 12, that aim to conserve threatened or endangered wildlife in general, become of increasing relevance and importance, as more marine species become threatened. Since most of these conventions are based on a system whereby the substantive articles of the treaty are used to express the general conservatory obligations but the particular species whose immediate protection or survival requires that measures be taken, are listed on amendable appendices to the convention, it is possible to add endangered marine species, such as marine mammals and amphibians, or such other species as may be threatened, to these appendices as required. The status for conservation purposes of such species then becomes discussable in forums other than fishery commissions and regulations can be developed by conferences or councils of states which will include states other than coastal or fishing states and thus enhance the pressure for conservation, as in the IWC. As experience in the IWC indicates, however, progress is likely to be slow in redefining, or defining more specifically the content of the obligation to conserve living resources and if the balance between conservation and economic interests is not well maintained exploiting states are likely to threaten withdrawal. The general acceptance of the need for sustainable development, however, has also enhanced acceptance of a legal obligation to conserve living resources for this purpose, especially fisheries.

Though it can be deduced from the practice outlined in this chapter that most states consider that they are under a duty to co-operate in conservation

---

[194] *Times* (24 Jan. 1991); see also Moore, in *Essays in Memory of Jean Carroz*.

of fisheries, this opinion is not universally shared; certainly many states, even in the EC, do not apparently consider themselves to be under an obligation *effectively* to conserve fish stocks, either by agreeing to quotas based on scientific advice (which may be uncertain) or stringently enforcing quotas, especially on their own nationals. Thus, the goals of the strategies and principles are not being achieved. Proposals for holistic or multi-species management are, in the light of this evidence, unlikely to be implemented.[195] Thus there is some support for abandoning government controlled fishing licensing systems and awarding rights to take these resources to private owners, who, it is argued, would then themselves have an interest in effectively regulating their own activities since they would otherwise devalue the worth of their private property rights; such a scheme has been introduced in New Zealand but appears to be leading to creation of monopolies of corporate right holders.[196] Such solutions, in any case, may not work well elsewhere, where there are many fishermen, from many different countries, with long-standing fishing practices and overlapping jurisdictional zones, as in the North Sea, Mediterranean, or Baltic.

The problem centres, even for states that clearly accept a duty to conserve living resources, in the lack of clear definition of the concept or term 'conservation' and the factors involved. Its expression in UNCLOS, Article 61, in terms of OSY modified by economic and developmental as well as environmental factors allows too much scope for avoidance of scientific advice. As Kwiatkowska points out these principles 'are not of a norm-creating character; but constitute what could be called '*obligationes imperfectae*', simplified guidelines that states may apply according to their circumstances.[197] This problem is exacerbated by the uncertainties inherent in scientific advice when scientific data is lacking. Steps are slowly being undertaken to remedy this, in FAO and through creation of new *ad hoc* multilateral scientific bodies such as the Pacific International Council for Exploration of the Sea (PICES),[198] but questions are arising concerning the whole approach to fisheries regulation by quotas based on uncertain scientific advice which allows them continually to be set too high and there is likely to be more resort to limitation of effort by the licensing of all fishing vessels, to take specified quantities of fish, at least in developed states; artisanal fisheries in developing states, however, would be less susceptible to such controls. There is also increasing perception that certain species, areas, or impacts require specific and special measures of protection; for example, Article 194(5) of the UNCLOS requires parties to

[195] Gulland, 11 *Marine Policy* (1987), 259; id., 8 *Marine Policy* (1984), 137–50, esp. 142–5; Juda and Burroughs, 14 *Marine Policy* (1990), 23–35.
[196] Pearse, 11 *Jnl. of Bus. Admin.* (1980), 185–209; Neher, Arnson, and Mollett (eds.), *Rights Based Fishing* (Dordrecht, 1989), esp. 117–45.
[197] Kwiatkowska, *The Exclusive Economic Zone*, 93.
[198] *OPN* (Aug. 1991), 3 and 6.

take measures to protect and preserve rare or fragile ecosystems, as well as the habitat of depleted, threatened, or endangered species and other forms of marine life, and similarly Article 196(1) requires that they prevent the intentional or accidental introduction of alien or new species to a particular part of the marine environment which may cause significant and harmful changes thereto. Environmental impact assessment, now increasingly required for potentially polluting activities and further elaborated by the new ECE Convention,[199] should include their effect on fisheries, as a recent proposal to pipe to California water from Alaskan rivers in which salmon spawn exemplifies; the effect on salmon migration has been overlooked.[200]

FAO has indicated that the 'sustainability' required by the environmental and development strategies implies that resources can be reduced by fishing to some agreed level at which their existence, that is, their reproductive capacity, is not threatened. 'Conservation' in relation to fisheries as perceived in the UNCLOS and other relevant treaties implies that this level can be fixed by determining the MSY on the basis of scientific findings and then modifying it by social, economic, and environmental factors, including interrelationship of species with their habitat and their interdependence with other species. As this chapter illustrates, this process is becoming both increasingly complex and increasingly politicized. It is thus unlikely that international law will provide any more specific definition of these terms in this context. However, though it still remains for states to elaborate through their practice the content of 'conservation' and to balance the factors involved, whether this is applied in their EEZs, EFZs, or on the high seas, to straddling stocks or highly migratory species of various kinds, they will, if the new EIA Convention is widely ratified, be unable to avoid acceptance of an obligation to co-operate and to undertake assessment of environmental effects if both environment and development are to be sustained. The Code of Conduct for Sustainable Fishing being developed by FAO following UNCED should also enhance this.

[199] 1991 Convention on Environmental Impact Assessment, *supra*, Ch. 3.
[200] *FNI* (Aug. 1991), 8.

14
Conclusions

A sceptic assessing the present state of international environmental law might make three main criticisms: that it remains preponderantly 'soft' in character, unsystematic and insufficiently comprehensive in scope, and weak in its enforcement and implementation. As we have seen, there are some grounds for such criticisms. Nevertheless, they overlook the significance of the broad framework for further development of the law to protect the environment that has now been established, and in certain respects fail to take account of what has been achieved since 1972.

Proponents of the view that international environmental law is still largely 'soft' in character and lacks the evidence of state practice and sufficiently widespread international support to generate rules of customary law binding on all states, or at least on most of them,[1] tend to emphasize the scarcity and particularity of judicial precedents, the difficulty of drawing conclusions from environmental treaties, and the unhelpful generality of such rules of customary law as can be identified, including the obligation to reduce and prevent environmental harm, or the requirement of consultation and co-operation on transboundary issues. Much of this sort of criticism frequently betrays unfamiliarity with the range of material on which this book has drawn, and a failure to devote sufficient attention to identifying the content of the rules in question. Moreover, although customary rules do often have an unhelpful generality, this criticism ignores the interplay of custom and treaty regimes, which has become, as we have seen, the major means of giving specific content to otherwise amorphous principles.[2] This is as true in the case of pollution as it is for wildlife conservation.

Critics who point to the piecemeal and unstructured development of the law in this field draw attention to the fact that much *ad hoc* lawmaking has occurred in response to environmental disasters such as Chernobyl or loss of the *Torrey Canyon*. But this characteristic also reflects the diversity of regional lawmaking and the conflicts of interest this reveals, particularly between North and South. The consequent lack of a global codification of basic principles adds to the belief that at present international environmental law is neither sufficiently coherent nor comprehensive in scope to support a policy of

---

[1] See e.g. Schachter, 'The Emergence of International Environmental Law', in *International Law in Theory and Practice* (Boston, 1991).

[2] See Ch. 3.

sustainable development or to facilitate the integration of environmental and developmental concerns sought by the UNCED.

The third group of critics observes the generally poor record of states in implementing and enforcing environmental treaties, even when widely ratified, and the inadequacy of the international legal system in dealing with the enforcement of international environmental law. The ICJ's limited jurisdiction, the lack of opportunity for public interest representation, in particular by NGOs, and the excessive reliance on political forms of international accountability lead on this view to a weak system of law of limited effectiveness.

How one responds to these criticisms is largely a function of one's views on the nature of international law and the way in which the international legal system functions. The authors of this book have taken a predominantly conservative approach to international lawmaking, and have not sought to invest policy statements, conference declarations, or 'soft-law' guidelines and recommendations with greater authority than, in their view, they can bear. Such instruments are best treated as affording some evidence of *opinio iuris* in appropriate cases, and as exerting a potential influence over state practice and the development of international law, but not as constituting law itself. An attempt has therefore been made to pay particular attention to state practice, in so far as that can be observed, and to the bilateral and especially the multilateral treaties which have formed the bulk of new international law in this field. Although evaluation of the precise character of existing customary rules, and even more so of general principles of law from which it is permissible to draw inferences, is not without difficulty, and is in the final analysis a matter of judgement, as stressed in Chapter 1, there is today rather more evidence for the existence of customary rules, including those discussed in Chapter 3, than sceptics have in the past suggested. Certainly, there is no doubt that the content of customary international environmental law today is much less modest than was true in 1972.[3] Even if in practice customary environmental law has not been the subject of much judicial elaboration or of widely accepted codification, it has exercised an influence, both in structuring the resolution of environmental disputes, such as those involving watercourses or fisheries conservation, and as a basis for negotiation of treaty regimes. That it has been the subject of attention in a number of ILC topics, in the work of the UNCED, and more recently in the programme of the ILA, is indicative of its evolution.[4] Moreover, the UN General Assembly gave the UNCED a specific mandate to promote the further development of international environmental law and to examine the feasibility of elaborating 'general rights and obligations of states, as appropriate, in the field of the environment, and

---

[3] Brownlie, 'A Survey of International Customary Rules of Environmental Protection', 13 *NRJ* (1973), 179.
[4] See Ch. 3.

taking into account relevant existing international legal instruments'.[5]

For this purpose, the Rio Declaration on Environment and Development,[6] adopted by UNCED in June 1992, is particularly important because of the widespread international support which it indicates for many of the existing or emerging principles of international environmental law considered in this book. The Declaration can best be seen in part as a codification of the subject, and in this respect the Conference has gone significantly beyond what could be achieved at Stockholm in 1972. This fact in itself indicates the measure of UNEP's success in developing international environmental law since then.

Principle 2 of the Rio Declaration reiterates the wording of Principle 21 of the earlier Stockholm Declaration; Principle 10 accords individuals the right to 'appropriate' access to environmental information and participation in decision-making and judicial and administrative proceedings; Principle 15 provides that the 'precautionary approach' shall be 'widely' applied and that lack of full scientific certainty will not be used to postpone cost-effective measures to prevent serious or irreversible environmental degradation; Principle 16 calls for national authorities to endeavour to internalize environmental costs by making the polluter 'in principle' bear the cost of pollution; Principle 17 provides that environmental impact assessment shall be undertaken for proposed activities likely to have a significant adverse impact on the environment; Principle 18 requires immediate notification to be given of disasters or emergencies likely to harm other states; Principle 19 requires prior and timely notification and consultation regarding activities that may have a significant adverse transboundary environmental effect; Principle 24 reiterates the need for respect for international law protecting the environment in times of armed conflict.

Underlying this consensus on principles of international law, however, is a continuing political conflict between developed and developing states,[7] which the Rio Declaration also addresses. It recognizes that the right to development must 'equitably' meet the developmental and environmental needs of present and future generations, that environmental protection constitutes an integral part of the development process, that states must enact effective environmental legislation, and that the special situation of developing countries should be reflected in the application and implementation of environmental

---

[5] UNGA Res. 44/228 (1989). See Sand, 'International Law on the Agenda of the UNCED', in Alexander (ed.), *Contemporary International Law Issues* (Dordrecht, 1992), 28–32, and id., 3 *CJIEL and P* (1992), 1.

[6] For preparatory work and the text of the Declaration, see UNCED, Prepcom, UN Doc. A/CONF. 151/PC/WG.111/L.8/Rev. 1. (1991); A/CONF. 151/5 (1992); UNEP, Report of the Meeting of Senior Government Officials Expert in Environmental Law for the Review of the Montevideo Programme, UNEP/Env.Law/2/3 (1991).

[7] For the position of developing states, see South Centre, *Environment and Development: Towards a Common Strategy of the South* (Dar-es-Salaam, 1991).

law. For their part developed states acknowledge their particular responsibility for sustainable development in view of the demands they place on the global environment and the technical and financial resources they command. Although UNCED did succeed in adopting the Rio Declaration, Conventions on Global Climate Change and Biological Diversity and an extensive programme for future action ('Agenda 21'), the political difficulties engendered by the problems referred to in our opening chapter and throughout this work occasioned many compromises which are reflected in particular in the two framework conventions. These are replete with so-called 'constructive ambiguities' which will require further interpretation by state practice and continuing negotiation of additional protocols.

Nevertheless, it must be accepted that the main part of international environmental law comprises the treaty regimes which have been the main subject of the second half of the present study. The impact of these, both on customary law, and in themselves, should not, however, be exaggerated. As we have seen, some of these treaties, such as the 1974 Nordic Convention, have had practically no effect, despite their entry into force and full participation by all relevant states. Many others are too poorly ratified, or have encountered significant objections from too many parties, to act as the basis for detailed and fully effective lawmaking. Widespread failure to implement and adequately to enforce such treaties remains therefore a serious weakness, and points to the need for a fuller evaluation of the factors which underlie this phenomenon. A review of this problem has been one of UNCED's more important tasks, despite the difficulty of formulating criteria by which effectiveness can be measured, and of assembling the information necessary for such an evaluation.[8] Many of the reasons for this failure are economic, social, and political, and thus technically outside the scope of this work, but they point to the importance of UNCED's attempt to integrate the needs of environmental protection and economic progress, particularly in developing countries, and the great difficulty this is likely to pose, not only for lawyers but also for other relevant disciplines.

What these treaties have done, however, as argued in Chapter 3, is to change the basis and perspective of international environmental law. Having started as a system of rules limited largely to liability for transboundary damage, resource allocation, and the resolution of conflicting uses of common spaces, international law now accommodates a preventive, and in this sense precautionary, approach to the protection of the environment on a global level. This is a necessary and inevitable development if international environmental law is to address major global and regional environmental issues; it involves

---

[8] Sand, 'International Law on the Agenda of the UNCED', and see UNCED, Prepcom, 4th Session, New York, 1992, UN Doc. A/CONF/151/PC.103: Survey of Existing International Agreements and Instruments and its Follow Up.

much greater emphasis on environmental regulation, and gives less prominence to liability for damage as the law's main response to environmentally harmful activities. To this extent, the development of contemporary international law reflects a comparable transformation during this century in national environmental law throughout much of the developed, industrialized world. As a consequence, the most convincing characterization of international environmental law is no longer that of neighbourly relations, but of environmental trusteeship, with certain institutional similarities to the protection of social and economic human rights, and a comparable concern for community interests at a global level, and not merely those of states *inter se*. These considerations help explain the increasing use of institutional supervision as the primary form of environmental dispute resolution, regulation, and supervision, and the relatively limited resort to judicial bodies.[9] Thus any examination of the functioning of the international legal system as regards protection of the environment must start with the realization that the role of courts is inevitably secondary in this context, limited to the settling of bilateral problems, or to providing judicial review of the operation of treaty regimes and international institutions. While international courts could be given greater power to act in the public interest in environmental matters, for example in the protection of common spaces, this should preferably be done at the behest of international organizations such as the UN General Assembly, UNEP, ECOSOC,[10] or of regional groupings of states, rather than by NGOs, whose authority to act in a *parens patriae* capacity is limited. But even if their role is widened in this way it is still difficult to envisage courts doing more than supplementing the work of other international institutions. Thus the primary concern of future development should properly be to address the deficiencies of existing institutions, not to introduce radical innovations in the judicial machinery and process.

From this perspective, the problems of environmental lawmaking and enforcement are essentially political and institutional in character. They are best seen as a reflection of the difficulties of securing international co-operation on global environmental management within a complex and diffuse structure of political authority and of the deeply conflicting priorities among developed and developing states. As Hurrell and Kingsbury perceptively argue:

Collective environmental management poses a severe and therefore politically sensitive challenge because it involves the creation of rules and institutions that embody notions of shared responsibilities and shared duties that impinge very heavily on the domestic structures and organization of states, that invest individuals and groups within states with rights and duties and that seek to embody some notion of a common good for the planet as a whole.[11]

---

[9] See Ch. 4.   [10]See ibid. nn. 105–6.
[11] Hurrell and Kingsbury, *The International Politics of the Environment* (Oxford, 1992), 6.

Tentative steps have been made, as we saw in Chapters 2 and 4, towards the creation of international institutions with supranational authority in the environmental sphere. Some environmentalists have argued for the radical restructuring of international authority along these lines, abandoning the present model of co-operation between sovereign states in favour of some form of majoritarian decision-making. Perhaps the most far-reaching proposal in this respect is to invest the UN Security Council, or some other UN organ, with power to act in the interests of 'ecological security',[12] taking universally binding decisions in the interests of all mankind and the environment.

Yet the major virtue of the present international political system is precisely that in matters of global interdependence, such as protection of the environment, it compels negotiation of a balance of interests and requires consensus if a framework of rules is to attain global acceptance. No group of states, including developing nations, are deprived of influence in this system, as they might well be under a majoritarian model of decision-making; competing priorities, including those of economic development, must also be fully accommodated. In this sense the attempt to negotiate the 1982 UNCLOS on a consensus basis does represent the kind of bargaining process which is arguably essential if global environmental needs are to command a global response,[13] despite the problems of acceptance by developed states the 1982 UNCLOS has subsequently encountered. Moreover, as the experience of the European Community illustrates, it is by no means clear that a supranational model of interstate regulation necessarily leads to better environmental management in the face of equally pressing claims to higher priority for other issues, or that it generates environmental law more quickly than the present decentralized international system. It has, for example, taken the EC longer to decide how to implement the 1989 Basel Convention in EC law than it took for the convention itself to be drafted, negotiated and enter into force, and similar problems have been encountered in attempts to negotiate a directive on ocean dumping.

If states have generally preferred to avoid resort to supranational law-making institutions, or supranational enforcement, it does not follow that their sovereignty has remained unaffected by the growth of international environmental law and the emergence of the environment as an issue of global concern. What is clear is not only that states are now subject to obligations of restraint and control in the use of their territory and in the exploitation of common spaces, as implied in Principle 21 of the Stockholm Declaration, but, more significantly, notions of common heritage, common interest, common concern and inter-generational equity have extended the scope of international law, and the legitimate interest of other states, into the management of every state's domestic environment, at least in respect of certain issues such as

---

[12] Ibid. 37 n. 54.   [13] See Buzan, 75 *AJIL* (1981) 324.

global climate change and conservation.[14] Moreover, the characterization of
the environment as a human rights issue, potentially affording individuals a
claim to protection in national and international law against their own government and those of other states, is likely to effect another radical transformation in the nature of so-called sovereignty or sovereign rights over natural
resources and the environment in general.[15] These developments, although
tentative at present and still largely *lex ferenda*, indicate that while sovereignty
may remain a focus of conflict and resistance to further encroachments on
national autonomy, it is no longer a decisive objection.

The development of modern international environmental law, starting
essentially in the 1960s, has been one of the most remarkable exercises in
international lawmaking, comparable only to the law of human rights in the
scale and form it has taken. The system which has emerged from this process
is neither primitive nor wholly without effect, though equally it has many
weaknesses, as we have seen. It is, of course, possible to argue that other
approaches to environmental management might be more desirable, and more
efficacious. But to say that economic models of control and assistance have as
much or more to offer than international law is merely to observe that
protecting the environment is not exclusively a problem for lawyers. Similarly,
it would be naïve to expect international law to remedy problems of the
complexity the world's environment now faces without an underlying political,
scientific, and technical commitment on the part of states, and a corresponding response in national legal and political systems. It has not been the
purpose of this book to explore the place of international law within this
broader context; it will be sufficient to observe the reality that international
environmental law has provided the framework for much political and scientific
co-operation, for measures of economic assistance and distributive equity, for
the resolution of international disputes, and for the adoption and harmonization of a great deal of national environmental law. These developments have
clearly not been without considerable significance, and have laid the foundations of a new system of global environmental order.

[14] See Ch. 3.   [15] See Ch. 5.

INDEX

1881